Software Fundamentals

Software Fundamentals

Collected Papers by
DAVID L. PARNAS

Edited by

Daniel M. Hoffman

David M. Weiss

ADDISON-WESLEY

An imprint of Addison Wesley Longman, Inc.

Boston • San Francisco • New York • Toronto • Montreal • London • Munich
Paris • Madrid • Capetown • Sydney • Tokyo • Singapore • Mexico City

The publisher offers discounts on this book when ordered in quantity for special sales. For more information, please contact:

Pearson Education Corporate Sales Division
One Lake Street
Upper Saddle River, NJ 07458
(800) 382-3419
corpsales@pearsontechgroup.com

Visit AW on the Web: www.awl.com/cseng/

Library of Congress Cataloging-in-Publication Data

Parnas, David Lorge.
   Software fundamentals: collected papers by David L. Parnas/edited by
Daniel M. Hoffman, David M. Weiss.
       cm.
   Includes bibliographical references and index.
   ISBN: 0-201-70369-6
Computer software. I. Hoffman, Daniel M. II. Weiss, David M., 1945– III. Title.
   QA76.754.P365 2001
   005.3—dc21   00-066351

ISBN 0-201-70369-6
Text printed on recycled paper
1 2 3 4 5 6 7 8 9 10—DOC—04030201
First printing, March 2001

Contents

12 p17.

Foreword

Jon Bentley

If you work in computing, you've already learned a lot from Dave Parnas. His insights have changed the way that you specify, design, document, build, and maintain software. His techniques have changed modern programming languages. His wisdom has steered our field.

When you read this book, you're going to learn even more from him—about all of those topics and more. But let's follow the design principles that he has taught us, and move from the *what* to the *how*. How do we learn from Dave Parnas? He has changed our professional lives in many different roles.

Author. As you probably know now, and will certainly know in the next few minutes, Dave's papers are fun to read. I was very familiar with many of them when I agreed to write this foreword. Even so, I asked to see some of the papers. I thought I would skim a few of them, but once I started, I couldn't stop. I ended up reading almost half the book. If you're opening this book for the first time, move right now to a comfortable chair.

Thinker. Dave's papers are good because they are well written; they are great because they contain great ideas. Dave questions assumptions the rest of us have overlooked, distills the best ideas in the field, studies the appropriate mathematics, consults his decades of experience, and tastefully mixes the brew to produce elegant insights that are admired by academics and useful for practitioners.

Lecturer. Dave is an excellent speaker. At many conferences, the most important talks take place in the corridors while speakers are standing in lecture halls in front of small, bored audiences. When Dave talks, those corridors empty as people stream in to hear him. If you are lucky enough to be there, follow the crowd to learn something new.

Teacher. Dave has had a lifelong passion for instruction. His contributions range from developing new courses (for universities and for industry) to designing and implementing accredited engineering curricula, in accordance with his strong belief that software development should be an engineering discipline. Chapter 22 of this book was written with a student; Chapter 6 was written by one of Dave's students. Read Kathryn Heninger's introduction to Chapter 6 to learn more about Professor Parnas.

Colleague. Dave's colleagues describe him with words such as *brilliant, creative,* and *ethical;* working with him, they say, is exciting, and a joy. His constant habit of challenging your basic assumptions can sometimes be frustrating; the fact that he is frequently correct (and knows it) can occasionally make him insufferable. His numerous coauthors show that Dave is a prized colleague, though, and the numerous repeat coauthors show that they keep coming back for more.

Wordsmith. Dave has a wonderful way with words. He arrived at the University of North Carolina at Chapel Hill as a professor when I was finishing my Ph.D. there. When the final requirements fell into place, I decided at the last minute to apply for a master's degree. The department was befuddled, and the university was traumatized by the idea of awarding a master's degree after a doctorate. David captured the complex situation in a few words: "You're going through our program backwards!"

Consider "Using Documentation as a Software Design Medium" (reference 71 in the bibliography). The title alone is a profound phrase and gave me a feeling that I've had with many of Dave's papers: *So clear! So obvious! Why didn't I think of that?* The paper fleshes out the insight into a software design method. I've used both the detailed approach and the general idea on several industrial-strength software projects. Be sure to take the time to think hard about phrases like *program families* in Chapter 10 and *software aging* in Chapter 29.

Dave's passion for precision with words helps us to explore some of the fundamental assumptions of our field. His analysis of the phrase *hierarchical structure* in Chapter 8 offers seven distinct interpretations, each with its own strengths and weaknesses for designers. In Chapters 28, 31, 32, and 33, Dave offers similar insight into the word *engineer.*

Builder. Dave has applied his elegant theories to real systems in applications as diverse as avionics (Chapter 6), telecommunications, and nuclear power plants (Chapter 19). His real-world experience shows in his sensitivity to the complete software life cycle, and the importance of families of software. A theme of his career is the critical role that documentation plays in software from requirements through implementation and test.

Citizen. Dave has always made substantial contributions to his institution, to his field (Chapters 28–33), and to society as a whole (Chapters 26 and 27). He takes seriously his role as a citizen, and as a scientist-engineer-citizen. You may recall his famous protest against our ability to build SDI software that would be trustworthy, motivated by a sense of outrage as a citizen and ethics as a software engineer. Part of his objective was to show those who aspire to be software engineers what their ethical standards should include. For this stand, he won the Norbert Wiener Award for Professional and Social Responsibility from Computing Professionals for Social Responsibility. At the request of his government, he helped assure the validity and correctness of the shutdown software for the Darlington Nuclear Power Plant, incidentally inventing new verification techniques as part of the project [Chapter 19]. In recent years he has led the fight to professionalize software engineering both by demanding licensing for software engineers and by creating a software engineering curriculum. Both efforts stem from his view that some software applications are critical to public safety, and that those who create them should be treated the same way as engineers in any discipline who create artifacts and products that are critical to public safety. By becoming a licensed professional engineer, he is practicing what he preaches.

Author. Let's return to the role that produced this book. How does Parnas write such excellent papers? A colleague of his explains: "Dave creates outlines for papers by listing the questions he wants each section of the paper to answer. This is a technique that he taught me and that I have taught others. It has stood me in good stead for many years." In Chapter 7, Dave will teach you to use similar responsibility assignments in your code.

If you sample a few of these papers, I have no doubt that you will be enticed into reading most of this book. When you first read a paper (or re-read one of his classics), you'll focus on the technical insights, and how they might change your professional life. After you have soaked up the content of this book, though, let me encourage you to study the form of one of your favorite papers. Analyze the structure of the document, and how it is decomposed into sections. Identify the fundamental assumptions, careful definitions, and precise use of words. Consider the larger context of the chapter, whether that is a complex system or an important social issue. After you learn the primary lesson of the paper, go back and savor the work of a designer. Enjoy!

Preface

Daniel M. Hoffman and David M. Weiss

Why Create a Book Around Dave Parnas's Work?

It is sometimes said that progress in a scientific discipline can be measured by how quickly its founders are forgotten. Software development, sometimes called software engineering, is not a scientific discipline and is still young: Many of those who formulated fundamental principles in the field are still active in it. Unfortunately, we have the worst of both worlds: Our founders seem dimly remembered, and we are making little progress towards becoming a discipline. Fundamental ideas, such as information hiding and abstraction, are only vaguely understood by those who need them most and are constantly reinvented. Those who practice software development and those who teach software engineering seem uneducated in, and unaware of, the history of their profession.

This book is our attempt to provide a view of the work of one of the grandmasters of our field, highlighting the fundamental ideas that he and his colleagues invented and expounded. We hope to provide a reference for those who teach and those who do, giving them both an historical record, a clear explanation of fundamental ideas that will help them in their work, and a set of examples to use and emulate. David L. Parnas is both a clear and creative thinker and an extraordinary expositor of seminal ideas. The issues that he addresses are at the heart of software engineering today; his explanations are still relevant and his solutions, trialed on real systems, transfer to today's software development organizations and environments.

Do you need to understand how to organize your software into modules so it can be easily maintained and so that your modules are reusable, whether they are expressed as classes, packages, or other forms? Dave Parnas identified the information hiding principle and showed how to to use it to construct workable, reusable modular structures that are stable over time. (See Chapters 2 and 16.)

Are you struggling to create APIs to make your software useful to application programmers? Dave Parnas devised the idea (and coined the term) for *abstract interfaces,* and showed how to design interfaces that provide services without revealing their implementations. (See Chapter 15.) Languages like C++ and Java directly support this idea with abstract classes.

Are you wondering how to create your software as a set of layers that define a hierarchical structure that meets your requirements, lets you build your system a few layers at a time, and lets others add to the structure that you have created? Dave Parnas clearly explained what a hierarchical structure is, what some of the important hierarchical structures that we use are, why people often confuse them, and how to create a layered structure that meets your needs. (See Chapter 8.)

Do you know that your software is going to exist in many different versions, but are having difficulty designing your software not just to accommodate the different versions, but to take advantage of your situation to make your development process more efficient? Dave Parnas defined program families to help with just this situation and showed how to create them in a cost-effective way. (See Chapters 10 and 14.)

Dave has been busy in more than just technical areas. His work includes commentary on the social responsibility of software engineers, both by exposition and by example. His stance on our inability to create trustworthy software for the Strategic Defense Initiative is represented (Chapters 26 and 27), as well as his thoughts on how to teach software engineering (Chapter 31 and 32), and how to make software engineering a profession (Chapters 28 and 33).

Why Did We Pick These Papers?

The preceding are just a few examples of the ideas described in the papers that constitute this book. Out of the more than two hundred papers that Dave has published, we selected thirty-two, plus one special one that he did not write, but strongly influenced. We picked technical papers that expressed fundamental ideas that were groundbreaking when they were published, that have an enduring message, and that are models of exposition, and nontechnical papers that had an influence on the opinions of the time. Some were controversial when published and remain so.

An outstanding aspect of Dave's career is his insistence that his ideas be tested on real problems, where one cannot define away the complexity of the world in the interest of devising an elegant solution. Perhaps the best known examples are the operational flight program (OFP) for the U.S. Navy's A-7E aircraft and the shut-down software for the Darlington nuclear power plant.

The A-7E project, also known as the Software Cost Reduction (SCR) project, was conducted by Dave and colleagues at the U.S. Naval Research Laboratory (NRL). It was a demonstration of how to apply ideas such as information hiding, abstraction, cooperating sequential processes, deterministic scheduling, program families, formal specification, hierarchical structuring, and undesired event handling to the design of a hard-real-time system. Many of the same approaches now appear in modern designs and modern languages under different names; a few diverse examples are exception handling (Chapter 12) and the observer pattern (Chapter 22).

Several years of Dave's time and effort were directed at making the SCR software and its documentation an engineering model of how to develop and document software. The papers derived from the project that appeared in the research literature; such as Chapters 6, 12, 15, 16, 17, 18, and 22, only tell part of the story. The complete set of requirements and design documentation (including what we now term architecture), was published as technical reports by NRL and serve as detailed guides and templates for those wishing to use the ideas.

How Is the Book Organized?

This book contains thirty-three papers divided into four sections. Dave has written a short introduction to each section and we have invited a guest author to write an introduction to each paper.

Specification and Description contains six papers, focusing on the most important kinds of software engineering documentation and the roles that they play. Relational and tabular documentation are presented in depth, including both the underlying mathematical basis and practical notations suitable for use by working programmers.

Design contains thirteen papers, covering the principles and techniques that have been central to Dave's work for the past three decades. Information hiding is emphasized, including the role of information hiding in abstract interfaces, its application in complex systems, and its implications in the design of program families.

Concurrency and Scheduling contains two early papers on the use of semaphores and two more recent papers on new approaches to synchronization and scheduling. The latter focus on achieving both good performance and a module structure that supports maintainability and comprehensibility.

Finally, *Commentary* contains ten papers on a wide variety of topics including education, social issues, the role of the engineer, and the status of software engineering as an engineering profession.

In the interests of preserving the historical record and of leaving Dave's writing style unperturbed, we have tampered as little as possible with the papers that appear here, only correcting a few typographical errors in most papers.

Why Have Guest Introductions?

The papers span the period from the 1970s through the 1990s. Some use old examples and notations that may not seem relevant to today's Internet world. We asked leading members of our field to write short introductions to the papers to explain the papers' historical and modern relevance. Right from the start, we knew that the introductions must be fun to read and worth reading. They must tell the reader something worth knowing that is not in the paper or is not obvious from reading the paper.

We were most fortunate in gathering an impressive collection of authors. Some have been involved with Dave since his work at NRL and earlier. Others participated in the SCR Workshops that continued the NRL work. Some have never directly collaborated with Dave. All are excellent writers with special insights about the significance of the papers both at the time of writing and today. All wrote with enthusiasm and skill. The thirty-three paper introductions are an important contribution in their own right. The fact that these people were all willing, indeed eager, to contribute speaks highly of Dave's work.

Dave collaborated with us on the selection of the papers in this book. On several occasions he commented that we were likely to get people angry once again. That is the nature of the man and his ideas: insightful, creative, stimulating, provocative. We hope you find that the papers in this book have the same qualities. It is our present to Dave on his sixtieth birthday.

Acknowledgments

We would like to say that we had the idea for this book on our own, but it actually originated with Brad Appleton. Thanks, Brad, for giving us the chance to carry out the idea. Organizational and production details for a book of this sort can get quickly out of hand without an experienced professional editor to guide you. Debbie Lafferty at Addison-Wesley has been a cheerful, steadfast guide for us, appreciating the idea for the book from the first, and working with us to make it happen. During the course of production, all of the papers contained herein were retyped. Dorene Brummel happily took on the job of proofreading them, for which we are very grateful.

Joanne Glazer Weiss showed outstanding forebearance and support when her husband plunged into this project immediately after finishing his first book. He thanks and loves her.

Duck Bay, British Columbia
September, 2000

Description
and Specification

DAVID LORGE PARNAS, P. ENG

1. Software Documents

The papers in this section deal with various approaches to producing software documents. I consider documentation to be the most neglected area of computer science. We all recognise that the software documentation that we deal with is vague, badly structured, inaccurate, and difficult to read, but few people have conducted serious research into how we can use our understanding of computer science to improve the way documentation is produced.

I have found it useful to distinguish three types of software descriptions: constructive descriptions, behavioural descriptions, and behavioural specifications.

1. *Constructive descriptions* show how a program is constructed from primitive or previously constructed programs. The notations used for constructive descriptions are commonly called programming languages. These descriptions are the products of programmers and are vital for both inspection and "maintenance".

2. *Behavioural descriptions* provide <u>complete</u> information about the externally visible effects of programs, preferably without providing information about the way they have been constructed. Descriptions detail the actual behaviour of a product; they make no statement about whether that behaviour is desirable.

3. *Behavioural specifications* state the requirements, that is, restrictions on the behaviour of a program. The acceptability of a product can be determined by comparing its behavioural description with a behavioural specifica-

tion. It is common today to make a (vague) distinction between "functional requirements" and "nonfunctional requirements". Whatever that distinction may be, both must be part of what I call a behavioural specification.

In engineering it is very important not to confuse descriptions with specifications, but some members of the computer science community have consistently identified models and constructive descriptions as specifications because they did not know how to write precise and complete behavioural specifications or descriptions. Much of my research has been directed at discovering how best to write descriptions of software. The papers in this section discuss some of the approaches that I have considered.

2. Types of Products

In my early research, I failed to recognise that one cannot unambiguously describe all types of software products the same way or with the same notation. When providing a behavioural description of modules or classes that are supposed to "hide" (or abstract from) data structures, one cannot mention the data structures being used inside those modules. In contrast, when describing the effects of a program (part of a module), one must provide a description in terms of the actual data structure. In dealing with programs in which the complete state representation is part of the interface with other programs, one can write descriptions and specifications in terms of before/after descriptions, that is, by describing the relation between the starting state and the termination state. When dealing with products in which part of the state is "hidden", behaviour descriptions must be expressed in terms of sequences of externally visible events (traces). These descriptions turn out to be much less intuitive for most programmers. Algebraic specifications and the Trace Assertion Method have found much less acceptance than precondition/postcondition methods.

3. Ad Hoc Notation Versus Mathematics

In my first papers on specification, I followed the "style" that is common in Computer Science and invented a language. I designed this language by looking at examples of what we were trying to do and introducing "features" that allowed me to handle the examples. This ad hoc approach frequently leads to notations with basic flaws. For example, my early specification notation could not describe modules with hidden state information, that is, modules in which one had to know more than the currently accessible information to predict future behaviour. An ad hoc extension was added to enable us to handle a stack [4]. This extension grew slowly and became the basis of my next approach to module specification. [1, 5].

With more experience, I began to understand that classical mathematics provides well-honed tools for solving many modern problems. Module specifications and descriptions, for example, can be viewed as predicates on event sequences, and this can become the basis of a much more systematic and general approach to specification than any early attempts. Program specifications could be viewed as relations or as predicates on state pairs. These observations lead to far nicer notations than many specially designed languages. If I were writing my early papers today, I would avoid inventing notation wherever possible and instead would apply existing mathematical concepts. Most of these have been honed by many generations of well-educated mathematicians and, as a result, have a headstart on many computer science efforts.

4. New Mathematical Notation

While classical mathematical concepts are very helpful, classical mathematical notation has always evolved as new classes of functions become relevant to those who apply mathematics. The growing importance of software has made discrete functions and piecewise continuous functions more important than they were previously. A combination of practical experience and theoretical analysis has convinced me that the old idea of using a (one-dimensional) string of characters to describe functions and relations is no longer adequate. Much of my recent work has been devoted to the definition of multidimensional expressions, called tabular expressions. Several colleagues and I have given precise definitions of the meaning of these notations and have found new forms of tabular expressions. I am convinced that we have just scratched the surface of this area and that much more work can be done. I am particularly impressed by the work of R. Janicki and others who are looking at general models of multidimensional notations; these will help us to find better notations and to build tools that are capable of working with a wide variety of tabular expressions.

5. Documentation-Driven Tools

Precise documentation of complex products is inherently complex and will always take considerable time and effort to produce. Many people in our highly competitive industry will question whether it is worth the effort to provide documentation that is accurate and complete. They will point out that they always have a constructive description (the programs) and that this may be enough for most practical purposes.

In the short run a constructive description may suffice, especially if the program is small. However, a constructive description will not be useful when we have large programs or in situations where determination of requirements requires interaction with future users or their representatives. Most subject-matter experts cannot read programs, nor are they optimal when programs must be maintained by someone other than the original authors.

In most cases, people who understand the requirements will not want to deal with constructive descriptions, even if they are available. They will want precise and complete behavioural documentation.

Furthermore, for most successful programs it will cost more after they are constructed than it costs to produce the first version. In many areas maintenance is a major burden for companies. I often hear the developers say that they don't need documentation; however, those who have to correct and modify the programs complain loudly about the lack of precise, accurate documentation.

It is very hard to get software developers to invest in something that will help someone else only in the far future. There are two ways to make investment in documentation more likely:

- Make it easier to produce precise documentation.
- Make the documentation more valuable.

My colleagues and I have decided that tools are the key to both approaches. With the help of staff and graduate students, we have developed the Table Tool System (TTS) framework for software documentation [6, 7, 8]. The kernel of this system contains a component that stores tabular expressions in an abstract form (without semantic or format information) as well as other components that can be used to store additional (semantic) information about the expressions. Other components allow convenient input and formatting of tabular expressions, and still other components perform completeness checks and type checks on the expressions. All of these components make it easier to produce precise documentation.

Other TTS tools are intended to be used in testing. For example, a specification can be translated into a test oracle, that is, an implementation of the "acceptability" predicate. For simple classes of specifications, code can be generated from the specifications and used for simulation or even production work. Specifications and descriptions can also be the input to tools that are used to evaluate the coverage of test data. The specifications can also become the basis of a set of tools that assist in the inspection/verification of software.

Only one of the papers in this section deals with constructive descriptions. I have found the notation it describes (heavily based on work by E. W. Dijkstra) to be extremely useful as a pseudocode. It helps designers take a "divide and conquer" approach to program design and makes it easier to inspect programs. It has also been the basis of a graphical notation that allows programmers to "zoom" in on the parts of the program that are relevant to them. I have long believed that the notation could be made into a very useful practical programming language, but I have never taken the time to implement a compiler for this language.

6. The Future

Researchers often bemoan the fact that practitioners do not use mathematical or formal description methods. Papers frequently call for more effective technology transfer, so authors need to look closer to home. When the notations and tools are really useful, practitioners will pick them up without a conscious technology transfer effect. The response to a better mousetrap is proverbial; rather than work on technology transfer, we need to work on improving our notation and tools. Technology transfer will then be easy.

Most of today's formal methods and tools fail a very simple test. The documentation for a program is not easier to read or use than the actual program text. Most programmers still find it easier to answer a question by looking at the code or talking with the author than by looking at formal descriptions. Our research results will not be used until that is no longer true.

One approach to making documentation more readable can be found in [2]. In this work we have reconsidered the most basic assumption of trace-based methods; that is, the canonical representation of a class of equivalent traces should be one of those traces. Dookhan explores the possibility of using other representations (sets, sequences, etc.) to make the documentation easier to understand.

Another approach was explored by Hu [3]. Descriptions of the state of a complex data structure are inevitably complex. Hu provides a notation for defining dynamically evaluated aliases. The alias, a short string, identifies key elements of the data structure that could otherwise be identified only by a lengthy expression. This allows more compact descriptions of program behaviour.

We are long past the point where we should be concerned with theoretical issues; the theoreticians have provided us with an adequate basis for program documentation. We must now turn our attention to readability but make sure that we do not lose the ability to provide precise descriptions that can be used as input to tools.

References

1. Bartussek, W., Parnas, D.L., "Using Assertions About Traces to Write Abstract Specifications for Software Modules", UNC Report No. TR77-012, December 1977.
2. Dookhan, A., "Improvements to the Trace Assertion Method for Software Engineering", CRL Report 372, Communications Research Laboratory, McMaster University, March 1999.

3. Hu, J., "Use of Aliases in Tabular Expressions", SERG Report 381, McMaster University, Dept. of Computing and Software, Software Engineering Research Group (SERG), September 1999.

4. Parnas, D.L., "A Technique for Software Module Specification with Examples", *Communications of the ACM*, 15, pp. 330–336, 5 May 1972.

5. Parnas, D.L., "The Use of Precise Specifications in the Development of Software", *Proceedings of the IFIP Congress '77*, North Holland Publishing Company, pp. 861–867, 1977.

6. McMaster University Software Engineering Research Group, "Table Tool System Developer's Guide", CRL Report 339, McMaster University, CRL (Communications Research Laboratory), TRIO (Telecommunications Research Institute of Ontario), January 1997.

7. McMaster University Software Engineering Research Group, "Appendices to the Table Tool System Developer's Guide", CRL Report 340, McMaster University, CRL (Communications Research Laboratory), TRIO (Telecommunications Research Institute of Ontario), January 1997.

8. Parnas, D. L., Peters, D. K., "An Easily Extensible Toolset for Tabular Mathematical Expressions", in *Proceedings of the Fifth International Conference on Tools and Algorithms for the Construction and Analysis of Systems (TACAS '99)*, Amsterdam, Netherlands, 22–26 March 1999.

Introduction

John McLean

Dave Parnas has often recommended that the specification of a software module abstract away from implementation details. Specifications should focus on what a module should do rather than how a module should do it.

Abstract specifications provide the programmer with the maximum amount of freedom in choosing the best implementation of a module and free both the programmer and the system engineer, who must incorporate the module into a larger system, from having to separate specification essential from specification artifact. Abstract specifications also help prevent unnecessary modular coupling. If a programmer writing a module A that must use another module B is given only an abstract specification for B, the programmer will not be able to make use of any implementation details about B. If, on the other hand, the programmer of A had to examine the implementation of module B to determine how to use the module, this would be almost sure to induce unnecessary coupling between modules A and B. This last advantage is particularly important to the overall Parnas design philosophy where one's choice of modularization should hide implementation details that are likely to change over time. The result is software that is easier to change and easier to maintain.

Dave was also an early advocate of formal specifications. Specifications stated in a formal language are free from the ambiguities of informal specification and can be supported by both software tools and mathematical techniques that perform specification analysis, code verification, test case generation, rapid prototyping, automatic implementation, and so on.

Given the advantages of formal, abstract specification, one wonders why the software community had not embraced it from the beginning. The reason lies in the difficulty of formally specifying the abstract behavior of a program. When this paper was written, the two most prevalent specification techniques were pseudocode and natural language. Pseudocode had some of the benefits of formal specification, but it forced the specifier to give up abstraction. If one were exceedingly careful, one could be abstract using natural language—but only at the expense of giving up formalism.

This paper introduced a formal specification method that allowed one to give a completely abstract characterization of a module's required behavior. The paper represents a departure from Parnas's earlier work on software specification, which dated from his 1972 paper [4], in that it incorporated ideas from the then emerging use of algebraic techniques in software specification.

The essence of the trace technique is to specify those system traces (sequences of procedure calls) that are legal and then to specify the value of those legal traces that end in a function call. To simplify the specification, the trace language also contains an equivalence relation that holds between traces that are indistinguishable with respect to current and future legality and with respect to all future values for legal traces ending in a function call.

Since this paper first appeared in 1977, it has been the basis of several research efforts aimed at further securing and expanding the formal foundation for the method [2] and at developing tools and techniques to make the specification method more useful for practical systems [1, 5]. Almost 25 years later, the paper has aged very well, and it still plays an important role, for example, in computer security research [3]. The exact technique described in the paper has never attained widespread use throughout the computer science community, possibly because of the size of trace-based specifications as compared, for example, to object-oriented programming, which typically limits its interface specifications to just signatures. Nonetheless, the paper's insistence on the advantages of formal, abstract specification has proven to be both correct and fruitful.

References

1. Hoffman, D.M., Snodgrass, R., "Trace Specifications: Methodology and Models," *IEEE Transactions on Software Engineering,* Vol. 14, No. 9, pp. 1243–1252, September 1988.

2. McLean, J., "A Formal Foundation for the Abstraction of Software," *Journal of the ACM,* Vol. 31, No. 3, pp. 660–627, July 1984.

3. McLean, J., "Proving Noninterference and Functional Correctness Using Traces," *Journal of Computer Security,* Vol. 1, No. 1, pp. 37–57, 1992.

4. Parnas, David L., "A Technique for Software Module Specification with Examples," *CACM 15,* pp. 330–336, 5 May 1972.

5. Parnas, D.L., Wang, Y.A., "Simulating the Behavior of Software Modules by Trace Rewriting," *IEEE Transactions on Software Engineering,* Vol. 19, No. 10, pp. 750–759, October 1994.

Using Assertions About Traces to Write Abstract Specifications for Software Modules

Wolfram Bartussek and David L. Parnas

1.1 Introduction

1.1.1 The Role of Specifications in Software Design

We are concerned with the building of software products that are so large that we cannot manage the task unless we reduce it to a series of small tasks. We further assume that each of the subtasks (which we call modules) will focus on one portion of the design and hide the details of that aspect of the design from the rest of the system. This has become known as the "information hiding principle", encapsulation, data abstraction, etc. [10, 12, 18]. The design process will only go smoothly if the intermodule interfaces are precisely defined. Ideally, the interface description states only the requirements that the component must satisfy and does not suggest any other restrictions on the implementation. We term such a description of the requirements a *specification* [13]. We also note that any software product is but a module in a still larger system; its requirements should be specified as precisely as each of its components.

For a trouble-free development process it is also necessary that one be able to verify the reasonableness of decisions before proceeding to make further decisions. If we reverse one of our decisions later (or find that it was inadequately described), we may have to discard all work done subsequent to that decision. If we have written a formal specification for a module, we should be able to verify that the specification has such basic properties as consistency and completeness. These aspects will be discussed later in this paper.

1.1.2 What Are Specifications?

A fair amount of confusion has been caused by the fact that the word "specification" is used with two distinct meanings in the computer literature. The dictionary definitions of the word "specification" cover any communication which provides additional information about the object being described—any communication that makes the description of the object more specific. In engineering usage, the word has a narrower meaning. A specification is a precise statement of the requirements that a product must satisfy. A description of the number of ones in the binary representation of a computer program is a specification in the general sense, but it is rarely a specification in the engineering sense.

1.1.3 Brief History of Work on Specifications

We distinguish two classes of specifications for software, which we shall denote as P/P (Precondition-Postcondition) and DA (Data Abstract). P/P specification techniques are based on the pioneering work of Floyd [3] and subsequent work by Hoare [7], Dijkstra [1], and others. P/P techniques describe the effect of a program in terms of predicates that describe acceptable states of data structures. The *Precondition* is a predicate that describes the states in which the program may be started. The *Postcondition* describes the states after program termination. Dijkstra's predicate transformers replace both of these predicates by a rule for transforming a postcondition into a precondition. [1, 2]. P/P specifications describe the change of state that the program must effect, but not how to effect it. Usually, the effect of each individual program is described separately and in terms of the data structure accessed by the program.

In DA specifications the specification of a module does *not* refer to the data structure used within a module. That data structure is not part of the requirement; it is part of the solution. It does not belong in a statement of requirements because it depends on implementation decisions. Early work on specifications that "hide" implementation data structures was done by Parnas [11]; more recent work by Guttag [4, 6] put a sounder mathematical basis behind the work and suggested some notational improvements.

The DA specification work is motivated by a desire to give a "black-box" description of a software module. The user is told only of a set of programs that access the data structure within the module. Some of these (here termed *V-functions*) return values that give information about parts of the data structure. Others (here termed *O-functions*) change the internal data. In most cases, the execution of an O-function will *eventually* cause a change in the value of a V-function. The effects of the calls of the O-function may not be visible in terms of V-function values until some other O-functions have been executed.

Parnas's early work was done on an *ad hoc* basis. The notation was developed to meet the needs of specific examples [11]. The early examples had the property that the effects of O-functions were immediately visible and could be described in terms of the new values of the V-functions. Only in later examples did Parnas and Handzel [14] seek to extend these techniques to cases where there were delayed effects.

The problem of delayed effects led Price and Parnas [20, 16, 17] to include "hidden" functions in their specifications. The "hidden" functions are not available outside the black box. They need not be implemented: their purpose is purely descriptive. The effects of O-functions are described in terms of the values of the hidden functions. These hidden functions are still in use at SRI [21] and elsewhere.

In spite of all disclaimers, the hidden functions do suggest data structures and possible implementations of the program. Liskov and Berzins [8] and others have suggested writing specifications simply by giving possible implementations—i.e., by giving a program whose behavior would be acceptable and asking that the programs produced be "equivalent."

The equivalent program approach and the hidden functions disturb us. They violate the basic motivation for DA specifications by providing information that is not a requirement. Some of the properties of a hypothetical implementation may not be required of the actual program. "One must be very careful not to read too much into such specifications" [8].

Guttag's method does not rely on hidden functions to describe delayed effects. His papers [4, 6] describe a systematic way of writing the specification. However, there were cases that he could not handle without the introduction of hidden functions. One of those examples, the stack with overflow, will be used later in this paper [6].

In this paper, we propose yet another approach. It allows the specification of modules with delayed or hidden effects without any reference to internal data structures. The only statements made are about the effects of calls on user accessible O-functions or user accessible V-functions.

1.1.4 When Is a D/A Specification Complete?

For simplicity, we assume that our modules are always created in the same initial state and could be returned to that state (reinitialized). We further assume that for each access program (O-function or V-function) there is an *applicability condition*. If this condition holds, the program may be called. In states where the condition does not hold, the module will "trap" or refuse to return through the normal exit [19]. Values of V-functions after a trap occurs will not be discussed in this paper.

A *trace* of a module is a description of a sequence of calls on the functions starting with the module in the initial state. A trace is termed a *legal trace* if calling the functions in the sequence specified in the trace with the arguments given in the trace when the module is in its initial state will not result in a trap. A specification *completely determines the externally visible behavior of a module* if for every legal trace ending with a call of a V-function, the value returned by that V-function can be derived from the specification. We term such a specification *complete*. A specification is *consistent* if only one value can be derived.

There are situations in which one may want a specification that is *not* complete in the above sense. In this paper, however, we will concern ourselves with the problem of recognizing complete and consistent specifications.

1.2 A Formal Notation for Specification Based on Traces

A specification will consist of two main parts. The first part, which we call *syntax*, gives the names of all of the access programs, and the type of each of the parameters. For O-functions we will indicate that it changes an object of the type being specified. For V-functions we will give the type of value that it delivers. This information is necessary for recognizing whether a program using the functions could be compiled by a typical compiler. The notation used is that used by Guttag [4, 6].

The second part of the specification will be called the *semantics*. It consists of three types of assertions.

1. *Assertions about trace legality.* These assertions identify a subset of the set of legal traces, that is a set of traces such that calling the functions as described in the trace (starting with a module in its initial state) will not result in traps. Additional legal traces may be implied by the equivalence assertions (see below). Any traces that cannot be shown to be legal using these assertions will be considered illegal traces.

2. *Assertions about equivalence of traces.* These assertions specify an equivalence relation on traces, such that (1) equivalent traces have the same legality (either both are legal or both are not legal) and (2) they have the same externally visible effect on the module or data item. These assertions of equivalence often enable us to extend the class of traces known to be legal. Equivalence is usually weaker than equality. Two traces are *equal* if they are identical in every respect (the same sequence of function calls with the same parameters).

3. *Assertions about the values returned by V-functions at the end of traces.* These statements describe the values delivered by V-functions for a subset of the set of legal traces. The traces discussed directly in this section of a specification are called *normal form* traces. Using the equivalence statements, one can derive the values of V-functions at the end of other traces by finding an equivalent normal form trace.

Remarks: In our examples, we have assumed that equality is defined for values of the types returned by the V-functions. In the unlikely event that we have no equality operator, V-function values would have to be described in terms of the operators that are available.

Since assertions about values of V-functions are made only using normal form traces, assertions about equivalence of traces will also be used to show that any legal trace can be transformed to a normal form trace.

The three classes of assertions together with the syntax definition form a specification or statement of requirements. An implementation will be considered correct if and only if the assertions are true of it. Any property that one can deduce from the assertions must be a property of any correct implementation.

A program that uses the module in such a way that the program's correctness depends *only* on properties of the module that can be deduced from the specification's assertions will be able to use any correct implementation of the module.

1.2.1 Notation

1. *Notation for describing the syntax* (taken from Guttag)

   <Function Name>:<type of parameter> × ... × <type of parameter> → <type of results>

2. *Notation for describing traces*

   A trace will be represented as a string from the language described by the following syntax. The parsing of a trace into component subtraces is deliberately ambiguous. The trace denotes execution of the functions named in a left-to-right sequence.

   <subtrace> ::= Ø|<syntactically correct function call> | <subtrace>.<syntactically correct function call>

   <trace> ::= Ø(|<subtrace[.<subtrace>] *

   [<T>]*   denotes any number of occurrences of <T>.

   "Ø"   denotes an empty trace. *Note that the symbol "Ø" never occurs in a trace.*

   We will sometimes use the following shorthand notation.

   Let p_i, $m \leq i \leq n$, be a list of actual parameters and $X(p_i)$ a syntactically correct function call. Then $X_M^N(p_i)$ denotes the same as

   $$X(p_M).X(p_{M+1}). \ ... \ .X(p_{N-1}).X(p_N)$$

If the list of parameters is empty, then X_M^N is simply X.X. ... .X with $n - m + 1$ repetitions of X. If $M > N$, then X_M^N denotes the empty trace. For $N \geq 1$ we write $X_1^N(p_i)$ as $X^N(p_i)$.

It is always assumed that a function call correctly adheres to the rules of the syntax section.

3. *Describing legality of sequences*

We introduce the predicate $\lambda(T)$ where T is a trace. $\lambda(T)$ is true if T is a legal trace. The appearance of the assertion $\lambda(T)$ in a specification is a requirement that calling the functions as described in T will not result in a trap.

Assuming that the module will not "trap" if it is not used, we *always* assume $\lambda(\varnothing)$ = *true*. (The empty trace is always legal.) It follows from our discussion of traces that if T is a trace and S is a subtrace, then

$$\lambda(T.S) \Rightarrow \lambda(T)$$

In other words, the prefix of any legal trace is a legal trace.

4. *Describing the values of V-functions at the end of traces*

If T is a legal trace, X is a syntactically correct call on a V-function, and $\lambda(T.X)$ is TRUE, then $V(T.X)$ describes the value delivered by X when called after an execution of T.

5. *Describing equivalence of two traces*

If T_1 and T_2 are traces then $T_1 \equiv T_2$ is an assertion that:

for any subtrace S (including the empty subtrace), $\lambda(T_1.S) - \lambda(T_2.S)$,

and

for any subtrace S (including the empty subtrace) and V-function X,

$$\lambda(T_1.S.X) \Rightarrow V(T_1.S.X) = V(T_2.S.X)$$

Then " $\equiv$ " is an equivalence relation. Note that the equivalence of two traces does not imply that they are the same in every respect, only in those respects specified above. For example, one may *not* conclude that two equivalent traces have the same length or that the prefixes of equivalent traces are equivalent. Note too that the above does not define a particular equivalence relation; that is done in each specification.

In the following specifications we have omitted universal quantifiers for variables representing traces (T) and values of specific types.

1.3 Some Simple Examples

(To be explained and discussed in the next section)

Example 1. A Stack for Integer Values

Syntax

PUSH:	<integer> × <stack> → <stack>	
POP:	<stack> → <stack>	
TOP:	<stack> → <integer>	
DEPTH:	<stack> → <integer>	

Legality

1. $\lambda(T) \Rightarrow \lambda(T.\text{PUSH}(a))$
2. $\lambda(T.\text{TOP}) = \lambda(T.\text{POP})$

Equivalences

3. $T.\text{DEPTH} \equiv T$
4. $T.\text{PUSH}(a).\text{POP} \equiv T$
5. $\lambda(T.\text{TOP}) \Rightarrow T.\text{TOP} \equiv T$

Values

6. $\lambda(T) \Rightarrow V(T.\text{PUSH}(a).\text{TOP}) = a$
7. $\lambda(T) \Rightarrow V(T.\text{PUSH}(a).\text{DEPTH}) = 1 + V(T.\text{DEPTH})$
8. $V(DEPTH) = 0$

Example 2. An Integer Queue

Syntax

ADD:	<integer> × <queue> → <queue>	
REMOVE:	<queue> → <queue>	
FRONT:	<queue> → <integer>	

Legality

1. $\lambda(T) \Rightarrow \lambda(T.ADD(a))$
2. $\lambda(T) \Rightarrow \lambda(T.ADD(a).\text{REMOVE})$
3. $\lambda(T.\text{REMOVE}) = \lambda(T.FRONT)$

Equivalences

4. $\lambda(T.\text{FRONT}) \Rightarrow T.FRONT \equiv T$
5. $\lambda(T.\text{REMOVE}) \Rightarrow T.ADD(a).\text{REMOVE} \equiv$ $T.\text{REMOVE}.\text{ADD}(a)$
6. $ADD(a).\text{REMOVE} \equiv \emptyset$

Values

7. $V(ADD(a).\text{FRONT}) = a$
8. $\lambda(T.\text{FRONT}) \Rightarrow V(T.ADD(a).\text{FRONT}) = V(T.\text{FRONT})$

The above specification assumes that only one queue exists and omits the queue parameter in the calls on the access programs.

Example 3. Sorting Queue (SQUEUE)

Syntax

$$
\begin{aligned}
\text{INSERT:} &\quad \text{<integer>} \times \text{<squeue>} \rightarrow \text{<squeue>}\\
\text{REMOVE:} &\quad \text{<squeue>} \rightarrow \text{<squeue>}\\
\text{FRONT:} &\quad \text{<squeue>} \rightarrow \text{<integer>}
\end{aligned}
$$

Legality

1. $\lambda(T) \Rightarrow \lambda(T.INSERT(a))$
2. $\lambda(T) \Rightarrow \lambda(T.INSERT(a).REMOVE)$
3. $\lambda(T.FRONT) = \lambda(T.REMOVE)$

Equivalences

4. $\quad \lambda(T.FRONT) \Rightarrow T.FRONT \equiv T$
5. $T.INSERT(a).INSERT(b) \equiv T.INSERT(b).INSERT(a)$
6. $INSERT(a).REMOVE \equiv \varnothing$
7. $\lambda(T.FRONT)$ **cand** $(V(T.FRONT) \leq b) \Rightarrow$
   $\qquad\qquad T.INSERT(b).REMOVE \equiv T$

Values

8. $V(INSERT(a).FRONT) = a$
9. $\lambda(T.FRONT)$ **cand** $V(T.FRONT \leq b \Rightarrow$
   $\qquad\qquad V(T.INSERT(b).FRONT) = b$

Note the value of X cand Y is *false* if X is *false*, and the value of X cand Y is the value of Y if X is *true*. Y need not have a defined value if X is *false*.

Example 4. Stack That Overflows (Stac)

Syntax

$$
\begin{aligned}
\text{PUSH:} &\quad \text{<stac>} \times \text{<integer>} \rightarrow \text{<stac>}\\
\text{POP:} &\quad \text{<stac>} \rightarrow \text{<stac>}\\
\text{VAL:} &\quad \text{<stac>} \rightarrow \text{<integer>}
\end{aligned}
$$

Legality

For all T, $\lambda(T)$

Equivalences

$O < N \leq 124 \Rightarrow PUSH^{N}(a_i).POP \equiv PUSH^{N-1}(a_i)$
$PUSH(a_o).PUSH_I^{124}(a_i) \equiv PUSH_I^{124}(a_i)$
$T.VAL \equiv T$
$N \geq O \Rightarrow POP^{N}.PUSH(a) \equiv PUSH(a)$

Values

$V(T.PUSH(a).VAL) = a \bmod 255$

Example 5. Alternative Formal Specifications (Guttag Type) for STAC

This alternative includes two "hidden functions," which are marked in the syntactic specifications with asterisk.

Type

stac

Syntactic Specification

NEWSTAC:	$\rightarrow$ <stac>	
PUSH(s, l):	<stac> $\times$ <integer> $\rightarrow$ <stac>	
POP(s):	<stac>	$\rightarrow$ <stac>
VAL(s):	<stac>	$\rightarrow$ <integer>
SPSLFT(s):	<stac>	$\rightarrow$ <integer>
*ADD(s, l):	<stac> $\times$ <integer> $\rightarrow$ <stac>	
*DEQ(s):	<stac>	$\rightarrow$ <stac>

Semantic Specification

SPSLFT(NEWSTAC) = 124
SPSLFT(ADD(s, l)) = SPSLFT(s) − 1
POP(NEWSTAC) = NEWSTAC
POP(ADD(s, l)) = s
DEQ(NEWSTAC) = NEWSTAC
DEQ(ADD(s, l) = **if** SPSI.FT(s) = 124
                   then s
                   else ADD(DEQ(s),l)
PUSH(s, l) = **if** SPSLFT(s) > 0
                   then ADD(s, l)
                   else ADD(DEQ(s),l)
VAL(NEWSTAC) = undefined
VAL(ADD(s, l)) = l **mod** 255

where * denotes a hidden function

1.4 Discussion of the Simple Examples

Example 1 is the classic example for abstract specifications. It is a stack with unlimited capacity. The legality section shows that any sequence of PUSH operations is a legal trace. The first statement in the value section shows the value of TOP after any trace that ends with a PUSH. (7) shows that PUSH always increments the value of DEPTH. (8) specifies the initial value of DEPTH to be zero. The equivalence section allows us to reduce any legal trace with PUSH, TOP, and POP to one that is equivalent but contains only PUSH operations. We will be able to determine the value of the V-functions for any legal trace by making such reductions.

In Example 2 (an integer queue) the "legality" section allows traces that consist of any number of ADDs, but each occurrence of REMOVE or FRONT must be preceded directly by an ADD. However, the equivalence statements allow other traces because the sequence ADD.REMOVE may be either replaced by REMOVE.ADD or (at the start of a trace) deleted, resulting in a trace equivalent to the original one. The value section shows the value of FRONT after (a) an item is added to an empty queue and (b) an item is added to the queue that already has a value of FRONT (same as before). To find the value of FRONT after a trace that has REMOVEs in it, one must apply (5) and (6) repeatedly until one has an equivalent trace that does not contain a REMOVE. Each application of (5) can move a REMOVE to the left one place. When REMOVE follows the first ADD directly, both can be deleted using (6).

In Example 3 we have a queue that always shows the largest item at the front. The largest object is also the one removed by REMOVE. The legal traces are the same as those in Example 2 (except for an obvious change of function names). The most important difference is (5) in which it is asserted that the order of two consecutive inserts is irrelevant. Assertion (7) shows the effect of a REMOVE after an INSERT that had a parameter larger than the value at the front of the SQUEUE. In that case it simply cancels the effect of the INSERT. However, because of (5), we can always rearrange the order of INSERTs so that the last one is the one that inserts the largest value. This allows us to use (7) for any REMOVE at the end of a trace with at least two inserts in it. (6) describes the effect of REMOVE in the case that it is preceded by only one INSERT. The value section shows us the value of FRONT after an INSERT in an empty queue and after inserting a value that is greater than the value of FRONT.

The discussion of the first three examples is intended to show that the formal specifications do correspond to our intuitive notions of the way that these modules perform. The correspondence with intuition must, of necessity, remain informal. The demonstration of completeness can be performed systematically. This will be discussed later on.

The fourth example is the problem that John Guttag could not specify without the use of hidden functions [5] (which follows from restrictions of the mathematical model underlying his technique). His specification is included as Example 5. We believe that the brevity of our specification shows the advantages of the trace method. This is a situation in which the values of V-functions for some legal traces are deliberately *not* defined. Any syntactically correct trace is legal. The module will never "trap." However the value of VAL initially (or after a POP on an "empty stack") is not defined. The implementation can deliver any value in these situations without violating the specifications. If a value, I, greater than 255, is inserted, only I mod 255 will be stored.

The above examples show a number of advantages over previous methods of DA specifications. There appears to be no need for hidden functions; the specifications are quite compact and the individual statements are simple. The derivations needed to demonstrate completeness are sometimes quite involved but they need not be performed during the implementation or during the verification that an implementation is correct.

The ideas are rather new and we are aware of a number of important unanswered questions. Nonetheless, we believe that this report demonstrates that the method is as good as any of the previously published ones and can help to discover design errors early in the design process.

1.5 A Compressed History of the Development of an Abstract Specification

In this section we present the history of the development of an abstract specification for a "table/list" (T/L) module. The programs offered by this module support the processing of linearly ordered data structures, regardless of whether they are implemented as tables or lists. This module is currently implemented to help in generating address translation tables as we need them for a virtual memory mechanism within a family of operating systems [15]. It is also expected that this specification can be used for various other table or list handling purposes.

1.5.1 An Informal Picture of the T/L Module

Because it is the purpose of this report to introduce a method of describing such modules, we must begin with an intuitive description of our example. One physical implementation of this module would be by means of a set of children's blocks where it is possible to write one "entry" on the upper surface. The blocks are arranged in a single row and covered with an opaque lid with a single window. Through this window one may read the entry on a single block, insert and remove blocks, or change the entry written on the block that shows through the window. The entry on the block that shows through the window is referred to as the *current entry*. Because the cover is opaque it is not possible to tell how many blocks are currently under it, but the cover is fitted with signals that tell whether or not there is a block to the right of the current entry, whether or not there is a block to the left of the current entry, and whether there are any blocks under the cover at all.

The operations that we want to perform include reading the value of the current entry, moving the lid one place to the right, moving the lid one place to the left, moving the lid and all blocks at the right-hand side of the current block to the right so that a new current block may be inserted through the window, and removing the current block (moving the lid and all blocks to the right of the deleted block one place to the left).

It was our goal that all operations that could be easily performed with the physical model described above be allowed by our specification.

In our specification we will have five operations (O-functions): INSERT, DELETE, ALTER, GOLEFT, and GORIGHT. ALTER will just be a shorthand for a sequence of DELETE and INSERT. The first two indicators mentioned above will be named EXLEFT (EXist entries to the LEFT) and EXRIGHT, and the third is represented by EMPTY. The current entry will be available through the V-function CURRENT. The precise relationship among the V-functions and the way that their values are changed by the module's operations will be described in the specifications.

Example 6. (Incorrect) Version of a Specification for a Table/List Module

Syntax of Functions

O-Functions:	INSERT(e):	<entry> × <TL> → <TL>
	DELETE:	<TL> → <TL>
	ALTER(e):	<entry> × <TL> → <TL>
	GOLEFT:	<TL> → <TL>
	GORIGHT:	<TL> → <TL>
V-Functions:	CURRENT:	<TL> → <entry>
	EMPTY:	<TL> → <boolean>
	EXLEFT:	<TL> → <boolean>
	EXRIGHT:	<TL> → <boolean>

Legal Traces

1. $\lambda(T) \Rightarrow \lambda(T.INSERT(e))$
2. $\lambda(T) \Rightarrow \lambda(T.INSERT(e).CURRENT)$
3. $\lambda(T.CURRENT) \Rightarrow \lambda(T.EXLEFT)$
4. $\lambda(T.CURRENT) \Rightarrow \lambda(T.EXRIGHT)$
5. $\lambda(T.CURRENT) \Rightarrow \lambda(T.ALTER(e))$
6. $\lambda(T.CURRENT) \Rightarrow \lambda(T.INSERT(e).GOLEFT)$
7. $\lambda(T.GOLEFT) \Rightarrow \lambda(T.GOLEFT.GORIGHT)$

Equivalences

8. $T.EMPTY \equiv T$
9. $T.INSERT(e).DELETE \equiv T$
10. $T.GOLEFT.GORIGHT \equiv T$
11. $T.ALTER(e) \equiv T.DELETE.INSERT(e)$
12. $\lambda(T.CURRENT) \Rightarrow T.CURRENT \equiv T$
13. $\lambda(T.EXLEFT) \Rightarrow T.EXLEFT \equiv T$
14. $\lambda(T.EXRIGHT) \Rightarrow T.EXRIGHT \equiv T$

Values

15. $V(EMPTY) = $ true
16. $\lambda(T) \Rightarrow V(T.INSERT(e).CURRENT) = e$
17. $\lambda(T) \Rightarrow V(T.INSERT(e).EMPTY) = \mathit{false}$

18. $\lambda(T)$ **cand** $(V(T.EMPTY) = true) \Rightarrow V(T.INSERT(e).EXLEFT)$
    $= false$

19. $\lambda(T)$ **cand** $V(T.EMPTY) = false \wedge V(T.EXLEFT) = false \Rightarrow$
    $V(T.INSERT(e).EXLEFT) = true$

20. $\lambda(T) \Rightarrow V(T.INSERT(e).EXRIGHT) = V(T.EXRIGHT)$

21. $\lambda(T.GOLEFT) \Rightarrow V(T.GOLEFT.EXRIGHT) = true$

22. $\lambda(T.GORIGHT) \Rightarrow V(T.GORIGHT.EXLEFT) = true$

23. $\lambda(T.ALTER(e)) \Rightarrow V(T.ALTER(e).CURRENT) = e$

24. $\lambda(T.ALTER(e)) \Rightarrow V(T.ALTER(e).EMPTY) = V(T.EMPTY)$

25. $\lambda(T.ALTER(e)) \Rightarrow V(T.ALTER(e).EXLEFT) = V(T.EXLEFT)$

26. $\lambda(T.ALTER(e)) \Rightarrow V(T.ALTER(e).EXRIGHT) =$
    $V(T.EXRIGHT)$

27. $V(T.INSERT(e).GOLEFT.CURRENT) = V(T.CURRENT)$

28. $V(T.INSERT(e).GOLEFT.EXLEFT) = V(T.EXLEFT)$

1.5.2 The First Version (Example 6)

We do not display the original specification but instead present a translation using traces. We were not using traces for specification purposes at the time that the original was written. The use of traces makes many deficiencies in the first version obvious. They were originally discovered after much hard labor. We show an abbreviated history of the development to provide evidence controverting the claim that abstract specifications state "only the obvious."

The "syntax" section is as in the earlier examples. We use elements of a type "entry" only to store them into the data structure of the T/L module or to fetch them. We assume that the relation of equality over entries is defined elsewhere.

Statements (3) through (5) tell us that V-functions EXLEFT and EXRIGHT and O-function ALTER(e) have the same applicability condition as CURRENT.

The "equivalences" section should allow the reader to transform any legal trace to one shown to be legal by (1) through (7). The alert reader will notice that this section does not satisfy this requirement. This will be investigated in some detail later.

Statement (8) is unconditional because a call on EMPTY can always be added to or removed from any trace without making the module trap.

Statements (9) and (10) say that subtraces INSERT(e).DELETE and GOLEFT.GORIGHT have no effect. Statement (11) is supposed to tell us that a call on ALTER has the same effect as two consecutive calls on DELETE and INSERT, provided that INSERT has the same actual parameter as ALTER. Statements (12) through (14) tell us that V-functions CURRENT, EXLEFT and EXRIGHT can be removed from a legal trace to get an equivalent trace.

Statement (15) gives the initialization of the module. Statements (16) through (20) describe the effects of INSERT at the end of a legal trace on the values of EMPTY, CURRENT, EXLEFT and EXRIGHT.

Statements (23) through (26) define the effects of ALTER at the end of a trace on the four V-functions. Note that only CURRENT is changed.

Statements (27) and (28) say that two consecutive calls on INSERT and GOLEFT have no effect on the values of CURRENT and EXLEFT.

1.5.3 Discussion of Flaws in the First Version of the T/L Module Specification

The use of traces and the way in which the present specifications are divided into sections allow us to discuss flaws in version 1 of the T/L module in a straightforward way and to omit two or three intermediate stages of the original development. However, all errors below were actually included in the original design of the T/L module (where a different method of specification was used) and allowed to remain in the design after formal discussion among the members of our group.

1.5.3.1 Incompleteness

In examining the first specification we first attempt to make certain that the specification is complete. We will (by definition) consider the specification to be incomplete if there are some traces ending in calls on V-functions which can be shown to be legal but for which no value can be derived.

One example of incompleteness concerns the value of the function EXRIGHT. Only (20) and (26) make any statement about the value of EXRIGHT and these make no statement about the initial value of EXRIGHT or $V(\text{INSERT}(e).\text{EXRIGHT})$ which can be shown to be legal.

The specification is similarly incomplete with respect to EXLEFT.

Another form of incompleteness can be found by attempting to derive the value of $V(\text{INSERT}(a).\text{INSERT}(b).\text{GOLEFT}.\text{EMPTY})$. There is no statement about the value of EMPTY when immediately preceded by GOLEFT and no equivalence assertion that would allow us to remove GOLEFT.

1.5.3.2 Specification Versus Intuitive Understanding

In addition to the instances of incompleteness that have been demonstrated, we can show that the number of statements in the "legal trace" section and "equivalences" section do not meet our intuitive expectations. There is a problem with the legality of traces beginning with a call on GOLEFT. For example, we would expect that a call on GOLEFT before the first entry has been inserted into the data structure should not be permitted. However, the value of $\lambda\,(\text{GOLEFT}.\text{GORIGHT})$ can by statement (10) always be calculated to be $\lambda(\varnothing)$, which is (by definition) "true." Since by definition $\lambda(\text{T}.\text{X}) \Rightarrow \lambda(T)$

we can conclude that (for T ≡ GOLEFT and X = GORIGHT) we have λ(GOLEFT) = true. A similar problem exists concerning the legality of traces ending with a call on GOLEFT.

Statements (2) and (6) eliminate the possibility of insertion to the left of the leftmost entry. We can move the window in our cover over to the leftmost entry but not farther. An insert would then make EXLEFT true again (statement (19)) but we would have inserted to the *right* of the leftmost entry.

The mnemonic "EMPTY" was an obstacle to a straightforward solution. Imagine that one moves left from the left end. By statement (18), EMPTY would become true although there are entries in the data structure.

We will eliminate these problems by renaming "EMPTY" to "OUT" and allowing one move to the left beyond the left end. The value of CURRENT is then undefined, while OUT is true, EXLEFT is false, and EXRIGHT is true. This is in contrast to the new initial state (no entries in the data structure) where EXRIGHT is false.

A problem that initiated the development of the specification technique presented in this paper is best formulated by posing the following question.

> How can the designer be sure that he specified the effects of all traces that he wants to be executable programs?

Or, put in another way and applied to our example, how do we determine the subset of

$$(INSERT(e), DELETE, ALTER(e), GOLEFT, GORIGHT, CURRENT,$$
$$OUT, EXLEFT, EXRIGHT) *,$$

(where "∗" is the Kleene star) that comprises the set of executable, i.e., legal traces? (Rules for including V-functions are easy to find and are therefore not considered now.)

We now note some quantitative properties of such traces: Let $|X|$ denote the number of calls on X in a given trace. Then for all legal traces:

$$|GOLEFT| > |GORIGHT|$$
$$|INSERT| > |GOLEFT| - |GORIGHT|$$
$$|INSERT| > |DELETE| + |GOLEFT| - |GORIGHT|$$

These relations alone, however, help little. The obviously unreasonable trace

$$GORIGHT.GOLEFT.GOLEFT.INSERT(a).INSERT(b)$$

satisfies the above inequalities.

We therefore have to make some additional assertions to characterize the set of legal traces.

The specification of Example 6 did not capture the language of the module, as we intuitively understand it. For example:

$$\lambda(\text{INSERT(a).INSERT(b).GOLEFT.GOLEFT)} = \text{false}$$

Other examples can easily be found.

Example 7. Table/List Module with Unlimited Capacity

Syntax

O-Functions:	INSERT:	\<entry\> × \<TL\> → \<TL\>
	ALTER:	\<entry\> × \<TL\> → \<TL\>
	DELETE:	\<TL\> → \<TL\>
	GOLEFT:	\<TL\> → \<TL\>
	GORIGHT:	\<TL\> → \<TL\>

V-Functions:	CURRENT:	\<TL\> → \<entry\>
	OUT:	\<TL\> → \<boolean\>
	EXLEFT:	\<TL\> → \<boolean\>
	EXRIGHT:	\<TL\> → \<boolean\>

Legal Traces

1. $\lambda(T) \Rightarrow \lambda(\text{T.INSERT(a)})$
2. $\lambda(T) \Rightarrow \lambda(\text{T.INSERT(a).GOLEFT})$
3. $\lambda(T.GOLEFT) \Rightarrow \lambda(\text{T.CURRENT})$

Equivalences

4. $\text{T.OUT} \equiv T$
5. $\text{T.EXLEFT} \equiv T$
6. $\text{T.EXRIGHT} \equiv T$
7. $\lambda(\text{T.CURRENT}) \Rightarrow \text{T.CURRENT} \equiv T$
8. $\lambda(\text{T.GOLEFT}) \Rightarrow \text{T.GOLEFT.GORIGHT} \equiv T$
9. $\text{T.INSERT(a).DELETE} \equiv T$
10. $\text{T.INSERT(a).GOLEFT.DELETE} \equiv$
    $\text{T.DELETE.INSERT(a).GOLEFT}$
11. $\lambda(T) \Rightarrow \text{T.INSERT(a).INSERT(b).GOLEFT} \equiv$
    $\text{T.INSERT(b).GOLEFT.INSERT(a)}$
12. $\text{T.ALTER(a)} \equiv \text{T.DELETE.INSERT(a)}$

Values

13. $V(\text{OUT}) = \text{true}$
14. $V(\text{EXLEFT}) = V(\text{EXRIGHT}) = \text{false}$
15. $\lambda(T) \Rightarrow V(\text{T.INSERT(a).CURRENT}) = a$
16. $\lambda(T) \Rightarrow V(\text{T.INSERT(a).OUT}) = \text{false}$
17. $\lambda(T) \Rightarrow V(\text{T.INSERT(a).EXLEFT}) = \text{not } V(\text{T.OUT})$
18. $\lambda(T) \Rightarrow V(\text{T.INSERT(a).EXRIGHT}) = V(\text{T.EXRIGHT})$
19. $\lambda(\text{T.CURRENT}) \Rightarrow V(\text{T.INSERT(a).GOLEFT.CURRENT})$
    $= V(\text{T.CURRENT})$

20. $\lambda(T) \Rightarrow V(T.INSERT(a).GOLEFT.OUT) = V(T.OUT)$
21. $\lambda(T) \Rightarrow V(T.INSERT(a).GOLEFT.EXLEFT) = V(T.EXLEFT)$
22. $\lambda(T.GOLEFT) \Rightarrow V(T.GOLEFT.EXRIGHT) = true$

1.5.4 The Current Specification for the T/L Module

After discovering the above errors (over a period of several months), we made an observation that allowed us to write the specification given in Example 7.

Any legal trace for the T/L module must be equivalent to a trace in which there is a (possibly empty) sequence of INSERTs followed by any number of repetitions of the sequence INSERT.GOLEFT. This observation is based on our intuitive model of the object that we are trying to specify. (We have no other possible basis.) We could create the table contents $a_0, a_1, \ldots, a_i, \ldots, a_N$, where a_i is the current entry, by successively inserting $a_0, a_1, \ldots, a_i$ and then executing $INSERT(a_j).GOLEFT$ for $j = n, n - 1, \ldots, i + 1$. Each $INSERT(a_j).GOLEFT$ sequence leaves CURRENT unchanged but inserts a block to the right of CURRENT.

Traces in this form are the *normal form* traces of this module. We will therefore have to provide a set of assertions that allow to transform any legal trace to such a normal form trace.

The assertions labeled "legal traces" in Example 7 ((1)–(3)) state that all traces in normal form (and some additional traces) are legal. We also indicate that CURRENT may be called whenever a GOLEFT would be allowed.

The assertions (4)–(7) state that the V-functions do not effect any changes on the module. (8) and (9) give the obvious facts that GOLEFT can be canceled by a GORIGHT that follows it and that an INSERT can be canceled by a DELETE that follows it. Note that (8) only applies when GOLEFT is legal.

If our specification is a good one, we should be able to show that every legal trace is equivalent to a trace in normal form. The V-functions can be trivially deleted. We are able to delete a DELETE if it immediately follows an INSERT and a GORIGHT if it immediately follows a GOLEFT. Using statement (11) we can move a GOLEFT right or left through a sequence of INSERTs to get an equivalent trace. That will allow us to remove instances of DELETE by bringing an INSERT up to them if only GOLEFTs intervene. Using assertion (10) one may transform sequences containing GOLEFT.DELETE and DELETE.GOLEFT into equivalent sequences where either the DELETE has been moved to the left (bringing it closer to the INSERT that it cancels) or the GOLEFT has been moved to the right (bringing it closer to any GORIGHT that would cancel it). Assertion (12) allows the removal of all occurrences of ALTER. Repeated application of these rules allows the removal of all functions except INSERT and GOLEFT.

1.5.4.1 Completeness of the Current Specification

To demonstrate completeness we examine primarily the value section (13)–(22). (13) and (14) specify the initial values of all V-functions except CURRENT. The failure to specify an initial value for CURRENT is not an instance of incompleteness because CURRENT is not a legal trace. Using (15)–(18) we have specified the values of all four V-functions for traces containing only INSERT.

Using (19)–(22) we can determine the values of the V-functions for any trace of the form T.INSERT(a).GOLEFT provided that we know the values of those functions after T. It follows that we know the values for any trace in the normal form. Since the equivalence statements allow any legal trace to be reduced to an equivalent trace in that form, the specification is complete.

1.5.4.2 Consistency

Demonstration of consistency is more complex. It is quite clear that the value section (13–22) is in itself consistent, but it is necessary to show that the transformations allowed by the equivalence section that produce a trace ending in a given V-function result in traces with the same value. Such a proof is beyond the scope of this paper.

1.6 Conclusions

It is clear that when we entered into the design of the T/L module interface we did not expect the difficulties that we encountered. Each proposal seemed intuitively obvious and the formal specifications that we wrote appeared to correspond to our intuition. Several people examined the specifications (which were written using weakest preconditions); all thought that they were acceptable. The types of difficulties described in connection with the first version of the T/L module specification came as a complete surprise. We had expected that writing the formal specifications was "only a formality" for so simple a module.

Our first conclusion then is simply that writing the formal specifications is useful *even* for simple modules. Had we been forced to make the change from the first version to the second version *after* coding was under way, it would have been expensive in terms of the amount of code (both in the module and in programs that use the module) needing revision.

Once we became aware of the difficulties, we found attempts to convince ourselves of the correctness of new versions to be extremely frustrating. The specifications that were written (using predicate transformers for programs consisting of calls on the functions) did not lend themselves well to examination for completeness and consistency. The mathematical model underlying those specifications is complex and there were difficulties intrinsic in the decision to talk about programs rather than traces. Although we have not yet produced a complete formal proof that this specification is complete and consistent, the intuitive justifications are far more convincing than our more formal arguments about the old specifications. Our second conclusion therefore is that the concept seems to be superior to other forms of data abstract specification known to us.

It is becoming popular among software specialists to speak of "front end" investment. The proposal is that by investing time and intellectual energy in the early design phase one can reduce the overall systems costs because of time saved at the later stages. A weakness of the majority of such proposals is that they provide little in the way of specific suggestions about what to do at those early stages. There is little evidence that the effort invested in the early stages will actually pay off. There is lots of evidence that just writing vague statements of good intentions ("the system will have a user-oriented interface") will *not* pay off. In this paper we have made a specific proposal for the use of that "front end" energy. We have shown how to write such specifications and indicated how one may evaluate them for completeness and consistency.

Further work on verifying properties of these specifications is clearly necessary. As Price has shown [20], there are clear advantages to doing as much verification as possible before implementation begins. Similar views are found in [9] but Price includes some (machine assisted) proofs.

References

1. E.W. Dijkstra, "Guarded commands, nondeterminacy, and formal derivation of programs," *CACM*, Vol. 18, no. 8, pp. 453–457, Aug. 1975.

2. E.W. Dijkstra, *A Discipline of Programming*, Prentice-Hall, 1976.

3. R.W. Floyd, "Assigning meaning to programs," Mathematical Aspects of Computer Science, J.T. Schwartz, editor, Proc. Symp. in Applied Math., Vol. 19, pp. 19–32, American Mathematical Society, Providence, R.I.

4. J.V. Guttag, *The Specification and Application to Programming of Abstract Data Types*, Ph.D. Dissertation, Report No. CSRG-59, Computational Sciences Group, Univ. of Toronto, 1975.

5. J. Guttag, Private communication, 1976.

6. J.V. Guttag, "Abstract data types and the development of data structures," CACM, Vol. 20, no. 6, pp. 396–404, 1977.

7. C.A.R. Hoare, "An axiomatic basis for computer programming," *CACM*, Vol. 12, no. 10, pp. 576–583, 1969.

8. B.H. Liskov, V. Berzins, "An appraisal of program specifications," In *Research Directions in Software Technology*, Peter Wegner, editor, MIT Press, pp. 276–301, 1979.

9. P.G. Neumann, R.S. Boyer, R.S. Feiertag, K.N. Levitt, R.S. Robinson, "A provably secure operating system: the system, its applications and proofs," Final Report, Stanford Research Institute, pp. 11, February 1977.

10. D.L. Parnas, "Information distribution aspects of design methodology," *Proc. of IFIP Congress*, Ljubljana, Yugoslavia, pp. 26–30, 1971.

11. D.L. Parnas, "A technique for the specification of software modules with examples," *CACM*, Vol. 15, no. 5, pp. 330–336, May 1972.

12. D.L. Parnas, "On the criteria to be used in decomposing systems into modules," *CACM*, Vol. 15, no. 2, pp. 1053–1058, Dec. 1972.

13. D.L. Parnas, "The use of precise specifications in the development of software," *Proc. IFIP Congress*, North-Holland, pp. 861–867, 1977.

14. D.L. Parnas, G. Handzel, "More on specification techniques for software modules," Technical Report, Technische Hochschule Darmstadt, Darmstadt, West Germany, 1975.

15. D.L. Parnas, G. Handzel, H. Wurges, "Design and specification of the minimal subset of an operating system family," *IEEE Transactions on Software Engineering*, Vol. SE-2, no. 4, pp. 301–307, December 1976.

16. D.L. Parnas, W.R. Price, "The design of the virtual memory aspects of a virtual machine," *Proc. ACM SIGARC-SIGOPS Workshop on Virtual Computer Systems*, March 1973.

17. D.L. Parnas, W.R. Price, "Using memory access control as the only protection mechanism," *Proc. International Workshop on Protection in Operating Systems*, pp. 13–14, March 1974.

18. D.L. Parnas, J.E. Shore, D. Weiss, "Abstract types defined as classes of variables," *Proc. Conf. on Data: Abstraction, Definition and Structure*, Salt Lake City, Utah, March 1976.

19. D.L. Parnas, H. Wurges, "Response to undesired events in software systems," *Proc. 2nd International Conference on Software Engineering*, pp. 437–437, San Francisco, CA, 1976.

20. W.R. Price, *Implications of a Virtual Memory Mechanism for Implementing Protection in a Family of Operating Systems*, Technical Report (Ph.D. Thesis), Carnegie-Mellon University, 1973.

21. O. Roubine, L. Robinson, *Special Reference Manual* (2nd edition), Technical Report CSG-45, Stanford Research Institute, Menlo Park, CA, 1977.

Acknowledgments

The authors are grateful to Professor D. Stanat for his advice on the research for and the writing of this paper. David Weiss, Lou Chmura, John Shore, and Janusz Zamorski also made helpful comments. This research was supported by the U.S. Army under contract #DAAG 29-76-G-0240. W. Bartussek was also supported by the German Academic Exchange Service (DAAD) under stipend #4-USA-CDN-AUS-NZ-3-EB.

Introduction

William Wadge

The paper presented here is being published for the first time—even though it was written about fifteen years ago. It is the followup to Dave's "A generalized control construct and its formal definition" [4], in which he introduced the `it-ti` construct.

On a purely technical level, these papers present this construct as a generalization of Dijkstra's `do-od` guarded command, together with a simple relational semantics. However Dave makes it clear from the start, in his first paper, that this is done to support three very general and very important points:

- that language semantics should use simple mathematics,
- that one good general structure can be better than many specialized ones, and,
- that nondeterministic programs can be simpler than deterministic ones that solve the same problem.

Each of the three points passes Dave's own "tautology" test: If we negate them, the results are not obviously and trivially false.

For example, many people are firmly convinced that programming language semantics absolutely require the most sophisticated tools of modern mathematics: nonstandard topologies, category theory, linear logic, infinite games, and the like.

Furthermore, current programming languages typically offer a bewildering variety of similar constructs. Loops are a good example: for, while, until, and repeat, often with exit and loop back commands, with each language (C, Java, Perl, etc.) offering its own idiosyncratic selection.

Finally, it has become almost the conventional wisdom that nondeterminism (and concurrency) are inherently complex and to be avoided if possible.

I met Dave about the time the first `it-ti` paper appeared, when I arrived at the University of Victoria to join the Computer Science Department where he was already a member. Dave, who likes to practice what he preaches, was teaching a special section of the introductory programming course using the `it-ti` construct in the context of a formal specification-based methodology. Since I would be teaching the course as well, he gave me a copy of the lecture notes, which I proceeded to examine under a mathematical microscope, using my background in pure mathematics and formal semantics.

My attention was eventually drawn to the restriction on guarded commands of the form $g \rightarrow p$, which required that p terminate in every state for which g is true. The only problem with this otherwise reasonable requirement is that (according to the somewhat informal notes) it had to hold in isolation, i.e., for *all* values of the program variables, not just those that arise during the execution of the program in which the guarded command appears. For example, if p involves dividing by n, then g must test that n is nonzero, even if n has just been assigned the value 2. Strict adherence to the rule as written would force programmers to pad their guards with obviously unnecessary tests.

When I consulted the paper itself, I discovered that the notes were in fact faithful to the official formal semantics. However, many of the example programs in the same paper lacked the required redundant tests. They were not legal programs; they were semantically meaningless, and the formal conclusions drawn about them were null and void.

Dave took the criticism in the constructive spirit in which it was intended, and we worked together to try to understand how much was really lost; the result was the short note that appeared in May 1984 [5].

The note explains the problem very clearly but is somewhat terse in describing the solution. There is no real problem changing the semantics so that the example programs become meaningful (without altering them). The changes, however, complicate the way in which the meaning of an it-ti construct depends on the meaning of the parts. The root of the problem, as I would describe it, is that it turns out to be impractical (impossible, if there are infinitely many states) to include LD union as a language construct, except on an unreasonably restricted class of operands.

Of course, there was always one simple solution, which was to abandon LD relations and (following other researchers) use only a simple relational approach. However, in the presence of nondeterminism, simple relations have the (in my mind) fatal flaw that they are unable to distinguish between programs that might terminate and programs that must terminate. With LD relations this is not an issue, because the competence set specifies those starting states that always lead to termination. Dave deserves credit for not taking the easy way out.

Our short note was not, in fact, the end of the story. Dave and I worked together on the full-length followup paper. We were quite happy with the final result but the referees were not. We both had other priorities and the "lost paper" never saw the light of day. I very much regretted this, because (as you will see) the followup paper does not merely rework the it-ti semantics; it also describes Dave's very clever solution to the (pragmatic) problem of it-ti programmers having to duplicate guards. Briefly, he extended the language to allow explicit reference to a value stack, including interpreting "#" as the top of the stack. At the time this looked very odd (in spite of a simple semantics). Now, however, popular languages like Perl use similar devices that are syntactically and semantically much more complex. In my opinion, Dave's it-ti provides another example of his being well ahead of his time. So perhaps the world is ready for the almost-lost second it-ti paper!

Less Restrictive Constructs for Structured Programs

David L. Parnas and William Wadge

2.1 Abstract

The syntax and formal semantics of new control constructs that resemble Dijkstra's guarded commands [1] is given. Like programs built using the standard "structured programming" constructs, programs built using these constructs are easily parsed into a hierarchy of components and the meaning of the constructed program is a simple function of the semantics of its components. Program structures that were previously considered heretical by advocates of structured programming, such as multiple-entrance programs and side-effects in boolean expressions, are shown not to complicate either the syntax or the semantics. The use of the new constructs is illustrated on some small examples.

2.2 Introduction

"Structured" control constructs have a very useful property; programs constructed using them can be decomposed into a hierarchy of easily understood parts using simple parsers—without even distinguishing one identifier from another. The semantics of the total program can be determined from the semantics of those parts, using simple set-theoretic operations [4]. Further, the semantics of the program can be determined in a simple order, evaluating inner parts first and constructs at the same level either left to right or right to left as one prefers. In contrast, the use of `goto` and arbitrary transfers makes it difficult to find a decomposition in which the components have simple semantics.

This property is important because it makes it possible to study a large structured program a small part at a time and to do so without a previous understanding of the overall structure of that program. When a program is constructed using labels and unrestricted jumps, some understanding of the program is needed to decompose the program into parts that can be studied in isolation. We consider a construct to be a *structured construct* if it permits syntactic decomposition as described above.

It is well known that restricting the programmer to the use of standard structured constructs can result in an increase in the space or time requirements of the program. The constructs described in this paper result from a search for structured constructs that do not force such inefficiencies. They are less restrictive than the constructs described in [4, 5].

The meaning of the new constructs is defined using LD-relations [4].

2.3 The State of a Computing Machine

Our presentation of these constructs is based on viewing digital computers as finite state machines in the form introduced by Huffman, Mealy and Moore. It is conventional to view the state as consisting of two components, a data state and a control state. The data state can be represented as a vector in which each element represents the state of one of the program variables. The control state includes any additional information that is needed to determine the future behaviour of the machine. As Mills [3] has shown, this conventional distinction is arbitrary and language-dependent. In the sequel, when we talk of the state of a machine, we mean its complete state—all information that determines its future behaviour. Where we mean the data state or the control state, we will say so explicitly. For the languages in this paper, "data state" means the state of the declared variables; "control state" refers to all other state information.

2.4 Programs

We view a program as a text describing a set of state-change sequences. A special class of programs consists of "non-procedural" programs. These describe only the relation between initial and final states without describing intermediate states. We can view "non-procedural" programs as program specifications and translators for such programs as automatic programming systems.

Following Dijkstra, we allow nondeterminism in programs [1]. Two programs are considered *the same* if they have the same text. Two programs are said to describe the same *algorithm* if they use the same representation of the data state and describe the same state change sequences.

2.5 Program Specifications

When a computing machine is started, the program is represented as part of its initial state. The machine will go through a sequence of state changes. If, for a given starting state, that sequence is finite, we say that the execution of the program terminates or, more simply, that the program terminates. In this paper we shall restrict our attention to situations in which the behaviour of programs before they terminate and, consequently, the sequence of state transitions of non-terminating executions, is not of interest. For those starting states in which termination of the execution is guaranteed, we only want to know the possible final states. If the execution might not terminate, we want to know any possible final states and the fact that non-termination is a possibility. Under these conditions the effect of executing a program may be described by an LD-relation on the set of complete states of the machine.

By including the complete state of the machine, LD-relations can even be used to describe self-modifying programs, i.e., programs that modify the portion of the state that we conventionally think of as the program.

Familiarity with LD-relations is a prerequisite for complete understanding of the remainder of this paper. They are defined in Appendix 2.B of this paper. A set of LD-relations may be used as a specification of a program. Below are two useful interpretations of a specification that consists of a single LD-relation.

(a) A program P satisfies an LD-relation S if the competence set of S is a subset of the competence set of the LD-relation of P, and the relation component of the LD-relation of P is a subset of the relation component of S.

(b) A program P satisfies an LD-relation S if the competence set of S is a subset of the competence set of the LD-relation of P, and the relation component of the LD-relation of P, restricted to the domain of the relation component of S, is a subset of the relation component of S.

We use (a) if we wish to require non-termination outside the domain of a specification. Definition (b) makes behaviour outside the domain a "don't care" condition.

If the specification consists of a set of LD-relations, a program satisfies that specification if it satisfies any member of the set.

In this paper we write a specification by giving the characteristic predicates of the components of the LD-relations. In describing the characteristic predicate of the relation component, we will denote the value of the program variable x before execution of the program by 'x and the value of that variable after execution of the program by x'. The notation is taken from [2] but the interpretation of the predicates is different.

If the competence set of an LD-relation is identical to the domain of the relation component, we give only the relation component.

2.6 Primitive Programs

With every programming language we are given a set of built-in programs. The built-in programs are considered primitive because we do not examine how they are constructed. Common examples are programs to perform arithmetic operations and programs to assign new values to variables.

2.7 Control Constructs and Constructed Programs

In addition to the primitive programs, programming languages contain *control constructs,* which are not programs themselves but allow the construction of new programs from previously defined programs. We call the resulting programs *constructed programs.*

2.8 Defining the Semantics of Constructed Programs

We assume that the LD-relations of each of the primitive programs will be known. The definition of the control constructs defines the LD-relation of the constructed programs as a function of the LD-relation of the programs from which it is constructed.

2.9 The Value of a Program

In this paper, a value is associated with every execution of every program. These values are part of the machine state but are not considered part of the data state. Arithmetic expressions are the most familiar example of the use of such values. While evaluating an arithmetic expression may change the explicit data state (such a change is often called a side-effect), the evaluation also computes a value. That value may not be recorded in the data state, but it is available for use in the next program to be executed. To define that value we introduce #, a function from the set of machine states to the set of possible program values; #(s) is the value computed by the program whose execution terminated in s. In the languages we describe in this paper, variables and constants are treated as primitive programs that do not change the data state; they have their usual values. The value of all constructed programs is determined by the definition of the constructs used to build them.

   In the examples in this paper, we allow programs to refer to this value using the symbol "#". We will also define and use a mechanism for stacking these values.

2.10 The Syntax of the Constructs

In this section we give the syntax of the control constructs. Nonterminals are enclosed in angle brackets. Characters enclosed in single quotes are meant to be taken literally, not as meta-characters used for syntax definition.

```
<simple program>  ::=
    <primitive program>
  | (<program>)
```

```
        |  (<limited component list>)
        |  it <program> ti

<guard>  ::= <simple program>

<limited component>  ::=
        <guard>→<simple program>

<limited component list>  ::=
        <limited component>
        |  <limited component list>  ' | '  <limited component>

<composed program>  ::=
        <simple program>  ;  <simple program>
        |  <composed program>  ;  <simple program>

<program>  ::= <simple program>  |  <composed program>

<key>  ::= stop  |  go
```

<primitive program> is not fully defined by this syntax. We give only examples.

```
<primitive program>  ::= <expression>  |  <assignment>  |  init  |
                           <key>  |  }  |  #  |  {  ...
```

2.11 Notation

We use R_L and C_L to denote the relation and competence set components of an LD-relation L.

If p is a program, we define:

L_p as the LD-relation of p,
C_p as the competence set of L_p,
R_p as the relation component of L_p.

2.12 Guard Semantics

Any simple program may be a guard. Guards are used in constructing limited components as discussed below. We call a guard *easy* if it does not change the data state when its value is `FALSE`. Programming languages in which the guards are restricted to easy guards can be implemented much more efficiently than the general constructs that we will define below. Our definitions are valid for those restricted languages as well.

The reader should note that we allow guard values other than `TRUE` and `FALSE`. All guard values other than `FALSE` will be treated as `TRUE`.

2.13 The Semantics of a Limited Component

Consider the limited component g→p where g is a guard, and p is any program. We define the LD-relation K as follows:

$C_K = \{x: \#(x) \text{ is not } `\text{FALSE}´\}$

$R_K = \{(x,x): x \text{ is in } C_K\}$

We define $L_{g→p}$ as $L_g \bullet K \bullet L_p$.
We define $D_{g→p}$ to be:

$\{x: x \text{ is not in } C_g \text{ or}$
        there is a y such that (x,y) is in R_g, $\#(y)$ is not $`\text{FALSE}´$, and y is not in $C_p\}$

$D_{g→p}$ is the set of states in which executing g, or executing p when g has a value other than `FALSE´, can lead to abortion (inability to terminate). Because no practical implementation can always avoid abortion in such states, they must be excluded from the competence set of constructed programs.

2.14 The Semantics of Limited Component Lists

If the limited component list is a single *<limited component>*, the semantics are those of the *<limited component>*.

Consider the component list A | B, where A is a limited component and B a limited component list; we define its meaning as follows:

$R_{A \mid B} = R_A \cup R_B$

$D_{A \mid B} = D_A \cup D_B$

$C_{A \mid B} = (C_A \cup C_B) \cap {\sim}D_{A \mid B}$

The competence set of A | B cannot include states that are in either D_A or D_B even if those states are in C_A or C_B.

2.15 The Semantics of ";"

$L_{A;B} = L_A \bullet L_B$

2.16 The Semantics of "stop", "go" and "init"

These programs are used to control the behaviour of iterative programs as described in section 2.17.

Keys are programs that affect hidden portions of the control state. Execution of a key leaves all other aspects of the state, including the value, unchanged. The two keys are "stop" and "go".

To define the semantics of the keys and the iteration construct we introduce a partial function on the set of states, $\$(s)$. The range of $\$$ is {GO, STOP, START}. We define L_{go} by:

C_{go} = {x: x is a state}

R_{go} = {(x,x'): x' is identical to x in all respects except, possibly, the value
of $\$(x')$. $\$(x')$ = GO.}

We define L_{stop} by:

C_{stop} = {x: x is a state}

R_{stop} = {(x,x'): x' is identical to x in all respects except, possibly, the value
of $\$(x')$. $\$(x')$ = STOP.}

For all primitive programs other than `stop` and `go`, $\$$ in the stopping state is the same as $\$$ in the starting state.

We define `init` as a primitive program with:

C_{init} = {x: x is a state}

R_{init} = {(x,x'): x' is identical to x in all respects except, possibly, the value of #.
#(x') is true if and only if $\$(x)$ = START.}

2.17 Semantics of the Iterative Construct (`it ti`)

An iterative program consists of the brackets "`it`" and "`ti`" surrounding a program, which we call the *body*. The LD-relation of the body can be determined without consideration of the context in which it appears.

`it B ti` is an iterative program with body B.

The definition below states that if the range of R_B contains a state s with $\$(s)$ = START, the program may abort.

We will define $L_{it\,B\,ti}$ in terms of L_B.

We define LD-relations N, G, and S (independent of L_B) as follows:

C_N = {x: x is a state}

R_N = {(x,x'): x' is identical to x in all respects except, possibly, the value
of $\$(x')$. $\$(x')$ = START.}

C_G = {x: $\$(x)$ = GO}

R_G = {(x,x): x is in C_G}

C_S = {x: $\$(x)$ = STOP}

R_S = {(x,x): x is in C_S}

N is the LD-relation of a program that leaves the data state unchanged but stops in a state s with $(s) = START. G is the LD-relation of a program that does nothing if $ in the starting state is GO, but aborts otherwise. S is the LD-relation of a program that does nothing if $ in the starting state is STOP, but aborts otherwise.

Let the LD-relation K be the union $K_0 \cup K_1 \cup K_2 \cup \ldots$, with

$K_0 = S$ and

$K_{i+1} = S \cup G \bullet L_B \bullet K_i$

In words, K_i describes the possible effect of executing the body at most i times in states with $=GO before terminating in a state with $= STOP. K describes the union of those possibilities.

Let M be $N \bullet L_B \bullet K$. We define $L_{it\,B\,ti}$ by

$C_{it\,B\,ti} = C_M$

and

$R_{it\,B\,ti} = \{(x,y'): (x,y)$ is in R_M and y' is identical to y except, possibly the value of $(y'). $(x) = $(y')\}$

In words, when the constructed program is executed, $ in any stopping state will be the same as $ in the starting state.

The use of `stop` and `go` outside of the `it ti` brackets has no visible effect except that the value of `init` will become `FALSE`. The value of `init` outside of `it ti` brackets is not defined.

2.18 The Semantics of Parentheses

For any program or limited component list p,

$L_{(p)} = L_p$

Note that if p is a limited component list, its semantics are described by a set D in addition to the LD-relation. However, when we convert p to a program by enclosing it in parentheses, D is no longer of interest.

2.19 The Value of "#"

The effect of a primitive program on # must be defined as part of its semantics. Because # is a function of the state, the value of constructed programs is implied by the definitions above. For the convenience of the reader we provide an informal description here.

- The value of an assignment statement is the value assigned.
- The value of a (*<program>*) is the value of *<program>*.

- When # appears in a limited component, the value is independent of any other components in the limited component list.
- The value of the limited component g→p is determined by p started in the state in which g terminates.
- The value of a limited component list is determined by one of those components whose guard is not `FALSE`.
- The value of A; B is determined by B started in the state in which A terminates.
- The value of an it ti is the value of the final execution of the body.
- No value is defined if a program aborts.

2.20 The Value Stack

In the examples below, " { " denotes a program that saves the value of # on a stack. The value of # is not affected. We denote by " } " a program that pops the value stack. The value of } is the value removed from the stack. To avoid notational clutter, we may omit "; " before or after these symbols.

- The use of } when the stack is empty is not allowed and the behaviour is not defined.
- For any composed program p that does not contain parentheses, let $N(p)$ be the number of occurrences of " { " minus the number of occurrences of " } " in p.
- For any limited component, let $N(g{\to}p)$ be $N(g) + N(p)$.
- For any limited component list $c_1 \ldots c_n$ let N be $MAX(N(c_1), \ldots, N(c_n))$.
- If p is a program, $N((p)) = N(p)$.
- $N(\text{it } B \text{ ti}) = N(B)$.
- If N is zero for every it ti constructed program, and if all elements of a limited component list have the same value of N, the stack depth at any point in the program can be computed before execution and efficient code can be compiled.

2.21 Exits and Entrances

One of the surprising implications of the simple syntax and semantics described above is that it allows multiple entry, multiple exit programs. Recall that the distinction between program and data and between data state and control state is arbitrary. For example, we could consider the instruction counter as a variable. Alternatively, the value of a program can often be usefully interpreted as a "transfer of control". Both are changes to the control state. A guard of the form #=x, where x is a constant, can be interpreted as a label. A program that begins with a limited component list in which there are three guards of the form just described can be viewed as a three entrance program. A program with three possible values on termination can be viewed as a three exit program. Such a multiple exit program can be connected by " ; " to a multiple entrance program. The semantics specifies exactly the behaviour that one would expect. The body of an it ti, and the constructed program that results, can also have several entrances and exits. It is clearly within our compiler capabilities to generate machine code that implements such programs using direct transfer from exit to entrance rather than tests and branches. Surprisingly, allowing more than one exit or entrance does not complicate either the syntax or the semantics. Neither changes. In some cases, viewing a program as a multi-entrance multi-exit program makes it easier to explain.

2.22 A Very Simple Example Done Three Ways

Some examples are given in the next two sections. These examples include arithmetic expressions. The formal semantics of a class of expressions is given in Appendix 2.B. The primitive program entier returns as its value the largest whole number in its argument.

The following programs add an amount to x depending on whether the value of x is even or odd, nonpositive or nonnegative. More formally, we wish to write a program that satisfies the following specification:

$$(odd(`x) \land `x \geq 0 \land x´ = `x+1) \lor$$

$$(\sim odd(`x) \land `x \geq 0 \land x´ = `x+2) \lor$$

$$(odd(`x) \land `x \leq 0 \land x´ = `x+3) \lor$$

$$(\sim odd(`x) \land `x \leq 0 \land x´ = `x+7) \lor$$

(a) In this program we use # to avoid writing a guard twice as would be necessary in other languages based on Dijkstra's guarded commands. The information obtained from the first comparison is stored in the variable L for future use.

```
entier(x/2)*2=x;
(#→L:=`EVEN´|¬#→L:=`ODD´);
x>0;
( #→(L=`EVEN´→x:=x+2 | L=`ODD´→x:=x+1)
| ¬#→(L=`EVEN´→x:=x+7 | L=`ODD´→x:=x+3)
)
```

(b) Below, the value stack is used instead of the variable L. The program may be understood by looking at the first two lines as a two exit program, with exits `EVEN´ and `ODD´. The limited component lists

```
(#=`EVEN´ → x:=x+2 | #=`ODD´ → x:=x+1)
```

and

```
(#=`EVEN´ → x:=x+7 | #=`ODD´ → x:=x+3)
```

may each be each viewed as two-entrance programs with entrance labels `EVEN´ and `ODD´. The use of the brackets makes it possible to combine these programs in a limited component list and produce a two-entrance program with the same entrances.

```
entier(x/2)*2=x;
(#→`EVEN´|¬#→`ODD´);
({x>0;
     ( #→(}(#=`EVEN´→x:=x+2 | #=`ODD´→x:=x+1) )
     | ¬#→(}(#=`EVEN´→x:=x+7 | #=`ODD´→x:=x+3))
     )
)
```

(c) In this version `EVEN´ and `ODD´ are not used. The first line constitutes a two exit program with values `TRUE´ and `FALSE´. The other limited component lists are two-entrance programs with labels `TRUE´ and `FALSE´.

```
entier(x/2)*2=x;
({x>0;
     ( #→(}(#→x:=x+2 | ¬#→x:=x+1))
     | ¬#→(}(#→x:=x+7 | ¬#→x:=x+3))
     )
)
```

2.23 The DEED Problem

We are to write a program that will output DEED if INPUT contains two d's and two e's, NO DEED otherwise. To specify the program we assume a predicate "hasit" which is `TRUE´ if the input stream contains two d's and two e's. The symbol "||" indicates concatenation of strings. The problem is to write a program whose LD-relation is characterised by:

hasit ∧ OUTPUT′ = `OUTPUT || `DEED' ∨

¬hasit ∧ OUTPUT′ = `OUTPUT || `NO DEED'

This problem was used in [4] to illustrate a restricted version of these constructs. Here we show a program that evaluates expressions less often than the best solution given there. In this example, "next(input)" is a primitive program that sets # to the next character in the input stream. The value of input is `EMPTY´ if and only if there are no more data to be read. The body of the it ti can be understood as consisting of two sections. The first has two exits. `FOUND´ is taken if we have found the required d's and e's,

`ONWARD` is taken otherwise. The second portion of the body has two entrances. It produces the requisite output and determines whether or not the iteration should continue.

```
(d:=0;e:=0);
it
init;
( #  →  `ONWARD´
| ¬# →(data = `D´;
        (# → d := d+1
        | ~#→( data = `E´;
               (# → e := e+1 | ~#→ `FALSE´)
           )
        );
        ( #→ (((d < 2) ∨ (e < 2)); (# → `ONWARD´ | ¬# → `FOUND´))
        |¬# → `ONWARD´
        )
   )
);

( #=`ONWARD´→ ((input = `EMPTY´);
        (¬#→ (data := next(input); go)
        | #  → (output := output ∥ `NODEED´ ; stop )
        )
   )
| #= `FOUND´  → (output := output ∥ `DEED´ ; stop )
)
ti
```

2.24 Conclusions

There has been a long-standing and widespread assumption that improving the structure of programs costs time and space. We believe that to be false. Previous conclusions have been based on a syntactic definition of "structured". This paper's definition is based on a practical need, the ability to decompose a program into comprehensible parts without first understanding how it is intended to work. We have found that we can satisfy this constraint and still allow side effects in guards and programs with more than one entrance or exit without complicating our semantics. Side effects in `FALSE` guards are expensive in terms of run-time computer resources, but the semantics are clear and simple. Side effects in guards when the guard evaluates to `TRUE` are useful and cause no problems at all. In part, the earlier opinions were based on an unjustified distinction between, program and data. Mills has shown how arbitrary such a distinction is [3]. The interchangeability of program and data can be used to reduce the complexity of a language without introducing restrictions.

References

1. Dijkstra, Edsger Wybe. *A Discipline of Programming.* Prentice Hall, Englewood Cliffs, NJ, USA. 1976, 217 pages.

2. Hehner, E.C.R. "Predicative Programming, Part 1," *Comm. ACM 27,* 2 February, 1984, pp. 134–143.

3. Mills, H.D. "Function Semantics for Sequential Programs," *IFIP Congress Series Information Processing 80,* volume 8, North-Holland Publishing Company, 1980, pp. 241–250.

4. Parnas, D.L. "A Generalized Control Structure and Its Formal Definition," *Comm. ACM 26,* 8 August, 1983, pp. 572–581.

5. Parnas, D.L. and Wadge, W. "A Final Comment Regarding 'An Alternative Control Structure and Its Formal Definition'" (Technical Correspondence), *Comm. ACM 27,* 5 May, 1984, pp. 499, 522.

Acknowledgments

J.W.J. Williams stimulated this research by pointing out some restrictions in the constructs proposed in [4]. Paul Clements, Stuart Faulk, Bruce Labaw, and John McLean have provided many helpful comments on earlier versions of this paper. Harlan Mills has influenced this work in many ways and has made helpful comments on earlier versions of this paper.

Appendix 2.A

Semantics of a Class of Expressions

For the purposes of the examples in this paper, we define the meaning of a class of expressions. These expressions are built up from constants, variables, and # using unary and binary operators.

A constant denotes a program that always terminates, and whose only effect is to return the indicated value. Thus, $C_{`string`}$ is {x: x is a state} and $R_{`string`}$ is

((x,x'): x is a state and x' is identical to x in all respects except, possibly, the value of #.

$\qquad$ #(x') = `string`.}

A variable denotes a program that always terminates, and whose only effect is to return the indicated value. Thus (for example) C_{count} is {x:x is a state} and R_{count} is

{(x,x'): x is a state and x' is identical to x except, possibly, the value of #(x').

$\qquad$ #(x') = the value of count in x}.

The meaning of # is the identity LD-relation, defined by

$\qquad$ $C_{\#}$ = {x:x is a state}

$\qquad$ $R_{\#}$ = {(x,x):x is a state}

Let A be a program and O be a unary operation. Then OA is a program like A, except that the value returned by OA is the result of applying O to the value returned by A. More precisely, C_{OA} is

{x in C_A : if (x,y) is in R_A then #(y) is in the domain of O}

and R_A is

{(x,y'): for some y, (x,y) is in R_A, #(y) is in the domain of O, and

$\qquad$ y' is identical to y except, possibly the value of #(y'). #(y') = O#(y)}

Finally, let A and B be any two programs and let Δ be a binary operator. $R_{A\Delta B}$ is

{(x,z'): for some y and z, (x,y) is in R_A, (y,z) is in R_B, (#(y),#(z)) is in the

$\qquad$ domain of Δ, and z' is identical to z except, possibly, #(z').

$\qquad$ #(z') = #(y)Δ#(z).}

The competence set $C_{A\Delta B}$ is

{x in $C_{A;B}$: for all y, z such that (x,y) in R_A and (y,z) in R_B, (#(y),#(z))

$\qquad$ is in the domain of Δ}

For any expression X, $L_{(X)} = L_X$.

The meaning of $A_1 \Delta A_2 \Delta \ldots A_n$ is the meaning of $A_1 \Delta (A_2 (\Delta \ldots \Delta A_n) \ldots)$.

These definitions do not allow one to mix operators without the use of parentheses to indicate operator precedence.

One must be very careful about using # in expressions. For example, #>4 and 4<# are not the same. The latter will never be `TRUE´. (2+3) ; #=5 is a constructed program with value `TRUE´. If x and y are variables, (x+y) ; 5=# always has value `TRUE´. (x+y) ; #=5 has value `TRUE´ only if x+y has value 5.

Appendix 2.B

Limited Domain Relations

The following definitions are used in defining the control constructs. The first four are standard and are included for completeness. This appendix is an extract from [4].

2.B.1 Universe

In the following, we assume the existence of a set known as the universe, U. All elements discussed below are members of U. We also assume that the concept of an ordered pair of elements from U and the usual set theoretic concepts are understood.

2.B.2 Relation

A relation R is a set of ordered pairs; both elements of the pair are members of U. We indicate that a pair (x,y) is in R by the notation, $(x,y) \in R$.

2.B.3 Domain

The domain of a relation R, denoted Dom_R, is defined by:

$$Dom_R = \{ \, x : \text{there is a } y \in U \text{ such that } (x,y) \in R \}$$

2.B.4 Limited Domain Relation (LD-Relation)

A limited domain relation L is an ordered pair (R_L, C_L) where R_L is a relation and C_L is a subset of Dom_R. We call C_L the competence set of L.

For any two LD-relations, A and B,

$A = B$ iff $R_A = R_B$ and $C_A = C_B$.

$A \subseteq B$ *iff* $R_A \subseteq R_B$ and $C_A \subseteq C_B$.

2.B.5 The Union of Two LD-Relations

For any two LD-relations, A and B, we define $A \cup B$ by:

$R_{A \cup B} = R_A \cup R_B$

$C_{A \cup B} = C_A \cup C_B$.

2.B.6 Composition of LD-Relations

Let A and B be LD-relations. A•B is defined by:

$$R_{A \bullet B} = \{(x,y): \text{there exists a } z \text{ such that } (x,z) \in R_A \wedge (z,y) \in R_B \}$$

In other words, $R_{A \bullet B} = R_A \bullet R_B$.

$$C_{A \bullet B} = \{x : x \in C_A \text{ and for all } y \text{ such that } (x,y) \in R_A, y \in C_B\}$$

Readers should note that the convention for relational composition is not consistent with the convention often used for functional composition. The order is reversed!

2.B.7 Some Theorems About LD-Relations

Let A,B and L be LD-relations,

$$A \cup (B \cup C) = (A \cup B) \cup C$$

$$A \cup B = B \cup A$$

$$C \bullet (A \cup B) \supseteq C \bullet A \cup C \bullet B$$

$$(C \bullet A) \bullet B = C \bullet (A \bullet B)$$

2.B.8 LD-Relations and Programs

When we use LD-relations to describe programs, U is the set of machine states. The relation component of an LD-relation describing a program is the set of states (x,y) such that when the program is executed starting in state x it may terminate in state y. The competence set of that LD-relation is the set of states in which the program described is guaranteed to terminate.

Introduction

Martin van Emden

Parnas on Logic

This paper is concerned with the difficulty exemplified by defining in logic $\sqrt{x}$ without using the absolute-value function. That should be simple enough. However, the intuitive $((x > 0) \wedge (y = \sqrt{x})) \vee ((x \leq 0) \wedge (y = \sqrt{-x}))$ does not work, as the left disjunct is undefined when x is negative, while the right disjunct is undefined when x is positive. Dave solves the difficulty by defining a new system of logic.

We should have gotten a logician to introduce Dave's system, but I don't think we would have been successful. I am not a logician, but my impression is that logicians are *conservative*. This may go back to the 1930s when W.V.O. Quine published a system of predicate logic, an honourable challenge for a logician at the time; after all, this was the decade when Church and Kleene wrote their great treatises. To Quine's embarrassment, the system was found to be inconsistent. Church had a similar experience. Since then the angels have been treading rather carefully.

Here we have Dave rushing in: Change predicate logic to allow functions to be partial, to do away with the resulting truth value "undefined". And, by the way, we don't really need truth values: they can just be individuals in the domain of discourse; that gives a nice simplification of the language, because we don't have formulas any more, as they have turned into terms. . . .

All this may be a bit wild for logicians, but logic is too important to be left to them. Artificial intelligencers, software engineers, and others are clamoring for logics for all kinds of applications. Their requirements tend to clash with the logic that developed during the first decades of the last century with the formalization of mathematics as intended application. For reasons that are unimportant here, this application lost support. Did logic then disappear? No, it had become a pretty piece of mathematics in its own right. This is what logicians study. When you come to them with Dave's problem, they'll quickly see that yes, if logic had been set up in a different way, this difficulty would not arise. But such a variant would not tell them anything new about logic itself, so they are not interested.

It is not surprising that Dave and others find that logic does not suit their purpose. And bravo to them for throwing out challenges such as this paper. Dave goes about it in the proper way: Basic Definitions, Syntax of Logic Expressions, Meaning of Logical Expressions, ... This is the proper way, but it is also the way Quine and Church came to grief. Maybe there are other ways.

Software engineers are interested in concise and intuitively appealing presentations of specifications of conditions with many different cases: if necessary, page upon page of tables. Logic programmers found themselves in a similar position: They were interested in specifying, and executing, theories taking up many pages. The logic of logic was never intended for practical applications. Their formulas are toy formulas. Their flagship theory, Zermelo-Fraenkel Set Theory, is a toy compared to what logic programmers want to write. Software engineers should follow the example of logic programmers and define a version of logic suited for their specific, practical, purposes. Dave's paper is a pioneering step in this direction.

Predicate Logic for Software Engineering

David Lorge Parnas

3.1 Abstract

The interpretations of logical expressions found in most introductory text-books are not suitable for use in software engineering applications because they do not deal with partial functions. More advanced papers and texts deal with partial functions in a variety of complex ways. This paper proposes a very simple change to the classic interpretation of predicate expressions, one that defines their value for all values of all variables, yet is almost identical to the standard definitions. It then illustrates the application of this interpretation in software documentation.

3.2 Introduction

Professional engineers can often be distinguished from other designers by the engineers' ability to use mathematical methods to describe and analyze their products. Although mathematics is not commonly used by today's programmers, many researchers are developing mathematical methods that are intended for use in software development. We hope that these methods will do for software engineering what differential and integral calculus did for other areas of engineering. The shared basis of all these proposals is mathematical logic. In the future, a solid understanding of logic will be essential for anyone who hopes to be recognized as a software engineer.

In [8], we have shown how the contents of key computer systems documents can be defined in terms of mathematical functions and relations. We also reminded our readers that (1) functions and relations can be viewed as sets of ordered pairs; (2) sets can be characterized by predicates and described by logical expressions; (3) predicates can be represented in a more readable way using multidimensional (tabular) expressions whose components are logical expressions and terms; and (4) the meaning of these tables can be defined by rules for translating those tables into more conventional expressions. A complete discussion of these tabular expressions can be found in [6]. The most recent illustration of their use can be found in [9].

In our approach to software development, it is essential to have a precise meaning for logical expressions, one that unambiguously yields a value of _**true**_ or _**false**_ for every assignment of values to the variables that appear in an expression. Our documents represent predicates on the observable behavior of programs. If we want to know whether an observed behavior satisfies a specification, we want a definite "yes" or "no," not "maybe."

Because our goal is to make a change in industrial practice, we have to pay attention to the size (and perceived complexity) of the expressions. We have had extensive experience in the use of mathematical methods working with industrial practitioners (e.g., [7]). It is clear that practitioners do not want to use methods that require them to use many symbols to say simple things. They will not read expressions that are lengthy or deeply nested. If we tell them that the increased complexity is necessary, "in order to be formal," most will reject the concept of formality. Rather than follow burdensome rules, they will take shortcuts, inventing ad hoc abbreviations at will, if a formalism requires that they write down a lot of conditions, variable definitions, etc. that do not seem to carry much information. These "on-the-fly" inventions are often ambiguous and cannot be the basis of sophisticated support tools. A full, formal definition of a logic that permits concise expressions is a prerequisite for practical use.

The most conventional formal interpretations of logical expressions (e.g., [5]) assume that all functions are *total*, i.e., defined on a domain that includes all possible values of their arguments. Those interpretations are not intended to deal with *partial* functions, functions whose value has not been defined for certain values of the arguments. Under conventional interpretations, a logical expression that includes partial functions will have a defined value only if the values assigned to the arguments of each function are within that function's domain; in other words, the predicate described by the expression is partial. Such interpretations are of limited usefulness when describing software because we frequently use partial functions to describe the behavior of programs. This paper proposes an interpretation of predicate expressions that is as close as possible to the standard interpretations but makes all predicates total.

Figure 3.1 contains a simple example that illustrates the problem that motivates this work. More interesting software-related examples will be found later in this paper.

3.3 The Structure of This Paper

Section 3.4 discusses the goals of this paper and compares them with the goals of other papers on the subject. Section 3.5 reviews the definitions of some basic concepts. Section 3.6 defines the class of expressions that we call predicate expressions and then gives precise meaning to these expressions by associating each with a set of n-tuples. The formal definition uses basic set theory and assures that the logical connectives have the expected behavior. The first paragraphs of Section 3.7 explain the implications of the formal definition; some readers may prefer to skip the formal definition on first

Assume that $\sqrt{}$ represents a function that is defined on a domain containing only non-negative real numbers. A software designer may write boolean expressions such as:

$$((x > 0) \wedge (y = \sqrt{x})) \vee ((x \leq 0) \wedge (y = \sqrt{-x})) \tag{1}$$

to describe the behavior of a computer program. The writer's intent seems to be to write an expression that is equivalent to:

$$y = \sqrt{|x|} \tag{2}$$

The usual rules for evaluating such expressions require evaluation of all of the functions and relational operators before application of the logical operators to the truth-values that result. For every value of x other than 0, some component of expression (1) is undefined. With the standard interpretation of logical operators, which are defined only for two-value logics, the value of (1) is not defined except when x is assigned the value of 0.

Those who think in terms of programming languages might consider replacing (1) with:

$$((x > 0) \rightarrow (y = \sqrt{x})) \wedge ((x \leq 0) \rightarrow (y = \sqrt{-x})) \tag{3}$$

because implications look like conditional statements. However, (3) is exactly equivalent to (1).

Figure 3.1   *A-7 Requirements table of contents.*

reading. Section 3.8 illustrates the way that we use this logic and explains its advantages in these applications. In Section 3.9 we offer some observations about reasoning, e.g., formula simplification, formula comparison and formal proof, with this interpretation.

3.4 Comparison with Other Work

The problem illustrated in Figure 3.1 is well known. There is a huge and complex literature on the subject of logic with partial functions. A discussion of recent work on this subject from a computer science point of view is given in [1]. Another, more philosophical, survey and analysis can be found in [3].[1] In fact, long before computer scientists became interested in this problem, it was discussed by most of the great philosophers and mathematicians who wrote about logic. It is not the purpose of this paper to duplicate the discussions of

---

1. Insight into the complexity and extent of the literature on this subject can be obtained by comparing the references cited in these two surveys. They have few authors, and fewer papers, in common.

alternatives that are found in the literature. Our goals are more pedestrian. This paper presents a specific proposal and illustrates its use. The proposal presented is close to Farmer's proposal (in [3]), but the presentation can be simpler because of our intended application and audience. The proposal made in this paper is one of a class of proposals called "disconcerting," and not given serious consideration in [1]. Although the proposal will be controversial, we have found it to be useful.

This paper's treatment of the subject can be different from that in the papers cited because it is intended for a specific application. By limiting our attention to software engineering, we are able to limit our domains to finite sets of elements, *n*-tuples of elements drawn from a finite and fixed universe. We are able to evade many of the deeper philosophical issues that complicate other papers and to provide a formal definition that is very close to the classical definitions for logics that are limited to total functions.

As our primary focus is on the use of mathematics for precise documentation of software and not on program verification, we present a formal semantics but do not present axioms or rules of inference for the logic. This allows a precise definition that is accessible to anyone with knowledge of "naïve" set theory [4].

Because of these simplifications, this paper will not satisfy everyone's needs and is not intended to do so. The logic proposed is not optimal for all applications. For example, when discussing the evaluation of the Boolean expressions that appear in programs, one may want to turn to three-valued logics. Those interested in the more general discussions will have to turn to the surveys included in the references.

Some proposals extend the conventional propositional and predicate calculus with new symbols, or change the meaning of the conventional ones. For example, it is common to define conditional versions of "∧" and "∨" (e.g., the well-known "**cand**" [2]) to allow the use of such partial functions. These conditional operators are defined by describing an evaluation procedure, one that depends on the values of subexpressions. Dijkstra's **cand**, and similar operators, are asymmetric. The value of the left operand determines whether or not the right operand will be evaluated. With such rules, subexpressions cannot be properly understood outside of the context in which they appear. This is unfortunate because it means that lengthy expressions must be understood as a whole rather than piece by piece. In other approaches to the problem conventional two-valued logic is replaced by a three-valued logic in which the third value is understood as "undefined." Three-valued logics were deemed to be unsuitable for our applications, for reasons discussed earlier.

The interpretation for predicate expressions proposed here neither specifies the order of evaluation nor introduces new symbols into the logic. All logical connectives retain their familiar meanings. Instead of changing the meaning of the connectives, we restrict the set of primitive predicates. A side effect of our restriction is that some common relational operators cannot be primitive in our logic. However, relational operators with the expected properties can be constructed from the primitive operators. We return to this issue in Section 3.9.

Another approach to the problem of partial functions has been the introduction, as part of the basic definitions, of bounded quantification, i.e., quantification on limited domains. We have experimented with this alternative and concluded that it complicates the expressions more than the approach presented in this paper. Bounded quantification can be introduced as an abbreviation in the logic defined in this paper if desired, but when introduced as an abbreviation, bounded quantification does not make a substantive change in the properties of the logic. We discuss this alternative further in Section 3.8.

Some researchers assume that what some people call the "axiom of reflection" (namely, that for all functions f, the value of $(f(x) = f(x))$ must always be *true*) is essential.

This intuitively appealing rule seems fine but leads to further deliberations about whether $f(x) = f(y)$ should be *true* when x and y are distinct but both outside of the domain of f. In the approach presented in this paper, we have consciously abandoned reflection as a universal property. In this interpretation, for any primitive relation, "=", $(x) = f(x)$ would be *false* if x is not the domain of f. It is possible to define a nonprimitive equivalence relation that satisfies the stated "axiom," but we do not believe that doing so is useful. We return to this issue in Section 3.9.

3.5 Basic Definitions

This section explains some well-known mathematical concepts used in the sequel, namely tuple, simple tuple, relation, function, predicate, characteristic predicate, domain, argument, and range.

3.5.1 Tuples

We assume the existence of a finite[2] set of values called U. U must include the truth-values (represented by "*true*" and "*false*"), a distinguished value (represented by "***"), and all other values of interest.

A *simple tuple* is an ordered list of one or more members of U. A *simple n-tuple* is an ordered list of n members of U. We make no distinction between a simple 1-tuple and a member of U.

A *tuple* is an ordered list of one or more simple tuples. An *n-tuple* is a tuple containing n elements, each of which is a simple tuple. A 1-tuple whose element is a simple n-tuple is the same as that simple n-tuple.

---

2. We restrict ourselves to finite sets, not because it is strictly necessary to be so restrictive, but because they are all that we need for our application.

When representing specific tuples, we separate the elements with commas and enclose tuples in <brackets> to make their structure clear. For example, "*<true,false,true,false>*" represents a simple 4-tuple, and "*<<true,false>,true,false>*" represents a 3-tuple that is not a simple 3-tuple. The strings "*true*," "*<true>*," and "*<<true>>*" all represent the same simple 1-tuple and member of *U.*

S^k is the set of all simple *k*-tuples; S^1 is *U. S* is the union of $S^1, S^2, ..., S^u$; *u* is the length of the longest tuple needed to apply the semantic model developed below.[3]

T^k is the set of all *k*-tuples. T^1 is *S.* T^k includes $S^k.$ *T* is the union of $T^1, T^2, ..., T^u.$

3.5.2 Relations, Functions, Predicates, and Characteristic Predicates

We define a *relation* to be a set of tuples, a subset of *T.* If the set consists entirely of pairs (2-tuples), we call the relation a *binary relation.* The set of values that appears as the first element of a pair in a binary relation is called the *domain* of that relation. The set of values that appears as the second element of a pair is called the *range* of that relation.

A *function* is a binary relation with one additional property: for any given simple tuple, *x,* in its domain, there is only one pair (x, y) in the function. If <*a, b*> is in the function *F, b* is called the *value* of the function at *a;* we may write "*F(a)*" to represent *b.* A procedure determining the value of *F* at *a* is called an *evaluation* of *F* at *a.* If there is no pair <*a, b*> in *F, F(a)* is not defined (i.e., *F* cannot be evaluated) at *a.* Note that the domain and range of a function can include simple tuples, and it may make sense to write "*F(a, b),*" "*F(a, b, c),*" and "*F(F(a, b, c)).*"[4]

We refer to functions whose domain is a proper subset of *S* as *partial functions* and functions whose domain includes all members of *S* as *total functions.* All of the functions that arise in software engineering are partial functions in the sense of this paper.[5]

A *predicate* is a function whose range contains no members other than **true** and **false**.

---

3. *u* will be the size of the set of variables.

4. We allow functions with varying "arity," both because it simplifies our definitions and because programmers often ask for such facilities.

5. Because we allow functions of varying arity, our definition of "partial" must be weaker than the usual definitions. Usually, a function whose domain was S^k (for fixed *k*) would be considered total.

For any set of simple tuples, X, the *characteristics predicate* of that set is a predicate whose domain is S, and whose value, for a simple tuple b, is ***true*** if and only if b is a member of X.

3.6 The Syntax of Logical Expressions

This section describes the class of expressions that is the subject of this paper. Readers will find our syntax very close to the standard ones. The semantics of these expressions is described in Section 3.7.

3.6.1 Primitive Functions and Predicates

We assume that the strings $f_1, \ldots, f_k$ are the names of functions and that $R_1, \ldots, R_m$ are the names of characteristic predicates of sets of simple tuples. Viewing the functions as sets of pairs and the predicates as characterizing sets of simple tuples, we require that the distinguished member of U, $*$, not appear in any of the tuples in those sets.

3.6.2 Terms

Expressions are constructed using a finite indexed set of mathematical variables, $x_1, \ldots, x_u$ and a finite set of constants, C. The constants are strings representing the members of U but no member of C represents $*$. For example, "***true***" is a constant that represents ***true***; "***false***" in an expression represents ***false***. The symbol "V" will be used to stand for a comma-separated list of terms (see below). If all the elements of V are constants, V represents a simple tuple.

A *function application* is a string of the form $f_j(V)$. Nothing else is a function application. The elements of V are called the *arguments* of the function application.

A term is either a member of C, a variable, or a function application. Nothing else is a term.

3.6.3 Primitive Expressions

A *primitive expression* is a string of the form $R_j(V)$. Nothing else is a primitive expression. The elements of V are called *arguments* of the primitive expression.

3.6.4 Predicate Expressions

All primitive expressions are *predicate expressions*. If P and Q are predicate expressions and x_k is a variable, then $\forall(x_k, P)$, (P), $(P) \wedge (Q)$, $(P) \vee (Q)$, and

$\neg(P)$ are *predicate expressions*. There are no other predicate expressions, but extensions of this work could introduce additional propositional connectives and quantifiers (see Section 3.7.6).

3.7 The Meaning of Logical Expressions

This section defines the meaning of the expressions described in the previous section in such a way that if we evaluate a primitive expression, $R_j(V)$, and some elements of V include applications of partial functions, and the values of the arguments of any function are not in the domain of that function, the value of the primitive expression will be ***false***.

A full formal definition is important because experience has shown that the simple description in the previous paragraph is unclear for some. Some specialists have expressed doubt that a logic with this property can preserve the standard meaning of the logical connectives. Further, some implications of the informal description are not immediately obvious. However, some readers may wish to skip the definitions on first reading. The examples provided in later sections can be understood without using the detailed definition.

To define the meaning of these expressions, we will interpret each predicate expression as denoting a set, which we call its *denotation*. These denotations will be subsets of S^u, where u is the number of variables that may appear in the expressions whose meaning is being defined. Each simple u-tuple will be called an *assignment*.

3.7.1 Evaluating Terms for a Given Assignment

We define a mapping *val*, which associates pairs, comprising a term and an assignment, with members of S by the following rules. For a term, t, and assignment, A:

1. if t is a constant representing t' (a member of U), $val(t, A)$ is t',
2. if t is a variable, x_k, $val(t, A)$ is the kth element of the assignment A,
3. if t is a function application, $f_k(V)$, let
   a. n be the length of V,
   b. V_i be the ith element of V, and
   c. V', be the simple tuple $<val(V_1, A), \ldots, val(V_i, A), \ldots, val(V_n, A)>$, and distinguish the following two cases:
      i. if V' is in the domain of f_k, $val(t, A)$ is $f_k(V')$.
      ii. if V' is not in the domain of f_k, $val(t, A)$ is $*$.

3.7.2 Evaluating Primitive Expressions for a Given Assignment

We define a mapping *tval*, which associates pairs, comprising a primitive expression and an assignment, with either **_true_** or **_false_** by the following rule.

For a primitive expression, $R_j(V)$, and assignment, A, let

- X_j be the set of simple tuples characterized by R_j,
- n be the length of V,
- V_i be the ith element of V, and
- V' be the simple tuple $<val(V_1, A), ..., val(V_i, A), ..., val(V_n, A)>$,

and distinguish the following two cases:

1. If V' is in X_j, $tval(R_j(V), A)$ is **_true_**.
2. If V' is not in X_j, $tval(R_j(V), A)$ is **_false_**.

3.7.3 The Denotation of Primitive Expressions

For a primitive expression, p, the denotation of p is the set of all assignments, A, such that $tval(p, A)$ is **_true_**.

3.7.4 The Denotation of Predicate Expressions

If A is an assignment, $A[k \rightarrow c]$ stands for an assignment, A', that is identical to A except that the kth element of A' is the member of U that is represented by c. If P and Q are predicate expressions,

1. the denotation of $(\forall x_k, P)$ is the set of all assignments, A, such that if c represents any value in U other than $*$, $A[k \rightarrow c]$ is in the denotation of P and
2. the denotation of (P) is the denotation of P and
3. the denotation of $(P) \wedge (Q)$ is the intersection of the denotations of P and Q and
4. the denotation of $(P) \vee (Q)$ is the union of the denotations of P and Q and
5. the denotation of $\neg (P)$ is the set of all members of S^u that are not in the denotation of P.

3.7.5 Satisfaction of an Expression

The denotation of any predicate expression is defined above.

Expressions that denote the empty set are said to be **_false_**; those that denote all of S^u are said to be **_true_**. An expression, e, is said to be *satisfied* by an assignment, A, if A is a member of the denotation of e.

3.7.6 Notational Conveniences

Existential quantification ("$\exists$") and implication ("$\Rightarrow$") can be introduced as abbreviations. "$(\exists x_k, P)$" can be written instead of "$\neg (\forall x_k, \neg (P))$". "$(P \Rightarrow Q)$" can be written instead of "$(\neg (P)) \vee (Q)$". It is usual to introduce operator precedence and eliminate many of the parentheses.

As most expressions include only a few variables, it is useful to describe sets of assignments by listing the values of some variables and not specifying values for the others. For example, a list such as "$x_2 : 4, x_{24} : 96$" represents all assignments in which the second element is 4 and the 24th element is 96.

It is also convenient to introduce other variables (e.g., *cat, y*), and conventional symbols representing the functions and relations. None of these conveniences would mean a substantive change in the interpretation of these expressions.

3.8 Examples of the Use of This Logic in Software Documentation

This section illustrates the use of our logic by discussing some simple examples.

For increased readability, we have developed tabular representations of functions and use the logic described above within the tables. The meaning of the tables is the subject of [6]; here we discuss only the logical expressions that appear in the tables. These expressions are used to partition the domain of a relation (each partition corresponding to a column) and to describe the conditions that values must satisfy.

Both of the examples given below describe programs that deal with an array, *B*, with indices $1 \cdots N$. Like many others, we treat such arrays as partial functions whose domain consists of the integers $1 \cdots N$. The value of the array (partial function) is not defined for other values.

Figure 3.2 documents the behavior of a program that must search the array *B*, looking for an element with value of the program variable *x*.[6] To describe the behavior of this program completely, we must distinguish two cases depending on whether or not there is such an element. The table describes the required properties of the values of *j'* and present' in each case. We further indicate that the variables *x* and *B* should not change (by writing "$NC(x, B)$").

The key predicate expression in Figure 3.2 is that in Figure 3.3.

---

6. In these tables, ___true___ and ___false___ are predicate values, while **true** and **false** represent the values of program variables. "|" is read "such that" and indicates that the value of the variable must satisfy a predicate given in the appropriate column.

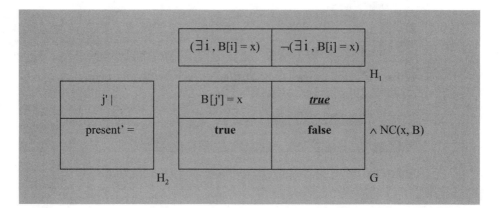

Figure 3.2 *Relational description of a program that searches B for the value of x.*

$$(\exists i , B[i] = x)$$

Figure 3.3 *Is the value of x to be found in B?*

A logic not designed for partial functions would leave the expression in Figure 3.3 undefined because there are values of i for which $B[i]$ is not defined. Other logics, e.g., some of those that introduce a third value, would assign that third value to this expression whether or not the value of x could be found in B. Neither of these interpretations would be consistent with the intended meaning of this table. We want one, and only one, of the two expressions in the column headers to evaluate to ***true***. Other alternatives introduce bounded quantification, i.e., quantification over an explicitly described set, allowing expressions like "$(\exists i : 0 < i \leq n, B[i] = x)$" and "$(\forall i : 0 < i \leq n, B[i] = x)$."[7] The use of bounded quantification as a primitive concept could solve this problem, but the expressions would always be longer, and more complex than Figure 3.3. The complexity can become especially troublesome if the arrays in an expression do not have the same index set. Consider the expression in Figure 3.4.

For this example, if we were depending on bounded quantification, the quantification would have to take place over the intersection of the index sets of B and C. Now, consider Figure 3.5; if we were using bounded quantification, and the index sets of the three arrays *A, B,* and *C* were distinct but over-

---

7. It is important *not* to define these as abbreviations for "$(\exists i, 0 < i \leq n \wedge B[i] = x)$" and "$(\forall i, 0 < i \leq n \Rightarrow B[i] = x)$," respectively. Bounded quantification must be primitive.

$$(\exists i, C[i] = B[i])$$

Figure 3.4   *Looking for matching elements in two arrays.*

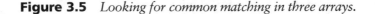

$$(\exists i, (A[i] = B[i]) \vee (A[i] = C[i]))$$

Figure 3.5   *Looking for common matching in three arrays.*

lapping, the expression in Figure 3.5 would have to be rewritten as the disjunction of two separate quantified expressions.

The logic proposed in this paper gives exactly the answers that would be wanted in such cases. When the value of i is outside the index set of either B or C, the value of $C[i] = B[i]$ is *false*.

The slightly more complex example in Figure 3.6 is introduced to show that we get the desired results when universal quantification is used. Figure 3.6 would document a program that examines an array, B, looking for a palindrome of length n.

If there is such a palindrome, its presence and location are indicated by the values of present′ and l'. If a palindrome is present, the value of l' must satisfy the expression in Figure 3.7.

This expression gives the desired results even though the implication is evaluated outside the domain (index set) of B; that domain is characterized by the left-hand side of the implication. When the expression is evaluated outside of the index set, the left-hand side of the implication is *false* and the

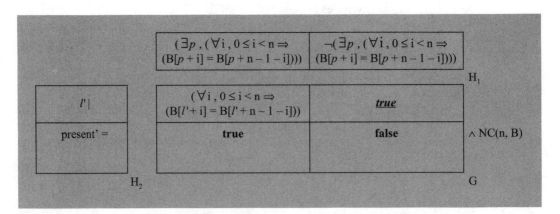

Figure 3.6   *Relational description of a program checking for palindromes.*

$$(\forall i\,,\,0 \le i < n \Rightarrow (B[l' + i] = B[l' + n - 1 - i]))$$

Figure 3.7 *Is there a palindrome of length n beginning at l'?*

implication is **_true_**. With universal quantification, our interpretation requires an explicit statement of the domain of interest, but we do not need to introduce bounded quantification as a primitive concept.

3.9 Conclusions

The meaning of expressions like the one presented in Figure 3.1 can be defined in terms of well-understood set-theoretic operations. As a result, the logical connectives have properties analogous to the corresponding set of theoretic operators, and the proposed definition is consistent with the intuitive meaning of these operators. It is not necessary to introduce either a third value or conditional operators in order to deal with partial functions.

Some researchers have proposed avoiding the problem of partial functions by avoiding the concept of function completely. It is possible to work entirely with relations and not use the "$f(x)$" notation. If F is the characteristic predicate of the function f, one can replace each use of "$y = f(x)$" with "$F(x, y)$". However, engineers have found the use of functional notation to be very valuable, and we are reluctant to discard it. One nice property of our proposal is that it gives exactly the same results that one would get if one avoided functions by using the corresponding relations.

Not only is our introductory example (1) fully defined using this interpretation, so is the simplified form in Figure 3.8.

This form, in which there are no "guarding" expressions, has exactly the same denotation as (1) and (2). The interpretation of logical formulae presented here allows us to simplify many expressions substantially. Obtaining the most compact readable formulation possible is essential if these notations are to be used to describe real programs.

Extensive discussions of axioms and rules of inference for logics similar to the one described here can be found in [1], [3] and the papers that they reference. Many of the usual axioms apply only to functions that are total. For

$$(y = \sqrt{x}) \vee (y = \sqrt{-x}) \qquad (4)$$

Figure 3.8 *Simplified version of (1).*

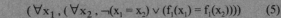

$$(\forall x_1, (\forall x_2, \neg(x_1 = x_2) \vee (f_1(x_1) = f_1(x_2)))) \quad (5)$$

Figure 3.9   *"Axiom" of reflection, which does not hold in this interpretation.*

example, we often assume that the expression in Figure 3.9 evaluates to ***true*** for any function, f_1. However, (5) is equivalent to ***true*** if, and only if, the domain of f_1 includes all values in $U - \{ * \}$.[8] If x_1 is outside of the domain of f_1, $f_1(x_1) = f_1(x_1)$ would have the value ***false***.

Some expressions that are normally assumed to represent complementary predicates would not do so in our interpretation if the relations are included in the set of primitive relations. For example, if both ">" and "≤" are primitive, "$\sqrt{x} > \sqrt{y}$" would not denote the complement of the denotation of "$\sqrt{x} \leq \sqrt{y}$"; both evaluate to ***false*** when either x or y is assigned negative values. We can define two *nonprimitive* ordering relations that are complementary by defining **one** of them to be true if both of the primitive relations are false. This would be an arbitrary choice and probably not useful.

It should be noted that our definitions do not treat equality differently from any of the other relations used in the expressions. Equality would be included in $\{ R_1, \ldots, R_m \}$ and should be defined to be the smallest symmetric, transitive, reflexive, binary relation on its domain; the domain should be $U - \{ * \}$. If this definition is used, the expression "$\sqrt{a} = \sqrt{a}$" cannot be replaced by "***true***" if U includes negative values. If U is the set of real numbers, "$\sqrt{a} = \sqrt{a}$" can be replaced by "$a > 0$," which characterizes the domain of the function applied in the expression.[9] Because this is contrary to our habitual assumptions and could lead to careless errors, the properties of the functions that we use must be stated precisely. Conventional simplification rules, and hence some automatic simplifiers and verifiers, must be either modified or used with caution; they are often based on the implicit assumption that functions are total.

The interpretation proposed here can be simpler than some proposed elsewhere because some of the complexities of dealing with partial functions have been kept out of the general interpretation; the complexity will reappear in the axiomatic definitions of the functions actually used. Simplification has also been obtained by insisting that all primitive predicates evaluate to ***false*** whenever one or more of their arguments are not defined. We believe that these are the proper decisions because (1) keeping the logic simple is essential

8. "−" denotes set difference.

9. The primitive predicates can be used to construct other predicates if desired. For example, it is possible to define $E(a, b)$ to be $(a = b) \vee (\neg((a = b) \vee (a \neq b)))$.

to practical application, (2) the assigned meanings are consistent with intuitive interpretations, and (3) the formulae that result are relatively simple for cases arising frequently in our use of the logic.

References

1. J.H. Cheng and C.B. Jones, "On the Usability of Logics Which Handle Partial Functions," in *Proc. Third Refinement Workshop,* C. Morgan and J. Woodcock, eds. Heidelberg, Germany: Springer-Verlag, 1991.

2. E.W. Dijkstra, *A Discipline of Programming.* Englewood Cliffs, NJ: Prentice-Hall, 1976.

3. William F. Farmer, "A Partial Functions Version of Church's Simple Theory of Types." *J. Symbolic Logic,* pp. 1269–1291. September 1990.

4. P.R. Halmos, *Naïve Set Theory.* New York: Van Nostrand Rheinhold, 1960.

5. E. Mendelson, *Introduction to Mathematical Logic,* Third Ed. Pacific Grove, CA: Wadsworth and Brooks, 1987.

6. D.L. Parnas, "Tabular Representation of Relations," *CRL Report 260,* McMaster University, TRIO (Telecommunications Research Institute of Ontario), October 1992.

7. D.L. Parnas, G.J.K. Asmis, and J. Madey, "Assessment of Safety-Critical Software in Nuclear Power Plants," *Nuclear Safety,* Vol. 32, no. 2, pp. 189–198. April–June 1991.

8. D.L. Parnas and J. Madey, "Functional Documentation for Computer Systems Engineering (version 2)," *CRL Report 237,* McMaster University, Hamilton, Canada, TRIO (Telecommunications Research Institute of Ontario), September 1991.

9. D.L. Parnas, J. Madey, and M. Iglewski, "Formal Documentation of Well-Structured Programs," *CRL Report 259,* McMaster University, TRIO (Telecommunications Research Institute of Ontario), September 1992.

Acknowledgments

I am grateful to Professors M. Iglewski, J. Madey, A. Kreczmar, W. Lukaszewicz, J. Zucker, P. Gilmore, M. van Emden, J. Ludewig, and Dr. J. McLean for helpful comments on earlier drafts of this paper. Careful reading and provocative remarks by Ramesh Bharadwaj, Philip Kelly, Yabo Wang, and Delbert Yeh were also very helpful. Several of the referees helped me to explain why I chose to add one more paper on this subject to the already immense literature.

Introduction

Joanne Atlee

Dave Parnas is one of the few software engineering researchers whose work focuses on coping with software's essential complexity. He continually reflects on what it means to *engineer* software systems and uses engineering philosophy and principles to guide his research program. He is not interested in shortcuts or quick fixes. His research groups have always taken a principle-centered approach to research: first identifying the fundamental principles behind good software design and engineering, then discovering practices that adhere to the principles, and finally inventing notations and techniques that codify such practices. His work has resulted in substantial and lasting contributions to software engineering.

This paper summarizes the 25-year evolution of one such contribution: "Parnas Tables". The paper begins by arguing that the full power of mathematical relations is needed to represent precisely how a software system or its environment behaves. Because such software relations can be large and discontinuous and because attempts to use conventional relational notations resulted in long parenthetical expressions, Dave and his colleagues experimented with tabular expressions for visualizing relational definitions. One can use a table's rows and columns to separate the relation's definition into cases, where each table entry specifies either the relation's value for some case or a condition that partially identifies some case. Such a format helps the reader to see clearly how various conditions affect the relation's output and helps the writer to ensure that cases don't overlap and that no case is overlooked. The first half of this paper recounts how Parnas Tables evolved through their use in several industrial applications. The second half presents a theory that not only formalizes the semantics of common Parnas Tables but suggests new types that software developers might find useful.

It is equally interesting to treat this paper as a lesson on how to incorporate a new formal method into engineering practice. While other researchers criticize the software industry for not using more formal methods in their development processes, Dave strives to develop mathematical notations and methods that match the needs and expertise of software developers. The history of Parnas Tables epitomizes his views on how mathematical methods for software development should evolve. Notations are invented when new needs that cannot be satisfied by existing methods arise. With repeated use, the notation evolves and matures, becoming simpler over time (rather than monotonically incorporating new features). If the mathematical method is found to be useful, practitioners willingly adopt it. Eventually, researchers formalize the mathematical method into a theory so they can explore its limits and discover new and varied uses. Finally, as the method's use becomes more prevalent, it is incorporated into undergraduate curricula.

So where do Parnas Tables reside in the above method-maturity spectrum? There are some early adopters that use mathematical relations and tabular expressions in practice:

- As noted in this paper, the A-7E experience was "an experiment in programming methods" that used as a case study the software for the U.S. Navy A-7E aircraft (see Paper 6). The software manager for the A-7D aircraft—a U.S. Air Force plane that used the same airframe but had many different weapons and instruments—was so impressed with the tabular specifications that he had his team modify the A-7E document to reflect the A-7D requirements. Thereafter, any change to the A-7D software was first documented as a change to the A-7D specification; the edited pages of the specification were then given to the programmers for them to implement [3].

- Since the Darlington project (described in this paper), Ontario Hydro and Atomic Energy of Canada Limited (AECL) have been incorporating Parnas Tables into their own domain-specific notations, documents, processes, and tools for developing nuclear-related software. The goal is to improve and streamline the software development and inspection processes without sacrificing software safety [2].

- Researchers at the University of British Columbia developed a higher-order-logic variant of Parnas Tables, and they used this notation to formalize and analyze an air traffic control document that specified, in natural language, the separation minima for aircraft flying in the North Atlantic region [1]. After the researchers presented their work, a member of the audience criticized the notation as being too mathematical for air traffic controllers. An air traffic controller who also saw the presentation disagreed, saying that the documents should have been written using tables in the first place.

As further evidence of the maturity of Parnas Tables, Dave's research groups have shown how they can be used in many phases of software development, from specifying system and software behaviour to documenting code fragments to generating test oracles and monitors. They have developed a formal theory that unifies the definitions and semantics of various types of Parnas Tables, thereby enabling the development of support tools. Finally, Parnas Tables are taught in several university software engineering courses and are used extensively in the software engineering program at McMaster University. Thus, while Parnas Tables are not yet in widespread use, they are mature enough to be formulated and packaged for undergraduate education, and students have demonstrated that they can use them effectively.

For more than 30 years, software professionals have dreamed of being able to estimate and control the quality, cost, and time-to-market of software products. There have been attempts to codify developers' expertise into general software-development methods. Unfortunately, most of these methods promote simplistic and undefined modeling notations and analysis techniques and enable developers to avoid grappling with essential details and complexity. At best, they help experienced developers to communicate familiar problems among themselves. But they cannot help even expert designers to understand new problems, and they are worthless when used by practitioners who do not appreciate the principles encoded in the methods. In contrast, Parnas Tables help developers construct and understand realistic descriptions of software systems. Like most of Dave's work, they help the developer manage a software system's essential complexity, instead of merely attacking some of its accidental complexity.

References

1. Nancy A. Day, Jeffrey J. Joyce, and Gerry Pelletier, "Formalization and Analysis of the Separation Minima for Aircraft in the North Atlantic Region", in *LFM97: Fourth NASA Langley Formal Methods Workshop*, NASA Conference Publication 3356, September 1997.

2. P.K. Joannou, J. Harauz, D.R. Tremaine, N. Ichiyen, "The Ontario Hydro/AECL Approach to Real-Time Software Engineering Standards", *Reliability Engineering and System Safety Journal*, Vol 43, No. 2, pp 143–150, 1994.

3. D. Weiss, P. Clements, D. Parnas. Personal communication, July 2000.

Tabular Representations in Relational Documents

Ryszard Janicki, David Lorge Parnas, Jeffery Zucker

4.1 Abstract

In this paper the use of relations, represented as tables, for documenting the requirements and behaviour of software is motivated and explained. A formal model of tabular expressions, defining the meaning of a large class of tabular forms, is presented. Finally, we discuss the transformation of tabular expressions from one form to another and illustrate some useful transformations.

4.2 A Relational Model of Documentation

More than 30 years ago, managers of large software projects began to understand the importance of having precise documentation for software products. The industry was experiencing the frustration of trying to get software to work; most of the many "bugs" that delayed completion and led to unreliable products were caused by misunderstandings that would have been alleviated by better documentation. Since that time, hundreds of "standards" have been proposed; each was intended to improve the consistency, precision, and completeness of natural language documents. In spite of these efforts, documentation is still inadequate. Because of the vagueness and imprecision of natural languages, even the best software documentation is unclear. Because informal documentation cannot be analyzed systematically, it is usually inconsistent and incomplete as well.

Software engineering, like other forms of engineering, can benefit from the use of mathematics. Mathematical notation is commonly used in engineering documents. Only through the use of mathematics can we obtain the precision that we need. In computer science, there has been a great deal of discussion about the use of mathematics to verify the correctness of software. Before program verification becomes practical, the use of mathematics in documentation must be well established. Specifications and design documents state the theorems that should be proven about programs.

The state of the art among software developers is such that there is no agreement on the contents of the various documents. It is quite common to hear developers arguing about whether or not a certain fact should be included in some given document. Often information is included in several documents or not found in any. The first step in using mathematics in this context is to find mathematical definitions of the contents of the documents.

In [13] the contents of a number of standard documents are defined by stating that each document must contain a representation of one or more binary relations. Each relation is a set of pairs. If the document contains enough information to determine whether or not any pair is included in the specified relation, it is complete. No additional information should be included. Below we give two examples of such document definitions, one for a system requirements document, the other for a program specification.

4.2.1 The System Requirements Document

The first step in documenting the requirements of a computer system is the identification of the environmental quantities to be measured or controlled and the association of those quantities with mathematical variables. The environmental quantities include physical properties (such as temperatures and pressures) and the readings on user-visible displays, etc. The association of these quantities with mathematical variables must be carefully defined, and coordinate systems, signs, etc. must be unambiguously stated.

It is useful to characterise each environmental quantity as monitored, controlled, or both. *Monitored* quantities are those that the user wants the system to measure. *Controlled* quantities are those whose values the system is intended to control. For real-time systems, time can be treated as a monitored quantity. We will use m_1, m_2, ..., m_p to denote the monitored quantities, and c_1, c_2, ..., c_q to denote the controlled ones.

Each of these environmental quantities can be considered as a function of time. When we denote a given environmental quantity by v, we will denote the time-function describing its value by v^t. Note that v^t is a function whose domain consists of real numbers; its value at time τ is written "$v^t(\tau)$". The vector of time-functions $(m_1^t, m_2^t, ..., m_p^t)$ containing one element for each of the monitored quantities, will be denoted by "$\underline{m}^t$"; similarly $(c_1^t, c_2^t, ..., c_q^t)$ will be denoted by "$\underline{c}^t$".

A *systems requirements document* should contain representations of two relations. NAT describes the *environment*. REQ describes the effect of the system when it is installed.

4.2.2 The Relation NAT

- Domain(NAT) is a set of vectors of time-functions containing exactly the instances of $\underline{m}^t$ allowed by the environmental constraints,
- Range(NAT) is a set of vectors of time-functions containing exactly the instances of $\underline{c}^t$ allowed by the environmental constraints,
- $(\underline{m}^t, \underline{c}^t) \in$ NAT if and only if the environmental constraints allow the controlled quantities to take on the values described by $\underline{c}^t$, if the values of the monitored quantities are described by $\underline{m}^t$.

4.2.3 The Relation REQ

- Domain(REQ) is a set of vectors of time-functions containing those instances of $\underline{m}^t$ allowed by environmental constraints,
- Range(REQ) is a set of vectors of time-functions containing only those instances of $\underline{c}^t$ considered permissible, i.e., values that would be allowed by a correctly functioning system.
- $(\underline{m}^t, \underline{c}^t) \in$ REQ if and only if the computer system should permit the controlled quantities to take on the values described by $\underline{c}^t$ when the values of the monitored quantities are described by $\underline{m}^t$.

NAT and REQ are used to guide the programmers, inspectors, and testers.

4.2.4 Program Descriptions

We use the term *program* to denote a text describing a set of state sequences in a digital (finite state) machine. Each of those state sequences will be called an *execution* of the program. Often, we do not want to document the intermediate states in the sequence. For each starting state, *s*, we want to know only:

1. Is termination possible, i.e., are there finite executions beginning in *s*?
2. Is termination guaranteed, i.e., are all executions that begin in *s* finite?
3. If termination is possible, what are the possible final states?

This information can be described by an LD-relation [8, 11]. An LD-relation comprises a relation and a subset of the domain of that relation, called the *competence set*. The competence set, in a description of a program, is the set of starting states for which termination is guaranteed. (This is sometimes called the "safe set" for that program or the initial part.) The set of starting states for which termination is possible is the domain of the relation. An ordered pair (*x,y*) is in the relation if it is possible that the program's execution would terminate in state *y* after being started in state *x*.

4.3 Industrial Experience with Relational Documentation

The need for relational documentation and tabular representations became apparent in attempts to apply the ideas above to describe programs that were in use in military and civilian applications. We now describe three of those experiences.

4.3.1 The A-7 Experience

An early version of this relational requirements model was used in 1977 at the U.S. Naval Research Laboratory to write a software requirements document for the Onboard Flight Program used in the U.S. Navy's carrier-based attack aircraft, the A-7E. The software was being redesigned as an experiment on programming methods, but the design team was inexperienced in that application area. They set out to produce a document that could be used as the exclusive source of information for programmers. At the same time, it was essential that the document could be carefully reviewed by people who understood the requirements, i.e., pilots. This document was reviewed by pilots (who found hundreds of detail errors in the first versions) and then guided the programmers for several years. A description of the A-7 requirements document (with samples) can be found in [3]; the complete document was published as [4]. It has been used as a model for many other requirements documents (cf. [5, 12]). Further discussion of requirements documents can be found in [17].

4.3.2 The Darlington Experience

The relational requirements model and the program documentation model were used in a multimillion dollar effort to inspect safety-critical programs for the Darlington Nuclear Power Generating Station in Ontario, Canada. A relational requirements document, modeled on the A-7 document [4], was written by one group after the English document was shown to have dangerous ambiguities. A second group wrote relational descriptions of the programs. The third group compared the two descriptions. A fourth group audited the process. In all, some 60 people were involved. Although the code had been under test for six years, numerous discrepancies were found and many had to be corrected. This experience is discussed in more detail in [10, 12].

4.3.3 The Bell Labs (Columbus, Ohio) Experience

An earlier experience with relational documentation is reported in [5]. In this experience, the time invested in producing a precise statement of the requirements was paid back when the system received its first on-site test. The test period was the shortest in the lab's history because most of the misunderstandings that usually become apparent during testing had been eliminated when the relational requirements document was reviewed. Another unique characteristic of this project was the use of the formal mathematical documentation in preparing informal user documentation. It was found that the informal documentation could imitate the structure of the formal documentation and that its quality was greatly enhanced by basing it on the formal document.

4.4 Why Use Tabular Representations of Relations?

In all of these experiences, we found that conventional mathematical expressions describing the relations were too complex and hard to parse to be really useful. Instead, we began to use two-dimensional expressions, which we call *tables*. Each table is a set of cells that can contain other expressions, including tabular ones.

No single notation is well suited for describing all mathematical functions and relations. The history of mathematics and engineering shows clearly that when we become interested in a new class of functions, we also invent new notations that are well suited for describing functions in that class. The functions that arise in the description of computer systems have two important characteristics. First, digital technology allows us to implement functions that have many discontinuities, which can occur at arbitrary points in the domain of the function. Unlike the designers of analogue systems, we are not constrained to implement functions that are either continuous or exhibit exploitable regularity in their discontinuities. Second, the range and domain of these functions are often tuples whose elements are of distinct types; the values cannot be described in terms of a typical element. The use of traditional mathematical notation, developed for functions that do not have these characteristics, often results in function descriptions that are complex, lengthy, and hard to read. As a consequence of this complexity, mathematical specifications are often incorrect, and, even more often, misunderstood. This has led many people to conclude that it is not practical to provide precise mathematical descriptions of computer systems. However, our experience shows that the use of tabular representations makes the use of mathematics in these applications practical.

4.4.1 Discovering the First Tables

The need for new notation for software documentation first became apparent when producing the requirements document for the A-7. Attempts to write the descriptions in English were soon abandoned because we realized that our turgid prose was no better than that of others. Attempts to write mathematical formulae were abandoned because they quickly developed into parentheses-counting nightmares. We tried using the notations that are commonly used in hardware design, but found that they would be too large in this application. The present table types evolved to meet specific needs. In this work, the tables were used in an ad hoc manner, i.e., without formal definition.

4.4.2 Use of Program Function Tables at Darlington

In the Darlington experience, the requirements document was prepared using the notation developed in the A-7 project. However, for this experience, it was necessary to describe the code. New table formats were introduced for this purpose. Once more the tables were used without formal definition. This time, the lack of formal definition caused some problems. During the inspection process heated discussions showed that some of the tables had more than one possible interpretation. This led to a decision to introduce formal definitions for the tables, but this work had to be postponed until the inspection was completed. The first attempt to formalize the meaning of tabular expressions was [9].

4.4.3 Why We Need More Than One Type of Table

The initial experience with tables on the A-7 went smoothly for a few weeks. Then we encountered an example that would not fit on one piece of paper. In fact, there were so many different cases that we used four large pieces of paper, taped to four physical tables, to represent one table. In examining this monster, we found that although there were many cases to consider, there were only a few distinct expressions that appeared in the table. This led us to invent a new form of table ("inverted tables") that represented the same information more compactly. The various types of tables will be discussed more extensively in later sections.

4.4.4 Tables Help in Thinking

To people working in theoretical computer science or mathematics, the use of tabular representations seems a minor matter. It is fairly easy to see that the use of tabular representations does not extend the expressive power of the notation. Questions of decidability and computational complexity are not affected by the use of this notation.

However, our experience on a variety of projects has shown that the use of this notation makes a big difference in practice. When someone sets out to document a program, particularly when one sets out to document requirements of a program that has not yet been written, they often do not know what they are about to write down. Writing, understanding, and discovery go on at the same time. Document authors must identify the cases that can arise and consider what should be done one case at a time. If the program controls the values of many variables of different types, they will want to think about each of those variables separately. They may have to consult with users, or their representatives, to find out what should be done in each case. Tabular notations are of great help in situations like this. One first determines the structure of the table, making sure that the headers cover all possible cases, then turns one's attention to completing the individual entries in the table. The task may extend over weeks or months; the use of the tabular format helps to make sure that no cases get forgotten.

4.4.5 "Divide and Conquer"—How Tables Help in Inspection

Tabular notations have also proven to be of great help in the inspection of programs. Someone reviewing a program will have to make sure that it does the right thing in a variety of situations. It is extremely easy to overlook the same cases that the designers failed to consider. Moreover, the inspection task is often conducted in open review meetings and stretch over many days. Breaks must be taken, and it is easy to "lose your place" when there is a pause in the middle of considering a program.

In the Darlington inspection, the tables played a significant role in overcoming these problems. Inspectors followed a rigid procedure. First, they made sure that the set of columns was complete and that no case was included in two columns. Second, they made sure that the set of rows was complete and that there were no duplications or overlaps. Then we began to consider the table column by column proceeding sequentially down the rows. A break could be taken at the end of any entry's consideration; a simple marker told us where to begin when we returned. For a task that took many weeks, the structure provided by the tabular notation was essential.

4.5 Formalisation of a Wide Class of Tables

The industrial applications of tabular expressions were conducted on an ad hoc basis, i.e., without formal syntax or semantics. New types of tables were invented when needed and the semantics was intuitive. The first formal syntax and semantics of tabular expressions (or simply tables) was proposed in [9]. Several different classes of tables, all invented for a specific practical application, were defined and for each class a separate semantics was provided. A different approach was proposed in [7]. Instead of many different classes and separate semantics, one general model was presented. The model covered all table classes in [9] as well as some new classes that had not been considered before. The new model followed from the topology of an abstract entity called "table", and per se, was application independent. In this section we will present the basic concepts of this model using very simple examples. For more interesting examples, the reader is referred to [13]. We shall not, here, make a distinction between relations and functions, as we view functions as a special case of relations. (However, in those cases where our relations are, in fact, functions, we shall generally use functional notation.)

Let us consider the two following definitions of functions, $f(x,y)$ and $g(x,y)$.

$$f(x, y) = \begin{cases} 0 & \text{if } x \geq 0 \wedge y = 10 \\ x & \text{if } x < 0 \wedge y = 10 \\ y^2 & \text{if } x \geq 0 \wedge y > 10 \\ -y^2 & \text{if } x \geq 0 \wedge y < 10 \\ x+y & \text{if } x < 0 \wedge y > 10 \\ x-y & \text{if } x < 0 \wedge y < 10 \end{cases}$$

$$g(x, y) = \begin{cases} x+y & \text{if } (x < 0 \wedge y \geq 0) \vee (x < y \wedge y < 0) \\ x-y & \text{if } (0 \leq x < y \wedge y \geq 0) \vee (y \leq x < 0 \wedge y < 0) \\ y-x & \text{if } (x \geq y \wedge y \geq 0) \vee (x \geq 0 \wedge y < 0) \end{cases}$$

If we were to describe $f(x,y)$ using classical predicate logic, we would write an expression like:

$$(\forall x, (\forall y, ((x \geq 0 \wedge y = 10) \rightarrow f(x, y) = 0) \wedge ((x < 0 \wedge y = 10) \rightarrow f(x, y) = x) \wedge$$
$$((x \geq 0 \wedge y > 10) \rightarrow f(x, y) = y^2) \wedge ((x \geq 0 \wedge y < 10) \rightarrow f(x, y) = -y^2) \wedge$$
$$((x < 0 \wedge y > 10) \rightarrow f(x, y) = x + y) \wedge ((x < 0 \wedge y < 10) \rightarrow f(x,y) = x - y)))).$$

Such classical mathematical notation is not very readable, even though the functions are very simple ones. The description becomes much more readable when tabular notation, even without a formal semantics, is used (see Figures 4.1 and 4.2).

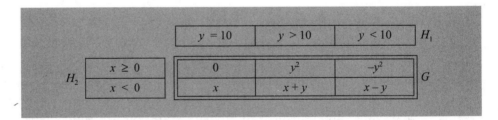

H_2		$y = 10$	$y > 10$	$y < 10$	H_1
	$x \geq 0$	0	y^2	$-y^2$	G
	$x < 0$	x	$x+y$	$x-y$	

Figure 4.1 *A (normal) table defining f.*

H_2		$x + y$	$x - y$	$y - x$	H_1
	$y \geq 0$	$x < 0$	$0 \leq x < y$	$x \geq y$	G
	$y < 0$	$x < y$	$y \leq x < 0$	$x \geq 0$	

Figure 4.2 *An (inverted) table defining g.*

We must now compare these two examples. What are the differences and similarities between the two tables? They both have the same *raw skeleton,* as illustrated in Figure 4.3, which in both cases consists of two *headers,* H_1 and H_2, and the grid, G. However, in Figure 4.1 the formulae giving the final value is in the main grid, while in Figure 4.2 the final formula to be evaluated is in header H_1.

Formally, a *header* is an indexed set of cells, say $H = \{h_i | i \in I\}$, where $I = \{1, 2, ..., k\}$ (for some k) is an index set. We treat *cell* as a primitive concept that does not need to be explained. A grid G indexed by headers $H_1, \cdots, H_n$, with $H_j = \{h_i^j | i \in I^j\}$, $j = 1, \cdots, n$, is an indexed set of cells G, where $G = \{g_\alpha | \alpha \in I\}$, and $I = I^1 \times \cdots \times I^n$. The set I is the index set of G. A *raw table skeleton* is a collection of headers plus a grid indexed by this collection.

The first step in expressing the semantic difference between the two types of tables is to define the *Cell Connection Graph* (CCG in short), which characterises *information flow* ("where do I start reading the table and where do I get my result?"). A CCG is a *relation* that could be interpreted as an *acyclic directed graph* with the grid and all headers as the nodes. The only requirement is that *each arc must either start from or end at the grid G*. There are four different types of CCGs. They are all illustrated in Figure 4.4 for $n = 3$. When the number of headers is smaller than 3, type 3 disappears. Type 1 is called *normal,* and type 2 is called *inverted.* These are the two most popular types in practice. The CCG divides the cells into relation cells and predicate cells. A cell is a *relation cell* if no arc starts from it, otherwise it is a *predicate cell.* In Figure 4.4 (as well as in Figure 4.1) all relation cells are represented by double boxes. Headers and a grid, together with a CCG graph, define a *medium table skeleton.* Each predicate cell defines the domain of a subset of the relation defined; the relation cells define possible values within each domain. However, we *still* do not have enough semantics. How do we determine the domain and values? Let us take the upper table

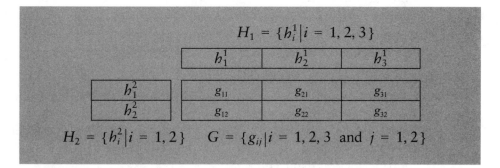

Figure 4.3 *A raw table skeleton of tables from Fig. 4.1 and Fig. 4.2.*

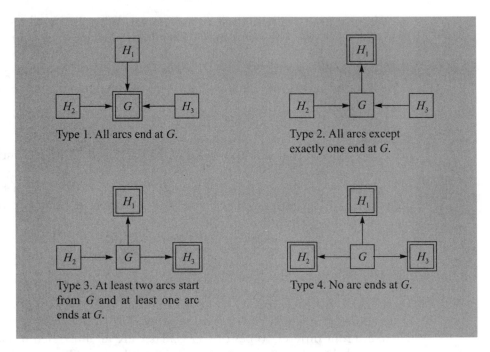

Figure 4.4 *Four different types of cell connection graphs.*

from Figure 4.3, and the cells h_1^1, h_1^2, g_{11}. If this table represents the function $f(x, y)$, then the CCG (together with the contents of the cells) restricted to these cells should represent the expression $(x \geq 0 \wedge y = 10) \Rightarrow f(x, y) = 0$. But why $(x \geq 0 \wedge y = 10)$? Why not, for example, $(x \geq 0 \vee y = 10)$, or $(\neg(x < 0 \vee y = 10))$, etc.?

There is no explicit information in the table that indicates conjunction. A medium table skeleton does not provide any information on how the domain and values of the relation (function) specified are determined; such information must be added. The domain is determined by a *table predicate rule*, P_T, and the value is determined by a *table relation rule*, r_T. A medium table skeleton together with table predicate and relation rules is called a *well-done table skeleton*. Figure 4.5 illustrates two well-done table skeletons. The left-hand one is of type 1, the domain is defined as the conjunction of the predicates contained in appropriate cells of the headers H_1 and H_2, while the value is defined just by an expression held in the appropriate cell of the grid G. The right-hand one is of type 4; the domain is defined by the predicate held in the appropriate cell of the grid G, while the value of the defined relation is the set union of the relations defined by appropriate expressions held in the headers H_1 and H_2.

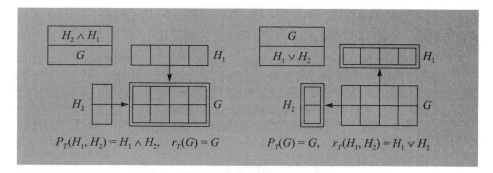

Figure 4.5 *Two examples of well-done table skeletons.*

To get the *full tabular expression* we need to enrich a well-done table skeleton by a mapping which assigns a predicate expression to each predicate cell, and a relation expression to each relation cell. Figures 4.6 and 4.7 show tabular expressions describing the functions *f* and *g*.

Summing up, the indexing scheme determines a *raw table skeleton*, where a table is a set of sets of cells. The *cell connection graph* shows "information flow". A *table predicate rule* and a *table relation rule* provide the remaining information.

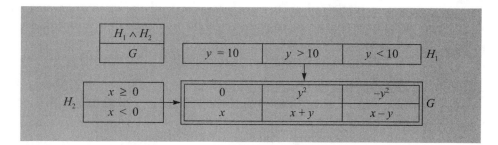

Figure 4.6 *A tabular expression describing the function f.*

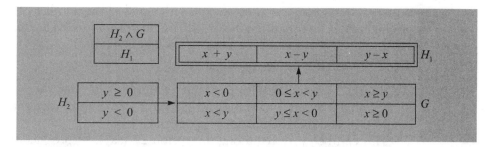

Figure 4.7 *A tabular expression describing the function g.*

4.6 Transformations of Tables of One Kind to Another

As we have seen above, many kinds of tables have been found to be useful. Many questions arise naturally: Given a function, what is the best kind of table to represent it? Given two tables (of the same or different kinds), can we see whether they define the same function? Can we (or under what conditions can we) perform certain useful manipulations on tables, such as transforming a table to a "simplest" form of the same kind, or transforming one kind of table to another?

These questions are the subject of ongoing research by the authors and their collaborators at McMaster University (Hamilton, Ontario, Canada). The present section focuses on the last question, on which significant progress has been made [16, 19]. We consider two of the kinds of tables discussed above, namely *normal function tables* and *inverted function tables*, with conjunction as the predicate rule. (We also revert from the relational to the functional formalism.)

We study various methods for effectively transforming one kind of table to the other. This section gives an informal overview; see also [19].

We are interested in transforming tables to other, semantically equivalent tables, which may be easier to work with. We will consider transformations φ of tables from one kind to another, which satisfy the following two properties: (i) φ is semantics preserving, and (ii) φ is computable. We will consider three examples of such transformations: *changing the dimensionality* of a table, *inverting* a normal table, and *normalizing* an inverted table.

4.6.1 Changing the Dimensionality of a Table

Note first that any n-dimensional (normal or inverted) table can be trivially transformed to an $(n + 1)$-dimensional table, by adding an $(n + 1)^{\text{th}}$ coordinate header with a single entry, "true".

More interestingly; given an n-dimensional table, we can transform it to an $(n - 1)$-dimensional table, by "combining" two of the dimensions, i.e., combining two of the headers into a single header.

By iterating this procedure, we can transform any table to a 1-dimensional table—albeit very long (with length equal to the number of cells in the original table), so that the value of such a transformation in general is unclear.

4.6.2 Inverting a Normal Table

We illustrate inversion with a simple example. Consider the case of a 2-dimensional 3×3 normal table, as in Figure 4.8. (The header entries c_i are conditions, and the grid entries t_i^j are terms.)

This can be "inverted along dimension 2" (say), to produce the table in Figure 4.9.

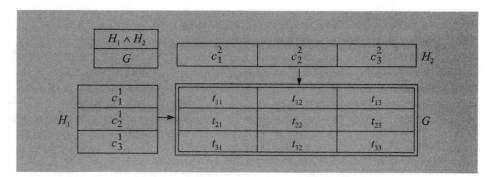

Figure 4.8 *A two-dimensional 3×3 normal table.*

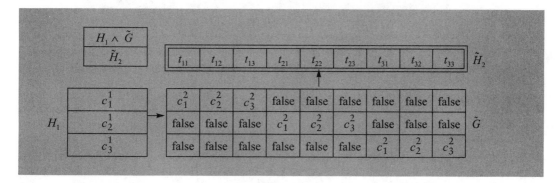

Figure 4.9 *Inversion of the table in Figure 4.8.*

In general, a normal table can be inverted along any dimension k to produce an inverted table with value header $\tilde{H}_k$, and the other headers unchanged. The practical value of this transformation is, however, dubious, since the new table is much bigger than the original. (The length of the value header in the new table is equal to the number of cells in the original table!)

In [19] a second method for inversion is also considered, which leads to better (i.e., smaller) inverted tables assuming there are not many distinct terms.

4.6.3 Normalising an Inverted Table

Here the situation is less satisfactory. We can transform an inverted table to a 1-dimensional normal one, but not (in general) to a many-dimensional one (apart from the trivial many-dimensional version of a 1-dimensional table described in Section 4.5). As a simple example, consider the 2-dimensional 2 $\times$ 3 inverted table T shown in Figure 4.10, with value header H_2.

Figure 4.10 can be normalised "along dimension 2" to a 1-dimensional table as shown in Figure 4.11. Note that the header of the transformed table

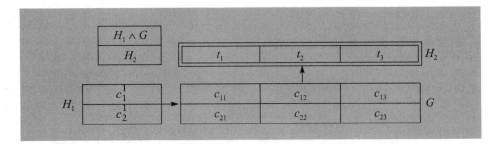

Figure 4.10 *Two-dimensional inverted table.*

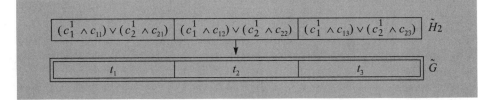

Figure 4.11 *Normalisation of the table in Figure 4.10.*

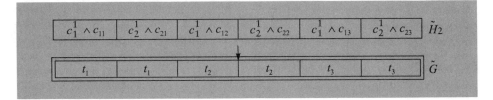

Figure 4.12 *Another normalisation of the table in Figure 4.10.*

of Figure 4.11 has the same length as H_2, but the conditions in this header are quite complicated. We can, however, effect a trade-off between complexity of conditions and header length by "splitting" disjunctions, as in Figure 4.12.

Another (more complex) normalisation algorithm for inverted tables, which preserves dimensionality, was reported in [16].

4.6.4 Interrelationship Between Transformations

We can find a connection between the three types of transformation considered above (changing dimensionality, inverting, and normalising), as follows. First we need some definitions.

An *elementary transformation* is any one of the following operations: permuting components of a conjunction or disjunction (in a cell), distributing a conjunction over a disjunction, simplifying conditions '$c \wedge$ **false**' to '**false**' and '$c \vee$ **false**' to 'c', repeating rows by "splitting disjunctions," permuting rows, and deleting rows with '**false**' in the header. (Note that by "rows" we mean rows in any dimension, i.e., rows or columns for two-dimensional tables.) *Elementary equivalence* of tables is the equivalence relation generated by the class of elementary transformations.

Theorem 4.5.1 (*See* [19])

i. If T is a normal table, then the result of an inversion of T followed by a normalisation is elementarily equivalent to the 1-dimensional transform of T.

ii. If T is an inverted table, then the result of a normalisation of T followed by an inversion is elementarily equivalent to the 1-dimensional transform of T.

4.7 Conclusions

During the practical work discussed earlier, it became clear that working with tabular relational documents was often dull, mechanical, and exacting. The work discussed in this paper provides the basis for tools to assist people when using these notations. We are now engaged in a project to produce a set of prototype tools. The kernel of our system is a "table holder" that creates objects representing uninterpreted tables. Other programs can use this kernel to store and communicate tabular expressions. The tables are stored as abstract data structures and without formatting information.

Separate tools will assist a user to create tables, which are stored in table-holder objects, and to print tables. The printing tool is designed for use by people who do not necessarily understand the expressions. Although the operator of this tool has control over the appearance of the table when printed, the contents cannot be changed by this tool. We are also designing tools to perform basic checks on tabular expressions.

A tool for evaluating and simplifying tabular expressions is being designed. We are also studying the problem of finding a tabular representation of the composition of two relations represented by given tables.

A tool that generates test oracles from tabular program specifications has been produced [15]. The transformation algorithms discussed above have been implemented [16] to provide a prototype tool that assists designers in transforming tables. Much work remains to be done in finding transformation algorithms which are simple and also produce compact transformed tables.

Related work is going on at the University of Quebec (Hull) [1, 2], Warsaw University [6], and Swansea University [18].

We believe that the idea of tabular representations of relations is an area deserving attention from both theoretical and practical computer specialists. Although tabular notations were useful before they were formalised [4, 10], the formalisation discussed in this paper has eliminated misunderstandings and made tools possible.

References

1. J. Bojanowski, M. Iglewski, J. Madey, A. Obaid, "Functional Approach to Protocols Specification", *Proceedings of the 14th International IFIP Symposium on Protocol Specification, Testing and Verification,* PSTV'94, Vancouver, B.C., 7–10 June 1994, pp. 371–378.

2. B. Desrosiers, M. Iglewski, A. Obaid, "Utilisation de la methode de traces pour la definition fromelle d'un protocole de communication", *Electronic Journal on Networks and Distributed Processing,* No. 2, September 1995, pp. 57–73.

3. K.L. Heninger, "Specifying Software Requirements for Complex Systems: New Techniques and Their Application", *IEEE Transactions Software Engineering,* Vol. SE-6, No. 1, January 1980, pp. 2–13.

4. K.L. Heninger, J. Kallander, D.L. Parnas, J.E. Shore, "Software Requirements for the A-7E Aircraft", *NRL Memorandum Report 3876,* United States Naval Research Laboratory, Washington DC, November 1978.

5. S.D. Hester, D.L. Parnas, D.F. Utter, "Using Documentation as a Software Design Medium", *Bell System Technical Journal,* Vol. 60, No. 8, October 1981, pp. 1941–1977.

6. M. Iglewski, J. Madey, "Software Engineering Issues Emerged from Critical Control Applications", *IFAC Workshop on Safety and Reliability in Emerging Control Technologies,* Daytona Beach, Florida, USA, 1–3 November 1995. To be published in conference proceedings by Pergamon–Elsevier Science.

7. R. Janicki, "Towards a Formal Semantics of Parnas Tables", *Proceedings of the 17th International Conference on Software Engineering,* Seattle, WA, 1995, pp. 231–240.

8. D.L. Parnas, "A Generalized Control Structure and Its Formal Definition", *Communications of the ACM,* Vol. 26, No. 8, August 1983, pp. 572–581.

9. D.L. Parnas, "Tabular Representation of Relations", *CRL Report 260,* Mc-Master University, Communications Research Laboratory, TRIO (Telecommunications Research Institute of Ontario), October 1992.

10. D.L. Parnas, "Inspection of Safety Critical Software Using Function Tables", *Proceedings of IFIP World Congress 1994, Volume III,* August 1994, pp. 270–277.

11. D.L. Parnas, "Mathematical Descriptions and Specification of Software", *Proceedings of IFIP World Congress 1994, Volume I,* August 1994, pp. 354–359.

12. D.L. Parnas, G.J.K. Asmis, J. Madey, "Assessment of Safety-Critical Software in Nuclear Power Plants", *Nuclear Safety,* Vol. 32, No. 2, 1991, pp. 189–198.

13. D.L. Parnas, J. Madey, "Functional Documentation for Computer Systems Engineering (Version 2)", *CRL Report 237,* McMaster University, TRIO (Telecommunications Research Institute of Ontario), September 1991. To be published in *Science of Computer Programming* (Elsevier) *25* (1995), pp. 41–61.

14. D.L. Parnas, J. Madey, M. Iglewski, "Precise Documentation of Well-Structured Programs", *IEEE Transactions on Software Engineering,* Vol. 20, No. 12, December 1994, pp. 948–976.

15. D. Peters, D.L. Parnas, "Generating a Test Oracle from Program Documentation", *Proceedings of the 1994 International Symposium on Software Testing and Analysis (ISSTA),* August 17–19, 1994, pp. 58–65.

16. H. Shen, "Implementation of Table Inversion Algorithms", M. Eng thesis, McMaster University, Communications Research Laboratory, December 1995.

17. A.J. van Schouwen, D.L. Parnas, J. Madey, "Documentation of Requirements for Computer Systems", *Proceedings of '93 IEEE International Symposium on Requirements Engineering,* San Diego, CA, 4–6 January 1993, pp. 198–207.

18. A.J. Wilder and J.V. Tucker, "System Documentation Using Tables—A Short Course", *CRL Report 306,* McMaster University, Communications Research Laboratory, TRIO (Telecommunications Research Institute of Ontario), May 1992. Also published as *Report CSR 11-95,* Computer Science Department, University of Wales, Swansea, 1995.

19. J.I. Zucker, "Transformations of Normal and Inverted Function Tables", *Formal Aspects of Computing,* Vol. 8, 1996, pp. 679–705.

Introduction

Ali Mili

1. Maintaining Perspective

At the end of the twelfth century A.D., the Moroccan-born Jewish mathematician and medical scholar Al Samawal Ibn Yahya Ibn Yahuda Al Maghribi wrote a book in Arabic titled *Al Qiwami fil Hisab al Hindi*, in which he gives an algorithm for the extraction of the fifth root of a fraction written in base 60. This work highlights three premises that epitomize twelfth century mathematics perhaps as much as today's software engineering research:

- *The algorithm is rather complex and requires a great deal of ingenuity on the part of its designer.* It takes a great deal of ingenuity to derive the fifth root algorithm by analogy with the second root and third root algorithms, which is how the fifth root algorithm seems to have been derived. Al Samawal seems to have had some empirical understanding of the main rationale of the algorithm (the binomial formula of $(a + b)^5$), but this was neither clearly formulated nor codified; also, while the binomial formula is necessary to understand the algorithm, it is not sufficient. The stepwise extraction of the consecutive digits of the root are modeled as the resolution of a sequence of equations [1]. This is further complicated by the use of base 60 and by the fact that the algorithm applies to fractions rather than integers.

- *Much of the complexity stems from a lack of perspective, rather than intrinsic complexity of the problem.* The use of the sexagesimal notation, the need for a separate algorithm for fractions, and the assignment of different meanings to the various digits of a fraction (discussed below), are all due to a single premise: As ingenious as they were, mathematicians of the period had failed to see that the decimal expansion of the fractional part of a number is a mere extension of the decimal representation of its integer part. As a result, they treated the integer parts and fractional parts separately, and they introduced the sexagesimal numeration for its convenience to represent fractions.

- *Some modeling conventions of the time made it virtually impossible to gain the necessary perspective.* The different positions in the fraction are interpreted to represent different units of angular measurement (degrees, minutes, seconds, . . .); this makes it even harder for the mathematician to discover, as the various digits are not seen to represent distinct orders of magnitude of the same number, but quite distinct quantities altogether. In particular, this places the focus of the algorithm on (sexagesimal) digits, rather than on whole numbers.

The situation that Dave laments in this paper is similar to that which prevailed at the time of Al Samawal: *There is no shortage of ingenuity, but there is a shortage of perspective*. Then, as now, talented scholars grappled with seemingly insurmountable problems; then, as now, they had to resort to complex, convoluted solutions; then, perhaps as now, their brave efforts yielded only small advances because they lacked perspective and were, in effect, solving the wrong problems. Work such as Dave's, questioning as it does widely held beliefs and attitudes, is most likely to enhance our perspective and reorient our efforts toward more fruitful pursuits.

2. On the Role of Documentation

In this paper, Dave argues that, while many researchers focus on the problem of program proofs, the bottleneck in today's practice is not the lack of proof methods, but rather the lack of precise methods to document programs. Further, he downplays the language aspects of this issue, arguing that the main issue in program documentation is *what* information to represent about a program, not *how* to represent it. To this effect, he introduces and contrasts four terms: *description, specification, model,* and *prototype*; then he focuses on the first two, whereby *description* characterizes what a program does, and *specification* characterizes what a program is required to do. Orthogonally to the distinction *description vs. specification*, Dave introduces the distinction *constructive vs. behavioral*, which distinguishes between a focus on structural properties (constructive) and a focus on functional properties (behavioral). He offers LD-relations (*limited-domain relations*) as a tool for representing behavioral descriptions and behavioral specifications. A limited domain relation is defined by a binary relation and a subset of its domain, called the *competence set*. Limited domain relations support the representation of nondeterministic descriptions and specifications, and their algebra supports the interpretation of description and specification compositions.

3. Historical Context

The field of software engineering research has always been prone to fads; this may be added to the wide range of paradoxes that characterize this field and distinguish it from more traditional engineering disciplines. In 1983, when Dave first introduced LD-relations, we were in the tail end of the *structured* wave, where prefixing the qualifier *structured* to your favorite idea (structured programming, structured design, structured analysis) greatly enhanced its chances of being funded and published. We have gone through two more fads since then, labeled respectively *knowledge-based* and *object-oriented*. It is refreshing to see prominent researchers remain on message and resist the temptation to join the latest fad. If nothing else, this reflects the recognition that because the promises that were touted for the *structured* wave, for example, were never fulfilled; the problems that were raised remain relevant. This also reflects a healthy, realistic attitude toward the potential of new research ideas: The discipline will most likely evolve through long-term, focused, painstaking effort, rather than through revolutionary changes. Speaking about software reuse, P. Bassett [2] characterizes this contrast in the following terms: "Software reuse is not a magic weight-loss pill. It is a diet and exercise program". Hearing all the claims made about the benefits of the latest wave (*Object-Oriented Programming*), one may be forgiven for losing sight of this simple premise.

By reiterating, in 1997, the premise that LD-relations were a viable tool for the documentation of programs, Dave made two statements, which were made all the more convincing by fourteen years of hindsight:

- *LD-relations are adequately expressive.* In the fourteen years that have elapsed since he first introduced LD-relations, Dave found them to be sufficiently powerful to deal with the variety of situations that he encountered.

- *LD-relations are adequately scalable.* After experimenting with LD-relations for so long, he has found them to be simple enough to scale up to nontrivial applications.

All the researchers that use similar models (focused on simplicity) will find the endorsement invaluable.

References

1. R. Rashed. L'extraction de la racine nieme et l'invention des fractions decimales (xieme-xiieme siecles). *Archive for the History of Exact Sciences*, 18:191–244, 1978.

2. P. Bassett. Keynote Talk: Software Reuse—Experience from the Field. In *Proceedings of the Symposium on Software Reuse*, M.T. Harandi, editor, Boston, MA, May 1997.

Precise Description and Specification of Software

D.L. Parnas

5.1 Abstract

Precise descriptions and specifications of software products can be very useful if they are simpler than the products that they describe. No new mathematical concepts are needed for this task; we can use old math in new ways. This paper discusses the difference between descriptions of programs, specifications of programs, and models of programs, suggesting that these important distinctions are being neglected by the "formal methods" community. We also discuss the distinction between programs, modules, objects, and real-time systems and the descriptive methods appropriate to each.

5.2 On Foundational Research

As an engineer, I recognize the importance of having a solid foundation for practical work and note with dismay that most software developers work in an ad hoc way, without solid foundations. At the same time, I harbor great doubts about the directions taken by foundation research in general and formal methods research in particular.

An analogy[1] may be the best way to illustrate these doubts. Suppose that we wish to erect a house in a marsh; we need a foundation. One approach would be to wade around in the marsh until we stumble over some solid rocks. An alternative would be to sketch the shape of the house we wish to build and then look for ways to erect foundations where they are needed for the house. Often it seems to me that computer scientists swarm around the solid rocks in the marsh without asking if these are in the appropriate places for the structures that they are trying to erect.

In formal methods, we see many researchers focusing on the problems of proof. While nobody can deny the attractiveness of the idea of program verification, examination of the needs of practitioners reveals that, in most cases, there are interesting research problems that must be solved before formal program verification could be of any help at all. For example, until we can write mathematical descriptions of program requirements that can easily be

---

1. The analogy is due to Professor Donald Loveland, logician and computer scientist.

read by those who know the requirements, proof will be of little value. We would end up proving the wrong theorems.

Denotational semantics of programming languages is another area where we see swarms of academic researchers trying to sharpen a "rock" that is in the wrong place. Rather than solve the problem of defining the semantics of languages that developers find useful, they work on the definition of languages whose semantics are easier to define. Although this work is interesting and potentially useful, it has resulted in a growing gap between theory and practice.

Although this paper discusses the problem of mathematical description of software, it is neither about verification nor about language semantics. We focus on the very practical problem of documenting programs. Rather than present a set of axioms for a programming language fragment, we assume that the programmer understands the available tools and ask how a creator's understanding of a program can best be recorded for future use. Rather than concern ourselves with formal proof, the problem for the next century, we ask only how program documentation can be organized so that it facilitates systematic inspection of programs.

Our goal is to be able to write program documentation that is sufficiently complete and precise that programmers can use the programs on the basis of the documentation alone, i.e., without needing to read the code itself. Of course, the descriptions we produce must be easier to read than the programs; otherwise the documentation will not be used. We also want to be able to describe requirements for programs that have yet to be written and to do so without unnecessarily restricting the set of acceptable solutions.

5.3 Language Is Not the Issue

Discussions of mathematical methods for software developers have a tendency to degenerate into discussions of specification languages. Language is not the issue that needs to be discussed first. In fact, the use of the term "language" seems to be something that has seriously misled our field. A *language* is a set of signals, symbols and conventions for formulating, communicating, and recording facts, or ideas, about the world, between people. Algol-60 was originally intended to fit this definition, but things like FORTRAN, C, Modula, and ADA have another purpose. They are the input to program generation tools, not conventions for discussing the world. Natural languages grow by an exception handling process; we add features when we need them. Program construction tools should not grow that way. Restrictions must be removed before features are added. Current computer "languages" have grown like natural languages and we suffer for it. The so-called "specification languages" seem to grow the same way.

Before we talk about language or notation, it is essential to agree on the information that should be presented in our documents. Once we have done that, we can turn our attention to the relatively simple issues of notation.

The use of the term "language" has led computer scientists to discuss "semantics." I find it useful to note that electrical engineers do not use that term to explain their use of differential equations in the analysis of circuits. They recognize that the equations are simply abstract descriptions of physical objects. Rather than talk about semantics, in this paper we try to show how mathematics can be used to describe programs in the same way that differential equations can describe a large class of circuits.

Just as engineers have long recognized that it takes several drawings to describe their products, we recognize that we will not seek complete descriptions of programs. Instead we shall look at a set of partial descriptions, each showing one aspect or view of the programs.

5.4 A Polemic About Four Words

Engineers distinguish between *descriptions*, *specifications*, *models*, and *prototypes* of their products.

- A *description* is a statement of some of the *actual* attributes of a product, or a set of products. A description is considered faulty if it contains information that is not true of the actual product.

- A *specification* is a statement of some of the properties *required* of a product, or a set of products. A product is considered faulty if the statements made in its specification are not true of that product.

- A *model* is a simplified or reduced size version of a product. Models have some, but not all, of the properties of the "real product" and are used because they are easier to study than the actual product. Discrepancies between models and products are normal and neither the model nor the product is necessarily faulty. The relation of the model to the product, i.e., which properties of the model are also properties of the product must be clearly stated; otherwise the model may be misused.

- A *prototype* is an early (often the first), full-scale version of a product. A prototype can actually be used to perform the functions that the future (production version) product will be intended to perform. Prototypes, unlike models, are expected to have *all* the essential properties of the real product.

We often speak of "mathematical models," which are not actually models in the sense described above. *Mathematical models* are sets of mathematical equations or axioms that are simplified descriptions of a mechanism that might be present in a system or product. Like models and prototypes, mathematical models can be used to predict the behavior of a proposed product. Like physical models, they have some properties of the actual product but may not be completely accurate. With the aid of an interpreter (usually a computer, but possibly a human), mathematical models may be used as models. Mathematical models may also be used to construct physical models, for example, using analog computing techniques.

A description may include attributes that are not required, i.e., incidental properties. For example, a description of a program may include the number of ones in its binary representation; usually there is no requirement to have any particular ratio of zeros to ones. A specification may include attributes that a (faulty) product does not possess. The statement that a product satisfies a given specification constitutes a description of the product. Perhaps it is this fact that leads some to confuse descriptions and specifications.

Any list of attributes can be interpreted *either* as a description or as a specification. "A volume of more than 1 cubic meter" may be either an observation about a specific box that has been measured or a requirement for a box that is about to be purchased. While a specification may allow a choice of attributes, a description of a specific object will contain only the actual attributes. It follows that a list of attributes should be accompanied by a statement of intent to indicate whether it is to be interpreted as a description, or as a specification.

When talking about aircraft and other physical products, we seldom have trouble distinguishing between "model," "prototype," "specification," and "description." A model 747 fits on my desk and is unable to fly. In contrast, a prototype 747 would have held more than 350 people and would have been able to fly. A specification of the 747 would tell us, among other things, that it must be able to carry 350 persons a certain distance. The statement "has a funny looking bump on top at the front" could be part of a description, but I doubt that it was part of a specification. When talking about mathematical products, such as programs, the distinction seems to get lost. Specifications, descriptions, models, prototypes, and even the final product are all abstract, mathematical in nature, and usually represented as text. Consequently, many tend to forget the distinction between real things and their descriptions.

We often try to use models as descriptions or specifications by accompanying a model with a statement such as, "It looks like this but is 100 times larger" or "Make it look like this." Before Floyd's paper [3], several researchers proposed using one program to specify another and thus to accomplish proofs of correctness by proving equivalence. In discussions of communication protocols, researchers and developers often present finite state machines that conform to a protocol as if they were specifications of the protocols. In fact, these are simply mathematical models, descriptions of mechanisms that purportedly satisfy unstated requirements. I see the same tendency to use models as if they were specifications in most current work on "formal methods."

These distinctions are important because we want software developers to be able to distinguish between incidental and required properties of products. If we use models or descriptions as specifications, they will be unable to do so.

5.5 Four Types of Software Products

Just as it would be unrealistic to expect that chemicals would be described using the same notation as hardware, it is unrealistic to expect that we could describe all kinds of software products in the same way. In this paper, we distinguish four types of computer system products.

5.5.1 Real-Time and Interactive Systems

These computer systems, sometimes called real-time systems, are controlled by nonterminating programs, observe an effectively infinite sequence of inputs, and produce an effectively infinite sequence of outputs. We have found that models based on those used in control theory are useful in describing these systems. Further discussion of the documentation of these systems can be found in [11, 12]. We will not describe them further in this paper.

5.5.2 Terminating Programs

These programs, often used as components of larger programs are initiated, run for some time and then terminate, leaving their results as part of the data state of the invoking program. We will describe them by describing their effect on the state of a data structure.

5.5.3 Modules

We use the term "module" to describe a collection of programs, usually a work assignment for a programmer or a group of programmers, that hides (abstracts from) the details of a shared (internal) data structure [9]. Because we wish to avoid describing that data structure, the methods that can be used for individual terminating programs are not appropriate. Instead we will have to describe the set of observable event sequences (traces) observable at the interface of the module. We discuss these further in Section 5.12.

5.5.4 Objects (Created by Modules)

In recent years, it has become popular to use modules to produce many copies of its data structure, each of these known as an object. The descriptions of the creating modules describe the essential properties of those objects, but we must allow for the fact that some operations will affect several objects. We discuss this further in Section 5.11.

5.6 Programs and Executions

This section presents a treatment of terminating programs that allows us to write useful descriptions and specifications of such programs. This approach was most heavily influenced by the work of Mills [6, 7] as well as private communications with N.G. de Bruijn, but there have been many similar approaches. Many of these ideas were developed some years ago and presented in [8, 13], but there are some valuable refinements and clarifications in this version.

A digital computer can usefully be viewed as a finite state machine and a program as a description of a behavior pattern for that machine. In this paper we have no need to exploit the fact that the number of states is finite, but in any practical application of these ideas the user must bear the finiteness in mind and be sure that this limitation is reflected in the descriptions of the programs and objects of interest. Otherwise, the descriptions will be inaccurate and it could be dangerous to use them.

> **Definition 1.** *A finite state machine is a machine that is always in exactly one of a finite set of stable states, S, and whose operation consists of a sequence of state changes, i.e., transitions from state to state. These machines have a finite set of input symbols, called the input alphabet, and a finite set of output symbols, the output alphabet.*

It would be a mistake to confuse the physical machine with its description, for example, by saying "a machine is an n-tuple."

> **Definition 2.** *An execution is a sequence (either finite or infinite) of states.*

> **Definition 3.** *A program is an initial state of a machine that determines a set of executions, sometimes called the executions of that program. The set of all executions of P is denoted Exec(P,S).*

> **Definition 4.** *The subset of Exec(P,S) that begins with the state x, (x ∈ S), is denoted by $e_P(x)$, and x is called the starting state of those executions.*

> **Definition 5.** *If there exists an execution in $e_P(x)$ that is finite and its last state is z, then we may write   <x, ..., z> ∈ $e_P(x)$, say that this execution terminates (in z), and call z the final state (of this execution). We will also say that the program P may start in x and terminate in z.*

> **Definition 6.** *An infinite sequence in $e_P(x)(<x, ... >)$ is called a nonterminating execution.*

Definition 7. *If there exists a state x, (x ∈ S), such that $e_P(x)$ contains two or more distinct executions, then P is called a nondeterministic program.*

Definition 8. *If for a given state x, (x ∈ S), every member of $e_P(x)$ is finite, x is called a safe state of P. The set of safe states of P is noted S_P.*

5.7 A Mathematical Interlude: LD-Relations

Definition 9. *A binary relation R on a given set U is a set of ordered pairs with both elements from U, i.e., $R \subseteq U \times U$. The set U is called the Universe of R. The set of pairs, R, can be described by its characteristic predicate, R(p,q), i.e., $R = \{(p,q):U \times U | R(p,q)\}$. The domain of R is denoted Dom(R) and is $\{p|\exists q[R(p,q)]\}$. The range of R is denoted Range(R) and is $\{q|\exists p[R(p,q)]\}$.*

Below, "relation" means "binary relation."

Definition 10. *A limited-domain relation (LD-relation) on a set, U, is a pair, $L = (R_L, C_L)$, where*

- *R_L, the relational component of L, is a relation on U, i.e., $R_L \subseteq U \times U$, and*
- *C_L, the competence set of L, is a subset of the domain of R_L, i.e., $C_L \subseteq Dom(R_L)$.*

5.8 Program Construction Tools

We treat compilers as program construction tools. For each such tool, we can identify two components: primitive programs and constructs (or constructors).

Definition 11. *A program is a primitive program with respect to a program-construction tool if it was produced without the tool. Primitive programs cannot be constructed using the tool but are used as building blocks to construct programs with the tool.*

In conventional tools (for example, Pascal compilers), the primitive programs include assignment of values to variables, arithmetic computations, tests of boolean variables, access of variables, etc. Some interesting tools contain unusual primitive programs, for example, list processing languages have primitive programs deemed useful for working with symbolic lists.

Definition 12. *Constructs are "templates," strings with one or more places to insert programs, that take one or more programs and produce new programs from them. Each construct is a function mapping from a tuple of programs to a program. There is one function argument for each of the "program places" in the templates.*

For example, " if...then...else..." is a construct that takes three programs and combines them to produce a single program. Each construct can be defined by saying how to determine a description of the constructed program from descriptions of the component programs.

5.9 Describing Programs

Engineers have been describing their products precisely for centuries. In their work:

- They use mathematics, not just words, to describe their products.
- They use a variety of descriptions rather than attempt one "complete" description.
- There is never a complete description of a product. Each product description is intended for a different purpose, and each is an accurate description of some aspects of the product. However, even taken together, these descriptions need not constitute a complete description.

5.9.1 Constructive Descriptions of Programs

The texts that we conventionally call programs are constructive descriptions of programs.

Definition 13. For a given program construction tool, a constructive description of a program is either the name of a primitive program or a construct with the program places filled with constructive descriptions of programs.

In other words, we can get a constructive description of a program by taking a construct and putting primitive programs, or constructive descriptions of programs, in its places. Simple programming languages are defined in this way in [8, 13].

Constructive descriptions are the primary product of the people that we call programmers. However, for larger programs, we need other kinds of descriptions because the constructive descriptions are hard to understand.

5.9.2 Behavioral Descriptions of Programs

Definition 14. Behavioral descriptions describe some aspects of the executions of a program; they generally do not describe how the program is constructed from component programs.

For example, performance models are behavioral descriptions.

Those who are going to use, not inspect or modify, a program need behavior descriptions far more than they need constructive descriptions of programs. They do not want to know the details of program construction; they want to know what the program will do. Even programmers need behavioral descriptions of programs when they are trying to debug or modify a program. They need them to be able to change one part of a program without understanding the constructive details of the other parts.

5.9.2.1 Before/After Descriptions

Before/after descriptions are behavioral descriptions that are used when the intermediate states of an execution are not important. For each state, s, they must describe (a) whether or not s is safe and (b) the final states of executions in $ep(s)$.

5.9.2.2 Using LD-Relations as Before/After Descriptions

Definition 15. Let P be a program, let S be a set of states, and let $L_P = (R_P, C_P)$ be an LD-relation on S, such that $(x,y) \in R_P$ if and only if $<x, ...,y> \in Exec(P,S)$, and $C_P = S_P$. L_p is called the LD-relation of P.[2]

By convention, if C_P is not given explicitly, it is, by default, $\text{Dom}(R_P)$. The following are some of the consequences of this definition:

- If P starts in x and $x \in C_P$, P always terminates; if $(x,y) \in R_P$, y is a possible termination state when P is started in state x.
- If P starts in x and $x \in (\text{Dom}(R_P) - C_P)$, the termination of P is non-deterministic; in this case, if $(x,y) \in R_P$, when P is started in x, y is one of the possible termination states, but the program may not terminate.
- If P starts in x, and $x \notin \text{Dom}(R_P)$, then P will not terminate.
- If P is a deterministic program, the relational component, R_P is Mills' program function and C_P (which will be the same as $\text{Dom}(R_P)$) need not be written. Hence, our approach is "upward compatible" with Mills [6, 7].

LD-relations have practical advantages over some more popular before/after descriptions.

- They provide complete before/after descriptions of nondeterministic programs.

---

2. Note that C_P is not the same as the precondition used in VDM [4]. S_P is the safe set of P.

■ They can be described by giving the characteristic predicates of R_P and C_P; those predicates can be expressed in terms of values of program variables. Illustrations can be found in [1, 10].

5.9.2.3 Other Kinds of Behavioral Descriptions of Programs

The before/after descriptions offered by LD-relations are not complete descriptions or suitable for all purposes. For example, they do not describe whether or not certain conditions were "invariant" in an execution of a program, or the length of an execution. This section discusses a few of the more popular alternatives and explains our choice.

5.9.2.4 The VDM Alternative

VDM is also based on a model that represents programs by a set and a relation, but the set is a precondition rather than the set of safe states. VDM [4] does not describe the behavior of a program if the precondition does not hold. Consequently, the VDM model does not allow one to distinguish certain programs that have distinct before/after behavior.

5.9.2.5 The "Pure" Relational Alternative

Many people have suggested representing programs by a relation alone, using a special symbol to denote nontermination. These models are theoretically equivalent[3] to LD-relations, but introducing an element that is not a state means that the sets cannot be characterized in terms of variable values alone. The nonstate requires special treatment and complicates the use of this model. N.G. de Bruijn used such a model when representing programs in his Automath system [2]. Another well-written paper that uses such a model is [5], which gives precise definitions of Dijkstra's predicate transformers in relational terms.

Since most of the programs encountered in practice are deterministic, we value the fact that Mills' model, which has been found practical for deterministic programs, is compatible with this more general model. The competence set is very convenient when dealing with nondeterministic programs.

5.10 Specifying Programs

When writing specifications for programs, we want to be able to allow behavior that need not actually be exhibited by a satisfactory program. For example, if we want a square root program we may be willing to accept either the positive or the negative root, but would be satisfied with a program

---

3. It is always possible to determine the pure relation corresponding to the LD-relation and vice versa.

that always gave the positive root. We may want to require termination for certain starting states, but do not care about what happens in some of the others. The following definitions allow us to write such specifications.

5.10.1 Before/After Specifications

When we are concerned only about the starting and stopping states of the executions, we should write before/after specifications.

5.10.2 Using LD-Relations for Before/After Specifications

We can use LD-relations to specify programs. The conditions under which a program satisfies an LD-relation used as a specification differ from those under which an LD-relation can be said to describe a program.

> **Definition 16.** *Let $L_p = (R_P, C_P)$ be the LD-relation of a program P. Let S, called a specification, be a set of LD-relations on the same universe, and let $L_S = (R_S, C_S)$ be an element of S. We say that (1) P satisfies the LD-relation L_S, iff $C_S \subseteq C_P$ and $R_P \subseteq R_S$, and (2) P satisfies the specification S, iff P satisfies at least one element of S. Often, S has only one element.*

If $S = \{L_S\}$ is a specification, then we can informally call L_S a specification. The following are implications of Definition 16.

- An acceptable program must not terminate if started in states outside $\text{Dom}(R_S)$.
- An acceptable program must terminate if started in states in $C_S(C_S \subseteq \text{Dom}(R_P))$.
- An acceptable program may terminate only in states that are in $Range(R_S)$.
- A deterministic program can satisfy a specification that would also be satisfied by a nondeterministic program.

It is important to note the following differences between the description and the specification of a program:

- There is only one LD-relation describing a program, but that program may satisfy many distinct specifications described by different LD-relations.
- An acceptable program need not exhibit all of the behavior allowed by R_S $(R_P \subseteq R_S)$.
- An acceptable program may be certain to terminate if started in states that are outside C_S but are in $\text{Dom}(R_S)$ $(C_S \subseteq C_P)$.

5.10.3 Constructive Specifications of Programs

One may want to put restrictions on the way that programs are constructed. For example, one may want to restrict the use of certain constructs, or primitive programs. It should be clear that constructive specifications are quite different from constructive descriptions; constructive specifications restrict the way that programs can be constructed, but do not describe the way a particular program has been constructed.

5.11 Objects Versus Programs

It is wise to design software by designing a set of objects. Each object is implemented by a *module* (a set of programs) using a data structure that is "hidden from" (never accessed directly by) programs outside the module. Changing the state of the object, or getting information about the object's state, is always done by invocations of programs from the module. For example, a stack is an object implemented by a module that includes accessible programs. PUSH, POP, TOP, and DEPTH might be programs in the module that are accessible in external programs and PUSH(x,3), PUSH(x,5), and POP(x) are operations on an object named x, created by that module.

> **Definition 17.** *An object is a finite state machine. The input alphabet of the object is the set of operations that one can perform upon the object. The output alphabet of the object is the set of values that can be returned by such operations.*

Describing or specifying objects is very different from describing or specifying programs. It is best to provide "black box" descriptions of objects, descriptions that do not reveal the hidden data structure used to represent the state. For such descriptions, LD-relations on the data structure that is changed by the program would be inappropriate as would be any method that describes an internal data structure for the module.

5.12 Descriptions and Specifications of Objects

There are many possible descriptions of objects. One can describe them by giving the next state and output functions or by describing their data structure and programs. For black box descriptions of finite state machines, the only information that we should mention is the externally visible events, i.e., sequences of inputs and outputs. We call such sequences *traces*.

> **Definition 18.** *A trace of a finite state machine is a finite sequence of pairs, each containing a member of the input alphabet and a member of the output alphabet. A trace, T, is considered possible for machine M, if*

M could react to the sequence of inputs in T by emitting the sequence of outputs in T.

Descriptions and specifications of objects can be written as predicates on classes of traces. LD-relations are not needed if we can assume that operations on objects always terminate.

5.13 Conclusions

The mathematics of program descriptions can be kept quite simple without losing utility. However, the definitions must be done very carefully. We have seen that "minor" changes can remove descriptive power. The difference between program description and program specification can be made precise, even though the same mathematical formalism can be used for both. As most programs encountered in practice are deterministic, this special class of programs can be described using a special class of LD-relations. The simplicity of these ideas must be viewed as a feature. In many years of participation in practical software development, I have seen many places where "theory" or mathematics was useful, but it was *always* simple theory. When theories get complex, they are not likely to be useful or used.

References

1. Bauer, B. and Parnas, D.L. Experience with the use of precise documentation. *Proc. of the Tenth Ann. Conf. on Computer Assurance*, 273–285, 1995.

2. De Bruijn, N.G. Computer program semantics in space and time. *Selected Papers on Automath Series—Studies in Logic and the Foundations of Mathematics*, Editors: R.P. Nederpelt, J.H. Geuvers, and R.C. de Vrijer, 113, North-Holland, 1983.

3. Floyd, R.W. Assigning meanings to programs. *Proc. of the Sym. of Applied Maths., 19*. Also in *Mathematical Aspects of Computer Science*, (1967), Editor: J.T. Schwartz, American Mathematical Society, 19–32, 1968.

4. Jones, C.B. *Systematic Software Development Using VDM*, Prentice-Hall, 1986.

5. Majster-Cederbaum, M.E. A simple relation between relational and predicate transformer semantics for nondeterministic programs. *Information Processing Letters*, 11, 190–192, 1980.

6. Mills, H.D. The new math of computer programming. *Comm. ACM*, 18, 43–48, 1975.

7. Mills, H.D. Function semantics for sequential programs. *Proc. of the IFIP Congress*, North Holland, 241–250, 1980.

8. Parnas, D.L. A generalized control structure and its formal definition. *Comm. ACM*, 26, 572–581, 1983.

9. Parnas, D.L., Clements, P. and Weiss, D. The modular structure of complex systems. *IEEE Transactions on Software Engineering*, SE-11, 259–266, 1985.

10. Parnas, D.L., Madey, J. and Iglewski, M. Precise documentation of well-structured programs. *IEEE Transactions on Software Engineering*, 20, 948–976, 1994.

11. Parnas, D.L. and Madey, J. Functional documentation for computer systems engineering. *Science of Computer Programming*, Elsevier, 25, 41–61, 1995.

12. Van Schouwen, A.J., Parnas, D.L., and Madey, J. Documentation of requirements for computer systems. *Proc. of '93 IEEE Int. Sym. on Requirements Engineering*, San Diego, CA, 198–207, 1993.

13. Parnas, D.L. and Wadge, W.W. Less restrictive constructs for structured programs. *Technical Report 86–186*, Queen's, C&IS, Kingston, Ontario, Canada, 16, 1986.

Acknowledgments

Work with William Wadge, Jan Madey, and Michal Iglewski has strongly influenced this paper. Comments by Dennis Peters, Yabo Wang, Jim Horning, Jeff Zucker, and John Tucker on earlier drafts were very helpful. Anders Ravn and Victoria Stavridou made very helpful suggestions when editing the final version.

Introduction

Kathyrn Heninger Britton

This paper is an instance of serendipity. In 1978, I was a member of a small team at the Naval Research Laboratory that embarked on a software engineering experiment led by Dave Parnas. Dave worked part-time with us in addition to his job as a university professor. We did not start out with any theories about requirements specification that we wanted to demonstrate to the world. Our sights were on a different goal: demonstrating the utility of a collection of software engineering ideas, most of them Dave's, by rebuilding an existing piece of software according to the discipline of information hiding, cooperating sequential processes, and other ideas featured in this book. We had established a partnership with a group of engineers at the Naval Weapons Center (NWC) in China Lake, California, who were willing to give us a chance to demonstrate that these design practices could make software easier to maintain and extend. But before we got started on the real project, we had to have a description of the software that both sides, the research team from the Naval Research Laboratory and the operational team from the Naval Weapons Center, could agree constituted an acceptable replacement software system. The pencil-annotated flowcharts that served as the NWC documentation did not suit. Not only did they unnecessarily restrict our freedom to create a new implementation, but also we were cautioned not to put too much trust in them; only the code was really accurate.

The project was called Software Cost Reduction (SCR), a name that evokes the widespread anxiety in military circles that the software required to drive weapons and communications systems was plagued by monumental cost overruns, generally absorbed by the taxpayer. As systems became more complex and took over more of the work, they also became very expensive to modify and extend. We chose the avionics software for the A-7E aircraft for this project, both because of the cooperative relationship that we had established with NWC engineers and because the software was small enough that a research team could dream of completing it. At the time, each release of new software for the A-7E required 6 months of simulator and flight tests before it was released to the fleet. We joked that if the Navy tested the F18 software to the same level of confidence, it would take 12 years for each new release, given the relative size and complexity of the software. This off-the-cuff extrapolation represented a growing fear that software complexity was getting beyond our capabilities, tools, and procedures.

The Software Cost Reduction project addressed the ongoing technology transfer problem. How do ideas created by research and academia become usable by practicing programmers and software engineers who are building big systems? I remember thinking at the time that I would never really believe in formal specifications until I saw them used on something bigger and messier than stacks and queues. I could see the same skepticism in the representatives from the various Navy laboratories who attended the two-week software engineering course that we gave with Dave's help. One of the skeptical course attendees, Dennis Farrell, was our entree to the Naval Weapons Center. He challenged us to come to his lab and try out our ideas on a real avionics program. The technology transfer problem exists because research has to focus on problems that look new and that fit within research budgets, semester time frames, or journal paper limits. At the same time, people in the field are dealing with big, messy problems, changing requirements, and tight schedules that do not include much "think time." I've been on both sides of technology transfer now, and I have sympathy for the field programmers, who often do not believe that ideas from research scale to real systems or perform acceptably or even address the problems that are really difficult. The Software Cost Reduction project was based on the idea that successful technology transfer required both sides to meet in the middle, with the research going past small demonstrations of technology to complete solutions for real problems.

It took us eight months to finish the A-7E software requirements, with lots of suggestions and feedback from Dave. It was primarily an exercise in organization and common sense. We took information from a wide variety of sources, including field manuals, interviews, sketches on blackboards, pencil-annotated flowcharts, and answers to questions addressed to people using the A-7E flight simulator. The task was to present the information in a form that supported quick reference for a follow-on implementation and then to get on with the implementation.

The challenge was to state the necessary externals precisely, without including information that would rule out a completely different implementation. I've seen many people founder on the difficulty of separating essential externals from modifiable internals. I was very fortunate to have a chance to practice where the decision criteria were so clear: Do we have to replicate this feature in the new A-7E software in order to pass simulator and flight tests?

The work on the A-7E requirements took on a life of its own. We received a surprisingly large number of requests for the requirements document itself, given that it was 500 pages long. The fact that we had accidentally achieved something of value in its own right stimulated me to write this paper. I wanted to summarize what we'd learned and to tie it to the design disciplines that Dave had established for the entire project. The requirements document itself was updated more than once as the project continued, and there has been ongoing work extending and formalizing the tabular techniques that we created.

A number of avionics projects have used SCR-style requirements [1]. A team at NRL has created the SCR* toolset to provide automated support for creating and verifying SCR-style requirements [2]. The SCR model has become the standard for research in model checking of requirements documents [3]. I still get e-mail from Professor John Knight of the University of Virginia, who uses the paper in his software engineering laboratory course. Serendipity led us into the requirements specification field. One of the joys of research is the chance to generate new ideas in side issues like this one.

So why is this paper included in this book even though Dave Parnas is not listed as a coauthor? Twenty-two years ago, I thought long and hard about inviting Dave Parnas to be a coauthor. We had worked together on the requirements statement, with me slogging through all the details and Dave appearing every six weeks or so to critique and make suggestions. I decided that I was in danger of becoming an also-ran on my own paper if Dave's name joined mine in the author list. But I've never felt completely right about the decision. For one thing, a brief acknowledgment does not express the role that Dave played as mentor and partner. For another, I've now had much more experience suggesting ideas that other people carry out. I know that both glimmers and legwork are needed, and Dave contributed many glimmers to the requirements work. So I am honored that the paper is included in this collection of Dave's work.

References

1. S.R. Faulk, L. Finneran, J. Kirby, Jr., S. Shah, and J. Sutton, "Experience Applying the CoRE Method to the Lockheed C-130J," *Proc. 9th Ann. Conf. Computer Assurance (COMPASS94),* p. 38, Gaithersburg, MD, June 1994.

2. C. Heitmeyer, J. Kirby, B. Labaw, and R. Bharadwaj, "SCR*: A Toolset for Specifying and Analyzing Software Requirements," *Proc. 10th Ann. Conf. Computer-Aided Verification (CAV'98),* Vancouver, Canada, 1998.

3. T. Sreemani and J.M. Atlee, "Feasibility of Model Checking Software Requirements: A Case Study," *Proc. 11th Ann. Conf. Computer Assurance (COMPASS96),* pp. 77–88, June 1996.

Specifying Software Requirements for Complex Systems: New Techniques and Their Application

Kathryn L. Heninger

6.1 Abstract

This paper concerns new techniques for making requirements specifications precise, concise, unambiguous, and easy to check for completeness and consistency. The techniques are well suited for complex real-time software systems; they were developed to document the requirements of existing flight software for the Navy's A-7 aircraft. The paper outlines the information that belongs in a requirements document and discusses the objectives behind the techniques. Each technique is described and illustrated with examples from the A-7 document. The purpose of the paper is to introduce the A-7 document as a model of a disciplined approach to requirements specification; the document is available to anyone who wishes to see a fully worked-out example of the approach.

6.2 Introduction

Much software is difficult to understand, change, and maintain. Several software engineering techniques have been suggested to ameliorate this situation, among them modularity and information hiding [11, 12], formal specifications [4, 9, 10, 13, 16, 20], abstract interfaces [15], cooperating sequential processes [2, 18, 21], process synchronization routines [2, 8], and resource monitors [1, 6, 7]. System developers are reluctant to use these techniques both because their usefulness has not been proven for programs with stringent resource limitations and because there are no fully worked-out examples of some of them. In order to demonstrate feasibility and to provide a useful model, the Naval Research Laboratory and the Naval Weapons Center are using the techniques listed above to redesign and rebuild the operational flight program for the A-7 aircraft. The new program will undergo the acceptance tests established for the current program, and the two programs will be compared both for resource utilization and for ease of change.

The new program must be functionally identical to the existing program. That is to say, the new program must meet the same requirements as the old program. Unfortunately, when the project started there existed no requirements documentation for the old program; procurement specifications, which were originally sketchy, are now out-of-date. Our first step was to produce a complete description of the A-7 program requirements in a form that would facilitate the development of the new program and that could be updated easily as the requirements continued to change.

Writing down the requirements turned out to be surprisingly difficult in spite of the availability of a working program and experienced maintenance personnel. None of the available documents was entirely accurate; no single person knew the answers to all our questions; some questions were answered differently by different people; and some questions could not be answered without experimentation with the existing system. We found it necessary to develop new techniques based on the same principles as the software design techniques listed above to organize and document software requirements. The techniques suggested questions, uncovered ambiguities, and supported crosschecking for completeness and consistency. The techniques allowed us to present the information relatively concisely, condensing several shelves of documentation into a single, 500-page document.

This paper shares some of the insights we gained from developing and applying these techniques. Our approach can be useful for other projects, both to document unrecorded requirements for existing systems and to guide software procurers as they define requirements for new systems. This paper introduces the techniques and illustrates them with simple examples. We invite anyone interested in more detail to look at the requirements document itself as a complete example of the way the techniques work for a substantial system [5].

First this paper addresses the objectives a requirements document ought to meet. Second it outlines the general design principles that guided us as we developed techniques; the principles helped us achieve the objectives. Finally it presents the specific techniques, showing how they allowed us to achieve completeness, precision, and clarity.

6.3 A-7 Program Characteristics

The A-7 flight program is an operational Navy program with tight memory and time constraints. The code is about 12,000 assembler language instructions and runs on an IBM System 4 PI model TC-2 computer with 16K bytes of memory. We chose this program because we wanted to demonstrate that the run-time overhead incurred by using software engineering principles is not prohibitive for real-time programs and because the maintenance personnel feel that the current program is difficult to change.

The A-7 flight program is part of the Navigation/Weapon Delivery System on the A-7 aircraft. It receives input data from sensors, cockpit switches, and a panel with which the pilot keys in data. It controls several display devices in the cockpit and positions several sensors. Twenty-two devices are connected to the computer; examples include an inertial measurement set providing velocity data and head-up display device. The head-up display projects symbols into the pilot's field of view, so that he sees them overlaying the world ahead of the aircraft. The program calculates navigation information, such as present position, speed, and heading; it also controls weapon delivery, giving the pilot steering cues and calculating when to release weapons.

6.4 Requirements Document Objectives

For documentation to be useful and coherent, explicit decisions must be made about the purposes it should serve. Decisions about the following question affect its scope, organization, and style: (1) What kinds of questions should it answer? (2) Who are the readers? (3) How will it be used? (4) What background knowledge does a reader need? Considering these questions, we derived the following six objectives for our requirements document:

1. *Specify external behavior only.* A requirements document should specify only the external behavior of a system, without implying a particular implementation. The user or his representative defines requirements using his knowledge of the application area, in this case aircraft navigation and weapons delivery. The software designer creates the implementation, using his knowledge of software engineering. When requirements are expressed in terms of a possible implementation, they restrict the software designer too much, sometimes preventing him from using the most effective algorithms and data structures. In our project the requirements document must be equally valid for two quite different implementations: the program we build and the current program. For our purposes it serves as a problem statement, outlining what the new program must do to pass acceptance tests. For those maintaining the current program, it fills a serious gap in their documentation: They have no other source that states exactly what the program must do. They have pilot manuals, which supply user-level documentation for the entire avionics system, of which the program is only a small part. Unfortunately, the pilot manuals make it difficult to separate the activities performed by the computer program from those performed by other devices and to distinguish between advice to the pilot and restrictions enforced by the program. The maintainers also have implementation documentation* for the current program: mathematical algorithm analyses, flowcharts, and 12,000 lines of sparsely commented assembler code. But the implementation documents do not distinguish between the aspects that are dictated by the requirements and those that the software designer is free to change.

2. *Specify constraints on the implementation.* In addition to defining correct program behavior, the document should describe the constraints placed on the implementation, especially the details of the hardware interfaces. As is

usually the case with embedded systems,[1] we are not free to define the interfaces to the system, but must accept them as given for the problem. A complete requirements description should therefore include the facts about the hardware devices that can affect the correctness of the program.

3. *Be easy to change.* Because requirements change, requirements documentation should be easy to change. If the documentation is not maintained during the system life cycle, control is lost over the software evolution; it becomes difficult to coordinate program changes introduced by maintenance personnel.

4. *Serve as a reference tool.* The primary function of the document is to answer specific questions quickly, rather than to explain in general what the program does. We expect the document to serve experienced programmers who already have a general idea about the purpose of the program. Precision and conciseness are valued. Indispensable reference aids include a glossary, detailed table of contents, and various indices. Since tutorial material has different characteristics, such as a narrative style, it should be developed separately if it is needed.

5. *Record forethought about the life cycle of the system.* During the requirements definition stage, we believe it is sensible to exercise forethought about the life cycle of the program. What types of changes are likely to occur [22]? What functions would maintainers like to be able to remove easily [17]? For any software product some changes are easier to make than others; some guidance in the requirements will help the software designer assure that the easy changes correspond to the most likely changes.

6. *Characterize acceptable responses to undesired events.* Undesired events [14], such as hardware failures and user errors, should be anticipated during requirements definition. Since the user knows the application area, he knows more than the software designer about acceptable responses. For example, a pilot knows better than a programmer whether a particular response to a sensor failure will decrease or increase his difficulties. Responses to undesired events should be stated in the requirements document; they should not be left for the programmer to invent.

6.5 Requirements Document Design Principles

Our approach to requirements documentation can be summarized by the three principles discussed below. These principles form the basis of all the techniques we developed.

---

1. An embedded system functions as a component of a significantly larger system. Parnas [15] has a discussion of embedded system characteristics.

1. *State questions before trying to answer them.* At every stage of writing the requirements, we concentrated first on formulating the questions that should be answered. If this is not done, the available material prejudices the requirements investigation so that only the easily answered questions are asked. First we formulated the table of contents in Figure 6.1 order

	Chapter	Contents
0	Introduction	Organization principles; abstracts for other sections; notation guide
1	Computer Characteristics	If the computer is predetermined, a general description with particular attention to its idiosyncrasies; otherwise a summary of its required characteristics
2	Hardware Interfaces	Concise description of information received or transmitted by the computer
3	Software Functions	What the software must do to meet its requirements, in various situations and in response to various events
4	Timing Constraints	How often and how fast each function must be performed. This section is separate from section 3 since "what" and "when" can change independently.
5	Accuracy Constraints	How close output values must be to ideal values to be acceptable
6	Response to Undesired Events	What the software must do if sensors go down, the pilot keys an invalid data, etc.
7	Subsets	What parts of the program should be easy to remove
8	Fundamental Assumptions	The characteristics of the program that will stay the same, no matter what changes are made
9	Changes	The types of changes that have been made or are expected
10	Glossary	Most documentation is fraught with acronyms and technical terms. At first we prepared this guide for ourselves; as we learned the language, we retained it for newcomers.
11	Sources	Annotated list of documentation and personnel, indicating the types of questions each can answer

Figure 6.1 *A-7 Requirements table of contents.*

to characterize the general classes of questions that should be answered. We wrote it before we looked at the A-7 at all, basing it on our experience with other software. Then we generated questions for the individual sections. Like any design effort, formulating questions requires iteration: We generated questions from common sense, organized them into forms, generated more questions by trying to fill in the blanks, and revised the forms.

2. *Separate concerns.* We used the principle of "separation of concerns" [3] to organize the document so that each project member could concentrate on a well-defined set of questions. This principle also serves the objective of making the document easy to change, since it causes changes to be well confined. For example, hardware interfaces are described without making any assumptions about the purpose of the program; the hardware section would remain unchanged if the behavior of the program changed. The software behavior is described without any references to the details of the hardware devices; the software section would remain unchanged if data were received in different formats or over different channels.

3. *Be as formal as possible.* We avoided prose and developed formal ways to present information in order to be precise, concise, consistent, and complete.

The next two sections of the paper show how these principles are applied to describe the hardware interfaces and the software behavior.

6.6 Techniques for Describing Hardware Interfaces

6.6.1 Organization by Data Item

To organize the hardware interfaces description, we have a separate unit, called *a data item,* for each input or output that changes value independently of other inputs or outputs. Examples of input data items include barometric altitude, radar-measured distance to a point on the ground, the setting of the inertial platform mode switch, and the inertial platform ready signal. Examples of output data items include coordinates for the flight path marker on the head-up display, radar antenna steering commands, and the signal that turns on and off the computer-failed light. The A-7 computer receives 70 input data items and transmits 95 output data items.

In order to have a consistent approach, we designed a form to be completed for each data item. We started with an initial set of questions that occurred to us as we read about the interfaces. How does the program read or write these data? What is the bit representation of the value? Can the computer tell whether a sensor value is valid? As we worked on specific data items, new questions occurred to us. We added these questions to the form, so that they would be addressed for all data items. The form is illustrated in Figures 6.2 and 6.3 at the end of this section.

6.6.2 Symbolic Names for Data Items and Values

The hardware section captures two kinds of information about data items: *arbitrary details* that might change if a device were replaced with a similar device, and *essential characteristics* that would be shared by similar devices. The bit representation of a value is an arbitrary detail; the semantics of the value is an essential characteristic. For example, any barometric altitude sensor provides a reading from which barometric altitude can be calculated— this information is essential. But the resolution, representation, accuracy, and timing might differ between two types of barometric altitude sensors—this information is arbitrary.

Essential information must be expressed in such a way that the rest of the document can use it without referencing the arbitrary details. For example, each data item is given a mnemonic name, so that it can be identified unambiguously in the rest of the document without reference to instruction sequences or channel numbers. If a data item is not numerical and takes on a fixed set of possible values, the values are given mnemonic names so that they can be used without reference to bit encodings. For example, a switch might be able to take the values "on" and "off." The physical representation of the two values is arbitrary information that is not mentioned in the rest of the document in case it changes. The names allow the readers and writers of the rest of the document to ignore the physical details of input and output, and are more visually meaningful than the details they represent.

We bracket every mnemonic name in symbols indicating the item type, for example /input-data-items/, //output-data-items//, and $nonnumeric-values$. These brackets reduce confusion by identifying the item type unambiguously, so that the reader knows where to find the precise definition. Moreover, the brackets facilitate systematic cross-referencing, either by people or computers.

6.6.3 Templates for Value Descriptions

The values of the numerical data items belong to a small set of value types, such as angles and distances. At first we described each data item in an ad hoc fashion, usually imitating the descriptions in the documents we referenced. But these documents were not consistent with each other and the descriptions were not always complete. We made great progress when we developed informal templates for the value descriptions, with blanks to be completed for specific data items. For example, the template for angles might read:

angle (?) is measured from line (?) to line (?) in the (?) direction, looking (?)

For example, *magnetic heading* is measured from *the line from the air-craft to magnetic north* to *the horizontal component of the aircraft X axis,* in the *clockwise* direction looking *down.*

Although templates were not used as hard-and-fast rules, their existence made values easier to describe, made the descriptions consistent with each other, and helped us apply the same standards of completeness to all items of the same type.

6.6.4 Input Data Items Described as Resources, Independent of Software Use

When describing input data items, we refrain from mentioning how or when the data is used by the software, to avoid making any assumptions about the software function. Instead, we describe the input data items as if taking inventory of the resources available to solve a problem. We define numerical values in terms of what they measure. For example, the value of the input data item called /RADALT/ is defined as the distance above local terrain as determined by the radar altimeter. Many nonnumerical inputs indicate switch positions; these are described without reference to the response the pilot expects when he changes the switch, since the response is accomplished by the software. For example, when the pilot changes the scale switch on the projected map display, he expects the map scale to change. Since the response is achieved by the software, it is not mentioned in the input data item description, which reads, *"/PMSCAL/ indicates the position of a two-position toggle switch on the projected map panel. This switch has no hardware effect on the projected map display."*

6.6.5 Example of an Input Data Item Description

Figure 6.2 shows the completed form for a nonnumerical input data item. The underlined words are the form headings. <u>Value encoding</u> shows how the mnemonic value names used in the rest of the document are mapped into specific bit representations. "Switch nomenclature" indicates the names of the switch positions as seen by the pilot in the cockpit. <u>Instruction sequence</u> gives the TC-2 assembler language instructions that cause the data to be transmitted to or from the computer. We are not usurping the programmer's job by including the instruction sequence because there is no other way to read in this data item—the instruction sequence is not an implementation decision for the programmer. The channel number is a cross reference to the computer chapter where the general characteristics of the eight channels are described. <u>Data representation</u> shows the location of the value in the 16-bit input word. Notice how the <u>Comments</u> section defines the value assumed by the switch while the pilot is changing it. This is an example of a question we asked about all switches, once it had occurred to us about this one.

Input Data Item: IMS Mode Switch

Acronym: /IMSMODE/

Hardware: Inertial Measurement Set

Description: /IMSMODE/ indicates the position of a six-position rotary switch on the IMS control panel.

Switch nomenclature: OFF; GND ALIGN; NORM; INERTIAL; MAG SL; GRID

Characteristics of Values

Value Encoding:

$Offnone$	(00000)
$Gndal$	(10000)
$Norm$	(01000)
$Iner$	(00100)
$Grid$	(00010)
$Magsl$	(00001)

Instruction Sequence: READ 24   (Channel 0)

Data Representation: Bits 3–7

Comments: /IMSMODE/ = $Offnone$ when the switch is between two positions.

Figure 6.2 *Completed input data item form.*

6.6.6 Output Data Items Described in Terms of Effects on External Hardware

Most output data items are described in terms of their effects on the associated devices. For example, the description of the output data items called //STEERAZ// and //STEEREL// shows how they are used to communicate the direction to point the antenna of the radar. This section does not explain how the software chooses the direction. For other output data items we define the value the peripheral device must receive in order to function correctly. For example, the description of the output data item called //FPANGL// shows that the radar assumes the value will be a certain angle which it uses to determine the climb or dive angle the aircraft should use during terrain following. We avoid giving any meaning to an output value that is not a characteristic of the hardware.

6.6.7 Example of an Output Data Item Description

Figure 6.3 shows the completed form for a numerical output data item. Notice how the value is described in terms of its effect on a needle in a display, rather than in terms of what the needle is supposed to communicate to

Output Data Item: Steering Error

Acronym: //STERROR//

Hardware: Attitude Direction Indicator (ADI)

Description: //STERROR// controls the position of the vertical needle on the ADI. A positive value moves the pointer to the right when looking at the display. A value of zero centers the needle.

Characteristics of Values

    Unit: Degrees

    Range: -2.5 to +2.5

    Accuracy: ± .1

    Resolution: .00122

Instruction Sequence: WRITE 229 (Channel 7)
                               Test Carry Bit = 0 for request acknowledged
                               If not, restart

Data Representation: 11-bit two's complement number, bit 0 and bits 3-12
                               scale = 512/1.25 = 409.6
                               offset = 0

( )		(		INDICATED VALUE									)		
Not used													0	0	0
0	1	2	3	4	5	6	7	8	9	10	11	12	13	14	15

BIT

Timing Characteristics: Digital to DC voltage conversion. See Section 1.5.7.

Comments: The pointer hits a mechanical stop at ± 2.5 degrees.

Figure 6.3 *Completed output data item form.*

the pilot. The value is characterized by a standard set of parameters, such as range and resolution, which are used for all numerical data items. For <u>Data representation</u>, we show how the 16-bit output word is constructed, including which bits must be zero, which bits are ignored by the device, and which bits encode the output value. Since the actual output value is not in any standard units of measurement, we also show how it can be derived from a value in standard units, in this case degrees. The relation between output values and values in standard units is given by the equation

$$\text{output value} = \text{scale} \times (\text{standard value} + \text{offset})$$

Since the same equation is used for all numerical data items, we need only provide the scale and offset values for a particular data item. Thus the output value for the data item //STERROR// in Figure 6.3 is derived from a value in degrees by the following expression:

$$\text{output value} = 409.6 \times (\text{standard value} + 0)$$

The Timing considerations section contains a pointer to another section; since many output data items have the same timing characteristics, we describe them once, and include cross-references. The comment shows a physical limit of the device.

6.7 Techniques For Describing Software Functions

6.7.1 Organization by Functions

We describe the software as a set of functions associated with output data items: Each function determines the values for one or more output data items, and each output data item is given values by exactly one function. Thus every function can be described in terms of externally visible effects. For example, the function calculating values for the output data item //STERROR// is described in terms of its effects on a needle in a display. The meaning conveyed to the pilot by the needle is expressed here.

This approach, identifying functions by working backward from output data items, works well because most A-7 outputs are specialized; most output data items are used for only a small set of purposes. The approach breaks down somewhat for a general-purpose device, such as a terminal, where the same data items are used to express many different types of information. We have one general-purpose device, the computer panel, where the same set of thirteen seven-segment displays can display many types of information, including present position, wind speed, and sensor status. We handled this situation by acting as if each type of information had its own panel, each controlled by a separate function. Thus we have forty-eight panel functions, each described as if it always controlled a panel, and a set of rules to determine which function controls the real panel at any given moment. This approach, creating *virtual panels,* allows us to separate decisions about what the values are from decisions about when they are displayed. It also causes the description to be less dependent on the characteristics of the particular panel device than it otherwise would be.

Software functions are classified as either demand or periodic. A *demand function* must be requested by the occurrence of some event every time it is performed. For example, the computer-failed light is turned on by a demand function when a computer malfunction is detected. A *periodic function* is performed repeatedly without being requested each time. For example, the coordinates of symbols on the head-up display are updated by periodic functions. If a periodic function need not be performed all the time, it is started and stopped by specific events. For example, a symbol may be removed from the head-up display when a certain event occurs.

This distinction is useful because different performance and timing information is required for demand and periodic functions. To describe a demand function one must give the events that cause it to occur; an appropriate timing question is *"What is the maximum delay that can be tolerated between request and action?"* To describe a periodic function, one must give the events that cause it to start and stop and the conditions that affect how it is performed after it is started; an appropriate timing question is *"What are the minimum and maximum repetition rates for this function?"*

6.7.2 Output Values as Functions of Conditions and Events

Originally we thought we would describe each output as a mathematical function of input values. This turned out to be a naïve approach. We found we could seldom describe output values directly in terms of input values; instead we had to define intermediate values that the current program calculated, but that did not correspond to any output values. These in turn had to be described in terms of other intermediate values. By the time we reached input values, we would have described an implementation.

Instead, we expressed requirements by giving output values as functions of aircraft operating conditions. For example, the output data item named //LATGT70// should change value when the aircraft crosses 70° latitude; how the program detects this event is left to the implementation. In order to describe outputs in terms of aircraft operating conditions, we defined a simple language of conditions and events. *Conditions* are predicates that characterize some aspect of the system for a measurable period of time. For example, /IMSMODE/ = $Gndal$ is a condition that is true when the IMS mode switch in the cockpit is set to the GND ALIGN position (see Fig. 6.2). If a pilot expects a certain display whenever the switch is in this position, the function controlling the display is affected by the value of /IMSMODE/. An *event* occurs when the value of a condition changes from true to false or vice versa. Events therefore specify instants of time, whereas conditions specify intervals of time. Events start and stop periodic functions, and they trigger demand functions. Events provide a convenient way to describe functions where something is done when a button is first pushed, but not if the pilot continues to hold it down. Before we distinguished clearly between events and conditions, situations of this sort were very difficult to describe simply.

6.7.3 Consistent Notation for Aircraft Operating Conditions

6.7.3.1 Text Macros

To keep the function descriptions concise, we introduced over two hundred terms that serve as text macros. The terms are bracketed in exclamation points and defined in an alphabetical dictionary. A text macro can define a quantity that affects an output value, but that cannot be directly obtained from an input. An example is "!ground track angle!", defined as "the angle measured from the line from the aircraft to true north to !ground track!, measured clockwise looking down." Although the derivation of such values is left to the implementation, text macros provide a consistent, encapsulated means to refer to them while specifying function values.

Text macros also serve as abbreviations for compound conditions that are frequently used or very detailed. For example, !Desig! is a condition that is true when the pilot has performed a sequence of actions that designates a target to the computer. The list of events defining !Desig! appears only in the dictionary; while writing or reading the rest of the document, these events need not be considered. If designation procedures change, only the definition in the dictionary changes. Another example of a text macro for a compound condition is !IMS Reasonable!,[2] which represents the following bulky, specific condition:

$$!IMS \text{ total velocity!} \leq 1440 \text{ fps AND}$$
$$\text{change of !IMS total velocity! from .2 seconds ago} \leq 50 \text{ fps}$$

Even though this term is used many times in the function descriptions, only one place in the document need be changed if the reasonableness criteria change for the sensor.

The use of text macros is an application of stepwise refinement: while describing functions, we give names to complicated operating conditions or values, postponing the precise definitions. As the examples above show, we continue introducing new terms in the definitions themselves. This allows us to limit the amount of detail we deal with at one time. Furthermore, like the

---

2. This text macro represents the condition that the values read from the inertial measurement set are reasonable; i.e., the magnitude of the aircraft velocity vector, calculated from inertial measurement set inputs, is less than or equal to 1440 feet per second and has changed less than 50 feet per second from the magnitude 0.2 seconds ago.

use of /, //, and $ brackets in the hardware descriptions, the use of ! brackets for text macros indicates to the reader that reference is being made to something that is defined precisely elsewhere. This reduces the risk of ambiguity that usually accompanies prose descriptions (e.g., !Desig! versus designated).

6.7.3.2 Conditions

We represent these predicates as expressions on input data items, for example, /IMSMODE/=$Gndal$, or expressions on quantities represented by text macros, for example, !ground track angle! = 30°. A condition can also be represented by a text macro, such as !IMS Reasonable!. Compound conditions can be composed by connecting simple conditions with the logical operators AND, OR, and NOT. For example, (!IMS Reasonable! AND /IMSMODE/=$Gndal$) is true only when both the component conditions are true.

6.7.3.3 Events

We use the notation@T(condition 1) to denote the occurrence of condition 1 becoming *true* and @F(condition 2) to denote the occurrence of condition 2 becoming *false*.

For example, the event @T(!ground track angle! < 30°) occurs when the !ground track angle! value crosses the 30° threshold from a larger value. The event @T(!ground track angle!=30°) occurs when the value reaches the 30° threshold from either direction. The event @T(/IMSMODE/ = $Gndal$) occurs when the pilot moves the switch to the GND ALIGN position. In some cases, an event only occurs if one condition changes when another condition is true, denoted by

$$@T(condition\ 3)\ WHEN\ (condition\ 4).$$

Thus, @T(/ACAIRB/=Yes) WHEN (/IMSMODE/=$Gndal$) refers to the event of the aircraft becoming airborne while the IMS mode switch is in the GND ALIGN position, while @T(/IMSMODE/=$Gndal$) WHEN (/ACAIRB/=Yes) refers to the event of the IMS mode being switched to GND ALIGN while the airplane is airborne.

6.7.4 Using Modes to Organize and Simplify

Although each function is affected by only a small subset of the total set of conditions, we still need to organize conditions into groups in order to keep the function descriptions simple. To do this, we define *modes* or classes of system states. Because the functions differ more between modes than they do within a single mode, a mode-by-mode description is simpler than a general description. For example, by setting three switches, deselecting guns, and keying a single digit on the panel, the pilot can enter what is called the visual navigation update mode. In this mode, several displays and the radar are dedicated to helping him get a new position estimate by sighting off a local landmark. Thus the mode affects the correct behavior of the functions associated with these displays. The use of modes has an additional advantage: If something goes wrong during a flight, the pilot is much more likely when he makes the trouble report to remember the mode than the values of various conditions.

Each mode is given a short mnemonic name enclosed in asterisks, for example, *DIG* for Doppler-inertial-gyrocompassing navigation mode. The mode name is used in the rest of the document as an abbreviation for the conditions that are true whenever the system is in that mode.

The current mode is defined by the history of events that have occurred in the program. The document shows this by giving the initial mode and the set of events that cause transitions between any pair of modes. For example, the transition list includes the entry

DIG TO *DI*

@T(!latitude! > 70°)

@(/IMSMODE/=$Iner$) WHEN (!Doppler coupled!)

Thus the system will move from *DIG* mode to Doppler-inertial (*DI*) mode either if the aircraft goes above 70° latitude or if the inertial platform mode switch is changed to INERTIAL while the Doppler Radar is in use.

The table in Figure 6.4 summarizes conditions that are true whenever the system is in a particular navigation mode. Thus in *DIG* mode the inertial platform mode switch is set to NORM, the aircraft is airborne, the latitude is less than 70°, and both the Doppler Radar and the inertial platform are functioning correctly. "X" table entries mean the value of that condition does not matter in that mode.

The mode condition tables are redundant because the information can be derived from the mode transition lists. However, the mode condition tables present the information in a more convenient form. Since the mode condition tables do not contain all the mode transition information, they do not uniquely define the current mode.

6.7.5 Special Tables for Precision and Completeness

In an early version of the document, function characteristics were described in prose; this was unsatisfactory because it was difficult to find answers to specific questions and because gaps and inconsistencies did not show up. We invented two types of tables that helped us express information precisely and completely.

Condition tables are used to define some aspect of an output value that is determined by an active mode and a condition that occurs within that mode. Figure 6.5 gives an example of a condition table. Each row corresponds to a group of one or more modes in which this function acts alike. The rows are

Mode	/IMSMODE/	/ACAIRB/	!latitude!	Other
DIG	$Norm$	Yes	<70°	!IMS Up! AND !Doppler Up!
DI	$Norm$ OR $Iner$	Yes	<80°	!IMS Up! AND !Doppler Up! AND !Doppler Coupled!
I	$Iner$	X	<80°	!IMS Up!
IMS fail	X	X	X	!IMS Down!

Figure 6.4 *Section from the navigation mode condition table.*

Condition Table: Magnetic heading (//MAGHDGH//) output values		
MODES	CONDITIONS	
DIG, *DI*, *I*, *Mag sl*, *Grid*	Always	X
IMS fail	(NOT /IMSMODE/=$Offnone$)	/IMSMODE/=$Offnone$
//MAGHDGH// value	angle defined by /MAGHCOS/ and /MAGHSIN/	0 (North)

Figure 6.5 *Example of a condition table.*

mutually exclusive; only one mode affects the function at a time. In each row are a set of mutually exclusive conditions; exactly one should be true whenever the program is in the modes denoted by the row. At the bottom of the column is the information appropriate for the interval identified by the mode-condition intersection. Thus to find the information appropriate for a given mode and given condition, first find the row corresponding to the mode, find the condition within the row, and follow that column to the bottom of the table. An "X" instead of a condition indicates that information at the bottom of the column is never appropriate for that mode.

In Figure 6.5, the magnetic heading value is 0 when the system is in mode *IMS fail* and the condition (/IMSMODE/=$Offnone$) is true. Whenever the system is in *IMS fail* mode, the following condition is true, showing that the row is complete:

(/IMSMODE/=$Offnone$ OR(NOT /IMSMODE/=$Offnone$))

and the following statement is false, showing the row entries are mutually exclusive:

(/IMSMODE/=$Offnone$ AND(NOT/IMSMODE/=$Offnone$))

Condition tables are used in the descriptions of periodic functions. Periodic functions are performed differently in different time intervals; the appropriate time interval is determined by the prevailing mode and conditions. Each row in the table completely characterizes the intervals within a mode that are meaningful for that function. The conditions must be mutually exclusive, and together they must describe the entire time the program is within the mode. These characteristics ensure that condition tables be complete, that is, all relevant intervals are indicated. They also ensure that condition tables be unambiguous, that is, given the aircraft operating conditions, the correct interval can be determined.

Event tables show when demand functions should be performed or when periodic functions should be started or stopped. Each row in an event table corresponds to a mode or group of modes. Table entries are events that cause an action to be taken when the system is in a mode associated with the row. The action to be taken is given at the bottom of the column.

The event table in Figure 6.6 specifies that the autocalibration light controlled by output data item //AUTOCAL// be turned on when the two listed modes are entered and off when they are exited. We use the symbol ":=" to denote assignment. The event @T(In mode) occurs when all the conditions represented by the mode become true, i.e., when the mode is entered.

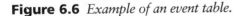

Event Table: When AUTOCAL Light Switched on/off		
MODES	**EVENTS**	
Lautocal *Sautocal*	@T(In mode)	@F(In mode)
ACTION	//AUTOCAL// : = On	//AUTOCAL// : = Off

Figure 6.6 *Example of an event table.*

@F(In mode) occurs when any one of the conditions represented by the mode becomes false, i.e., when the system changes to a different mode.

6.7.6 Function Description Examples

Figures 6.7 and 6.8 illustrate the forms we created for demand and periodic functions, respectively. All function descriptions indicate the associated output data items, thereby providing a cross-reference to the hardware description. The list of modes gives the reader an overview of when the function is performed; the overview is refined in the rest of the description.

The event table in Figure 6.7 shows both the events that request the function and the values output by the function at different times. For example, if the //IMSSCAL// value is $Coarse$ when the *Landaln* mode is entered, the function assigns it the value $Fine$. Notice how the table uses the symbolic names introduced in the hardware section for data items and data item values.

In Figure 6.8 the initiation and termination section gives the events that cause this periodic function to start and stop. This function starts when

Demand Function Name: Change scale factor

  Modes in which function required:
       Lautocal, *Sautocal*, *Landaln*, *SINSaln*, *HUDaln*, *Airaln*

Output data item: //IMSSCAL//

Function Request and Output Description:

Event Table: When the Scale Factor Is Changed

MODES	EVENTS	
Lautocal *Landaln*	@T(In mode) WHEN (//IMSSCAL// = $Coarse$)	X
HUDaln	@T(In mode) WHEN (//IMSMODE// = $Gndal$ AND //IMSSCAL// = $Coarse$)	@T(In mode) WHEN (NOT (/IMSMODE/ = $Gndal$) AND //IMSSCAL// = $Fine$)
Sautocal *SINSaln* *Airaln*	X	@T(In mode) WHEN (//IMSSCAL// = $Fine$)
ACTION	//IMSSCAL// : = $Fine$	//IMSSCAL// : = $Coarse$

Figure 6.7 *Completed demand function form.*

Periodic Function Name: Update Flight Path Marker coordinates

Modes in which function required:
DIG, *DI*, *I*, *MAG SL*, *Grid*, *IMS fail*

Output data item: //FPMAZ//, //FPMEL//

Initiation and Termination Events:
Start: @T(//HUDVEL// = On)
Stop: @T(//HUDVEL// = Off)

Output description:

The Flight Path Marker (FPM) symbol on the head-up display shows the direction of the aircraft velocity vector. If the aircraft is moving straight ahead from the nose of the aircraft, the FPM is centered on the display. The horizontal displacement from display center shows the lateral velocity component and elevation displacement shows the vertical velocity component.

Although the means for deriving Flight Path Marker position varies as shown in the table below, the position is usually derived from the current !System velocities!. The velocities are first resolved into forward, lateral, and vertical components. Then FPM coordinates are derived in the following manner:

//FPMAZ// shows $\dfrac{\text{Lateral velocity}}{\text{Forward velocity}}$ //FPMEL// shows $\dfrac{\text{Vertical velocity}}{\text{Forward velocity}}$

Condition Table: Coordinates of the Flight Path Marker

MODES	CONDITIONS		
DIG, *DI*	X	Always	X
I	/ACAIRB/ = No	/ACAIRB/ = Yes	X
Mag sl, *Grid*	/ACAIRB/ = No	!ADC Up! AND /ACAIRB/ = Yes	!ADC Down! AND /ACAIRB/ = Yes
IMS fail	/ACAIRB/ = No	X	/ACAIRB/ = Yes
FPM COORDINATES	//FPMAZ// : = 0 //FPMEL// : = 0	based on !System velocities!	//FPMAZ// : = 0 //FPMEL// : = /AOA/

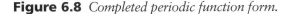

Figure 6.8 *Completed periodic function form.*

another output data item, //HUDVEL//, is assigned the value On, and stops when //HUDVEL// is assigned the value Off. The function positions a symbol on a display device. The position of the symbol usually represents the direction of the aircraft velocity vector, but under some conditions the output data items are given other values. The output description consists of two parts: a brief prose description of the usual meaning of the symbol and a condition table that shows what will happen under different conditions. Notice that every mode in the mode list is accounted for in the table. The relevant conditions for this function are !ADC Up! Or !ADC Down!, (the operating status of the air data computer sensor which provides a measurement of true airspeed) and /ACAIRB/=Yes and /ACAIRB/=No (whether the aircraft is airborne). Thus, if the system is in the inertial mode (*I*) and the aircraft is not airborne (/ACAIRB/=No is true), both coordinates of the symbol are set to zero.

6.8 Techniques for Specifying Undesired Events

6.8.1 Lists of Undesired Events

In order to characterize the desired response of the system when undesired events occur, we started with a list of undesired events and interviewed pilots and maintenance programmers to find out both what they would like to have happen and what they considered feasible. The key was the list of possible undesired events. To derive this list, we used the classification scheme shown in Figure 6.9 as a guide.

For example, in the class "Resource failure—temporary," we include the malfunctioning of each sensor since the sensors tend to resume correct functioning; in the class "Resource failure—permanent," we include the loss of areas of memory.

```
1   Resource Failure
        1.1 Temporary
        1.2 Permanent

2   Incorrect input data
        2.1 Detected by examining input only
        2.2 Detected by comparison with internal data
        2.3 Detected by user realizing he made a mistake
        2.4 Detected by user from incorrect output

3   Incorrect internal data
        3.1 Detected by internal inconsistency
        3.2 Detected by comparison with input data
        3.3 Detected by user from incorrect output
```

Figure 6.9 *Undesired event classification derived from Parnas [19].*

6.9 Techniques for Characterizing Types of Changes

In order to characterize types of changes, we looked through a file of change requests and interviewed the maintainers. To define requirements for a new system, we would have looked at change requests for similar systems. We also made a long list of fundamental assumptions that we thought would always be true about the system, no matter what. In a meeting with several maintenance system engineers and programmers, all but four of the fundamental assumptions were rejected; each rejected assumption was moved to the list of possible changes! For example, the following assumption is true about the current program, but may change in the future: "The computer will perform weapon release calculations for only one target at a time. When a target is designated, the previously designated target is forgotten." By writing two complementary lists—possible changes and fundamental assumptions—we thought about the problem from two directions, and we detected many misunderstandings. Producing a list of fundamental assumptions forced us to voice some implicit assumptions, so that we discovered possible changes we would have omitted otherwise. One reason for the success of this procedure is that it is much easier for a reviewer to recognize an error than an omission.

Listed below are examples of feasible changes:

1. Assignment of devices to channels may be changed.
2. The rate of symbol movement on the display in response to joystick displacement might be changed.
3. New sensors may be added. (This has occurred already in the history of the program.)
4. Future weapons may require computer control after release.
5. Computer self-test might be required in the air (at present it is required only on the ground).
6. It may be necessary to cease certain lower priority functions to free resources for higher priority functions during stress moments. (At present the program halts if it does not have sufficient time to perform all functions, assuming a program error.)

6.10 Discussion

We expect the document to be kept up-to-date as the program evolves because it is useful in many ways that are independent of our project. The maintainers of the current program plan to use it to train new maintenance personnel, since it presents the program's purpose in a consistent, systematic way. It is the only complete, up-to-date description of their hardware interfaces. One of the problems they now face when making changes is that they cannot tell easily if there are other places in the code that should be changed to preserve consistency. For example, they changed the code in one place to turn on a display when the target is twenty-two nautical miles away; in another place, the display is still turned on when the target is twenty nautical miles away. The unintended two-nautical-mile difference causes no major problems, but it adds unnecessary complexity for the pilot and the programmer. Inconsistencies such as this show up conspicuously in the function tables in our document. Besides using the document to check the implications of small changes, the maintenance staff want to modify it to document the next version of the program. They expect major benefits as they prepare system tests, since the document provides a description of acceptable program behavior that is independent of the program. In the past, testers have had to infer what the program is supposed to do by looking at the code. Finally they also intend to derive test cases systematically from the tables and mode transition charts.

The usefulness of these ideas is not limited to existing programs. They could be used during the requirements definition phase for a new product in order to record decisions for easy retrieval, to check new decisions for consistency with previously made decisions, and to suggest questions that ought to be considered. However, a requirements document for a new system would not be as specific as our document. We can describe acceptable behavior exactly because all the decisions about the external interfaces have been made. For a new program a requirements document describes a set of possible behaviors, giving the characteristics that distinguish acceptable from unacceptable behavior. The system designer chooses the exact behavior for the new product. The questions are the same for a new system; the answers are less restrictive. For example, where we give a specific number for the accuracy of an input, there might be a range of acceptable accuracy values for a new program.

6.11 Conclusions

The requirements document for the A-7 program demonstrates that a substantial system can be described in terms of its external stimuli and its externally visible behavior. The techniques discussed in this paper guided us in obtaining information, helped us to control its complexity, and allowed us to avoid dealing with implementation details. The document gives a headstart on the design phase of our project. Many questions that usually would be left to programmers to decide or to discover as they build the code are answered precisely. Since the information is expressed systematically, we can plan for it systematically, instead of working each detail into the program in an ad hoc fashion.

All of the techniques described in this paper are based on three principles: formulate questions before trying to answer them, separate concerns, and use precise notation. From these principles we developed a disciplined approach including the following techniques:

Symbolic names for data items and values

Special brackets to indicate type of name

Templates for value descriptions

Standard forms

Inputs described as resources

Outputs described in terms of effects

Demand versus periodic functions

Output values given as functions of conditions and events

Consistent notation for conditions and events

Modes for describing equivalence classes of system states

Special tables for consistency and completeness checking

Undesired event classification

Complementary lists of changes and fundamental assumptions

This paper is only an introduction to the ideas that are illustrated in the requirements document [5]. The document is a fully worked-out example; no details have been left out to simplify the problem. Developing and applying the techniques required approximately seventeen man-months of effort. The document is available to anyone interested in pursuing the ideas. Most engineering is accomplished by emulating models. We believe that our document is a good model of requirements documentation.

References

1. P. Brinch Hansen, *Operating Systems Principles*. Englewood Cliffs, NJ: Prentice-Hall, 1973.

2. E.W. Dijkstra, "Co-operating Sequential Processes," in *Programming Languages,* F. Genuys, Ed. New York: Academic, 1968, pp. 43–112.

3. E.W. Dijkstra, *A Discipline of Programming*. Englewood Cliffs, NJ: Prentice-Hall, 1977.

4. J.V. Guttag, "Abstract Data Types and the Development of Data Structures," *Commun. Ass. Comput. Mach.,* Vol. 20, pp. 396–404, June 1976.

5. K. Heninger, J. Kallander, D. L. Parnas, and J. Shore, *Software Requirements for the A-7E Aircraft,* Naval Res. Lab., Memo Rep. 3876, Washington, DC, November 27, 1978.

6. C.A.R. Hoare, "Monitors: An Operating System Structuring Concept," *Commun. Ass. Comput. Mach.*, Vol. 17, pp. 549–557, October 1974.

7. J. Howard, "Proving Monitors," *Commun. Ass. Comput. Mach.*, Vol. 19, pp. 273–279, May 1976.

8. R. Lipton, *On Synchronization Primitive Systems,* Ph.D. dissertation, Pittsburgh, PA: Carnegie-Mellon Univ., 1973.

9. B. Liskov and S. Zilles, "Specification Techniques for Data Abstractions," *IEEE Trans. Software Eng.*, Vol. SE-1, pp. 7–19, March 1975.

10. B. Liskov and V. Berzins, "An Appraisal of Program Specifications," in *Proc. Conf. on Research Directions in Software Technology,* pp. 13.1–13.24, October 10–12, 1977.

11. D.L. Parnas, "Information Distribution Aspects of Design Methodology," in *Proc. Int. Fed. Inform. Processing Congr.*, Vol. TA-3, pp. 26–30, 1971.

12. D.L. Parnas, "On the Criteria to Be Used in Decomposing Systems into Modules," *Commun. Ass. Comput. Mach.*, Vol. 15, pp. 1053–1058, December 1972.

13. D.L. Parnas and G. Handzel, *More on Specification Techniques for Software Modules,* Darmstadt, W. Germany: Fachbereich Informatik, Technische Hochschule Darmstadt, 1975.

14. D.L. Parnas and H. Würges, "Response to Undesired Events in Software Systems," *in Proc. 2nd Int. Conf. Software Eng.*, pp. 437–446, 1976.

15. D.L. Parnas, *Use of Abstract Interfaces in the Development of Software for Embedded Computer Systems,* Naval Res. Lab., Rep. 8047, Washington, DC, 1977.

16. D.L. Parnas, "The Use of Precise Specifications in the Development of Software," in *Proc. Int. Fed. Inform. Processing Congr.*, 1977.

17. D.L., "Designing Software for Ease of Extension and Contraction," *in Proc. 3rd Int. Conf. Software Eng.*, May 1978.

18. D.L. Parnas and K. Heninger, "Implementing Processes in HAS," in *Software Engineering Principles,* Naval Res. Lab., Document HAS.9, course notes, Washington, DC, 1978.

19. D.L. Parnas, "Desired System Behavior in Undesired Situations," in *Software Engineering Principles,* Naval Res. Lab., Document UE.1, course notes, Washington, DC, 1978.

20. O. Roubine and L. Robinson, *SPECIAL Reference Manual,* 3rd ed., Stanford Res. Inst., Menlo Park, CA: SRI Tech. Rep. CSL-45, SRI project 4828, 1977.

21. A.C. Shaw, *The Logical Design of Operating Systems.* Englewood Cliffs, NJ: Prentice-Hall, 1974.

22. D.M. Weiss, *The MUDD Report: A Case Study of Navy Software Development Practices,* Naval Res. Lab., Rep. 7909, Washington, DC, 1975.

Acknowledgments

The techniques described in this paper were developed by the author together with D. Parnas, J. Shore, and J. Kallander. The author thanks E. Britton, H.S. Elovitz, D. Parnas, J. Shore, and D. Weiss for their careful and constructive reviews of the manuscript.

Software Design

DAVID LORGE PARNAS, P. ENG

1. Introduction

My teaching career began with design courses in Electrical Engineering. Because of the sudden death of a colleague who taught programming in another department, I was asked to teach there. I was surprised by the difference in the way design in Engineering and programming were taught. In Engineering we were teaching design methods based on solid and substantive mathematics and science. For example, we could show students how to design a circuit with a specified resonant frequency, how to design a transformer, or how to design a computer adder. Engineering courses explained how to apply mathematics and physics when designing. In contrast, programming courses spent a lot of time on such arbitrary and artificial trivia as the syntax of a programming language, in my case, GATE.[1] Rather than teach design principles, we showed them programs that we thought were well designed.

After a while, I realised that software design principles were not taught because they had not been formulated. People learned programming the way we seem to learn natural languages; students saw programs and wrote programs with the same patterns as the ones they had seen. Rather than design in a disciplined, systematic way, they would "think like the computer", writing instructions in the order they would be executed.

Programming was seen as a matter of style, much like writing fiction, rather than an opportunity to apply engineering principles. In fact, attempts

---

1. GATE was an extension of GAT, which in turn was a successor of IT. IT had been used in FORTRANSIT, one of the first FORTRAN translators. Nobody uses any of these tools today, and knowledge of them is of no value to those who took courses about them.

to tell people how they could improve their programs were viewed as infringements on freedom of speech. That view is still heard today; I am told that nobody should tell anyone else how to write a program any more than he should tell authors what to say. Because programs affect the safety of others, I consider that view inappropriate. Engineers' work has long been regulated to protect the public.

2. What Makes a Design "Clean" or "Elegant"?

The importance of having design principles became even clearer to me when I worked at the Philips Computer Division in Apeldoorn, Holland. There was much controversy about the software design decisions that were being made, and there were no principles that could be used to settle disagreements. In fact, the lack of design principles resulted in some very poorly designed software. When I would identify what I believed to be "dirty" code, I discovered that my coworkers did not accept the criticism. They did not understand what I meant by "dirty" and felt that as long as it worked, or appeared to work, anything was acceptable. Our department manager asked me to explain what I meant by such terms.

My papers on design were an effort to respond to his request, that is, to explain why some software looked "clean" or elegant while others were considered "dirty" or "spaghetti code". It was clear to me that there were important issues beyond functionality. Some programs are much easier to change, inspect, or reuse than others. These were real substantive concerns, not merely matters of style or taste. The design principle that is now known as "Information Hiding" was my effort to enunciate principles that, if followed, would make programs more maintainable. This principle, which is now so well known that it is often mentioned in books or papers without either a reference or a definition, was controversial when first formulated. A reviewer explained his rejection of my best-known paper on the subject by writing, "Obviously Parnas does not know what he is talking about because nobody does it that way". Only a decade later, however, a textbook stated, "Parnas only wrote down what all good programmers did anyway". A logician would conclude that the set of good programmers was empty; that set is still very small.

Although the principle of Information Hiding underlies newer ideas such as abstract data types, object orientation, and component orientation, it is often not understood and applied. I commonly find programs in both academia and industry in which arbitrary design decisions are implicit in intermodular interfaces making the software unnecessarily hard to inspect or change. I frequently meet "Software Engineers" who have never heard the idea.

Information Hiding is actually quite subtle. For example, my early example of Information Hiding, a KWIC index program, contained a violation of the principle. The fact that the program was sorting strings using standard alphabetisation rules was revealed to the programmers of modules that could have been written properly without that information. They used the information and thereby prevented the introduction of an important and practical speed-up technique. While many people have studied this example, very few people have noticed this mistake. Given the same problem, most of today's programmers would not apply Information Hiding, and the majority of those who did would repeat the mistake in my paper. This should not be interpreted as saying that Information Hiding is too difficult to apply. Even when the design is not perfect, a design that is based on information hiding will be better than one that is not.

The principle of Information Hiding is mentioned in very many textbooks, but it is treated in a very shallow manner. I still consider it the most important and basic software design principle and believe that if my students learn only one thing about software design, they should learn how to use that principle. The principle can be explained in 40 minutes, but it really takes at least a semester of practice to learn how to use it. Even then, you may subconsciously be using an assumption that you should have hidden.

3. Program Families or Product Lines

Other papers in this collection tried to remind developers that they were designing program families or product lines not single programs. If you are developing a family of programs, you must do that consciously, or you will incur unnecessary long-term costs.

Fred Brooks was among the first to apply the family concept when he and his colleagues wrote about the IBM S/360 family of machines. Their idea was a family of machines with a common programmer interface. That idea can be generalised to apply to software and to apply to programs that have other commonalities, not just their user interface. Although there is now growing academic interest and some evidence of real industrial success in applying this idea, the majority of industrial programmers seem to ignore it in their rush to produce code. The only source of real guidance is the book by Weiss and Lai [3].

4. Error Handling

In many real programs, the code that deals with the normal case is but a small fraction of the program. Much more code is devoted to checking for, and dealing with, undesired events or values. Frequently, this "exception handling" code is added in an ad hoc way as the program evolves. As a result, even the best structured program turns into "spaghetti code". In the 70s, Harald Würges and I described a more systematic approach to error handling, but I remain unsatisfied with this approach because there are difficult flow-of-control issues; it must be possible to either return to the point where the error was detected or transfer control elsewhere. I suspect that we will not find a good solution until we start to consider multientrance, multiexit programs as a normal situation. At the moment, most programmers believe, and most gurus preach, that each program should have just one normal entry point and one normal exit. Error response requires an exceptional mechanism. That assumption is a bit of programmer folklore that deserves to be questioned.

5. Software Inspections

The newest paper in this section deals with the difficult question of software quality assurance. Bugs are still considered the norm in software; in fact, the ACM Council recently suggested that it was impossible to write programs without bugs.

Proofs of correctness for programs have been discussed for more than 30 years and are, in theory, possible. In fact, they are very rare, difficult, and arduous. This is one of the areas where research is really needed, but it seems to have declined in popularity in recent years. I cannot teach my students that proof of correctness is practical today, only that they should understand it and use it in the appropriate circumstances in the future.

On the other hand, it is possible to describe a practical procedure for systematic inspection of software. Of necessity, such procedures must take a "divide and conquer" approach and allow inspectors to focus on small amounts in each inspection session. The process must be highly systematic in order to provide assurance that no part of the program and no situation are overlooked. Unfortunately, the word "inspection" is sometimes used to denote a kind of group reading experience in which programs are read from top to bottom, and it is easy to overlook many serious errors.

The inspection method discussed in [1, 2] is time-consuming and requires the production of detailed documentation. More study is needed to find tools and methods that will reduce the cost of inspections without reducing their effectiveness.

6. Other Structural Design Decisions

In the 70s there were many papers and debates about software structure. However, the terms used in those papers and debates were never precisely defined. Any diagrams that were drawn appeared precise, but the meaning of the boxes and arrows was fuzzy; it was quite easy for two people to draw the same diagram with very different intent. As David Weiss has pointed out, a picture may be worth a thousand words, but in software it will take a thousand words to explain what it really means.

The lack of definition led to heated debates that seemed destined to continue forever. Several of my papers were devoted to understanding the meaning of the diagrams and studying the implications of imposing restrictions (such as forbidding loops) on the structures. At that time it was possible to clarify a few issues, but the bad habit of using loosely defined terms and diagrams continues, and nobody seems to be able to clarify the new ones. There is now a whole class of undefined modeling languages (UMLs) that will add to the misunderstandings. Even the advocates of such languages admit that they are not well defined but believe that someone else will define them later.

The myth that it is useful to describe the syntax of a design notation and let others define the concepts later seems widespread, but it never works. Pictures and notations whose meaning is not precisely defined will usually do more harm than good. Making useful design decisions requires that they be precisely documented and that the implications of those decisions be precisely understood.

Today, designers are building on sand when they use buzzwords and buzz diagrams. UMLs are a bad idea.

7. Conclusions

The papers in this section seem to have withstood the passage of time. The advice they offer is still useful today, nearly three decades since the earliest of them was written. I attribute this to the fact that the papers were not tied to a particular technology. They deal with perennial issues and offer methods that can be applied with almost any language, any operating system, and any application.

On the other side, the advice that these papers offer is quite incomplete. Most students can read the papers and then get lost trying to apply the principles. We need to make the design principles more precise and to provide more illustrative examples. I undertook the redesign of the A-7E software as a research project that would provide more examples. Although that project is still alive (now known as SCR) more than two decades later, I still see a strong lack of good examples. Other such projects would be a worthwhile investment.

References

1. D.L. Parnas, "Inspection of Safety Critical Software Using Function Tables", *Proceedings of IFIP World Congress 1994, Volume III,* August 1994, pp. 270–277.

2. D.L. Parnas, "Using Mathematical Models in the Inspection of Critical Software", in *Applications of Formal Methods*, M.G. Hinchey and J.P. Bowen (eds.), Prentice-Hall International Series in Computer Science, 1995, pp. 17–31.

3. David M. Weiss and Chi Tau Robert Lai, *Software Product Line Engineering*, Addison-Wesley, 1999.

Introduction

David M. Weiss

What makes a paper revolutionary? Is it the breadth and depth of the new ideas it presents? Is it the cogency of the arguments? Is it the effect it has on its audience? Is it its durability? Is it that the paper opens new areas of research? Most important, is it the paper's ability to change the way its readers think about the world? This paper does all of the above. I have read it perhaps 10 times in the nearly 30 years since it was written. Every time it sparkles with ideas that are cogent and relevant and, incidentally, that are continually being rediscovered. Forthwith, some of the sparklers.

Idea: A module is a work assignment. Before this paper, many programmers considered, and many still do, that a module is a set of routines that are related in some way, usually vaguely specified. Perhaps the routines may together provide some functionality or a step in processing. In contrast, Dave says that a module is an assignment of responsibility and that every module is characterized by its knowledge of a design decision that it hides from all others. Later this knowledge became known as the secret of the module, a terminology that many in the Department of Defense found amusing or distressing. Dave called this design principle "information hiding," but it is often misinterpreted and strait-jacketed with the misnomer "data hiding." Well-established object-oriented approaches point to information hiding as fundamental to good class design.

Dave not only explains information hiding, but he describes its benefits for different role-players in software development. For the manager the benefit is shortened development time since modules can be developed independently. For the marketer it is product flexibility since one should be able to change modules independently and quickly. For the programmer it is comprehensibility since one should be able to understand one module at a time. This discussion of benefits also suggests the notion of families, a topic explored in Papers 10 and 14 and an idea considered essential to today's explorations of product-line engineering.

Idea: At runtime, one might not be able to distinguish what criteria were used to decompose the system into modules. To the thoughtful reader, this is a stunning idea. The implication is that a module may be a design-time entity or a load-time entity or an entity created at some other time. Binding time becomes a critical ally in the battle to create maintainable programs that are also efficient. *When* we make a decision becomes nearly as important as *what* decision we make. We can hear the fans of macros cheering on the sidelines. Aspect-oriented programming, a current vogue in programming technique, appears to be a rediscovery of the use of binding time in creating modular designs.

Idea: Every information hiding module should have an interface that provides the only means to access the services provided by the module. The interface hides the module's implementation and thereby preserves the secret of the module. Does this sound like the methods of a class? Paper 15 gives a systematic method for designing such interfaces, where they are known as abstract interfaces. This idea has now been absorbed into the everyday language of the software designer. I see it appear in papers by authors who have condemned themselves to repeat its invention.

Idea: The way to evaluate a modular decomposition, particularly one that claims to rest on information hiding, is to ask what changes it accommodates. Here is the seed of how to perform the maintainability part of a design review, although these days we might call it an architecture review. One compares the list of changes that the design easily accommodates with a list of expected changes. This leads also to quantifiable measures of the goodness of a design and to cost estimation. Looking deeper, one could also compare business goals with easily accommodated changes and base architecture evaluation on product-line planning. This idea, dubbed strategic software engineering, is now starting to appear in some university courses.

Idea: Hierarchical structuring and modular decomposition are two different concepts. Modular decomposition leads to a hierarchy, but it is only one of several different hierarchies that are important in software design. Implicit is the idea of using different design structures to separate different concerns. The meaning of hierarchical structuring and its importance for the software designer are explored more deeply in Paper 8.

The preceding ideas, and a myriad of others, along with a convincing example of the application of information hiding and a list of common violations that a good designer should avoid are contained in six lucid pages. Thus began what I think of as the Parnas era in software engineering.

You might wonder why the revolution started with the KWIC index example whose two different modularizations form the heart of the paper. Dave's first intention was to use a compiler as an example. He was discouraged from this by people who told him that standard designs for compilers already existed and that there was no point in redesigning them. Not easily dissuaded, Dave included a section that hints at a design for a family of programs that includes both compilers and interpreters and that significantly differs from the conventional design for either. It is also true that the KWIC index example was easily explained to students and made a good class exercise. It was a good, simple example to introduce the notion of information hiding, faithful to Einstein's dictum that "Everything should be as simple as possible, but no simpler."

On the Criteria to Be Used in Decomposing Systems into Modules

D.L. Parnas

7.1 Abstract

This paper discusses modularization as a mechanism for improving the flexibility and comprehensibility of a system while allowing the shortening of its development time. The effectiveness of a "modularization" is dependent upon the criteria used in dividing the system into modules. A system design problem is presented and both a conventional and unconventional decomposition are described. It is shown that the unconventional decompositions have distinct advantages for the goals outlined. The criteria used in arriving at the decompositions are discussed. The unconventional decomposition, if implemented with the conventional assumption that a module consists of one or more subroutines, will be less efficient in most cases. An alternative approach to implementation which does not have this effect is sketched.

7.2 Introduction

A lucid statement of the philosophy of modular programming can be found in a 1970 textbook on the design of system programs by Gouthier and Pont [1, ¶ 10.23], which we quote below.[1]

> A well-defined segmentation of the project effort ensures system modularity. Each task forms a separate, distinct program module. At implementation time each module and its inputs and outputs are well-defined, there is no confusion in the intended interface with other system modules. At checkout time the integrity of the module is tested independently; there are few scheduling problems in synchronizing the completion of several tasks before checkout can begin. Finally, the system is maintained in modular fashion; system errors and deficiencies can be traced to specific system modules, thus limiting the scope of detailed error searching.

Usually nothing is said about the criteria to be used in dividing the system into modules. This paper will discuss that issue and, by means of examples, suggest some criteria which can be used in decomposing a system into modules.

---

1. Reprinted by permission of Prentice-Hall, Englewood Cliffs, NJ.

7.3 A Brief Status Report

The major advancement in the area of modular programming has been the development of coding techniques and assemblers which (1) allow one module to be written with little knowledge of the code in another module, and (2) allow modules to be reassembled and replaced without reassembly of the whole system. This facility is extremely valuable for the production of large pieces of code, but the systems most often used as examples of problem systems are highly modularized programs and make use of the techniques mentioned above.

7.4 Expected Benefits of Modular Programming

The benefits expected of modular programming are (1) managerial—development time should be shortened because separate groups would work on each module with little need for communication; (2) product flexibility—it should be possible to make drastic changes to one module without a need to change others; (3) comprehensibility—it should be possible to study the system one module at a time. The whole system can therefore be better designed because it is better understood.

7.5 What Is Modularization?

Below are several partial system descriptions called *modularizations*. In this context "module" is considered to be a responsibility assignment rather than a subprogram. The *modularizations* include the design decisions which must be made *before* the work on independent modules can begin. Quite different decisions are included for each alternative, but in all cases the intention is to describe all "system level" decisions (i.e., decisions which affect more than one module).

7.6 Example System 1: A KWIC Index Production System

The following description of a KWIC index will suffice for this paper. The KWIC index system accepts an ordered set of lines, each line is an ordered set of words, and each word is an ordered set of characters. Any line may be "circularly shifted" by repeatedly removing the first word and appending it at the end of the line. The KWIC index system outputs a listing of all circular shifts of all lines in alphabetical order.

This is a small system. Except under extreme circumstances (huge data base, no supporting software), such a system could be produced by a good programmer within a week or two. Consequently, none of the difficulties motivating modular programming are important for this system. Because it is impractical to treat a large system thoroughly, we must go through the exercise of treating this problem as if it were a large project. We give one modularization which typifies current approaches, and another which has been used successfully in undergraduate class projects.

7.6.1 Modularization 1

We see the following modules:

- **Module 1: Input.** This module reads the data lines from the input medium and stores them in core for processing by the remaining modules. The characters are packed four to a word, and an otherwise unused character is used to indicate the end of a word. An index is kept to show the starting address of each line.

- **Module 2: Circular Shift.** This module is called after the input module has completed its work. It prepares an index which gives the address of the first character of each circular shift, and the original index of the line in the array made up by module 1. It leaves its output in core with words in pairs (original line number, starting address).

- **Module 3: Alphabetizing.** This module takes as input the arrays produced by modules 1 and 2. It produces an array in the same format as that produced by module 2. In this case, however, the circular shifts are listed in another order (alphabetically).

- **Module 4: Output.** Using the arrays produced by module 3 and module 1, this module produces a nicely formatted output listing all of the circular shifts. In a sophisticated system the actual start of each line will be marked, pointers to further information may be inserted, and the start of the circular shift may actually not be the first word in the line, etc.

- **Module 5: Master Control.** This module does little more than control the sequencing among the other four modules. It may also handle error messages, space allocation, etc.

It should be clear that the above does not constitute a definitive document. Much more information would have to be supplied before work could start. The defining documents would include a number of pictures showing core formats, pointer conventions, calling conventions, etc. All of the interfaces between the four modules must be specified before work could begin.

This is a modularization in the sense meant by all proponents of modular programming. The system is divided into a number of modules with well-defined interfaces; each one is small enough and simple enough to be thoroughly understood and well programmed. Experiments on a small scale indicate that this is approximately the decomposition which would be proposed by most programmers for the task specified.

7.6.2 Modularization 2

We see the following modules:

- **Module 1: Line Storage.** This module consists of a number of functions or subroutines which provide the means by which the user of the module may call on it. The function call $CHAR(r,w,c)$ will have as value an integer representing the cth character in the rth line, wth word. A call such as $SETCHAR(r,w,c,d)$ will cause the cth character in the wth word of the rth line to be the character represented by d (i.e., $CHAR(r,w,c) = d$). $WORDS(r)$ returns as value the number of words in line r. There are certain restrictions in the way that these routines may be called; if these restrictions are violated the routines "trap" to an error-handling subroutine which is to be provided by the users of the routine. Additional routines are available which reveal to the caller the number of words in any line, the number of lines currently stored, and the number of characters in any word. Functions $DELINE$ and $DELWRD$ are provided to delete portions of lines which have already been stored. A precise specification of a similar module has been given in [3] and [8] and we will not repeat it here.

- **Module 2: Input.** This module reads the original lines from the input media and calls the line storage module to have them stored internally.

- **Module 3: Circular Shifter.** The principal functions provided by this module are analogs of functions provided in module 1. The module creates the impression that we have created a line holder containing not all of the lines but all of the circular shifts of the lines. Thus the function call $CSCHAR(l,w,c)$ provides the value representing the cth character in the wth word of the lth circular shift. It is specified that (1) if $i < j$ then the shifts of line i precede the shifts of line j, and (2) for each line the first shift is the original line, the second shift is obtained by making a one-word rotation to the first shift, etc. A function $CSSETUP$ is provided which must be called before the other functions have their specified values. For a more precise specification of such a module see [8].

- **Module 4: Alphabetizer.** This module consists principally of two functions. One, $ALPH$, must be called before the other will have a defined value. The second, ITH, will serve as an index. $ITH(i)$ will give the index of the circular shift which comes ith in the alphabetical ordering. Formal definitions of these functions are given [8].

- **Module 5: Output.** This module will give the desired printing of the set of lines or circular shifts.
- **Module 6: Master Control.** Similar in function to the modularization above.

7.6.3 Comparison of the Two Modularizations

7.6.3.1 General

Both schemes will work. The first is quite conventional; the second has been used successfully in a class project [7]. Both will reduce the programming to the relatively independent programming of a number of small, manageable programs.

Note first that the two decompositions may share all data representations and access methods. Our discussion is about two different ways of cutting up what *may* be the same object. A system built according to decomposition 1 could conceivably be identical *after assembly* to one built according to decomposition 2. The differences between the two alternatives are in the way that they are divided into the work assignments, and the inter-faces between modules. The algorithms used in both cases *might be* identical. The systems are substantially different even if identical in the runnable representation. This is possible because the runnable representation need only be used for running; other representations are used for changing, documenting, understanding, etc. The two systems will not be identical in those other representations.

7.6.3.2 Changeability

There are a number of design decisions which are questionable and likely to change under many circumstances. This is a partial list:

1. Input format.
2. The decision to have all lines stored in core. For large jobs it may prove inconvenient or impractical to keep all of the lines in core at any one time.
3. The decision to pack the characters four to a word. In cases where we are working with small amounts of data it may prove undesirable to pack the characters; time will be saved by a character per word layout. In other cases we may pack, but in different formats.
4. The decision to make an index for the circular shifts rather than actually store them as such. Again, for a small index or a large core, writing them out may be the preferable approach. Alternatively, we may choose to prepare nothing during *CSSETUP*. All computation could be done during the calls on the other functions such as *CSCHAR*.

5. The decision to alphabetize the list once, rather than either (a) search for each item when needed, or (b) partially alphabetize as is done in Hoare's FIND [2]. In a number of circumstances it would be advantageous to distribute the computation involved in alphabetization over the time required to produce the index.

By looking at these changes we can see the differences between the two modularizations. The first change is confined to one module in both decompositions. For the first decomposition the second change would result in changes in every module! The same is true of the third change. In the first decomposition the format of the line storage in core must be used by all of the programs. In the second decomposition the story is entirely different. Knowledge of the exact way that the lines are stored is entirely hidden from all but module 1. Any change in the manner of storage can be confined to that module!

In some versions of this system there was an additional module in the decomposition. A symbol table module (as specified in [3]) was used within the line storage module. This fact was completely invisible to the rest of the system.

The fourth change is confined to the circular shift module in the second decomposition, but in the first decomposition the alphabetizer and the output routines will also know of the change.

The fifth change will also prove difficult in the first decomposition. The output module will expect the index to have been completed before it began. The alphabetizer module in the second decomposition was designed so that a user could not detect when the alphabetization was actually done. No other module need be changed.

7.6.3.3 Independent Development

In the first modularization the interfaces between the modules are the fairly complex formats and table organizations described above. These represent design decisions which cannot be taken lightly. The table structure and organization are essential to the efficiency of the various modules and must be designed carefully. The development of those formats will be a major part of the module development and that part must be a joint effort among the several development groups. In the second modularization the interfaces are more abstract; they consist primarily in the function names and the numbers and types of the parameters. These are relatively simple decisions and the independent development of modules should begin much earlier.

7.6.3.4 Comprehensibility

To understand the output module in the first modularization, it will be necessary to understand something of the alphabetizer, the circular shifter, and the input module. There will be aspects of the tables used by output which will only make sense because of the way that the other modules work. There will be constraints on the structure of the tables due to the algorithms used in the other modules. The system will only be comprehensible as a whole. It is my subjective judgment that this is not true in the second modularization.

7.6.4 The Criteria

Many readers will now see what criteria were used in each decomposition. In the first decomposition the criterion used was to make each major step in the processing of a module. One might say that to get the first decomposition one makes a flowchart. This is the most common approach to decomposition or modularization. It is an outgrowth of all programmer training which teaches us that we should begin with a rough flowchart and move from there to a detailed implementation. The flowchart was a useful abstraction for systems with on the order of 5,000–10,000 instructions, but as we move beyond that it does not appear to be sufficient; something additional is needed.

The second decomposition was made using "information hiding" [4] as a criterion. The modules no longer correspond to steps in the processing. The line storage module, for example, is used in almost every action by the system. Alphabetization may or may not correspond to a phase in the processing according to the method used. Similarly, circular shift might, in some circumstances, not make any table at all but calculate each character as demanded. Every module in the second decomposition is characterized by its knowledge of a design decision which it hides from all others. Its interface or definition was chosen to reveal as little as possible about its inner workings.

7.6.5 Improvement in Circular Shift Module

To illustrate the impact of such a criterion let us take a closer look at the design of the circular shift module from the second decomposition. Hindsight now suggests that this definition reveals more information than necessary. While we carefully hid the method of storing or calculating the list of circular shifts, we specified an order to that list. Programs could be effectively written if we specified only (1) that the lines indicated in the circular shift module's current definition will all exist in the table, (2) that no one of them would be included twice, and (3) that an additional function existed which would allow us to identify the original line given the shift. By prescribing the order for the shifts we have given more information than necessary and so unnecessarily restricted the class of systems that we can build without changing the definitions. For example, we have not allowed for a system in which the circular shifts were produced in alphabetical order, *ALPH* is empty, and *ITH* simply returns its argument as a value. Our failure to do this in constructing the systems with the second decomposition must clearly be classified as a design error.

In addition to the general criteria that each module hides some design decision from the rest of the system, we can mention some specific examples of decompositions which seem advisable.

1. A *data structure,* its internal linkings, *accessing procedures, and modifying procedures* are part of a single module. They are not shared by many modules as is conventionally done. This notion is perhaps just an elaboration of the assumptions behind the papers of Balzer [9] and Mealy [10]. Design with this in mind is clearly behind the design of BLISS [11].

2. *The sequence of instructions necessary to call a given routine and the routine itself are part of the same module.* This rule was not relevant in the FORTRAN systems used for experimentation but it becomes essential for systems constructed in an assembly language. There are no perfect general calling sequences for real machines and consequently they tend to vary as we continue our search for the ideal sequence. By assigning responsibility for generating the call to the person responsible for the routine we make such improvements easier and also make it more feasible to have several distinct sequences in the same software structure.

3. The *formats of control blocks* used in queues in operating systems and similar programs *must be hidden* within a "control block module." It is conventional to make such formats the interfaces between various modules. Because design evolution forces frequent changes on control block formats such a decision often proves extremely costly.

4. *Character codes, alphabetic orderings, and similar data should be hidden* in a module for greatest flexibility.

5. The *sequence* in which certain items will be processed *should* (as far as practical) *be hidden within a single module.* Various changes ranging from equipment additions to unavailability of certain resources in an operating system make sequencing extremely variable.

7.6.6 Efficiency and Implementation

If we are not careful the second decomposition will prove to be much less efficient than the first. If each of the functions is actually implemented as a procedure with an elaborate calling sequence there will be a great deal of such calling due to the repeated switching between modules. The first decomposition will not suffer from this problem because there is relatively infrequent transfer of control between modules.

To save the procedure call overhead, yet gain the advantages that we have seen above, we must implement these modules in an unusual way. In many cases the routines will be best inserted into the code by an assembler; in other cases, highly specialized and efficient transfers would be inserted. To successfully and efficiently make use of the second type of decomposition will require a tool by means of which programs may be written as if the functions were subroutines, but assembled by whatever implementation is appropriate. If such a technique is used, the separation between modules may not be clear in the final code. For that reason additional program modification features would also be useful. In other words, the several representations of the program (which were mentioned earlier) must be maintained in the machine together with a program performing mapping between them.

7.6.7 A Decomposition Common to a Compiler and Interpretor for the Same Language

In an earlier attempt to apply these decomposition rules to a design project we constructed a translator for a Markov algorithm expressed in the notation described in [6]. Although it was not our intention to investigate the relation between compiling and interpretive translators of a language, we discovered that our decomposition was valid for a pure compiler and several varieties of interpretors for the language. Although there would be deep and substantial differences in the final running representations of each type of compiler, we found that the decisions implicit in the early decomposition held for all.

This would not have been true if we had divided responsibilities along the classical lines for either a compiler or interpretor (i.e., syntax recognizer, code generator, run-time routines for a compiler). Instead the decomposition was based upon the hiding of various decisions as in the example above. Thus register representation, search algorithm, rule interpretation, etc. were modules and these problems existed in both compiling and interpretive translators. Not only was the decomposition valid in all cases, but many of the routines could be used with only slight changes in any sort of translator.

This example provides additional support for the statement that the order in time in which processing is expected to take place should not be used in making the decomposition into modules. It further provides evidence that a careful job of decomposition can result in considerable carryover of work from one project to another.

A more detailed discussion of this example was contained in [8].

7.7 Hierarchical Structure

We can find a program hierarchy in the sense illustrated by Dijkstra [5] in the system defined according to decomposition 2. If a symbol table exists, it functions without any of the other modules, hence it is on level 1. Line storage is on level 1 if no symbol table is used or it is on level 2 otherwise. Input and Circular Shifter require line storage for their functioning. Output and Alphabetizer will require Circular Shifter, but since Circular Shifter and line holder are in some sense compatible, it would be easy to build a parameter-ized version of those routines which could be used to alphabetize or print out either the original lines or the circular shifts. In the first usage they would not require Circular Shifter; in the second they would. In other words, our design has allowed us to have a single representation for programs which may run at either of two levels in the hierarchy.

In discussions of system structure it is easy to confuse the benefits of a good decomposition with those of a hierarchical structure. We have a hierar-chical structure if a certain relation may be defined between the modules or programs and that relation is a partial ordering. The relation we are con-cerned with is "uses" or "depends upon." It is better to use a relation be-tween programs since in many cases one module depends upon only part of another module (e.g., Circular Shifter depends only on the output parts of the line holder and not on the correct working of *SETWORD*). It is conceiv-able that we could obtain the benefits that we have been discussing without such a partial ordering, e.g., if all the modules were on the same level. The partial ordering gives us two additional benefits. First, parts of the system are benefited (simplified) because they use the services of lower[2] levels. Second, we are able to cut off the upper levels and still have a usable and useful prod-uct. For example, the symbol table can be used in other applications; the line holder could be the basis of a question answering system. The existence of the hierarchical structure assures us that we can "prune" off the upper levels of the tree and start a new tree on the old trunk. If we had designed a system in which the "low level" modules made some use of the "high level" mod-ules, we would not have the hierarchy, we would find it much harder to remove portions of the system, and "level" would not have much meaning in the system.

Since it is conceivable that we could have a system with the type of decomposition shown in version 1 (important design decisions in the inter-faces) but retaining a hierarchical structure, we must conclude that hierarchi-cal structure and "clean" decomposition are two desirable but *independent* properties of a system structure.

7.8 Conclusions

We have tried to demonstrate by these examples that it is almost always incorrect to begin the decomposition of a system into modules on the basis of a flowchart. We propose instead that one begins with a list of difficult design decisions or design decisions which are likely to change. Each module is then designed to hide such a decision from the others. Since, in most cases, design

---

2. Here "lower" means "lower numbered."

decisions transcend time of execution, modules will not correspond to steps in the processing. To achieve an efficient implementation we must abandon the assumption that a module is one or more subroutines, and instead allow subroutines and programs to be assembled collections of code from various modules.

References

1. Gauthier, Richard, and Pont, Stephen. *Designing Systems Programs,* Prentice-Hall, Englewood Cliffs, NJ, 1970.

2. Hoare, C.A.R. Proof of a program, FIND. *Comm. ACM* 14, 1 (Jan. 1971), 39–45.

3. Parnas, D.L. A technique for software module specification with examples. *Comm. ACM 15,* 5 (May,1972), 330–336.

4. Parnas, D.L. Information distribution aspects of design methodology. Tech. Rept., Dept. Computer Science, Carnegie-Mellon U., Pittsburgh, PA, 1971. Also presented at the IFIP Congress 1971, Ljubljana, Yugoslavia.

5. Dijkstra, E.W. The structure of "THE"-multiprogramming system. *Comm. ACM 11,* 5 (May 1968), 341–346.

6. Galler, B., and Perlis, A.J. *A View of Programming Languages,* Addison-Wesley, Reading, MA, 1970.

7. Parnas, D.L. A course on software engineering. *Proc. SIGCSE Technical Symposium,* Mar. 1972.

8. Parnas, D.L. On the criteria to be used in decomposing systems into modules. Tech. Rept., Dept. Computer Science, Carnegie-Mellon U., Pittsburgh, PA, 1971.

9. Balzer, R.M. Dataless programming. *Proc. AFIPS 1967 FJCC,* Vol. 31, AFIPS Press, Montvale, NJ, pp. 535–544.

10. Mealy, G.H. Another look at data. *Proc. AFIPS 1967 FJCC,* Vol. 31, AFIPS Press, Montvale, NJ, pp. 525–534.

11. Wulf, W.A., Russell, D.B., and Habermann, A.N. BLISS, A Language for systems programming. *Comm.* ACM 14, 12 (Dec. 1971), 780–790.

Introduction

Paul C. Clements

I love this paper! When I take my seat at the keyboard to try to put a few modest thoughts in writing, it is this paper that goads me on and nags at me to write more clearly, to try harder, to convey my ideas more effectively, to do better. Not only does it carry a message of fundamental importance, but it's impeccably structured, unfolding its case in devastatingly methodical style and smooth prose. I have yet to meet its standard. And just as the best actors do not ever appear to act, the paper reads as though it were effortlessly written. It's hauntingly good.

I admire this paper principally for three reasons. First, it laid out a fundamental and timeless principle of software engineering, to my knowledge, for the first time: Software has many structures. In 1974, when this paper appeared, structure was primarily used to mean the code structure of programs, referring to the appearance of the flowchart that accompanied the program. While "top-down programming" and "structured programming" were all the rage in 1974, they both referred to practices in which getting to code was clearly the end game. (Contrast this to the current object- or component-oriented world in which we concentrate on services provided, not statements executed.) In 1974, code was king. This was only two years after Dave's timeless "On the Criteria" paper appeared, which held that how you structured the code into work assignments was a question worthy of careful consideration. Software, Dave pointed out, had other important qualities besides just computing the correct answer, and the key to these other qualities (such as the effort it took to make modifications) lay in structures beyond that of the code. The fact that there were such structures was heady stuff. In the "Buzzword" paper, Dave expanded that concept and identified (and carefully and clearly defined) the module structure, the uses structure, the process structure, the calls structure, and several structures unique to operating systems. After this paper, never again would we be justified in referring to "the" structure of the system. Many people still do, but now we can (we should!) ask innocently and sincerely: "Which structure do you mean?" If this stops a conversation or presentation dead in its tracks, it means that the speaker was not as expert as his or her terminology suggested. A tool to uncover such a thing early is a valuable (not to mention entertaining) tool indeed.

The second reason I admire this paper is because it's prescient. Building on contemporary work (not the least of which was Dave's own) in the structuring and design of programs, it lays the groundwork for the field of software architecture, which would not come into vogue until a decade or two later. "The word 'structure,'" it says, "refers to a partial description of a system showing it as a collection of parts and showing some relations between the parts." Compare that to the following:

> The structure of the components of a program/system, their interrelationships, and principles and guidelines governing their design and evolution over time. [2]

Garlan and Shaw write that software architecture is a level of design concerned with issues

> . . . beyond the algorithms and data structures of the computation; designing and specifying the overall system structure emerges as a new kind of problem. Structural issues include gross organization and global control structure; protocols for communication, synchronization, and data access; assignment of functionality to design elements; physical distribution; composition of design elements; scaling and performance; and selection among design alternatives. [3]

My favorite, not surprisingly because it's partly mine, is this one:

> The software architecture of a program or computing system is the structure or structures of the system, which comprise software components, the externally visible properties of those components, and the relationships among them. [1]

The "structure or structures" passage is a direct and intentional homage to this paper. Like so many ideas in software engineering, including those with and without a limited shelf life, Dave got there first.

And the third reason I admire this paper is because it takes dead aim at sloppy thinking and thoroughly shreds it in a disarmingly witty manner. Unless you explain what structure you mean, it says, the term 'hierarchical structure' "carries no information at all." This is Dave playing the role of the little boy who points out that the emperor is wearing no clothes. Along the way, he witheringly dispatches the phrase "high level," which unfortunately has invaded current speech and writing like a vile weed. "It would be nice," he writes laconically, "if the next person to use the phrase 'higher level language' in a paper would define the hierarchy to which he refers." Yes, or "high level" anything, for that matter: Does "high level of detail" refer to information that is more detailed or more abstract?

Our field needs more papers like this one. People who use terms because they are in vogue, but who don't have an understanding of what the terms mean, need to have their errors publicized. We all need to be goaded to think more clearly and deeply and nagged to write more clearly, to try harder, to convey ideas more effectively, to do better. We need to be haunted.

References

1. Bass, L., Clements, P., and Kazman, R., *Software Architecture in Practice,* Addison-Wesley Longman, 1998.

2. Garlan, D. and Perry, D., "Introduction to Special Issue on Software Architecture," *IEEE Transactions on Software Engineering,* April 1995.

3. Garlan, D. and Shaw, M., *An Introduction to Software Architecture,* Technical report CMU/SEI-94-TR-21, 1994.

On a "Buzzword": Hierarchical Structure

David Parnas

8.1 Abstract

This paper discusses the use of the term "hierarchically structured" to describe the design of operating systems. Although the various uses of this term are often considered to be closely related, close examination of the use of the term shows that it has a number of quite different meanings. For example, one can find two different senses of "hierarchy" in a single operating system [3] and [6]. An understanding of the different meanings of the term is essential, if a designer wishes to apply recent work in Software Engineering and Design Methodology. This paper attempts to provide such an understanding.

8.2 Introduction

The phrase "hierarchical structure" has become a buzzword in the computer field. For many it has acquired a connotation so positive that it is akin to the quality of being a good mother. Others have rejected it as being an unrealistic restriction on the system [1]. This paper attempts to give some meaning to the term by reviewing some of the ways that the term has been used in various operating systems (e.g., T.H.E. [3], MULTICS [12], and the RC4000 [8]) and providing some better definitions. Uses of the term, which had been considered equivalent or closely related, are shown to be independent. Discussions of the advantages and disadvantages of the various hierarchical restrictions are included.

8.3 General Properties of All Uses of the Phrase "Hierarchical Structure"

As discussed earlier [2], the word "structure" refers to a partial description of a system showing it as a collection of parts and showing some relations between the parts. We can term such a structure *hierarchical*, if a relation or predicate on pairs of the parts $(R(\alpha,\beta))$ allows us to define levels by saying that

1. Level 0 is the set of parts α such that there does not exist a β such that $R(\alpha,\beta)$, and

2. Level i is the set of parts α such that
   a. there exists a β on level i–1 such that $R(\alpha,\beta)$ and
   b. if $R(\alpha,\gamma)$ then γ is on level i–1 *or lower.*

This is possible with a relation R only if the directed graph representing R has no loops.

The above definition is the most precise reasonably simple definition, which encompasses all uses of the word in the computer literature. This suggests that the statement "our Operating System has a hierarchical structure" carries no information at all. *Any* system can be represented as a hierarchical system with one level and one part; more importantly, it is possible to divide *any* system into parts and contrive a relation such that the system has a hierarchical structure. Before such a statement can carry any information at all, the way that the system is divided into parts and the nature of the relation must be specified.

The decision to produce a hierarchically structured system may restrict the class of possible systems, and may, therefore, introduce disadvantages as well as the desired advantages. In the remainder of this paper we shall introduce a variety of definitions for "hierarchical structure", and mention some advantages and disadvantages of the restrictions imposed by these definitions.

8.3.1 The Program Hierarchy

Prof. E.W. Dijkstra in his paper on the T.H.E. system and in later papers on structured programming [3] and [4] has demonstrated the value of programming using layers of abstract machines. We venture the following definition for this program hierarchy. The parts of the system are subprograms, which may be called as if they were procedures.[1] We assume that each such program has a specified purpose (e.g., FNO :: = find next odd number in sequence or invoke DONE if there is none). The relation "uses" may be defined by USES(p_i,p_j) *iff* p_i calls p_j *and* p_i will be considered incorrect if p_j does not function properly.

With the last clause we intend to imply that, in our example, FNO does *not* "use" DONE in the sense defined here. The task of FNO is to invoke DONE; the purpose and "correctness" of DONE is irrelevant to FNO. Without excepting such calls, we could not consider a program to be higher in the hierarchy than the machine, which it uses. Most machines have "trap" facilities, and invoke software routines, when trap conditions occur.

A program divided into a set of subprograms may be said to be hierarchically structured, when the relation "uses" defines levels as described above.

---

1. They may be expanded as macros.

The term "abstract machine" is commonly used, because the relation between the lower level programs and the higher level programs is analogous to the relation between hardware and software.

A few remarks are necessary here. First, *we* do not claim that the only good programs are hierarchically structured programs. Second, we point out that the way that the program is divided into subprograms can be rather arbitrary. For *any* program, some decompositions into subprograms may reveal a hierarchical structure, while other decompositions may show a graph with loops in it. As demonstrated in the simple example above, the specification of each program's purpose is critical!

The purpose of the restriction on program structure, implied by this definition, is twofold. First, the calling program should be able to ignore the internal workings of the called program; the called program should make no assumptions about the internal structure of the calling program. Allowing the called program to call its user, might make this more difficult since each would have to be designed to work properly in the situations where it could be called by the other.

The second purpose might be termed "ease of subsetting". When a program has this "program hierarchy", the lower levels may always be used without the higher levels, when the higher levels are not ready or their services are not needed. An example of nonhierarchical systems would be one in which the "lower level" scheduling programs made use of the "high level" file system for storage of information about the tasks that it schedules. Assuming that nothing useful could be done without the scheduler, no subset of the system that did not include the file system could exist. The file system (usually a complex and "buggy" piece of software) could not be developed using the remainder of the system as a "virtual machine".

For those who argue that the hierarchical structuring proposed in this section prevents the use of recursive programming techniques, we remind them of the freedom available in choosing a decomposition into subprograms. If there exists a subset of the programs, which call each other recursively, we can view the group as a single program for this analysis and then consider the remaining structure to see if it is hierarchical. In looking for possible subsets of a system, we must either include or exclude this group of programs as a single program.

One more remark: please, note that the division of the program into levels by the above discussed relation has no *necessary* connection with the division of the programs into modules as discussed in [5]. This is discussed further later (Section 8.3.6).

8.3.2 The "Habermann" Hierarchy in the T.H.E. System

The T.H.E. system was also hierarchical in another sense. In order to make the system relatively insensitive to the number of processors and their relative speeds, the system was designed as a set of "parallel sequential processes". The activities in the system were organized into "processes" such that the sequence of events within a process was relatively easy to predict, but the sequencing of events in different processes was considered unpredictable (the relative speeds of the processes were considered unknown). Resource allocation was done in terms of the processes and the processes exchanged work assignments and information. In carrying out a task, a process could assign part of the task to another process in the system.

One important relation between the processes in such a system is the relation "gives work to". In his thesis [6] Habermann assumed that "gives work to" defined a hierarchy to prove "harmonious cooperation". If we have an Operating System we want to show that a request of the system will generate only a finite (and reasonably small) number of requests to individual processes before the original request is satisfied. If the relation "gives work to" defines a hierarchy, we can prove our result by examining each process separately to make sure that every request to it results in only a finite number of requests to other processes. If the relation is not hierarchical, a more difficult, "global" analysis would be required.

Restricting "gives work to" so that it defines a hierarchy helps in the establishment of the "well-behavedness", but it is certainly not a necessary condition for "harmonious cooperation".[2]

In the T.H.E. system the two hierarchies described above coincided. Every level of abstraction was achieved by the introduction of parallel processes and these processes only gave work to those written to implement lower levels in the program hierarchy. One should not draw general conclusions about system structure on the basis of this coincidence. For example, the remark that "building a system with more levels than were found in the T.H.E. system is undesirable, because it introduces more queues" is often heard because of this coincidence. The later work by Dijkstra on structured programming [21] shows that the levels of abstraction are useful when there is only one process. Further, the "Habermann hierarchy" is useful, when the

---

2. This restriction is also valuable in human organizations. Where requests for administrative work flow only in one direction things go relatively smoothly, but in departments where the "leader" constantly refers requests "downward" to committees (which can themselves send requests to the "leader") we often find the system filling up with uncompleted tasks and a correspondingly large increase in overhead.

processes are controlled by badly structured programs. Adding levels in the program hierarchy need not introduce new processes or queues. Adding processes can be done without writing new programs.

The "program hierarchy" is only significant at times when humans are working with the program (e.g., when the program is being constructed or changed). If the programs were all implemented as macros, there would be no trace of this hierarchy in the running system. The "Habermann hierarchy" is a restriction on the run time behavior of the system. The theorems proven by Habermann would hold even if a process that is controlled by a program written at a low level in the program hierarchy "gave work to" a process which was controlled by a program originally written at a higher level in the program hierarchy. There are also no detrimental effects on the program hierarchy provided that the programs written at the lower level are not written in terms of programs at the higher level. Readers are referred to "Flatland" [7].

8.3.3 Hierarchical Structures Relating to Resource Ownership and Allocation

The RC4000 system [8] and [9] enforced a hierarchical relation based upon the ownership of memory. A generalization of that hierarchical structure has been proposed by Varney [10] and similar hierarchical relationships are to be found in various commercial operating systems, though they are not often formally described.

In the RC4000 system the objects were processes and the relation was "allocated a memory region to". Varney proposes extending the relation so that the hierarchical structure controlled the allocation of other resources as well. (In the RC4000 systems specific areas of memory were allocated, but that was primarily a result of the lack of virtual memory hardware; in most systems of interest now, we can allocate quantities of a resource without allocating the specific physical resources until they are actually used.) In many commercial systems we also find that resources are not allocated directly to the processes which use them. They are allocated to administrative units, who, in turn, may allocate them to other processes. In these systems we do not find any loops in the graph of "allocates resources to", and the relation defines a hierarchy, which is closely related to the RC4000 structure.

This relation was not a significant one in the T.H.E. system, where allocating was done by a central allocator called a BANKER. Again this sense of hierarchy is not strongly related to the others, and if it is present with one or more of the others, they need not coincide.

The disadvantages of a nontrivial hierarchy (the hierarchy is present in a trivial form even in the T.H.E. system) of this sort are (1) poor resource utilization that may occur when some processes in the system are short of resources while other processes, under a different allocator in the hierarchy, have an excess; (2) high overhead that occurs when resources are tight. Requests for more resources must always go up all the levels of the hierarchy before being denied or granted. The central "banker" does not have these disadvantages. A central resource allocator, however, becomes complicated in situations where groups of related processes wish to dynamically share resources without influence by other such groups. Such situations can arise in systems that are used in real time by independent groups of users. The T.H.E. system did not have such problems and as a result, centralized resource allocation was quite natural.

It is this particular hierarchical relation which the Hydra group rejected. They did not mean to reject the general notion of hierarchical structure as suggested in the original report [1] and [11].

8.3.4 Protection Hierarchies á la MULTICS

Still another hierarchy can be found in the MULTICS system. The conventional two level approach to operating systems (low level called the supervisor, next level the users) has been generalized to a sequence of levels in the supervisor called "rings". The set of programs within a MULTICS process is organized in a hierarchical structure, the lower levels being known as the inner rings, and the higher levels being known as outer rings. Although the objects are programs, this relation is not the program hierarchy discussed in Section 1. Calls occur in both directions and lower level programs may use higher level ones to get their work done [12].

Noting that certain data are much more crucial to operation of the system than other data, and that certain procedures are much more critical to the overall operation of the system than others, the designers have used this as the basis of their hierarchy. The data to which the system is most sensitive are controlled by the inner ring procedures, and transfers to those programs are very carefully controlled. Inner ring procedures have unrestricted access to programs and data in the outer rings. The outer rings contain data and procedures that affect a relatively small number of users and hence are less "sensitive". The hierarchy is most easily defined in terms of a relation "can be accessed by" since "sensitivity" in the sense used above is difficult to define. Low levels have unrestricted access to higher levels, but not vice versa.

It is clear that placing restrictions on the relation "can be accessed by" is important to system reliability and security.

It has, however, been suggested that by insisting that the relation "can be accessed by" be a hierarchy, we prevent certain accessibility patterns that might be desired. We might have three segments in which A requires access to B, B to C, and C to A. No other access rights are needed or desirable. If we insist that "can be accessed by" define a hierarchy, we must (in this case) use the trivial hierarchy in which A, B, C are considered one part.

In the view of the author, the number of pairs in the relation "can be accessed by" should be minimized, but he sees no advantage in insisting that it define a hierarchy [13] and [14].

The actual MULTICS restriction is even stronger than requiring a hierarchy. Within a process, the relation must be a complete ordering.

8.3.5 Hierarchies and "Top Down" Design Methodology

About the time that the T.H.E. system work appeared, it became popular to discuss design methods using such terms as "top down" and "outside in" [15], [16], and [17]. The simultaneous appearance of papers suggesting how to design well and a well-designed system led to the unfounded assumption that the T.H.E. system had been the result of a "top down" design process. Even in more recent work [18] top down design and structured programming are considered almost synonymous.

Actually "outside in" was a much better term for what was intended, than was "top down"! The intention was to begin with a description of the system's user interface, and work in small, verifiable steps towards the implementation. The "top" in that hierarchy consisted of those parts of the system that were visible to the user. In a system designed according to the "program hierarchy", the lower level functions will be used by the higher level functions, but some of them may also be visible to the user (store and load, for example). Some functions on higher levels may not be available to him (Restart system). Those participants in the design of the T.H.E. system with whom I have discussed the question [19] report that they did not proceed with the design of the higher levels first.

8.3.6 Hierarchical Structure and Decomposition into Modules

Often one wants to view a system as divided into "modules" (e.g., with the purpose outlined in [5] and [20]). This division defines a relation "part of". A group of subprograms is collected into a module, groups of modules collected into bigger modules, etc. This process defines a relation "part of" whose graph is clearly loop-free. It remains loop-free even if we allow programs or modules to be part of several modules—the part never includes the whole.

Note that we may allow programs in one module to call programs in another module, so that the module hierarchy just defined need not have any connection with the program hierarchy. Even allowing recursive calls between modules does not defeat the purpose of the modular decomposition (e.g., flexibility) [5], provided that programs in one module do not assume much about the programs in another.

8.3.7 Levels of Language

It is so common to hear phrases such as "high level language", "low level language", and "linguistic level" that it is necessary to comment on the relation between the implied language hierarchy and the hierarchies discussed in the earlier sections of this paper. It would be nice, if, for example, the higher level languages were the languages of the higher level "abstract machines" in the program hierarchy. Unfortunately, this author can find no such relation and cannot define the hierarchy that is implied in the use of those phrases. *In moments of skepticism* one might suggest that the relation is "less efficient than" or "has a bigger grammar than" or "has a bigger compiler than", however, none of those phrases suggests an ordering, which is completely consistent with the use of the term. It would be nice, if the next person to use the phrase "higher level language" in a paper would define the hierarchy to which he refers.

8.4 Summary

The computer system design literature now contains quite a number of valuable suggestions for improving the comprehensibility and predictability of computer systems by imposing a hierarchical structure on the programs. This paper has tried to demonstrate that, although these suggestions have been described in quite similar terms, the structures implied by those suggestions are not necessarily closely related. Each of the suggestions must be understood and evaluated (for its applicability to a particular system design problem) independently. Further, we have tried to show that, while each of the suggestions offers some advantages over an "unstructured" design, there are also disadvantages, which must be considered. The main purpose of this paper has been to provide some guidance for those reading earlier literature and to suggest a way for future authors to include more precise definitions in their papers on design methods.

References

1. Wulf, Cohen, Coowin, Jones, Levin, Pierson, Pollach, *Hydra: The Kernel of a Multiprogramming System*, Technical Report, Computer Science Department, Carnegie-Mellon University.

2. David L. Parnas, Information Distribution Aspects of Design Methodology, *Proceedings of the 1971 IFIP Congress*, Booklet TA/3, 26–30.

3. E.W. Dijkstra, The Structure of the T.H.E. Multiprogramming System, *Communications of the ACM,* vol. 11, no. 5, May 1968, 341–346.

4. E.W. Dijkstra, Complexity controlled by Hierarchical Ordering of Function and Variability, *Software Engineering,* NATO.

5. David L. Parnas, On the Criteria to Be Used in Decomposing Systems into Modules, *Communications of the ACM,* vol. 15, no. 12, December 1972, 1053–1058.

6. A.N. Habermann, On the Harmonious Cooperation of Abstract Machines, Doctoral Dissertation, Technische Hogeschool Eindhoven, The Netherlands.

7. Edwin A. Abbott, *Flatland, the Romance of Many Dimensions,* Dover Publications, Inc., New York, 1952.

8. Per Brinch Hansen, The Nucleus of a Multiprogramming System, *Communications of the ACM,* vol. 13, no. 4, April 1970, 238–250.

9. RC4000 Reference Manuals for the Operating System, Regnecentralen Denmark.

10. R.C. Varney, Process Selection in a Hierarchical Operating System, *SIGOPS Operating Review,* June 1972.

11. W. Wulf, C. Pierson, Private discussions.

12. R.W. Graham, Protection in an Information Processing Utility, *Communications of the ACM,* May 1968.

13. W.R. Price and David L. Parnas, The Design of the Virtual Memory Aspects of a Virtual Machine, *Proceedings of the SIGARCH-SIGOPS Workshop on Virtual Machines,* March 1973.

14. W.R. Price, Doctoral Dissertation, Department of Computer Science, Carnegie-Mellon University, Pittsburgh, PA.

15. David L. Parnas and Darringer, SODAS and Methodology for System Design, *Proceedings of 1967 FJCC.*

16. David L. Parnas, More on Design Methodology and Simulation, *Proceedings of the 1969 SJCC.*

17. Zurcher and Randell, Iterative Multi-Level Modeling, *Proceedings of the 1968 IFIP Congress.*

18. F.T. Baker, System Quality through Structured Programming, *Proceedings of the 1972 FJCC.*

19. E.W. Dijkstra, A.N. Habermann, Private discussions.

20. David L. Parnas, Some Conclusions from an Experiment in Software Engineering, *Proceedings of the 1972 FJCC.*

21. E.W. Dijkstra, A Short Introduction to the Art of Programming, in O.-J. Dahl, E.W. Dijkstra, and C.A.R. Hoare, *Structured Programming,* Academic Press, New York, 1972.

Acknowledgments

The author acknowledges the valuable suggestions of Mr. W. Bartussek (Technische Hochschule Darmstadt) and Mr. John Shore (Naval Research Laboratory, Washington, D.C.). Both of these gentlemen have made substantial contributions to the more precise formulation of many of the concepts in this paper; neither should be held responsible for the fuzziness, which unfortunately remains.

Introduction

Daniel Siewiorek

I arrived at Carnegie-Mellon University in January 1972. Shortly thereafter Dave Parnas invited me to provide a hardware example for a paper he was working on to define the concept of transparency. In the hardware realm, the concept of an Instruction Set Architecture (ISA) was being fully exploited by industry. With the introduction of the IBM system/360 in 1964, IBM defined the instruction-set level of abstraction, thereby separating architecture from implementation. In 1971, Gordon Bell and Allen Newell's classic textbook *Computer Structures: Readings and Examples* extended IBM's concepts into a comprehensive hierarchy ranging from the circuit level all the way up through the networking level. Primitive components and a language to compose those components into primitives at the next higher level of the hierarchy were identified, and two new notations—Instruction Set Processor (ISP) and Processor, Memory, Switch (PMS)—were introduced for the instruction-set architecture and networking level. Software design was focusing on "programming in the small." The concepts of abstractions and modularity, as exemplified by information hiding in exportation of functions, were beginning to appear in the research literature.

This paper introduced the concept of transparency between a base machine and a virtual machine. The paper states, "If the virtual machine and its implementation were completely transparent, any base machine state and any sequence of base machine states which we could obtain by programming the base machine would also be obtainable by programming the virtual machine. In the more common situation, where some base machine sequences cannot be obtained by programming the virtual machine, we term the missing state sequences the loss of transparency." The architect's job is to define operations at the virtual machine level that are simpler to comprehend than the sequence of functions on the base machine required to implement the functionality. In the process of defining these abstractions, the architect should not preclude useful sequences on the base machine. By introducing virtual machine abstractions, the architect might make it exceedingly difficult to do on the base machine a simple operation that is useful to application programmers. If the missing functions would be frequently used, the application programmer might be motivated to seek shortcuts to circumvent the architecture, thereby jeopardizing its modularity and portability.

The concept of transparency is even more relevant in today's highly layered architectures. Often there is no feedback to the application programmer or user with respect to the cost of performing individual functions and composition of functions. For example, the cost and complexity of a search on the

World Wide Web appear the same to the user whether the contents are locally stored in a cache or require a search spanning a multitude of machines.

The paper also envisioned several future research areas. One example described how virtual memory makes the hierarchy of main memory and secondary storage appear as one large random access memory. However, there was no way for a user to indicate that a page would not be used again and hence need not be saved to secondary storage. The paper suggested that the user might give hints that could be used by the operating system to optimize performance. Such hints are utilized today to assist virtual memory systems.

In another example, it was suggested that the same base machine for the hardware could be used to describe a virtual machine with a load/store architecture with enhanced addressing modes and a rich set of register operators. This was a precursor to the RISC architectures of the mid-1970s and beyond.

Use of the Concept of Transparency in the Design of Hierarchically Structured Systems

D.L. Parnas and D.P. Siewiorek

9.1 Abstract

This paper deals with the design of hierarchically structured programming systems. It develops a method for evaluating the cost of requiring programmers to work with an abstraction of a real machine. A number of examples from hardware and software are given as illustrations of the method.

9.2 Introduction

The starting point of this paper is the goal of constructing systems with a hierarchical structure of the type first illustrated by E.W. Dijkstra in [1, 2]. Each level in such a system provides a virtual machine which hides (or abstracts from) some aspects of the machine below it. In designing such a system, we repeatedly face a question which a hardware designer faces only once: "How do I know that the instruction set provided by this machine is suitable for the programs which users will want to run upon it?" There is a risk in freezing the design of a level, the risk that we may force some inefficiency upon our final system. We may even eliminate some essential capability.

The purpose of this paper is to introduce a concept which appears to be useful in the design of hierarchically structured systems. For purposes of comparison, we shall review an approach which was suggested earlier, then introduce and illustrate the main concepts of this paper.

9.3 The "Top Down" or "Outside In" Approach

Several papers [3, 4, 5] suggest that the solution to software design problems lies in beginning with a precise description of the desired system and deriving the internal structure from it. This would prevent design decisions which remove necessary capabilities and eliminate the risk of constructing a system with unexpected undesirable properties. The papers referenced were all concerned with providing simulation tools which could be used to verify that each decision was an adequate one. The approach was called "top down" or "outside in."

In this paper we shall refer to this approach as "outside in" rather than "top down" because the latter appellation often leads to a confusion of this approach with the levels introduced by Dijkstra [1]. The "outside in" approach and that of Dijkstra cannot be compared as they are addressing quite different questions. Dijkstra was not discussing the sequence in which design decisions were made, he was discussing the structure of the final product. Higher levels in Dijkstra's sense are not necessarily "closer to the outside" in our sense. Some low level features may appear on the "outside."

The "outside in" approach has been discussed in several places (e.g., [6]) and found to involve a number of difficulties.

1. The necessary specification of the "outside" is often difficult to obtain. In addition to the obvious difficulty in making such design decisions, it is difficult to express those decisions precisely without implying additional, internal, design decisions.

2. The derivation of a design from such a specification is often not feasible. The set of possible internal structures for a given external specification is so large that one needs some additional constraints before a search can be begun. These constraints are usually information about the "inside" (e.g., the hardware).

3. In attempting to follow the "outside in" procedure it is quite easy to specify internal mechanisms which would simplify implementation of the desired outside but would themselves be impractical to implement.

4. It is difficult to apply this method if one is actually designing a set of systems whose only description is "general purpose."[1]

5. As was pointed out in [7], the application of this method may result in a piece of software which is unnecessarily inflexible (see also [8]).

6. It is quite common to design software in a situation where the inside is already fixed (e.g., the hardware for an operating system, or the operating system for a piece of application software).

It is for these reasons that we have found it necessary to abandon the pure "outside in" approach and adopt some additional procedures which are actually of an "inside out" or "bottom up" nature. We do not propose the following as a procedure to be used instead of the "outside in"; we propose these as complementary approaches which must be used in some judicious combination according to the needs of the situation.

---

1. We are indebted to C.W. Koot of NV Philips-Electrologica (Apeldoorn, The Netherlands), who was the first to point out to us the difficulties introduced when "general purpose" is included in the description of a future product.

9.4 "Transparency" of an Abstraction

We wish to consider a typical stage in a "bottom up" design process. We assume that we have a well defined lower level and are considering the design of the next highest level. The lower level may be either hardware or an intermediate level in our software design. We shall refer to either as the *base machine*. We assume that we are considering a proposal for a new abstraction to result in a new programmable machine which we shall refer to as the *virtual machine*.

We must determine the set of states which is possible for the base machine under arbitrary programs in the "language" of the base machine. Also of interest is the set of state *sequences* which can be obtained by arbitrary base machine language programs.

For any given implementation of our virtual machine we can determine a set of base machine states and sequences of base machine states which is obtainable by running programs written for the virtual machine.

If the virtual machine and its implementation were *completely transparent,* any base machine state and any sequence of base machine states which we could obtain by programming the base machine would also be obtainable by programming the virtual machine. In the more common situation, where some base machine sequences cannot be obtained by programming the virtual machine, we term the missing state sequences the *loss of transparency.*

In the above we have defined transparency as a property of a triple consisting of the base machine, the virtual machine, and the implementation of the virtual machine on the base machine. In many cases, however, we can find that there is a loss of transparency for the virtual machine, base machine, and any conceivable or likely to be used implementation. In such cases we shall speak loosely of the transparency of the virtual machine for a given base machine.

In fact, in many cases we can ascertain a lack of transparency for a given virtual machine and any base machine likely to be considered. In those cases we can speak very loosely about the transparency of the virtual machine without reference to a specific base machine.

For the purposes of the present paper it is sufficient to rely on our intuitive understandings of what the properties of reasonable base machines and certain virtual machine propositions are. For many interesting software design problems there is no need to resort to formal models.

9.5 Preliminary Example

The following example is intended to illustrate the concept of transparency and to make the point that a loss of transparency is often one of the goals of a design.

Figure 9.1 shows a diagram of a low level portion of a four-wheeled vehicle. Note that each front wheel is connected to two strings and should a driver use such a vehicle, he would control the steering by pulling on a total of four strings.

It is probably feasible for well-coordinated people to learn to use such a control mechanism, but it is certainly not convenient or pleasant. Figure 9.2 shows the addition of a higher level mechanism which uses the mechanism of Figure 9.1 to provide a more convenient virtual machine for the driver. The ropes have been wrapped around a steering wheel and attached so that now the vehicle can be controlled by the more easily learned mechanism of turning the wheel in the desired direction. If this is properly done, it is a very good abstraction from the real machine. (If it is not properly done, it may introduce all sorts of inefficiencies, including excessive tire wear and poor driving characteristics.)

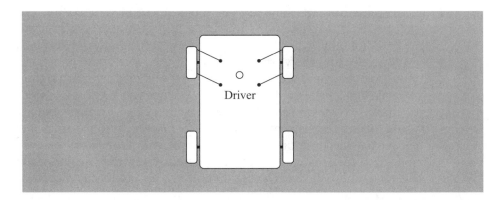

Figure 9.1

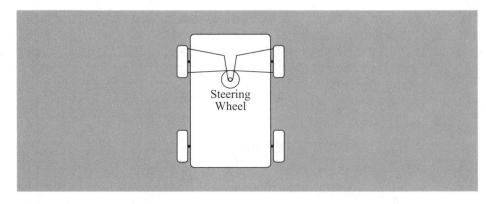

Figure 9.2

The point of this example, however, is that even if this is done in an ideal way, the abstraction is not transparent in the sense just defined. Figure 9.3 shows some of the states which were possible with the lower level control mechanism. Positions (a) and (b) will be possible by the use of any reasonably designed steering wheel implementation. Positions (c) and (d) will no longer be possible with reasonable implementation. Very sharp turns (e) could be eliminated by some designs and permitted by others.

If the steering wheel were an abstraction proposed in a "bottom up" design process, we would ask that the designer use the concept of transparency in evaluating the validity of the proposed design. In this particular case the lack of transparency with regard to (c) and (d) would be considered acceptable because situations in which those positions are useful are extremely rare. The lack of transparency for those cases can be considered a desirable feature of the abstraction; one of the purposes of introducing certain abstractions is to prevent the occurrence of undesirable states. The loss of (e) is more difficult to evaluate; it is undesirable, but it might be acceptable if the turning circle would be adequate anyway or if there was a cost decrease obtained by eliminating this extreme position.

The fundamental assumption behind our proposed "bottom up" approach is that the primitive mechanisms from which one builds a system have the ability to perform all the functions finally expected of the system. (If that is not true, the project is hopeless from the start.) If we evaluate each level by examining the loss of transparency as illustrated above and make certain that nothing desirable is lost, we may be assured that the upper levels will still have the desired capabilities.

The remainder of this paper will be devoted to examples from the field of computer systems.

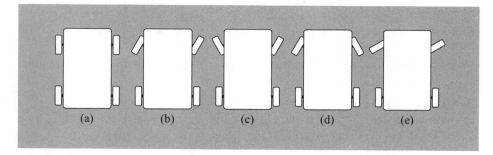

Figure 9.3 *Some states possible with the lower level control mechanism.*

9.6 "Register" for Markov Algorithm Machine

Figure 9.4 is a specification of a module developed for use in a Markov algorithm interpreter or compiler. One can view this module as providing a virtual machine which has a register which has essentially the same capabilities

INTEGER PROCEDURE: LENGTH
possible values: an integer $0 \leq LENGTH \leq 1000$
effect: no effect on values of other functions
parameters: none
initial value: 0

INTEGER PROCEDURE: CHAR (I)
possible values: an integer $0 \leq CHAR \leq 255$
parameters: I must be an integer
effect: no changes to other functions in modules
    if $I \leq 0 \vee I >$ 'LENGTH' **then** a procedure call to a user written routine RGERR
    is performed (program cannot be assembled without such a routine).
initial value: undefined

PROCEDURE: INSERT (I, J)
possible values: none
parameters: I must be an integer
         J must be an integer
effect:
    if $I < 0 \vee I >$ 'LENGTH' $\vee J < 0 \vee J > 255$ **then** a subroutine call to a user
    written routine INSAER is performed (routine required).
    else LENGTH = 'LENGTH' + 1 **if** LENGTH ≤ 1000 a subroutine call to user
    written function LENGER is performed.
    CHAR (K) =
        if $K \leq I$, 'CHAR (I)'
        if $K = I + 1$, J
        if $K > I + 1$, 'CHAR (K – 1)'

PROCEDURE: DELETE (I, J)
possible values: none
parameters: I, J must be integers
effect:
    if $I \leq 0 \vee J < 1 \vee I + J >$ 'LENGTH' + 1 **then** a procedure call to a user written
    routine DELERR is performed.
    else
        LENGTH = 'LENGTH' – J.
    CHAR (K) = **if** $K < I$ **then** 'CHAR (K)'
                if $K \geq I$ **then** 'CHAR (K + J)'

Figure 9.4 *Definitions.*

as that in the idealized Markov algorithm machine. Characters may be inserted and deleted at any point in the string, etc. The one fundamental difference is that, because this is a specification for a real piece of software, there are limits to its capacity.

Informally, the four operations provided can be described as follows:

"LENGTH"   reveals the number of characters in the register.
"CHAR(I)"   gives the Ith character in the register if $I \leq$ length.
"INSERT(I,J)" places a new character at the specified point in the register.
"DELETE(I,J)" removes a character in the register.

At first glance this appears to be a good design. In fact, it was used unsuspectingly and, for quite a while, the faults were not apparent to any of those involved in the project. The fault is easily noticed as a loss of transparency.

Such a module has many possible implementations. We list just a *few* of the more interesting or useful ones:

1. *Register is an array.* Access is by indexing; inserts and deletions require shifting.
2. *Register is a one-way linked list.* Access is by linear search counting for the Ith item requested. Inserts and deletions require list processing operations—no large shifts.
3. *Register is a two-way linked list.* Access is by search from either end or from the last point accessed. Insertions require list processing operations.
4. *Register is a linked list with an "index"* pointing to a number of points within the list to reduce searching.
5. *Register is a linked list of small arrays.* Most small changes can be done on a single small array as in implementation (1). Larger changes require addition or removal of one or more small arrays. (The small arrays might be machine words in which up to six characters are packed.)

Each implementation would be good under some set of operating conditions and costs (e.g., (1) is the minimal coding time version).

We can easily imagine having designed an abstract machine which contained operators which could be used for one of the above implementations. We refer to that machine as the *"base" machine.* On *any* likely base machine there will be simple sequences (e.g., a single store operation) which replace a single character in the register with another single character. These sequences involve no shifting in implementations (1) or (5) and no linked list operations in implementations (2) through (5). *These sequences cannot be evoked by calling the "virtual machine" operations defined above.* Thus, this design has a loss of transparency because there are sequences on the base machine which cannot be evoked by commands given to the virtual machine. Further,

PROCEDURE: ALTER (I, J)
possible values: none
parameters: I, J must be integers
effect:

       if $I \leq 0 \vee I >$ 'LENGTH' $\vee J < 0 \vee J > 255$ **then** a subroutine call to a user
       written routine ALTERERR is performed.

      CHAR (K) = **if** $K \neq I$ **then** 'CHAR (K)'
                  if $K = I$ **then** J

Figure 9.5 *Definition of ALTER.*

we see that the lack of transparency is undesirable because (1) the missing sequences are both harmless and useful, (2) the work they accomplish can only be performed by much more expensive sequences evoked by the higher level.[2]

The above loss of transparency can easily be corrected by the addition of the "alter" command specified in Figure 9.5. In our experimental project we did this during the project. Because of the "upward compatible" nature of the improvement, old programs continued to work but new ones could be written to be more efficient. In no case did we have to reveal the inner workings of a module to gain in efficiency.

For some time we considered the amended design to have the proper degree of transparency, but further reflection has indicated an additional problem. In most of the base machines there exist sequences which efficiently insert several characters at a given point in the register. For example, in implementation (1), if we wished to insert four characters, we could do so (on the base machine) by shifting the information right four places and then inserting the four characters. By calling the commands proposed, the base machine would *probably* perform four one place shifts instead of the single four place shift.

At this point there appear to be three fundamentally distinct solutions to this design problem. Each has advantages and disadvantages, and we are unable to make a general choice among them.

---

2. Even if we were willing to accept the loss of efficiency, we would have difficulties because of the psychological nature of good professional programmers. Most feel such revulsion at the writing of inefficient programs that they would seek some way of going beneath the interface of the base machine in order to improve performance. In that case, the modular structure would be lost. Such behavior is readily apparent in much production software.

1. *A more sophisticated implementation.* The word "probably" occurs in the above paragraph because there do exist possible implementations which would not incur the loss of efficiency described. For example, "Insert" might be implemented so that it would not actually perform the insertions in the basic data structure until a call was made to insert at a different point. In this way the module could "store" commands until it had enough information to determine the most efficient way to perform the insertion series. Deletes are also possible in this way.

2. *String parameters.* We could modify the routines defined so that they accepted strings as parameters. In this way the insertion of a string could be specified as a single operation.

3. *Use of "open."* We could add an "open" instruction which would essentially mark a place in our register. Subsequent insert and delete operations would have the marked place as their implicit positional parameter. Modifications of the fundamental data structure could be postponed until a "close" command or another call of "open."

The first solution forces the module to make decisions which might not pay off. For example, such an implementation would be relatively slow if used for random insertions of single characters. The primary advantage of the first solution is that it has the same specification as the earlier solutions so that one could freely choose between a simple or a sophisticated implementation without changing the rest of the system.

The second solution's primary disadvantage is that it requires a more complex interface between the module and the rest of the system. Some format for the passing of string parameters must be agreed on. This is undesirable from the point of view of [9]. It might also result in a great deal of excess computation being done since strings might be assembled twice: once in the module and once in the parameter format. A good implementation in this direction is not impossible, but it certainly is difficult.

The third solution offers the greatest efficiency potential, but it is a little more revealing of internal structure. In a sense, this solution shifts the burden assumed by the module in solution (1) to the program which uses the module. Although all the solutions have situations in which they would be appropriate, this is probably the best "general" solution.

The above discussion permits us to discuss a fundamental "tradeoff" which exists between transparency and flexibility of a design. In the above examples we made the point that the lack of transparency introduced was true for *all* reasonable implementations of the proposed design. There are, however, situations in which a proposed virtual machine would be adequately transparent for some base machines, but would have a distinct loss of transparency for others. A design which would increase the transparency for one machine may pose great implementation difficulties or inefficiencies for another base machine. We can offer no better advice than that the designer must be alert for such situations and be prepared to make a difficult decision.

9.7 A Hardware Example

As an example of a loss of transparency at the hardware level consider the Hewlett-Packard 2116. The HP 2116 is a 16-bit, general purpose minicomputer. A simplified block diagram is shown in Figure 9.6. The HP 2116 contains six registers: memory buffer (MB), memory address (MA), program counter (P), two accumulators or general purpose registers (A and B), and an instruction register (I).

The read/write memory cycle is divided into eight minor cycles. In each minor cycle one or more micro-operations can be performed. For example, the A register can be read to the R Bus during one minor cycle. A partial list of the micro-operations which can be performed in a minor cycle is given in ISP notation in Table 9.1 [15].

To see how these micro-operations may be combined to form a machine instruction, consider the timing diagram for the RAL (rotate A register left one bit) shown in Figure 9.7.

The ISP code describes the RAL instruction execution as follows:

```
RAL → (
      T0:  (MB ← 0); next
      T1:  (I ← 0); next
      T2:  (I ← MB⟨15 : 10⟩); next
      T3:  (R_Bus ← A); next
           (T_Bus ← R_Bus × 2); next
           (A ← T_Bus); next
      T6:  (R_Bus ← P); (S_Bus ← 1); next
           (T_Bus ← R_Bus + S_Bus); next
           (P ← T_Bus))
```

The base machine for the HP 2116 can perform a combination of the micro-operations listed in Table 9.1 during one minor cycle. Eight minor cycles can be "stacked" together to form a machine instruction. Note, however, there are some physical limitations imposed by the structure of the base machine. First, the data read from memory during the current memory cycle isn't available until halfway through T2. This effectively limits instruction execution to T3–T7. Also for data to be entered into memory it has to be in the MB by the middle of T3. The bus structure also limits some operations. For example, the A and B registers cannot be used during the same minor cycle because they both are connected to the R Bus. Finally some sequence of operations might be essentially a no-operation (NOP) such as ((R_Bus ← A) next; (T_Bus ← R_Bus ∧ S_Bus)). Since there is no store operation the A register remains unchanged.

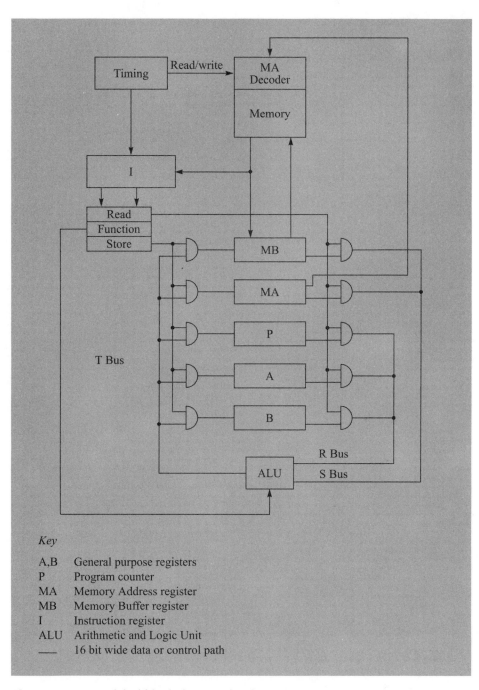

Figure 9.6 *Simplified block diagram for the HP 2116.*

Table 1.1   *Partial List of Micro-operations for the HP 2116*

	Micro-operations
Read	S_Bus ← MB
	S_Bus ← MA
	S_Bus ← 1
	R_Bus ← P
	R_Bus ← A
	R_Bus ← B
Store	MB ← 0
	MB ← T_Bus
	MA ← T_Bus
	P ← T_Bus
	A ← T_Bus
	B ← T_Bus
	I ← 0
	I ← MB(15 : 10)
Function	T_Bus ← R_Bus ∧ S_Bus
	T_Bus ← R_Bus ∨ S_Bus
	T_Bus ← R_Bus + S_Bus
	T_Bus ← R_Bus × 2
	T_Bus ← R_Bus / 2

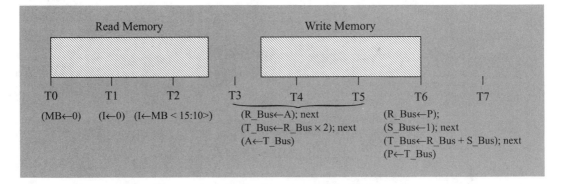

Figure 9.7   *The timing diagram for rotation of A register.*

When we look at the instruction code provided to the user we find that some of the micro-operation sequences which were possible at the base machine level cannot be obtained by sequences of machine instructions.

Consider, for example, the shift-rotate instruction group. In addition to the restrictions imposed by the base machine structure the following manufacturer imposed rules apply to all instructions in the group:

1. Minor Cycles T3, T4, T5 are used for instruction execution. The other minor cycles are used for housekeeping chores such as instruction decode, incrementing program counter, etc.

2. All shifts and rotates take place in T3 and T5.

3. All skip conditions are checked during T4. If the skip condition is met a flag is set so that two is added, instead of one, during the update of the program counter.

Since the machine instruction set allows at most two one-bit shifts per instruction, two machine instructions are required to perform a multiply by eight. The base machine can perform the multiply by eight in one machine instruction as indicated by the following ISP.

```
RAL8 → (
        T0: (MB ← 0); next
        T1: (I ← 0); next
        T2: (I ← MB⟨15 : 10⟩); next
        T3: (R_Bus ← A); next
            (T_Bus ← R_Bus × 2); next
            (A ← T_Bus); next
        T4: (R_Bus ← A); next
            (T_Bus ← R_Bus × 2); next
            (A ← T_Bus); next
        T5: (R_Bus ← A); next
            (T_Bus ← R_Bus × 2); next
            (A ← T_Bus); next
        T6: (R_Bus ← P); (S_Bus ← 1); next
            (T_Bus ← R_Bus + S_Bus); next
            (P ← T_Bus))
```

As another example of a loss of transparency consider a memory reference instruction. The instruction in Figure 9.7 was a register reference instruction and could be executed in one major cycle time. In contrast, a memory reference instruction requires at least two major cycle times: the first to fetch the instruction, the second to fetch the operand. During the instruction fetch major cycle of every memory reference instruction the address portion of the memory word is loaded into the memory address register. This can occur any time after T2 when the instruction is known to be a memory reference instruction. During this time a predesignated register could be added to the address portion of the memory reference instruction. Thus base-displacement (using one of the two accumulator registers as a base register) or relative addressing (using the program counter as the added register) could be performed by the base machine. The ISP for the fetch portion of a memory reference instruction using base-displacement addressing is as follows:

```
Fetch → (
        T0: (MB ← 0); next
        T1: (I ← 0); next
        T2: (I ← MB⟨15 : 10⟩); next
        T3: (R_Bus ← A); (S_Bus ← MB⟨9 : 0⟩); next
            (T_Bus ← R_Bus + S_Bus); next
            (MA ← T_Bus))
```

Whereas the multiply by eight sequence of micro-operations would be relatively cheap to add to the machine language level machine (add some extra decoding to select an unused bit pattern as the op-code) the cost of enhanced addressing modes may be higher. An alternate design using the same base machine might use a limited memory reference class of instruction (e.g., Load, Store) with enhanced addressing modes and a large class of register reference operations. Yet another design would use double words for memory reference instructions. The first word could contain the op-code and addressing information, the second the address portion. It is not clear which of these three virtual machines is more desirable.

9.8 An Unsolved Transparency Problem from the Operating System Area

The following example is a problem which we consider to be an important unsolved research problem.

One of the most difficult items in the programming of an operating system is the coordination and synchronization of many concurrent activities. The handling of interrupts (the hardware device available for coordinating concurrent activities) is very difficult for a programmer and likely to introduce errors. For this reason, several operating system designers have introduced an abstract machine for which interrupts no longer exist. Instead, the machines are provided with "process synchronization primitives" which can be used to allow synchronization and communication between several cooperating processes which are, at least conceptually, operating asynchronously and in parallel. Among the better known of these are those of Dijkstra [1, 10], Saltzer [11], and P.B. Hansen [12, 13]. If all process synchronization at all levels (except the lowest which implements the primitives) are to be handled in terms of the primitives, their transparency is an extremely important issue. The loss of any of the fundamental abilities to coordinate concurrent activities would seriously interfere with the usefulness of the operating system.

It is difficult to make a precise determination of the transparency of such primitives because we do not have a precise expression of the essential capabilities of the base machine. We can, however, discuss two of the mentioned primitive systems with respect to a "typical" interrupt system. For both cases some lack of transparency can be shown, but the question of "undesirable" lack of transparency remains a matter of opinion.

Consider first the following situation: We wish to have two cooperating administrative units operating in parallel at least part of the time. One of them is primarily computation and occasionally determines that it needs certain records from the disk. Fortunately, it determines the name of the record it needs well in advance of the time that it must have the record in order to continue. It sometimes determines the names of many records (e.g., 10 or 12) simultaneously. In those cases it must process the records one at a time (an error would be introduced if two were processed at once), but the order in which they are processed is irrelevant. The other process (or perhaps a group of processes) can care for the finding of the records on the disk and bringing them to core. The computational process will proceed until it needs one of the records requested, and if it is not available, will then wait for it. The disk handling process or processes should bring the records to core in an order unpredictable by the computational process. For optimum use of processing resources, etc., we should like to see the computational process send *one* message to the others with the names of the requested records but receive a "signal" as *each* record arrives so that it will not have to wait for all the records to arrive before beginning its work.

On any reasonable base machine it would be possible to set up such signaling (using the primitives from the T.H.E. system, for example). Using the primitives used by Hansen and his colleagues in the RC4000 system [12] we *cannot* set up such conventions. That system has a restriction on interprocess communication so that there is a reply for every message (1:1). In this way the computational process must either send 12 messages or wait for a single reply. (An even more expensive possibility is to send one message, wait for reply, then receive 12 messages and send 12 replies.) The fact that there is a lack of transparency is clear; whether or not it is an undesirable one is a matter of opinion. Hansen has stated [14] that the restriction was introduced as a means of detecting certain common errors and that the restriction was not significant in the situations for which the system was intended.

Another lack of transparency in [12] results from a decision to transmit an eight character message with each synchronization signal. Thus sequences on the base machine with simply synchronization but without such a message are not available through the virtual machine or nucleus. This was a decision based on knowledge that, in the intended application areas, synchronization without communication of a message would not be needed. Apparently the system was not intended to be able to handle teletype communication on a character at a time basis at the nucleus level. It would be unfortunate if each character arriving were handled with an eight character message and similar reply; some lower level mechanism must be used.

It is interesting to note that the primitives used by Dijkstra in T.H.E. do not have this particular lack of transparency. From another point of view it is possible to make certain programming errors with those primitives that would be detected by the RC4000 system nucleus [14].

The authors of this paper believe the transparency of Dijkstra's primitives is an open question; in fact, it is a question which required careful definition. We have seen statements of the problem which would yield a negative answer [16]. On closer investigation, it appeared that the statement of the problem eliminated solutions which would be acceptable on practical grounds [17]. The heart of the difficulty lies in our ability to reassign operating system tasks among processes (e.g., to increase the number of processes) to avoid an apparent limitation of the primitive scheme. Since we abstract from the concept of interrupt, supply the synchronizing primitives, and introduce the concept of process simultaneously, the set of achievable computations is very hard to characterize.

From a practical point of view, the ability to stop a process which is not executing a synchronization primitive seems available on the base machine, seems essential, and seems to be missing with Dijkstra's primitives. All attempts to go beyond this statement have failed to date. This example is included in the hope that others will see fit to investigate it further.

9.9 "Suggestive Transparency"

One example of a lack of transparency which resulted in a performance difficulty occurred in the design of virtual memory mechanisms. Usually the virtual machine provided no means of indicating to the mechanism that a segment contained useless information. As a result, many old save areas and similar useless items were moved between core and backup store.

This is one of many situations in which a weaker form of transparency is important. It is often necessary that a mechanism be able to receive *suggestions* about certain base machine sequences although the virtual machine user is not able to cause those sequences. The user of a virtual memory mechanism should be able to *suggest* removal of a segment by indicating that he will not need it again. He must not be able to cause such removal since there may be other users of the segment or the optimal time for removal may not occur until later.

9.10 "Misleading Transparency"

A related problem occurs when the design of the virtual machine suggests that certain virtual machine programs are efficient although they are actually expensive on the base machine. A virtual memory mechanism which simulates a very large random access memory is an example of such a design. To use such a virtual machine efficiently one must have certain additional information. It is often possible and preferable to design a virtual machine in which the expensive sequences are either impossible or difficult to evoke.

9.11 Outside In and Bottom Up Procedures in Combination

Advocation of design from the outside in is based on the engineering rule that one should not begin to design an object that is not fully specified. It is difficult to reject this precept. Whenever one begins to build an object with only a muddy view of what it will be, one gets a muddy object.

The difficulties with the outside in approach come because of a number of peculiar characteristics of software engineering.

1. The economics of the industry are such that one is seldom designing a single object; we are usually designing a family of related objects. (Only a proper subset of that family will actually ever exist.)

2. Because of our limited experience with man-machine symbiosis it is often impossible to specify the outside before construction and not want to change it afterwards. As was pointed out in [7] the outside in procedure often adds difficulties in such a change.

In software we begin with a specification of the *family* of objects one wishes to construct. The technique described in [18] allows one to describe parameterized families of objects, but the members must be highly similar items. To describe a broad family of objects we must describe a set of lower level mechanisms which will be common to all members. The family being designed consists of all possible "tops" for that lower level structure. It is at this point that the concept of transparency becomes important. By use of this concept we may assure ourselves that the class of tops which can be built upon the lower level structure includes the family of objects that we set out to design.

References

1. Dijkstra, E.W., The structure of the "THE" operating system, *Comm. ACM 11, 5* (May 1968), 341–346.

2. Dijkstra, E.W. Notes on structured programming. *Report of the Technische Hoogschool Eindhoven*, Eindhoven, The Netherlands.

3. Parnas, D.L., and Darringer, J.A. SODAS and a methodology for system design. *Proc. AFIPS 1967 FJCC,* Vol. 31, AFIPS Press Montvale, NJ, pp. 449–474.

4. Zurcher, F.W., and Randell, B. Multi-level modeling—A methodology for computer system design. *Proc. IFIP Cong.,* 1968.

5. Parnas, David L. More on simulation languages and design methodology for computer systems. *Proc. AFIPS 1969 SJCC,* Vol. 34, AFIPS Press, Montvale, NJ, pp. 739–743.

6. Gill, S. Thoughts on the sequence of writing software. In *Software Engineering,* report of a conference in Garmisch, Germany, Oct. 1968.

7. Parnas, D.L. Information distribution aspects of design methodology. *Proc. IFIP Cong.,* 1971.

8. Braden, et al. An implementation of MVT, UCLA report.

9. Parnas, D.L. On the criteria to be used in decomposing systems into modules. *Comm. ACM 15,* 12 (Dec. 1972), 1053–1058.

10. Dijkstra, E.W. Cooperating sequential processes. *Report of Technische Hoogschool Eindhoven,* Eindhoven, The Netherlands.

11. Saltzer, G. Traffic control in a multiplexed computer system. MIT Thesis.

12. Hansen, P.B. The nucleus of a multiprogramming operating system. *Comm. ACM 13,* 4 (Apr. 1970), 238–241.

13. Hansen, P.B., *RC4000 Reference Manual.* Regnecentralen, Copenhagen, Denmark.

14. Hansen, P.B., private discussions.

15. Bell, C.G., and Newell, A. *Computer Structures: Readings and Examples.* McGraw-Hill, New York, 1971.

16. Patil, S.S. Limitations and capabilities of Dijkstra's semaphore primitives for coordination among processes. *Proj. MAC,* Computat. Structures Group Memo 57, Feb. 1971.

17. Parnas, D.L. On a solution to the cigarette smoker's problem (without conditional statements). *Comm. ACM 18,* 3 (Mar. 1975), 181–183.

18. Parnas, D.L. A technique for software module specification with examples. *Comm. ACM 15,* 5 (May 1972), 330–336.

Introduction

Ralph Johnson

It is popular to talk about program families now. The most recent version of this topic is "product-line software," [3] but "domain analysis" has been a popular topic since the early 1980s, and object-oriented frameworks provide the foundations for producing members of program families [1]. Any serious study of reusable software must consider program families (called "application families" by Jacobson, Griss, and Jonsson [2]). However, there was once a time that people did not think of families of programs.

"On the Design and Development of Program Families" was the first paper to focus on program families. Dave describes three possible ways to make a program family. The "classical method" had been in use for a long time, though always informally and usually unconsciously. It consisted of producing a complete, working version of a program and then modifying its code as necessary to produce other versions. He proposed two alternative ways, one using stepwise refinement and one using module specification. Stepwise refinement was based on a top-down procedural derivation of a program, while module specification required dividing a program into a set of information-hiding modules, each of which hid a design decision that could be changed for the various family members. His conclusion was that these ways were complementary, not equivalent or contradictory. Module specification was more powerful, but more expensive. He thought stepwise refinement would be more widely used, but module specification would have an important place.

Twenty-five years later, the classical method is still the most widely used, still used mostly unconsciously. However, the module specification method is commonly used to design program families, and stepwise refinement is rarely used for that purpose. It is not clear why the module specification method is more successful than stepwise refinement for making reusable software. One reason might be that module specification fits in better with object-oriented programming, which has become popular with those trying to write reusable software. Objects are not quite the same as modules, since modules can contain classes and can also contain procedures that are independent of any class. However, the module specification method applies very well to object-oriented programs. The module specification method assumes that the interface can be separated from the implementation of a module and that one module can replace another if its interface is compatible. This is true of classes, too.

For example, a Java applet is a subclass of Applet. An applet has a set of components that represent its user interface widgets, but the only semantics these components have is that they are subclasses of Component. A subclass of Applet will have a custom initialization method that creates its components. It also has an interface that lets it be used inside an internet browser. This lets Applet describe the family of applets. This family is much broader and less precisely specified than Dave meant in his paper. Nevertheless, the module specification method can be used to develop families like it. Stepwise refinement cannot, since it focuses on control flow, which is a secondary part of the design of Applet.

One of the differences between module specifications and class interfaces is that class interfaces usually contain only type information, while module specifications also define behavior. Class interfaces in Java or C++ contain less information than module specifications, permit a larger range of behaviors to users (most of them wrong), and are easier to write. In other words, even if class interfaces are compatible, one class cannot necessarily be replaced by another. Programmers sometimes get in trouble because of this, and so many people have advocated enhancing interfaces with behavioral specifications. Eiffel is the best-known language whose interfaces can define preconditions and postconditions on operations, not just types. Those who use Eiffel like this benefit, but assertions have been slow to creep into other languages. Language designers don't seem to be convinced that the benefit is worth the cost. So, perhaps another reason for the success of the module specification method is that class interfaces are a weaker form of module specification but are easier for most developers to learn and use.

One of the great things about reading a paper like this is that it focuses on essentials instead of getting caught up in a particular technology. The design of a programming family is based more on hiding design decisions than on whether we are using C or Java. The principles and techniques that Dave describes have stood the test of time and have survived major changes in programming style. Although we have to adapt his examples for the programming language that we use, it is well worth the effort.

References

1. Mohamed E. Fayad, Douglas C. Schmidt, Ralph E. Johnson (editors), *Building Application Frameworks: Object-Oriented Foundations of Framework Design*, Wiley, 1999.

2. Ivar Jacobson, Martin Griss, and Patrik Jonsson, *Software Reuse: Architecture, Process and Organization for Business Success*, ACM Press, 1997.

3. David M. Weiss and Chi Tau Robert Lai, *Software Product-Line Engineering: A Family-Based Software Development Process*, Addison-Wesley, 1999.

On the Design and Development of Program Families

David L. Parnas

10.1 Abstract

Program families are defined (analogously to hardware families) as sets of programs whose common properties are so extensive that it is advantageous to study the common properties of the programs before analyzing individual members. The assumption that, if one is to develop a set of similar programs over a period of time, one should consider the set as a whole while developing the first three approaches to the development, is discussed. A conventional approach called "sequential development" is compared to "stepwise refinement" and "specification of information hiding modules." A more detailed comparison of the two methods is then made. By means of several examples it is demonstrated that the two methods are based on the same concepts but bring complementary advantages.

10.2 Introduction

We consider a set of programs to constitute a *family*, whenever it is worthwhile to study programs from the set by *first* studying the common properties of the set and *then* determining the special properties of the individual family members. A typical family of programs is the set of versions of an operating system distributed by a manufacturer. While there are many significant differences between the versions, it usually pays to learn the common properties of all the versions before studying the details of any one. Program families are analogous to the hardware families promulgated by several manufacturers. Although the various models in a hardware family might not have a single component in common, almost everyone reads the common "principles of operations" manual before studying the special characteristics of a specific model. Traditional programming methods were intended for the development of a single program. In this paper, we propose to examine explicitly the process of developing a program family and to compare various programming techniques in terms of their suitability for designing such sets of programs.

10.3 Motivation for Interest in Families

Variations in application demands, variations in hardware configurations, and the ever-present opportunity to improve a program mean that software will *inevitably* exist in many versions. The differences between these versions are unavoidable and purposeful. In addition, experience has shown that we cannot always design all algorithms before implementation of the system. These algorithms are invariably improved experimentally after the system is complete. This need for the existence of many experimental versions of a system is yet another reason for interest in "multiversion" programs.

It is well known that the production and maintenance of multiversion programs is an expensive problem for software distributors. Often separate manuals and separate maintenance groups are needed. Converting a program from one version to another is a nontrivial (and hence expensive) task.

This paper discusses two relatively new programming methods which are intended explicitly for the development of program families. We are motivated by the assumption that if a designer/programmer pays conscious attention to the family rather than a sequence of individual programs, the overall cost of development and maintenance of the programs will be reduced.[1] The goal of this paper is to compare the methods, providing some insight about the advantages and disadvantages of each.

10.4 Classical Method of Producing Program Families

The classical method of developing programs is best described as *sequential completion*. A particular member of the family is developed completely to the "working" stage. The next member(s) of the family is (are) developed by modification of these working programs. A schematic representation of this process is shown by Figure 10.1. In this figure a node is represented as a circle, if it is an intermediate representation on the way to producing a program, but not a working program itself. An X represents a complete (usable) family member. An arc from one node to another indicates that a program (or intermediate representation of a program) associated with the first node was modified to produce that associated with the second.

Each arc of this graph represents a design decision. In most cases each decision reduces the set of possible programs under consideration. However, when one starts from a working program, one generally goes through a

---

1. Some preliminary experiments support this assumption [1], [2], but the validity of our assumption has not yet been proved in practice. Readers who do not want to read about programming techniques based on this unproved assumption should stop reading here.

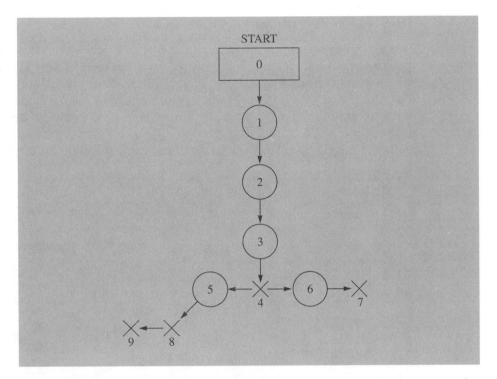

Figure 10.1 *Representation of development by sequential completion. Note: nodes 5 and 6 represent incomplete programs obtained by removing code from program 4 in preparation for producing programs 7, 8, and 9.*

Symbols: □ *is the set of initial possibilities;* O *is the incomplete program;* × *is the working program.*

reverse step, in which the set of possible programs is again increased (i.e., some details are not decided). Nodes 5 and 6 are instances of this.

When a family of programs is produced according to the above model, one member of the family can be considered to be an ancestor of other family members. It is quite usual for descendants of a given program to share some of its ancestor's characteristics which are not appropriate to the purpose of the descendants. In bringing the earlier version to completion, certain decisions were made which would not have been made if the descendant program had been developed independently. These decisions remain in the descendant program only because their removal would entail a great deal of reprogramming. As a result, later versions of the program have performance deficiencies, because they were derived by modifying programs designed to function in a different environment or with a different load.

10.5 New Techniques

Figure 10.2 shows the common basic concept of newer methods. Using these methods one never modifies a completed program to get a new family member; one always begins with one of the intermediate stages and continues from that point with design decisions, ignoring the decisions made after that point in the development of the previous versions. Where in the classical method one can say that one version of the program is the ancestor of another, here we find that the two versions have a common ancestor [3].

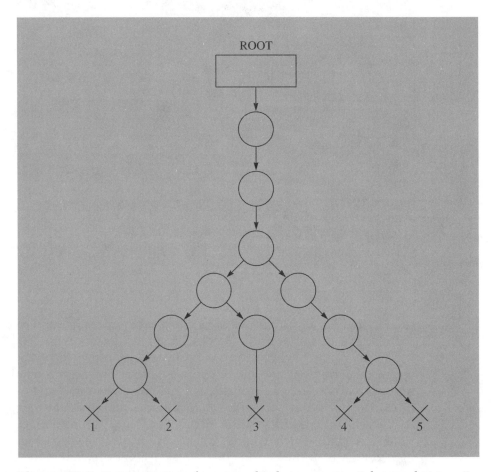

Figure 10.2 *Representation of program development using "abstract decisions."*
Symbols: □ is the set of initial possibilities; O is the incomplete program; × is the working program.

The various versions need not be developed sequentially. If the development of one branch of the tree does not use information from another branch, the two subfamilies could be developed in parallel. A second important note is that in these methods the order in which decisions are made has more significance than in the classical method. Recall that all decisions made above a branch point are shared by all family members below that point. In our motivation of the family concept, we emphasized the value of having much in common among the family members. By deciding as much as possible before a branch point, we increase the "similarity" of the systems. Because we know that certain differences must exist between the programs, the aim of the new design methods is to allow the decisions, which can be shared by a whole family, to be made before those decisions, which differentiate family members. As Figure 10.2 illustrates, it is meaningful to talk of subfamilies which share more decisions than are shared by the whole family.

If the root of the tree represents the situation before any decisions are made, then two programs, which have only the root as common ancestor, have nothing in common.

We should note that representing this process by a tree is an oversimplification. Certain design decisions can be made without consideration of others (the decision processes can be viewed as commutative operators). It is possible to use design decisions in several branches. For example, a number of quite different operating systems *could* make use of the same deadlock prevention algorithm, even if it was not one of the decisions made in a common ancestor.

10.6 Representing the Intermediate Stages

In the classical method of producing program families, the intermediate stages were not well defined and the incomplete designs were not precisely represented. This was both the cause and the result of the fact that communication between versions was in the form of completed programs. If either of the two methods discussed here is to work effectively, it is necessary that we have precise representations of the intermediate stages (especially those that might be used as branch points). Both methods emphasize precision in the descriptions of partially designed programs. They differ in the way that the partial designs are represented. We should note that it is not the final version of the program, which is our real product (one seldom uses a program without modification); in the new methods it is the well-developed but still incomplete representation that is offered as a contribution to the work of others.

10.7 Programming by Stepwise Refinement

The method of "stepwise refinement"[2] was first formally introduced by Dijkstra [3] and has since been further discussed by a variety of contributors [4]–[6]. In the literature the major emphasis has been on the production of correct programs, but the side effect is that the method encourages the production of program families. One of the early examples was the development of a program for generation of prime numbers in which the next to the last program still permitted the use of two quite different algorithms for generating primes. This incomplete program defined a family of programs which included at least two significantly different members.

In "stepwise refinement" the intermediate stages are represented by programs, which are complete except for the implementation of certain operators and operand types. The programs are written as if the operators and operands were "built into" the language. The implementation of these operators in the actual language is postponed to the later stages. Where the (implicit or explicit) definition of the operators is sufficiently abstract to permit a variety of implementations, the early versions of the program define a family in which there is a member for each possible implementation of the unimplemented operators and operands. For example, a program might be written with a declaration of a data type *stack* and operators *push* and *pop*. Only in later versions would the stack representation and procedures to execute *push* and *pop* be introduced. We illustrate the technique of stepwise refinement with two examples, which will be used in a later comparison.

10.7.1 Example 1: Dijkstra's Prime Program

Dijkstra [3] has described the development of a program to print numbers. The first step appears as follows:

```
begin variable table p;
        fill table p with first thousand prime numbers;
        print table p;
end
```

In this program Dijkstra has assumed an operand type "table" and two operators. The representation of the table, the method of calculating the primes, and the printing format are all left undecided. In fact, the only binding decisions (common characteristics of the whole family of programs) are that *all* the primes will be developed before *any* are printed, and that we will always want the first thousand primes. Dijkstra then debates between implementing table or elaborating "fill table." Eventually he decides that "table"

---

2. The reader should note that although stepwise refinement is often identified with "goto less programming," the use and abuse of the goto is irrelevant in this paper.

should be implemented, and all members of the remaining family share the same table implementation. A branch of the family with an alternative table implementation is mentioned, but not developed. Later members of the family are developed by considering various possible methods of computing the prime numbers.

10.7.2 Example 2: Wulf's KWIC Index Program

Wulf [5] presents a proposed stepwise refinement development of a KWIC index production program as follows:

Step 1: PRINTKWIC

We may think of this as being an instruction in a language (or machine), in which the notion of generating a KWIC index is primitive. Since this operation is not primitive in most practical languages, we proceed to define it:

Step 2: PRINTKWIC: generate and save all interesting circular shifts
                     alphabetize the saved lines
                     print alphabetized lines

Again we may think of each of these lines as being an instruction in an appropriate language; and again, since they are not primitive in most existing languages, we must define them, for example:

Step 3a: generate and save all interesting circular shifts:

```
for each line in the input do
    begin
    generate and save all interesting
       shifts of "this line"
    end
```

etc.

For purposes of later comparison, we note the decisions that must be shared by the remaining members of the family:

1. All shifts will be stored;
2. All circular shifts will be generated and stored before alphabetization begins;
3. Alphabetical ordering will be completed before printing is started;
4. All shifts of the one line will be developed before any of the shifts for another line;
5. "Uninteresting" shifts will be eliminated at the time that the shifts are generated.

In the best-known examples of programming by stepwise refinement the definitions of the operators have been informal. All of the published examples have been designed as tutorial examples, and the operators are kept "classical" so that one's intuitive understanding of them suffices for the correct understanding of the program development. The only exception known to the author is [11].[3] Formal definition of the operators can be included by application of the predicate insertion technique first introduced by Floyd for the purpose of program verification. As Dijkstra has suggested, we can think of the operators as "predicate transformers" (rules which describe how a predicate which describes the state of the program variables after application of the operator can be transformed into a predicate describing the state of the program variables before the operator is executed [7]).

10.8 Technique of Module Specification

Another technique for the design of program families has been described in [8], [9]. This method is distinguished from the method of stepwise refinement in that the intermediate representations *are not* incomplete programs. Instead, they are "specifications" of the externally visible collective behavior of program groups called modules.[4] These intermediate representations are not written in a programming language, and they never become part of the final system.

To illustrate this method we compare the development of the KWIC program described in [8], [9] with the development by stepwise refinement discussed earlier in this paper.

In the method of "module specification" the design decisions which *cannot* be common properties of the family are identified and a module (a group of programs) is designed to hide each design decision. For our example, the following design decisions were identified:

1. The internal representation of the data to be processed;

2. The representation of the circular shifts of those lines and the time at which the shifts would be computed;

3. The method of alphabetization, which would be used, and the time at which the alphabetization would be carried out;

4. The input formats;

5. The output formats;

6. The internal representation of the individual words (a part of decision 1).

---

3. In this example the method failed to produce a correct program because the intuitive understanding of the operators was too vague.

4. Naur has called a similar concept "action clusters" [10].

To hide the representation of the data in memory, a module was provided which allows its users to simply write CHAR (line, word, c) in order to access a certain character. Data were "stored" in this module by calling SETCHAR (line, word, c, d). Other functions in the module would report the number of lines, the number of words in a given line, and the number of characters in a word. By the use of this group of programs the rest of the program could be written in a way that was completely independent of the actual representation.

A module quite similar in appearance to the one described above hid the representation of the circular shifts, the time at which they were computed, even whether or not they were ever stored. (Some members of the program family reduced storage requirements by computing the character at a given point in the list of shifts whenever it was requested.) All of these implementations shared the same external interface.

Still another pair of programs hid the time and method of alphabetization. This (2 program) module provided a function ITH (i) which would give the index in the second module for the i-th line in the alphabetic sequence.

The decisions listed above are those which are not made, i.e., postponed. The decisions which were made are more difficult to identify. The design has placed restrictions on the way that program parts may refer to each other and has, in that way, reduced the space of possible programs.

The above description is intended as a brief review for those who already have some familiarity with the two methods. Those who are new to the ideas should refer to the original articles before reading further.[5]

10.9 Comparison Based on the KWIC Example

To understand the differences in the techniques the reader should look at the list of decisions which define the family of KWIC programs whose development was started by Wulf. All of the decisions which are shared by the members of Wulf's family are hidden in individual modules by the second method and can therefore differentiate family members. Those decisions about sequencing of events are specified early in Wulf's development but have been postponed in the second method.

Lest one think that in the second method no decisions about implementation have been made, we list below some of the common properties of programs produced using the second method.

---

5. For symmetry we remark that while stepwise refinement was developed primarily to assist in the production of correct programs and has a pleasant side effect in the production of program families, module specification was developed for the production of program families but helps with "correctness" as discussed in [14].

1. All programs will have access to the original character string during the process of computing the KWIC index.

2. Common words such as THE, AND, etc., would not be eliminated until the output stage (if ever).

3. The output module will get its information one character at a time.

The astute reader will have noted that these decisions are not necessarily good ones. Nonetheless, decisions have been made which allow work on the modules to begin and progress to completion without further interaction between the programmers. In this method the aim of the early work is not to make decisions about a program but to make it possible to postpone (and therefore easily change) decisions about the program. Later work should proceed more quickly and easily as a result [1].

In the stepwise refinement method we progressed quickly toward a relatively narrow family (limited variations in the family). With modules we have prepared the way for the development of a relatively broad family.

10.10 Comparative Remarks Based on Dijkstra's Prime Program

We now take a second look at the Dijkstra development of the prime number program.

In his development Dijkstra is moved to make an early decision about the implementation of TABLE in order to go further. All members of the family developed subsequently share that implementation. Should he decide to go back and reconsider that decision, he would have to reconsider all of the decisions made after that point. The method of module specification would have allowed him to postpone the table implementation to a later stage (i.e., to hide the decision) and thereby achieve a broader family.

10.11 Comparative Remarks Based on an Operating System Problem

We consider the problem of core allocation in an operating system. We assume that we have a list of free core areas and data that should be brought to core storage. Writing a program that will find a free spot, and allocate the space to the program needing it, is trivial. Unfortunately there are many such programs, and we cannot be certain which of them we want. The programs can differ in at least two important ways, policy and implementation of the mechanism. By "policy" we mean simply the rule for choosing a place, if there are several usable places; by "implementation of the mechanism" we mean such questions as, how shall we represent the list of free spaces, what operations must we perform to add a free space to the list, to remove a free space? Should the list be kept in a special order? What is the search procedure? etc.

The decisions discussed above are important in that they can have a major impact on the performance of a system. On the other hand, we cannot pick a "best" solution; there is no best solution!

On the policy side there have been numerous debates between such policies as "first fit"—allocate the first usable space in the list, "best fit" —find the smallest space that will fit, "favor one end of core," "modified best fit" —look for a piece that fits well but does not leave a hopelessly small fragment, etc. It is clear to most who have studied the problem that the "best" policy depends on the nature of the demand, i.e., the distribution of the requested sizes, the expected length of time that an area will be retained, and so on.

Choosing an implementation is even more complicated because it depends in part on the policy choice. Keeping a list ordered by size of fragment is valuable if we are going to seek a "best fit" but worse than useless for a policy which tends to put things as low in core as possible.

The following "structured programming" development of such an algorithm illustrates the construction of an abstract program which has the properties of all of those that we are interested in and does not yet prejudice our choice.

```
stage 1:
   bestyet :=null;
while not all spaces considered do

   begin
    find next item from list of free spaces (candidate)
    best yet := bestof(bestyet,candidate)
   end
       if bestyet = null then erroraction
     allocate (best yet); remove (best yet)
```

Strictly following the principles of writing well-structured programs we should now verify that the above is correct or write down the conditions under which we can be certain that it is correct.

Correctness Assumptions:

1. "bestyet" is a variable capable of indicating a free space; null is a possible value of this variable indicating no space.

2. "not all spaces considered" is a predicate which will be *true* as long as it is possible that a "better" space is still to be found but will be *false* when all possible items have been considered.

3. "candidate" is a variable of the same type as bestyet.

4. "find next item from list of free spaces" will assign to its parameter a value indicating one of the items on the free space list. If there are *n* such

5. items on the list, n calls of the procedure will deliver each of the n items once.

6. No items will be removed from or added to the list during the execution of the program.

7. "bestof" is a procedure which takes two variables of the type of bestyet and returns (as a value of the same type) the better of the two possible spaces according to some unspecified criterion. If neither place is suitable, the value is "<u>null</u>," which is always unsuitable.

8. "error action" is what the program is supposed to do if no suitable place can be found.

9. "remove" is a procedure which removes the space indicated by its parameter from the list of free spaces. A later search will not find this space.

10. "allocate" is a procedure which gives the space indicated by its parameter to the requesting program.

11. Once we have begun to execute this program, no other execution of it will begin until this one is complete (mutual exclusion).

12. The only other program which might change the data structures involved is one that would add a space to the free space list. Mutual exclusion may also be needed here.

10.12 Design Decisions in Stage 1

Although this first program appears quite innocuous, it does represent some real design decisions which are best understood by considering programs which do not share the properties of the above abstract program.

1. We have decided to produce a program in which one is not allowed to add to the free space list *during* a search for a free space.

2. We have not allowed a program in which two searches will be conducted simultaneously.

3. We are considering only programs where a candidate is not removed from the free space list while it is being considered. Perfectly reasonable programs could be written in which the "bestyet" was not on the list and was reinserted in the list when a better space was discovered.

4. We have chosen not to use a program in which a check for possible allocation is made before searching the list. Some reasonable programs would have a check for the empty list, or even a check for the size of the largest available space before the loop so that no time would be spent searching for an optimum fit when no fit at all was possible. In our program, an assignment to "bestyet," an evaluation of the termination con-

dition, plus an evaluation of "bestyet=<u>null</u>" will take place every time the program is called.

The programs omitted from the family of programs which share the abstract program of stage 1 are not significant omissions. If they were, we would not have chosen to eliminate them at such an early stage in our design. We have discussed them only so that the reader will see that writing the program of stage 1 has not been an empty exercise.

We now consider a subfamily of the family of programs defined in stage 1. In this subfamily we will decide to represent the list by a two-dimensional array in which each row represents an item in the free space list. We assume further that the first free space is kept in row 1, that the last is in row *N,* and that all rows between 1 and *N* represent valid free spaces. We make no assumptions about the information kept in each row to describe the free space nor the order of rows in the array. This allows us to write the following:

```
stage 2:
        bestyet := 0;
        candidate := 0;
    while candidate ≠ N do
      begin
        candidate := candidate + 1;
        bestyet := bestof(bestyet,candidate)
      end
    if bestyet = 0 then erroraction;

    allocate (bestyet)
    remove (bestyet).
```

We have been able to allow the variables "bestyet" and "candidate" to be integers to implement the test for "not all spaces considered" as an integer test on the value of "candidate" because of our assumptions. Our assumptions do not yet permit us to elaborate the operations on the table rows or to implement our policy decision in "best of." We cannot even implement "remove," because we do not know if we are going to allocate all of the space found or allocate only that part needed and leave the rest on the free space list.

10.13 Stage 3

We now skip several stages in a "proper" structured programming development in order to show one of the possible "concrete" family members. In this program we have decided that the entries in each row of the array will give the first and last locations of each free space and that when we allocate a space we will allocate the whole space so as to avoid having to keep track of an ever increasing set of small fragments. We also assume a policy of "best fit" which means that we pick the smallest of the suitable free spaces.

```
                    bestyet := 0;
                    candidate := 0;
                    OLDT := ∞

while candidate ≠ N do

        begin
            candidate := candidate + 1

            T := (end(candidate)-start(candidate))
            if T ≥ request Λ T < OLDT then begin
                    bestyet := candidate
                    OLDT := T end;
        end;
            if bestyet = 0 then erroraction;
        allocate (bestyet)
            N := N - 1;
         for I := bestyet step 1 until N do begin

            END[I] := END[I+1];
            START[I] := START[I+1];
        end;
```

To understand the value of structured programming in producing programming families, we now have to consider what would happen if, instead of the program developed in stage 3, we wanted a program in which (1) we did *not* allocate the *smallest suitable* space but only that part of it that was needed and (2) we represented the free spaces by giving the *start address* and the *length* rather than *start and end* addresses. We consider making this change in two situations:

Situation 1: We wrote the program shown in stage 3 in the classical way, i.e., we wrote that program directly without writing down the intermediate stages.

Situation 2: We used the structured programming development as shown above.

In situation 1 we would have to modify the programs shown in the section in stage 3. We would have nothing else. As you can see, it would take some effort to identify which lines in the program could remain and which could or should be changed. Even on this rather simple example it would require a fairly careful study of the program to determine which changes should be made unless the person making the changes was very familiar with the program (e.g., unless he personally had just written it).

In situation 2, however, we have the option of returning to the program labeled "stage 2." All the assumptions made in stage 2 are still valid and the program itself is still valid, only incomplete. Completing the program shown in stage 2 in order to produce the new nonabstract program is as straightforward as the original modification of stage 2 to get stage 3. It can be done by someone new. In this situation the new final program is obtained not by modifying the old working program but by modifying the closest common ancestor.

If the organization in charge of maintaining the system wishes to keep both versions in active use, they can use the stage 2 documentation as valid documentation for both versions of the program and even consider some changes for both versions by studying stage 2.

This example was intended to demonstrate why structured programming is such a valuable tool for those who wish to maintain and develop families of programs such as operating systems. The reader must keep in mind that this is a small and simple example; the benefits would be even greater for larger programs developed in this way.

Although we have shown an advantage for development of program families by using structured programming we have also revealed a fundamental problem. Progress at each stage was made by making design decisions. Going back to stage 2 was possible in our case because we had in stage 2 all of those design decisions which we wanted to keep and none of those which we wanted to discard. Unless we were able to predict in advance exactly which decisions we would change and which we would keep, we are not likely to be so lucky in practice. In fact, even with the ability to see into the future, there might not be any decision making sequence which would allow us to backtrack without discarding the results of decisions which will remain unchanged. The results of perfectly valid design decisions may have to be recoded, because the code that implements those decisions was designed to interact with the code that is being changed.

It is to get around these difficulties that the division into "information hiding" modules can be introduced. Rather than continually refine step by step a single program, as is done in stepwise refinement, we break the program up into independent parts and develop each of them in ignorance of the implementation of the other. In contrast to classical programming methods, these parts are not the subprograms which are called from a main program; they are collections of subprograms.

In our example we would have a free space list module, allocation module, and a selection criterion module. The free space list module would consist of

1. The code which implemented the variable bestyet and any other variable that could represent a place in a list as well as the representation of the constant <u>null</u>;

2. The program "not all spaces considered";

3. The program "find next item from the list of free spaces";

4. The program "remove";

5. A program to add items to the free space list (this program is not called in the above program, but must be called elsewhere in the system and would be considered a part of the free space list module);

6. Programs to give the essential characteristics of a space on the list (e.g., start and end address).

The selection criterion module would consist of

1. bestof;

2. Some other programs which will be called elsewhere, such as programs to choose a victim (a space to be removed from its owner and made available).

The allocation module consists of "allocate" and other programs not discussed above. Each of these modules would have to contain an initialization section which would be called from the main program so that the additional temporary variables introduced in implementing the programs would not be visible in the main program. For some implementations of a module the initialization section would be empty, but its call would be written in the main program so that the main program would not have to be changed if the new implementation included variables which had to be initialized.

This division into modules and independent implementation will only result in a working program if the external characteristics of each module were sufficiently well specified so that the code could be written without looking at the implementation of other modules [1], [9]. This is clearly an extra effort which is not needed if only the stepwise refinement method is used. In return for this effort one would gain the ability to reverse the decision about table representation made in stage 2 without even considering the code written to implement the policy introduced in stage 3. One also gains the ability to develop the two parts of the program without any communication between the groups developing each one. This can lead to a shorter development time and the ability to develop several versions of the system simultaneously.

10.14 How the Module Specifications Define a Family

Members of a family of programs defined by a set of module specifications can vary in three principal ways.

1. *Implementation methods used within the modules.* Any combination of sets of programs which meets the module specifications is a member of the program family. Subfamilies may be defined either by dividing each of the main modules into submodules in alternative ways, or by using the method of structured programming to describe a family of implementations for the module.

2. *Variation in the external parameters.* The module specifications can be written in terms of parameters so that a family of specifications results. Programs may differ in the values of those parameters and still be considered to be members of the program family.

3. *Use of subsets.* In many situations one application will require only a subset of the functions provided by a system. We may consider programs which consist of a subset of the programs described by a set of module specifications to be members of a family as well. This is especially important in the development of families of operating systems, where some installations will require only a subset of the system provided for another. The set of possible subsets is defined by the "uses" relation between the individual programs [16].

10.15 Which Method to Use

By now it should be clear that the two methods are neither equivalent nor contradictory. Rather they are complementary. They are both based on the same basic ideas (see historical note which follows): 1) precise representations of the intermediate stage in a program design, and 2) postponement of certain decisions, while continuing to make progress toward a completed program.

Stepwise refinement (as practiced in the literature) encourages one to make decisions about sequencing early, because the intermediate representations are all programs. Postponement of sequencing decisions until runtime requires the introduction of processes [13]. The method of module specification is not usually convenient for the expressing of sequencing decisions. (In our KWIC index project sequencing had to be described by writing a brief "structured" "Main Program," which was one of several possible ways that the module could have been used to produce a KWIC index. It was written last!)

Stepwise refinement has the significant advantage that it does not add to the total amount of effort required to design the first complete family member. By keeping complexity in control, it usually reduces the total amount of effort. In contrast, the module specifications represent a very significant amount of extra effort. Experience has shown that the effort involved in writing the set of specifications can be greater than the effort that it would take to write one complete program. The method permits the production of a broader family and the completion of various parts of the system independently, but at a significant cost. It usually pays to apply the method only when one expects the eventual implementation of a wide selection of possible family members. In contrast, the method of stepwise refinement is always profitable.

10.16 Relation of the Question of Program Families to Program Generators

A common step taken by industrial maintainers of multiversion programmers is the construction of system generation programs. These programs are given a great deal of data describing the hardware configuration and software needs of the users. Built into the generator is a description of a large family of programs and the generator causes one member of the family to materialize and be loaded on the target hardware.

The methods described in this paper are not intended to replace system generators. Since these methods are applied in the design stage and generators are useful when a specific family member must be produced. Stepwise refinement and the method of module specification can simplify the work to be done by a system generation program.

System generators would be completely unnecessary if we wished to build a program which at runtime could "simulate" any member of the family. Such a program would be relatively inefficient. By removing much of this variability at the time that the program is generated, increases in productive capacity are made possible.

Often a family of programs includes small members in which certain variables are fixed and larger members in which these factors may vary. For example, an operating system family may include some small members where the number of processes is fixed and other members where dynamic creation and deletion are possible. The programs developed for the larger members of the family can be used as part of the "generator," which produces a smaller member.

10.17 Conclusions

Another way of comparing the two methods is to answer the following often-heard questions:

1. When should we teach structured programming or stepwise refinement to our students?

2. When should we teach about modules and specifications?

To the first question we can respond with another question: "When should we teach unstructured programming?" The second question, however, requires a "straight answer": module design specifications should only be taught to students who have learned to program well and have decided to proceed further and learn methods appropriate to the production of software packages [12].

One of the difficulties in applying the recent concepts of structured programming is that there are no criteria by which one may evaluate the structure of a system on an objective basis. Aspiring practitioners must go to a famous artist and ask for an evaluation. The "master" may then indicate whether or not he considers the system "tasteful."

The concept of program families provides one way of considering program structure more objectively. For any precise description of a program family (either an incomplete refinement of a program or a set of specifications or a combination of both) one may ask which programs have been excluded and which still remain.

One may consider a program development to be good, if the early decisions exclude only uninteresting, undesired, or unnecessary programs. The decisions which remove desired programs would be either postponed until a later stage or confined to a well delimited subset of the code. Objective criticism of a program's structure would be based upon the fact that a decision or assumption which was likely to change has influenced too much of the code either because it was made too early in the development or because it was not confined to an information hiding module.

Clearly this is not the only criterion which one may use in evaluating program structures. Clarity (e.g., ease of understanding, ease of verification) is another quite relevant consideration. Although there is some reason to suspect that the two measures are not completely unrelated, there are no reasons to assume that they will agree. For one thing, the "ease" measures mentioned above are functions of the understander or verifier, the set of programs being excluded by a design decision can be interpreted objectively. Of course, the question of which decisions are likely to require changing for some family member is again a question which requires judgment and experience. It is, however, a somewhat more concrete and more easily discussed question than ease of comprehension.

10.18 Historical Note

In closing this comparison, I want to make a comment on the origin and history of some of the ideas found in this paper. I recently reread one of the papers in which Dijkstra introduced the ideas of structured programming [3]. This paper is unusual in that it seems better each time you read it. The root of *both* methods of producing program families and the concept of family itself is in this original work by Dijkstra. The concept of the division into modules is somewhat differently formulated, but it is present in the concept of the design of the abstract machines, the notion of information hiding is implicit (in the discussion of the thickness of the ropes tying the pearls together). Module specification is not discussed. (Naur introduced a concept quite similar to that of the module when he discussed action clusters [10], but the concept of information hiding was not made specific and the example does not correspond exactly to what this principle would suggest.) For various reasons the concept of division into modules and the hiding of information seems to have attracted less attention, and later works by other authors [4], [5] have emphasized only the stepwise refinement of programs, ignoring the order of the steps or the question of the thickness of the ropes.

References

1. D.L. Parnas, "Some conclusions from an experiment in software engineering techniques," in *1972 Fall Joint Computer Conf., AFIPS Conf. Proc.,* vol. 41. Montvale, NJ: AFIPS Press, 1972, pp. 325–329.

2. H. Mills, "Mathematical foundations of structured programming," IBM Federal Systems Div., No. FSC72-6012, pp. 1–62, Feb. 1972.

3. E.W. Dijkstra, "Structured programming," in *Software Engineering Techniques,* J.N. Buxton and B. Randell, Ed. Brussels, Belgium: NATO Scientific Affairs Division, 1970, pp. 84–87.

4. N. Wirth, "Program development by stepwise refinement," *Commun. ACM,* vol. 14, pp. 221–227, Apr. 1971.

5. W.A. Wulf, "The GOTO controversy: A case against the GOTO," *SIGPLAN Notices,* vol. 7, pp. 63–69, Nov. 1972.

6. C.A.R. Hoare, "Monitors: An operating system structuring concept," *Commun. ACM,* vol. 17, pp. 549–557, Oct. 1974.

7. E.W. Dijkstra, "On the axiomatic definition of semantics," *EWD 367,* privately circulated.

8. D.L. Parnas, "On the criteria used in decomposing systems into modules," *Commun.* ACM, vol. 15, pp. 1053–1058, Dec. 1972.

9. ———, "A technique for software module specification with examples," *Commun. ACM* (Programming Techniques Dept.), pp. 330–336, May 1972.

10. P. Naur, "Programming by action clusters," *BIT,* vol. 9, pp. 250–258, 1969.

11. P. Henderson and R. Snowdon, "An experiment in structured programming," *BIT,* vol. 12, pp. 38–53, 1972.

12. D.L. Parnas, "A course on software engineering techniques," in *Proc. ACM SIGCSE,* 2nd Tech. Symp., Mar. 24–25, 1972.

13. E.W. Dijkstra, "Co-operating sequential processes," *Programming Languages,* F. Genuys, Ed. New York: Academic Press, 1968, pp. 43–112.

14. W.R. Price, "Implications of a virtual memory mechanism for implementing protection in a family of operating systems," Ph.D. dissertation, Carnegie-Mellon Univ., Pittsburgh, PA, 1973.

15. B. Randell and F.W. Zurcher, "Iterative multi-level modelling—A methodology for computer system design," in *Proc. IFIP Congr.,* 1968.

16. D.L. Parnas, "On a 'buzzword' hierarchical structure," in *Proc. IFIP Congr.,* 1974, pp. 336–339.

Acknowledgments

I am grateful for opportunities to discuss the subject with members of I.F.I.P. Working Group 2.3 on Programming Methodology. These discussions have helped me to clarify the points in this paper. I am also grateful to W. Bartussek of the Technische Hochschule Darmstadt, for his thoughtful comments on an earlier version of this paper, to Dr. H. Mills of the IBM Federal Systems Division who found a rather subtle error in a recent draft, and to Dr. L. Belady of the IBM T.J. Watson Research Laboratory who made a number of helpful comments.

Introduction

John Shore

Dave and I often attended presentations together when he was a consultant at the United States Naval Research Laboratory. Those who presented to him learned quickly that they wouldn't get far unless key terms and notation were defined precisely. If the presenter showed a block diagram, Dave would ask about the semantics—the meaning of different block shapes; the meaning of different line widths; the meaning of an arrow; whether an unfilled arrow meant something different than a solid, filled arrow; and so on. Usually these visual frills had no meaning. They certainly didn't aid careful analysis, and they often got in the way. To this day, I think of Dave when I draw diagrams.

This entire paper is devoted to defining the word "type", as used in discussions of type-extensible programming languages. The approach is to explain why existing definitions are inadequate, to outline the main motivations for having user-defined types in programming languages (abstraction, redundancy and compile-time checking, abbreviation, and portability), and then to offer a definition based on equivalence classes of variables that can be legally and meaningfully substituted for one another. In re-reading the paper today, I still find the approach to be persuasive and valuable.

Devoting so much attention to a definition was characteristic of Dave. He felt strongly that software engineering should be based on sound scientific reasoning and mathematical principles, which often means starting with precise definitions and notations. (See also Paper 33, "Who Taught Me About Software Engineering Research", and Paper 8, "On a 'Buzzword': Hierarchical Structure".)

11

Abstract Types Defined as Classes of Variables

Abstract Types Defined as Classes of Variables

D.L. Parnas, J.E. Shore, and D.M. Weiss

11.1 Introduction

The concept of *type* has been used without a precise definition in discussions about programming languages for 20 years. Before the concept of user-defined data types was introduced, a definition was not necessary for discussions of specific programming languages. The meaning of the term was implicit in the small list of possible types supported by the language. There was even enough similarity between different languages so that this form of definition allowed discussions of languages in general. The need for a widely accepted definition of type became clear in discussions of languages that allow users to add to the set of possible types without altering the compiler. In such languages the concept of type is no longer implicitly defined by the set of built-in types. A consistent language must be based on a clearer definition of the notion of type than we now have.

11.2 Previous Approaches

We have found the following five approaches to a definition of type in the literature (sometimes implicitly):

- *Syntactic*. Type is the information that one gives about a variable in a declaration. If in old languages one could write "VARIABLE X IS INTEGER" and one can now write "VARIABLE X IS ***," then *** is a type. Such an approach only avoids the problem. The basic need of a definition appears when one tries to decide what should go under ***.

- *Value Space*. A type is defined by a set of possible values. One may therefore discuss unions, cartesian products, and other mathematically acceptable topics [1, 2].

- *Behavior*. A type is defined by a value space and a set of operations on elements of that space [3].

- *Representation*. A type is determined by the way that it has been represented in terms of more primitive types [4, 5]. This determination is repeated until one reaches primitive data types that are usually hardware (or compiler) implemented.

- *Representation Plus Behavior.* A type is determined by a representation plus the set of operators that define its behavior; these operators are defined in terms of a set of procedures operating on the representation [6–8].

We have been unable to use any of these approaches to produce a definition of type in an "extensible" language that allowed us to achieve both certain practical goals (such as strong compile-time type checking of arrays with dynamic bounds) as well as the aesthetic goal of having a simple language with a clear and simple set of semantic rules. Each simple set of rules led to the exclusion of cases of practical importance; the inclusion of those cases invariably resulted in a set of exceptions that made the basic semantics of the language hard to understand.

As a result of these experiences we have taken a new approach. We consider the notion of a variable and its permitted contexts within a program as primitive, and we define types as equivalence classes of variables. We do not include a precise definition of a variable, since variables have essentially the same meaning in all commonly used programming languages, and since there is no evidence of any practical difficulty resulting from the lack of a definition. As a result we feel justified in taking the concept of variable to be primitive and using that concept as a basis of our definition of mode and type. For this purpose we consider constants and temporary variables for the storage of intermediate results to be variables as well.

11.3 Motivations for Type Extensions

We begin with a brief discussion of the reasons for including user-defined types, sometimes called type extensions, in a programming language. Including a type definition facility in a language will not increase the class of functions that can be computed by programs in the language, nor will it make possible the generation of better machine code than was possible before. We believe however that type extension can support the following four goals:

- *Abstraction.* An abstraction is a concept that can have more than one possible realization. The power of abstraction, in mathematics as well as in programming, comes from the fact that by solving a problem in terms of the abstraction one can solve many problems at once. The user-defined data type is generally an abstraction from many possible structures of more primitive data elements and many possible procedure implementations. Languages that allow the definition of abstract data types support the use of such programming methodologies as "structured programming," "stepwise refinement," and "information hiding" [9–12].

- *Redundancy and Compile Time Checking.* In defining new types and declaring variables to be of those types, one is providing additional information about the intended use of the data, thereby restricting the set of meaningful operations on the data. In a correct program this information is redundant, but for programs being developed it allows more checking and error detection by the compiler. It is widely believed that such redundancy will lead to more reliable programs and lower program development costs.

- *Abbreviation.* If a program is written in terms of operations on data types and structures defined by the user, it can be shorter than an equivalent program written in terms of data types defined for general purposes. The shorter program is easier to write, understand, prove correct, modify, etc. The source text requires less storage space. Code sharing can occur if the user-defined data elements and their associated operations are suitable for use in more than one program or in more than one "module" of a large program. Extensive abbreviation and code sharing in programs was made possible by the invention of the subroutine. Data abstractions are the next step.

- *Data Portability.* Often a programmer is faced with using or producing data defined according to a data organization not under his control. Sometimes the programmer must process data independently produced in several systems using different formats. The ability to define data types and write programs in terms of those data types should help reduce the amount of program rewriting made necessary by the introduction of new data or new data organizations. In many important applications the data may be self-describing, so that its characteristics can be completely determined only at the time of actual processing. Extensible languages should be helpful in this situation as well.

In our opinion languages currently being discussed have not achieved the foregoing goals. Current trends seem to favor strongly typed languages that use a representation approach or representation plus behavior approach to type definition [5,7,8]. The definition of types in terms of representation plus behavior interferes with the goal of abstraction, because a technique for handling more than one implementation of an abstraction at a time in one program has not been developed. The desire for compile-time checking interferes with abbreviation and code sharing, because strong type checking tends to prevent code developed to work with data of one type from use on data of another type, even when its application is meaningful. One reason APL programs can be so short is the "everything goes" attitude taken toward the types of variables expected by operators. A definition of type in terms of value spaces interferes with the goal of compile-time checking, since variables that count pears and variables that count light bulbs have the same value space. (Because so many distinct properties of objects can be described with the same value space, it has proven necessary to use the concept of units. We see support for the definition of the units in which a quantity is expressed as being an obligation of the concept of user-defined types. We also note that units as such are often inadequate for our purposes. Very different properties, such as length and height of an object, may be measured in the same units.)

11.4 A New Approach

The extent to which a programming language supports the goals discussed in the previous section depends almost entirely on the situations in which one variable may be substituted for another. Abstraction from the differences between two variables is achieved when one variable may be substituted for the other without making the program illegal or meaningless. Compile-time type checking prohibits the substitution of one variable for another in certain contexts.

All of the practical difficulties that we have encountered in our attempts to use the five approaches to a definition of type previously listed appeared because each definition placed certain restrictions on the context in which variable substitutions were allowed. Those restrictions then prevent the achievement of one or more of the four goals outlined. As a result we have chosen to consider a less restricted definition in which the concept of variable is considered primitive and types are defined as various equivalence classes of variables that may be legally and meaningfully substituted for one another. To explore such a definition, we need to introduce the concept of a variable's *mode*. (The use of the terms *type* and *mode* here is not consistent with that found in the literature, which is itself inconsistent in the use of these terms. In particular the use of these terms here is different from the use adopted in [13].)

11.4.1 The Mode of a Variable

When a variable is declared in conventional programming languages, such as FORTRAN, ALGOL 60, or PASCAL, the compiler is given enough information to determine how the data referred to by means of the variable is to be represented and which procedures are allowed to operate on the representation. We refer to all variables that are identical with respect to data representation and access as being of the same mode. Once the mode of a variable is determined, the compiler has enough information to produce machine code that will operate on the machine representation of the variable.

Mode defines an equivalence class on variables. Any value that can be stored in one variable of a given mode can be stored in another of the same mode. Any program that operates correctly on a variable of a given mode will operate on any other variable of the same mode under exactly the same conditions (initial values, etc.).

11.4.2 Types as Classes of Modes

Each mode defines a simple class of variables, namely, variables whose substitution for each other in any context will not result in a compile-time error. We introduce the concept of type in order to define classes of variables whose substitution for each other is permitted by the compiler only in some restricted contexts. Since we need never distinguish between two variables of the same mode, types can be thought of as classes of modes.

We are unwilling to restrict ourselves to types that consist of a single mode because of our goals of abstraction and abbreviation. In a practical language it should be possible to write programs that can be applied to variables of more than one mode. (Generic procedures are currently often used to solve this problem.) On the other hand the goal of increased redundancy and type checking forbids allowing the compiler to compile code whenever a meaningful interpretation can be imagined. Such an approach is often euphemistically called automatic type conversion. Because we have never seen a system of automatic type conversions that performed all conversions that agreed with our intended use of the data and refused to perform any others, we favor languages that have no automatic conversions. The alternative to types consisting of a single mode is to define types as classes of modes and to specify in terms of types the set of permissible operands for newly defined operators. This allows the programmer who defines a new type to determine the set of permissible operator/operand combinations and requires that he define the meaning of expressions involving his type. Additional burdens are thereby placed on the definer of a data type, but the user of that type is relieved from the onerous task of writing explicit calls on conversion routines in many situations.

In our view the term *abstract data type* is properly applied to the preceding concept of type; that is, a data type deserves the name *abstract* only if it includes more than one mode and if one can deal with all members of the mode class without distinguishing among them.

One can combine modes into types for a variety of reasons, such as to support the goals of abstraction, abbreviation, and code sharing without sacrificing type checking. In the following sections we will discuss examples of situations in which modes should be grouped into types. These examples should not be interpreted as a refinement of the basic definition. The language user should be able to group modes into types almost arbitrarily. The situations we will describe are merely those which we expect to occur most often. Any language that will not allow us to define types in the situations we describe is not satisfactory.

11.4.3 Types Consisting of Modes with Identical Externally Visible Behavior (Spec-Types)

For any mode defined by a representation and a set of permissible operators, one can describe those characteristics that can be observed by operating on the representation using only the operators provided. This black-box picture of the mode can be termed its specification [14]. If this specification of the mode contains less information than is contained in a description of its implementation, other modes also satisfy the specification. As an example the specification for modes used to implement complex numbers need not define whether the internal representation is in terms of real and imaginary parts or in terms of argument and magnitude.

The set of modes that satisfies a given specification constitute an important class, which we call a *spec-type*. Any program that is written to operate on variables of a spec-type *and* that can be proven correct without assuming more information about the type than is given in the specification will be correct for another variable of that type even if the mode is different. When the mode is changed, recompilation may be needed, but the program text need not be changed. Given a procedure with a parameter specified to be of a given spec-type, it should be possible for the compiler to verify that the parameter is operated on only as permitted by the type specification. The compiler can then permit the procedure to be shared by anyone who wishes to call it with a variable whose mode is a member of the given spec-type.

11.4.4 Types Consisting of Modes with Identical Representations (Rep-Types)

It is common to find data with quite different meanings having the same representation. For example integers and real numbers are often represented by a single machine word. A user may choose to represent both a two-dimensional position and a complex number by a structure with two real elements. A frequent complaint about languages with strong type checking is that one cannot use the common properties of two modes. These restrictions have been introduced in part to prevent the writing of programs whose correctness depends on implementation details that are not part of the language definition. (Such programs could become incorrect if a compiler change is made.) Unfortunately the restrictions extend beyond the protection of implementation details. Many operations (such as storage management) can be usefully applied (with the same meaning) to all modes having the same representation. A program may also be useful when applied to variables of different modes that have common representations even though interpretation of the effect of that program may be quite different in each case.

For example the same program could calculate distance from origin for a point in two-dimensional cartesian space and the magnitude of a complex number whose representation is in terms of real and imaginary parts. However nice the aesthetic properties of a language may be, if it forces users to write duplicate programs or forces the code generated to be larger than otherwise necessary, the language will have difficulty gaining acceptance by organizations with strong cost, time, and memory constraints. Under pressure the users of such a language will resort to the dirtiest of dirty tricks to meet their time and space constraints.

From these considerations we conclude that a user should be able to declare as a type a group of modes that have the same representation and to define a set of operations on variables of that type in terms of that representation. We call such a type a *rep-type*. We do *not* want a compiler to recognize common representations. Membership in a rep-type should be declared explicitly in such a way that the compiler can detect undeclared representation dependence. The decision to have a representation-dependent program should be explicit, and the points at which representation dependence is introduced should be easily recognized.

11.4.5 Types Consisting of Modes That Are Invocations of Parameterized Mode Descriptions (Param-Types)

One of our goals is the achievement of code sharing, that is, the ability to use the same code to operate on variables of different types. With current computers, compilers, and macro generators it is easy to write code that can be applied to variables that are alike except for the value of one or more descriptive parameters. For example the same code can invert a matrix whether it be 5 by 5 or 60 by 60. As the CLU language shows [7, 8], it is also possible to write code that will implement a stack of integers or a stack of variables of type complex. These are examples of the use of parameterized mode descriptions. Both are descriptions in which certain symbols are designated to be parameters. Defining values of those parameters completes the mode description. Thus *integer array* [M:N], where M and N are parameters, defines the mode *integer array* [2:3] if M has the value 2 and N the value 3. Similarly TYP *array* [M:N], where TYP is considered to be a parameter, can generate integer arrays, real arrays, etc. The class of all modes that can be obtained by assigning values to the parameters of a parameterized mode description can be considered as a type. Code sharable by all members of this type can then be written, because it can refer to the parameters.

An example of a language that does not allow code sharing in such situations is PASCAL, which excludes even dynamic arrays as they were known in ALGOL 60. There have been several proposals to make a special case of such arrays. Rather than recognize one or two special cases, we choose to allow the user to declare modes to be members of the same type if they can be generated by assigning values to the parameters of a mode description. We call this type a *param-type*.

11.4.6 Types Consisting of Modes with Some Common Properties (Variant-Types)

A weaker form of spec-types is needed for situations in which a variety of modes do not have identical specifications but have some common properties that one wants to exploit. (This example of a type can be regarded as a catch-all, since it allows handling of anything not falling into any of the previous situations.) Consider a personnel records system. There may be many different modes for representing employees, because the data kept for each class of employee may be quite different. However all of these will have a birthdate. An organization may want to invite its employees to a free dinner on their birthdays and will want a program that goes through the personnel records and produces a file sorted according to birthdate containing only the name, address, and (in Germany) titles and degrees, so that a proper invitation can be issued a few days before the birthday. This program should be written so that it ignores (abstracts from) those aspects of the personnel record that are irrelevant to the program. It should be possible to declare a type that includes all personnel records and makes them all appear to have only those attributes needed by this program. The program need not be changed when it is applied to new modes. It is only necessary to include the new mode in the abstract type for which the program was written. This type is also defined by a specification, and the operators specified to be common to all variables of the mode must be implemented for the new type in accordance with those specifications. We call such a type a *variant-type*.

11.4.7 Modes Belonging to More Than One Type

An advantage of our basic definition of type is that there are no conceptual difficulties involved in considering one variable to be of more than one type. That arises whenever one mode is a member of more than one class of modes. Types may also be declared to be subsets of other types, or a set of types may be combined because of some common property and considered (for some programs) as a single type.

For example one may have two forms of strings that are members of a spec-type defining the meaningful set of string operations. One of these modes keeps the strings tightly packed for storage efficiency; the other keeps them in a form more suitable for changes. For convenience exactly the same set of string operations is defined for both of them, so that certain programs can be written to operate on variables of either mode (on any variable whose mode is a member of the spec-type) without converting one into the other.

The representations of these two modes will not be the same, and if a rep-type is declared for one of the modes, there will be programs that can operate on one but not on the other. These programs will be shared with other members of the rep-type but not with other members of the spec-type. Efficiency requires that we allow such differences to exist; the dictates of structured programming and modularity require that we confine knowledge of those differences to small parts of the system [9–11].

A language that allows a variable to be of more than one type might be regarded as unstructured (unrestricted), because it allows one to write a program that will be correct for one variable of a given type but not for another variable of the same type. It is clear that abuse of this facility could lead to programs that are hard to understand and maintain. Our position is that representation or machine-dependent programs will be written whenever cost considerations demand it; it is better to provide a mechanism that allows the control of such dependency than to force the programmer to use dirty tricks.

11.4.8 The Times at Which Code Sharing May Occur

If two variables are members of the same spec-type, they may share the source code of a program but not necessarily the compiled code. This allows source code to be shared among versions of the programs [15]. If several members of the spec-type are expected to be operated on by the same piece of compiled code, then either the code compiled must contain a branch on the mode of the variable or the procedures required to satisfy the spec-type's specifications must be passed with the variable at runtime. If the program is written so that the mode of the variable can be determined at compile time, more efficient code can be compiled than if the program is left more general (if only the spec-type is known).

11.4.9 Need for a General Equivalence Facility

If the concepts in this paper are to be used, it will be necessary to have programs in which one data item appears to be of two different types in two different programs. One program will operate on a variable as a variable of type "personnel record," and another will operate on it as a variable of type "officer record." Some part of the system must be responsible for making sure that the same record is operated on in both cases and that the changes are kept consistent. This can be achieved by representing both variables with the same data item. This is an equivalencing facility—but one without all of the dangerous properties of the FORTRAN EQUIVALENCE statement. In FORTRAN, the users of a variable declare the EQUIVALENCE. In our proposal, only the program responsible for implementing the abstract types can make two variables equivalent. Users of the modes cannot. The responsibility for consistency rests with one implementor rather than with all possible users of the data.

11.4.10 Description of Formal Parameters for Procedures, Macros, and More

In a language based on the concepts discussed it is vital that the description of a formal parameter given with the declaration of a procedure be permitted in terms of types as well as modes. It is worth remembering that in the ALGOL 60 reference language [3] formal parameter descriptions, although syntactically similar to variable declarations, were referred to as specifications and did not always provide as much information as needed in a declaration. (Implementations of ALGOL 60 often require that the parameter specification include information allowed but not required by the reference language.) The clear distinction between parameter specifications and variable declarations in ALGOL 60 is often lost because of the syntactic similarity in the two. Allowing user-defined types makes the distinction vital. A parameter specification may be any kind of type, but a variable declaration must always determine a mode.

Allowing the full range of possibilities suggested by this report would appear to require some new or unusual compiling techniques. We view the issues involved in parameter bindings to be among the most important and most difficult remaining problems for developers of languages that allow user-defined data types.

11.5 Applying These Concepts to Designing a Language

Although we feel that the preceding view of types provides a clearer conceptual basis for a language design than the others that we have considered, we have not yet developed a language syntax that embodies our concepts. Syntaxes to accommodate some of these ideas within the context of database-management systems have been proposed (as in [16]). We know that the declaration of a mode will resemble languages such as PASCAL and CLU, but we expect the declaration of a type to look quite different. It must be possible to define a type by enumerating the member modes (or types) or by making a declaration of the required properties of member modes or by some combination of the two techniques. For some types a set of operations will exist that must be defined for all modes that are of that type; the compiler must then check that the necessary operators are available for each member mode. Since we do not expect to be able to check for correctness, the compiler is required to check only that an operator of the proper name and form (parameters, etc.) exists. We believe that the syntax for parameterized mode descriptions should resemble the syntax for procedures, which we view as parameterized statements.

References

1. C.A.R. Hoare, "Note on Data Structuring," in *Structured Programming,* O.-J. Dahl, E.W. Dijkstra, and C.A.R. Hoare, Academic Press, 1972.

2. B. Wegbreit, "The Treatment of Data Types in EL 1," *Communications of the ACM* 17 (No. 5), 251–264 (May 1974).

3. P. Naur, editor, "Revised Report on the Algorithmic Language ALGOL 60," *Communications of the ACM,* 6 (No. 1), 1–17 (Jan. 1963).

4. A. Van Wijngaarden et al., "Report on the Algorithmic Language ALGOL 68," *Numerische Mathematik* 14, Feb. 1969.

5. N. Wirth, "The Programming Language PASCAL (revised report)," Berichte der Fachgruppe Computer—Wissenschaften, Eidgenossische Technische Hochschule, Zurich, Dec. 1973.

6. O-J. Dahl, B. Myrhaug, and K. Nygaard, "Simula 67, Common Base Language," Norwegian Computing Center, Oslo, Norway, 1968.

7. B. Liskov and S. Zilles, "Programming with Abstract Data Types," *SIGPLAN Notices* 9, 50–59 (Apr. 1974).

8. B. Liskov, "A Note on CLU," *Computation Structures Group* Memo 112, MIT, Project MAC, Nov. 1974.

9. E.W. Dijkstra, "Notes on Structured Programming," in *Structured Programming,* O.-J. Dahl, E.W. Dijkstra, and C.A.R. Hoare, Academic Press, 1972.

10. D.L. Parnas, "On the Criteria to be Used in Decomposing Systems into Modules," *Communications of the ACM* 15 (No. 12), 1053–1058 (Dec. 1972).

11. N. Wirth, "Program Development by Stepwise Refinement," *Communications of the ACM* 14 (No. 4), 221–227 (Apr. 1971).

12. J.M. Aiello, "An Investigation of Current Language Support for the Data Requirements of Structured Programming," *MAC Technical Memorandum* 51, MIT, Project MAC, Sept. 1974.

13. "CS-4 Language Reference Manual," Oct. 1975; available from the Naval Electronics Laboratory Center, Code 5200, San Diego, Calif. 92152.

14. D.L. Parnas, "A Technique for Software Module Specification with Examples," *Communications of the ACM* 15 (No. 5), 330–336 (May 1972).

15. D.L. Parnas, "On Methods for Developing Families of Programs," Technical Report, Forschungsgruppe Betriebssysteme (I), Technische Hochschule Darmstadt, Darmstadt, West Germany.

16. R. Boyce and D. Chamberlin, "Using a Structured English Query Language as a Data Definition Facility," IBM Technical Report RJ 1318, IBM Research Laboratory, San Jose, California, Dec. 1973.

Acknowledgments

The authors are grateful to Mr. Warren Loper of the Naval Electronics Laboratory Center and Drs. James Miller and John Nestor of Intermetrics, Inc., for many useful discussions. We are especially grateful to Prof. Dr. Hoffmann of the Technische Hochschule Darmstadt for constructive suggestions. We also thank the referees for pointing out the lack of clarity in earlier versions of this report.

The ideas expressed in this report have been stimulated by the authors' involvement in the Navy's design of a new programming language (CS-4) [13].

Introduction

Stuart Faulk

Parnas and Würges's "Response to Undesired Events in Software Systems" (UEs) was one of those papers sufficiently ahead of its time that its essential insights were often missed or misunderstood. History, however, has provided any vindication necessary. Not only has the concept of "undesired events" passed into common usage, but exception handling in today's distributed and Web-based applications follows the conceptual structures first laid out in this paper.

At the time this paper was published, the prevailing academic focus was on developing "correct" programs. The general view was that programs exhibited only two kinds of behavior: correct and incorrect. Incorrect behavior represented "bugs" or "errors," that is, things that could have and should have been fixed before a program was deployed. Research emphasized methods for achieving program correctness by building correct programs, detecting errors, or proving correctness. It followed that if one could develop correct programs, exception-handling code was unnecessary. This view, that one could abstract away idiosyncrasies of a program's run-time execution environment, was a natural assumption at a time when a program's execution and I/O typically occurred in the context of a single machine.

In contrast, this paper recognized the essentially undependable nature of real-world execution environments. Its key insight was that there will always be aspects of a program's execution environment that do not behave as we would wish: Things go wrong, things fail, things change, or we make incorrect assumptions. These are not problems that arise from programming errors but are unavoidable consequences of executing programs in any real-world environment.

Likewise, these are not problems that arise from unforeseen circumstances but from the normal, often stochastic, behavior of the real world. More than one colleague was treated to Dave's tender mercies for substituting the word "unexpected" for "undesired." The very goal is to anticipate what can go wrong and make accommodations in advance.

The key lesson of the paper is that we can maintain the structural integrity of a well-engineered program only if we plan for UEs and build our systems accordingly. By planning for UEs and building separate code to detect and handle them, we can maintain appropriate modularization, information hiding, and separation of concerns.

History has proven these insights durable. With the explosion of network-based computing, client-server architectures, and distributed applications, the uncertainties of the execution environment have become a driving issue in developing effective applications. Delays in communication, synchronization, or execution are so central a part of the overall problem that much of the development effort for such systems necessarily addresses undesired event issues.

The paper proposes an approach to handling UEs based on the concept of hardware "traps" for error detection and recovery. On machines implementing hardware traps, detection of an error (e.g., divide-by-zero) results in the transfer of control to a user-supplied routine. Parnas extends this notion to software-detected events by viewing UEs as the trap mechanism for an abstract machine. The approach inherits key features of hardware traps: the ability to separate the code handling undesired events and treat it as a distinct concern and the ability to invoke different event handling routines depending on the error context.

One sees the same conceptual structures in today's programming languages. For example, the exception handling paradigms of C++ and Java follow the conceptual model first enunciated in this paper. Their notions of "throwing" exceptions and "catching" them supply the mechanisms necessary to separate concerns for program behavior in the normal case and program behavior in the exceptional case. In Java and C++, there are no "error routines": Catch blocks are arbitrary pieces of code. As first discussed in "Response to Undesired Events in Software Systems," this approach helps preserve the modularization and encapsulation of object-oriented designs.

Response to Undesired Events in Software Systems

D.L. Parnas and H. Würges

12.1 Abstract

This paper discusses an approach to handling run-time errors in software systems. It is often assumed that in programs which can be proven correct, errors will not be a problem. This paper is predicated on the assumption that, even with correct programs, undesired events at run-time will continue to be a problem. Routines to respond to these undesired events (UEs) must be provided in reliable systems.

This paper describes a program organization which aims at satisfying the following criteria:

1. UE response routines are written by each programmer in terms of the abstract machine which he uses for his normal case code. UEs are reported in those terms. He is never forced to use information about the implementation of other modules in the system.

2. Programs can be written so that the code for UE detection, UE correction, and normal case, are lexically separate and can be modified independently.

3. The system can evolve from an initial version that does little recovery to one which uses sophisticated recovery techniques without a change in the structure of the system.

4. Even with unsophisticated recovery procedures, the task of locating the module containing a bug discovered at run-time does not require internal knowledge of many modules.

5. Costs incurred because of the recovery techniques are low as long as no UE occurs.

12.2 Introduction

Perhaps because structured programming is advocated as a means of eliminating errors in programs, programs written to demonstrate structured programming (e.g., [3, 5]) are written assuming that each subprogram will always perform correctly. Moreover, each program is written on the assumption that it itself will never behave incorrectly.

Four justifications for questioning this assumption are:

1. Even the best of "structured programmers" occasionally err;

2. The machines which we use occasionally fail and may cause a program to fail (either directly or by causing a change in code or data);

3. In practice, programs are changed and errors appear which had not appeared before;

4. Incorrect or inconsistent data may be supplied to the system.

If this assumption is valid, then it would be foolhardy to make early design decisions on the assumption that errors or other undesired events will not occur. As explained in [10], the early decision (e.g., the interfaces between the various independently developed components) will be the hardest to change. In real world situations certain undesired events occur frequently, they are expected by the user, and he can define programs to take corrective action when they occur. Often such programs can only be added after a period of use, but the structure of the system must allow for such a likely change or addition to the program. The overall reliability of a system can be significantly increased by the addition of programs which respond to or "handle" UEs.

The term "undesired event" (UE) is introduced, because (1) we want to include all events that result in a deviation from normal behavior, and (2) the term "error" often led to the objection that "errors" should not be handled, but "corrected."

This paper suggests a design approach which we believe can increase reliability. It is not particularly concerned with detecting UEs; it is concerned with the response to detected UEs. We are not primarily concerned with debugging (the programmer's response to a detected error); we are concerned with *the program's* response to an UE. Such responses include attempts at self-diagnosis, saving of partial results, printing of diagnostic information, retry, use of alternative resources, etc.

This paper does not present an algorithm for recovery from UEs. The paper does present a scheme for program organization which facilitates the introduction of recovery and diagnostic algorithms. It also presents a list of guidelines to help the designer in anticipating the types of UEs which might occur.

The concept proposed in Section 12.9 aids in specifying reaction to UEs and enables the user of an abstract machine to state explicitly which UEs he is prepared to "handle" and what he regards as "correct" UE handling.

12.3 Difficulties Introduced by a "Leveled Structure"

To understand the proposal of this paper, one must understand the concept of a hierarchically structured system [8, 9]. One must recall that the lower levels must function without the presence of the upper levels, and they can be used by a variety of upper level programs. It follows that the lower levels cannot use any knowledge about the higher levels. However, recovery usually requires the combined action of several levels. An UE will be detected by a lower level, but information available elsewhere determines the appropriate action.

This is a special case of the observation that structured systems compartmentalize knowledge and any action which requires knowledge from several compartments may require more effort as a result of the extra communication needed.

12.4 The Effect of Undesired Events on Code Complexity

A straightforward machine language program to write on a tape is usually naïve. The probability of an UE in peripherals is high; the code needed for error detection and correction makes the programs quite complex. As a result, a change in the normal case procedure is difficult.

Such complications can occur in all parts of a system. They are most apparent in the I/O modules because the probability of UEs is higher there, but the problems are not essentially different for other modules.

To keep the code for the normal case separate from the code concerned with UEs, we propose that modules in a structured system make use of a software analog of a "trap." Most computer hardware is designed to detect commonly occurring UEs and transfer control to a specified location upon detecting such an UE. Typical trap conditions are "divide by zero" and "memory bounds violation." Traps simplify code, because one need not include checks for those UEs in the program. Traps also decrease the probability of such UEs going undetected.[1]

In the examples given in [1], the modules are specified to transfer control to user-provided routines under conditions which we interpret as UEs. In fact, this is the only way that restrictions on the use of these functions are specified! The user of those functions may write his code without checks for

---

1. It has been suggested that traps provide a convenient mechanism for reporting infrequent events to programs which would otherwise need to make frequent checks. UEs, the subject of this paper, are only special cases of that class of situations [7].

violations of the "applicability conditions." The code concerned with recovery from UEs is called by means of a trap. This organization achieves lexical separation of normal use, detection, and correction procedures, thereby easing changes.

Our first suggestion: *Assign responsibility for the detection of attempts to violate its specifications to the "abstract machine"; it calls a trap routine upon detection of such an UE. Other errors, failures of the virtual machine, will also be reported by traps.* The remainder of this paper assumes such an organization.

Every group of programmers, writing programs using an abstract machine, provides additional programs that will be executed if the abstract machine fails to execute that program correctly. Only these programmers know what their program was intended to do and what should be done in case of an UE. They also know which message should be given to the user of their program, if recovery is not successful or if the UE was caused by a forbidden application of their program.

Routines for UE handling use the same abstract operations and operands as the normal case program, i.e., they use the same abstract machine. This guarantees that no knowledge about lower level programs and about the implementation of the abstract machine is used in UE handling. Otherwise a change in those programs may lead to "incorrect UE handling."

12.5 Impossible Abstractions

In this paper we are assuming that systems are structured according to the recommendations of [2, 8] and [9, 10]. Each program is written in terms of abstractions of the code that it calls upon. This section illustrates that the need to make appropriate responses to UEs often severely limits the abstractions that we may use.

The structure of a program will be less clear if the user of an abstract machine cannot write *all* of his code in terms of the abstract model [4]. Consequently, we cannot abstract from facts which should be used to recover from (or diagnose) an UE.

As an example, consider an abstract machine which provides instructions which perform "simultaneous" string substitutions on every line of a file. The substitutions can be irreversible (one cannot tell where the change was made by looking at the file afterwards). Let us further assume that the specification given to the users of this machine completely hides the processing sequence (giving the appearance that all lines are processed simultaneously).

Execution of the machine "instruction" will extend over a measurable period of time and might be interrupted by an UE. If the file is partially processed, recovery will depend on the user's ability to know which parts of his file have been operated upon. When this depends upon the sequence of processing, he must know "hidden" information.

One solution would be to keep, within the "abstract machine," information sufficient to restore the file to its original state [11]. This solution usually has a very high cost. If one made a module with such a specification, there would be many situations in which one could not afford to use it.

Often a practical solution is to make the module somewhat *less abstract*. The specification must admit to the possibility of UE and provide information to assist in recovery. The set of "degraded" designs includes designs which specify the sequencing as well as designs that mark unchanged and erroneous parts of the file. Unless we abandon the idea of abstraction completely, no design *always* presents all of the information usable for recovery. We can, however, prepare for the most frequent UEs by defining a set of abstract UEs.

The above brings out the second suggestion of this paper: *Do not specify a module to have properties which UEs will frequently violate.* One must include in the interface the necessary operations to communicate about the occurrence of UEs. An example can be found in Appendix 12.A.

12.6 Error Types and Direction of Propogation

An UE detected at any given level in a system may be propagating either downward (violating the specified restrictions on the virtual machine) or upward. The upward propagating UE represents either failure of a mechanism which has been used correctly, or it represents "reflection" of an UE which had previously propagated downward. We shall deal with these cases in turn.

When detected, a downward propagating UE should be returned to the level above. Responsibility for diagnosis and possible recovery must be assigned to the higher levels, because the lower level program does not have sufficient knowledge to determine what was desired. (See Appendix 12.B for examples.) With the "trap" mechanism this results in a transfer of control to a routine designated by the last caller. Thus, when a downward propagating UE is detected, it is *reflected* to higher levels.

An upward propagating UE is reported by "trapping" to an UE handling routine. If the routine responds to a reflected error it should first determine whether or not the original error occurred at its own level. If it determines that the "error of usage" occurred at a higher level, it must adjust its external state,[2] and report the UE to its user. If it is determined that the UE has

---

2. We elaborate on this later.

returned to its original level, the program may either attempt recovery or inform the next higher level of an "error of mechanism" (by use of a trap).

When a level is informed of a failure of the machine below it, it may either attempt recovery or adjust its external state and report the UE still higher. Any of these routines may also produce diagnostics for programmers as side effects.

The lower levels of a system should never abort the job in the event of a failure of mechanism. Recovery or loss minimization procedures may be available elsewhere. *Job abortion occurs only as a last resort* (e.g., when the trap mechanism fails).

To summarize, upon detecting an UE in a hierarchically structured piece of software, the UE is first reflected and control passed to the level where it originated. At this point it is either corrected or reflected still higher as a "defective virtual machine." At every level, either recovery is attempted or the UE is reported still higher. At each level, the UE handling routines have the responsibility of restoring the state of the virtual machine used by the level above to one which is consistent with the specifications. All possible efforts are made to assure that no program is given control with its virtual machine in an "impossible" state.[3]

12.7 Continuation After UE "Handling"

The above is only a skeleton into which various recovery and diagnostic policies may be fit. The meta-structure proposed has four advantages:

1. It allows each UE handling procedure to be written at the level where the necessary knowledge exists and in terms of the virtual machine. This does not violate the "information hiding" principle" [4].

2. "Uses" still defines a hierarchy allowing usable subsets [8, 9].

3. *It provides for the evolution of a system toward increased reliability without major revisions.* Usually, when a system is first assembled, the UE handling routines are primitive. They may do no more than print their name. As the development progresses, increased experience and understanding allows these routines to be replaced with more sophisticated diagnostic and loss-minimization routines.

4. The use of even the trivial versions of the trap routines greatly simplifies debugging once the system has been "integrated." When a system has

---

3. With a precisely defined machine (real or virtual) certain relations between the functions may be "proven" by taking the specification as a set of axioms. A state in which those relations do not hold is termed "impossible."

been produced by the cooperation of many programmers, no one knows the complete system well. When a bug appears, it is a difficult job to determine which programmer should study the problem. In our experience, in testing systems whose UE policies approximate those suggested in this paper, UE routines which do no more than print out their own name usually indicate which module (and which programmer) is at fault. We make great efforts to avoid having bugs which show up after the modules are combined, but when we fail, the UE routines become very useful.

12.8 Specifying the Error Indications

When a module is designed and specified, we specify all the limitations of the program and all the UEs which will occur in the event that those applicability conditions are violated. We also specify routines to be called in the event of certain classes of internal failures. The following is a list of considerations which must enter into the construction of the list. It may be viewed as an aid to the UE anticipation.

12.8.1 Limitations on the Values of Parameters

Since any piece of software has a limited range of parameters which it can handle, a trap should occur if these are violated. These can be omitted if it is impossible to violate them at run-time, because "compile time" checks are feasible.

12.8.2 Capacity Limitations

Since any module which stores information will have finite storage capacity, traps should occur when that capacity is exceeded. The specification must enable users to predict when such a trap will occur (i.e., to determine the capacity).

12.8.3 Requests for Undefined Information

Any module which provides a memory function must be designed in the light of the possibility that information will be requested before it has been inserted or after it has been deleted. Traps should be specified for all such conditions.

12.8.4 Restrictions on the Order of Operations

Efficiency, ease of implementation, or a desire to detect probable programming errors may dictate a restriction on the order of calls on a module's functions. For example, most file systems require "opening" a file before one may access it. Traps should be specified for violation of these restrictions. It is sometimes useful to add functions to a module in order to simplify the specification of the conditions under which such traps occur. In the file example a predicate "OPENED" would be appropriate. (See also Appendix 12.B.)

12.8.5 Detection of Actions Which Are Likely to Be Unintentioned

Experience has shown us a common class of programming errors which result in certain "strange" actions. For example, the opening of a file which is already open is often indicative of an error. Many pieces of software use the unlikely action as a way of encoding some other operation (e.g., the closing of the file). We prefer to specify traps for such occurrences and provide alternative means of performing the other operation. Then a user has the option of specifying the alternative operation as the body of his UE routine. This particular recommendation is a question of taste. Modules designed in this way often have restrictions that some find annoying. Some people prefer executing OPEN for an OPEN file to checking to see whether or not it is already opened.

12.8.6 Sufficiency

The above lists of applicability conditions could be summarized as follows: The set of trap conditions specified should be *sufficient to guarantee* that, if none of them applies, the change specified as the effect of calling the routine could be carried out without violating any module limitations. Further, the fact that no trap occurs, should guarantee that the value of the function (if any) will not be "undefined."

12.8.7 Priority of Traps

A single erroneous call may violate several of the applicability conditions mentioned above. It is usually not useful to trap to several UE routines. Instead, we assign a priority to each trap and specify that only the highest priority "enabled" trap will occur. (In [1] the priority was indicated by the sequence of the calls in the text.) Priority assignment becomes essential when the value of some functions in the applicability conditions might be undefined in an erroneous call. The priority of the traps must guarantee that there will be an enabled trap with a higher priority than any UE condition which mentions undefined functions (see Appendix 12.A).

12.8.8 Size of the "Trap Vector"

The structure and efficiency of the individual trap routines can be improved by restricting the class of UEs they handle. The analysis done by the routine to determine the exact UE often computes information which was known to the "trapping" program. However, one must also avoid specifying a very large number of distinct UE routines. One can combine several similar conditions to reduce the number of distinct routines. The optimal "trade-off" is a function of (1) the sophistication of the UE diagnosis being attempted (which determines the number of routines which would actually be different), and (2) a complex space-time tradeoff. A practical compromise is to combine similar conditions and pass a parameter providing additional UE information.

12.8.9 State After the Trap

Programming is simplest when the module did not change state if an UE occurred. When it is not practical to adhere to such a rule, the trap should not occur until sufficient information to determine the state change is made available to the users.

12.8.10 Errors of Mechanism

Reporting a failure by the module is inherently more difficult than reporting the violation of applicability conditions. The actual UE can only be accurately described in terms of information which has been hidden from the user. He could not use an accurate report. We want to give him abstract information (i.e., to classify the UE) which may help him in recovering; we are again faced with a trade-off between the simplicity of the design and the accuracy or detail of the abstract report. At one extreme we use a single trap name to report "failure" and require that the user of the module run diagnostic programs on his virtual machine to determine the extent of the damage. Experience with hardware diagnostic programs teaches us that this is quite a difficult task. In the case of a software-implemented "virtual machine" there are many types of failures in which the module has the capability of delivering quite a detailed analysis of the damage to the virtual machine. For example, a file system is usually capable of giving its users a list of damaged records and even a list of "commands" which no longer work correctly. However, some failures are so catastrophic that the information is not available. In the example given in Appendix 12.A we have chosen a design in which the "failure" trap routines pass a parameter which classifies the type of failure. These classifications allow the user to answer such questions as:

1. Did the command which failed change the value of any function?
2. Is it possible that a retry would work?
3. Were functions other than that which was called affected?
4. Was the module able to restore functions to a state consistent with the specifications or is the machine in an "impossible" state?

Information of this sort can be mentioned in the specifications where a means for communicating supplementary information can be defined. We considered an alternative which was further towards the fully detailed extreme. In this alternative we would have added a predicate associated with each function; the predicate would be true if the failure had affected proper functioning of its associated function. There would also have been a predicate which would be true if the module had been unable to set the value of the previously mentioned predicates properly. This predicate would have been true in catastrophic failures. (There would always be the possibility of a catastrophe so great that even the last predicate could not be properly set.) In an extreme alternative, the predicates had as many parameters as their associated functions and would provide true or false indications for each possible call.

We rejected these alternatives, because:

1. It seemed unlikely that one would want to make an implementation which was sufficiently redundant that it would be able to provide such detailed information.

2. It seemed unlikely that a user program would be written to use such information.

Our decision we made was based upon a certain expected set of applications and would be wrong for some. We present it only as an example of one solution to this class of problems.

12.9 Redundancy and Efficiency

Modules designed as described above can be thought of as highly insulated external programs; the traps can be viewed as a wall protecting the module from damage. In a system constructed with such a view, much of the system resources are applied to maintaining the walls. For example, as a particular value is passed through several modules, it will be repeatedly checked against the same limits. Such redundancy is extremely valuable in the early testing stages, but when the system is reliable, the inefficiency introduced by the redundant checking becomes significant.

When UEs are quite rare, we can eliminate some of the *redundant* checks.

Here one can discern two extreme approaches.

1. Retain the upper level checks, eliminate the lower level checks assuming that no UE will affect the variable on its way down.

2. Retain the lower level checks, use the trap routines at the intermediate levels to pass the UE back up to the point where it originated.

The second is usually preferable, but there are exceptions. It may be difficult to effect the "backing up" which is sometimes needed in the second approach; the first approach can detect UEs before irreversible changes are made.

12.10 Degrees of Undesired Events

In [12] Krakowiak and Kaiser distinguished two types of errors: incidents and crashes. Incidents are events which, although undesired, were expected and where recovery attempts were successful.

All other errors are called crashes. This distinction may be refined to allow several degrees of UEs. Each degree corresponds to a set of predicates which must be satisfied if recovery is to be considered successful. Degree 0 describes normal behavior of the program. If the requirements for degree i cannot be met, the system attempts to satisfy degree i+1. An UE that is successfully handled by satisfying the requirements of degree i is termed "an UE of degree i."

Distinguishing several degrees of UEs enables a programmer to exactly define (1) what he expects his program to do, (2) what he wants to treat as an incident which he is prepared to handle, and (3) what he means by "correct UE-handling." By this means system specifications, which normally define desired behavior only, may be extended to include response to those undesired events which are expected to happen and which the system should be prepared to handle.

Examples

1. If a deadlock occurs in an operating system (e.g., because of a defect in an external device) this is usually regarded as a normal undesired event. (Note that such a deadlock is possible in spite of a mechanism for deadlock prevention.) Degree 1 may require delaying the processes involved in the hope that continuation will be possible within a short (and fixed) period of time. If this is not possible, degree 2 requires storing the blocked processes on secondary storage so that they may be restarted at a later point of time. If this cannot be achieved (because of a lack of free storage), degree 3 may allow deleting one or more processes.

2. Assume that a program for matrix inversion fails due to "division by zero." A program on degree 1 that works with greater precision may succeed in case of near singularity. Degree 2 may require an error message.

3. Assume that the alphabetical order of a sorted textfile is destroyed. Degree 1 may try to re-establish alphabetical ordering. If this is not possible, e.g., because the separately stored keys are destroyed too, degree 2 may use an old copy and a list of operations that were executed since the copy was

made. If this too fails, e.g., because such a list does not exist or is no longer accessible, degree 3 may make the old copy available to the user (together with an apology).

12.10.1 Why Different Degrees?

There are two basic factors which determine the degree of an UE.

1. The degree of an UE is determined by its basic cause. As an example, consider a read error by a card reader. If this UE was caused by a transient error in the power supply, it is usually sufficient to re-read the card. With a permanent defect, however, this does not work. One has to use another card reader or wait until the first one is repaired. Another cause might be a damaged card or an invalid card code.

In many cases the easiest way to determine the cause of the UE is to try several recovery actions. The order of "tries" usually depends on their "cost." One starts with the simplest or cheapest recovery action and only when it fails, one tries the next one.

2. The degree of an UE depends on the situation at the time the UE occurs. This can be illustrated using the example given above (device failure). In a situation where not all devices are allocated, a failure of one device need not cause a deadlock. One may switch to another device and retry the interrupted operation. Under heavy load, however, this is not possible and a deadlock may occur. Similarly, success or failure of degree 2 (storing the processes involved on secondary storage) depends on the availability of storage.

12.10.2 Order of Degrees

When we tried to solve the question of whether we should try all degrees of one level before we go to the next level or execute the first degree of all levels before trying the second degree, we faced the problem of defining an ordering between degrees. What does it mean that degree i is lower (i.e., has a lower number) than degree j? In the example shown above we stated that some actions are "simpler" or "less costly" than others. But what does that mean and how can simplicity and costliness be determined? In the following some criteria for determining the ordering of degrees are considered.

12.10.3 Order of Aims

By definition recovery actions associated with degree i are tried only if it is impossible to satisfy the requirements associated with degree i–1, i–2, etc. From this one can conclude that the situation achieved by degree i is less desirable than the aims of lower degrees. Clearly, "less desirable" depends upon the goal or purpose the user wants to achieve. A young boy traveling by bike would always fix a flat tire before continuing his journey. That is the cheapest way for him to "handle" this undesired event. If the same happens to a racing cyclist during the Tour de France, he replaces the bike. This is the "cheapest way" for him to handle such an event. Similarly, it must be left to the user of an operating system to decide whether he wants to wait until a defective device (e.g., disc) comes into operation again or to use another device (e.g., tape). The order of recovery actions and thus the order of degrees may be different for different users according to their goals and purposes.

Sometimes not only the ordering may be different, but some situations are not desirable at all. For example, storing a process on secondary storage and restarting it at a later point in time may not be sensible for some processes, either because the results produced by that process are useless after a certain point in time or because restarting that process may be cheaper.

12.10.4 Order of Actions

Even if all degrees lead to the same situation but use different methods with different costs to achieve this situation, the order of degrees may be different for each user. For some applications (weather prediction, air traffic control) time is the most critical resource, and all other resources (storage, paper, etc.) are regarded as less expensive. A program for editing text files will view costs differently. Therefore the decision as to which degree should be tried first must be left to the user. He is the only one who knows which situations are less desirable and which actions are less costly with respect to his task.

From this we may conclude that recovery from an UE requires cooperation of both levels: the user knows which situations are useful and which costs are acceptable; the programs of the lower level know how these situations may be achieved (e.g., how to store processes) and which costs will arise.

12.10.5 Possible Solutions

To achieve this cooperation, two basic concepts may be used:

1. Several different versions of a module [2] are provided; the difference between these versions lies in their preparation for and recovery from UEs. For example, one version of a module for file management provides additional operations for copying a file and contains a mechanism for recording operations that change the contents of this file. A second version works without this mechanism and thus offers less security. It is up to the user to decide which version he wants to use. This possibility may be applied to modules that are used within large (operating) systems where a unique interface is not necessary.

2. Another solution is to provide the recovery actions as operation of the abstract machine. The specification of these operations describes the requirements these operations try to fulfill and the costs that result from executing them. These specifications can be used by higher level programs to determine a response suitable for their purposes. This procedure does not exclude the alternative: some recovery operations are tried before the higher level is informed. This may be useful if costs for reporting an UE are higher than costs for trying that degree (e.g., repeating an I/O operation).

12.11 Examples

Appendix 12.A gives an example of a module specified in accordance with this paper. The notes annotating the example indicate which sections of the paper gave rise to particular decisions in the specification. Appendix 12.B is a narrative of an UE traversing several levels.

Space does not permit us to discuss a whole system in great detail. The reader might wish to look at [2] where all the modules of a small system are presented. In that example we are forced to ignore "errors of mechanism," because the lowest level was a commercial Fortran implementation which did not permit the fielding of errors by user provided software.

12.12 Conclusions

We find it unfortunate that our conclusions are based on small scale systems. This limited experience supports the following conclusions:

1. Proper handling of UEs requires that a systematic approach to UE handling be taken in *every* part of the system. Most of the difficulties with UEs that we have experienced occurred because our "lowest" level, the commercial system that we were using, did not follow our approach.

2. Our ability to use abstract interfaces does not appear excessively restricted by the necessity of considering UEs in designing the abstraction.

3. Reflection of downward traveling UEs and the passing of failures upward appears, on the basis of very limited trials, to be workable and useful. Reflection provides a means of eliminating redundant checks except in the (hopefully) rare case of actual occurrence of an UE.

4. The consideration of UE possibilities requires half and sometimes more than half of a designer's effort in writing specifications in our present efforts. In our own evaluation this is a reasonable price for the potentially increased reliability of the system.

5. The TRAP-function and the functions for resuming normal execution should form a separate module, the details of communication between

levels are hidden from both levels. This module may be implemented differently for different levels. Thus additional facilities available at higher levels may be used.

6. Information determined by UE routines of one level and given to the user of this level support user's reaction to UEs. It is important, however, that this information is consistent with the abstraction defined by that level. Otherwise it will only be meaningful to users that know "hidden" information.

7. The "uses" hierarchy can be maintained even in case of UEs [8].

8. We feel that an organization similar to the one proposed is an essential step towards the production of highly reliable systems.

References

1. Parnas, D.L., "A Technique for Software Module Specification With Examples," *CACM*, May 1972.

2. Parnas, D.L., "On the Criteria for Decomposing Systems into Modules," Carnegie-Mellon University Technical Report, 1971; *CACM*, vol. 15, 12 (Dec. 1972).

3. Dijkstra, E.W., "Notes on Structured Programming," T.H.E., Eindhoven, The Netherlands.

4. Parnas, D.L., "Information Distribution Aspects of Design Methodology," *Proc. of IFIP Congress* 71, 1971.

5. Wirth, N., "Programming by Stepwise Refinement," *CACM*, vol. 14, 4 (April 1971).

6. Parnas, D.L., "Some Conclusions from an Experiment in Software Engineering Techniques," Carnegie-Mellon University Technical Report, *Proc. FJCC*, 1972, AFIPS Press.

7. Jones, A., Private communication.

8. Parnas, D.L., "Some Hypotheses About the "Uses" Hierarchy for Operating Systems," *Forschungsbericht BS* I 76/1, Technische Hochschule Darmstadt (Germany), March 1976.

9. Parnas, D.L., "On a 'Buzzword': Hierarchical Structure," *Proc. of IFIP Congress* 74, 1974, North-Holland Pub. Co.

10. Parnas, D.L., "On the Design and Development of Program Families," *Forschungbericht* BS I 75/2, Technische Hochschule Darmstadt (Germany), IEEE Transactions on Software Engineering, March 1976.

11. Randell, B., "System Structure for Software Fault Tolerance," *Proc. of 1975 Int. Conf. On Reliable Software*, Los Angeles, CA, April 1975.

12. Kaiser, C., Krakowiak, S., "An Analysis of Some Run-Time Errors in an Operating System," *Colloques IRIA*, Rocquencourt, April 23–25, 1974.

Acknowledgments

We are grateful to P.J. Courtois, H.D. Wactlar, Dr. James S. Miller, A. Newell, A. Jones, J. King, and the other members of the Research Group Betriebssysteme I for helpful comments on versions of this paper. Many of the ideas in this paper were suggested by the work of systems programmers who informally organized parts of this program this way. The assistance of their examples in suggesting the guidelines offered here is acknowledged.

Appendix 12.A

Annotated Example of Module Design in the Light of Errors

Introduction

Figure 12.A.1 is a module specification using the technique described in [1]. The module specified is a modification of an example from that paper. With one minor exception all changes from the earlier version are a consequence of the considerations in this paper. The notes below refer to markings in Figure 12.A.1.

1. This function has no parameters and may always be called. The only trap provided is for the case that the module fails. The function represents the number of nodes which may yet be added to the tree and is included so that the user of the module may predict when the trap EC41 or EC46 will occur. See also (8) below.

2. The only limitation on this function call is the size of the parameter (i.e., the maximum integer which may be a node identifier) as discussed in section 12.8.1 of the paper.

3. Here we have an illustration of the ordering suggested by the priority considerations in section 12.8.7. If EC4 does not occur, the value of EC5 should be defined. Trap EC6 only makes sense, if EC4 or EC5 need not be issued.

4. The function VALDEFD (<u>Val</u>ue <u>def</u>ine<u>d</u>) is included in order to specify a trap, if someone attempts to read a value stored at a node in the tree (by calling VAL) before setting that value (by calling SVAL). This is according to the considerations in section 12.8.3.

5. Functions ELS and ERS (<u>E</u>xists <u>L</u>eft <u>S</u>on and <u>E</u>xists <u>R</u>ight <u>S</u>on) are included so that the user can predict the conditions under which EC20 and EC24 would occur.

6. The inclusion of the separate functions SVAL and CVAL (Set VAL and Change VAL) is an example of the attempt to trap probable user errors as discussed in section 12.8.5. The design makes the assumption that setting a value for a node which already has a value is, in many applications, an error and requires a distinct function CVAL for that case (alternatively we could require deletion of the node, but that would introduce great inefficiency). In most programs this would cause no inconvenience. If it did, the reaction to EC28 could be a call on CVAL. This, of course, is an external change of design which is less efficient than the corresponding internal change would have been.

7. We have specified a module in which deletion of a node which still has descendants is illegal. This is certainly a debatable design decision. It might trap some UEs, but it can force inefficiency when it is desired to delete a whole subtree. Were this to become a problem, we would add a distinct function to delete a whole subtree.

```
Function SPSLFT
        possible values: integer
        parameters: none
(1)    initial values: p2
        effect:
(11)        call EC1 (k)  if failure
Function Exists
        possible values: true, false
        parameters: integer i
        initial values: Exists(0) = true;
            Exists (1:p1)=false; all others undefined
        effect:
(2)         call EC2 if i<0 or i>p1
(11)        call EC3 (k)  if failure
Function FA
        possible values: integer
        parameters: integer i
        initial values: FA(0)=0;
          all others undefined
        effect:
            call EC4 if i<0 or i>p1
(3)         call EC5 if 'Exists'(i)=false
(11)        call EC6(k)  if failure
Function VALDEFD
        possible values: true,false
        parameters: integer i
(4)    initial values: VALDEFD(0)=false;
          all others undefined
        effect:
            call EC7 if i<0 or i>p1
            call EC8 if 'Exists'(i)=false
(11)        call EC9(k)  if failure
Function VAL
    possible values: integer
    parameters: integer i
    initial values: undefined
    effect:
            call EC10 if i<0 or i>p1
            call EC11 if 'Exists'(i)=false
            call EC12 if 'VALDEFD'(i)=false
(11)        call EC13(k)  if failure
Function ELS
        possible values: true,false
        parameters: integer i
        initial values: ELS(0)=false;
          all others undefined
        effect:
            call EC48 if i<0 or i>p1
            call EC14 if 'Exists'(i)=false
(11)        call EC15(k)  if failure
```

Figure 12.A.1

```
Function ERS
      possible values: true,false
      parameters: integer i
      initial values: ERS(0)=false;
         all others undefined
   effect:
              call EC49 if i<0 or i>p1
              call EC16 if 'Exists'(i)=false
(11)          call EC17(k)  if failure

Function LS
      possible values: integer
      parameters: integer i
      initial values: undefined
      effect:
              call EC18 if i<0 or i>p1
              call EC19 if 'Exists'(i)=false
              call EC20 if 'ELS'(i)=false
(11)          call EC21(k)  if failure

Function RS
      possible values: integer
      parameters: integer i
      initial values: undefined
      effect:
              call EC22 if i<0 or i>p1
              call EC23 if 'Exists'(i)=false
              call EC24 if 'ERS'(i)=false
(11)          call EC25(k)  if failure

Function SVAL
      possible values: none
      parameters: integer i,v
      initial values: not applicable
      effect:
              call EC26 if i<0 or i>p1
              call EC27 if 'Exists'(i)=false
(6)           call EC28 if 'VALDEFD'(i)=true
(11)          call EC29(k)  if failure
          VAL(i)=v
          VALDEFD(i)=true

Function CVAL
      possible values: none
      parameters: integer i,v
      initial values: not applicable
      effect:
              call EC30 if i<0 or i>p1
              call EC31 if 'Exists'(i)=false
              call EC32 if 'VALDEFD'(i)=false
(11)          call EC33(k)  if failure
          VAL(i)=v
```

Figure 12.A.1 *continued*

Function DEL
    possible values: none
    parameters: integer i
    initial values: not applicable
    effect:
        call EC34 if i<0 or i>p1
        call EC35 if 'Exists'(i)=or
(7)   call EC36 if 'ELS'(i)=false
                'ERS'(i) = true
(11)   call EC37(k) if failure
        FA(i) is undefined
        VAL(i) is undefined
        ERS(i) is undefined
        ELS(i) is undefined
        VALDEFD(i) is undefined
        Exists(i)=false
        if i='LS'('FA'(i)) then
          [LS('FA'(i)) is undefined
            ELS('FA'(i)) = false]
        if i='RS'('FA'(i)) then
          [RS('FA'(i)) is undefined
            ERS('FA'(i)) = false]
(8)   SPSLFT = 'SPSLFT'+1

Function SLS
    possible values: none
    parameters: integer i
    initial values: not applicable
    effect:
        call EC38 if i<0 or i>p1
        call EC39 if 'Exists'(i)=false
        call EC40 if 'ELS'(i)=true
(10)   call EC41 if 'SPSLFT'=0
(11)   call EC42(k) if failure
        there exists k such that
        [0<k<p1
          'Exists'(k)=false
          Exists(k)=true
          LS(i)=k
          ELS(i)=true
          ELS(k)=ERS(k)=false
          VALDEFD(k)=false
           FA(k)=i]
(8)   SPSLFT='SPSLFT''−1

Figure 12.A.1 *continued*

```
Function SRS
      possible values: none
      parameters: integer i
      initial values: not applicable
      effect:
              call EC43 if i<0 or i>p1
              call EC44 if 'Exists'(i)=false
              call EC45 if 'ERS'(i)=true
(10)          call EC46 if 'SPSLFT'=0
(11)          call EC47(k)  if failure
            there exists k such that
              [0<k<p1
(9)            'Exists'(k)=false
               Exists(k)=true
               RS(i)=k
             VALDEFD(k)=false
             ELS(k)=ERS(k)=false
               ERS(i)=true
               FA(k)=i]
(8)          SPSLFT='SPSLFT'–1
```

Values of k in calls of EC1, EC3, EC6, EC9, EC13, EC15, EC17, EC21, EC25, EC29, EC33, EC37, EC42, EC47

k=0   value of SPSLFT,Exists,FA,VALDEFD,VAL,ELS, ERS,LS,RS unchanged. Successful retry possible.

k=1   value of SPSLFT,Exists,FA,VALDEFD,VAL,ELS, ERS,LS,RS unchanged. Successful retry possible

k=2   value of function called lost or changed, no other changes. "possible state". Successful retry possible.

k=3   value of function called lost or changed, no other changes. "impossible state". Continuation impossible.

k=4   value of function called lost or changed, no other changes. "possible state". Successful retry impossible.

k=5   value of functions other than that called changed. "possible state". Successful retry possible.

k=6   value of functions other than that called have been changed. "impossible state". Successful retry impossible.

k=7   value of functions other than that called have been changed. "impossible state". Continuation impossible.

Notes
1. k=2, 3, 4, only possible in EC1, EC3 . . . EC25.
2. k=0 or k=1 suggest that information is not lost but growth or change of tree is restricted.
3. "possible state" and "impossible state" are defined in the paper.
4. The design makes the assumption that if the module is unable to restore its external appearance to a "possible state" it cannot continue.
5. "successful retry possible" does not guarantee successful retry. It only means that successful retry is not known to be impossible. This value would be given if the module experienced difficulties which might be resolved externally to the module and suffered no internal damage to its data structures.
6. If not stated otherwise, "continue" is always possible.

Figure 12.A.1 *continued*

8. The three points marked "(8)" illustrate a difficulty in trying to make the traps completely predictable, yet not reveal the implementation. Our manipulation on SPSLFT makes the assumption that space for storing VAL is allocated when the node is created. Further, we assume that the space is limited by the number of nodes. In some implementations that would not be so. For example, the real limitation might be maximum depth. For those implementations the specifications will require traps EC41 or EC46 in some cases when space is actually still available. If, however, we took the obvious alternative and made separate changes to SPSLFT for creating a node and SVAL, we would be restricting our implementation to one which made separate allocations. Such implementations would use more space and would be undesirable, if SLS or SRS were always followed directly by SVAL. Note that the elimination of space limitations would violate Sections 12.8.2 and 12.8.6.

9. Note that the specification does not specify the value of LS(i); only some properties of it. Further note that this specification is acceptable only on the very reasonable assumption that p1 (the maximum number of node names) is not less than p2 (the maximum number of nodes). If that assumption were violated, we would have to introduce traps for the situations where there does not exist a value of k with the properties specified.

10. Note that it would be quite reasonable to reduce the size of the trap vector by combining EC41 and EC46. See section 12.8.8.

11. The traps EC1, EC3, EC6, EC9, . . . report failures of mechanism rather than an incorrect call. We have chosen to have each of these pass a parameter k which will indicate the class of failure which has occurred. The values of k are defined as part of the specifications.

The important thing to note is that the meaning of each particular possible value of k is defined in terms of external properties of the module. If the user had kept redundant records he would be able to determine which value of k applied by diagnostic testing. We pass the value of k so that he will not need to keep such records and on the assumption that reasonable implementations will be able to determine the proper value under all but the most catastrophic of failures. The last value is an escape for such cases.

As mentioned in section 12.8.10, this particular design is but one point on a scale which includes many possibilities. We gave it as a reasonable but not necessarily optimal design.

Examples of Possible Error Degree Specifications

When the user of this tree module specifies just exactly what he wants implemented, he must specify not just the desired behavior when everything goes well, he must provide information about his preferences in case of mishap. He can do this by describing various degrees of damage, *from his viewpoint*. He *might*, for example, define 4 degrees as described below.

Degree 0: Through the use of extra data maintained by the module, the tree is reconstructed. The user is only aware of a delay.

Degree 1: The user is informed of the root of the deleted subtree. All functions are updated to indicate that the lost subtree does not exist.

Degree 2: The user is informed that some data has been lost, but not which subtree. Functions are updated as in degree 1.

Degree 3: The user is informed that some data has been lost. Functions are not updated and the user may find the tree in an "impossible" state. He may, however, continue to insert data.

Degree 4: The user is informed that he may make no further changes to the tree, that some data may have been lost, and that the tree may be in an impossible or inconsistent state.

Although this set of degrees appears reasonable, it certainly does not correspond to the wishes of every possible user. For some users with strict real time demands, the delay involved in degree 0 may be unacceptable, it may be preferable to lose the data and proceed as in degree 1. For other users, the cost of maintaining the redundant data necessary to satisfy the requirements stated in degree 1 may not be worth it, they may prefer degree 2.

The very fact that such differences in goals can exist emphasizes the need for a specification of the degrees. The behavior of the module when something goes wrong should not be left as a random result of implementation decisions made by a programmer. The programmer should be informed of the way that purchaser or user ranks damage so that the programmer may be guided by that information.

Appendix 12.B

Examples in Which UE Messages Must Be Passed Between Levels

It may not be obvious to some readers that UEs in a hierarchically structured system must be handled at levels other than those at which they are detected. We present two examples as a means of showing why the detecting level may not have the information necessary to perform the proper action.

Example 1. Bad Tape Block

An unreadable tape block will be detected at the lowest level, because the hardware will signal its presence. The low level program, which has been ordered to read a given tape block, has no knowledge of the intended use of the information and can take no corrective action. Some levels higher, we have a program providing a simple sequential access method. This program knows that the block was part of a given file but no more. Still higher we *might* find a program managing a large data base. This program might know that the block in question was part of a summary file which had just been computed from a master file and the record could be recomputed. Alternatively, the system might not be that sophisticated, but the UE could be passed higher to the user who is able to give instructions for recovery.

Example 2. Out-of-Date Directory

Due to a software error a file is changed while a copy of its directory still exists. A program using that old directory attempts to read the file and ultimately receives an UE due to some hardware violation. If the UE is passed up to the level which used the incorrect directory, it can check its copy against the master copy and try again. Recovery at the intermediate levels was impossible. If this sophistication were not present, the UE could be passed upward to some higher level which would attempt a retry. If the retry involves getting a new copy of the directory, we may well have success.

In these two examples we have tried to show both "errors of usage" and "errors of mechanism." We have also shown that the considerations are important for both hardware and software errors. In all the situations outlined an attempt to handle the UEs at the incorrect level would have failed due to lack of proper knowledge, the system would have a poorer reliability than necessary. The alternative solution is to introduce the necessary knowledge to the lower level. This clearly would reduce the advantage we have gained from the hierarchical structure and from decomposition into "information hiding" modules.

Introduction

James Horning

It is rare to find a twenty-year-old software engineering paper that seems fresh and relevant to contemporary practice or makes me want to launch into a dialog with the author as I read. "Some Software Engineering Principles" does both. In a concise and readable fashion it summarizes a number of the central contributions that Dave Parnas made to software engineering ("the multiperson construction of multiversion programs") in the previous decade.

I do not recall seeing this paper when it came out. As an Infotech State of the Art Report, its circulation, I suspect was fairly limited. However, many of the papers it cites and summarizes were more widely available at the time. I remember reading, discussing, and being impressed by many of them. I still find the ideas interesting and largely persuasive.

This paper focuses on issues of modularity: what it means, how it can be realized and exploited, and why it is important. The key tools are decomposition and specification. The key idea is that "the connections between program parts are the assumptions that the parts make about each other." This definition of "interface" is, like Algol 60, "an improvement on most of its successors."

Another theme, which occurs repeatedly in Parnas's work, is the imposition and use of various kinds of structure (cf. "On a 'Buzzword': Hierarchical Structure," Chapter 8).

Because the exposition in this paper is stripped to its bare bones, the reader is repeatedly challenged to flesh out the argument—and sometimes left to splutter mentally, "but, but, but, . . ." to the author. I leave it as an exercise for the reader to find the flaws, if any, in Parnas's argument.

It is somewhat of a puzzle to me why these ideas have not had more influence on the practice of software engineering. There is much common-sense good advice here; it seems that present day projects would benefit greatly by following it. It may be that most organizations are still not willing to pay the cost of doing the job properly, despite the demonstrated costs of not doing it properly. Or it may be that Parnas has simply been more successful as an innovator than as a salesman.

Some Software Engineering Principles

David L. Parnas

13.1 Abstract

Software Engineering is defined as the multi-person construction of multi-version programs. After discussing the meaning of the word "structure" in discussions of software, the following topics, of particular relevance in software engineering situations, are discussed:

1. The decomposition of programming projects into work assignments (modules)
2. Precise specification of the work to be done
3. Designing systems so that they are easily contracted or extended
4. Designing abstract interfaces for modules.

This paper is intended to provide an introductory overview. The bibliography includes more thorough discussions of each topic.

13.2 Introduction

Software engineering is the design of useful programs under one or both of the following conditions:

1. More than one person is involved in the construction and/or use of the program, and
2. More than one version of the program will be produced.

The above definition emphasizes the fact that the distinguishing characteristics of software engineering do *not* depend on the function of the program being produced. We are not distinguishing systems programs from applications programs. Our definition excludes only the design of one program by one man who is also its only user. The latter situation can be called *solo-programming*.

In multiperson programming we find three problems that are not significant in the solo-programming situation:

1. How to divide the job of producing the software among the programmers
2. How to specify the exact behavior required of each program component
3. How to communicate to all the people involved information about the occurrence of run-time errors among the system components and to the user.

These problems are not present in the "solo-programming" situation; classical programming textbooks do not treat them. The third problem is particularly vexing; even with the latest in programming techniques, programs are designed on the assumption that everything will go well.

In multi-version programming we find three additional problems that are not present if we are going to write a single program:

4. How to write programs that are easily modified. Programs in which a change of one design decision does not require changes in many parts of the program.

5. How to write programs with useful subsets. If we only need a subset of the services performed by a program we should be able to quickly remove unneeded parts without having to rewrite the remainder. If we are unable to complete or use certain functions, we would like a reduced set of capabilities to be available.

6. How to write programs that are easily extended. We should like to be able to add new capabilities to programs without rewriting the programs that are already present. This, too, is a fail soft goal; build a subset to meet a deadline, then extend as time permits.

This paper reviews some techniques that have been developed for software engineering situations, and the results of preliminary experiment to evaluate the value of those techniques. These results are not new, having been presented in more detail in the papers cited in the bibliography. They are repeated here as concisely as possible.

13.3 What Is a Well-Structured Program?

Before we can proceed we must explore the use of the word "structure" when discussing programs.

"Structure" refers to a partial description of a system. A structure description shows the system divided into a set of parts, and specifies some connections between those parts. Because any given system admits many such descriptions, our usage of "part" does not allow a precise definition (parallel to that of "subroutine" in software and of "card" in hardware). The definitions of the latter words delineate a restricted class of objects in a way that the definition of "part" does not. Nevertheless, "part" is useful in the same manner that "unit" is in military or economic discussions.

The term "connection" is often accepted without definition. Many assume that the "connections" are control transfer points, passed parameters, shared data for software, and wires or other physical connections for hardware. Such a definition of "connection" is a highly dangerous over-simplification, one which results in misleading structure descriptions.

The connections between program parts are the assumptions that the parts make about each other. In most systems we find that these connections are much more extensive than the calling sequences and control block formats that are usually shown in system structure descriptions.

The meaning of the above definition of connection can be clarified by considering two situations in which the structure of a system is terribly important: (1) making of changes in a system, and (2) proving system correctness. (I will neither argue the necessity of proving programs correct, nor support the necessity of making changes. I wish to use those hypothetical situations to exhibit the meaning of "connection.")

Correctness proofs for programs can become so complex that their own correctness is in question (e.g., [7], [8]). For large systems we would be forced to exploit the structure of the programs in producing the proofs. We must examine each part separately. For each part we will identify (1) the system properties that it is required to guarantee, and (2) the properties that it expects other parts to satisfy. The correctness proof for each part will take (1) as the set of theorems to be proven, and (2) as a set of axioms that may be used in the proof. Eventually the theorems proven about each part will be used in proving the correctness of the whole system. The task of proving system correctness will be facilitated by this process if and only if the amount of information in the statement sets (1) and (2) is significantly less than the information in the complete description of the programs that implement the parts.

We can also consider making a change in the completed system. We ask, "What changes can be made to one part without involving change to other parts?" We may make only those changes that do not violate the assumptions that other parts make about the part being changed. In other words, a single part may be changed only if the "connections" still "fit."

In both cases we have a strong argument for making the connections contain as little information (in the information theoretic sense) as possible. Systems in which the connections between parts contain little information are termed well structured.

13.4 What Is a Module?

The word module is one of the buzzwords of the computer industry. It always refers to parts that can be put together to make a complete system. However, during the preparation of software, there are several times at which parts are joined together. For example:

1. The products of various programmers are put together.
2. Subroutines are "linked" together.
3. Segments of a system are loaded into memory.
4. Programs to perform various functions are combined.

This variety of occasions on which parts are put together has led to a variety of distinct meanings for modules. "Module" sometimes refers to a programmer work assignment, a subroutine, a memory load, or a functional component. One must be very careful not to make the assumption that all of these meanings are the same. The criteria that are useful in a decomposition into work assignments can be very different from the criteria appropriate for a decomposition into modules of the other types.

In this paper, because of our interest in multi-person programming, we will use "module" to mean the work assignment given to a programmer or group of programmers. Because of our interest in multi-version programming, this will also be the unit of change. Whenever we have to make a change in the system, it is best if we can confine the change to the work of just one programmer.

13.5 Two Techniques for Controlling the Structure of Systems Programs

To produce well-structured systems programs, there are two basic functions that the designer must perform very carefully. The first of these is the division of the project into modules or work assignments (*decomposition*); the second is the precise *specification* of those modules.

Some informal experiments have revealed that there is a remarkable consistency in the way that programmers will divide systems into modules. For example, I have often asked programmers how they would go about dividing the project of producing a KWIC index program into modules (work assignments). With very rare exceptions the programmers suggested a decomposition based on a flowchart of the system. They are following the lessons that they received in their early training in programming. Programmers are taught that the first step in producing a program is to write a "rough" flowchart and then proceed to detail each of the boxes in it. This is often an excellent strategy for a "solo" programming project, but, as demonstrated in [2], it is seldom a good procedure for dividing a project into work assignments. One conclusion of the previous sections was that a well-structured program was one with minimal interconnections between its modules. Because information must be passed in large chunks (and using fixed conventions) between the various phases (boxes in the flowchart) the conventional approach results in modules that have quite strong interconnections. As was indicated in [2], systems that result from such a design are quite difficult to change. We can, however, forget our flowcharts and attempt instead to define our modules "around" assumptions that are likely to change. One then designs a module (a collection of subroutines or macros) that "hides" or contains each one. Such modules have abstract interfaces that are relatively unlikely to change. If we succeed in defining interfaces that are sufficiently "solid" (i.e., they will not change), changes in the system can be confined to one module. The reader is referred to [2, 24] for deeper discussions of this point including detailed examples. Teaching experience described in [9] has shown that, at this point in time, such skills can only be taught by the use of many examples.

The second function of the designer is that of specification. There is good reason to believe [6] that the designer can obtain a system with the structure he suggested only if he has a way of precisely describing the assumptions that the designers of one module are permitted to make about other modules. In describing those assumptions (writing specifications for each module), the designer is walking a tightrope. If the programmer has too little information about the other modules, he will be unable to produce an efficiently working system. The need for sufficient information is obvious to almost everyone. The surprising side of the tightrope is that it is also wrong to provide too much information. If the excess information is used (i.e., if additional assumptions are made), the structure of the program will not be that intended by the designer. These will be additional (unintended) assumptions. The most common approach to software module specification is to reveal a rough description of the internal structure of the module. The next most common approach is to reveal a description of a "hypothetical" implementation of the module. Almost invariably we are told the structure of some real or imagined table (or procedure) to which the user of the module does not have access. Both of these approaches are fraught with danger. In the first, the system becomes hard to change if the correctness of the interfacing programs depends upon the internal information that was revealed. In the second case the program may *never* work correctly, because the correctness depended on some aspect of the "hypothetical" implementation that was never true. It is extremely difficult to reveal some part of an implementation (in order to be precise) and then instruct the reader as to precisely which parts of the revealed information he must not use.

We have had some experience with a specification technique whose goal is the precise specification of externally visible aspects without suggesting internal constructions. The specifications relate the externally visible value functions to each other rather than to a (real or imagined) lower level machine. In syntax these specifications resemble programs. It is the refusal to mention lower level (or internal) mechanisms that distinguishes them from programs. The reader is referred to [3, 14–19] for more discussion and detailed examples.

13.6 Results

On the basis of the above considerations we have obtained very good results in small scale experiments. For example, in the fall of 1971 we produced 192 quite distinct versions of a KWIC index program using 15 modules produced by 15 students. (Each module satisfied one of 5 module specifications.) (We set out to produce 45 versions using 20 students, but five of the students produced modules that failed to meet specifications.) Of the 15 that passed the preliminary testing, we could have had 192 distinct combinations. We selected only 25 of these for testing (for economy reasons), but all of the 25 ran successfully. All students worked independently and had no advance knowledge of the combinations that would be tested. The actual testing was carried out by graduate students with no knowledge of the internal behavior of any program module. The only changes made during integration were the elimination of excessive memory requests. Similar experiments have been repeated several times—all have been successful in producing easily changed systems. The method has become known as information hiding—the modules as information hiding modules.

13.7 Error Handling

In a sense, the treatment of run-time errors is made more difficult by the information hiding approach to structuring programs. When an error is detected, the information about what has gone wrong is originally expressed in terms of data structures and programs that are not known in most of the system. The information needed to understand the cause of the error and the procedure for corrective action are likely to be in other modules. If the information about the error is communicated in terms of the hidden program structures, the structure of the resulting system will be destroyed by the distribution of the additional assumptions.

In [10, 20] an approach to solving this problem has been outlined. This approach was used, in a primitive form, in the experiment described above. Even in this form it had the advantage that, when an error was discovered, it took no detailed knowledge of any module to identify the module that had caused the error. This was a great advantage in managing the project and a complete change from the author's earlier experience in other multi-person projects. Identifying the module at fault is often the major problem in correcting an error.

More recently the approach has been used in a small operating system project and a compiler. In both experiments, the developers found that the preparation for the handling of undesired events became a significant proportion of the initial design and development. In both cases, some participants doubted that the effort was worthwhile. However, experience later in the project showed that the preparation did pay off in both reduced debugging times and increased system reliability. A complete report on this aspect of the operating system experience can be found in [21].

13.8 Hierarchical Structure and Subsetable Systems

A topic of interest to the academic community for a number of years is "hierarchical structure" in software systems. Hot debates have raged over the feasibility or practicality of such approaches, but it has been found that most of the disagreements stem from the fact that at least 10 distinct concepts have been discussed under that heading. One of these concepts, called the "uses" hierarchy in [22, 23], has been found to be of great practical significance. It determines the ease with which a software product can be extended or contracted.

"Uses" is a relation between independently callable programs. P_1 uses P_2 if a working copy of P_2 is needed in the system in order for P_1 to meet its specification. If the "uses" relation defines a hierarchy among the programs, it is easy to find useful subsets of the system. If, on the other hand, the graph of the uses hierarchy contains loops, we may find ourselves in the situation where nothing works until everything works.

We have found that it is important for software designers to design the "uses" hierarchy before coding begins. If not, the "uses" relation will be determined by the decisions of individual programmers and it is unlikely that the set of obtainable subsets will correspond to the needs of the possible users.

We have also found a simple rule of thumb that helps in the design of the "uses" hierarchy. The lower level programs should use data structures as if the size and part of the contents were fixed, but the upper level programs can alter those structures. The "why" and "how" behind that rather surprising proposal is to be found in [23].

13.9 Designing Abstract Interfaces

Above we have spoken blithely of modules having abstract interfaces that are less likely to change than the "secrets" that they hide. In fact, the design of that interface is quite difficult and requires both careful investigation and some creativity. We have, however, found a procedure that seems to be practical—even in real world situations. It breaks the design of the interface into two phases:

1. The development of a list of assumptions believed unlikely to change during the life cycle of the product, and
2. The specification of a set of interface functions whose implementability is guaranteed by those assumptions.

No design procedure is foolproof, but we have found that the first phase, which is the most difficult and time-consuming because many people must be consulted, eliminates a lot of errors that were made when it is skipped.

A new report [24] discusses the approach in great detail including the complete design of interfaces that have been used in further programming experiments.

13.10 Conclusions

One hears a great deal of discussion about spending more time in preliminary design in order to reduce the total life-cycle cost of software. Unfortunately, most of these discussions give little guidance as to what decisions should be made in those early phases. Further, they give few suggestions about the criteria to be used in making those early design decisions. Our experience with the design concepts discussed in this paper has convinced us that the issues dealt with here are the ones that must be addressed in the early phases of software design. We have also been convinced that the criteria and principles mentioned here give useful guidance during that time. Correct decisions during this phase require a great deal of foresight and errors cannot be eliminated. However, even when errors occur, our experience has been that the effort was worthwhile.

These ideas are clearly intended to be applied early in the design of a software product. They are, unfortunately, of little help to those who are burdened with the maintenance of software that was designed by more conventional approaches.

References

1. Parnas, D.L. "Some Conclusions from an Experiment in Software Engineering," *Proceedings of the 1972 FJCC.*

2. Parnas, D.L. "On the Criteria to be Used in Decomposing Systems into Modules," *Communications of the ACM (Programming Techniques Department),* December 1972.

3. Parnas, D.L. "A Technique for Software Module Specification with Examples," *Communications of the ACM (Programming Techniques Department),* May 1972.

4. Robinson, L., and D.L. Parnas. "A Program Holder Module," Technical Report, Carnegie-Mellon University, June 1973.

5. Robinson, L. "Design and Implementation of a Multi-Level System Using Software Modules," Technical Report, Carnegie-Mellon University, June 1973.

6. Parnas, D.L. "Information Distribution Aspects of Design Methodology," *Proceedings of IFIP Congress 1971.*

7. Balzer, Robert M. "Studies Concerning Minimal Time Solutions to the Firing Squad Synchronization Problem," Ph.D. Thesis, Carnegie Institute of Technology, 1966.

8. London, R. "Certification of Treesort 3," *CACM,* June 1970.

9. Parnas, D.L. "A Course on Software Engineering Techniques," included in the *Proceedings of the ACM SIGCSE, Second Technical Symposium*, March 24–25, 1972.

10. Parnas, D.L. "On the Response to Detected Errors in Hierarchically Structured Systems" Technical Report, Carnegie-Mellon University, 1972.

11. Price, W.R. "Implications of a Virtual Memory Mechanism for Implementing Protection in a Family of Operating Systems," Technical Report (Ph.D. Thesis), Carnegie-Mellon University, June 1973.

12. Parnas, D.L., and W.R. Price. "The Design of the Virtual Memory Aspects of a Virtual Machine," *Proceedings of the ACM SIGARCH-SIGOPS Workshop on Virtual Computer Systems*, March 1973.

13. Popek, G.J., and C. Kline. "Verifiable Secure Operating Systems Software," *AFIPS Conference Proceedings*, 1974, NCC AFIPS Press, Montvale, NJ, USA.

14. Parnas, D.L., and G. Handzel. "More on Specification Techniques for Software Modules," Technical Report, Technische Hochschule Darmstadt, Darmstadt, West Germany, February 1975.

15. Liskov, B., and S.N. Zilles. "Specification Techniques for Data Abstractions," *IEEE Transactions on Software Engineering*, Vol. SE-1, No. 1, March 1975.

16. Guttag, J. "The Specification and Application to Programming of Abstract Data Types," Ph.D. thesis, CSRG TR 59, University of Toronto, September 1975.

17. Guttag, J. "Abstract Data Types and the Development of Data Structures," SIGPLAN/SIGMOD Conference on DATA: Abstraction, Definition and Structure (to be published in *CACM*).

18. Parnas, D.L., Handzel, G., and H. Würges. "Design and Specification of the Minimal Subset of an Operating System Family," *IEEE Transactions on Software Engineering*, Vol. SE-2, No. 4, pp. 301–307, December 1976.

19. Parnas, D.L. "The Use of Precise Specifications in the Development of Software," to be published in *Proceedings of the IFIP 1977*. North Holland, pp. 861–867.

20. Parnas, D.L., and H. Würges. "Response to Undesired Events in Software Systems," *Proceedings of the 2ⁿᵈ International Conference on Software Engineering*, 13–15 October 1976, San Francisco, CA.

21. Würges, H. "Reaktion auf Unerwünschte Ereignisse in Hierarchisch Strukturierten Software-Systemen" ("Reaction to Undesired Events in Hierarchical Structured Software-Systems"), Ph.D. thesis, Technische Hochschule Darmstadt, Darmstadt, West Germany.

22. Parnas, D.L. "On a 'Buzzword': Hierarchical Structure," *Proc. IFIP Congress 1974*, North Holland Publishing Co., 1974.

23. Parnas, D.L. "Some Hypotheses About the 'Uses' Hierarchy for Operating Systems," Technical Report, Technische Hochschule Darmstadt, Darmstadt, West Germany, March 1976.

24. Parnas, D.L. "The Use of Abstract Interfaces in the Development of Software for Embedded Computer Systems," Technical Memorandum of the Naval Research Laboratory, Washington, DC 20375.

Introduction

Barry Boehm

I'm generally happy at the end of a professional conference if at least one presentation provides me with some experience or concept I feel excited about taking home and sharing or adopting. At ICSE 3 in Atlanta in 1978, David Parnas's "Designing Software for Ease of Extension and Contraction" definitely gave me that feeling.

At TRW, we had done all sorts of things with module size standards, coding standards, and documentation standards, but our software was still frustratingly hard to maintain. So was the software we got from other contractors.

It was clear that one of the main problems was that most contract software at the time was built by companies that had been the lowest bidder on a fixed set of requirements. The natural approach in such a case is to develop a point-solution design that implements just that set of requirements. However, knowing that this was the source of much of the problem was not equivalent to having a solution that we could teach designers and use in design reviews.

And there at ICSE 3, all of a sudden, was Dave's paper with a constructive, understandable approach to designing maintainable software that looked eminently teachable and usable. As with many paradigm-shifting concepts, it pointed out that we had been starting our search for solutions in the wrong places—not with code, documentation, or design, but with the requirements.

To design for ease of change, your requirements had to indicate not just what you thought they were now, but also in which directions you thought they were most likely to change. Once you had that starting point, you could apply Dave's previous work on modularity and information hiding to hide the sources of requirements change within your modules. Then when the changes came, you could accommodate them within that module, without the usual ripple effects across the rest of the software that had been causing the maintainability problems with point-solution designs.

Before I left ICSE 3, I asked Dave if he would be willing to consult for TRW and help us learn and apply these concepts. Fortunately, he was, and this led to a very stimulating time in which Dave taught and worked with TRW projects to help us learn and apply the techniques.

I personally found these concepts extremely helpful in organizing the architecture of the TRW Software Productivity System, our corporate software support environment. There we organized the design to accommodate both existing sources of variation (e.g., different design tools and configuration management systems to support) and future sources of variation (e.g., evolving workstations and local area networks). I've also found the technique useful in organizing artifacts other than software (e.g., in designing project organizations to anticipate shifts in institutional responsibility).

It's remarkable, however, how long it takes for good ideas to become common practice. Even now, most requirements documentation standards and requirements tools don't have a place to specify evolution requirements.

Designing Software for Ease of Extension and Contraction

David L. Parnas

14.1 Abstract

Designing software to be extensible and easily contracted is discussed as a special case of design for change. A number of ways that extension and contraction problems manifest themselves in current software is explained. Four steps in the design of software that is more flexible are then discussed. The most critical step is the design of a software structure called the "uses" relation. Some criteria for design decisions are given and illustrated using a small example. It is shown that the identification of *minimal* subsets and *minimal* extensions can lead to software that can be tailored to the needs of a broad variety of users.

14.2 Introduction

This paper is being written because the following complaints about software systems are so common.

1. "We were behind schedule and wanted to deliver an early release with only a <proper subset of intended capabilities>, but found that that subset would not work until everything worked."

2. "We wanted to add <simple capability>, but to do so would have meant rewriting all or most of the current code."

3. "We wanted to simplify and speed up the system by removing the <unneeded capability>, but to take advantage of this simplification we would have had to rewrite major sections of the code."

4. "Our SYSGEN was intended to allow us to tailor a system to our customers' needs but it was not flexible enough to suit us."

After studying a number of such systems, I have identified some simple concepts that can help programmers to design software so that subsets and extensions are more easily obtained. These concepts are simple if you think about software in the way suggested by this paper. Programmers do not commonly do so.

14.3 Software as a Family of Programs

When we were first taught how to program, we were given a specific problem and told to write one program to do that job. Later we compared our program to others, considering such issues as space and time utilization, but still assuming that we were producing a single product. Even the most recent literature on programming methodology is written on that basis. Dijkstra's *A Discipline of Programming* [1] uses predicate transformers to specify *the* task to be performed by *the* program to be written. The use of the definite article implies that there is a unique problem to be solved and but one program to write.

Today, the software designer should be aware that he is not designing a single program but a family of programs. As discussed in an earlier paper [2], we consider a set of programs to be a program family if they have so much in common that it pays to study their common aspects before looking at the aspects that differentiate them. This rather pragmatic definition does not tell us what pays, but it does explain the motivation for designing program families. We want to exploit the commonalities, share code, and reduce maintenance costs.

Some of the ways that the members of a program family may differ are listed below.

1. They may run on different hardware configurations.
2. They may perform the same functions but differ in the format of the input and output data.
3. They may differ in certain data structures or algorithms because of differences in the available resources.
4. They may differ in some data structures or algorithms because of differences in the size of the input data sets or the relative frequency of certain events.
5. Some users may require only a subset of the services or features that other users need. These "less demanding" users may demand that they not be forced to pay for the resources consumed by the unneeded features.

Engineers are taught that they must try to anticipate the changes that may be made, and are shown how to achieve designs that can easily be altered when these anticipated changes occur. For example, an electrical engineer will be advised that the world has not standardized the 60-cycle 110-V current. Television designers are fully aware of the differing transmission conventions that exist in the world. It is standard practice to design products that are easily changed in those aspects. Unfortunately, there is no magic technique for handling unanticipated changes. The makers of conventional watches have no difficulty altering a watch that shows the day so that it displays "MER" instead of "WED," but I would expect a long delay for redesign were the world to switch to a ten day week.

Software engineers have not been trained to design for change. The usual programming courses neither mention the need to anticipate changes nor do they offer techniques for designing programs in which changes are easy. Because programs are abstract mathematical objects, the software engineers' techniques for responding to anticipated changes are more subtle and more difficult to grasp than the techniques used by designers of physical objects. Further, we have been led astray by the other designers of abstract objects—mathematicians who state and prove theorems. When a mathematician becomes aware of the need for a set of closely related theorems, he responds by proving a more general theorem. For mathematicians, a more general result is always superior to a more specialized product. The engineering analogy to the mathematician's approach would be to design television sets containing variable transformers and tuners that are capable of detecting several types of signals. Except for the U.S. armed forces stationed overseas, there is little market for such a product. Few of us consider relocations so likely that we are willing to pay to have the generality present in the product. My guess is that the market for calendar watches for a variable length week is even smaller than the market for the television sets just described.

In [2] I have treated the subject of the design of program families rather generally and in terms of text in a programming language. In this paper, I focus on the fifth situation described above: families of programs in which some members are subsets of other family members or several family members share a common subset. I discuss an earlier stage of design, the stage when one identifies the major components of the system and defines relations between those components. We focus on this early stage because the problems described in the introduction result from failure to consider early design decisions carefully.

14.4 How Does the Lack of Subset and Extensions Manifest Itself?

Although we often speak of programs that are "not subsetable" or "not extensible," we must recognize that phrase as inaccurate. It is always possible to remove code from a program and have a runable result. Any software system can be extended (TSO proves that). The problem is that the subsets and extensions are not the programs that we would have designed if we had set out to design just that product. Further, the amount of work needed to obtain the product seems all out of proportion to the nature of the change. The obstacles commonly encountered in trying to extend or shrink systems fall into four classes.

14.4.1 Excessive Information Distribution

A system may be hard to extend or contract if too many programs were written assuming that a given feature is present or not present. This was illustrated by an operating system in which an early design decision was that the system would support three conversational languages. There were many sections of the system where knowledge of this decision was used. For example, error message tables had room for exactly three entries. An extension to allow four languages would have required that a great deal of code be rewritten. More surprisingly, it would have been difficult to reduce the system to one that efficiently supported only two of the languages. One could remove the third language, but to regain the table space, one would have had to rewrite the same sections of code that would be rewritten to add a language.

14.4.2 A Chain of Data-Transforming Components

Many programs are structured as a chain of components, each receiving data from the previous component, processing it (and changing the format), before sending the data to the next program in the chain. If one component in this chain is not needed, that code is often hard to remove because the output of its predecessor is not compatible with the input requirements of its successor. A program that does nothing but change the format must be substituted. One illustration would be a payroll program that assumed unsorted input. One of the components of the system accepts the unsorted input and produces output that is sorted by some key. If the firm adopts an office procedure that results in sorted input, this phase of the processing is unnecessary. To eliminate that program, one may have to add a program that transfers data from a file in the input format to a file in the format appropriate for the next phase. It may be almost as efficient to allow the original SORT component to sort the sorted input.

14.4.3 Components That Perform More Than One Function

Another common error is to combine two simple functions into one component because the functions seem too simple to separate. For example, one might be tempted to combine synchronization with message sending and acknowledgment in building an operating system. The two functions seem closely related; one might expect that for the sake of reliability one should insist on a "handshake" with each exchange of synchronization signals. If one later encounters an application in which synchronization is needed very frequently, one may find that there is no simple way to strip the message sending out of the synchronization routines. Another example is the inclusion of run-time type-checking in the basic subroutine call mechanism. In applications where compile-time checking or verification eliminates the need for the run-time type-check, another subroutine call mechanism will be needed. The irony of these situations is that the "more powerful" mechanism could have been built separately from, but *using*, simpler mechanisms. Separation would result in a system in which the simpler mechanism was available for use where it sufficed.

14.4.4 Loops in the "Uses" Relation

In many software design projects, the decisions about what other component programs to use are left to individual systems programmers. If a programmer knows of a program in another module, and feels that it would be useful in his program, he includes a call on that program in his text. Programmers are encouraged to use the work of other programmers as much as possible because, when each programmer writes his own routines to perform common functions, we end up with a system that is much larger than it need be.

Unfortunately, there are two sides to the question of program usage. Unless some restraint is exercised, one may end up with a system in which nothing works until everything works. For example, while it may seem wise to have an operating system scheduler use the file system to store its data (rather than use its own disk routines), the result will be that the file system must be present and working before any task scheduling is possible. There are users for whom an operating system subset without a file system would be useful. Even if one has no such users, the subset would be useful during development and testing.

14.5 Steps Toward a Better Structure

This section discusses four parts of a methodology that I believe will help the software engineer to build systems that do not evidence the problems discussed above.

14.5.1 Requirements Definition: Identifying
the Subsets First

One of the clearest morals in the earlier discussion about "design for change" as it is taught in other areas of engineering is that one must anticipate changes before one begins the design. At a past conference [3] many of the papers exhorted the audience to spend more time identifying the actual requirements before starting on a design. I do not want to repeat such exhortations, but I do want to point out that the identification of the possible subsets is part of identifying the requirements. Treating the easy availability of certain subsets as an operational requirement is especially important to government officials who purchase software. Many officials despair of placing strict controls on the production methods used by their contractors because they are forbidden by law to tell the contractor how to perform his job. They may tell him what they require, but not how to build it. Fortunately, the availability of subsets may be construed as an operational property of the software.

On the other hand, the identification of the required subsets is not a simple matter of asking potential users what they could do without. First, users tend to overstate their requirements. Second, the answer will not characterize the set of subsets that might be wanted in the future. In my experience, identification of the potentially desirable subsets is a demanding intellectual exercise in which one first searches for the *minimal* subset that might conceivably perform a useful service and then searches for a set of *minimal* increments to the system. Each increment is small—sometimes so small that it seems trivial. The emphasis on minimality stems from our desire to avoid components that perform more than one function (as discussed in Section 14.4.3). Identifying the minimal subset is difficult because the minimal system is not usually a program that anyone would ask for. If we are going to build the software family, the minimal subset is useful; it is not usually worth building by itself. Similarly, the maximum flexibility is obtained by looking for the smallest possible increments in capability: often these are smaller increments than a user would think of. Whether or not he would think of them before system development, he is likely to want that flexibility later.

The search for a minimal subset and minimal extensions can best be shown by an example. One example of a minimal subset is given in [4]. Another example will be given later in this paper.

14.5.2 Information Hiding: Interface and Module Definition

In an earlier section we touched upon the difference between the mathematician's concept of generality and an engineer's approach to design flexibility. Where the mathematician wants his product, a theorem or method of proof, to be as general as possible, i.e., applicable, without change, in as many situations as possible, an engineer often must tailor his product to the situation actually at hand. Lack of generality is necessary to make the program as efficient or inexpensive as possible. If he must develop a family of products, he tries to isolate the changeable parts in modules and to develop an interface between the module and the rest of the product that remains valid for all versions. The crucial steps are as follows.

1. Identification of the items that are likely to change. These items are termed "secrets."

2. Location of the specialized components in separate modules.

3. Designing intermodule interfaces that are insensitive to the anticipated changes. The changeable aspects or "secrets" of the modules are not revealed by the interface.

It is exactly this that the concept of information hiding [5], encapsulation, or abstraction [6] is intended to do for software. Because software is an abstract or mathematical product, the modules may not have any easily recognized physical identity. They are not necessarily separately compilable or coincident with memory overlay units. The interface must be general but the contents should not be. Specialization is necessary for economy and efficiency.

The concept of information hiding is very general and is applicable in many software change situations—not just the issue of subsets and extensions that we address in this paper. The ideas have also been extensively discussed in the literature [5–9]. The special implications for our problem are simply that, as far as possible, even the presence or absence of a component should be hidden from other components. If one program uses another directly, the presence of the second program cannot be fully hidden from its user. However, there is never any reason for a component to "know" how many other programs use it. All data structures that reveal the presence or number of certain components should be included in separate information hiding modules with abstract interfaces [10]. Space and other considerations make it impossible to discuss this concept further in this paper; it will be illustrated in the example. Readers for whom this concept is new are advised to read some of the articles mentioned above.

14.5.3 The Virtual Machine (VM) Concept

To avoid the problems that we have described as "a chain of data transforming components," it is necessary to stop thinking of systems in terms of components that correspond to steps in the processing. This way of thinking dies hard. It is almost certain that your first introduction to programming was in terms of a series of statements intended to be executed in the order that they were explained to you. We are goal oriented; we know what we start with and what we want to produce. It is natural to think in terms of steps progressing toward that goal. It is the fact that we are designing a family of systems that makes this "natural" approach the wrong one.

The viewpoint that seems most appropriate to designing software families is often termed the virtual machine approach. Rather than write programs that perform the transformation from input data to output data, we design software machine extensions that will be useful in writing many such programs. Where our hardware machine provides us with a set of instructions that operate on a small set of data types, the extended or virtual machine will have additional data types as well as "software instructions" that operate on those data types. These added features will be tailored to the class of programs that we are building. While the VM instructions are designed to be generally useful, they can be left out of a final product if the user's programs do not use them. The programmer writing programs for the virtual machine should not need to distinguish between instructions that are implemented in software and those that are hardware implemented. To achieve a true virtual machine, the hardware resources that are used in implementing the extended instruction set must be unavailable to the user of the virtual machine. The designer has traded these resources for the new data elements and instructions. Any attempt to use those resources again will invalidate the concept of virtual machine and lead to complications. Failure to provide for isolation of resources is one of the reasons for the failure of some attempts to use macros to provide a virtual machine. The macro user must be careful not to use the resources used in the code generated by the macros.

There is no reason to accomplish the transformation from the hardware machine to a virtual machine with all of the desired features in a single leap. Instead we will use the machine at hand to implement a few new instructions. At each step we take advantage of the newly introduced features. Such a step-by-step approach turns a large problem into a set of small ones and, as we will see later, eases the problem of finding the appropriate subsets. Each element in this series of virtual machines is a useful subset of the system.

14.5.4 Designing the "Uses" Structure

The concept of an abstract machine is an intuitive way of thinking about design. A precise description of the concept comes through a discussion of the relation "uses" [11, 12].

14.5.4.1 The Relation "Uses"

We consider a system to be divided into a set of programs that can be invoked either by the normal flow of control mechanisms, by an interrupt, or by an exception handling mechanism. Each of these programs is assumed to have a specification that defines exactly the effect that an invocation of the program should have.

We say of two programs A and B that A *uses* B if correct execution of B may be necessary for A to complete the task described in its specification. That is, A *uses* B if there exist situations in which the corrected functioning of A depends upon the availability of a correct implementation of B. Note that to decide whether A *uses* B or not, one must examine both the implementation *and* the specification of A.

The "uses" relation and "invokes" very often coincide, but *uses* differs from *invokes* in two ways:

- Certain invocations may not be instances of "*uses*." If A's specification requires only that A *invoke* B when certain conditions occur, then A has fulfilled its specification when it has generated a correct call to B. A is correct even if B is incorrect or absent. A proof of correctness of A need only make assumptions about the way to invoke B.

- A program A may use B even though it never invokes it. The best illustration of this is interrupt handling. Most programs in a computer system are only correct on the assumption that the interrupt handling routine will correctly handle the interrupts (leave the processor in an acceptable state). Such programs use the interrupt handling routines even though they never call them. "*Uses*" can also be formulated as "*requires the presence of a correct version of.*"

Systems that have achieved a certain "elegance" (e.g., T.H.E. [5], Venus [6]) have done so by having parts of the system "*use*" other parts in such a way that the "user" programs were simplified. For example, the transput stream mechanism in T.H.E. *uses* the segmenting mechanism to great advantage. In contrast, many large and complex operating systems achieve their size and complexity by having "independent" parts. For example, there are many systems in which "spooling," virtual memory management, and the file system all perform their own backup store operations. Code to perform these functions is present in each of the components. Whenever such components must share a single device, complex interfaces exist.

The disadvantage of unrestrained "usage" of each other's facilities is that the system parts become highly interdependent. Often there are no subsets of the system that can be used before the whole system is complete. In practice, some duplication of effort seems preferable to a system in which nothing runs unless everything runs.

14.5.4.2 The Uses Hierarchy

By restricting the relation "*uses*" so that its graph is loop free we can retain the primary advantages of having system parts "*use*" each other while eliminating the problems. In that case it is possible to assign the programs to the levels of a hierarchy by the following rules:

1. Level 0 is the set of all programs that *use* no other program.
2. Level i (i ≥ 1) is the set of all programs that *use* at least one program on level i – 1 and no program at a level higher than i – 1 .

If such a hierarchical ordering exists, then each level offers a testable and usable subset of the system. In fact, one can get additional subsets by including only parts of a level. The easy availability of these subsets is very valuable for the construction of any software systems and is vital for developing a *broad* family of systems.

The design of the "uses" hierarchy should be one of the major milestones in a design effort. The division of the system into independently callable subprograms has to go on in parallel with the decisions about *uses*, because they influence each other.

14.5.4.3 The Criteria to Be Used in Allowing One Program to Use Another

We propose to allow A "*uses*" B when all of the following conditions hold:

1. A is essentially simpler because it uses B.
2. B is not substantially more complex because it is not allowed to use A.
3. There is a useful subset containing B and not A.
4. There is no conceivably useful subset containing A but not B.

During the process of designing the "uses" relation, we often find ourselves in a situation where two programs could obviously benefit from using each other and the conditions above cannot be satisfied. In such situations, we resolve the apparent conflicts by a technique we call "sandwiching." One of the programs is "sliced" into two parts in a way that allows the programs to "use" each other and still satisfy the above conditions. If we find ourselves in a position where A would benefit from using B, but B can also benefit from using A, we may split B into two programs: B1 and B2. We then allow A to use B2 and B1 to use A. The result would appear to be a sandwich with B as the bread and A as the filling. Often, we then go to split A. We start with a few levels and end up with many.

An earlier report [11] introduced many of the ideas that are in this paper and illustrated them by proposing a "uses" relation for a family of operating systems. It contains several examples of situations where "sandwiching" led us from a "T.H.E.-like structure" [14] to a structure with more than twice as many levels. For example, the virtual memory mechanism was split into address translation and dynamic allocation of memory areas to segments.

The most frequent instances of splitting and sandwiching came because initially we were assuming that a "level" would be a "module" in the sense of Section 14.5.2. We will discuss this in the final part of this paper.

14.5.4.4 Use of the Word "Convenience"

It will trouble some readers that it is usual to use the word "convenience" to describe a reason for introducing a certain facility at a given level of the hierarchy. A more substantial basis would seem more scientific.

As discussed in [11] and [13], we must assume that the hardware itself is capable of performing all necessary functions. As one goes higher in the levels, one can lose capabilities (as resources are consumed)—not gain them. On the other hand, at the higher levels the new functions can be implemented with simpler programs because of the additional programs that can be used. We speak of "convenience" to make it clear that one could implement any functions on a lower level, but the availability of the additional programs at the higher level is useful. For each function we give the lowest level at which the features that are useful for implementing that function (with the stated restrictions) are available. In each case, we see no functions available at the next higher level that would be useful for implementing the functions as described. If we implemented the program one level lower we would have to duplicate programs that become available at that level.

14.6 Example: An Address-Processing Subsystem

As an example of designing for extensibility and subsets, we consider a set of programs to read in, store, and write out lists of addresses. This example has also been used, to illustrate a different point, in [10] and has been used in several classroom experiments to demonstrate module interchangeability. This example is intended as an integral part of this paper; several statements in the final summation are supported only in this section.

14.6.1 Our Basic Assumptions

1. The information items discussed in Figure 14.1 will be the items to be processed by all application programs.

The following items of information will be found in the addresses to be processed and constitute the only items of relevance to the application programs:

- Last name
- Given names (first name and possible middle names)
- Organization (command or activity)
- Internal identifier (branch or code)
- Street address or P.O. box
- City or mail unit identifier
- State
- Zip code
- Title
- Branch of service if military
- GS grade if civil service

Each of the above will be strings of characters in the standard ANSI alphabet, and each of the above may be empty or blank.

Figure 14.1 *Address information items.*

2. The input formats of the addresses are subject to change.

3. The output formats of the addresses are subject to change.

4. Some systems will use a single fixed format for input and output. Other systems will need the ability to choose from several input or output formats at run-time. Some systems will be required in which the user can specify the format using a format definition language.

5. The representation of addresses in main storage will vary from system to system.

6. In most systems, only a subset of the total set of addresses stored in the system need be in main storage at any one time. The number of addresses needed may vary from system to system, and in some systems the number of addresses to be kept in main memory may vary at run-time.

14.6.2 We Propose the Following Design Decisions

1. The input and output programs will be table driven: the table will specify the format to be used for input and output. The contents and organization of these format tables will be the "secrets" of the input and output modules.

2. The representation of addresses in core will be the "secret" of an address storage module (ASM). The implementation chosen for this module will be such that the operations of changing a portion of an address will be relatively inexpensive, compared to making the address table larger or smaller.

3. When the number of addresses to be stored exceeds the capacity of an ASM, programs will use an address file module (AFM). An AFM can be made upward compatible with an ASM; programs that were written to use ASMs could operate using an AFM in the same way. The AFM provides additional commands to allow more efficient usage by programs that do not assume the random access properties of an ASM. These programs are described below.

4. Our implementation of an AFM would use an ASM as a submodule as well as another submodule that we will call block file module (BFM). The BFM stores blocks of data that are sufficiently large to represent an address, but the BFM is not specialized to the handling of addresses. An ASM that is used within an AFM may be said to have two interfaces. In the "normal interface" that an ASM presents to an outside user, an address is a set of fields and the access functions hide or abstract from the representation. Table 14.1 is a list of the access programs that comprise this interface. In the second interface, the ASM deals with blocks of contiguous storage and abstracts

Table 14.1 *Access Function for "Normal Interface"*

Module: ASM				
Name of Access Program	**Input Parameters**			**Output**
ADDTIT*	asm	integer	string	asm ●
ADDGN	asm	integer	string	asm ●
ADDLN	asm	integer	string	asm ●
ADDSERV	asm	integer	string	asm ●
ADDBORC	asm	integer	string	asm ●
ADDCORA	asm	integer	string	asm ●
ADDSORP	asm	integer	string	asm ●
ADDCITY	asm	integer	string	asm ●
ADDSTATE	asm	integer	string	asm ●
ADDZIP	asm	integer	string	asm ●
ADDGSL	asm	integer	string	asm ●
SETNUM	asm	integer		asm* ●
FETTIT	asm	integer		string
FETGN	asm	integer		string
FETGN	asm	integer		string
FETLN	asm	integer		string
FETSERV	asm	integer		string
FETBORC	asm	integer		string
FETCORA	asm	integer		string
FETSORP	asm	integer		string
FETCITY	asm	integer		string
FETSTATE	asm	integer		string
FETZIP	asm	integer		string
FETGSL	asm	integer		string
FETNUM	asm			integer

* These are abbreviations: ADDTIT = ADD TITLE; ADDGN = ADD GIVEN NAME, etc.

from the contents. There are commands for the ASM to input and output "addresses" but the operands are storage blocks whose interpretation as addresses is known only within the ASM. The AFM makes assumptions about the association between blocks and addresses but not about the way that an address's components are represented as blocks. The BFM is completely independent of the fact that the blocks contain address information. The BFM might, in fact, be a manufacturer supplied access method.

14.6.3 Component Programs

Module: Address Input

INAD	Reads in an address that is assumed to be in a format specified by a format table and calls ASM or AFM functions to store it.
INFSL	Selects a format from an existing set of format tables. The selected format is the one that will be used by INAD. There is always a format selected.
INFCR	Adds a new format to the tables used by INFSL. The format is specified in a "format language." Selection is *not* changed (i.e., INAD still uses the same format table).
INTABEXT	Adds a blank table to the set of input format tables.
INTABCHG	Rewrites a table in the input format tables using a description in a format language. Selection is not changed.
INFDEL	Deletes a table from the set of format tables. The selected format cannot be deleted.
INADSEL	Reads in an address using one of a set of formats. Choice is specified by an integer parameter.
INADFO	Reads in an address in a format specified as one of its parameters (a string in the format definition language). The format is selected and added to the tables and subsequent addresses could be read in using INAD.

Module: Address Output

OUTAD	Prints an address in a format specified by a format table. The information to be printed is assumed to be in an ASM and identified by its position in an ASM.
OUTFSL	Selects a format table from an existing set of output format tables. The selected format is the one that will be used by OUTAD.
OUTTABEXT	Adds a "blank" table to the set of output format tables.
OUTTABCHG	Rewrites the contents of a format table using information in a format language.
OUTFCR	Adds a new format to the set of formats that can be selected by OUTFSL in a format description language.
OUTFDEL	Deletes a table from the set of format tables that can be selected by OUTFSL.
OUTADSEL	Prints out an address using one of a set of formats.

OUTADFO	Prints out an address in a format specified in a format definition language string, which is one of the actual parameters. The format is added to the tables and selected.

Module: Address Storage (ASM)

FET	(Component Name): This is a set of functions used to read information from an address store. Returns a string as a value. See Table 14.1.
ADD	(Component Name): This is a set of functions used to write information in an address store. Each takes a string and an integer as parameters. The integer specifies an address within the ASM. See Table 14.1.
0BLOCK	Takes an integer parameter, returns a storage block as a value.
1BLOCK	Accepts a storage block and integer as parameters. Its effect is to change the contents of an address store—which is reflected by a change in the values of the FET programs.
ASMEXT	Extends an address store by appending a new address with empty components at the end of the address store.
ASMSHR	"Shrinks" the address store.
ASMCR	Creates a new address store. The parameter specifies the number of components. All components are initially empty.
ASMDEL	Deletes an existing address store.

Module: Block File (BFM)

BLFET	Accepts an integer as a parameter and returns a "block."
BLSTO	Accepts a block and an integer and stores the block.
BFEXT	Extends BFM by adding additional blocks to its capacity.
BFSHR	Reduces the size of the BFM by removing some blocks.
BFMCR	Creates a file of blocks.
BFMDEL	Deletes an existing file of blocks.

Module: Address File (AFM)

This module includes implementations of all of the ASM functions except 0BLOCK and 1BLOCK. To avoid confusion in the diagram showing the uses hierarchy we have changed the names to:

AFMADD	(Component Name) defined as in Table 14.1
AFMFET	(Component Name) defined as in Table 14.1
AFMEXT	Defined as in BFM above
AFMSHR	Defined as in BFM above
AFMCR	Defined as in BFM above
AFMDEL	Defined as in BFM above.

14.6.4 Uses Relation

Figure 14.2 shows the *uses* relation between the component programs. It is important to note that we are now discussing the implementations of those programs, not just their specifications. The *uses* relation is characterized by the fact that there are a large number of relatively simple, *single-purpose* programs on the lowest level. The upper level programs are implemented by means of these lower level programs so that they too are quite simple. This *uses* relation diagram characterizes the set of possible subsets.

14.6.5 Discussion

To pick a subset, one identifies the set of upper level programs that the user needs and includes only those programs that those programs use (directly or indirectly). For example, a user who uses addresses in a single format does not need the component programs that interpret format description languages. Systems that work with a small set of addresses can be built without any BFM components. A program that works as a query system and never prints out a complete address would not need any Address Output components.

The system is also easily extended. For example, one could add a capability to read in addresses with self-defining files. If the first record on a file was a description of the format in something equivalent to the format description language, one could write a program that would be able to read in that record, use INTABCHG to build a new format table, and then read in the addresses. Programs that do things with addresses (such as print out "personalized" form letters) can also be added using these programs and selecting only those capabilities that they actually need.

One other observation that can be made is that the upper level programs can be used to "generate" lower level versions. For example, the format description languages can be used to generate the tables used for the fixed format versions. There is no need for a separate SYSGEN program.

We will elaborate on this observation in the summation.

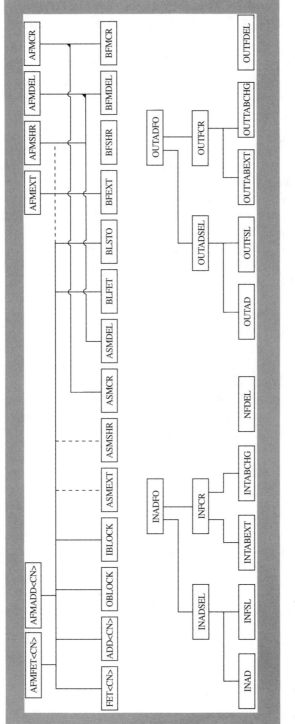

Figure 14.2 *Uses relation.*

14.7 Some Remarks on Operating Systems: Why Generals Are Superior to Colonels

An earlier report [11] discusses the design of a "uses" hierarchy for operating systems. Although there have been some refinements to the proposals of that report, its basic contents are consistent with the present proposals. This section compares the approach outlined in this paper and the "kernel" approach or "nucleus" approach to OS design [18]–[20]. It is tempting to say that the suggestions in this paper do not conflict with the "kernel" approach. These proposals can be viewed as a refinement of the nucleus approach. The first few levels of our system could be labeled "kernel," and one could conclude that we are just discussing a fine structure within the kernel.

To yield to that temptation would be to ignore an essential difference between the approaches suggested in this paper and the kernel approach. The system kernels known to me are such that some desirable subsets cannot be obtained without major surgery. It was assumed that the nucleus must be in every system family member. In the RC4000 system the inability to separate synchronization from message passing has led some users to bypass the kernel to perform teletype handling functions. In Hydra as originally proposed [19], "type-checking" was so intrinsic to the call mechanism that it appeared impossible to disable it when it was not needed or affordable.[1]

Drawing a line between "kernel" and the rest of the system, and putting "essential" services of "critical programs" in the nucleus yields a system in which kernel features cannot be removed and certain extensions are impractical. Looking for a *minimal* subset and a set of *minimal* independent incremental functions leads to a system in which one can trim away unneeded features. I know of no feature that is always needed. When we say that two functions are *almost* always used together, we should remember that "almost" is a euphemism for "not."

14.8 Summation

This chapter describes an approach to software intended to result in systems that can be tailored to fit the needs of a broad variety of users. The points most worthy of emphasis are as follows.

1. *The Requirements Include Subsets and Extensions.* It is essential to recognize the identification of usable subsets as part of the preliminaries to software design. Flexibility cannot be an afterthought. Subsetability is

---

1. Accurate reports on the current status and performance of that system are not available to me.

needed, not just to meet a variety of customers' needs, but to provide a fail-safe way of handling schedule slippage.

2. *Advantages of the Virtual Machine Approach.* Designing software as a set of virtual machines has definite advantages over the conventional (flow-chart) approach to system design. The virtual machine "instructions" provide facilities that are useful for purposes beyond those originally conceived. These instructions can easily be omitted from a system if they are not needed. Remove a major box from a flowchart and there is often a need to "fill the hole" with conversion programs.

3. *On the Difference Between Software Generality and Software Flexibility.* Software can be considered "general" if it can be used, *without change*, in a variety of situations. Software can be considered flexible, if it is *easily changed* to be used in a variety of situations. It appears unavoidable that there is a run-time cost to be paid for generality. Clever designers can achieve flexibility without significant run-time cost, but there is a design-time cost. One should incur the design-time cost only if one expects to recover it when changes are made.

Some organizations may choose to pay the run-time cost for generality. They build general software rather than flexible software because of the maintenance problems associated with maintaining several different versions. Factors influencing this decision include (a) the availability of extra computer resources, (b) the facilities for program change and maintenance available at each installation, and (c) the extent to which design techniques ease the task of applying the same change to many versions of a program.

No one can tell a designer how much flexibility and generality should be built into a product, but the decision should be a conscious one. Often, it just happens.

4. *On the Distinction Between Modules, Subprograms, and Levels.* Several systems and at least one dissertation [14–17] have, in my opinion, blurred the distinction between modules, subprograms, and levels. Conventional programming techniques consider a subroutine or other callable program to be a module. If one wants the modules to include all programs that must be designed together and changed together, then, as our example illustrates, one will usually include many small subprograms in a single module. It does not matter what word we use; the point is that the unit of change is not a single callable subprogram.

In several systems, modules and levels have coincided [14, 15]. This has led to the phrase "level of abstraction." Each of the modules in the example abstract from some detail that is assumed likely to change. In our approach there is no correspondence between modules and levels. Further, I have not found a relation, "more abstract than," that would allow me to define an abstraction hierarchy [12]. Although I am myself guilty of using it, in most cases the phrase "levels of abstraction" is an abuse of language.

Janson has suggested that a design such as this one (or the one discussed in [11]) contains "soft modules" that can represent a breach of security principles. Obviously an error in any program in one of our modules can violate the integrity of that module. All module programs that will be included in a given subset must be considered in proving the correctness of that module. However, I see no way that allowing the component programs to be on different levels of a "uses" hierarchy makes this process more difficult or makes the system less secure. The boundaries of our modules are quite firm and clearly identified.

The essential difference between this paper and other discussions of hierarchically structured designs is the emphasis on subsets and extensions. My search for a criterion to be used in designing the *uses* hierarchy has convinced me that if one does not care about the existence of subsets, it does not really matter what hierarchy one uses. Any design can be bent until it works. It is only in the ease of change that they differ.

5. *On Avoiding Duplication.* Some earlier work [21] has suggested that one needs to have duplicate or near duplicate modules in a hierarchically structured system. For example, they suggest that one needs one implementation of processes to give a fixed number of processes at a low level and another to provide for a varying number of processes at a user's level. Similar ideas have appeared elsewhere. Were such duplication to be necessary, it would be a sound argument against the use of "structured" approaches. One can avoid such duplication if one allows the programs that vary the size of a data structure to be on a higher level than the other programs that operate on that data structure. For example, in an operating system, the programs to create and delete processes need not be on the same level as the more frequently used scheduling operations. In designing software, I regard the need to code similar functions in two separate programs as an indication of a fundamental error in my thinking.

6. *Designing for Subsets and Extensions Can Reduce the Need for Support Software.* We have already mentioned that this design approach can eliminate the need for separate SYSGEN programs. We can also eliminate the need for *special*-purpose compilers. The price of the convenience features offered by such languages is often a compiler and run-time package distinctly larger than the system being built. In our approach, each level provides a "language extension" available to the programmer of the next level. We never build a compiler; we just build our system, but we get convenience features anyway.

7. *Extension at Runtime Versus Extension During SYSGEN.* At a later stage in the design we will have to choose data structures and take the differ-

ence between run-time extension and SYSGEN extension into consideration. Certain data structures are more easily accessed but harder to extend while the program is running; others are easily extended but at the expense of a higher access cost. These differences do not affect our early design decisions because they are hidden in modules.

8. *On the Value of a Model.* My work on this example and similar ones has gone much faster because I have learned to exploit a pattern that I first noticed in the design discussed in [11]. Low level operations assume the existence of a fixed data structure of some type. The operations on the next level allow the swapping of a data element with others from a fixed set of similar elements. The high level programs allow the creation and deletion of such data elements. This pattern appears several times in both designs. Although I have not designed your system for you, I believe that you can take advantage of a similar pattern. If so, this paper has served its purpose.

References

1. E.W. Dijkstra, *A Discipline of Programming.* Englewood Cliffs, NJ: Prentice-Hall, 1976.

2. D.L. Parnas, "On the design and development of program families," *IEEE Trans. Software Eng.*, vol. SE-2, pp. 1–9, Mar. 1976.

3. Second Int. Conf. Software Engineering, Oct. 13–15, 1976; also, *IEEE Trans. Software Eng.*, (Special Issue), vol. SE-2, Dec. 1976.

4. D.L. Parnas, G. Handzel, and H. Würges, "Design and specification of the minimal subset of an operating system family," presented at the 2nd Int. Conf. Software Engineering, Oct. 13–15, 1976; also, *IEEE Trans. Software Eng.*, (Special Issue), vol. SE 2, pp. 301–307, Dec. 1976.

5. D.L. Parnas, "On the criteria to be used in decomposing systems into modules," *Commun. Ass. Comput. Mach.*, Dec. 1972.

6. T.A. Linden, "The use of abstract data types to simplify program modifications," in *Proc. Conf. Data: Abstraction, Definition and Structure*, Mar. 22–24, 1976; also *ACM SIGPLAN Notices* (Special Issue), vol. II, 1976.

7. D.L. Parnas, "A technique for software module specification with examples," *Commun Ass. Comput. Mach.*, May 1972.

8. ———, "Information distribution aspects of design methodology," *in 1971 Proc. IFIP Congr.* Amsterdam, The Netherlands: North-Holland, 1971.

9. ———, "The use of precise specifications in the development of software," *in 1977 Proc. IFIP Congr.* Amsterdam, The Netherlands: North-Holland, 1977.

10. ———, "Use of abstract interfaces in the development of software for embedded computer systems," Naval Res. Lab., Washington, DC, NRL Rep. 8047, June 1977.

11. ———, "Some hypotheses about the 'uses' hierarchy for operating systems," Technische Hochschule Darmstadt, Darmstadt, West Germany, Tech. Rep., Mar. 1976.

12. ——, "On a 'buzzword': Hierarchical structure," in *1974 Proc. IFIP Congr.* Amsterdam, The Netherlands: North-Holland, 1974.

13. D.L. Parnas and D.L. Siewiorek, "Use of the concept of transparency in the design of hierarchically structured systems," *Commun. Ass. Comput. Mach.*, vol. 18, July 1975.

14. E.W. Dijkstra, "The structure of the 'T.H.E.'-multiprogramming system," *Commun. Ass. Comput. Mach.*, vol. 11, pp. 341–346, May 1968.

15. B. Liskov, "The design of the Venus operating system," *Commun. Ass. Comput. Mach.*, vol. 15, pp. 144–149, Mar. 1972.

16. P.A. Janson, "Using type extension to organize virtual memory mechanisms," Lab. for Comput. Sci., M.I.T., Cambridge, MA, MIT-LCS-TR167, Sept. 1976.

17. ——, "Using type-extension to organize virtual memory mechanisms," IBM Zurich Res. Lab., Switzerland, Res. Rep. RZ 858 (#28909), August 31, 1977.

18. P. Brinch Hansen, "The nucleus of the multiprogramming system," *Commun. Ass. Comput. Mach.*, vol. 13, pp. 238–241, 250, Apr. 1970.

19. W. Wulf, E. Cohen, A. Jones, R. Lewin, C. Pierson, and F. Pollack, "HYDRA: The kernel of a multiprocessor operating system," *Commun. Ass. Comput. Mach.*, vol. 17, pp. 337–345, June 1974.

20. G.J. Popek and C.S. Kline, "The design of a verified protection system," in *Proc. Int. Workshop Prot. In Oper. Syst.*, IRIA, pp. 183–196.

21. A.R. Saxena and T.H. Bredt, "A structured specification of a hierarchical operating system," in *Proc. 1975 Int. Conf. Reliable Software.*

Acknowledgments

The ideas presented in this paper have been developed over a lengthy period and with the cooperation and help of many collaborators. I am grateful to numerous Philips employees for thought-provoking comments and questions. Price's collaboration was invaluable at Carnegie-Mellon University. The help of W. Bartussek, G. Handzel, and H. Würges at the Technische Hochschule Darmstadt led to substantial improvements. Heninger, Weiss, and J. Shore at the Naval Research Laboratory helped me to understand the application of the concepts in areas other than operating systems. B. Trombka and J. Guttag both helped in the design of pilots of the address process system. Discussions with P.J. Courtois have helped me to better understand the relation between software structure and run-time characteristics of computer systems. Dr. E. Britton, H. Rettenmaier, L. Belady, Dr. D. Stanat, G. Fran, and Dr. W. Wright made many helpful suggestions about an earlier draft of this paper. If you find portions of this paper helpful, these people deserve your thanks.

Introduction

James Waldo

A Procedure for Designing Abstract Interfaces for Device Interface Modules

The most striking feature of this paper is how thoroughly modern (and relevant) it is. Even though it is a report of work done more than twenty years ago, the problems, approaches, and solutions described in the article are still instructive today.

The paper addresses the problem of defining an appropriate layer of abstraction between the hardware that makes up a system and the software that uses that hardware. What makes the problem more interesting is the particular kind of hardware and software that were being joined; this is a report on the embedded systems being designed for the Navy's A-7 aircraft avionics, an extremely complex embedded system meant to have a lifetime many times longer than the useful life of any of the individual components.

On the surface, the problem seems to be overconstrained. Because this was a hard real-time system where failures could endanger the pilot, it had to be possible to implement the interfaces efficiently with the minimum of software layering. But the interfaces needed to present a real level of abstraction, since upgrades would be required when newer and better components became available, even when those new components had new input requirements, new output capabilities, and perhaps even new functionality. Adding to the complexity of the definitional task was the requirement that all of the software in the layers above the interfaces could not be changed when the components were changed, since the customer (the Navy) required a single version of the system throughout the fleet.

The process that led to the solution and the solution itself are an elegant mixture of computer science theory and hard-headed engineering practice. Motivated by theory, the solution adopted was to define a set of abstract interfaces that could be implemented using the components available. These interfaces captured the functionality of the components without capturing the details of how the components offered that functionality. This enabled a level of abstraction that cut the tie between the user program and the actual devices themselves, allowing multiple devices to be (conceptually) combined or single devices to have separate representations, depending on what would be clearest to the programmer using the device. The effect is to change the collection of physical devices into a collection of abstract services, associated by their functionality rather than by the accidents of the component technology used.

The hard-headed engineering is evident in the trade-offs made between abstraction, conceptual clarity, and efficiency. A "pure" object-oriented design in which all values and parameters were abstracted into methods would have compromised the performance of the overall system or required an implementation that was too large and complex, and so a balance had to be struck between the abstractness of the design and the hard engineering needed to maintain system performance. Often this trade-off was made based on the taste and experience of the designers, in an iterative process, involving both the design team and the customers of that design.

If this paper were nothing more than a case study in such trade-offs, it would be well worth reading today. It is not often that we get explanations from master practitioners in our field on the whys of particular design decisions. But the paper is far more than that—it is an introduction to problems that used to be particular to fairly specialized areas of embedded systems, but that will soon be the province of much of distributed and networked computing.

As our systems become more and more network-centric, our reliance on the proper set of abstractions, expressed as interfaces, has increased. As our view of the computing world changes from single machines to networked entities that offer or consume services, the need for a way of expressing and accessing those services, no matter how they have been implemented, becomes more and more important. At the same time, the variety of ways of offering services is increasing to include specialized devices (both large and small) as well as software-based services running on generalized hardware. Systems like the Jini Connection Technology [1], Salutation [2], or Universal Plug and Play are all attempts at making such networked systems easier to build and more reliable.

All of these systems rely on the notion of abstracting away from a particular implementation of a service by expressing the service as a general interface. The problem is how to define that interface so that it scales over all of the various ways of providing the service, remains reasonably efficient, and yet provides an intuitive abstraction for programmers and a way of evolving the interface to allow new service providers, not yet designed, to work with the interface. These are precisely the problems discussed in this paper. This is the true indication of just how far ahead of its time this particular piece is, for it is more relevant now than it was when it was written.

In some ways, the article is still ahead of its time. While we have adopted some of the methodology outlined in the paper (most notably that having to do with defining abstract data types), we still lack a design methodology as sophisticated as the one described here. In particular, modern abstract interface design has no analog to the list of assumptions that was half of the specification used by the authors. Such a list allows checking a new implementation of a service for adherence to the requirements assumed by the interface and gives a first step toward an informal description of the semantics of the service. Such a technique is badly needed in service interface design today. Perhaps seeing this article again will spur current practitioners to continue this line of research.

References

1. K. Arnold, B. O'Sullivan, R. Scheifler, J. Waldo, and A. Wollrath, *The Jini Specification,* Addison-Wesley, 1999.
2. Salutation Home Page, *http: www.salutation.org.*

A Procedure for Designing Abstract Interfaces for Device Interface Modules

Kathryn Heninger Britton, R. Alan Parker, David L. Parnas

15.1 Abstract

This paper describes the abstract interface principle and shows how it can be applied in the design of device interface modules. The purpose of this principle is to reduce maintenance costs for embedded real-time software by facilitating the adaptation of the software to altered hardware interfaces. This principle has been applied in the Naval Research Laboratory's redesign of the flight software for the Navy's A-7 aircraft. This paper discusses a design approach based on the abstract interface principle and presents solutions to interesting problems encountered in the A-7 redesign. The specification document for the A-7 device interface modules is available on request; it provides a fully worked out example of the design approach discussed in this paper.

15.2 Introduction

15.2.1 Background

At the Naval Research Laboratory, we are redesigning the flight software for the Navy's A-7 aircraft in order to evaluate the applicability of new software engineering techniques for embedded software design. (An embedded software system is a single component of a significantly larger hardware or software system. For a more complete description, see Parnas's paper on abstract interfaces [5].) We intend to provide fully worked-out examples of both well-structured software and helpful documentation in order to help other designers apply the techniques that are found useful. For more information, see Heninger's paper about the project [1].

Much of the complexity of embedded real-time software is associated with controlling special-purpose hardware devices. Many designers seek to reduce this complexity by isolating device characteristics in software device interface modules, thereby allowing most of the software to be programmed without knowledge of device details. While these device interface modules generally do make the rest of the software simpler, their interfaces are usually the result of an ad hoc design process, and they fail to encapsulate the device details completely. As a result, device changes lead to changes throughout the software, rather than just in the device interface module. We developed a systematic procedure based on the abstract interface principle [5] to design the interfaces to A-7 device interface modules. We believe the resulting interfaces will successfully encapsulate device dependencies, so that replacing or modifying a device will require only changes in the device interface module, not in the rest of the software. This paper explains and illustrates this procedure.

15.2.2 Contents

Although the underlying principles described in this paper are not new, the design procedure is both new and a significant deviation from current practice. The procedure is a practical approach to a recurring problem. As a result, we expect the paper to be of more interest to practicing software engineers than to researchers interested in today's hot topics.

Section 15.3 discusses device interface modules and the goals designers hope to achieve by including them in a system. Although this material is not new, it is included because it motivates the rest of the paper.

Section 15.4 defines terms that are used in the rest of the paper. Although the definitions are not new [5], they are not widely known. The presentation of the procedure relies on precise use of these terms.

Section 15.5 describes and illustrates the systematic procedure. The illustration shows several stages in the development of an abstract interface for one of the A-7 device interface modules.

Even systematic procedures do not make software design easy. In the A-7 design we often had to make difficult trade-offs between flexibility and runtime efficiency. In retrospect, we identified several recurring problems. None of these problems forced us to change the basic procedure, but they did cause us to add some additional guidelines for device interface design. Section 15.6 describes some of these problems and the resulting guidelines.

15.3 Objectives

Embedded real-time software systems usually have complex and restrictive external interfaces. Since embedded software is usually a small component of a much larger system, the interfaces are seldom modified for the convenience of the software designer. The A-7 avionics software is typical: twenty-one devices are connected to the computer, including sensors, displays, and equipment controlled by the computer. Arbitrary interface characteristics, such as value encodings and timing quirks, are subject to change both during development and after initial deployment. Inadequacies may be discovered in the device specifications; a supplier may deliver a device that is judged adequate even though it does not exactly meet its specifications; a device may be replaced by an improved device; or new connections may be added between devices.

It is a common but undesirable property of embedded software that a change in a device interface requires widespread changes to the software because many programs are based on arbitrary interface details. If an interface changes, programs depending on it become invalid. Because these dependencies are seldom explicitly documented, interface changes often have surprising ramifications.

To avoid these problems it is common to divide the software into two groups of components: (1) the *device interface modules* containing the device-dependent code, and (2) the device-independent remainder of the software, including the *user programs*, so called because they use the device interface modules. Device interface modules provide *virtual devices*, that is, device-like capabilities that are partially implemented in software. For example, there is a virtual altimeter for the A-7 system. The virtual altimeter returns a value of type *range*, instead of the bitstring read in from the actual sensor. The raw data is read, scaled, corrected, and filtered within the altimeter device interface module. This software structure is illustrated in Figure 15.1.

Design of device interface modules has the following goals:

Confining changes: Designing device interface modules is a special case of the information-hiding approach [6]; hardware interface details are hidden within modules that should be the only system components requiring changes when devices are modified or replaced by others that can perform

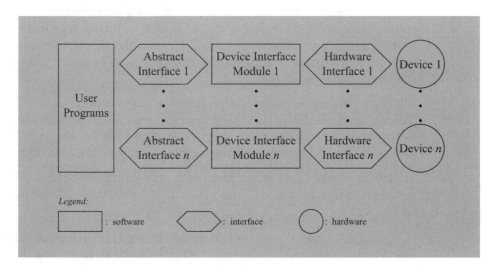

Figure 15.1 *Software designed with abstract interfaces.*

the same basic functions. Problems in confining change are caused by three types of errors:

1. The device interface module allows user programs to exploit special characteristics of a particular device so that user programs must be revised if the device is replaced.

2. The virtual device lacks essential capabilities, so that user programs must access the actual device directly; again user programs must be revised if the device is replaced.

3. Programs that are not necessarily device-dependent are included in the device interface module. As a result, the device interface module may need to be changed if the requirements change even if the device is not changed. Furthermore, the module will be harder to change when the device is changed.

In summary, a device interface module will ideally

1. be the only component that needs to change if a device is changed;

2. not need to change unless the device is changed; and

3. be relatively small and straightforward so that it is easy to change.

Simplifying the rest of the software: Embedded software is often hard to understand because its correctness depends on many arbitrary interface details. If these details are confined to device interface modules, user programs should be simpler, easier to write correctly, and easier to understand, than they would be if they used the hardware interfaces directly.

Enforcing disciplined use of resources: Software reliability is enhanced when all programs that access a device adhere to certain disciplines, such as regular checks for undesired events [7] and standard protocols for device sharing [3]. If these disciplines are built into the device interface modules, they are systematically enforced; programmers writing user programs need not be concerned with them.

Code sharing: When many programs access a device directly, they often contain similar subprograms performing the same device control functions. With device interface modules, this code need only be written once, saving programming, debugging, and testing time, and possibly computer storage.

Efficient use of devices: Independently written programs often cause devices to repeat actions unnecessarily. Centralizing device-access code should make it easier to avoid unnecessary operations.

To achieve these goals and to avoid the mistakes mentioned earlier, the interface between a device interface module and user programs should be an *abstract interface*, as defined in the next section.

15.4 Definitions

15.4.1 Interface

The interface between two programs consists of the set of assumptions that each programmer needs to make about the other program in order to demonstrate the correctness of his own program. For convenience, we use the phrase "assumptions made by program A about program B," to mean the properties of B that must be true in order for A to work properly. These assumptions are not limited to the calling sequences and parameter formats traditionally found in interface documents; they include additional information such as the meaning and limits of information exchanged, restrictions on the order of events, and expected behavior when undesired events occur. There is an analogous definition of the interface between a program and a device.

15.4.2 Abstraction

An abstraction of a set of objects is a description that applies equally well to any one of them. Each object is an instance of the abstraction. For a nontrivial abstraction, there is a one-to-many relationship between the abstraction and the objects it describes. Differential equations are an example of a mathematical abstraction representing systems as diverse as electrical circuits and collections of springs and weights.

An abstraction that is appropriate for a given purpose is easier to study than the actual system because it omits details that are not relevant for that purpose. A road map is an abstraction used to represent a road network; the graph represents the directions, relative lengths, and intersections of roads, but it does not show whether a road is made of asphalt or how it is banked. It is far easier to find a good route by studying a road map than by exploring the actual roads.

Any result obtained by studying an abstraction can be applied to any system represented by the same abstraction. Well-known graph theoretic results can be applied to a road map to determine the shortest route; the same methods have been applied to solve a wide variety of problems in other systems represented by directed graphs. Results may be misleading if they are obtained from an inappropriate abstraction, i.e., one that omits relevant details. For example, a road map is not sufficient to find the quickest route because it does not show other factors affecting driving time such as speed limits.

15.4.3 Abstract Interface

An abstract interface is an abstraction that represents more than one interface; it consists of the assumptions that are included in all of the interfaces that it represents. An abstract interface for a given type of device reveals some, but not all, properties of the actual device: it describes the common aspects of devices of that type, omitting the aspects that distinguish them from each other.

15.4.4 Device Interface Module

A device interface module is a set of programs that translate between the abstract interface and the actual hardware interface. The implementation of this module is possible only if all assumptions in the abstract interface are true of the actual device.

15.4.5 Secret

Secrets of a device interface module are assumptions about the actual device that user programs are not allowed to make. The secrets are information about the current device that need not be true of other devices with the same functions. Secrets must be taken into account somewhere in correctly working software; they are encapsulated in a device interface module.

15.4.6 Undesired Event Assumptions

The interface between programs A and B includes both the assumptions made by A about B and the assumptions made by B about A. Systems can be designed so that only one of two programs relies on the other meeting its specifications. A program can be designed so that it does not rely on user programs using it correctly; it can check for improper uses and signal undesired events when they occur. However, the error checking and reporting require extra instructions. In development versions of the A-7 software, the device interface modules will assume that undesired events *can* occur; they will contain code to check for errors made by user programs. In the production version there will not be room for that error-checking. The device interface modules will assume that improper uses will not occur; the error-checking code will be omitted to make the system smaller and faster. If a problem occurs during operation of the production system, the error-checking will be reinserted to help locate the cause. The software will be written in such a way that the error-checking code can be easily included or omitted when the program is assembled. This applies only to programming errors; error checks specified in the software requirements [2] will never be omitted.

15.4.7 Access Functions

An access function is a program that is part of one module and may be called by programs in other modules. There are different kinds of access functions: some return information to the caller; others change the state of the module to which they belong.

15.4.8 Events

Events are signals from a module to user programs indicating the occurrence of some state change within the module. They resemble hardware interrupts because they occur at unpredictable times and are not synchronized with the control flow of the user programs. In the A-7 system, modules will use a mechanism such as event counts [8] to signal the occurrence of an event to user programs that are waiting for it to occur.

15.5 Design Approach

This section describes a procedure for the design of abstract interfaces. The procedure is based on obtaining two partially redundant descriptions of the interface.

15.5.1 Description 1: Assumption List Characterizing the Virtual Device

For an application area such as avionics, many devices fall into standard types; all devices of a given type have many common characteristics. For example, as shown by advertisements in *Aviation Week* and *Space Technology*, computer panels vary little in the features seen by the pilot. For each hardware device, make a list of the characteristics that are not likely to change if the device is replaced by another device of the same type. To do so requires considerable study of devices that are available or being developed. The list of common characteristics is a description of the assumptions that user programs are allowed to make about the virtual device. The assumptions characterize device capabilities, modes, information requirements, behavior, and proper use of the device. A typical assumption might be:

"The device provides information from which barometric altitude can be determined."

We are quite certain that only devices satisfying this assumption will replace the current barometric altitude sensor. Note that this assumption does not describe the form of the information, which may vary from one device to another.

Many assumptions will appear innocuous, but they must be recorded anyway. During the A-7 design reviews, some seemingly innocuous assumptions were found to be false.

15.5.2 Description 2: Programming Constructs Embodying the Assumptions

The second description specifies the access functions and events that can be used by user programs. The access functions can be called by user programs to access the data or facility provided by the virtual device. For example, an interface might provide an access function "GET_BAROALT," which returns a barometric altitude value. For each access function, we specify the values returned, the limitations, and the effect it has on the virtual device to which it belongs. User programs can also use the events in order to be signaled when the virtual device changes state. For example, user programs may need to be signaled when a virtual sensor is no longer operational.

15.5.3 Why Two Descriptions?

These two descriptions are partially redundant, i.e., the specifications for the programming constructs imply the assumptions. For example, specifications for the access function "GET_BAROALT" imply the assumption that the device provides information from which barometric altitude can be determined. The access function specifications provide additional information, namely the form of the data exchange between the device interface module and the user programs. For example, rather than provide barometric altitude directly, the device interface module might provide two or three quantities from which it could be computed. Such a design change would require a change in the function specification but not in the assumption list.

The two versions of the interface have different purposes: (1) the assumption list *explicitly* states assumptions that are implicit in the function specifications, making invalid assumptions easier to detect, and (2) the programming constructs can be used directly in user programs. It is essential that the two descriptions be consistent. The assumptions should be embodied clearly in the programming construct specifications, and the programming construct specifications should not imply any capabilities that are not stated in the assumption list. The assumption list should be reviewed by programmers, users, and hardware engineers who have the knowledge necessary to check it for validity and generality. For example, the A-7 assumptions were reviewed by systems engineers and hardware engineers familiar with the A-7, A-6, and F-18 aircraft. Assumptions written in prose are easier for nonprogrammers to review. The specifications of the programming constructs should be reviewed by programmers who have worked with similar programs. These reviewers evaluate how well the abstract interface supports user programs and whether the device interface module can be implemented efficiently. The procedures and criteria used to review the A-7 device interface modules are described in the device interface document [4].

15.5.4 Design Procedure

Obtaining a correct and consistent dual description of an abstract interface is an iterative process. Although we attempted to list assumptions first, many of the necessary assumptions were quite subtle and only became apparent when we designed the programming constructs. Review of the assumption lists revealed errors in the programming constructs. The interfaces are the result of several cycles of review, both internally at NRL and by the A-7 maintenance team at the Naval Weapons Center (NWC). The first drafts were reviewed several times informally by the NRL A-7 team before they were submitted for an informal review at NWC. After further revisions within the NRL team, we held a formal review at NWC, resulting in the current version.

15.5.5 Illustration

As an example of this procedure, this section sketches the development of the abstract interface to the Air Data Computer (ADC). The ADC is a sensor that measures barometric altitude, true airspeed, and the mach number representation of airspeed.

Figures 15.2, 15.3 and 15.4 are excerpted from successive versions of the ADC abstract interface. Each figure includes an assumption list and tables showing the associated programming constructs. These figures are not the complete specifications; other tables define system generation parameters and specify the ranges and resolutions of values. In the access function tables, "I" indicates an input parameter whose value is supplied by user programs; "O" indicates an output parameter whose value is returned by the ADC module.

Although the early draft shown in Figure 15.2 seemed simple and reasonable to us, NRL and NWC reviewers found the following errors in it:

- The current ADC hardware and most replacement devices include a built-in test capability that cannot be accessed with the current interface.
- The description does not specify the values to be returned by the access functions while the ADC is in a failed state.
- The description does not specify the range of possible values for the measured quantities. The ranges are device-dependent, but they also affect user programs.
- The virtual ADC does not signal when it fails. User programs must poll the validity function to detect changes in reliability.

Assumption List

1. The ADC provides a measure of barometric altitude, mach number, and true airspeed.

2. The above measurements are based on a common set of sensors. Therefore an inaccuracy in one ADC sensor may affect any of these outputs.

3. The ADC provides an indication if any of its sensors are not functioning properly.

4. The measurements are made assuming a sea level pressure of 29.92 inches of mercury.

Access Function Table

Function Name	Parameter Type	Parameter Information
G_ADC_ALTITUDE	pl:distance;O	altitude assuming 29.92 inches sea level pressure
G_ADC_MACH_INDEX	pl:mach;O	mach
G_ADC_TRUE_AIRSPEED	pl:speed;O	true airspeed
G_ADC_FAIL_INDICATOR	pl:logical;O	true if ADC failed

Figure 15.2 *Excerpts from an early draft . . . of the ADC abstract interface.*

- The description does not make it clear whether the module performs device-dependent corrections to the raw sensor values.

After we corrected these errors, the interface shown in Figure 15.3 was reviewed formally at NWC. The following problems were pointed out:

- There is a device-dependent correction necessary for actual sea level pressure. The assumption of constant pressure is a poor one as it will force a device-dependent correction to be done by user programs. Future hardware may perform this correction automatically.

- Although the current hardware has one reliability indicator for all three values, replacement devices might not. In replacement devices the measurements might be made using independent sensors.

- We cannot assume that the minimum mach and true airspeed values are zero; some devices might not be capable of measuring such low values.

Figure 15.4 illustrates the product of the final revisions.

The development of the ADC abstract interface shows how the procedure supported our design efforts. Even the version in Figure 15.2 is a reasonable design; the errors it contains are typical of errors made in embedded software. As a result of our procedure, the erroneous assumptions were written explicitly in a form meant for review, rather than left implicit. Unwise assumptions, which might have escaped our notice until after the code was

Assumption List

1. The ADC provides measurements of the barometric altitude, true airspeed, and the mach number representation of the airspeed of the aircraft. Any known measurement errors are compensated for within the module. Altitude measurements are made assuming that the air pressure at sea level is 29.92 inches of mercury.

2. All of these measurements are based on a common set of sensors; therefore an inaccuracy in one ADC sensor will affect all measurements.

3. User programs are notified by means of an event when the ADC hardware fails. If the access functions for barometric altitude, true airspeed, and mach number are called during an ADC failure, the last valid measurements (stale values) are provided.

4. The ADC is capable of performing a self-test upon command from the software. The result of this test is returned to the software.

5. The minimum measurable value for mach number and true airspeed is zero. The minimum barometric altitude measurable is fixed after system generation time, as are the maximum value and resolution for all measurements.

Access Function Table

Function Name	Parameter Type	Parameter Information
G_ADC_BARO_ALTITUDE	pl:distance;O	corrected altitude assuming sea level pressure = 29.92 inches mercury
	pl:mach;O	corrected mach
G_ADC_MACH_INDEX	pl:logical;O	true if ADC reliable
G_ADC_RELIABILITY	pl:speed;O	corrected true airspeed
G_ADC_TRUE_AIRSPEED	pl:logical;O	true of ADC passed self test
TEST_ADC		

Event Table

Event	When Signaled
@T(ADC unreliable)	When "ADC reliable" changes from true to false

Figure 15.3 *Excerpts from draft of the ADC abstract interface used for formal NWC review.*

written, were caught when they could be corrected relatively easily. The current version of the ADC interface may not be perfect, but it is much better than it would have been if we had not followed the procedure. Having two partially redundant descriptions of the interface was very important. We have examined our records and found that some errors were found in the assumption lists and others in the programming construct specifications. Seldom was the same error found in both versions.

Assumption List

1. The ADC provides measurements of the barometric altitude, true airspeed, and the mach number representation of the airspeed of the aircraft (mach index). Any known measurement errors are compensated for within the module.

2. User programs are notified by means of events when one or more of the outputs are unavailable. A user program can also inquire about the reliability of individual outputs. If the access functions for barometric altitude, true airspeed, and mach number are called while the values are unreliable, the last valid measurements (stale values) are provided.

3. The ADC is capable of performing a self-test upon command from a user program. The result of this test is returned to the user program.

4. The minimum, maximum, and resolution of all ADC measurements are fixed after system generation time.

5. The ADC will compute its outputs on the basis of a value for Sea Level Pressure (SLP) supplied to it by a user program. If no value is provided, an SLP of 29.92 will be assumed.

Access Function Table

Function Name	Parameter Type	Parameter Information
G_ADC_ALTITUDE	p1:distance;O	corrected altitude assuming SLP=29.92 or user supplied SLP
	p2:logical;O	true if altitude valid
G_ADC_MACH_INDEX	p1:mach;O	corrected mach
	p2:logical;O	true if mach valid
G_ADC_TRUE_AIRSPEED	p1:speed;O	corrected true airspeed
	p2:logical;O	true if true airspeed valid
S_ADC_SLP	p1:pressure;I	sea level pressure
TEST_ADC	p1:logical;O	true if ADC passed self test

Event Table

Event	When Signaled
@T(altitude invalid)	When "altitude valid" changes from true to false
@T(airspeed invalid)	When "true airspeed valid" changes from true to false
@T(mach invalid)	When "mach valid" changes from true to false

Figure 15.4 *Excerpts from the final version of the ADC abstract interface.*

15.6 Design Problems

The design considerations mentioned earlier serve as design guidelines and as standards for judging results. Although they help considerably, it is not always easy to apply them. Conflicts arise among three design goals: small device interface modules, device-independent user programs, and efficiency. What if user programs could use a device more efficiently if they could exploit assumptions that are not valid for all possible replacement devices? What if encapsulation of assumptions that are not always valid makes a device interface module slower or bigger? Acceptable compromises must be based on estimates of the likelihood of future changes. This section shows tradeoff problems and how we resolved them, attempting to minimize the expected cost of the software over its entire period of use.

15.6.1 Problem 1: Major Variations Among Available Devices

Deciding how much capability to include in a device interface module is particularly difficult when there are major differences among replacement devices. For example, new Inertial Measurement Set (IMS) models produce present position data; other IMS devices produce velocity data; and the current A-7 IMS produces only velocity increments. In order to simulate an IMS that produces present position using the current IMS hardware, much of the navigation software would have to be inside the IMS device interface module; the result would be a very large module. One must choose between (a) confining major changes within the device interface module, and (b) keeping the device interface module small, so that minor but more likely changes are easier to make. Our compromise limits the range of devices represented by our virtual IMS, with the understanding that the remaining differences can be confined to a small set of user programs. Although our virtual IMS does not provide present position, it does provide velocities rather than velocity increments; the velocity increments are only used to compute velocities, and the velocities are widely used. The resulting virtual IMS is considerably easier to use than the hardware IMS, yet we expect the IMS module to be reasonably small.

15.6.2 Problem 2: Devices with Characteristics That Change Independently

Some devices have several sets of characteristics that can change independently. For example, the Projected Map Display Set (PMDS) consists of a set of filmstrips and a hardware drive that positions a filmstrip in a display. The same drive could be used with new filmstrips containing maps in a different format, and the same filmstrips could be used with a different drive.

According to the information-hiding principle, two independent sets of characteristics should be hidden in different modules so that they can be changed independently. However it is unnecessary for user programs to be aware of the separation. We chose to hide both sets of characteristics in one PMDS device interface module. The module will later be divided into two submodules, each insulated from changes in the other. Since the division is a secret of the PMDS device module, it is not apparent to user programs and is not presented in the interface specification.

15.6.3 Problem 3: Virtual Device Characteristics That Are Likely to Change

Some changeable device characteristics must be revealed to user programs so that they can exploit the device effectively. Examples include measurement resolutions, the number of positions on switches, and device limitations such as a maximum displayable value. Although we would like user programs to be insulated from all device changes, they *must* behave differently if such characteristics change. For example, user programs controlling the PMDS must behave differently if the virtual PMDS provides maps of three different scales instead of just two. We represent such characteristics by symbolic constants. Both user programs and device programs are written in terms of symbolic constants rather than actual values. At system generation time, code can be generated by conditional macro expansion based on the actual values of the parameters.

We defined system generation parameters for the range and resolution of input and output data because (1) range and resolution are highly likely to vary among different devices; and (2) this information is needed by user programs in order to perform arithmetic accurately and efficiently. User programs written in terms of system generation parameters do not need to be rewritten if the parameter values change.

Initially we assumed that all parameter values would be known at system generation time; i.e., we explicitly assumed that whenever a replacement device is introduced, a new version of the program will be generated and deployed with the device. This assumption was questioned at the design review. It is Navy policy not to have multiple versions of the software in the fleet, even though equipment changes cannot be made simultaneously. Furthermore, we cannot require a new system generation if a new device breaks down and is temporarily replaced by a device of the old type. As a result, some of the parameters must be changeable at run-time. In theory this is true for any of the parameters; in fact, changeover problems are more likely for some devices than others. The cost of run-time variability also differs among devices, depending on whether the parameter can be used to control code generation so that run-time tests can be avoided. If changes are unlikely, we are reluctant to give up the efficiency advantages of binding the values at system generation time; if binding the value early causes no significant savings, we are reluctant to give up flexibility. We decided each case individually, using the following guidelines:

1. Parameters with a low cost for variability are treated as run-time variables, whatever the likelihood of change. Access functions to store and retrieve values appear in the module interface. See problem 4 for an additional problem about these parameters.

2. Parameters with a low likelihood of change and a high cost for variability are bound at system generation time.

3. For parameters with both a high likelihood of change and a high cost for variability, there are two possible solutions:.

- They can be treated as run-time variables, with the option to bind them earlier by providing values at system generation time. This option allows us to delay the final choice until we have more information.

- We can find a conservative value that can be used for both devices, allowing us to bind the value at system generation time.

15.6.4 Problem 4: Device-Dependent Characteristics That Vary at Run-Time

In those circumstances, user programs must handle device-dependent data. For example, when one IMS is replaced by another of the same type, the software must be adjusted because of manufacturing variations. The IMS software is parameterized so that it can be tailored to fit a particular piece of hardware. It is a requirement that we be able to change these parameters without reassembly. The parameters are entered at run-time through the computer panel. To receive the data, the IMS module provides access functions, which are called by the user programs that read in the panel data. Unfortunately, the existence of a run-time parameter such as drift rate reveals a secret of the IMS module, i.e., that the actual device drifts out of alignment. An additional drawback is that a replacement device might require different calibration data, requiring a change in the interface. We restrict use of these access functions so that the software making use of them is limited and easily identified. The restricted assumptions and access functions are called *reconfiguration interfaces* and are appended to the normal interfaces.

15.6.5 Problem 5: Interconnections Between Virtual Devices

Ideally, virtual devices would be independent of each other, allowing the associated abstract interfaces to be designed independently of each other. However the A-7 system has device interdependencies introduced for hardware convenience. Some of these interdependencies are based on assumptions made by hardware designers about the software. For example, the Doppler and Ship Inertial Navigation Set might share a data path because someone assumed that the software will not need both devices simultaneously. We can hide the nature but not the existence of the interconnections; if we hid the interconnections, later changes in the user programs might result in attempts to access the devices incorrectly. The existence of interconnections is revealed in the assumption lists in terms of restrictions on the use of virtual devices. For example, there may be an assumption that two virtual devices cannot be used simultaneously. If the hardware interconnection is later removed, additional uses of one or both devices may become possible and desirable. Making such additions will inevitably require changes on *both* sides of the abstract interface: changes in user programs to exploit the new capabilities and changes in device interface modules to remove the restrictions. Since this cannot be avoided, there is no loss in revealing the restriction.

A similar problem can arise within a single device interface module if the present hardware does not allow two capabilities of the virtual device to be used at once. Again, we chose to reveal the restriction to user programs even though it might not be true of future devices.

Interconnection problems also arise where one device (the provider) provides information used by another (the receiver). There are two cases to consider:

1. The computer can detect the failure of the provider. If so, the virtual receiver signals a failure when the provider fails, even if the actual receiver does not detect the failure. The device interface module for the receiver can simulate detection of the failure, thereby hiding the interconnection.

2. The computer cannot detect the failure of the provider. The undetectable failure of the provider must be also considered an undetectable failure of the receiver. People writing user programs that rely on the virtual receiver must be aware that undetectable failures are possible, but they need not be aware of the interconnection.

15.6.6 Problem 6: Inconsistencies in the Hardware Interfaces

A hardware interface may provide similar functions in dissimilar ways. For example, the symbols on the head-up display (HUD) have three states: ON, OFF, and BLINKING. The HUD provides a hardware blink command for some symbols, but for others the software must simulate the BLINKING state by alternating the symbol between the ON and OFF states. Whenever the hardware interface provides some means to perform the action, we provide the feature consistently in the virtual device. The virtual HUD has commands to blink all symbols. However, when the hardware interface does not provide a way to perform an action, we were forced to reveal the inconsistency in the interface. For example, some HUD symbols have only two states: OFF and BLINKING.

Since there is no way to simulate the ON state, the virtual device cannot provide it. If the hardware limitation is removed in the future, the inconsistency can be removed from the virtual device. It is unavoidable that this change would require changes on *both* sides of the abstract interface: changes in user programs to exploit the new capability and changes in the device interface module to implement it.

15.6.7 Problem 7: Switch Nomenclatures

Many of the switches do nothing more than set a bit that the computer can read. The label on a switch is an easily changed characteristic and could be hidden. We could name the switches anonymously (e.g., with integers) and use non-mnemonic names for the settings. However, a change in switch nomenclature will most likely be accompanied by a change in the requirements. The expected cost of working with non-mnemonic names, i.e., more errors, is high. In line with our basic principle of trying to minimize the expected cost of the software over its whole period of use, we have chosen to reveal the nomenclature in switch names and mnemonic values for the switch settings. The names may suggest more than is actually stated in the assumptions; programmers are cautioned not to make assumptions about the switches beyond those that are explicitly stated in the interface documents.

15.6.8 Problem 8: Switches with Hardware Side Effects

When a switch also affects other devices, the meaning associated with it is not solely a software decision; major hardware changes would be required to use it for any other purpose. We consider such a switch part of the device that it affects, even if it is not physically located with the device. As far as user programs are concerned, the switch does not exist; the effects of the switch appear as changes in the operating mode of the virtual device. For example, the "Terrain Following" switch located on the master function panel affects the state of the Forward Looking Radar (FLR). Instead of appearing in the same interface description as the other master function switches, it is hidden within the FLR device interface module. User programs cannot read the switch, but they can call an access function that reveals the operating mode of the FLR.

15.6.9 Problem 9: Reporting Changes in Device State

User programs are often required to respond quickly to a change in device state. For example, user programs determining the current navigation mode need to know when the reliability status of the IMS sensor changes. The device interface module can either (1) provide an access function reporting the current state of the device, or (2) signal the state-change event. The choice of a mechanism depends on whether user programs base decisions on the current state or wait for the state to change. If we based the design on the requirements of user programs, changes in their requirements might result in changes in the device interface module, violating the design goal that the device module should not need to be changed unless the device is changed. We chose to specify both mechanisms in every case, but plan to implement only the ones that are actually needed. Thus requirements changes may require changes to device interface modules, but these changes will consist of implementing previously specified features. By specifying possible additions in advance, we expect to reduce the cost of later reprogramming.

15.6.10 Problem 10: Devices Requiring Information from the Software

Some hardware devices require information that is not calculated within the associated device interface module. For example, the current IMS device needs to know whether or not the aircraft is above 70° latitude, even though latitude is not calculated within the IMS module. One must choose between two ways to get the information to the device: (1) the device module can provide an access function that a user program calls in order to provide the information; or (2) programs in the device module can call other programs to get the information. Our decision is based on whether or not the information requirement is common to the class of replacement devices. If it is, the device interface module provides access functions for receiving the information. This solution results in added requirements for the rest of the software, and the user programs supplying the information must change if the information need changes. If the information need is peculiar to a particular hardware device, device interface programs call other programs to get the data. As long as the needed information is available from the rest of the system, no program outside the device interface module needs to change if the need for information disappears. We chose the latter solution for the IMS example because not all IMS devices require a signal from the computer at 70° latitude.

15.6.11 Problem 11: Virtual Devices That Do Not Correspond to Hardware Devices

Initially, we assumed that there would be one virtual device for each hardware device. We found that modeling the virtual devices on the actual devices does not always result in clear interfaces. Some related capabilities are scattered among several hardware devices; some unrelated capabilities occur in the same device for physical convenience; other groupings can only be explained in terms of historical development. For example, weapons-related capabilities in the A-7 are scattered among several devices. Some weapons data comes from the device that controls weapon release, some is stored in tables, and some is provided by the pilot through switches. Additionally, the weapons release device fills two distinct roles: it is both a source of input data and the device that releases a weapon under computer control. Our final design includes one virtual device for weapons release and one for weapon data. The virtual devices are much simpler to understand than the actual devices. It is important not to be unduly influenced by the physical location of hardware units.

15.7 Summary

We have applied a systematic procedure based on the abstract interface principle in the design of a substantial system. We find that the abstract interfaces make the system easier to code, and we expect to find that they make it easier to change in the future. Although the success of our abstract interface design cannot be judged until the A-7 implementation is complete and undergoing maintenance, our experiences so far have given us confidence to recommend the procedure to other designers.

This paper serves as an introduction to a more complete report [4]. Along with complete specifications for all the A-7 device interface modules, the report contains a description of the documentation organization and notation, a discussion of additional design problems, a description of the procedures, and questionnaires used for the major design review. The document is available from the authors.

References

1. K.L. Heninger, "Specifying Software Requirements for Complex Systems: New Techniques and their Application," *IEEE Trans. Software Eng.*, vol. SE-6, pp. 2–13, Jan. 1980.

2. K.L. Heninger, J. Kallander, D.L. Parnas, and J.E. Shore, *Software Requirements for the A-7E Aircraft,* Naval Research Lab., Washington, D.C., Memorandum Report 3876, 27 Nov. 1978.

3. C.A.R. Hoare; "Monitors: An Operating System Structuring Concept;" *Commun. of ACM,* vol. 17, no. 10; Oct. 1974.

4. R.A. Parker, K.L. Heninger, D.L. Parnas, and J.E. Shore, *Abstract Interface Specifications for the A-7E Device Interface Modules,* Naval Research Lab., Washington, D.C., Memorandum Report 4385, 20 Nov. 1980.

5. D.L. Parnas, *Use of Abstract Interfaces in the Development of Software for Embedded Computer Systems,* Naval Research Lab., Washington, D.C., Report 8047, 1977.

6. D.L. Parnas, "On the Criteria to be Used in Decomposing Systems into Modules," *Commun. Ass. Comput. Mach.,* vol. 15, no. 12, p. 1053–1058, Dec. 1972.

7. D.L. Parnas and H. Würges, "Response to Undesired Events in Software Systems," *Proc. Second Int. Conf. Software Eng.,* pp. 437–446, 1976.

8. D. Reed and R. Kanodia, "Synchronization with Eventcounts and Sequencers," *Commun. Ass. Comput. Mach.,* v. 22, no. 2, p. 115–123, Feb. 1979.

Acknowledgments

By reviewing interface specifications and discussing design problems, John Shore contributed greatly to the design of the A-7 abstract interfaces. Our collaborators at the Naval Weapons Center reviewed the A-7 abstract interface specifications, pointing out errors and helping us resolve the design problems. The authors also thank Edward Britton, Paul Clements, Constance Heitmeyer, and David Weiss for their careful reviews of an earlier version.

Introduction

David M. Weiss

Dave's foundational paper on information hiding (Paper 7) was published in 1972 and often met with skepticism from industrial software developers who thought that the technique was inefficient and didn't scale up. Academic researchers frequently lauded the work but didn't see the need for further exploration. In response, Dave and a team[1] from the United States Naval Research Laboratory, happily including me, embarked on a project to show how to use information hiding and other ideas in the design and implementation of a hard real-time system. The goal was to redesign and reimplement the operational flight program (OFP) for the Navy's A-7E jet aircraft.[2] The new software would have to meet the requirements of the original, including efficiency, and would be compared to the original with respect to changeability. In this goal we had the unreserved cooperation of the team that maintained the original A-7E OFP at the Naval Weapons Center (NWC) in China Lake, California. We were all confident enough of our ability to apply information hiding to a hard real-time system; Dave even claimed that he would fly in the backseat of the A-7E with the new software in operation.

Attaining the goal meant that we would have to deal with all of the complexities of developing a working program, including requirements that were tightly constraining, a computer that was designed to save weight and power but had few features designed to make the programmers' jobs easier, idiosyncratic devices, and other factors that one might ignore in a research environment. Adopting such a challenge has been characteristic of Dave: His goal has been to create a software engineering discipline and the associated engineering models that make the discipline usable and teachable. Explicit in his work is the theme that those who do research in engineering methods should both demonstrate that their methods work in a real engineering environment and provide standardizable ways of applying them.

The centerpiece of the A-7E OFP redesign was a modular structure based on information hiding. That structure and the means for organizing and documenting it meaningfully and usefully are described in this paper. It is one of a set of papers derived from the A-7 experience that together form a pattern for software engineering, addressing issues such as requirements elicitation

---

1. A complete list of the people who belonged to the team at one time or another is too long to provide here.
2. At the suggestion of a Navy program manager, the project was named Software Cost Reduction.

and specification, modular decomposition, interface design, concurrency, design of program families, use of abstraction, and design review.

As the design of the A-7E OFP proceeded, it became apparent that there would be many small modules: too many, in fact, to decide easily when the set was complete or to find one that hid a particular secret. The problem was how to help current and future A-7E programmers to navigate through the collection of modules. The solution was to form a hierarchy for classifying modules organized by type of secret. At the first level were three classes of modules that together contained all modules in the A-7E OFP. These were the behavior-hiding modules, the hardware-hiding modules, and the software decision-hiding modules. Dave, not known for his prowess at games of chance, occasionally offered to bet a nickel that these three modules could be used for the top-level design of 90 percent of all software systems. In the twenty or so years since I saw the module hierarchy created, I have been unable to claim that nickel. As one descended through the hierarchy, the secrets narrowed until, at the bottom, modules of the size and complexity of those described in the 1972 paper appeared. These lowest-level modules could then be fitted with abstract interfaces and assigned to a programmer for implementation.

Mirroring the module structure, a document called the module guide was created. It formed a road map to help a developer find his or her way through the module structure to locate modules of interest. Major parts of the module guide are reproduced verbatim in the paper. The point is to provide an engineering model of documentation. I have often handed the A-7E module guide to a designer and said, "Here, produce one of these for your system," thereby transitioning years of technology development at one stroke, while perhaps also converting another developer to the information hiding philosophy. Not only does the guide contain an archetypical structure, it also describes the criteria by which the structure was created. The paper also explains the goals of the modular structure, sowing the seeds for the questions that one should ask during a review of a modular structure.

The classification scheme used in the hierarchy helped ensure completeness by allowing the design team to focus on one set of concerns at a time, for example, "Have we considered all of the devices that the OFP may have to control?" It helped project newcomers find their way through the design, and it helped in reviewing the design. Most important, a module guide helps developers assess the effects of potential changes. It is the first place to look to answer questions such as "If this change is requested by the users, what modules must be modified?"

Exemplar architecture, decomposition tutorial, document template—no wonder that this paper, which first appeared in the International Conference on Software Engineering in 1984, was selected in 1994, in a ten-year retrospective, as the best paper of that earlier conference.

The story is not complete without some discussion of the results of the A-7E project. The OFP was organized into a series of subsets, some of which were developed and underwent testing on an NWC simulator. The first subset, known as the minimal useful subset, contained code for some of each of the behavior-hiding, hardware-hiding, and software decision-hiding module classes. I attended the integration testing, which took a week and uncovered nine bugs. In each case the bug was isolated to a single module within hours and was quickly fixed. We felt that a major advantage of information hiding was confirmed: Integration testing was a breeze. Although the completely redesigned OFP never flew on an aircraft (complete flight testing would have cost approximately $300,000), the results of the simulator tests left no doubt that it would have flown successfully. Sadly, we missed the opportunity to see Dave Parnas fly in the backseat of an A-7E.

The Modular Structure of Complex Systems

D.L. Parnas, P.C. Clements, and D.M. Weiss

16.1 Abstract

This paper discusses the organization of software that is inherently complex because of very many arbitrary details that must be precisely right for the software to be correct. We show how the software design technique known as information hiding, or abstraction, can be supplemented by a hierarchically structured document, which we call a module guide. The guide is intended to allow both designers and maintainers to identify easily the parts of the software that they must understand, without reading irrelevant details about other parts of the software. The paper includes an extract from a software module guide to illustrate our proposals.

16.2 Introduction

More than five years ago, a number of people at the Naval Research Laboratory became concerned about what we perceived to be a growing gap between software engineering principles being advocated at major conferences and the practice of software engineering at many industrial and governmental laboratories. The conferences and many journals were filled with what appeared to be good ideas, illustrated using examples that were either unrealistically simple fragments or complex problems that were not worked out in much detail. When we examined actual software projects and their documentation, few showed any use of the ideas and no successful product appeared to have been designed by consistent application of the principles touted at conferences and in journals. The ideas appeared to be easier to write about than to use.

We could imagine several reasons for the gap: (1) the ideas were, as many old-style programmers claim, simply impractical for real problems; (2) responsible managers were unwilling to bet on principles that had not been proven in practice, thus creating a start-up problem; (3) the examples used in the papers were too unlike the problems of the practitioners to serve as models; (4) the ideas might need refinement or extension before they could be used as guidelines for projects with the complexity and resource constraints found in the field; and (5) the practitioners were, as some academics claim, not intellectually capable of the tasks given them. Our familiarity with both the ideas and the practitioners led us to reject (1) and (5); we decided to see what could be done about (2) through (4).

Our decision was to take an undeniably realistic problem and to apply the "academic" ideas to it, so that if we succeeded, (1) there would be evidence of the feasibility for responsible managers; (2) there would be a model for use by others with similar problems; and (3) we could refine or supplement the ideas until they would work for systems more complex than those in the literature. We chose to build an exact duplicate of an existing system so that it would be possible to compare the system built by conventional techniques to one built in accordance with the new academic principles. The project chosen was the Onboard Flight Program (OFP) for the A-7E aircraft. The current program uses many dirty tricks, barely fits in its memory, and barely meets its real-time constraints. Consequently, we felt that this program, although much smaller than many programs, was a realistic test of the ideas. Because the current OFP is considered one of the best programs of its ilk, we considered the task sufficiently challenging that skeptics would not attribute our success to the poor quality of the program that we are trying to match.

Although the project is far from complete, we have already had some limited success in all three of our goals. Our ability to write a complete and precise requirements specification for the software has encouraged managers to try the same approach, and our document [9] has served as a model for those projects. We have also found useful refinements of the principles that we advocated before starting the project. For example, the concept of abstract interfaces, which we discussed in [1], has now been refined and illustrated in [2] and [3].

This paper presents another refinement of the principles that we set out to use. One of the most basic ideas in our approach was the use of the principle of information hiding [6] to decompose a project into work assignments or modules. This idea was an excellent example of the gap between academic software engineering and practice. While it has been considered self-evident by some academics, we could find no sizable product in which the idea had been consistently used. While some authors were treating the idea as "old hat," we could not persuade those charged with building real software to do something so radically different from what they had been doing.

When we tried to use the idea we found that while it was quite applicable, some additional ideas were necessary to make it work for systems with more than a dozen or so modules. This paper discusses the problems that we encountered and the additional ideas.

16.3 Background and Guiding Principles

16.3.1 Three Important Software Structures

A structural description of a software system shows the program's decomposition into parts and the relations between those parts. A-7E programmers must be concerned with three structures: (a) the module structure, (b) the uses structure, and (c) the process structure. This section contrasts these structures.

(a) A module is a work assignment for a programmer or programmer team. Each module consists of a group of closely related programs. The module structure is the decomposition of the program into modules and the assumptions that the team responsible for each module is allowed to make about the other modules.

(b) In the uses structure the components are programs, i.e., not modules but parts of modules; the relation is "requires the presence of." The uses structure determines the executable subsets of the software [5].

(c) The process structure is a decomposition of the run-time activities of the system into units known as processes. Processes are not programs; there is no simple relation between modules and processes. The implementation of some modules may include one or more processes, and any process may invoke programs in several modules.

The rest of this paper discusses the module structure.

16.3.2 Design Principle

Our module structure is based on the decomposition criterion known as information hiding [6]. According to this principle, system details that are likely to change independently should be the secrets of separate modules; the only assumptions that should appear in the interfaces between modules are those that are considered unlikely to change. Each data structure is used in only one module; it may be directly accessed by one or more programs within the module but not by programs outside the module. Any other program that requires information stored in a module's data structures must obtain it by calling access programs belonging to that module.

Applying this principle is not always easy. It is an attempt to minimize the expected cost of software and requires that the designer estimate the likelihood of changes. Such estimates are based on past experience, and may require knowledge of the application area, as well as an understanding of hardware and software technology. Because a designer may not have all of the relevant experience, we have developed formal review procedures designed to take advantage of others that do have that experience. These procedures are described in [2].

16.3.3 Goals of Modular Structure

The primary goal of the decomposition into modules is reduction of overall software cost by allowing modules to be designed and revised independently. Specific goals of the module decomposition are as follows:

1. Each module's structure should be simple enough to be understood fully.

2. It should be possible to change the implementation of one module without knowledge of the implementation of other modules and without affecting the behavior of other modules.

3. The case of making a change in the design should bear a reasonable relationship to the likelihood of the change being needed. It should be possible to make likely changes without changing any module interfaces; less likely changes may involve interface changes, but only for modules that are small and not widely used. Only very unlikely changes should require changes in the interfaces of widely used modules.

4. It should be possible to make a major software change as a set of independent changes to individual modules, i.e., except for interface changes, programmers changing the individual modules should not need to communicate. If the interfaces of the modules are not revised, it should be possible to run and test any combination of old and new module versions.

As a consequence of the goals above, our software is composed of many small modules. In previous attempts to use information hiding, we had seen systems with 5 to 20 modules. We know now that we will have hundreds of modules. With 25 or fewer modules it would not be difficult to know which modules would be affected by a change. With hundreds of modules that is not the case. With 25 or fewer modules, careful inspection may suffice to make sure that nothing has been overlooked. With hundreds of modules we found that impossible. We realized that the use of information hiding could backfire. With most maintainers ignorant about the internal structure of most of the modules, maintainers would have to search through many module documents to find the ones they had to change. We also feared working for some time before discovering that we had left out some major modules.

We concluded that we needed some additional discipline in applying the information hiding principle, and that special documentation was needed if we were really to reduce the cost of maintaining complex software systems. We had to find a way to work with small lists of modules so that we could prepare convincing arguments that each list was complete. We needed to prepare a software module guide that would assist the maintenance programmer in finding the modules that were affected by a change or could be causing the problem.

As a result of these considerations, the modules have been organized into a tree-structured hierarchy; each nonterminal node in the tree represents a module that is composed of the modules represented by its descendents. The hierarchical structure has been documented in a module guide [7]. The hierarchy and the guide are intended to achieve the following additional goals.

5. A software engineer should be able to understand the responsibility of a module without understanding the module's internal design.

6. A reader with a well-defined concern should easily be able to identify the relevant modules without studying irrelevant modules. This implies that the reader be able to distinguish relevant modules from irrelevant modules without looking at their components.

7. The number of branches at each nonterminal module in the graph should be small enough that the designers can prepare convincing arguments that the submodules have no overlapping responsibilities, and that they cover all of the responsibilities that the module is intended to cover. This is most valuable during the initial design, but it also helps when identifying modules affected by a change.

16.3.4 Restricted and Hidden Modules

We found that it was not always possible to confine information to a single module in a real system. For example, information about hardware that could be replaced should be confined, but diagnostic information about that hardware must be communicated to modules that display information to users or hardware maintainers. Any program that uses that information is subject to change when the hardware changes. To reduce the cost of software changes, the use of modules that provide such information is restricted. Restricted interfaces are indicated by "(R)" in the Guide. Often the existence of certain smaller modules is itself a secret of a larger module. In a few cases, we have mentioned such modules in this document in order to clearly specify where certain functions are performed. Those modules are referred to as hidden modules and are indicated by "(H)" in the documentation.

16.3.5 Module Description

The Module Guide shows how responsibilities are allocated among the major modules. Such a guide is intended to lead a reader to the module that implements a particular aspect of the system. It states the criteria used to assign a particular responsibility to a module and arranges the modules in such a way that a reader can find the information relevant to his purpose without searching through unrelated documentation. The guide defines the scope and contents of the individual design documents.

Three ways to describe a module structure based on information hiding are: (1) by the roles played by the individual modules in the overall system operation; (2) by the secrets associated with each module; and (3) by the facilities provided by each module. The module guide describes the module structure by characterizing each module's secrets. Where useful, a brief description of the role of the module is included. The detailed description of facilities for modules is relegated to other documents called "module specifications", e.g., [2]. The module guide tells you which module(s) will require a change. The module specification tells you both how to use that module and what that module must do.

For some modules we find it useful to distinguish between a primary secret, which is hidden information that was specified to the software designer, and a secondary secret, which refers to implementation decisions made by the designer when implementing the module designed to hide the primary secret.

In the Module Guide we attempted to describe the decomposition rules as precisely as possible, but the possibility of future changes in technology makes some boundaries fuzzy. Where this occurs we note fuzzy areas and discuss additional information used to resolve ambiguities.

16.3.6 The Illustrative Example

To show how our techniques work, we give a fairly large extract from the Module Guide for the A-7 OFP. We discuss the way that it helps during construction and maintenance after the extract.

The design that we present is the module structure of the A-7E flight software produced by the Naval Research Laboratory. The A-7E flight software is a hard real-time program that processes flight data and controls displays for the pilot. It computes the aircraft position using an inertial navigation system, and must be highly accurate. The current operational program is best understood as one big module. It is very difficult to identify the sections of the program that must be changed when certain requirements change. Our software structure is designed to meet the goals mentioned above, but must still meet all accuracy and real-time constraints.

What follows is an extract from the Module Guide for NRL's version of the software [7]. A complete copy of the guide or any of the other NRL reports can be obtained by writing to

Code 7590
Naval Research Laboratory
Washington, DC 20375 USA

16.4 A-7E Module Structure

16.4.1 Top Level Decomposition

The software system consists of the three modules described below.

16.4.1.1 Hardware-Hiding Module

The Hardware-Hiding Module includes the programs that need to be changed if any part of the hardware is replaced by a new unit with a different hardware-software interface but with the same general capabilities. This module implements virtual hardware that is used by the rest of the software. The primary secrets of this module are the hardware-software interfaces described in Chapters 1 and 2 of the requirements document [9]. The secrets of this module are the data structures and algorithms used to implement the virtual hardware.

16.4.1.2 Behavior-Hiding Module

The Behavior-Hiding Module includes programs that need to be changed if there are changes in the sections of the requirements document that describe the required behavior [9, Chapters 3 and 4]. The content of those sections is the primary secret of this module. These programs determine the values to be sent to the virtual output devices provided by the Hardware-Hiding Module.

16.4.1.3 Software Decision Module

The Software Decision Module hides software design decisions that are based upon mathematical theorems, physical facts, and programming considerations such as algorithmic efficiency and accuracy. The secrets of this module are *not* described in the requirements document. This module differs from the other modules in that both the secrets and the interfaces are determined by software designers. Changes in these modules are more likely to be motivated by a desire to improve performance than by externally imposed changes.

16.4.1.4 Notes on the Top-Level Decomposition

Fuzziness is present in the above classifications for the following reasons:

1. The line between requirements definition and software design has been determined in part by decisions made when the requirement documents are written; for example, weapon trajectory models may be chosen by system analysts and specified in the requirements document, or they may be left to the discretion of the software designers by stating accuracy requirements but no algorithms.

2. The line between hardware characteristics and software design may vary. Hardware can be built to perform some of the services currently performed by the software; consequently, certain modules can be viewed either as modules that hide hardware characteristics or as modules that hide software design decisions.

3. Changes in the hardware or in the behavior of the system or its users may make a software design decision less appropriate.

4. All software modules include software design decisions; changes in any module may be motivated by efficiency or accuracy considerations.

Such fuzziness would be unacceptable for our purposes. We can eliminate it by referring to a precise requirements document such as [9]. That document specifies the lines between behavior, hardware, and software decisions.

1. When the requirements document specifies an algorithm, we do not consider the design of the algorithm to be a software design decision. If the requirements document only states requirements that the algorithm must meet, we consider the program that implements that algorithm to be part of a Software Decision Module.

2. The interface between the software and the hardware is specified in the software requirements document. The line between hardware characteristics and software design must be based on estimates of the likelihood of future changes. If it is reasonably likely that future hardware will implement a particular facility, the software module that implements that facility is classified as a Hardware-Hiding Module; otherwise, the module is considered a software design module. We have consistently taken a conservative stance; the design is based on the assumption that drastic changes are less likely than evolutionary changes. If there are changes to the aspects of the hardware described in the requirements document, it will affect the corresponding hardware-hiding module. If there are radical changes that provide services previously provided by software, some of the software decision modules may be eliminated or reduced in size.

3. A module is included in the Software Decision Module only if it would remain useful, although possibly less efficient, when there are changes in the requirements document.

4. A module will be included in the software decision category only if its secrets do not include information documented in the software requirements document.

16.4.2 Second-Level Decomposition

16.4.2.1 Hardware-Hiding Module Decomposition

The Hardware Hiding Module comprises two modules.

16.4.2.1.1 Extended Computer Module

The Extended Computer Module hides those characteristics of the hardware-software interface of the avionics computer that we consider likely to change if the computer is modified or replaced.

Avionics computers differ greatly in their hardware-software interfaces and in the capabilities that are implemented directly in the hardware. For example, some avionics computers include a floating-point approximation of real numbers, while others perform approximate real-number operations by a programmed sequence of fixed-point operations. Some avionics systems include a single processor; some systems provide several processors. The Extended Computer provides an instruction set that can be implemented efficiently on most avionics computers. This instruction set includes the operations on application-independent data types, sequence control operations, and general I/O operations.

The primary secrets of the Extended Computer are the number of processors, the instruction set of the computer, and the computer's capacity for performing concurrent operations.

The structure of the Extended Computer Module is given in Section 16.4.3.1.

16.4.2.1.2 Device Interface Module

The Device Interface Module hides those characteristics of the peripheral devices that are considered likely to change. Each device might be replaced by an improved device capable of accomplishing the same tasks. Replacement devices differ widely in their hardware-software interfaces. For example, all angle-of-attack sensors measure the angle between a reference line on the aircraft and the velocity of the surrounding air mass, but they differ in input format, timing, and the amount of noise in the data.

The Device Interface Module provides virtual devices to be used by the rest of the software. The virtual devices do not necessarily correspond to physical devices, because all of the hardware providing a capability is not necessarily in one physical unit. Furthermore, there are some capabilities of a physical unit that are likely to change independently of others; it is advantageous to hide characteristics that may change independently in different modules.

The primary secrets of the Device Interface Module are those characteristics of the present devices documented in the requirements document and not likely to be shared by replacement devices.

The structure of the Device Interface Module is given in Section 16.4.3.2.

16.4.2.1.3 Notes on the Hardware-Hiding Module Decomposition

Parts of the hardware were considered external devices by those who designed the CPU, but they are treated as part of the processor by other documents. Our distinction between computer and device is based on the current hardware and is described in the requirements document. Information that applies to more than one device is considered a secret of the Extended Computer; information that is only relevant to one device is a secret of a Device Interface Module. For example, there is an analog-to-digital converter that is used for communicating with several devices; it is hidden by the Extended Computer, although it could be viewed as an external device. As another example, there are special outputs for testing the I/O channels; they are not associated with a single device. These are the responsibility of the Extended Computer.

If all the hardware were replaced simultaneously, there might be a significant shift in responsibilities between computer and devices. In systems like the A-7E, such changes are unusual; the replacement of individual devices or the replacement of the computer alone is more likely. Our design is based on the expectation that this pattern of replacement will continue to hold.

16.4.2.2 Behavior-Hiding Module Decomposition

The Behavior-Hiding Module consists of two modules: a Function Driver (FD) Module supported by a Shared Services (SS) Module.

16.4.2.2.1 Function Driver Module

The Function Driver Module consists of a set of individual modules called Function Drivers; each Function Driver is the sole controller of a set of closely related outputs. Outputs are considered closely related if it is easier to describe their values together than individually. For example, if one output is the sine of an angle and the other is the cosine of the same angle, a joint description of the two will be smaller than two separate descriptions. Note that the Function Driver Modules deal with outputs to the virtual devices created by the Hardware-Hiding Modules, not the physical outputs. The primary secrets of the Function Driver Module are the rules determining the values of these outputs.

The structure of the Function Driver Module is given in Section 16.4.3.3.

16.4.2.2.2 Shared Services Module

Because all the Function Drivers control systems in the same aircraft, some aspects of the behavior are common to several Function Drivers. We expect that if there is a change in that aspect of the behavior, it will affect all of the functions that share it. Consequently, we have identified a set of modules, each of which hides an aspect of the behavior that applies to two or more of the outputs.

The structure of the Shared Services Module is found in Section 16.4.3.4.

16.4.2.3 Notes on Behavior-Hiding Module Decomposition

Because users of the documentation cannot be expected to know which aspects of a function's behavior are shared, the documentation for the Function Driver Modules will include a reference to the Shared Services Modules that it uses. A maintenance programmer should always begin his inquiry with the appropriate function driver. He will be directed to the Shared Services Modules when appropriate.

16.4.2.4 Software Decision Module Decomposition

The Software Decision Module has been divided into (1) the Application Data Type Module, which hides the implementation of certain variables, (2) the Physical Model Module, which hides algorithms that simulate physical phenomena, (3) the Data Banker Module, which hides the data-updating policies, (4) the System Generation Module, which hides decisions that are postponed until system generation time, and (5) the Software Utility Module, which hides algorithms that are used in several other modules.

16.4.2.4.1 Application Data Type Module

The Application Data Type Module supplements the data types provided by the Extended Computer Module with data types that are useful for avionics applications and do not require a computer dependent implementation. These data types are implemented using the data types provided by the Extended Computer; variables of those types are used just as if the types were built into the Extended Computer.

The secrets of the Application Data Type Module are the data representation used in the variables and the programs used to implement operations on those variables. These variables can be used without consideration of units. Where necessary, the modules provide conversion operators, which deliver or accept real values in specified units.

Run-time efficiency considerations sometimes dictate that an implementation of an Application Data Type be based on a secret of another module. In that case, the data type will be specified in the application data type module documentation, but the implementation will be described in the documentation of the other module. The Application Data Type Module documentation will contain the appropriate references in such cases.

The structure of the Application Data Type Module is given in Section 16.4.3.5.

16.4.2.4.2 Physical Model Module

The software requires estimates of quantities that cannot be measured directly but can be computed from observables using models of the physical world. The primary secrets of the Physical Model Module are the physical models; the secondary secrets are the computer implementations of those models.

The structure of the Physical Model Module is given in Section 16.4.3.6.

16.4.2.4.3 Data Banker Module

Most data are produced by one module and "consumed" by another. Usually the consumers should receive a value as up-to-date as practical. The Data Banker Module acts as a "middle-man" and determines when new values for these data are computed. The Data Banker obtains values from producers; consumer programs obtain data from Data Banker access programs. The producer and consumers of a particular datum can be written without knowing whether or not the Data Banker stores the value or when a stored value is updated. In most cases, neither the producer nor the consumer need be modified if the updating policy changes.

The Data Banker is not used if consumers require specific members of the sequence of values computed by the producer, or if they require values associated with a specific time, such as the moment when an event occurs.

Some of the updating policies that can be implemented in the Data Banker are described in the following table, which indicates whether or not the Data Banker stores a copy of the item and when a new value is computed.

Name	Storage	When New Value Is Produced
on demand:	No	Whenever a consumer requests the value.
periodic:	Yes	Periodically. Consumers get the most recently stored value.
event-driven:	Yes	Whenever the data banker is notified, by the occurrence of an event, that the value may have changed. Consumers get the most recently stored value.
conditional:	Yes	Whenever a consumer requests the value, provided certain conditions are true. Otherwise, a previously stored value is delivered.

The choice among these and other updating policies should be based on the consumer's accuracy requirements, how often consumers require the value, the maximum wait that consumers can accept, how often the value changes, and the cost of producing a new value. Since the decision is not based on coding details of either consumer or producer, it is usually not necessary to rewrite a Data Banker Module when producer or consumer change.

16.4.2.4.4 System Generation Module

The primary secrets of the System Generation Module are decisions that are postponed until system-generation time. These include the values of system generation parameters and the choice among alternative implementations of a module. The secondary secrets of the System Generation Module are the method used to generate a machine-executable form of the code and the representation of the postponed decisions. Most of the programs in this module do not run on the on-board computer; they run on a more powerful computer used to generate the code for the on-board system. Some of the programs are tools provided with our system; others have been developed specifically for this project.

16.4.2.4.5 Software Utility Module

The primary secrets of this module are the algorithms implementing common software functions such as resource monitor modules, and mathematical routines such as square-root and logarithm.

16.4.3 Third-Level Decomposition

Note: For the purposes of this paper, only third-level modules whose descriptions are particularly illustrative are included. Ellipses indicate omissions.

16.4.3.1 Extended Computer Module Decomposition

16.4.3.1.1 Data Type Module

The Data Type Module implements variables and operators for real numbers, time periods, and bitstrings. The data representations and data manipulation instructions built into the computer hardware are the primary secrets of this module—specifically, the representation of numeric objects in terms of hardware data types; the representation of bitstrings; how to access a bit within a bitstring; and how times are represented for the hardware timers. The secondary secrets of this module are how range and resolution requirements are used to determine representation; the procedures for performing numeric operations; the procedures used to perform bitstring operations; and how to compute the memory location of an array element given the array name and the element index.

16.4.3.1.2 Computer State Module

The Computer State Module keeps track of the current state of the Extended Computer, which can be either operating, off, or failed, and signals relevant state changes to user programs. The primary secret is the way that the hardware detects and causes state changes. After the EC has been initialized, this module signals the event that starts the initialization for the rest of the software.

16.4.3.1.3 Diagnostics Module (R)

The Diagnostics Module provides diagnostic programs to test the interrupt hardware, the I/O hardware, and the memory. Use of this module is restricted because the information it returns reveals secrets of the Extended Computer, i.e., programs that use it may have to be revised if the avionics computer is replaced by another computer.

16.4.3.1.4 Virtual Memory Module (H)

The Virtual Memory Module presents a uniformly addressable virtual memory for use by DATA, I/O, and SEQUENCE submodules, allowing them to use virtual addresses for both data and subprograms. The primary secrets of the Virtual Memory Module are the hardware addressing methods for data and instructions in real memory; differences in the way that different areas of memory are addressed are hidden. The secondary secrets of the module are the policy for allocating real memory to virtual addresses and the programs that translate from virtual address references to real instruction sequences.

16.4.3.2 Device Interface Module Decomposition

The following table describes the Device Interface submodules (DIMs) and their secrets. The phrase "How to read . . ." is intended to be interpreted quite liberally, e.g., it includes device-dependent corrections, filtering, and any other actions that may be necessary to determine the physical value from the device input. All of the DIMs hide the procedures for testing the device that they control.

Section	Virtual Device	Secret: How to . . .
16.4.3.2.1	Air data computer	read barometric altitude, true airspeed, and Mach number
16.4.3.2.2	Angle of attack sensor	read angle of attack
16.4.3.2.20	Weapon release system	ascertain weapon release actions the pilot has requested; cause weapons to be prepared and released

16.4.3.3 Function Driver Module Decomposition

The following table describes the Function Driver submodules and their secrets:

Section	Function Driver	Secret
16.4.3.3.7	Head-up display functions	Where the movable HUD symbols should be placed. Whether a HUD symbol should be on, off, or blinking. What information should be displayed on the fixed-position displays.
16.4.3.3.8	Inertial measurement set functions	Rules determining the scale to be used for the IMS velocity measurements. When to initialize the velocity measurements. How much to rotate the IMS for alignment.
16.4.3.3.9	Panel functions	What information should be displayed on panel windows. When the enter light should be turned on.

16.4.3.4 Shared Services Module Decomposition

The Shared Services Module comprises the following modules.

16.4.3.4.1 Mode Determination Module

The Mode Determination Module determines system modes (as defined in the requirements document). It signals the occurrence of mode transitions and makes the identity of the current modes available. The primary secrets of the Mode Determination Module are the mode transition tables in the requirements document.

16.4.3.4.2 System Value Module

A System Value submodule computes a set of values, some of which are used by more than one Function Driver. The secrets of a System Value submodule are the rules in the requirements that define the values that it computes. The shared rules in the requirements specify such things as (1) selection among several alternative sources, (2) applying filters to values produced by other modules, or (3) imposing limits on a value calculated elsewhere.

This module may include a value that is only used in one Function Driver if the rule used to calculate that value is the same as that used to calculate other shared values.

Each System Value submodule is also responsible for signaling events that are defined in terms of the values it computes.

16.4.3.5 Application Data Type Module Decomposition
The Application Data Type Module is divided into two submodules.

16.4.3.5.1 System Data Type Module
The System Data Type Module implements variables of the following widely used types: accelerations, angles, angular rates, character literals, densities, Mach values, distances, pressures, and speeds. These modules may be used to implement types with restricted ranges or special interpretations (e.g., angle is used to represent latitude).

16.4.3.5.2 State Transition Event Module
The STE Module implements variables that are instances of finite state machines. Users can await the transition of a variable to/from a particular state value, cause transitions, and compare values for equality.

16.4.3.6 Physical Model Module Decomposition
The Physical Model Module comprises the modules described below.

16.4.3.6.1 Earth Model Module
The Earth Model Module hides models of the earth and its atmosphere. This set of models includes models of local gravity, the curvature of the earth, pressure at sea level, magnetic variation, the local terrain, rotation of the earth, coriolis force, and atmospheric density.

16.4.3.6.2 Aircraft Motion Module
The Aircraft Motion Module hides models of the aircraft's motion. They are used to calculate aircraft position, velocity, and altitude from observable inputs.

16.4.3.6.3 Spatial Relations Module
The Spatial Relations Module contains models of three-dimensional space. These models are used to perform coordinate transformations as well as angle and distance calculations.

16.4.3.6.4 Human Factors Module
The Human Factors Module is based on models of pilot reaction time and perception of simulated continuous motion. The models determine the update frequency appropriate for symbols on a display.

16.4.3.6.5 Weapon Behavior Module
The Weapon Behavior Module contains models used to predict behavior after release.

16.5 Conclusions

Any conclusions that we draw at this point must be considered tentative, as they have not been confirmed by the production of a running program. Nonetheless, we have been using the module guide for several years and it has proven remarkably stable. It plays a significant role in our development process; programmers and designers turn to it when they are unsure about where a certain program should reside. Numerous discussions have been resolved by this means, and relatively few and superficial changes have resulted from the discussions.

Our experience suggests that the use of information hiding in complex systems is practical, but only if the design begins with the writing of a module guide that is used to guide the design of the individual module interfaces. When we tried to work without the guide, numerous problems slipped between the cracks and responsibilities ended up either in two modules or in none. With the module guide, further progress on the design has revealed relatively few oversights. New programmers joining the project are able to get a quick grasp of the structure of our project without using much time talking to those who have been on the project longer. We feel that this will help to ameliorate Brooks' adage, "Adding more men then lengthens, not shortens, the schedule" [8].

We realize that the module guide that we are using as an illustration stops at an arbitrary point. Most of the modules mentioned in this guide are divided into submodules that are now shown in this guide. We found it more convenient to have separate module guides for the smaller modules than to keep extending this one. This module guide is the one document that all implementors must read; the others are for specialists. This one is less than 30 pages in length and we can afford to let everyone read it.

In writing this and other module guides, we have seen how important it is to focus on describing secrets rather than interfaces or roles of the modules. Where we have forgotten that (usually when we are rushing to meet a deadline), we have ended up with modules without clear responsibilities and eventually had to revise our design.

The Module Guide, like our requirements document, provides a clear illustration of the advantages of an approach that we call "Design through Documentation" [4]. Writing the document is our way of making progress in design. The document then serves to guide us and others in future designs.

In another paper [10], we have argued that this approach increases the likelihood that the software we produce will be reusable and reused. That paper uses the same example to argue rather different points.

References

1. D. Parnas, "Use of Abstract Interfaces in the Development of Software for Embedded Computer Systems," Naval Res. Lab., Washington, DC, NRL Rep. 8047, June 1977.

2. A. Parker, K. Heninger, D. Parnas, and J. Shore, "Abstract Interface Specifications for the A-7E Device Interface Module," Naval Res. Lab., Washington, DC. NRL Memo. Re. 4385, November 20, 1980.

3. K. Britton, A. Parker, and D. Parnas, "A Procedure for Designing Abstract Interfaces for Device Interface Modules," in *Proc. 5th Int. Conf. Software Eng.*, March 1981.

4. S. Hester, D. Parnas, and D. Utter, "Using Documentation as a Software Design Medium," *Bell Syst. Tech. J.*, vol. 60, pp. 1941–1977, October 1981.

5. D. Parnas, "Designing Software for Ease of Extension and Contraction," *in Proc. 3rd Int. Conf. Software Eng.*, May 1978; see also *IEEE Trans. Software Eng.*, vol. SE-5, March 1979.

6. ———, "On the Criteria to Be Used in Decomposing Systems into Modules," *Commun. ACM*, vol. 15, pp. 1053–1058, December 1972.

7. K. Britton and D. Parnas, "A-7E Software Module Guide," Naval Res. Lab., Washington, DC, NRL Memo. Rep. 4702, December 1981.

8. F. P. Brooks, Jr., *The Mythical Man Month—Essays on Software Engineering*. Reading, MA: Addison-Wesley, 1975.

9. K. Heninger, J. Kallander, D. Parnas, and J. Shore, *Software Requirements for the A-7E Aircraft;* Naval Res. Lab., Washington, DC, NRL Memo. Rep 3876, 27 November 1978.

10. P. Clements, D. Parnas, and D. Weiss, "Enhancing Reuseability with Information Hiding" *Proceedings of the Workshop on Reuseability in Programming*, September 1983.

Acknowledgments

K. Britton, now with IBM, Research Triangle Park, NC, is a coauthor of our software module guide. Parts of that guide have been included in this paper.

Introduction

Kathryn Heninger Britton

One of the most rewarding aspects of working with Dave on the A-7E software project was the way he challenged commonly held views. Out of these challenges came changes in thinking that frequently led to interesting new approaches. This paper is a prime illustration.

When we finished writing the A-7E specifications, we took them back to the U.S. Naval Weapons Center to have the Navy's engineers review them for completeness, accuracy, and usefulness. Like most people preparing for a review, I initially felt the fewer comments, the better. After all, comments translate to errors in the document, which translate to rework. I had the same feeling toward the documents that most graduate students have toward their theses: It is time to be finished with this job and get on to the next one. Many people then and now consider the smaller the number of comments during a review, the higher the quality of the work.

Dave turned this assumption on its head. In his view, a paucity of comments indicated a superficial review that had probably not achieved its purpose of validating the correctness of the document. An effective review did not mean a set of people reading the document from end to end. After all, who reads reference books that way? An effective review meant using the document as a reference to answer real questions, simulating future uses of the document. The purpose of the review was to evaluate both the correctness of the document and its effectiveness as a reference.

Taking the A-7E documents for review, we had the problem that the documents used formats unfamiliar to the reviewers. For an effective review, the reviewers needed to take time to get oriented to the way we organized information and the notation that we used to achieve an effective separation of concerns. Since the reviewers were participating because they wanted to help us, not because they needed the documents to pursue their own work, we knew we had to help them engage with the material. We designed multiple-day review meetings, organizing the reviewers according to interests and skills, providing them with appropriate questionnaires that required them to search through the documents for answers, and interviewing them afterwards to evaluate their experiences. In terms of evaluating the correctness of the answers, we relied on their subject expertise. In many cases, they could have answered the questions from their internalized knowledge. Did the documents yield results that were consistent with their expectations? I remember that many of the reviewers found, to their surprise, that the documents were useful to them after the reviews because of the large amount of information presented in small packages. Once they learned how to use our documents, many engineers started relying on them as reference sources.

Developers like the active review process because they receive a clear assignment that they can achieve mostly at their desks. The reviews tend to generate a wealth of comments. For example, when Dave Weiss introduced active reviews to Ada programmers at the Software Productivity Consortium, he reported that the volume of significant comments that authors received was far beyond their previous experiences with reviews [1].

The active design review process could be extended to include questionnaires written by people other than the document authors. For example, in our organization, a development group writes design documents to communicate with other developers, external test organizations, performance analysts, the technical writers of manuals and product helps, the usability team, and the people who manage translation testing for internationalization. Each group asks different questions: What test cases will be needed to flush out functional errors? Where is this design likely to break down? Can the design be made easier to test? How will this design affect the response of the system to heavy loads? Are there aspects of this design that will affect its performance or ability to scale to many users? Are there ways to instrument it so that performance problems can be more easily diagnosed? What information will users or administrators need to manage this system, and can I imagine writing it from the information in this document? Does this design require users to answer configuration questions that they won't know how to answer? Does it create restrictions that users will find onerous? How much translatable text will this design require? Does the design account for double-byte character sets and bi-directional presentation? For consistency and completeness, a rigorous active design review should include questionnaires written by all the groups that need the information, not just by the authors.

As it stands, the active design review process reflects a basic method that Dave Parnas uses in analyzing, writing, and teaching: He first identifies the set of questions of interest and only then proceeds to try to answer them. This keeps him from being satisfied with the answers to the easy questions.

Reference

1. Weiss, David, Personal communication.

Active Design Reviews: Principles and Practices

David L. Parnas and David M. Weiss

17.1 Abstract

Although many new software design techniques have emerged in the past 15 years, there have been few changes to the procedures for reviewing the designs produced using these techniques. This paper describes an improved technique, based on the following ideas, for reviewing designs.

1. The efforts of each reviewer should be focused on those aspects of the design that suit his experience and expertise.
2. The characteristics of the reviewers needed should be explicitly specified before reviewers are selected.
3. Reviewers should be asked to make positive assertions about the design rather than simply be allowed to point out defects.
4. The designers pose questions to the reviewers, rather than vice versa. These questions are posed on a set of questionnaires that require careful study of some aspect of the design.
5. Interaction between designers and reviewers occurs in small meetings involving 2–4 people rather than meetings of large groups.

Illustrations of these ideas drawn from the application of active design reviews to the Naval Research Laboratory's Software Cost Reduction Project are included.

17.2 Introduction

Although many new software design techniques have emerged from research in software engineering, there have been few changes to the procedures for reviewing the design before writing the code. This paper presents a new approach to reviewing a software design. We illustrate our ideas in terms of designs based on the information hiding principle, but the ideas can be applied to other designs as well. The principal innovation of our approach is the use of questionnaires to give the reviewers better defined responsibilities and to make them play a more active role. The technique has been used in the Naval Research Laboratory's Software Cost Reduction (SCR) project for several years with good results. The SCR project involves the experimental redevelopment of the operational flight program (OFP) for the Navy's A-7E aircraft. The examples used in this paper are taken from that project.

17.3 Objectives of Design Reviews

The purpose of all design reviews is to find errors in the design and its representation. The review should be designed to make it easy for the reviewers to find errors. If errors are present but escape the reviewers' attention, the review has failed. In theory, the errors found should be errors made in producing the documents that are being reviewed. In fact, errors are often found that were made earlier and were not caught. Such errors include unstated requirements, unnecessary requirements, obsolete requirements, and design and implementation decisions stated as requirements. Reviews should be designed to find both the errors made in specifying the latest design decisions and the errors made earlier.

Getting maximum benefit from a review requires that the objectives of the review be made explicit. To achieve the objectives of the review, a systematic review method is needed. This method must ensure that the design is covered completely and in detail by the review. The method should take maximum advantage of the skills and knowledge of the available reviewers.

17.3.1 Error Classification

To focus reviewers' attention properly, and to take advantage of their different skills and knowledge, we find it useful to classify design errors as follows:

1. Inconsistencies, i.e., places where the design won't work. For example, if two design statements make different assumptions about the "sense" of an angle, the design simply will not work.

2. Inefficiencies, i.e., places where the design imposes a barrier to efficient programming or use. For example, a programmer who is only interested in obtaining the latitude of a location from another programmer's module, but whose program is only able to request both latitude and longitude at the same time, is being forced to waste both time and space.

3. Ambiguities, i.e., places where the design specification may be interpreted in several different ways, or is not clear enough.

4. Inflexibilities, i.e., places where the design does not accommodate change well. For example, if the design assumes that there are exactly two sources of altitude information, it may be difficult to deal with an additional altimeter.[1]

---

1. Note that some inflexibilities may actually be requirements misunderstandings, particularly if the requirements specify changes that are likely to occur during the lifetime of the system. (See [1] for an example of a requirements specification containing likely changes.)

The purpose of this categorization is not to ensure that each error found falls into one and only one category, but rather to guide us in designing reviews that will find as many errors as possible.

17.3.2 Obtaining Detailed Coverage of the Design

When a set of reviewers that can provide complete design coverage is assembled, it is important to ensure that each reviewer focuses on areas relevant to him and that he can identify the decisions made in arriving at the design. It is also important to make the reviewer think hard about what he is reading rather than skim it for obvious errors.

To accomplish a detailed review, we believe it is necessary to force the reviewers to take an active role whether they agree or disagree with the design decisions that have been made. The reviewers must be asked to provide justification for accepting or rejecting design decisions.

Because using a document is often the best way to find its problems, we try to make the reviewers use the document that they are reviewing. We do this by asking them to answer a set of questions about the document—questions that can only be answered by careful study of the document. Some questions may ask them to write programs that would use the programs specified by the design.

Performing a good job as a reviewer is difficult work. It is important that the review be designed to give the reviewers a sense of participation and accomplishment. Lacking such a feeling they are unlikely to participate in future reviews.

17.4 Conventional Design Reviews

Conventional design reviews usually proceed as follows:

1. A massive quantity of highly detailed design documentation is delivered to the reviewers three to four weeks before the review.
2. The designated reviewers, many of them administrators who are not trained in software development, read as much of the documentation as is possible in the time allowed. Often this is very little.
3. During the review, a tutorial presentation of the design is given by the design team; during this presentation, the reviewers ask any questions they feel may help them to understand the design better.
4. After the design tutorial, a round-table discussion of the design is held. The result is a list of suggestions for the designers.

The design documentation for such reviews is usually an English prose description of the design in a prescribed format. Pseudo-code representations of many of the algorithms to be implemented are sometimes included.

Those attending the design tutorial include managers who are paying for the development, potential users, programmers who maintain similar systems, and those who will build or maintain the system under development.

17.4.1 Problems with Conventional Reviews

Conventional design reviews tend to be incomplete and shallow. They fail to uncover many of the errors and weaknesses in the design. The following circumstances contribute substantially to this failure:

1. The reviewers are swamped with information, much of which is not necessary to understand the design. Structural decisions are hidden in a mass of implementation details. Finding the relevant information is difficult and tedious. Even given sufficient time, reviewers are unlikely to extract the information they need. They rarely have the time.

2. Most reviewers are not familiar with all of the goals of the design and the constraints placed on it.

3. Responsibility for reviewing the design may rest with the review team as a whole, without individual reviewers having clear individual responsibilities. All reviewers may try to look at all of the documentation, with no part of the design receiving a concentrated examination.

4. The design team expects the reviewers to initiate action to uncover errors and weaknesses. Reviewers who have a vague idea of their responsibilities or the design goals, or who feel intimidated by the review process, can avoid potential embarrassment by saying nothing.

5. Interaction between individual reviewers and the design team is limited because the review is conducted as a large meeting. Detailed discussions of specific design issues become hard to pursue in this situation.

6. Often the wrong people are present. People who are mainly interested in learning the status of the project, or who are interested in learning about the purpose of the system may turn the review into a tutorial.

7. Reviewers are often asked to examine issues beyond their competence. They may be specialists in one aspect of the system, but they are asked to review the entire system.

8. There is no systematic review procedure and no prepared set of questions to be asked about the design. In the rush to prepare and read the mass of documentation, little thought is given to the conduct of the review.

9. As a result of unstated assumptions, subtle design errors may be implicit in the design documentation and go unnoticed.

There are many variations on conventional reviews, each of which changes some aspect of the approach in the hope of improving the process. Some of the currently popular variations are well described in [2] and [3]. Despite the popularity of these approaches, we believe that none of them solves the major problems of conventional reviews.

17.5 A More Effective Review Process

To avoid the problems just stated and to achieve the objectives stated in Section 17.3, we redesigned the design review process. Rather than conducting one large meeting, we identify several types of reviews, each designed to find different types of design errors. Since each review requires its own expertise, we identify different types of reviewers needed to perform the reviews. Instead of conducting the reviews as discussions, we devise questionnaires for the reviewers to answer using the design documentation. Responding to the questionnaire requires the reviewer to study the documentation carefully, and to make assertions about design decisions. The issues raised by the reviewers as a result of answering the questionnaires are discussed in small meetings between designer and each reviewer. There are no protracted group discussions involving all designers and all reviewers. Because our reviews are very tightly focused, we also ask a few people for overall reviews to decrease the chance that we overlook problems because we neglected to pose a question.

The remainder of this paper contains a more detailed description of the design properties that we believe a good review should cover, the properties of a reviewable design representation, the structure needed in the design documentation to facilitate the review process, the identification of the individual review types, the classification of reviewers, the design of the questionnaires, and the conduct of the reviews.

17.5.1 Making the Design Reviewable

Producing a reviewable design requires concern with both the design and the design documentation. We start with a discussion of design properties, and then discuss documentation issues.

17.5.1.1 Design Properties

Regardless of the object being designed, it should be possible to identify the desirable properties of a design. Our list of such properties follows.

1. Well structured. The design should be consistent with chosen principles, such as the principle of information hiding.
2. Simple. To paraphrase a statement often attributed to Albert Einstein, the design should be as simple as possible, but no simpler.
3. Efficient. The functions provided by the design should be computable with the available computing resources and the design should not interfere with meeting space and time requirements.

4. Adequate. The design should satisfy present requirements.

5. Flexible. The design should make it as easy as possible to respond to requirements changes.

6. Practical. Module interfaces should be sufficient for the job, neither providing unneeded capability nor requiring the user to perform functions that properly belong to the module being used.

7. Implementable. The functions offered by the design should be theoretically computable with the information available.

8. Standardized. The design should be represented using a standard organization for design documentation.

17.5.1.2 Making the Design Representation Reviewable

The design representation should make the design assumptions as explicit as possible. Including explicitly stated assumptions is a form of redundancy that makes the design easier to review, but also means that additional consistency checks must be performed.

17.5.1.2.1 Making Assumptions Explicit

The interface between two modules is the set of assumptions that the programmers writing one module make about the behavior of the other module. Such assumptions are embodied in the description of the module's access programs. Using the terminology and notation of [4], a module that offers to its users a function that returns a device's current mode of operation embodies the assumption that the software can detect the mode of that device. This assumption is implicit in the statement that such a program is included in the interface; it may go unnoticed and unquestioned by a reviewer. To make the assumption explicit, it must be included in the design documentation; to help the reviewer, it should be included in a section devoted to basic assumptions about the module.

Other types of assumptions that may be implicit are assumptions about operations that can be performed by the programs of the module, types of data provided to and returned by those programs, the effects of the programs on each other, the time at which information is available (compile time, load time, run time, when the module is in a particular state, etc.), the variability of data, and undesired events [5].

For example, the mode determination submodule of the OFP contains an access program, named IN_MODE, that takes as input the name of a mode of the system and returns a Boolean variable whose value indicates whether or not the system is currently in that mode. (Modes are classes of system states.) Included as basic assumptions about the module are the following:

1. The system is always in at least one mode. Changes in current modes can always be signaled to user programs.

2. This module can always determine if the system is in a particular mode.

3. Mode transitions may be considered to be instantaneous.

These assumptions are implicit in the specification of IN_MODE, but are explicitly stated in the design documentation for the mode determination submodule.

We do not advocate that every assumption that users can make about the module be explicitly specified. Assumptions that apply to all designs need not be included. An example is the assumption that it is possible to pass information to other modules using parameters or the assumption that a parameter designated as "Input," will not be assigned a new value.

17.5.1.2.2 Including Redundant Information in the Design Representation

A basic principle used in engineering is that redundant information is needed to perform error checking. The lists of assumptions included with the design documentation for each module are a form of redundancy; they represent the designer's intentions. They can be used to check that the designer stayed true to his intentions, and they can be read by non-programmers to check the adequacy and validity of his intentions.

Two lists of assumptions are included for each module. One is a list of basic assumptions about the module, i.e., information that designers of the module assume will never change. The second is a list of assumptions that describe incorrect usage of the module, i.e., usage that the designers assume should not occur.

The list of basic assumptions is redundant with the description of access programs and their externally visible effects. The list of incorrect-usage assumptions is redundant with the description of undesired events. For an example of an abstract interface representation see [6].

Omitted access programs, parameters, undesired events, and program effects are examples of missing information that we can detect by including redundancies. Contradictory assumptions and descriptions of program effects are examples of inconsistencies similarly detectable. Detection is accomplished by comparing the lists of assumptions, which appear in one section of the interface document, with the rest of the document. In the previous example, a reader of the interface can compare the definition of IN_MODE and its effects with the basic assumptions about the module. Were the third assumption omitted, the reviewer should question the use and meaning of invoking IN_MODE when the system is in transition from one mode to another.

17.5.1.3 Organizing Design Documentation for Review

Most of the SCR design documentation consists of abstract interface specifications for the modules that constitute the design. Each such specification is the subject of a separate review. For example, the module hierarchy for the A-7E OFP contains a device interface module (DIM) whose secret is those characteristics of the peripheral devices connected to the computer that are likely to change. This module comprises 23 submodules, each of which was specified in one section of [6]. During the review of the DIM, each of the sub-module interfaces was reviewed separately.

Because there is often information common to all the submodules of a higher level module, the abstract interfaces for the submodules are combined in a single design document, with the common information included only once. A set of cross-references and indices are supplied with the document. These aids permit the reviewers (and users) of these documents to find quickly modules, and access programs, locally defined data types, terms, undesired events, and symbols.

We also provide a set of instructions for reviewing the document. Discussion of these instructions follows.

17.5.2 Identifying Review Types

To give individual reviewers a focus and a clear area of responsibility, a set of specialized reviews should be designed. These reviews are categorized according to the properties of the design that the reviewer should be verifying. Each review must have a specified purpose and be intended for use by a reviewer with a particular expertise. The following briefly characterizes some of the reviews used for the Device Interface Modules.

1. *Review A: Assumption Validity.* For each device, check that all assumptions made are valid for any device that can reasonably be expected to replace the current device.

2. *Review B: Assumption Sufficiency.* For each device, check that the assumption lists contain all the assumptions needed by the user programs in order to make effective and efficient use of the device.

3. *Review C: Consistency Between Assumptions and Functions.* For each module, compare the assumptions to the function and event descriptions to detect whether (a) they are consistent, and (b) the assumptions contain enough information to ensure that the functions can be implemented, the events can be detected, and the module can be used as intended.

4. *Review D: Access Function Adequacy.* For each device, check that user programs can use the device efficiently and meet all requirements using only the access functions provided in the abstract interface.

Table 17.1 shows some of the questions comprising Review C.

Table 17.1   *Part of the Reviewer Questionnaire for Review C*

Review C: Consistency Between Assumptions and Functions
The assumptions should be compared to the function and event descriptions to detect whether (a) they are consistent, and (b) the assumptions contain enough information to ensure that the functions can be implemented and the events can be detected. If an access function cannot be implemented unless the device has properties that are not in the assumption list, there is a design error, i.e., either a gap in the assumption list or a function that cannot be implemented for some replacement device. The device interface specifications should be reviewed for this criterion by AVIONICS PROGRAMMER reviewers. After studying the assumptions, the design issues, and the functions and events, they should perform the following reviews.

Review C-1	
For each of the access functions the reviewer should answer the following questions:	
C1	Which assumptions tell you that this function can be implemented as described?
C2	Under what conditions may this function be applied? Which assumptions describe those conditions?
C3	Is the behavior of this function, i.e., its effects on other functions, described in the assumptions?

17.5.3 Classifying Reviewers

Just as several reviews each with different purpose are needed, several reviewers each with different expertise and perspective are needed. Among them are the following:

1. Specialists, such as a person with detailed knowledge of a particular class of device or of a particular application, such as avionics. These specialists should be capable of assessing the performance and feasibility aspects of the design.

2. Potential users of the system.

3. Those who are familiar with the design methodology used, even if they are not familiar with the application.

4. Those who are skilled at and enjoy finding logical inconsistencies and who may be used for performing systematic consistency checks, despite not being specialists in a particular area.

The DIM reviews required four kinds of reviewers, as described in Table 17.2.

To assure complete coverage of the design document, reviewers are assigned so that each kind of review is performed for each section of the document (Table 17.3). In scheduling our reviews we try not to require any one reviewer to perform one kind of review for all sections of the document. We try to keep the time expended by an individual reviewer from being more

Table 17.2   *Characteristics of Reviewers for the DIM Abstract Interfaces*

Point of View	Expertise Required
Device Expert	Familiarity with the device used on the A-7 and with similar devices found on other aircraft. These people ought to know about several devices of this type, about the technology used to build such devices, and about past changes and future trends in these devices. They need not be programmers; people involved with the design or purchase of such devices would be fine.
Device Programmer	Experience writing or modifying programs that deal with this device or others of the same type. They should be familiar with tricks to use the device effectively with minimum consumption of computing resources. If people with experience on the A-7 cannot be found, people who have used similar devices for other aircraft are acceptable.
Avionics Programmer	Good logical minds and familiarity with avionics programming in general. These people need not have experience writing programs for these specific devices. They will be asked to perform certain checks for *internal* consistency and completeness; consequently a lack of information on the specific devices may be advantageous.
A-7 Requirements Expert	Sufficient familiarity with the A-7 software requirements document [1] to be able to read the function descriptions that refer to the devices hidden in this module. Familiarity with the A-7 application beyond this document is not essential. We value the ability to make disciplined logical completeness checks above familiarity with the A-7. However, they should have experience writing programs similar to the A-7 software.

Table 17.3   *Correspondence of Reviews and Reviewers*

Review	Reviewer
A: Assumption Validity	Device Expert
B: Assumption Sufficiency	Device Programmer
C: Consistency Between Assumptions and Functions	Avionics Programmer
D: Access Function Adequacy	Device Programmer

than what is usually available for a design review. It is rare that one reviewer is able or asked to perform more than one kind of review.

17.5.4 Designing the Questionnaires

The instructions shown in Table 17.1 describe the properties for which the reviewer should check, the sections of the abstract interface to be studied, and include a questionnaire to be completed by the reviewer.

The questionnaires are designed to make the reviewers take an active stand on issues and to use the documentation. An example is question C1, which requires the reviewer to use the document to find assumptions that justify the inclusion of each access program in the interface. The question is phrased in an active way ("Which assumptions tell you . . . ?"), rather than "Is there an assumption that justifies the implementation of this function?" The passive phrasing would give the designer little assurance that the reviewer read, understood, and thought about the document. Using the passive phrasing makes it too easy to say yes.

17.5.5 Conducting the Review

The review schedule must include time for each reviewer to complete his questionnaire(s) and must also allow a chance for discussions between each reviewer and the designers, both during the time the reviewer is completing the questionnaire(s) and after he has completed them.

The discussions are either one-on-one sessions between a reviewer and designer, or include a small group of each. We found no need for protracted group discussions involving all designers and all reviewers.

Our reviews are conducted in three stages. In the first stage, a brief overview of the module being reviewed is presented. The overview consists of explaining the modular structure, if it is unfamiliar to the reviewers, showing where in the structure the module belongs, and describing the module's secrets. If previous assignments have not been made, reviewers are assigned to reviews and sections of the document. Reviewers are also assigned times during which they may raise any questions they have, and a time to meet with designers after the designers have read the completed questionnaires.

In the second stage, reviewers perform their reviews, meeting with designers to resolve questions they have about the design or about the review questionnaires.

In the third stage the designers read the completed questionnaires and meet with the reviewers to resolve questions the designers may have about the reviewers' answers to the questionnaires. The reviewers may be asked to defend their answers. This interaction continues until both designers and reviewers understand the issues, although agreement on those issues may not be reached. After the review the designers produce a new version of the documentation. A discussion of design issues, including those raised during the review, are contained in our documents.

17.6 Conclusions

Our results with active design reviews have convinced us that the technique is an effective way of achieving our review objectives. In addition to helping us find design errors, the technique is significantly effective in assuring that we use our design methodology consistently.

We believe our success with active reviews is a result of the following factors:

1. The technique helps us to select appropriate reviewers by requiring that we write down the characteristics of the reviewers needed.

2. The technique makes good use of the reviewers' skills by focusing their energies on those aspects of the design that they are best suited to evaluate.

3. The technique makes effective use of our reviewers' time by focusing their attention on the issues that they know about. The structure of the questionnaires allows the reviewers to concentrate on one concern at a time. Since there is no large continuing group review, each reviewer concentrates on his part of the review independently and in parallel with all other reviewers.

4. Each reviewer must make a considerable commitment of effort to the review. No reviewer merely observes the process without contributing. Reviewers who might hesitate to speak up in a large discussion group will often identify problems in a one-on-one meeting. All reviewers feel that they are contributing to the review process and that they are gaining an understanding of the design.

5. The conduct of the review fosters rapid focus on specific problems. Reviewers and designers both gain understanding of problems in the design. Designers are matched with reviewers with similar interests and backgrounds and are able to interact freely without distraction.

6. The structure of our documentation permits us to design the review questionnaires to focus attention on different concerns individually, and to provide the information needed to accomplish a complete, detailed review.

By focusing our reviewers' attentions and making them take an active role, we find many more errors than we would find in a conventional review.

References

1. K. Heninger, J. Kallander, D.L. Parnas, and J. Shore, "Software Requirements for the A-7E Aircraft," Memo Report 3876, Naval Research Laboratory, November 1978.

2. D. Freedman and G. Weinberg, *Ethnotechnical Review Handbook, Second Edition*, ETHNOTECH, INC., 1979.

3. M. Fagan, "Design and Code Inspection and Process Control in the Development of Programs," TR 21.572, IBM System Development Division, December 1974.

4. P.C. Clements, R.A. Parker, D.L. Parnas, J.E. Shore, and K.H. Britton, "A Standard Organization for Specifying Abstract Interfaces," NRL Report 8815, Naval Research Laboratory, June 1984.

5. D.L. Parnas and H. Würges, "Response to Undesired Events in Software Systems." *Proc. Second International Conference on Software Engineering*, 1976.

6. R.A. Parker, K.L. Heninger, D.L. Parnas, and J.E. Shore, "Abstract Interface Specifications for the A-7E Device Interface Module," Memo Report 4385, Naval Research Laboratory, November 1980.

Acknowledgments

We thank the many people who have acted as reviewers during the development of the active design review technique, in particular those people at the Naval Weapons Center, China Lake, and at the Naval Research Laboratory. Sandra Fryer and Robert Westbrook were particularly helpful in finding people and time to support the reviews carried out at NWC.

Bruce Labaw and Paul Clements contributed many valuable suggestions for improving an earlier draft of this paper. Several improvements were also suggested by Carl Landwehr and by Ken DeJong.

Introduction

Barry Boehm

Introducing this classic paper also gives me a chance to introduce one of my favorite charts about software engineering. Figure I18.1 summarizes one of a set of empirical studies on software design done by Raymonde Guindon. It charts the level of concern (lift scenario; requirement; high-, medium-, and low-level solution) versus time of a person solving "the elevator problem." This problem involves designing the logic of an elevator (or "lift") control system to respond effectively to any sequence of button pushes by people on the elevator or on any of the floors served by the elevator.

All of the designers in Guindon's study had time sequences that looked pretty much like Figure I18.1. It shows that the "rational design process" of hierarchical top-down design described by Parnas and Clements (and indicated by the dotted path in the figure) is definitely not the way we humans design real systems. Instead, we hop around from level to level, getting good solution insights (the light bulbs in Figure 1) at seemingly random times.

Although each designer's time sequence looked similar, none was anywhere near the same. This was also true of some empirical studies we did of stakeholder win-win requirements negotiation time sequences. This lack of in-detail human-to-human repeatability puts limits on the extent to which we should aspire to have fully repeatable processes when solving software requirements and design problems.

It also motivates the point of this Parnas–Clements paper. It would not help other designers very much if the designer in Figure I18.1 documented the design process shown, because other people's design instincts would have led them to different processes. Thus it's preferable to replace one of a number of messy design processes by a rational design process that can be more easily understood.

The "rational design process" described in the paper is actually a bit misleading. It does not specify a particular series of process steps, but rather the content of a set of artifacts that may be achieved incrementally and concurrently. At first glance, it looks like a sequential "first all the requirements, then all the design, then all the code" waterfall process. This is an irrational choice for projects involving commercial-off-the-shelf (COTS) components or high-risk elements, which need concurrent determination of requirements, design, and code to achieve an appropriate balance (my paper, "Anchoring the Software Process," in *IEEE Software,* July 1996, pp. 73–82, discusses this in more detail). However, Parnas and Clements are not prescribing a waterfall or any other detailed process. They are just defining a rational set of content and relationships for the process to establish for its requirements and design specifications.

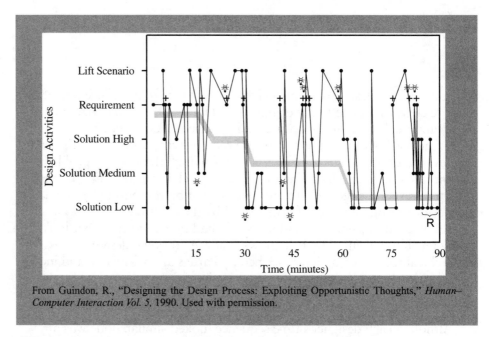

From Guindon, R., "Designing the Design Process: Exploiting Opportunistic Thoughts," *Human–Computer Interaction Vol. 5,* 1990. Used with permission.

Figure I18.1 *Example elevator (lift) control design scenario.*

With this caveat on the details of the process, I believe that the desired content of the requirements and design specifications in the Parnas and Clements paper, however arrived at, is appropriate to achieve. And I think that Parnas and Clements have done a valuable service by pointing out that faking some clean process for achieving this state is much better than documenting the actual messy process. (Here, "faking it" does not mean omitting parts or magically cheating in some way; it just means making it appear that one had followed an ideal process). Another good point made by Parnas and Clements is to document the alternatives one considered, as if one had done so in an analytic, foresightful way, instead of following a false trail for a while and then having to return to an earlier step and redo. Another is to document the likely changes in the requirements, as discussed in my introduction to Paper 14, "Designing Software for Ease of Extension and Contraction."

A Rational Design Process: How and Why to Fake It

David Lorge Parnas and Paul C. Clements

18.1 Abstract

Many have sought a software design process that allows a program to be derived systematically from a precise statement of requirements. This paper proposes that, although we will not succeed in designing a real product in that way, we can produce documentation that makes it appear that the software was designed by such a process. We first describe the ideal process, and the documentation that it requires. We then explain why one should attempt to design according to the ideal process and why one should produce the documentation that would have been produced by that process. We describe the contents of each of the required documents.

18.2 The Search for the Philosopher's Stone: Why Do We Want a Rational Design Process?

A perfectly rational person is one who always has a good reason for what he does. Each step taken can be shown to be the best way to get to a well-defined goal. Most of us like to think of ourselves as rational professionals. However, to many observers, the usual process of designing software appears quite irrational. Programmers start without a clear statement of desired behavior and implementation constraints. They make a long sequence of design decisions with no clear statement of why they do things the way they do. Their rationale is rarely explained.

Many of us are not satisfied with such a design process. That is why there is research in software design, programming methods, structured programming, and related topics. Ideally, we would like to derive our programs from a statement of requirements in the same sense that theorems are derived from axioms in a published proof. All of the methodologies that can be considered "top down" are the result of our desire to have a rational, systematic way of designing software.

This paper brings a message with both bad news and good news. The bad news is that, in our opinion, we will never find the philosopher's stone. We will never find a process that allows us to design software in a perfectly rational way. The good news is that we can fake it. We can present our system to others as if we had been rational designers and it pays to pretend to do so during development and maintenance.

355

18.3 Why Will a Software Design "Process" Always Be an Idealization?

We will never see a software project that proceeds in the "rational" way. Some of the reasons are listed below:

1. In most cases the people who commission the building of a software system do not know exactly what they want and are unable to tell us all that they know.

2. Even if we knew the requirements, there are many other facts that we need to know to design the software. Many of the details only become known to us as we progress in the implementation. Some of the things that we learn invalidate our design and we must backtrack. Because we try to minimize lost work, the resulting design may be one that would not result from a rational design process.

3. Even if we knew all of the relevant facts before we started, experience shows that human beings are unable to comprehend fully the plethora of details that must be taken into account in order to design and build a correct system. The process of designing the software is one in which we attempt to separate concerns so that we are working with a manageable amount of information. However, until we have separated the concerns, we are bound to make errors.

4. Even if we could master all of the details needed, all but the most trivial projects are subject to change for external reasons. Some of those changes may invalidate previous design decisions. The resulting design is not one that would have been produced by a rational design process.

5. Human errors can only be avoided if one can avoid the use of humans. Even after the concerns are separated, errors will be made.

6. We are often burdened by preconceived design ideas—ideas that we invented, acquired on related projects, or heard about in a class. Sometimes we undertake a project in order to try out or use a favorite idea. Such ideas may not be derived from our requirements by a rational process.

7. Often we are encouraged, for economic reasons, to use software that was developed for some other project. In other situations, we may be encouraged to share our software with another ongoing project. The resulting software may not be the ideal software for either project, i.e., not the software that we would develop based on its requirements alone, but it is good enough and will save effort.

For all of these reasons, the picture of the software designer deriving his design in a rational, error-free way from a statement of requirements is quite unrealistic. No system has ever been developed in that way, and probably none ever will. Even the small program developments shown in textbooks and papers are unreal. They have been revised and polished until the author has shown us what he wishes he had done, not what actually did happen.

18.4 Why Is a Description of a Rational Idealized Process Useful Nonetheless?

What is said above is quite obvious, known to every careful thinker, and admitted by the honest ones. In spite of that, we see conferences whose theme is the software design process, working groups on software design methods, and a lucrative market for courses purporting to describe logical ways to design software. What are these people trying to achieve?

If we have identified an ideal process, but cannot follow it completely, we can still follow it as closely as possible and we can write the documentation that we would have produced if we had followed the ideal process. This is what we mean by "faking a rational design process."

Below are some of the reasons for such a pretense:

1. Designers need guidance. When we undertake a large project we can easily be overwhelmed by the enormity of the task. We will be unsure about what to do first. A good understanding of the ideal process will help us to know how to proceed.

2. We will come closer to a rational design if we try to follow the process rather than proceed on an ad hoc basis. For example, even if we cannot know all of the facts necessary to design an ideal system, the effort to find those facts before we start to code will help us to design better and backtrack less.

3. When an organization undertakes many software projects, there are advantages to having a standard procedure. It makes it easier to have good design reviews, to transfer people, ideas, and software from one project to another. If we are going to specify a standard process, it seems reasonable that it should be a rational one.

4. If we have agreed on an ideal process, it becomes much easier to measure the progress that a project is making. We can compare the project's achievements to those that the ideal process calls for. We can identify areas on which we are behind (or ahead).

5. Regular review of the project's progress by outsiders is essential to good management. If the project is attempting to follow a standard process, it will be easier to review.

18.5 What Should the Description of the Development Process Tell Us?

The most useful form of a process description will be in terms of work products. For each stage of the process, this chapter describes

1. What product we should work on next.
2. What criteria that work product must satisfy.
3. What kind of persons should do the work.
4. What information they should use in their work.

Management of any process that is not described in terms of work products can only be done by mindreaders. Only if we know which work products are due and what criteria they must satisfy, can we review the project and measure progress.

18.6 What Is the Rational Design Process?

This section describes the rational, ideal software design process that we should try to follow. Each step is accompanied by a detailed description of the work product associated with that step.

The description of the process that follows includes neither testing nor review. This is not to suggest that one should ignore either of those. When the authors apply the process described in this paper, we include extensive and systematic reviews of each work product as well as testing of the executable code that is produced. The review process is discussed in [1] and [17].

18.6.1 Establish and Document Requirements

If we are to be rational designers, we must begin knowing what we must do to succeed. That information should be recorded in a work product known as a requirements document. Completion of this document before we start would allow us to design with all the requirements in front of us.

18.6.1.1 Why Do We Need a Requirements Document?

1. We need a place to record the desired behavior of the system as described to us by the user; we need a document that the user, or his representative, can review.
2. We want to avoid making requirements decisions accidentally while designing the program. Programmers working on a system are very often not familiar with the application. Having a complete reference on externally visible behavior relieves them of any need to decide what is best for the user.

3. We want to avoid duplication and inconsistency. Without a requirements document, many of the questions it answered would be asked repeatedly throughout the development by designers, programmers, and reviewers. This would be expensive and would often result in inconsistent answers.

4. A complete requirements document is necessary (but not sufficient) for making good estimates of the amount of work and other resources that it will take to build the system.

5. A requirements document is valuable insurance against the costs of personnel turnover. The knowledge that we gain about the requirements will not be lost when someone leaves the project.

6. A requirements document provides a good basis for test plan development. Without it, we do not know what to test for.

7. A requirements document can be used, long after the system is in use, to define the constraints for future changes.

8. A requirements document can be used to settle arguments among the programmers; once we have a complete and accurate requirements document, we no longer need to be, or to consult, requirements experts.

Determining the detailed requirements may well be the most difficult part of the software design process because there are usually no well-organized sources of information.

18.6.1.2 What Goes into the Requirements Document?

The definition of the ideal requirements document is simple: it should contain everything you need to know to write software that is acceptable to the customer, and no more. Of course, we may use references to existing information, if that information is accurate and well organized. Acceptance criteria for an ideal requirements document include the following:

1. Every statement should be valid for all acceptable products; none should depend on implementation decisions.

2. The document should be complete in the sense that if a product satisfies every statement, it should be acceptable.

3. Where information is not available before development must begin, the areas of incompleteness should be explicitly indicated.

4. The product should be organized as a reference document rather than an introductory narrative about the system. Although it takes considerable effort to produce such a document, and a reference work is more difficult to browse than an introduction, it saves labor in the long run. The information that is obtained in this stage is recorded in a form that allows easy reference throughout the project.

18.6.1.3 Who Writes the Requirements Document?

Ideally, the requirements document would be written by the users or their representatives. In fact, users are rarely equipped to write such a document. Instead, the software developers must produce a draft document and get it reviewed and, eventually, approved by the user representatives.

18.6.1.4 What Is the Mathematical Model Behind the Requirements Specification?

To assure a consistent and complete document, there must be a simple mathematical model behind the organization. The model described here is motivated by work on real-time systems but, because of that, it is completely general. All systems can be described as real-time systems—even if the real-time requirements are weak.

The model assumes that the ideal product is not a pure digital computer, but a hybrid computer consisting of a digital computer that controls an analog computer. The analog computer transforms continuous values measured by the inputs into continuous outputs. The digital computer brings about discrete changes in the function computed by the analog computer. A purely digital or purely hybrid computer is a special case of this general model. The system that will be built is a digital approximation to this hybrid system. As in other areas of engineering, we can write our specification by first describing this "ideal" system and then specifying the allowable tolerances. The requirements document treats outputs as more important than inputs. If the value of the outputs is correct, nobody will mind if the inputs are not even read. Thus, the key step is identifying all of the outputs. The heart of the requirements document is a set of mathematical functions described in tabular form. Each table specifies the value of a single output as a function of external state variables.

18.6.1.5 How Is the Requirements Document Organized?

Completeness in the requirements document is obtained by using separation of concerns to obtain the following sections:

1. *Computer Specification*: A specification of the machines on which the software must run. The machine need not be hardware—for some software this section might simply be a pointer to a language reference manual.

2. *Input/Output Interfaces*: A specification of the interfaces that the software must use in order to communicate with the outside world.

3. *Specification of Output Values*: For each output, a specification of its value in terms of the state and history of the system's environment.

4. *Timing Constraints*: For each output, how often, or how quickly, the software is required to recompute it.

5. *Accuracy Constraints*: For each output, how accurate it is required to be.

6. *Likely Changes*: If the system is required to be easy to change, the requirements should contain a definition of the areas that are considered likely to change. You cannot design a system so that everything is equally easy to change. Programmers should not have to decide which changes are most likely.

7. *Undesired Event Handling*: The requirement should also contain a discussion of what the system should do when, because of undesired events, it cannot fulfill its full requirements. Most requirements documents ignore those situations; they leave the decision about what to do in the event of partial failures to the programmer.

It is clear that good software cannot be written unless the above information is available. An example of a complete document produced in this way is given in [9] and discussed in [8].

18.6.2 Design and Document the Module Structure

Unless the product is small enough to be produced by a single programmer, one must give thought to how the work will be divided into work assignments, which we call modules. The document that should be produced at this stage is called a module guide. It defines the responsibilities of each of the modules by stating the design decisions that will be encapsulated by that module. A module may consist of submodules, or it may be considered to be a single work assignment. If a module contains submodules, a guide to its substructure is provided.

A module guide is needed to avoid duplication, to avoid gaps, to achieve separation of concerns, and most of all, to help an ignorant maintainer to find out which modules are affected by a problem report or change request. If it is kept up-to-date, this document, which records our initial design decisions, will be useful as long as the software is used.

If one diligently applies "information hiding" or "separation of concerns" to a large system, one is certain to end up with a great many modules. A guide that was simply a list of those modules, with no other structure, would help only those who are already familiar with the system. The module guide should have a tree structure, dividing the system into a small number of modules and treating each such module in the same way until all of the modules are quite small. For a complete example of such a document, see [3]. For a discussion of this approach and its benefits, see [6] and [15].

18.6.3 Design and Document the Module Interfaces

Efficient and rapid production of software requires that the programmers be able to work independently. The module guide defines responsibilities, but it does not provide enough information to permit independent implementation. A module interface specification must be written for each module. It must be formal and provide a black box picture of each module. Written by a senior designer, it is reviewed by both the future implementors and the programmers who will use the module. An interface specification for a module contains just enough information for the programmer of another module to use its facilities, and no more. The same information is needed by the implementor.

While there will be one person or small team responsible for each specification, the specifications are actually produced by a process of negotiation between implementors, those who will be required to use it, and others interested in the design, e.g., reviewers. The specifications include:

1. A list of programs to be made invokable by the programs of other modules (called "access programs");
2. The parameters for the access programs;
3. The externally visible effects of the access programs;
4. Timing constraints and accuracy constraints, where necessary; and
5. Definition of undesired events.

In many ways this module specification is analogous to the requirements document. However, the notation and organization used is more appropriate for the software-to-software interface than is the format that we use for the requirements.

Published examples and explanations include [1], [2], [5], and [11].

18.6.4 Design and Document the Uses Hierarchy

The "uses" hierarchy [13] can be designed once we know all of the modules and their access programs. It is conveniently documented as a binary matrix where the entry in position (A, B) is true if and only if the correctness of program A depends on the presence in the system of a correct program B. The "uses" hierarchy defines the set of subsets that can be obtained by deleting whole programs without rewriting any programs. It is important for staged deliveries, fail soft systems, and the development of program families [12]. The "uses" hierarchy is determined by the software designers, but must allow the subsets specified in the requirements document.

18.6.5 Design and Document the Module Internal Structures

Once a module interface has been specified, its implementation can be carried out as an independent task except for reviews. However, before coding, the major design decisions are recorded in a document called the module design document [16]. This document is designed to allow an efficient review of the design before the coding begins and to explain the intent behind the code to a future maintenance programmer.

In some cases, the module is divided into submodules and the design document is another module guide, in which case the design process for that module resumes at step 18.6.3 above. Otherwise, the internal data structures are described; in some cases, these data structures are implemented (and hidden) by submodules. For each of the access programs, a function [10] or LD-relation [14] describes its effect on the data structure. For each value returned by the module to its caller, another mathematical function, the abstraction function, is provided. This function maps the values of the data structure into the values that are returned. For each of the undesired events, we describe how we check for it. Finally, there is a "verification," an argument that programs with these properties would satisfy the module specification.

The decomposition into and design of submodules are continued until each work assignment is small enough that we could afford to discard it and begin again if the programmer assigned to do it left the project.

Each module may consist of one or more processes. The process structure of the system is distributed among the individual modules.

When one is unable to code in a readable high-level language, e.g., if no compiler is available, pseudocode must be part of the documentation. It is useful to have the pseudocode written by someone other than the final coder, and to make both programmers responsible for keeping the two versions of the program consistent [7].

18.6.6 Write Programs

After all of the design and documentation has been carried out, one is finally ready to write actual executable code. Because of the preparatory work, this goes quickly and smoothly. The code should not include comments that are redundant with the documentation that has already been written. It is unnecessary and makes maintenance of the system more expensive. Redundant comments increase the likelihood that the code will not be consistent with the documentation.

18.6.7 Maintain

Maintenance is just redesign and redevelopment. The policies recommended here for design must be continued after delivery or the "fake" rationality will disappear. If a change is made, all documentation that is invalidated must be changed. If a change invalidates a design document, it and all subsequent design documents must be faked to look as if the change had been the original design. If two or more versions are being maintained, the system should be redesigned so that the differences are confined to small modules. The short term costs of this may appear high, but the long term savings can be much higher.

18.7 What Is the Role of Documentation in This Process?

18.7.1 What Is Wrong with Most Documentation Today? Why Is It Hard to Use? Why Is It Not Read?

It should be clear that documentation plays a major role in the design process that we are describing. Most programmers regard documentation as a necessary evil, written as an afterthought only because some bureaucrat requires it. They do not expect it to be useful.

This is a self-fulfilling prophecy; documentation that has not been used before it is published, documentation that is not important to its author, will always be poor documentation.

Most of that documentation is incomplete and inaccurate, but those are not the main problems. If those were the main problems, the documents could be easily corrected by adding or correcting information. In fact, there are underlying organizational problems that lead to incompleteness and incorrectness and those problems, which are listed below, are not easily repaired.

18.7.1.1 Poor Organization

Most documentation today can be characterized as "stream of consciousness," and "stream of execution." "Stream of consciousness" writing puts information at the point in the text that the author was writing when the thought occurred to him. "Stream of execution" writing describes the system in the order that things will happen when it runs. The problem with both of these documentation styles is that subsequent readers cannot find the information that they seek. It will therefore not be easy to determine that facts are missing, or to correct them when they are wrong. It will not be easy to find all the parts of the document that should be changed when the software is changed. The documentation will be expensive to maintain and, in most cases, will not be maintained.

18.7.1.2 Boring Prose

Lots of words are used to say what could be said by a single programming language statement, a formula, or a diagram. Certain facts are repeated in many different sections. This increases the cost of the documentation and its maintenance. More important, it leads to inattentive reading and undiscovered errors.

18.7.1.3 Confusing and Inconsistent Terminology

Any complex system requires the invention and definition of new terminology. Without it the documentation would be far too long. However, the writers of software documentation often fail to provide precise definitions for the terms that they use. As a result, there are many terms used for the same concept and many similar but distinct concepts described by the same term.

18.7.1.4 Myopia

Documentation that is written when the project is nearing completion is written by people who have lived with the system for so long that they take the major decisions for granted. They document the small details that they think they will forget. Unfortunately, the result is a document useful to people who know the system well, but impenetrable for newcomers.

18.7.2 How Can One Avoid These Problems?

Documentation in the ideal design process meets the needs of the initial developers as well as the needs of the programmers who come later. Each of the documents mentioned above records requirements or design decisions and is used as a reference document for the rest of the design. However, the documents also provide the information that the maintainers will need. Because the documents are used as reference manuals throughout the building of the software, they will be mature and ready for use in the later work. The documentation in this design process is not an afterthought; it is viewed as one of the primary products of the project. Some systematic checks can be applied to increase completeness and consistency.

One of the major advantages of this approach to documentation is the amelioration of the Mythical Man Month effect [4]. When new programmers join the project they do not have to depend completely on the old staff for their information. They will have an up-do-date and rational set of documents available.

"Stream of consciousness" and "stream of execution" documentation is avoided by designing the structure of each document. Each document is designed by stating the questions that it must answer and refining the questions until each defines the content of an individual section. There must be one, and only one, place for every fact that will be in the document. The questions are answered, i.e., the document is written, only after the structure of a document has been defined. When there are several documents of a certain kind, a standard organization is written for those documents [5]. Every document is designed in accordance with the same principle that guides our software design: separation of concerns. Each aspect of the system is described in exactly one section and nothing else is described in that section. When documents are reviewed, they are reviewed for adherence to the documentation rules as well as for accuracy.

The resulting documentation is not easy or relaxing reading, but it is not boring. It makes use of tables, formulas, and other formal notation to increase the density of information. The organizational rules prevent the duplication of information. The result is documentation that must be read very attentively, but rewards its reader with detailed and precise information.

To avoid the confusing and inconsistent terminology that pervades conventional documentation, a system of special brackets and typed dictionaries is used. Each of the many terms that we must define is enclosed in a pair of bracketing symbols that reveals its type. There is a separate dictionary for each such type. Although beginning readers find the presence of !+terms+!, %terms%, #terms#, etc., disturbing, regular users of the documentation find that the type information implicit in the brackets makes the documents easier to read. The use of dictionaries that are structured by types makes it less likely that we will define two terms for the same concept or give two meanings to the same term. The special bracketing symbols make it easy to institute mechanical checks for terms that have been introduced but not defined or defined but never used.

18.8 Faking the Ideal Process

The preceding describes the ideal process that we would like to follow and the documentation that would be produced during that process. The process is "faked" by producing the documents that we would have produced if we had done things the ideal way. One attempts to produce the documents in the order that we have described. If a piece of information is unavailable, that fact is noted in the part of the document where the information should go and the design proceeds as if that information were expected to change. If errors are found, they must be corrected and the consequent changes in subsequent documents must be made. The documentation is our medium of design and no design decisions are considered to be made until their incorporation into the documents. No matter how often we stumble on our way, the final documentation will be rational and accurate.

Even mathematics, the discipline that many of us regard as the most rational of all, follows this procedure. Mathematicians diligently polish their proofs, usually presenting a proof very different from the first one that they discovered. A first proof is often the result of a tortured discovery process. As mathematicians work on proofs, understanding grows and simplifications are found. Eventually, some mathematician finds a similar proof that makes the truth of the theorem more apparent. The simpler proofs are published because the readers are interested in the truth of the theorem, not the process of discovering it.

Analogous reasoning applies to software. Those who read the software documentation want to understand the programs, not to relive their discovery. By presenting rationalized documentation we provide what they need.

Our documentation differs from the ideal documentation in one important way. We make a policy of recording all of the design alternatives that we considered and rejected. For each, we explain why it was considered and why it was finally rejected. Months, weeks, or even hours later, when we wonder why we did what we did, we can find out. Years from now, the maintainer will have many of the same questions and will find his answers in our documents.

An illustration that this process pays off is provided by a software requirements document written some years ago as part of a demonstration of the ideal process [9]. Usually, a requirements document is produced before coding starts and is never used again. However, that has not been the case for [9]. The currently operational version of the software, which satisfies the requirements document, is still undergoing revision. The organization that has to test the software uses our document extensively to choose the tests that it does. When new changes are needed, the requirements document is used in describing what must be changed and what cannot be changed. Here we see that a document produced at the start of the ideal process is still in use many years after the software went into service. The clear message is that if documentation is produced with care, it will be useful for a long time. Conversely if it is going to be extensively used, it is worth doing right.

18.9 Conclusion

It is very hard to be a rational designer; even faking that process is quite difficult. However, the result is a product that can be understood, maintained, and reused. If the project is worth doing, the methods described here are worth using.

References

1. D.L. Parnas, D.M. Weiss, P.C. Clements, and K.H. Britton, "Interface specifications for the SCR (A-7E) extended computer module," NRL Memo. Rep. 5502, December 31, 1984 (major revisions to NRL Rep. 4843).

2. K.H. Britton, R.A. Parker, and D.L. Parnas, "A procedure for designing abstract interfaces for device-interface modules," in *Proc. 5th Int. Conf. Software Eng.*, 1981.

3. K.H. Britton and D.L. Parnas, "A-7E software module guide," NRL Memo. Rep. 4702, December 1981.

4. F.P. Brooks, Jr., *The Mythical Man-Month: Essays on Software Engineering.* Reading, MA: Addison-Wesley, 1975.

5. P. Clements, A. Parker, D.L. Parnas, J. Shore, and K. Britton, "A standard organization for specifying abstract interfaces," NRL Rep. 8815, June 14, 1984.

6. P. Clements, D. Parnas, and D. Weiss, "Enhancing reusability with information hiding," in *Proc. Workshop Reusability in Program.*, September 1983, pp. 240–247.

7. H.S. Elovitz, "An experiment in software engineering: The architecture research facility as a case study," in *Proc. 4th Int. Conf. Software Eng.*, September 1979.

8. K.L. Heninger, "Specifying software requirements for complex systems: New techniques and their application," *IEEE Trans. Software Eng.*, vol. SE-6, January 1980, pp. 2–13.

9. K. Heninger, J. Kallander, D.L. Parnas, and J. Shore, "Software requirements for the A-7E aircraft," NRL Memo. Rep. 3876, November 27, 1978.

10. R.C. Linger, H.D. Mills, B.I. Witt, *Structured Programming: Theory and Practice.* Reading, MA: Addison-Wesley, 1979.

11. A. Parker, K. Heninger, D. Parnas, and J. Shore, "Abstract interface specifications for the A-7E device interface module," NRL Memo Rep. 4385, November 20, 1980.

12. D.L. Parnas, "On the design and development of program families," *IEEE Trans. Software Eng.*, vol. SE-2, March 1976.

13. ———, "Designing software for ease of extension and contraction," in *Proc. 3rd Int. Conf. Software Eng.*, May 10–12, 1978, pp. 264–277.

14. ———, "A generalized control structure and its formal definition," *Commun. ACM*, vol. 26, no. 8, August 1983, pp. 572–581.

15. D.L. Parnas, P. Clements, and D. Weiss, "The modular structure of complex systems," in *Proc. 7th Int. Conf. Software Eng.*, March 1984, pp. 408–417.

16. S. Faulk, B. Labaw, and D. Parnas, "SCR module implementation document guidelines," NRL Tech. Memo. 7590-072:SF.BL:DP, April 1, 1983.

17. D.L. Parnas and D.M. Weiss, "Active design reviews: Principles and practices," in *Proc. 8th Int. Conf. Software Eng.*, London, August 1985.

Acknowledgment

S. Faulk, J. Shore, D. Weiss, and S. Wilson of the Naval Research Laboratory provided thoughtful reviews of this paper. P. Zave and anonymous referees provided some helpful comments.

Introduction

A. John van Schouwen

People tend to have great difficulty in inspecting software and in reviewing traditional software documentation when detailed understanding and analysis are needed. This paper provides an overview of a feasible, systematic, and rigorous approach to manual software verification via inspection. The approach was applied to real software in a nuclear generating station that is currently in operation in Darlington, Ontario, Canada. The approach is built on the foundation of mathematical relations that describe program behavior. Inspection is made feasible and systematic by the use of tables in describing those relations.

Tables are well suited for communicating detailed design information among people: they present information organized in a way that is easier to use than the unstructured linear forms of description that are still typical in the software industry today. Equally important, they facilitate analysis for aspects such as completeness and consistency. Such tables provide strong support for software reviewers who must perform an exhaustive inspection in a way that gives them confidence that a system will perform as intended.

This work was done at a time when there was little experience in formally verifying or inspecting safety-critical software. Although it was common practice to use software in the reaction control systems of Canadian nuclear generating stations, this was the first time that a Canadian design used software in its safety shutdown systems. The regulator, the Canadian Nuclear Safety Commission, had serious concerns about the trustworthiness of these systems. The information-capture techniques and the verification process used by the licensee, and the inspection process used by the regulator were all undergoing development, and there were mounting financial and political pressures to get the plant into operation. All parties wanted assurance that the techniques were sound and practical and that they could be confident in the outcome. After the inspection had taken place, all parties were indeed confident that the power plant was licensable with respect to the computer systems. In fact, in subsequent lectures, Dave would comment on how he would have moved upwind from the plant if he hadn't been confident in the results.[1] I also spoke with a tester who raved about the new tabular notation used in the requirements documentation. What he liked so much

---

1. Of course, one has to wonder why he moved west of Darlington a couple of years later.

was that test cases were much easier to formulate and he could be confident that his test suite covered all of the requirements.

The techniques continue to be developed by Dave and his colleagues at McMaster University, as well as at the Université du Québec à Hull, Warsaw University, and the Naval Research Laboratory. Development continues independently in industry as well. Ontario Hydro and Atomic Energy of Canada Limited (AECL) have been further developing techniques, tools, and internal corporate procedures. Atlantic Nuclear Services has developed a CASE tool based on program-function tables. NASA has applied variants of the techniques to several systems, as has Lockheed and Nortel Networks.

As tool development progresses, the techniques are becoming more cost-effective to use. The Table Tools Project in progress at McMaster University aims to produce a generic software foundation for tools that manipulate tabular mathematical expressions efficiently, whether those tools support program functions, specifications for information-hiding modules and classes, or requirements specifications. As the tools mature, the anticipated increase in cost-effectiveness of software inspections should push rigorous' inspection techniques more broadly across the software industry.

Inspection of Safety-Critical Software Using Program-Function Tables

David Lorge Parnas

19.1 Abstract

Software whose failure could cause serious damage or loss of life must be carefully inspected before it enters service. To be confident that we have considered all cases and possible event sequences, we must follow a systematic procedure based on a sound mathematical model. This paper describes our experience with such a procedure.

19.2 Introduction

Papers on the problem of assuring safety in situations where a software error might cause severe damage, injury, or loss-of-life generally promote one of the following three approaches:

- *Reliability*—It is assumed that (a) to increase safety one must increase the reliability of software and (b) evaluating the safety of a software system means estimating the reliability of the system.

- *Rigour*—It is assumed that safety requires correctness and that safety and correctness can be achieved by the use of highly rigorous "formal" methods.

- *Hazard Analysis*—It is assumed that to assure the safety of a computer-based system one must identify the possible unsafe conditions (hazards) and then work backwards from a description of each hazard to determine whether or not that hazard has been eliminated, or its likelihood minimised, by the design of the system.

As so often happens in our field, advocates of each of the approaches sketched above often speak and write as if these were competing approaches; they imply that practitioners must choose one over the other two.[2] Hazard analysis is viewed as ad hoc and unscientific by some of the advocates of the other two approaches. Many in the rigour camp find the probabilistic

---

2. In this paragraph, I characterize the most extreme of these views in the hope of provoking some discussion leading to improved understanding. Many researchers espouse more moderate views.

approach inappropriate for software, because, in their view, it is either right or wrong not "probably right". Some of the reliability researchers, pointing to the very positive role that probabilistic approaches have played in other areas of engineering, regard the rigour approaches as unrealistic, and unproven. The advocates of various forms of hazard analysis stress that safety is not the same as either reliability or correctness and criticize the advocates of other methods for not looking specifically at safety.

While these approaches do compete for research funding, in practice the three approaches are actually complementary; they can be used together. Nobody should accept a safety-critical system unless it had been designed for high reliability and some evidence of that reliability had been provided. Whenever a safety-critical software system is being developed or inspected, one has a right to expect that the most rigorous practicable methods would be used. If there are well-identified hazards, it is only common sense to perform an analysis to determine whether or not those hazards are prevented by the system.

Work in the "reliability" approach can be further subdivided into

- *Reliability analysis*—techniques for predicting the reliability of a system, and
- *Redundant design*—techniques for increasing the reliability of a system (given components with fixed reliability) by including "extra" (redundant) components.

Clearly there is no conflict between these approaches either.

Work in the "rigour" category can be classified as

- *Rigorous construction*—methods of deriving programs from precise specifications, or
- *Verification*—methods for showing that a given program satisfies its specification.

It is often claimed that if one has used rigorous construction techniques, verification is not needed, but there is little evidence to support that claim.

Work on hazard analysis is more difficult to categorize; I see two schools of thought:

- Hazard analysis should be performed on the code itself, and
- Hazard analysis should be performed on abstractions derived from the code.

We return to this topic at the end of the paper.

This paper arises out of work developed over many years and applied as part of the licensing process for the Darlington (Canada) Nuclear Power Generating Station. The work was first reported in [1] and included all three of the approaches sketched above. This paper however does not discuss reliability-based techniques. It describes a rigorous approach to software inspection (verification) and concludes with a brief discussion of hazard analysis.

19.3 Safety-Critical Software in the Darlington Nuclear Power Generating Station

The Nuclear Power Generating Station in Darlington, Ontario, is one of the first in which the safety shutdown systems were computer controlled. Canadian nuclear stations must have three control systems, each one capable of shutting down the station if a serious problem is detected.

The reactivity control system is responsible for power adjustments under normal operating conditions, but is also required to initiate a shutdown when key parameters depart safe ranges. Reactivity control systems have long been computerized. However, because of their complexity, and a history of some failures, the AECB does not rely upon these systems in their safety analysis. They assume that these systems will fail and look for assurance that the plant will be safe even when the reactivity control system fails.

In addition to the reactivity control system, there are two systems, whose only job is to shut the system down in the event of an accident. They are completely separate and play no role in normal plant operations. Known as the safety systems or shutdown systems, they have no task other than their shutdown role and, consequently, are much simpler than the reactivity control system. Canadian regulations forbid giving them any functions that are not essential for the shutdown task. Any of the three systems can cause a shutdown even if the other two systems are not calling for such action. Each of the systems has its own sensors and control mechanisms. None of the systems can inhibit a shutdown initiated by another.

In Canadian nuclear plants built before Darlington, each safety system was a network of analog components and relays. At Darlington, the safety systems were computerized. The two shutdown systems used distinct computers, were programmed in different languages, and were done by different teams of programmers. This was intended to assure design diversity and reduce the likelihood of both systems failing simultaneously.

The Atomic Energy Control Board (AECB) is the governmental agency charged with certifying that nuclear plants are safe to operate. They customarily inspect design and construction carefully and it is quite normal for them to require changes. When they tried to inspect the software in the safety systems, they became concerned. Although the two programs were relatively simple (approximately 10,000 lines in a mixture of a compiler language and assembly code), they found them much more complex than the hardware systems that they were replacing. Although the two systems had been implemented by different teams, one shared design error had been found in an informal analysis. The AECB could not state, with confidence, that there were no errors in the code. They were unwilling to grant a license without further inspection.

A team comprising about 60 people conducted an inspection of the code over a period of nearly one year. During that inspection, a number of unsuspected discrepancies between the code and the requirements were discovered. Those that were found to be safety relevant were corrected and the plant is now operating.

The inspection was based on the preparation of precise mathematical documentation for the code. This paper will describe the method that was used.

19.4 Why Is Software Inspection Difficult?

Regulatory authorities routinely inspect safety-critical installations both while they are being designed and during construction; usually, the authorities are confident of their ability to detect safety-relevant flaws.

However, when software is involved that confidence evaporates. If you try to inspect all but the smallest programs, the complexity overwhelms you. You are faced with a large amount of detail without the clear structure usually obvious in physical mechanisms. You know that any detail in any part of the program could cause a serious failure. In commonly used programming languages, the interactions between code sections are unrestricted and, most often, undocumented. There are many cases that must be considered and it is hard to be confident that you have not overlooked something important.

Practical experience has shown that people cannot easily understand long programs. When asked to study such programs, we tend to focus on little details while making use of inaccurate descriptions of the overall structure. The combination of a large amount of detail with inaccurate or vague descriptions of the structure makes it quite common for serious errors to escape our attention.

When studying a long program, we must decompose it into small parts and then, provisionally, associate a function with each one. We must then convince ourselves that (1) if each part implements its assigned function, the whole program will be correct, and (2) each part implements its assigned function. Frequently, we find that our provisional assumptions were not exactly what the programmer intended. Then, after revising our initial division and function descriptions, we try again. In principle, this iterative process converges and we learn whether or not the program is correct. In practice, we usually give up before we have a complete and precise understanding of the program. The process terminates when we run out of time or patience.

In inspecting a safety-critical program, one cannot rely upon ad hoc inspections in which people stare at code until they run out of energy. One needs a systematic process in which it is possible to be sure that one has covered all cases and all possible paths.

19.5 Functional Documentation

In recent years a small group of collaborators has developed a general approach to software documentation, which we call "functional documentation" [2]. We define the required content of documents in terms of mathematical relations. Each of the documents must contain a representation of certain relations; if it does not, it is incomplete. If it contains additional information, we consider the document to be faulty; that information should have been placed elsewhere. These definitions are independent of the notation used.

The documents described in [2] include the "system requirements document", the "system design document", the "software requirements document", an optional "software behavior specification", the "module interface specification", and the "module internal design document". Hardware descriptions and communication protocol descriptions are discussed briefly.

In a separate paper, [3], we have discussed notation for representing relations in any of these documents. If our method of software documentation is to be practical, we need a representation of relations that is easily read. In practice, the use of conventional notation results in very complex, deeply nested, expressions that are difficult for anyone to use. Practitioners are quickly turned off by notations that require them to parse long expressions to learn simple facts. We have discovered that a multi-dimensional notation, tables whose entries can be mathematical expressions (including other such tables), results in precise notation that will be used by people in industry. There is no increase in theoretical expressive power over conventional expressions, but the tabular format has several practical advantages.

One of the goals of our research is to be able to use the same tabular notations in all of our documents. All of the documents describe mathematical relations, but the ranges and domains of those relations vary from document to document.

In the Darlington inspection process, we used two of the documents mentioned above. The first was a software requirements document written and reviewed by nuclear engineers, not software specialists. Like most such systems, the shutdown systems were written as a periodic loop. The requirements document could be interpreted as a description of the actions that must be taken on any pass through that loop.

The second document was a set of program-function descriptions derived from the code by software experts. These tables described the effects of the execution of the loop body. The ultimate goal was to have both documents describe the same functions and to be confident that those functions were the "right" functions.

19.6 Program-Function Tables

Another paper in these proceedings describes the mathematical foundations of our method for describing programs. It shows how LD-relations are used to describe and specify programs [4]. That paper describes an abstraction. It does not tell how to represent the LD-relations. Although LD-relations can be described by boolean expressions that describe the characteristic predicate of the sets involved, we have not found this to be satisfactory in practice. The programs that we encounter alter many variables and distinguish many different cases. The boolean expressions become long, deeply nested, and visually unapproachable. An early version of the tabular notations described in [3], the program-function table[3] was used in the inspection at Darlington. This section gives an informal introduction to program-function tables based on the example in Figure 19.1.

The table in Figure 19.1 describes a program that must search an array, B, to find an element whose value is that of the variable x. The program is to determine the value of two program variables called "j" and "present". The variable j, presumed to be an integer variable, is to record the index of one element of A whose value is the value of the variable x (if one exists). The variable called "present", presumed to be a boolean variable, is to indicate whether or not the desired value could be found in B. If B does not contain the value sought, the value of j is allowed to be any integer value.

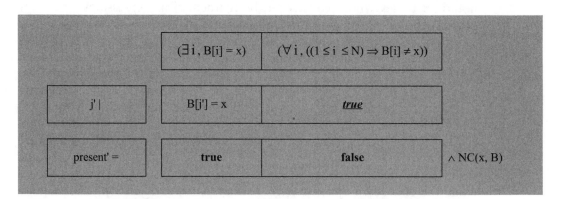

Figure 19.1 *Specification of a search program.*

---

3. Program-function tables are essentially mixed-vector tables [3].

The header at the top of the table in Figure 19.1 shows that two situations must be distinguished. The first column of the main grid (under the first element of the top header) describes the case where the value sought can be found in the array. The second column describes what the program must do if the value cannot be found.

Each row in the main grid of a program-function table corresponds to a program variable and describes the value that this variable must have upon termination. The header to the left of the table identifies the variable whose value is described in each row and also indicates how that variable will be described. A "|" in the vertical header indicates that the variable's value must satisfy a predicate given in the appropriate cell in the main grid. When "=" appears instead of "|", the grid elements in that row must be expressions that will evaluate to the value of the variable. The values of predicates are represented by "*true*" and "*false*". The symbols "*true*" and "*false*" represent the possible values of the boolean variable.

The table describes a predicate on a set of pairs representing the values of the variables before and after execution. The value of a variable, v, on termination is denoted by "'v". Its initial value is denoted "v'". The program must terminate in a state in which the predicate represented by the variable is *true*. The predicate "NC(x, B)" is *true* if x and B are not changed by the program ('x = x' ∧ 'B = B'). Because the table represents a predicate it can be part of a conjunction with another such table or any boolean expression.

The table in Figure 19.1 is equivalent to the boolean expression in Figure 19.2. In practice, program-function tables have many more rows and columns. In the Darlington inspection, programs that altered a dozen or more variables and for which 6–10 different cases had to be distinguished were common. However, in our Darlington experience quantifiers were not needed because the programs did not deal with conditions on arrays.

There is nothing that can be said with such a table that cannot be said using equivalent conventional boolean expressions. Figure 19.2 shows a boolean expression that is equivalent to Figure 19.1. However, the table parses the expression for the reader and presents the reader with a set of simpler boolean expressions instead of a single complex expression. Using the table, one can select the row and column of interest and need not understand the whole expression in order to find out what must happen in a specific case. The number of characters that appear in the tabular expression is usu-

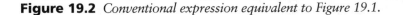

$$(((\exists\, i\,,\ B[i] = x) \wedge (B[j'] = x) \wedge (\text{present}' = \textbf{true})) \vee$$

$$((\forall\, i\,, ((1 \le i \le N) \Rightarrow B[i] \neq x)) \wedge (\text{present}' = \textbf{false}))) \wedge ('x = x' \wedge 'B = B')$$

Figure 19.2 *Conventional expression equivalent to Figure 19.1.*

ally smaller than the number of characters in the equivalent conventional expression because in the latter some of the expressions that appear once in one of the headers would have to be repeated several times in the conventional expression.[4] In spite of the fact that the tabular representation takes up more space on the paper, we all found the tables far easier to work with than the equivalent boolean expressions. On larger tables involving many cases, many variables, and longer identifiers, the advantages of the table format are more dramatic. More extensive discussions of these tables can be found in [2,3].

19.7 The Inspection Process

The inspection process was designed by the AECB to deal with the following facts:

- Inspectors looking for errors in a program need "quiet time" to think.
- The results of their inspection must be scrutinized carefully in open discussion.
- Lengthy inspections must be interrupted by breaks, evenings, and weekends.
- Inspection must focus on small amounts of the program at any one time.
- It is essential that all cases be considered and all parts of the program be inspected.

The program-function tables were well suited for this task. They were representations of the private analysis of inspectors that were well suited for scrutiny by others. The tabular format allows the inspectors to focus on simple cases, while suggesting a systematic procedure for covering all cases.

The AECB called for an inspection by four teams:

1. A requirements team, producing tabular representation of the requirements,

2. A code inspection team, producing program-function tables from the code,

3. A comparison team, establishing equivalence between requirements tables and program-function tables by showing step-by-step transformations from one to the other, and

4. An audit team that checked the work of team 3 on a "random sample" basis.

---

4. Note how "present'=" appears only once in the table, but twice in the conventional expression. The repetition gets more serious when there are more rows. More advanced forms of these tables reduce the repetition of subexpressions even more [3].

The requirements tables were based on [5]; more up-to-date descriptions of this method are to be found in [2, 6, 7]. Their output was a set of tables like those in [5]. It has been found that, although these tables are "formal" (i.e., they use mathematical notation), they can be read by engineers with no training in either computer science or abstract mathematics. For example, the A-7 requirements document [5] could be read by pilots assigned to advise the software team. The team that produced the requirements document for the Darlington shutdown system comprised people considered experts in nuclear safety, not programming. Most of the members of this team were employed by AECL, which make the equipment.

The second team comprised primarily software consultants who were *not* active in the nuclear power industry. They were chosen for their expertise in the programming language and had little knowledge of the requirements. They were hired as consultants by the owner of the plant, Ontario Hydro.

The third team contained people who had been trained to understand program-function tables. They did not look at the code; instead they worked from the program-function tables and the requirements tables. They had to show step-by-step transformations of the tables that would get both tables to look alike. Unfortunately for this team, in most cases the tables were not equivalent and no such sequence of transformations could be found. The team would report discrepancies.

The fourth team was hired by AECB, the regulator, and worked in Ottawa while the other teams were based in the Toronto area. They were primarily software experts.

When a discrepancy was first reported, the second team would be asked to check its work. They would not be told what the problem was, just asked to check their work again. If there was still a discrepancy it would be reported to a set of safety experts for evaluation. Evaluation usually revealed one of the following situations:

■ The requirements tables were wrong; they were corrected and the process repeated.

■ The programmers had added "something extra", thinking that they were improving things. In some cases, the "extra" was a positive change and was accepted.

■ There was a coding error, but it would not adversely affect safety. It was allowed to remain.

■ There was a coding error that did affect safety. It was corrected and the review was repeated.

The fourth team sampled the work of the first three, after those teams were satisfied that their work was correct. In the early phases, they found numerous problems. As skills developed the process became fairly routine and the audit found fewer problems.

Perhaps because the code had been tested for many years before the inspection,[5] the number of changes required was relatively small, but each change made was deemed important. Nonetheless, the main product of the inspection was confidence. The plant was allowed to go into service and all involved felt confident about the thoroughness of the inspection. Another view of the inspection process can be found in [8].

19.8 Hazard Analysis Using Functional Documentation

Ontario Hydro brought in its own consultant before this review was undertaken. She concluded that, in addition to the inspection discussed here, a form of hazard analysis was needed. The inspection described here showed that the requirements document and the code were consistent, but it did not show that there were no hazards. A particular form of hazard analysis, involving inspection of the code, was carried out and reported in [9].

It is the opinion of this author that, although a hazard analysis was necessary, it should not have been performed on the code. When applied to code, "fault-tree" analysis looks suspiciously like weakest-precondition analysis and duplicates the analysis that is required to derive the program-function tables. It is possible to perform a fault-tree analysis using the functional requirements document instead of the code. By using an abstraction of the code instead of the code itself, one saves a great deal of effort and can put more time and energy into defining hazards and investigating the ways that they might occur. Just as the program-function tables provided an abstraction of the code that was easier to work with than the code itself, the requirements tables provide an abstraction of the system that summarizes everything one needs to know for any analysis of the effects of the system on its environmental variables.

19.9 Conclusions

One important test of the value of any technology that has been transferred from the research lab or university to industry is whether the practitioners continue to use the technology when the researcher is no longer involved. Often an idea is used by newly graduated Ph.Ds on their first job, but their employer does not follow up and continues to use or develop the ideas. The experience with program-function tables has been quite different. None of the practitioners in the four teams mentioned had any previous contact with

---

5. Although the software was behind schedule, the physical plant was much further behind its schedule. This software should have been inspected much earlier.

the technology. Ontario Hydro and AECL were initially strongly opposed to using such a new method. All three organizations involved called in other experts looking for an alternative that was more mature. They reluctantly concluded that the approach described was the best one and completed the inspection described above. After the process was completed, the author was asked to give two one-week courses on Software Engineering to others in the Canadian nuclear industry. The organizations involved have since published widely (within the industry) on their experience with the method and have offered their expertise to others. Ontario Hydro has developed the methods further and incorporated them in a software development standard which has now been approved for trial use by the AECB. New software is being developed using program-function table methods. AECL has used the ideas on software being developed for Nuclear Power Plants being built in Korea. The AECB, apparently convinced that this approach is essential to the use of software in safety-critical applications, continues to study similar approaches in its own research program. The author, who introduced the ideas to those involved, has not been involved with the nuclear industry in the past few years, but the work goes on. This is the best evidence of success.

In the author's research group, we are continuing to refine the notation, and to develop tools that will make the techniques less expensive to use.

References

1. Parnas, D.L., Asmis, G.J.K., Madey, J., "Assessment of Safety-Critical Software in Nuclear Power Plants", *Nuclear Safety*, vol. 32, no. 2, April-June 1991, pp. 189–198.

2. Parnas, D.L., Madey, J., "Functional Documentation for Computer Systems Engineering (Version 2)", CRL Report 237, Communications Research Laboratory, McMaster University (also in *Science of Computer Programming*, October 1995, pp 41–61).

3. Parnas, D.L., "Tabular Representation of Relations", CRL Report 260, Communications Research Laboratory, McMaster University, October 1992, 17 pgs.

4. Parnas, D.L. "Mathematical Descriptions and Specification of Software", *Proceedings of IFIP World Congress 1994*, August 1994.

5. Heninger, K., Kallander, J., Parnas, D.L., Shore, J., "Software Requirements for the A-7E Aircraft", NRL Report 3876, November 1978, 523 pgs.

6. Van Schouwen, A.J., "The A-7 Requirements Model: Re-examination for Real-Time Systems and an Application to Monitoring Systems", *Technical Report 90-276*, Queen's C&IS, TRIO, Kingston, Ontario, Canada, May 1990, 93 pgs.

7. Van Schouwen, A.J., Parnas, D.L., Madey, J., "Documentation of Requirements for Computer Systems", presented at *RE '93 IEEE International Symposium on Requirements Engineering*, San Diego, CA, 4-6 January, 1993.

8. Archinoff, G.H., Hohendorf, R.J., Wassyng, A., Quigley, B., Borsch, M.R., "Verification of the Shutdown System Software at the Darlington Nuclear Generating

Station", International Conference on Control & Instrumentation in Nuclear Installations, Glasgow, May 1990.

9. Bowman, W.C., Archinoff, G.H., Raina, V.M., Tremaine, D.R., Leveson, N.G., "An Application of Fault Tree Analysis to Safety Critical Software at Ontario Hydro", Probabilistic Safety and Management Conference, February 1991.

Acknowledgments

I am indebted to Harlan D. Mills and N. G. de Bruijn who first introduced me to the concept of program functions/relations. A. J. van Schouwen contributed a great deal to the early work on these methods, and Jan Madey has helped to formalize the model behind them.

Concurrency and Scheduling

DAVID LORGE PARNAS, P. ENG

1. Why Make a Special Case of Concurrency?

This is the shortest section of the book, perhaps because it deals with the hardest problem. Software design is never easy, but it gets much harder when one has to deal with systems in which there are concurrent activities that must be coordinated.

In fact, most of the papers in this section were motivated by mistakes—other people's mistakes. When you see smart people making mistakes repeatedly, you know you are facing an interesting and difficult problem.

2. What We Should Be Able to Do but Cannot Yet Do

When dealing with sequential programs, we have a very useful mathematical basis. We can represent the effect of any program by a function or relation. When we combine several programs using constructors, such as ";" (sequential composition), "**if then else**", or "**while do**", we have rules that allow us to determine the function/relation representing the effects of the constructed program from the representations of the effects of the component programs. If we make a mistake, it is because we did not follow the rules, not because we don't know the theory.

I don't think we are anywhere near as fortunate in the case of concurrent programs. We don't know how to represent the effects of a nonterminating program as a single function or relation. I see this as the first step toward determining the semantics of a set of concurrent sequential processes whose individual semantics we can represent. We would need to represent the effects of a nonterminating program (a process) by a set of functions, each representing what that program can do in a single uninterruptable step. We need a way of representing the program state (instruction counter) of each process and the state of any shared variables that the component uses for communication with other such components. When we combine two processes for which we have such a representation, we need a way of determining the functional representation of the combination from the functional representations of the component processes.

We do not need to solve this problem in general, that is for arbitrary processes and interprocess communication. We can, and probably must, put restrictions on the behaviour of individual components and on the way they communicate. For example, we must decide if we are going to allow "true concurrency" (simultaneous actions) or restrict ourselves to interleaving the discrete steps of each process. Unfortunately, I don't think we even know the right restrictions. I have seen many interesting theories of concurrency, but none that seemed sufficient to handle the problems that I have seen in actual applications. The concurrency that is so important in our present systems is designed on an intuitive basis, and that intuition is often wrong.

3. Synchronisation

One way to simplify the constructive semantics of concurrency is to provide a restrictive mechanism for interprocess coordination and to restrict other forms of communication. E. W. Dijkstra pioneered this approach by introducing his well-known "P" and "V" operators and suggesting that they be used to protect shared data by implementing mutual exclusion for critical sections. Most people accepted his general approach, but many people doubted that "P" and "V" were the right operators. Countless other operators have been proposed, and it seems that each of these proposals can solve some problem better than some other proposals can solve those problems. For example, both the "Readers and Writers" (Paper 20), and the "Cigarette Smoker" (Paper 21), problems were introduced by people who claimed that those problems could not be solved with Dijkstra's primitive operations. In both cases, the original negative claims were wrong, but we do know that it is possible to define problems that cannot be solved exactly with these operators.

Although the debate has been going on for more than thirty years, I don't think we have found the solution yet. In fact, most people have lost interest in the discussion because it does not seem to be getting anywhere. However, it remains an important problem for practitioners. We know that the methods being used today (e.g., message passing) are far from ideal; they can have a very negative impact on performance when they are used. Even when message passing methods are used, it is remarkably easy to make mistakes and produce unreliable systems.

One approach, the one outlined in Paper 22, provides developers with a mechanism for defining the right synchronisation operators for their problem. This is appealing, but its practicality has not been proven in practice.

4. Scheduling

Scheduling is a problem that tends to be ignored in the community that worries about synchronisation, and the scheduling community often ignores synchronisation. We need them both because they provide "separation of concerns". With the proper synchronisation primitives, one can provide a kind of "logical correctness" in which a program is correct no matter what the relative speeds of the processors. This allows the scheduling programs to be developed without concern for the "logical correctness".

In the scheduling area one sees a surprising lack of awareness of the state of our knowledge in the majority of the computer science community. Most people seem to assume that one should assign priorities to processes and follow a discipline in which one assigns the processor to the highest priority waiting process. In some schemes, it is recognised that this will not work and priorities must be changed while the system is running.

I find this surprising because there is another community that has been interested in scheduling for many decades. These are people who are concerned with production maximisation in "job shops". In that situation, there are a fixed number of (sometimes specialised) resources and a variable number of jobs that require those resources. Situations are often much more complex than those we find in computer systems. In this context it has been long known [1] that priorities are not the solution. For reliable and close-to-optimal scheduling we need to work in terms of deadlines and resource requirements. Processors should be assigned to the process with the least "laxity" (spare time): priorities just get in the way [2].

Of course, many scheduling problems are extremely difficult to solve, and one tends to solve special cases. This is an area where much more research is needed, but relatively little is done.

5. Conclusion

I wish I had time to do a lot more study in this area. There is a real need for a textbook that deals with both scheduling and synchronisation and provides practical, technology-independent advice.

References

1. Lui, C.L. and Layland, J.W., "Scheduling algorithms for multiprogramming in a hard-real-time environment", *J. ACM*, vol. 20, January 1973.

2. Xu, J. and Parnas, D.L., "Priority scheduling versus pre-run-time scheduling", in *The International Journal of Time Critical Computing Systems,* 18, pp. 7–23 (2000), Kluwer Academic Publishers, Boston.

Introduction

Pierre-Jacques Courtois

It all began in the summer of 1970. Dave was in Brussels, visiting the M.B.L.E research laboratory, then one of the Philips research institutes. He had spent the previous months in The Netherlands, working as a consultant to Philips Computer Industries. It was during a visit to Electrologica, in Rijkswijk, that he first heard of readers and writers. He had seen a note on the problem written by Dijkstra with an argument that it was not solvable with the P and V semaphore operations. Dave had expressed doubts on the validity of this argument, and these doubts had excited our curiosity.

The apparent simplicity of the problem was deceptive. Each of us in turn proudly brandished one or more solutions, which were quickly dismissed as being incorrect by the others. We had to recognise, humbly, the great virtues of software-independent reviews at a time when they were not yet considered to be a standard and quite honourable practice.

We were going to give up this prolific production of faulty and clumsy programs when Frans Heymans came up with the idea of counting processes to differentiate first coming and last leaving readers and of making processes use what was later called a split semaphore. From then on, more acceptable solutions quickly emerged.

Today, the structure of the first solution may appear quite simple and natural. Not long ago I found this in a recent textbook on concurrent programming: "A *simple* way to *specify this synchronisation* is to count the number of each kind of process, then to constrain the counters. . . ." Taking this specification for granted, the textbook then goes to great lengths to construct the program by means of invariant predicates, pre- and post-conditions, and coarse- and fine-grained refinements. The author was not the only one to overlook the real difficulty, which was not to implement what he calls the *specification of the synchronisation*. The tricky bit was to ferret out this counting mechanism from the informal *Kaffeeklatsch* problem description, which was all we had. Even now, I still can't think of any programming language or arsenal of formal tools that could have helped to make that particular decisive design step.

The solution to the second problem, where priority is given to writers, is more complicated. Its merit was perhaps to have been one of the first to show that apparently simple synchronisation problems could not always be elegantly solved with P and V. This solution raised a wave of alternative propositions programmed with new synchronisation primitives, in an attempt to obtain programs simpler to understand and easier to validate; the conditional critical section from Brinch Hansen was just one of these primitives[1]. These solutions were not comparable. They solved another type of synchronisation problem and took advantage of what had been coined "busy waiting" by E. W. Dijkstra, an active state in which a waiting process keeps testing state conditions. Loose synchronisation of this type turned out to be easier to design and to understand than a tight coordination of processes active only whey they have access to the resources they need.

Studies prompted by this type of problem later showed that primitives like P and V are necessary and sufficient when mutual exclusion—and thus synchronisation—programs need to be associative (invariant under the number of parallel processes involved), without busy waiting, and with minimum process blocking or interrupt masking. The problem that readers can starve writers or vice versa also gave rise to various prevention algorithms.

It is worth noting that this second solution, despite its complexity, still allows one reader, but no more, to bypass all barriers and sneak in ahead of a writer. How this can occur, and whether or not it is avoidable are questions left to the reader as an exercise so that he can judge by himself whether Dijkstra was not perhaps right after all.

At the end of August, the paper was issued as a research report of the M.B.L.E laboratory and submitted for publication shortly afterwards when Dave was back in Pittsburgh. It was and still is one of the shortest of Dave's publications and, perhaps for that reason as he himself says, also one of the most quoted.

Reference

1. Courtois, P.J., Heymans, F., and Parnas, D.L., *Comments on "A Comparison of Two Synchronizing Concepts by P.B. Hansen,"* Acta Informatica, 1, 375–376, 1972.

Concurrent Control with "Readers" and "Writers"

P.J. Courtois, F. Heymans, and D.L. Parnas

20.1 Abstract

The problem of the mutual exclusion of several independent processes from simultaneous access to a "critical section" is discussed for the case where there are two distinct classes of processes known as "readers" and "writers." The "readers" may share the section with each other, but the "writers" must have exclusive access. Two solutions are presented: one for the case where we wish minimum delay for the readers; the other for the case where we wish writing to take place as early as possible.

20.2 Introduction

Dijkstra [1], Knuth [2], and de Bruijn [3] have discussed the problem of guaranteeing exclusive access to a shared resource in a system of cooperating sequential processes. The problem they deal with has been shown to have a relatively simple solution using the "P" and "V" operations of Dijkstra [4]. We discuss two related problems of practical significance in which we recognize two classes of processes wishing to use the resource. The processes of the first class, named *writers*, must have exclusive access as in the original problem, but processes of the second class, the *readers*, may share the resource with an unlimited number of other readers.

20.3 Problem 1

We demand of our solution that no reader be kept waiting unless a writer has already obtained permission to use the resource; i.e., no reader should wait simply because a writer is waiting for other readers to finish. In this case the solution presented is quite simple, but our experience has shown that it is not easily arrived at. Numerous solutions, which have quite unreasonable complexity, have been proposed. The following solution resulted from several cycles among the authors in which each simplified a solution shown him by another. We present it in hope that others may be spared the effort of solving again this rather common problem. See Figure 20.1.

 Please notice that w functions as a mutual exclusion semaphore for the writer but is only used by the first reader to enter the critical section and the

integer *readcount* ; (initial value = 0)
semaphore *mutex, w* ; (initial value for both = 1)

READER   WRITER
P(*mutex*) ;
readcount : = *readcount* + 1 ;
if *readcount* = 1 **then** P(*w*) ;
V(*mutex*) ;

                                            P(*w*) ;
            …   …
     reading is performed   writing is performed
            …   …
P(*mutex*) ;   V(*w*) ;
readcount : = *readcount* – 1 ;
if *readcount* = 0 **then** V(*w*) ;
V(*mutex*) ;

Figure 20.1 *Problem 1.*

last reader to leave it. It is ignored by readers who enter or leave while other readers are present. *mutex* ensures that only one reader will enter or leave at a time thereby eliminating the possibility of ambiguity about which process is responsible for adjusting *w*. *w* will be positive if and only if there are no readers and no writers present in the critical section.

20.4 Problem 2

Here we retain the requirement that writers must have exclusive access while readers may share, but we add the requirement that once a writer is ready to write, he performs his "write" as soon as possible. A solution to this problem cannot be a solution to Problem 1 because to meet this requirement a reader who arrives after a writer has announced that he is ready to write must wait *even if the writer is also waiting.* For the first problem it was possible that a writer could wait indefinitely while a stream of readers arrived. In this problem we give priority to writers and allow readers to wait indefinitely while a stream of writers is working. On general principles we require that the solution give priority to writers without making any assumptions about priority being built into the V routine. In other words, where several processes are waiting at a semaphore, we cannot predict which one will be allowed to proceed as the result of a V operation.

We propose the solution shown in Figure 20.2.

The reader should first note that the use of *mutex* 1 and *w* corresponds exactly to the use of *mutex* and *w* in the solution to Problem 1. The sema-

```
integer readcount, writecount ; (initial value = 0)
semaphore mutex 1, mutex 2, mutex 3, w, r ; (initial value = 1)

READER                              WRITER
P(mutex 3) ;                        P(mutex 2) ;
   P(r) ;                              writecount : = writecount + 1 ;
      P(mutex 3) ;                     if writecount = 1 then P(r)
      readcount = readcount + 1 ;      V(mutex 2) ;
      if readcount = 1 then P(w) ;     P(w) ;
      V(mutex 1) ;
   V(r) ;
V(mutex 3) ;

        ...                                   ...
   reading is done                      writing is performed
        ...                                   ...
P(mutex 1) ;                         V(w) ;
readcount : = readcount – 1 ;        P(mutex 2) ;
if readcount = 0 then V(w) ;         writecount : = writecount – 1 ;
V(mutex 1) ;                         if writecount = 0 then V(r)
                                     V(mutex 2) ;
```

Figure 20.2 *Problem 2.*

phore *r* is used to protect the act of entering the critical section in the same way that *w* is used to protect the shared resource in Problem 1. The first writer to pass P(r) will block readers from entering the section which manipulates *mutex* 1 and *w.mutex* 2 is used here for writers just as *mutex* is used for readers in Problem 1. *mutex* 3 is necessary because of our absolute insistence on priority for writers. Without *mutex* 3 we have the possibility that a writer and one or more readers will be simultaneously waiting for a V(r) to be done by a reader. In that event we could not guarantee priority to the writer. *mutex* 3 guarantees a reader exclusive access to the block of code from "P(r)" to "V(r)" inclusive. As a result there will be at most one process ever waiting at r, and the result of a V is clear.

20.5 Final Remarks

The reader will note that the above solutions do not guarantee a FIFO discipline for the writers. To provide such a guarantee we must either assume further properties of the V operation or make use of an array of *n* semaphores where *n* is the number of writers.

References

1. Dijkstra, E.W., Solution of a problem in concurrent programming control. *Comm. ACM 8*, 9 (September 1965), 569.

2. Knuth, D.W., Additional comments on a problem in concurrent programming control. *Comm. ACM 9*, 5 (May 1966), 321–322.

3. de Bruijn, N.G., Additional comments on a problem in concurrent programming control. *Comm. ACM 10*, 3 (March 1967), 137–138.

4. Dijkstra, E.W., The structure of the "THE"-multiprogramming system. *Comm. ACM 11*, 5 (May 1968), 341–346.

Acknowledgments

We are grateful to A.N. Habermann of Carnegie-Mellon University for having shown us an error in an earlier version of this report.

Introduction

Stuart Faulk

"On a Solution to the Cigarette Smoker's Problem" is quintessential Parnas in its analysis of the literature and its approach to providing a better software engineering solution. While I was a graduate student, Dave advised me on his approach to reading the literature effectively. As in much of his work, Dave distilled the essence of critical review down to principle. In brief, he held that the quality of most research depended on the quality of the underlying assumptions. He reasoned that most people could construct a sound argument given sound assumptions. What people find difficult, however, is critically examining their own assumptions. Thus the first task in critically examining our own work, or that of others, is to validate the assumptions.

Dave's analysis of Patil's work illustrates the effectiveness of the approach. Dave responds to Patil's assertion that the cigarette smoker's synchronization problem cannot be solved using Dijkstra's P/V operators. Rather than argue with the complex proof Patil presents, Dave questions the appropriateness of Patil's assumptions. In brief, he shows that Patil cannot find a solution because of the constraints he has put on the problem, that the constraints are unnecessary, and that a straightforward solution is possible if those constraints are relaxed.

Also vintage Parnas is his critique of the assumptions based on sound software engineering principles and the need for software engineers to address real (rather than artificial) problems. One sees this in the cigarette smoker's problem where Dave points out that Patil's more complicated replacements for P and V are no longer primitive in the practical and effective sense of "small and quickly executed"—a fundamental goal for synchronization primitives. Further, the operations are analogous to goto in that they "add nothing to the set of solvable problems and make it easier to write programs which should not be written."

While effective, Dave's approach is not always popular. I'll surprise no one by saying that most people do not enjoy having their assumptions criticized and that Dave's willingness to do so has earned him enmity in some quarters. This is particularly true where the critique has revealed deep structural flaws in cherished areas of research.

However, my own work with Dave has shown that the strength of his work is in no small part a result of his willingness to examine critically his own assumptions as well as to accept such critique from others. While I cannot say that it is easy to convince Dave that he is wrong about something, I can say that he will listen and, if the critique is valid, act upon it. This reflects what I believe to be an overriding principle of research—our first duty is to the truth.

On a Solution to the Cigarette Smoker's Problem (without conditional statements)

D.L. Parnas

21.1 Abstract

This report discusses a problem first introduced by Patil, who has claimed that the cigarette smoker's problem cannot be solved using the P and V operations introduced by Dijkstra unless conditional statements are used. An examination of Patil's proof shows that he has established this claim only under strong restrictions on the use of P and V. These restrictions eliminate programming techniques used by Dijkstra and others since the first introduction of the semaphore concept. This paper contains a solution to the problem. It also discusses the need for the generalized operators suggested by Patil.

21.2 Introduction

In a widely circulated and referenced memorandum [1, 2], Suhas Patil has introduced a synchronization problem called the "cigarette smoker's problem" and claimed that the problem cannot be solved using the P and V primitives introduced by Dijkstra [3] unless conditional statements are also used. On the basis of an elaborate proof in terms of Petri nets, it is concluded that the P and V primitives are not sufficiently powerful and that more complex operations are needed. This paper presents a solution to the cigarette smoker's problem without conditional statements, explicitly states an implicit assumption used in Patil's proof, and discusses the need for more powerful operations.

While a full introduction into the problem can be found in Patil [1], the aspects of the problem essential to this paper are related below.

There are three resource classes and also three processes using those resources. At a certain point in each process it must have one resource of each class in order to proceed. If it does not have all three, it must wait before proceeding. However, each of these processes has a permanent supply of one of the three resources. (No two of them have a permanent supply of the same resource.) There is a set of processes known as the agent which occasionally makes two of the resources available. The one process which has the remaining resource can then proceed. When it has finished with the three resources it is to notify the agent. The agent will not supply any more resources until it receives such notification.

In Patil's description of the problem the agent is considered to be an unchangeable part of the problem definition and is defined by the six processes shown below (notation is changed to be consistent with other *Communications* papers).

$$
\begin{array}{lll}
r_a : & P(s); & r_b : & P(s); & r_c : & P(s); \\
 & V(b); & & V(a); & & V(a); \\
 & V(c); & & V(c); & & V(b); \\
 & \textbf{go to } r_a; & & \textbf{go to } r_b; & & \textbf{go to } r_c; \\
\beta_x : & P(X); & \beta_y : & P(Y); & \beta_z : & P(Z); \\
 & V(s); & & V(s); & & V(s); \\
 & \textbf{go to } \beta_x; & & \textbf{go to } \beta_y; & & \textbf{go to } \beta_z;
\end{array}
$$

Note: Initially $s = 1$ and a, b, c, X, Y and $Z = 0$.

The semaphores, a, b, and c, are used by the agent to report the arrival of the three resources. Each semaphore denotes one of the resources. s is a mutual exclusion semaphore to assure that only one pair of resources is deposited at a time. X, Y, Z are to be used by the resource users to report that they are done with the resources.[1]

The problem is stated so as to allow the definition of any number of additional semaphores and processes and to use any number of P and V statements to write programs for the resource users which will use the resources and be free of deadlock. Conditional statements are not allowed in these programs. Patil states that this problem has no solution.

The Solution (processes and semaphores are in addition to the agent)

semaphore mutex; (initially 1)

integer t; (initially 0)

semaphore array $S[1 : 6]$; (initially 0)

$$
\begin{array}{lll}
\delta_a : & P(a); & \delta_b : & P(b); & \delta_c : & P(c); \\
 & P\,(\text{mutex}); & & P(\text{mutex}); & & P(\text{mutex}); \\
 & t \leftarrow t + 1; & & t \leftarrow t + 2; & & t \leftarrow t + 4; \\
 & V(S[t]); & & V(S[t]); & & V(S[t]); \\
 & V\,(\text{mutex}); & & V(\text{mutex}); & & V(\text{mutex}); \\
 & \textbf{go to } \delta_a; & & \textbf{go to } \delta_b; & & \textbf{go to } \delta_c; \\
\alpha_x : & P(S[6]); & \alpha_y : & P(S[5]); & \alpha_z : & P(S[3]); \\
 & t \leftarrow 0; & & t \leftarrow 0; & & t \leftarrow 0; \\
 & \cdots & & \cdots & & \cdots \\
 & V(X); & & V(Y); & & V(Z); \\
 & \textbf{go to } \alpha_x; & & \textbf{go to } \alpha_y; & & \textbf{go to } \alpha_z;
\end{array}
$$

---

1. In the present author's opinion, X, Y, and Z could be combined first with each other and then with s without essentially changing the problem. Then the three "beta" processes could be eliminated. We leave them unchanged because the problem definition has the agent unchanged.

Optional: If overflow is a problem,

δ_1: $P(S[1])$; δ_2: $P(S[2])$; δ_3: $P(S[4])$;
   go to δ_1 ;   **go to δ_2 ;**   **go to δ_3 ;**

The . . . stands for some operations performed by the process.

21.3 Comments

The last three processes are superfluous unless one worries about the ill-defined problem of semaphore overflow. The solution works by simulating a six-branch case statement using a semaphore array and simple arithmetic operations. The solution is simpler than the published solution [1] using conditionals. P.J. Courtois [6] has shown that the extra processes could be eliminated by decrementing those semaphores in other processes and adding a semaphore $s[0]$.

21.4 On Patil's Proof

Patil [1] gives a method of representing cooperating processes as Petri nets, stating that, "the 'transition' representing the instruction $P[S]$ has an additional arc from the place corresponding to semaphore S and from the transition corresponding to the instruction $V[S]$, there is an additional arc to the place corresponding to the semaphore S." Every element of a semaphore array must be represented by its own place. The transitions corresponding to V operations may now place markers in any one (but only one) of these places. The description of the action of a Petri net [1] states that a transition places markers on *all* of its output places.

It appears then that Patil has used (but not stated) an assumption that there are no semaphore arrays. Since these arrays appeared in the earliest literature on the subject [3], the limitation reported by Patil is not a limitation on the primitives as they were described by Dijkstra.

21.5 Patil's Result

Patil has obtained the following result: A solution to the cigarette smoker's problem cannot be composed given:

1. *P* and *V* operations on single semaphores—each operation appearing in the text operating on a specific semaphore determined by the text and fixed throughout execution of the program.
2. Algol-like sequencing rule with no conditional statements.
3. Assignment statements with arithmetic expressions (perhaps allowing quite restricted function calls), but no conditional expressions.
4. A set of parallel processes (any number) each written from elements (a)–(c) above.

This result, although more restricted than one would like, is a definite contribution to the state of our knowledge about *P* and *V*.

21.6 On a Complication Arising from the Introduction of Semaphore Arrays

The use of semaphore arrays does introduce one minor complication which has not been discussed in the literature. In a call of the form "*P(S[E])*" (where *E* represents an arbitrary integer valued expression), the evaluation of *E* must take place only once and *before* execution of the body of "*P*". The evaluation is not considered a part of the "primitive" *P*. (In other words, we must be able to consider the state of the system during evaluation of the expression, whereas we have no information about the state of a system during the execution of a "Primitive" such as "*P*" or "*V*". The semaphore value will be referenced at least twice. Those interested in programming languages might be intrigued by the fact that the classical parameter passing modes found in Algol 60 are inadequate for this purpose. Were we to want to write an appropriate "*P*" algorithm in Algol 60, it would require use of the format *P(s,E)* where *s* is a semaphore array. Only in this way could we call *E* by value while being able to refer to *s* by name. We consider this minor difficulty to be a quirk in the design of Algol 60 rather than any limitation of the concept of the semaphore.

21.7 On the Yet Unsolved Problem

It is not the purpose of this paper to suggest that there are no limitations to the capabilities of Dijkstra's semaphore primitives. There are limitations of the semaphore operations. While we disagree with the result claimed by Patil, we applaud his goal of a precise and substantial evaluation of the Dijkstra primitives.

It is important, however, that such an investigation not investigate the power of these primitives under artificial restrictions. By artificial we mean restrictions which cannot be justified by practical considerations. In this author's opinion, restrictions prohibiting either conditionals or semaphore arrays are artificial. On the other hand, prohibition of "busy waiting" is quite realistic.

The justifications given by Patil for eliminating conditional statements are not valid. Some characteristics of the definition of the agent are also artificial. In fact, the agent could be modified to make the problem more difficult by removing the restriction that the agent throws down only two resources and waits until they have been taken before adding more [6]. Although we do not have a solution to that more difficult problem (without conditional statements), we do not conclude that the problem is unsolvable.

An investigation of these questions is difficult because (1) we have no firm definition of the set of problems which we wish to be able to solve, and

(2) in using the *PV* system we have great freedom in the way that we assign tasks to processes and the way that we assign interpretations to the semaphores in use. Often problems which appear unsolvable are easily solved when additional processes or semaphores are introduced. It would be artificial to rule out such solutions in any investigation of the capabilities of semaphore primitives.

"*P*" and "*V*" are deliberately designed so that when there are several processes waiting for a "*V*" operation on a given semaphore, the choice of the process to be released by a "*V*" is not specified. This "nondeterminism" is advantageous in writing programs where schedulers are subject to change or programs are likely to be moved to another machine. On the other hand, it makes the solution of "priority problems" such as [4] more difficult. Perhaps exact solutions to some are impossible. The question remains open. Some recent work by Belpaire and Willmotte [8] and Lipton [9] has helped narrow the issues.

21.8 On More Powerful Primitives

Patil's paper ends with the introduction of a "more powerful" primitive than the "*P*" and "*V*" primitives. His P can simultaneously decrement several semaphores when *all* are passable! He suggests that the necessity of such a primitive is supported by the inability of "*P*" and "*V*" to solve the smoker's problem. Such proposals are not new—a similar proposal was made when *P* and *V* operations were believed insufficient for problems similar to those solved in [4].

Such arguments are invalid since the problems can be solved. Further, we note that the generalized operation can be programmed in a straightforward way using *P* and *V* (and conditionals).

In this author's opinion, the use of the word "primitive" to describe routines which might have been called "monitor routines" or "operating system service calls" suggests that the programs implementing the operations be small and quickly executed. There are obvious practical advantages to placing such restrictions on a code which is the uninterruptable "heart" of an operating system. "*P*" and "*V*" have the desired properties, the generalized operations do not.

There is no doubt that the generalized operations can be useful in describing certain processes. If one wants to describe such processes, one should build the operations, but they need not be built as "primitives." This attitude has been taken by the authors of [5] where some interesting new upper level operations are suggested.

Patil's generalized operations have been called "parallel" operations because they simulate simultaneous activities on many semaphore variables. They make it easy to describe a single process which does tasks which could have been done by several cooperating sequential processes. Often one finds possibilities for parallel execution within such processes; these possibilities cannot be exploited by a multiprocessor system because one does not assign two processors to the same process simultaneously.[2] Often, because of the potential parallelism within the process, the program describing the process becomes very complex. In this sense, the generalized operation is akin to the "go to" statement in programming languages. Both add nothing to the set of soluble problems; both make it easier to write programs which should not be written. Those who feel dissatisfied with the P,V primitive system could look at some "more primitive primitives" suggested by Belpaire and Willmotte [8] and Wodon (7).

Those interested in further discussions of the cigarette smoker's problem itself (including a correctness proof for the solution given here) should read [10].

References

1. Patil, S.S., Limitations and capabilities of Dijkstra's semaphore primitives for coordination among processes. Proj. MAC, Computational Structures Group Memo 57, February 1971.

2. Project MAC. Progress Report, 1970–71.

3. Dijkstra, E.W., Cooperating sequential processes. In *Programming Languages*, F. Genuys (Ed.), Academic Press, New York, 1968. [First published by T.H. Eindhoven, Eindhoven, The Netherlands, 1965.]

4. Courtois, P.J., Heymans, F., and Parnas, D.L., Concurrent control with readers and writers. *Comm. ACM 15* (October 1971), 667–668.

5. Vantilborgh, H., van Lamsweerde, A., On an extension of Dijkstra's semaphore primitives. Re. R192, MBLE, Laboratoire de Recherches, Brussels. Also published in *Information Processing Letters*, North Holland Pub. Co., Amsterdam.

6. Courtois, P.J., Private communication.

7. Wodon, P., Still another tool for synchronizing cooperating processes. Dept. Computer Sci. Rep., Carnegie-Mellon U., Pittsburgh, PA, 1972.

8. Belpaire, G., and Willmotte, J.P., Proc., 1973 European ACM Symposium, Davos, Switzerland.

9. Lipton, Richard., On synchronization primitives. Ph.D. Thesis, Carnegie-Mellon U., Pittsburgh, PA, June 1973.

10. Habermann, A.N., On a solution and a generalization of the cigarette smoker's problem. Techn. Rep., Carnegie-Mellon U., August 1972.

---

2. Such a restriction is the operational definition of "process" or "task" in most operating systems.

Acknowledgments

I am indebted to Wing Hing Huen for helping me to strengthen one of the arguments in this paper. I am also grateful to P. Wodon and P.J. Courtois for helpful comments. An anonymous referee is acknowledged for his lucid description of the proper conclusion of Patil's paper.

Introduction

Stuart Faulk

Do real programmers write in assembler?

At the time "On Synchronization in Hard-Real-Time Systems" was published, embedded, real-time systems remained one of the last bastions of hairy-chested assembly language programming. Asserting that tight resources and hard deadlines called for machine-level control, real-time programmers eschewed the use of "academic" software engineering practices including abstraction, modularization, information hiding, and even high-level languages. The resulting systems were typically so difficult to understand and maintain that writing one could provide the lucky programmer with lifetime job security.

Even into the 1980s, conventional wisdom held that advanced, "academic" software engineering principles and methods could not be used for embedded real-time applications, particularly those with mission- or safety-critical requirements. Developers asserted that such techniques introduced unacceptable overhead and abstracted away from code and timing details necessary to satisfy rigid timing constraints.

Embedded applications were developed in assembly language using hard-coded scheduling loops ("cyclic executive") to control run-time task scheduling. Since timing relationships between tasks were built into the code, even minor changes in the execution time of one task could cause otherwise unrelated tasks to miss their deadlines. The resulting systems were notoriously brittle and difficult to develop, understand, and change.

These problems had just begun to attract attention from the research community. I recall participating in early symposia on real-time systems and listening to lively debates on the meaning of the term "real time." Much of the audience remained convinced that "real time" was simply a euphemism for "fast" and that most, if not all, "real-time" problems would vanish with the advent of faster systems.

It is now well established that "temporal correctness," the ability for a program to deliver results within real-time limits, is a concern distinct from both program speed and logical correctness. "On Synchronization" was seminal in developing a conceptual framework and disciplined approach to writing temporally correct software.

A key contribution of the work was to show how to treat the design-time structure of a real-time program as a distinct concern from the run-time structure without sacrificing control of program efficiency or schedule. The approach describes how to develop a system as a set of cooperating sequential processes, then translate those processes into efficient in-line code.

Designing the software in terms of cooperating sequential processes allows each process to be created, understood, and maintained independently. Timing constraints and intertask dependencies can be defined in terms of timing, scheduling, and exclusion constraints between processes. A novel "pre-run-time" scheduler/loader then mapped the processes to in-line code consistent with timing and precedence constraints.

Since the approach attacked real-time system development in a completely new way, a number of novel techniques for writing real-time processes were developed including:

1. Real-time process synchronization. The paper introduces synchronization mechanisms with the properties that (a) processes do not wait unless they cannot do useful work, (b) waits are bounded, (c) processes do not consume resources (e.g., cpu cycles) when they must wait, and (d) mutual exclusion is implemented without need for waiting or for additional run-time mechanisms.

2. Pre-run-time scheduling. Schedules are determined in advance and then embedded in the code. Most run-time scheduling overhead is eliminated and optimal schedules can often be produced off-line.

3. Event observers. The synchronization approach separates concerns for which process detects an event from which processes react to an event— an approach that is now well known through its use in the "observer" design pattern.

The insights and methods described in the paper have demonstrated their endurance by their influence on subsequent work. Among others:

■ The State Transition Event mechanism showed that concurrent finite state machines could effectively model embedded system states. This result was extended in [2] to define a formal model for specifying system states and state transitions in software requirements and was influential in developing a complete formal model and tools for the SCR requirements method [3, 4, and 5].

■ The pre-run-time scheduling approach was extended by Parnas and Xu to address a number of previously unsolved real-time scheduling problems. This work showed that one could guarantee timing properties and even provide optimal schedules for scheduling problems that cannot be addressed with priority-based scheduling [6, 7, and 8].

■ The principle of separating design constraints from real-time scheduling constraints for real-time systems has subsequently influenced development of other specification methods (e.g., ASTRAL [1]).

The lessons of "On Synchronization" remain current in spite of the intervening years. One continues to hear debates over the efficiency of object-oriented designs and whether information hiding or abstraction will introduce too much overhead. Much of this confusion would be alleviated with a better understanding of the issues discussed in "On Synchronization."

References

1. Coen-Porisini, A., C. Ghezzi, and R. Kemmerer, "Specification of Real-time Systems Using ASTRAL," *IEEE TSE, v. 23,* no. 9, September 1997, pp. 572–598.

2. Faulk, Stuart R., "A State Machine Approach to State Determination in Hand-Embedded Systems," *NRL Memorandum Report 9199,* U.S. Naval Research Laboratory, Code 5540, Washington, DC, 1989.

3. Constance Heitmeyer, Bruce Labaw, and Daniel Kiskis, "Consistency Checking of SCR Style Requirements Specifications," In *Proceedings, International Symposium on Requirements Engineering,* York, England, March 26–27, 1995.

4. Heitmeyer, Constance L., Ralph D. Jeffords, and Bruce G. Labaw, "Automated Consistency Checking of Requirements Specifications," *ACM Trans. on Software Eng. and Methodology 5,* 3, July 1996, pp. 231–261.

5. Heitmeyer, C., J. Kirby, B. Labaw, and R. Bharadwaj, "SCR*: A Toolset for Specifying and Analyzing Software Requirements," *Proc. Computer-Aided Verification, 10th Ann. Conf. (CAV'98),* Vancouver, Canada, 1998.

6. Xu, Jai, and D. L. Parnas, "Scheduling Processes with Release Times, Deadlines, Precedence, and Exclusion Relations," *IEEE TSE, v. 16,* no. 3, March 1990, pp. 360–369.

7. Xu, Jai, and D.L. Parnas, "On Satisfying Timing Constraints in Hard-Real-Time Systems," *IEEE TSE, v. 19,* no. 1, January 1993, pp. 70–84.

8. Xu, Jai, and D.L. Parnas, "Multiprocessor Scheduling of Processes with Release Times, Deadlines, Precedence, and Exclusion Relations," *IEEE TSE, v. 19,* no. 2, February 1993, pp. 139–154.

On Synchronization in Hard-Real-Time Systems

Stuart R. Faulk and David L. Parnas

22.1 Abstract

The design of software for hard-real-time systems is usually difficult to change because of the constraints imposed by the need to meet absolute real-time deadlines on processors with limited capacity. Nevertheless, a new approach involving a trio of ideas appears to be helpful for those who build software for such complex applications.

22.2 Introduction

We use the term *hard real time* (HRT) to describe systems that must supply information within specified real-time limits. If information is supplied too early or too late, it is not useful. For systems that are not HRT, information that is delivered earlier than required is acceptable, and information that comes a little later than required is still usable. Many safety-critical systems are HRT systems. The class includes such applications as production control, robotics, flight control, traffic control, and embedded tactical systems for military applications.

Our work on synchronization in HRT systems has been performed as part of an ongoing experiment in software engineering at the Naval Research Laboratory called the Software Cost Reduction (SCR) Project. The purpose of the project has been to develop a disciplined approach to system development with an emphasis on producing software that is easy to understand and change. We have applied software engineering techniques such as formal specifications, information hiding modules, abstract interface specification, and cooperating sequential processes to the redevelopment of an existing HRT system, that is, the operational flight program for the Navy's A-7E aircraft. By redesigning an existing system, we are assured the approach addresses the concerns of a real application and has a standard against which the development products can be compared. The goal is both to demonstrate feasibility of the techniques and to provide a model of system development, including complete documentation. Previous publications have described our approach to documentation and design [10], formal specification of system requirements [15, 16], the modular structure of the system [26], and the formal specifications of module interfaces [7, 17]. In this article we discuss our approach to synchronization in an HRT system developed as a set of cooperating sequential processes. In the introductory sections, we motivate the need for a new approach to synchronization in HRT systems based on general principles such as separation of concerns. We then describe a two-level approach to synchronization and discuss constraints on choosing synchronization mechanisms appropriate to each level. Finally, a class of mechanisms for the upper level synchronization is introduced and illustrated. We then discuss an approach to process scheduling consistent with the constraints of HRT systems. Later sections justify the approach, give the results of our experience, and compare the techniques developed with other approaches.

22.3 The Need for a Separation of Concerns

A factor that often makes HRT systems difficult to understand or change is failure to separate concerns [25]. HRT systems often perform a variety of unrelated or loosely related tasks. For example, the embedded tactical system for an aircraft might be simultaneously maintaining a radar display, calculating weapon trajectories, performing navigation functions, etc. The need to share computing and data resources and perform simultaneously a variety of loosely related tasks while meeting real-time deadlines often results in code in which conceptually different functions are intertwined.

Typically in such systems, one sees that (1) the code implementing the various tasks is interleaved, making it difficult to understand; and (2) the timing dependencies are such that changing one section may affect whether many otherwise unrelated tasks meet their deadlines. This failure to separate concerns makes the software hard to understand or change.

In many situations the object code cannot be restructured to improve readability without reducing performance. System resources are scarce enough that any attempt to separate code segments along functional lines and transfer control by means of subroutine calls or gotos would incur unacceptable penalties in memory usage and processor time. Further, this would not lessen the timing dependencies between code segments or obviate the need to reconsider all the timing constraints when one of them changes.

It is unrealistic to expect such problems to vanish with further increases in processor speed or number of processors. Expectations tend to increase at least as quickly as the technology advances, and requirements for increased function tend to keep pace with engineering gains. Considerations such as size and weight also constrain the range of available hardware solutions in some classes of applications such as "smart" weapons or satellites. Finally, not all problems can be solved by increased processing power. Problems such as *deadlock* and *livelock* among processes are completely hardware independent. The policy for resource sharing among processes also affects the absolute timing characteristics of the software [20].

Even when the structure of the object code cannot be improved, the situation can be improved by taking advantage of the distinction between the source code and object code. If the source code can be organized so that a separation of concerns is achieved and if we can then transform it into object code with the structure necessary to meet time and memory constraints, then we have made a major step toward code that is easy to read, maintain, and change.

22.3.1 Using Processes to Achieve Separation of Concerns

A technique that supports the notion of a separation of concerns is designing and developing the system as a set of cooperating sequential processes [12]. A sequential process consists of operations that must be executed in a prescribed order. Most HRT systems perform a number of activities so loosely related that the order of events is not fully constrained. We view such systems as containing several processes. Each process in the system can be designed as if it had its own processor. In this way unrelated tasks can be developed independently of each other.

Although conceptually distinct concerns, such tasks are seldom completely unrelated. Information produced in one task may be used by another, and some of the tasks may share resources. Because the correctness of programs that depend on relative speeds of different processes is difficult to demonstrate and because such programs are sensitive to small changes in timing, there is a need for synchronization mechanisms to implement interprocess cooperation. In addition, the demand for processor time in an HRT system is typically high enough that processes without useful work cannot be allowed to consume processing resources. Such processes must be placed in a "wait" state in which they do not have access to a processor. Processes that detect changes in system state must be able to activate waiting processes and communicate those changes. Process synchronization schemes are used to perform these functions.

Although the literature abounds with process synchronization schemes, not all of them are equally suitable for HRT systems. Most mechanisms currently in use, such as semaphores [12], monitors [3, 18], and the "rendezvous" operators [1, 19], are based on *mutual exclusion*. There are many cases in which we wish to control the sequencing of execution in different processes, but do not require mutual exclusion. For instance, when processes monitor the system state and must broadcast changes to any number of processes, neither signaling nor waiting processes need exclude one another [27]. Where mutual exclusion is used, such processes may impede one another's progress unnecessarily. Additional timing constraints are introduced so the absolute timing characteristics of the code are harder to determine. Unnecessary use of mutual exclusion makes it more difficult to show that the software will meet real-time constraints.

Some schemes require more information to be shared by processes accessing the synchronization mechanism than others. For instance, they may require communicating processes to identify one another explicitly (e.g., [4, 19]). When information is shared, a change in one process can necessitate changes in all processes that interact with it. In contrast, schemes like Dijkstra's semaphores allow "anonymous" process synchronization; the cooperating processes are written without knowing how many other processes there will be.

22.4 A Two-Level Approach to Synchronization

Our system design is based on a "uses" hierarchy of abstract machines [23]. At the bottom of the hierarchy is the hardware machine interface. Using the operations provided by the hardware machine, we provide a virtual machine, which we call the *extended computer* [7]. By using the extended computer interface to hide machine-dependent characteristics, we intend to make upper level code more portable, abstract from machine idiosyncrasies, provide more readable code, and provide more uniform solutions to machine-dependent coding problems.

The extended computer interface is designed to include only those operations that would have a different machine-dependent implementation should the underlying computer be replaced by one of similar capabilities; these include process switching and synchronization operations. The object is to provide the minimal set from which efficient implementations of all useful operations can be constructed [24]. Minimizing the support provided minimizes the amount of machine-dependent software and the amount of software that must be rewritten to transport the system to a different machine.

Since the implementation of processes depends on such hardware considerations as the number of physical processors, the extended computer provides facilities for defining a set of cooperating sequential processes. A basic synchronization mechanism is also provided. We have found, however, that such primitive mechanisms are not convenient at higher levels where synchronization requirements tend to be complicated functions of system state. We have taken a two-track approach to synchronization; convenient synchronization operations of the upper level are implemented using the basic mechanisms provided by the extended computer.

22.5 Considerations at the Lower Level

One consideration at the extended machine level is the time and space efficiency of the operation provided. Another consideration is the amount of time the hardware must operate with interrupts masked out. The extended computer hides the distinction between hardware interrupts and software-generated events. That is, the mechanism provided by the extended computer to signal the occurrence of hardware-generated events such as I/O and device interrupts is also the mechanism used to signal software-generated events such as changes in system values detected by polling device inputs. Uniform handling of events allows the limitations of the interrupt system of a particular hardware architecture to be hidden from the portable portion of the software.

As a consequence, the software can be adapted easily if hardware replacements introduce interrupts for events that previously required software detection. For example, the design abstracts from the number of timers available in the hardware. The extended computer interface provides as many "timers" and "timer interrupts" as needed by the application software. At least one hardware timing mechanism is necessary to implement such timers, but the implementation can take advantage of additional hardware timers if they become available.

The synchronization mechanisms provided by the extended computer interface are used to implement the response to hardware interrupts and other events occurring in real time. Accordingly, the synchronization routines must have execution times that are short relative to the required response times so responses are not delayed or events missed. Further, the extended computer operations are used often in the code and occur frequently during execution so they must be memory- as well as time-efficient. For these reasons, the low-level mechanism must be simple.

The synchronization operations provided by the extended computer must be used to implement higher-level synchronization mechanisms. The operations selected must allow efficient implementation of more complex synchronization mechanisms.

22.6 The Lower-Level Synchronization Primitives

Our lower level synchronization operators are based on synchronization primitives proposed by Belpaire and Wilmotte [2]. Belpaire and Wilmotte propose three primitive synchronization operations, called *d-operations*, on an integer variable *semaphore*.

The *semaphore passage* operation allows a process to suspend execution. If a process attempts to execute a semaphore passage operation and the value of the semaphore is less than 0, the operation is not completed, and execution of the process is suspended until the semaphore becomes nonnegative. Unlike Dijkstra's P operation, this operation does not affect the value of the semaphore. If the value of the semaphore is 0 or greater, the semaphore passage has no effect on the program state. We use the notation pass(s) for semaphore passage on integer semaphore s.

The *semaphore closing* operation, down(s), decrements the value of the semaphore. Execution of the closing operation is always possible; its effect is to decrease the value of the semaphore by 1. Unlike Dijkstra's P operation, this operation cannot suspend the process that executes it.

The *semaphore opening* operation, up(s), increments the value of the semaphore. This is identical to Dijkstra's V operation. Execution of the opening operation is always possible; its effect is to increase the value of the semaphore by 1. While the semaphore value remains nonnegative, all processes waiting for that event can proceed.

22.6.1 Regions Versus Indivisibility

In the approach used by Belpaire and Wilmotte, d-operations can be combined to form more complex operators. Since allowing more than one process to execute a combined operation at the same time can produce unpredictable results, the combined operations are made indivisible; that is, no other action can occur while the operation is executing. If a combined operation includes semaphore passage operations, none of its parts can be executed until all are executable. For instance, the combination of a semaphore passage and semaphore closing into the single operation (written pass(s):down(s)) provides the same synchronization effect as Dijkstra's P operation (although the value of the semaphore differs) [2].

We found Belpaire and Wilmotte's use of indivisibility to be unsuitable for HRT systems. Lengthy indivisible operations can exclude operations needed to handle interrupts or other real-time events. Unacceptable delays in responding to events might be introduced.

We make use of a weaker mechanism, a facility for describing exclusion relations among code segments based on Belpaire and Wilmotte's "language of critical sections" [2]. One can designate sections of programs as *regions*. The relation *excludes* may then be defined on the set of regions. If region A excludes region B, no process will be allowed to enter region B while a process is executing within region A. The exclusion relation concept is a valuable generalization of the better-known concept of critical regions [3] because it allows nonsymmetric exclusion relations. The asymmetry permits better solutions when one class of processes must be treated differently from another (e.g., the reader-writer problem where writers require exclusive access to a critical section, but readers need only exclude writers, not other readers) [2].

The use of regions states the constraints on concurrent execution of critical sections directly. Other systems use synchronization primitives to enforce exclusion at run time. The critical sections are implicit in the placement of the synchronization primitives. It is then difficult to determine where synchronization operations are used to enforce exclusion and where they are used for other purposes. Making the exclusion regions explicit allows more efficient implementation.

We use regions and exclusion relations to make operations on a semaphore variable mutually exclusive. For instance, a P operation can be implemented by enclosing each pass(s); down(s) sequence on semaphore s inside a region and defining the regions for each semaphore to be mutually exclusive. An example of the use of such regions is given later.

The use of regions to enforce exclusive access to combined synchronization operations is *not* equivalent to indivisibility. For example, combining two pass operations inside a region will allow a process to execute each operation sequentially with the possibility that intervening operations will occur. With indivisibility, neither can be executed until both can be. The weaker mechanism, however, is sufficient for our needs and avoids the problems presented by indivisibility.

22.7 Considerations at the Upper Level

The d-operations are not a suitable mechanism for our upper level. The d-operations and other primitive mechanisms such as Dijkstra's P/V and its variations do not preserve separation of concerns. Several semaphores would be required to implement synchronization for any but the simplest set of state transitions. In HRT applications there is a need to signal and respond to complex events occurring in real time when responsibility for detecting the event may be distributed among several processes and more than one process may respond to the event. Providing the necessary synchronization while maintaining separation of concerns among all the processes signaling and responding to events is the driving problem at the upper level. A complex set of conventions governing the meaning and use of the mechanism would be required to achieve consistent interpretations of high-level synchronization in terms of the low-level mechanism. The upper level mechanisms should allow programmers to write in terms of transitions in the system state rather than operations on a semaphore.

Information characterizing system state and state changes can be captured using a language of *conditions* and *events*. A condition is a predicate that characterizes the system state for a measurable period of time. For instance, altitude < 500 feet, (x - y) < epsilon, and device ready might be conditions. More complex conditions can be described using Boolean expressions.

Condition values often change at unpredictable times. The change in value of a condition is called an *event*. Whereas conditions persist for measurable time intervals, events occur at single points in time. Events can be described as a relation between states before and after the change. For example, x becomes 3 refers to any state change in which the value of x was other than 3 before the state change and was 3 after the change. x incremented by 1 refers to any state change in which the new value of x is exactly 1 more than the old value of x.

The event of a condition C changing value from false to true is written @T(C); and similarly, the event of the condition changing value from true to false, @F(C). Thus, @T(device_ready) denotes the event associated with the condition device_ready becoming true. That certain conditions must hold at the time the change in value occurs is denoted by a **when** clause. For instance @T(device_ready) **when** (altitude > 500 m) indicates those moments at which the condition device_ready becomes true while the condition altitude > 500 m holds. It does not denote those moments at which the altitude surpasses 500 meters when the device is ready.

Adequacy of these techniques for describing system state information, and, indeed, system functional requirements, is demonstrated by Heninger [16]. Heninger gives a complete formal specification of the A-7E software as a function of the external system state where state information is specified using conditions and events.

22.7.1 A Real-Time Event

Problems encountered in signaling and responding to system state changes can be illustrated by considering the following event from the A-7E requirements specification (ACAIRB and IMSMODE are acronyms for input data items. The value of ACAIRB indicates whether or not the aircraft is currently airborne; IMSMODE gives the setting of the inertial navigation mode switch in the cockpit):

```
@T(ACAIRB = Yes OR IMSMODE = Iner) when (CL_stage_complete and
latitude > 80°).
```

This describes an event that occurs either if (1) the aircraft takes off, or (2) if the pilot switches a cockpit switch to the Iner position at a time when the inertial platform has been coarse leveled (CL_stage_complete) and the aircraft is above 80° latitude.

Often more than one process is used to determine the occurrence of such an event, and more than one process may wait for its occurrence. As in the example, there may be little in common among the programs for determining each of the condition values beyond the event itself. For instance, the code that detects when the aircraft is airborne can be expected to be written or changed completely independently of the code for determining the current latitude. Thus, code for each legitimately belongs in a separate module.[1] In addition, timing constraints such as the relative frequency with which differ-

---

1. The system software is decomposed into modules. The state of a module is accessible only through programs defined on the module interface. Two programs belong to the same module only if they are not likely to change independently.

ent values change require processes with different deadlines or periods of execution.

22.7.2 Desirable Characteristics of the Upper-Level Mechanisms

For a synchronization device to be appropriate for the upper level, it obviously must provide sufficient capability to implement all the necessary synchronization. In addition, it should have the following characteristics:

1. *Provide a useful abstraction.* Our driving concern is the need to signal and respond to changes in the system state. The upper-level mechanism should allow programmers to think and write in terms of the system state as it relates to the module they are developing, rather than in terms of process states or semaphores. Programs will be easier to understand and show correct; mapping to system requirements will also be simplified.

2. *Preserve separation of concerns.* We must develop a system as information hiding modules and cooperating sequential processes to preserve separation of concerns. If the characteristics of the synchronization mechanism are such that processes must share assumptions about others' state or absolute timing characteristics to use the mechanism, then it defeats the purpose. Processes that represent separate concerns should not interfere with one another or have to share assumptions about one another.

- Event-detecting processes should be able to signal events without having to wait for actions in processes that synchronize with the signals. Processes should be able to wait for state changes independently of those signaling the events. Processes should be able to check (read) the state without risking delay.

- Processes that signal events should not have to embody assumptions about how those signals are used, for instance, which or how many processes wait for an event. Programs that respond to events or use state information should not be required to embody assumptions about the processes that signal the events or about one another.

3. *Allow efficient implementation.* Since time and memory are often tight, we are concerned that the mechanism be as efficient as possible. The absolute efficiency obviously depends on implementation considerations below this level. Nevertheless, we can require of the upper level mechanism that it allow one to tailor the solution to the problem in the sense that it does not require more mechanism than is needed.

We found no single synchronization mechanism that solved all of our problems. Instead, we have identified a class of useful mechanisms and introduced a notation for describing a member of the class. Our class includes mathematically elegant devices such as (finite) semaphores, but also includes special-purpose mechanisms tailored to the ugly exigencies of real-world problems.

22.7.3 An Example System

Our example problem is a software module in an avionics system implementing a virtual radar device (see [22] for examples of device interface modules of this sort, and [6] for discussion). The problem is contrived in the sense that no actual physical device in our experience corresponds exactly to the one we describe here. No real problem in our experience illustrates all the kinds of synchronization problems one encounters and is small enough to be encompassed by the scope of this article. Nevertheless, the example is "real" in the sense that all the problems raised by the example occur in the flight program software we are writing for the Navy's A-7E aircraft.

We make the following assumptions about our example hardware device: The radar device has three modes of operation designated ranging, tracking, and standby, respectively. These modes are mutually exclusive. The characteristics of the radar inputs are such that ranging mode must be used during target acquisition and tracking mode used during air-to-air combat; either mode may be used during normal flight operation. In standby mode the radar performs only self-checking operations. Although initiated in hardware, changes in mode can be detected by the software.

Under certain operating conditions, usually temporary, data from the radar become unreliable. This condition can be detected by the software and may occur in any of the three modes. In addition, the radar hardware may fail completely. There are no useful inputs from the radar once it fails. Once a failure occurs, the radar never resumes operation. The observable states and state transitions of the radar are depicted in Figure 22.1. Our software mod-

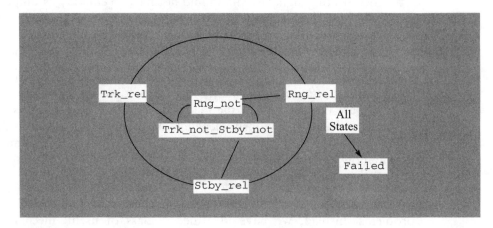

Figure 22.1 *Radar states.*

ule, called the radar set module, provides an abstract interface implementing a virtual version of our hardware radar. The module interface must provide access to input values from the radar (the details of which do not concern us), information about the current state of the radar, and signals indicating state changes. The externally visible characteristics of the state of the virtual radar are defined in Table 22.1.

Since radar inputs are useful only when the radar inputs are reliable and the mode is something other than `Stby`, the following conditions are also useful:

```
RS_down = (RS_mode = Stby or not RS_reliable or RS_failed)
  RS_up = not RS_down
```

We assume values from the radar set module are useful to a variety of tasks in our avionics system, so there are several processes that use information about the radar state. In particular, one or more processes may be required to run on the occurrence of any of the events describing externally visible changes in the radar state.

Processes outside the module wait for state changes and otherwise use the radar state; there are one or more processes inside the radar set module to keep track of the state and signal changes in it. The following three processes keep track of the radar state:

1. *Mode monitor.* This process polls the hardware register for changes to the radar mode and signals changes in its state.
2. *Reliability monitor.* This process does the calculation necessary to determine if radar inputs are reliable and signals any changes in the reliability of the inputs.
3. *Fault monitor.* This process detects and signals hardware failure of the radar.

The events signaled by these processes are shown in Table 22.2 Event signaling is supported by our high-level synchronization mechanism, state transition event (STE) synchronization.

Table 22.1 *Conditions Defining States of the Radar*

Condition	Description
`RS_mode = Track`	The radar set is in the tracking mode.
`RS_mode = Range`	The radar set is in the ranging mode.
`RS_mode = Stby`	The radar set is in the standby mode.
`RS_reliable`	The radar set input is reliable.
`RS_failed`	The radar set has failed.

Table 22.2 *Externally Visible Radar Events and the Processes That Detect Them*

Events		Signaling process
`@T(RS_mode = Track)`	`@F(RS_mode = Track)`	Mode monitor
`@T(RS_mode = Range)`	`@F(RS_mode = Range)`	Mode monitor
`@T(RS_reliable)`	`@F(RS_reliable)`	Reliability monitor
`@T(RS_down)`	`@F(RS_down)`	Fault monitor
`@T(RS_failed)`		

22.8 The STE Synchronization Mechanisms

Our higher level synchronization is provided by operations on a type of variable we call STE variables.

Each STE type is a class of equivalent finite state machines. An STE variable is one instance of the class of finite state machines where the current state of the machine is considered the value of the variable. An STE type declaration defines the set of possible states, the set of possible state transitions, and the characteristics of the operations permitted on instances of the type. The **state**, **relation**, and **set** parameters defining the characteristics of the underlying state machine and the operations of an STE type are referred to as *attributes* of the type. After a type has been defined, the implementation makes available a set of operations on instances of the type we refer to *as access programs*. Programmers may use these operations to declare and use instances of an STE type just as variables of other system types are declared and used.

22.8.1 Defining the Finite State Machine

The *state* and *relation* attributes define the states of the class of machines and the possible state transitions, respectively. We illustrate using our radar set example.

Since the radar may be reliable or unreliable in any of the three modes, all possible combinations of conditions may occur, making six states. We do not care about the mode or reliability when the radar is failed, and there is no recovery once it has failed. Thus, the radar is either failed or in one of the six states described.

The first step in defining a synchronization mechanism for the radar set is to define an STE type with one state representing each possible state of our virtual device. The STE state/condition correspondence is defined in Table 22.3.

Table 22.3 *States of the Radar*

State	Condition
Trk_rel	(RS_mode=Track AND RS_reliable AND NOT RS_failed)
Rng_rel	(RS_mode=Range AND RS_reliable AND NOT RS_failed)
Stby_rel	(RS_MODE=Stby AND RS_reliable AND NOT RS_failed)
Trk_not	(RS_MODE=Track AND NOT RS_reliable AND NOT RS_failed)
Rng_not	(RS_MODE=Range AND NOT RS_reliable AND NOT RS_failed)
Stby_not	(RS_MODE=Stby AND NOT RS_reliable AND NOT RS_failed)
Failed	(RS_failed)

The STE states for our example may then be defined as follows:[2]

```
dcl_type(radar,
  (state(Trk_rel, Rng_rel, Stby_rel, Trk_not, Rng_not, Stby_not,
  Failed))).
```

The header specifies the name of the STE type as `radar`. The *state* attribute specifies seven literal STE values corresponding to the seven system states. These are the only possible values of an STE variable of type `radar`.

22.8.2 Representing State Transitions

Transitions among system states are represented by transitions among the states of an STE variable. Possible transitions are defined by defining relations on the set of STE states. In our example the radar changes state whenever `RS_mode` or one of the conditions `RS_reliable` or `RS_failed` changes value. Each of these sets of state transitions describes a relation on the states. We define these transitions by enumerating the elements of each relation as follows:

```
(relation(reliable,
    ((Rng_not, Rng_rel), (Trk_not, Trk_rel), (Stby_not,
    Stby_rel)))),

(relation(unreliable,
    ((Rng_rel, Rng_not), (Trk_rel, Trk_not), (Stby_rel,
    Stby_not)))),
```

---

2. The "list" syntax is unattractive and not intended as a model for future programming languages. We use it here because it is the syntax we began with and that in which our system has been written.

```
(relation(track,
    ((Rng_not, Trk_not), (Rng_rel, Trk_rel), (Stby_not, Trk_not),
     (Stby_rel, Trk_rel)))),

(relation(range,
    (Trk_not, Rng_not), (Trk_rel, Rng_rel), (Stby_not, Rng_not),
     (Stby_rel, Rng_rel)))),

(relation(standby,
    (Trk_not, Stby_not), (Trk_rel, Stby_rel), (Rng_not, Stby_not),
     (Rng_rel, Stby_rel)))),

(relation(failure,
    ((Trk_rel, Failed), (Rng_rel, Failed), (Stby_rel, Failed),
     (Trk_not, Failed), (Rng_not, Failed), (Stby_not, Failed)))).
```

For each relation attribute, the identifier (e.g., reliable) gives the name of the relation. Each ordered pair (x, y) in the next list specifies a transition from state x to state y. For instance, the relation `reliable` specifies transitions from state `Trk_not` to state `Trk_rel`, `Rng_not` to `Rng_rel`, and `Stby_not` to `Stby_rel`. These represent all the possible changes in state when the event `@T(RS_reliable)` occurs. The relation `unreliable` defines the inverse.

22.8.3 The State Transition Operations

State transition operations on variables of an STE type are given by the *relation* attributes defined on the type. The name of the attribute becomes the name of the corresponding transition program, as in

```
relation(p1)
```

where *relation* is the name of the relation, and $p1$ is a variable of the type. For instance, `reliable()` is the transition access program corresponding to relation *reliable*.[3]

Let the ordered pair of states $(s1, s2)$ be an element of the relation R. Then invoking the transition operation corresponding to R with an STE variable whose current state is $s1$ causes a transition in the state of the variable from $s1$ to $s2$. If $s1$ is the first element of more than one ordered pair, the transition may be to any of the second states of the pair. It is an error if $s1$ is not a first element of any ordered pair of the relation.

---

3. We avoid program name conflicts by using the type name as a prefix. There is nothing new in this, and other techniques common in the literature would work as well, so the prefixes are omitted herein to improve readability.

Suppose RS is declared to be an STE variable of type radar. Then, if the current value of RS is Rng_not, the program invocation

```
reliable(RS)
```

changes the value of RS to Rng_rel. A subsequent invocation of the program

```
track(RS)
```

would change the value of Trk_rel. A second invocation of reliable(RS) at this point would be an error since the current state of RS (i.e., Trk_rel) is not a first element of any pair in the relation reliable.

22.8.4 State Inquiry Operations

The current value (state) of an STE variable may be read at any time or assigned to other variables of the same type. In addition, there are state inquiry operations corresponding to each *relation* and each *set* attribute specified in the type declaration as follows:

1. *Relation inquiry programs.* Corresponding to each *relation* attribute is a state inquiry operation of the form

```
is_relation(p1, p2, b)
```

where formal parameters $p1$ and $p2$ must be replaced by STE entities and b by a Boolean actual parameter. If the values of the actual parameters replacing $p1$ and $p2$ are $s1$ and $s2$, respectively, and the ordered pair $(s1, s2)$ is an element of the relation, the effect of the invocation is to set b to true; otherwise, b is set to false.

This facility allows the user to determine information about the current state of the system relative to other states. For instance, suppose we wish to assign priorities to the radar modes such that priority from highest to lowest is tracking, ranging, and standby, respectively. For simplicity, it is assumed we are only interested in the priority when the radar is reliable. Then the priority relation can be defined as

```
(relation(has_priority
   ((Trk_rel, Rng_rel), (Trk_rel, Stby_rel), (Rng_rel,
   Stby_rel))))).
```

Then, the invocation

```
is_has_priority(RS, Rng_rel, b)
```

will set b to true if the current state of RS has priority over Rng_rel (i.e., is Trk_rel), and false otherwise.

2. *Set inquiry programs.* The *set* attribute is used to define named sets of states. There are corresponding state inquiry programs that report whether the current value of a state variable is a member of the set. For instance, if we

are interested in inquiring whether the condition RS_down defined earlier holds or not, we define a set consisting of those states for which the condition RS_down holds; that is,

```
(set(down,
    (Trk_not, Rng_not, Stby_rel, Stby_not, Failed))).
```

A state inquiry operation is of the form

```
set(p1, b),
```

where *set* is the name of a set attribute, and *p*1 must be replaced by an entity of the type being defined and *b* by a Boolean actual parameter. The state inquiry program down is defined on the type radar so that the invocation

```
down(RS, b)
```

assigns *b* the value true if the current state of RS is a member of set down, and false otherwise.

22.8.5 The Synchronization Operations

We have identified the need for our synchronization mechanism to provide facilities to wait for complex changes in the system state. Where the transition and inquiry operations provide the means for recording changes in the current state and reading related values, the synchronization operations provide facilities that allow programmers to implement processes synchronized with changes in the system state. The declaration of an STE type may be used to define any of five kinds of synchronization operations on variables of the type. There are three synchronization operations corresponding to each *relation* attribute and two corresponding to each *set* attribute. These are defined in the next two sections and summarized in Table 22.4.

22.8.5.1 Synchronization on Relations

1. *Wait on transition event.* The transition event operations permit a process to wait for an event corresponding to a transition relation. For each *relation* attribute, an operator may be defined that allows a process to wait until an STE variable changes state from *s*1 to *s*2 such that the ordered pair (*s*1, *s*2) is an element of the relation. For instance, the invocation

```
await@reliable(RS)
```

would cause the executing program to suspend execution until the variable RS changes state from one indicating unreliability (Trk_not, Rng_not, or Stby_not) to another indicating reliability (any of Trk_rel, Rng_rel, or Stby_rel).

2. *Wait conditional.* The conditional await programs are used if a process should wait under some circumstances, but not in others. For each *rela-*

Table 22.4 *Summary of Synchronization Operations*

Operation	Form	Interpretation	Example
Wait on transition event	`await@`*relation*`(p1)`	Wait until STE $p1$ changes state	`await@reliable(RS)`
Wait conditional	`await.T.`*relation* `(p1, p2)` `await.F.`*relation* `(p1, p2)`	Wait if relation does not (/does) hold between $p1$ and $p2$	`await.T.has_priority` `(RS,Stby_rel)` `await.F.has_priority` `(RS,Stby_rel)`
Wait on call	`await@=`*relation*`(p1)`	Wait for program call	`await@=track(RS)`
Wait conditional on set membership	`await.T.`*set*`(p1)` `await.F.`*set*`(p1)`	Wait if STE value is not (/is) a member of the set	`await.T.down(RS)` `await.F.down(RS)`
Wait on set	`await@`*set*`(p1)`	Wait until state changes to an element of the set	`await@down(RS)`

tion attribute, two access programs may be defined, one that allows a process to wait only if the specified relation does not hold for the current state of an STE variable, and the other, if the relation currently holds. For instance, using the relation `has_priority`, the invocation

```
await.T.has_priority(RS, Stby_rel)
```

will cause the executing program to wait if the current state of `RS` is anything other than `Trk_rel` or `Rng_rel`, that is, until `RS` has a state with priority higher than `Stby_rel`. The call has no effect on the executing process if the relation holds at the time of the call (i.e., `RS` has the value `Trk_rel` or `Rng_rel`). Similarly, the invocation

```
await.F.has_priority(RS, Stby_rel)
```

will cause the executing program to wait if `Trk_rel` or `Rng_rel` is the current state, and not otherwise. Execution resumes when the state changes so that the relation holds.

3. *Wait on call.* For each relation an operator may be defined that allows a process to wait until the transition program corresponding to that relation is executed with actual parameter values equal to the parameter values specified in the program call. For instance, the invocation

```
await@=track(RS)
```

will cause the invoking program to wait until another program executes the transition operation `track(RS)`. This type of synchronization is useful where we want to distinguish between a transition caused by one particular transition program and the same transition caused by other operators.

22.8.5.2 Set Synchronization Programs

4. *Wait conditional on membership.* Like the "wait on condition" operators for relations, these programs may be used to choose between stopping and not stopping an executing process depending on the value of a condition. For each *set* attribute, two synchronization operators may be defined. These operators allow programs to wait for transitions to or from a set of states. The T (true) form causes the executing process to wait if and only if the state of *p*1 is not a member of *set* at the time the operation is executed. For instance, operations can be defined on the set down to allow processes to wait until the condition RS_down holds or, if the condition already holds, to continue execution. The invocation

```
await.T.down(RS)
```

will cause the executing program to wait until the radar is down (i.e., it will wait if and only if the value is Trk_rel or Rng_rel). A process suspended in execution of the operation will continue when the value of RS becomes a member of down. If the value of RS is already a member of down, the call has no effect, and the executing program continues. The program

```
await.F.down(RS)
```

waits for the converse condition to hold or has no effect if it already holds.

5. *Wait on set.* For each set attribute, an operator may be defined to wait (unconditionally) until an STE variable changes value from a state outside the designated set to one inside the set.[4] For instance, executing the operator

```
await@down(RS)
```

causes the executing process to be suspended until there is a transition from a state outside the set down to a state that is a member of the set. If the current state is a member of the set, the waiting process will pause until both a transition outside the set and a transition back into the set have occurred.

22.8.6 Combined Operations

For each synchronization operator that can be defined on an STE type, there is a corresponding combined operation that serves for both synchronization and state inquiry. The combined operation is formed by writing .g.*relation*, where *relation* appears in the synchronization declaration (the .g. stands for *get*). An additional output parameter of the STE type must be provided at the end of the parameter list. For instance, assume RS2 is declared to be of type

---

4. The "wait on set" operations are redundant in the sense that equivalent programs can be provided using the relation attribute. The relation definitions rapidly become unwieldy, however, as the cardinality of the set increases.

`radar`. Given the relations and sets of our previous examples, the following sorts of combined operators can be defined:

```
await@.g.reliable(RS, RS2)
await@=.g.track(RS, RS2)
await@.g.down(RS, RS2)
await.T.g.down(RS, RS2)
```

The effect of executing a combined operation is that of executing the corresponding synchronization operation with the output parameter assigned the value of the STE at the time the operation is allowed to complete. That is, if the process is suspended in the `await` operation and a transition from state *s*1 to *s*2 allows it to proceed, the value of RS2 becomes *s*2. These forms of the `await` operation are provided because we found that we often needed to write programs that performed different actions depending on the state change that initiated the program. By providing the combined operation, we can write programs of this sort without worrying about cases where the state can change between the time the program is enabled to run and the time it executes.

22.8.7 Interprocess Synchronization with STEs

To describe the need for an upper level mechanism, we identified a set of characteristics that the mechanism should have. In the following, we discuss how the STE mechanism meets those goals:

1. *Provide an appropriate abstraction.* Each STE type is a direct model of the problem it is intended to solve. Users are not concerned with the way the primitive synchronization mechanism is used, only with the characteristics of their problem.

2. *Permit separation of concerns.* Processes do not signal other processes; they access operations on a commonly defined STE type. Waiting processes do not wait for signals from specific processes; they wait for certain state changes in an STE variable. The processes that cause the state changes need not wait for the other processes to react. In this way interaction between processes that signal changes and those that wait for them can be minimized.

Knowledge of a common STE type definition is all that is required to write programs that signal state changes or wait for them using STEs. There are no shared data among processes accessing an STE variable except those accessible through the interface programs defined on the type. All state information is contained within the state of the STE variable. A programmer need not have knowledge of which or how many other processes use the interface to signal events.

3. *Efficiency.* The design of the STE mechanism allows efficient implementation because the implementation need only provide the access programs that are actually used for a given type. The STE implementation need not provide unnecessary operations, and the representative can be fine-tuned to achieve the required efficiency. Obviously, the complexity of the implementation will differ from type to type depending on the underlying state machine and the operations provided. Nevertheless, improvements in the implementation of an STE variable type will not affect programs that use the operations on variables of that type.

22.9 Implementation in Terms of the Lower-Level Mechanism

In considering the implementation of STE types, two distinct concerns are identifiable: The first relates to the representation of the STE state machine and those parts of the access program implementations that depend on that representation. The second relates to synchronization required to allow different processes to perform concurrent operations on the same STE variable. A general treatment of the representation of state machines is outside the scope of this article. The second concern, how the synchronization of the upper-level mechanism is realized using the lower level operations, is relevant to our concerns.

Although there are a number of different kinds of `await` operations, there are only two different classes of underlying synchronization: One class consists of the "conditional `await`" programs that suspend the executing process only if a certain condition holds. This includes all programs of the form `await.T` and `await.F`. The other class consists of the "unconditional `await`" programs that always result in the suspension of the executing process. These include all access programs of the form `await@`. Each class requires a different solution in terms of our lower level mechanisms, but within a class, the implementation is the same across types.

The general implementation of the class of conditional `await`s is shown in Table 22.5 Since the values of different STE variables change independently and since, in general, two different `await` access programs provided for an STE type will not have the same synchronization effect in relation to the state of the STE variable, one semaphore is generally required for each type of `await` operation on each STE variable. There are only two possible states of the condition so the `await` can be implemented with a binary semaphore. The initial value of the semaphore should be −1 if the condition corresponding to the `await` does not hold (processes should wait), and 0 otherwise. If the value of the STE is changed so that the condition holds and all processes executing the conditional `await` operation should proceed, then the d-operation `up(s)` is executed on the corresponding semaphore. Conversely, if the state changes so that the condition does not hold, a down(s) must be executed. The synchronization part of this class of await operations is implemented simply as a pass(s). If the semaphore is negative at the time the pass(s) is executed, a process waits until an up(s) operation is executed. If the semaphore is nonnegative, the pass(s) has no effect. Thus, a process waits only if the condition does not hold, and then only until it holds, as required by our definition of the conditional await operations.

Implementation of the unconditional await operations is slightly more complex. By definition, all processes executing a pass operation are suspended inside the pass if the value of the semaphore is negative, and will proceed when its value becomes nonnegative. Thus, we can cause all the processes waiting on semaphore *s* to proceed by executing the (divisible) sequence of operations up(s); down(s). The remaining problem is that nothing will prevent a process from executing a pass(s) between the time the semaphore is raised and the time it is again lowered. Since we do not have general indivisibility for our d-operations, regions must be used to prevent concurrent execution of these operations. This is done by declaring a region R1 around each up(s); down(s) pair implementing the release of an unconditional await operation corresponding to semaphore *s*. Each instance of the await operation is then translated as a pass(s) inside of a region R2, and an exclusion relation is defined to include the ordered pair (R1, R2). The interpretation is that region R1 excludes R2; it does not imply that R2 excludes R1. The example in Table 22.5 shows such a definition with regions await and signal defined for the corresponding implementations. Now, if a process is executing inside of region signal (the up(s); down(s) sequence), no process can begin executing await (the pass(s)). Conceptually, a process that attempts to execute the pass(s) while the semaphore is being manipulated will be stopped outside the enclosing region. Thus, a process executing an unconditional await will be suspended until the corresponding event is signaled, and only those processes that are waiting at the time the signal is initiated will be allowed to proceed, as required by the definition of unconditional awaits.

Doubtless, primitive mechanisms other than ours could also implement the necessary synchronization. Nevertheless, the simplicity of this solution exploits both the ability to separate semaphore passage from semaphore closing and the ability to define asymmetric exclusion relations. Further, in our solution one can add or remove processes from the system without concern about other processes using the synchronization mechanisms.

Table 22.5 *Implementation of* `signal` *and* `await`

Conditional `signal` *and* `await`		
Await	**Condition** `true`	**Condition** `false`
`pass(s)`	`up(s)`	`down(s)`
Unconditional `signal` *and* `await`		
Translation of `await`		**Translation of** `signal`

```
await region                          signal region
    pass(s)                               up(s)
    end_region(await)                     down(s)
                                          end_region(signal)
                excludes((signal,await))
```

22.10 The Pre-Run-Time Scheduler

Although programs are developed as if each process had its own processor, typically there will be fewer processors than processes. Where there are fewer processors than processes, parallel processing must be simulated by allocating processor time among the system processes. Since the system must respond to events within real-time deadlines, ongoing processes cannot simply be allowed to run to completion. We must be able to interrupt (preempt) and restart processes as necessary.

Most previous systems modeled on the process concept (e.g., [13, 28]) have not been required to schedule programs to meet HRT deadlines. Although priority schedulers are often adequate without real-time deadlines, more sophisticated scheduling schemes are needed for deadline scheduling [21]. Further, most implementations of processes do scheduling at run time. This consumes run-time resources and, more important, makes it difficult to guarantee in advance that real-time deadlines will be met. Consequently, the scheduling approach used in previous systems is often unacceptable for an HRT system.

Earlier systems designed as a set of processes have chosen a representation of processes that was easily identified in the data structures at run time. Usually there is a data structure containing a process image; processes can be suspended only if the current values of any volatile data (e.g., values in registers) are saved. The operations associated with saving the image of a preempted process and loading the image of a preempting process are known as *context switching*. Where the number of processes in a system is large or transfers of control between processes frequent, the system memory needed to save images and the processor time required for context switching can be substantial.

One of the advantages of the use of regions and exclusion relations rather than semaphores is that the cost of both run-time scheduling and run-time context switching can be reduced by providing a pre-run-time scheduler. The code for each process is decomposed into sections (scheduling blocks) that must be run to completion. The pre-run-time scheduler is given the set of scheduling blocks along with sequencing and timing constraints. The scheduling program uses the information on sequencing and timing constraints to interleave the scheduling blocks so that the interleaved code satisfies the constraints of the component processes. The output is object code in which the schedule is embedded in the code organization. In most cases, exclusion constraints can be satisfied by not interleaving code where an exclusion relation exists; there need be no run-time synchronization mechanism to implement such exclusion. The division into scheduling blocks can be done to minimize the amount of context switching, and one can take advantage of knowledge of the code to optimize any required context-switching code.

In many HRT applications, the bulk of the computation can be confined to processes that are executed periodically. Periodic processes can be written without the use of semaphores, and a schedule for the least-common multiple of the periods can be produced in advance.

Because the system must respond to external events, the schedule cannot be completely determined ahead of time. A small run-time scheduler must be provided to allocate processor time among the processes that run in response to external events. In our application the amount of computation required for these processes is small, and "worst-case" scheduling is feasible. By making scheduling decisions before run time, the amount of run-time scheduling is reduced. Usually, run-time scheduling decisions can be reduced to a small set of alternative schedules allowing run-time scheduling to be performed by table lookup. Algorithms for developing schedulers of this sort are discussed in detail in [21]. Although the problem of finding optimal schedules quickly becomes NP-hard except under a limited set of combinations of constraints, optimal schedules are only required when no suboptimum schedule meets the constraints. Ad hoc methods have been used successfully, and routines exist for searching for less-than-optimal schedules.

When programs are written as cooperating sequential processes, timing information need not be embodied in the programs that describe the sequence of events. Instead, one can provide a description of which processes are periodic and which sporadic, along with timing parameters for each of the processes. A periodic process is activated at regular intervals, whereas a sporadic process is activated only on demand. This timing information is used by the scheduler. The effects of changes in timing or timing constraints

can be restricted to changes in the parameters or modification of the algorithm used by the scheduler.

22.11 Why Another Synchronization Mechanism?

Since the appearance of Dijkstra's pioneering synchronization work in the
mid-1960s, there have been dozens of proposed variations on it. In addition
to systems based on communication by shared variables, there have been
many proposals to avoid shared variables by the use of message passing.
There are also many proposals for language concepts that are designed to
allow packages of programs to have exclusive access to shared data. A
proper survey and discussion of the mechanisms that have been considered
would require an article far longer than the present one.

One of the basic reasons behind our decision to add one more animal to
the synchronization zoo was our belief that efficient real-time systems
depend ultimately on the availability of shared variables. Even message-
passing systems must be implemented using shared variables (hard wires can
be considered a form of shared variable). The problems of shared variables
are not avoided by such schemes, but only pushed back a level at the cost of
introducing additional mechanisms and possibly additional synchronization
constraints. This is not to say message-passing mechanisms are not useful.
Rather, the added resource costs and delays associated with message processing make them an inappropriate substitute for the sorts of shared-variable
mechanisms discussed here.

We also felt all of the proposals were attempting to do too much with
one mechanism. The required generality must be achieved by very simple, but
unrestricted, mechanisms such as d-operations. Such mechanisms, however,
are not very convenient for higher level applications. In fact, none of the
many types of synchronization variables is suitable for all the problems that
we encountered. It was the recognition of the fact that we needed more than
one type of synchronization variable that led us to define the STE class of
variables and the notation for defining individual types within that class.

The decision to use the exclusion regions as a mechanism rather than as a
problem specification notation was motivated by our desire to be able to do
synchronization by means of pre-run-time scheduling. Without that ability it
is difficult to produce trustworthy real-time systems. No other mechanism
directly met that need.

22.12 Experience and Results

The approach described has been applied in our redevelopment of the operational flight program (OFP) for the Navy's A-7E aircraft. The program is typ-

ical of a class of HRT systems: It (1) performs a variety of tasks including navigation, maintenance of pilot displays, control of and communication with a variety of special-purpose hardware, weapons delivery, and so on; (2) must meet HRT deadlines; and (3) executes under tight time and memory constraints. The target computer is an IBM TC-2 4Pi with 16K memory of 16-bit words and a minimum cycle time of 2.5 μs.

The system design has been completed by the SCR research staff. The product of the design phase is a guide to the modular decomposition of the system [5] and a set of abstract formal specifications of the module interfaces [7, 8, 9, 11, 22]. A useful subset consisting of about half of the complete system functions has been implemented in a high-level pseudocode [14]. Approximately 80 percent of the coding has been done by contractor personnel working directly from the formal module specifications. Those working as coders had no previous experience in concurrent programming. About half of the useful subset has been translated into TC-2 assembly code. To avoid consuming precious project resources developing translators, the translation process is only partially automated. The part of the code that has been translated into TC-2 assembly code is currently undergoing testing.

The system above the level of the extended computer has been written entirely as processes. The subset under test includes some 75 periodic and 172 (usually small) demand (asynchronous) processes. All the synchronization except those events signaled by the extended computer is implemented using STEs. Most demand processes wait on state change events signaled using STEs. There are some 21 different type classes of STEs defined, about two-thirds of which are dedicated to specific devices as in our example. The remaining third are "generic." The synchronization required in the remainder of the system does not differ in kind from that required for the implemented subset.

The biggest problem encountered by coders using STEs was an initial difficulty in understanding how to translate a specification written using conditions and events into an STE type specification. Once coders became experienced in translating the set of possible states implied by the conditions into the states of a finite state machine and, hence, more or less directly into the states of an STE, they reportedly found the mechanism easy to use. The STE in turn is translated by hand into lower level code. Translation of those parts of the STEs that vary from one STE type to the next (e.g., the state representation and the implementation of the access programs) is done on a case-by-case basis. Common macros written in terms of the d-operations are used to implement the synchronization required. Translation of the d-operations into TC-2 code is automated.

The automated pre-run-time scheduler remains an unsolved problem. For testing purposes we have devised a small real-time scheduler that is specifically designed to allow us to add and remove processes easily from the set of processes being tested. A fundamental difference between the scheduler used and that proposed is that the pre-run-time scheduling is done by hand and embedded in a table rather than automated by the scheduler and embedded in the code. Nevertheless, the essential features of the target code remain. Code from different processes is interleaved in time following a schedule determined before run time and may be interleaved physically in the load module. Exclusion among regions is implemented by interleaving code so there is no additional run-time cost. The lower-level synchronization is implemented by the scheduler, which makes run/no-run decisions based on semaphore values at run time. The implementation of regions by interleaving code applies to the lower level synchronization operations, including those implementing STEs, so indivisibility is not required. Enough of the code has been tested to establish that these mechanisms perform as expected. This is sufficient to establish feasibility of the approach, but is not enough for the implementation of real systems. Automation of the pre-run-time scheduler remains to make the approach complete.

22.13 Summary

The STE mechanism allows processes to share information about the system state and changes in the system state without sharing information about each other. Different processes can wait for the same event, wait for different events in the same STE variable, cause state transitions in a variable, or use the state inquiry programs for an STE variable without needing to know which other processes are using the same interface. The only shared assumptions are those about the meaning of the states.

   With Dijkstra's P/V, and similar mechanisms, communicating processes interfere with each other. For example, if one process is waiting for an event, a second process waiting for the event can cause the delay of the first. If a semaphore is used to synchronize several processes that are waiting for an event, the implementation of signaling processes must embody assumptions about how many processes will wait. A process cannot delay another without the possibility that it, too, will be delayed. With STEs, all necessary information is encoded in the logic of the finite state machine, and programs are concerned with the state of a variable, not with the states of other processes. Processes using STE operations are only delayed for the time it takes to update one STE variable.

   The STE mechanism provides the facilities needed to handle events occurring in real time. There are necessarily implementation-dependent delays between the time an event occurs and the time responding processes are awakened. Representing events as transitions in a state machine allows us to overcome the transient nature of real-time events by preserving their occurrence in the state of an STE variable. For instance, processes can use synchronization mechanisms like "wait on condition" to respond to events that occur while they are busy, and the "get" forms of the `await` programs to preserve volatile state information until the process can act on it. Conversely, in the case where an action is no longer needed because of interim change, the current state can be determined from the state of the STE.

In addition to its other advantages, the STE mechanism permits a more efficient implementation of our programs than other synchronization mechanisms. The ability to reserve information using a state machine makes it unnecessary for processes that respond to events to reevaluate conditions to determine which event has occurred or what the current state is. This need be done only by the processes that detect events. Since operations on an STE need be provided only if requested for the type, resources need not be expended for facilities not needed.

The design and implementation of our two-level synchronization mechanism propose some new solutions to the synchronization problem and employ some old solutions in novel ways. In summary, these are (1) the use of Belpaire and Wilmotte's d-operations as synchronization primitives; (2) the use of Belpaire and Wilmotte's critical regions as a synchronization mechanism; (3) the use of exclusion relations in the source code, so exclusion need not be implemented explicitly using synchronization operations, and our more complex synchronization operators can be built without requiring indivisibility; (4) the use of the pre-run-time scheduler in implementing exclusion relations; (5) a clear separation of concerns through the separation of the hardware-dependent implementation of semaphore operations from the machine-independent implementation of higher-level mechanisms such as monitors; and (6) the STE synchronization mechanism.

Problems that remain to be solved include automatic translation of STE specifications and the design and automation of the pre-run-time scheduler. For the scheduler, basic questions remain open, such as what are the dependencies between the scheduling algorithms used and the characteristics of the underlying machine architecture. Such questions must be answered before basic issues such as correctness with respect to timing constraints and portability can be resolved.

References

1. Ada Joint Program Office. Ada programming language. ANSI/MILSTD-1815A, U.S. Dept. of Defense, Washington, DC, January 1983.

2. Belpaire, G., and Wilmotte, J.P., A semantic approach to the theory of parallel processes. In *Proceedings of the 1973 European ACM Symposium* (Davos, Switzerland). ACM, New York, 1973, pp. 159–164.

3. Brinch Hansen, P., *Operating Systems Principles.* Prentice-Hall, Englewood Cliffs, NJ, 1973.

4. ———, Distributed processes: A concurrent programming concept. *Commun. ACM 21,* 8 (November 1978), 934–941.

5. Britton (nee Heninger), K., and Parnas, D., A-7E software module guide. Memo. Rep. 4702, Naval Research Laboratory, Washington, DC, December 1981.

6. Britton (nee Heninger), K., Parker, A., and Parnas, D., A procedure for designing abstract interfaces for device interface modules. In *Proceedings of the 5th International Conference on Software Engineering* (San Diego, Calif., March 9–12). ACM, New York, 1981, pp. 195–204.

7. Britton (nee Heninger), K., Clements, P., Parnas, D., and Weiss, D. Interface specifications for the A-7E (SCR) extended computer module. Memo. Rep. 4843, Naval Research Laboratory, Washington, DC, January 6, 1983. (Updated version available as Memo. Rep. 5502, Naval Research Laboratory, Washington, DC, December 31, 1984.)

8. Clements, P., Interface specifications for the SCR (A-7E) function driver module. Memo. Rep. 4659, Naval Research Laboratory, Washington, DC, November 27, 1981.

9. ———, Interface specifications for the SCR (A-7E) shared services module. Memo. Rep. 4863, Naval Research Laboratory, Washington, DC, September 8, 1982.

10. Clements, P., and Parnas, D., A rational design process: How and why to fake it. *IEEE Trans. Softw. Eng. SE-12.* (February 1986), 251–257.

11. Clements, P., Faulk, S., and Parnas, D., Interface specifications for the SCR (A-7E) application data types module. Memo. Rep. 8734, Naval Research Laboratory, Washington, DC, August 23, 1983.

12. Dijkstra, E.W., Cooperating sequential processes. In *Programming Languages*, F. Genuys, Ed. Academic Press, New York, 1968, pp. 43–112.

13. Dijkstra, E.W., The structure of the 'THE"-multiprogramming system, *Commun. ACM 11*, 5 (May 1968), 341–346.

14. Faulk, S., Pseudo-code language for the SCR (A-7E) operational flight program. Tech. Memo. 7590–261:SF, Naval Research Laboratory, Washington, D.C., Nov. 1980.

15. Heninger, K., Specifying software requirements for complex systems: New techniques and their application. *IEEE Trans. Softw. Eng. SE-6*, 1 (January 1980), 2–13.

16. Heninger, K., Kallander, J., Parnas, D., and Shore, J., Software requirements for the A-7E aircraft. Memo. Rep. 3876, Naval Research Laboratory, Washington, DC, November 27, 1978.

17. Hester, S.D., Parnas, D.L., and Utter, D.F., Using documentation as a software design medium. *Bell Syst. Tech. J. 60*, 8 (October 1981), 1941–1977.

18. Hoare, C.A.R., Monitors: An operating system structuring concept. *Commun. ACM 17*, 10 (October 1974), 549–557.

19. ———, Communicating sequential processes. *Commun. ACM 21*, 8 (August 1978), 666–677.

20. Mok, A.K., The design of real-time programming systems based on process models. In *Proceedings of the IEEE Real-Time Systems Symposium* (Austin, TX, December 4–6). IEEE Press, New York, 1984, pp. 5–17.

21. Mok, A.K., and Dertouzos, M.L., Multiprocessor scheduling in a hard real-time environment. *In Proceedings of the 7th IEEE Texas Conference on Computing Systems* (Houston, TX, October 30–November 1). IEEE Press. New York, 1978, pp. 5.1–5.12.

22. Parker, A., Britton, K.H., Parnas, D.L., and Shore, J., Abstract interface specification for the A-7E device interface module. Memo. Rep. 4385, Naval Research Laboratory, Washington, DC, November 1980.

23. Parnas, D.L., On a "Buzzword"; Hierarchical structure. In *Proceedings of the IFIP Congress*. North-Holland, Amsterdam, 1974.

24. ———, On the design and development of program families. *IEEE Trans. Softw. Eng. SE-2*, 1 (March 1976), 1–9.

25. ———, A new approach to the structuring of avionics software. Tech. Memo. 5403–107, Naval Research Laboratory, Washington, D.C., March 29, 1977.

26. Parnas, D.L., Clements, P., and Weiss, D., The modular structure of complex systems. *IEEE Trns. Softw. Eng. SE-11*, 3 (March 1985), 259–266.

27. Reed, D.P. and Kanodia, R.K., Synchronization with eventcounts and sequencers. *Commun. ACM 22*, 2 (February 1979), 115–123.

28. Ritchie, D.M., and Thompson, K., The UNIX time-sharing system. *Commun. ACM 17*, 7 (July 1974), 365–375.

Acknowledgments

We are indebted to Paul Clements and Grady Campbell who contributed greatly to the design and development of the STE interface. We are grateful to Paul Clements, Kevin Jeffay, Bruce Labaw, Michael Levy, John McLean, Eugene Margulis, Alan Shaw, John Shore, and David Weiss for the many helpful comments on earlier drafts.

Introduction

Aloysius Mok

I became aware of Dave's interest in real-time scheduling problems as early as 1979 when I was working on my doctoral dissertation at MIT. Dave invited me to visit the Naval Research Laboratory (NRL) in Washington D.C. to help formulate the problem of constructing the cyclic executive for the A-7E aircraft. At the time, he and a team at NRL working on the Software Cost Reduction (SCR) project were focusing on the problem of capturing the functional and performance requirements of the A-7E by means of various types of tables, a task that is far more daunting than would first appear to the lay person. Eventually, they produced an inch-thick document that, for the first time, in a semiformal way, recorded what the A-7E avionics was supposed to do. Even before the requirements capture was completed, however, Dave was already looking toward the future. The problem was not just to capture the A-7E requirements in a rigorous fashion but also to use the requirements actually to reimplement the avionics software for the A-7E in a disciplined way. As people who make Dave's acquaintance ought to know, he is a hard-driving leader who rides herd on his team as if his life depends on it. Well, this is close enough to the truth in the case of the A-7E project since Dave had volunteered to ride in the backseat of the A-7E that was to fly with the to-be-reimplemented avionics software from the SCR requirements specification. As far as I know, Dave has never gone to parachute school.

To translate the SCR table-based requirements into a software implementation, a key step is to set up a task model for CPU scheduling considerations. The A-7E requirements specification, which describes only the required behavior, does not lend itself directly to this purpose. This is as it should be since the requirements specification should not completely determine how the functions are to be partitioned and implemented by software entities. This means that the real-time task scheduling problem was underdefined, but even back then Dave had some ideas about what the task model should look like. After he moved to a Canadian University, he went on to work with Professor Jia Xu of York University on the definition of the task model and the associated real-time scheduling problem. One result of this collaboration is the paper "Scheduling Processes with Release Times, Deadlines, Precedence, and Exclusion Relations."

The problem considered in the Xu-Parnas paper is to compute a "cyclic executive" that satisfies the performance requirements of a set of periodic processes. This is a standard problem in the implementation of avionics software. A single CPU is to be time-shared by a set of processes, each of which must be executed repeatedly at its own specified frequency. For scheduling purposes, each process can be regarded as the composition of a chain of "segments" (blocks of computer instructions). The CPU timesharing problem is complicated by certain precedence relations (some segments must execute before others) and mutual exclusion relations (some segments must not be preempted by others) in addition to meeting the individual deadlines of the periodic processes. The Xu-Parnas paper discusses an algorithm for sequencing the segments from all the processes in a finite schedule that can then be repeated ad infinitum by the CPU scheduler to perform the required avionics functions in real time.

As I have shown in my own work, the cyclic executive construction problem is an NP-hard problem which means that in general some kind of search strategy is needed to determine a solution. A key idea in the Xu-Parnas paper is to make use of the precedence and mutual exclusion relations to compute a lower bound on the lateness of a segment in the exploration of the search tree. This strategy results in a reduction in search time. Since the Xu-Parnas paper, there have been a number of papers by other authors who adopt the search paradigm in the Xu-Parnas paper and use other search-tree pruning techniques. More sophisticated task models have also been adopted to deal with other timing requirements. The Xu-Parnas paper is still being cited today in the literature in connection with cyclic executive construction.

I think Dave's key contribution in the real-time scheduling area is not so much the solution technique, which primarily is his coauthor Professor Jia Xu's expertise, but rather his recognition that a formal approach with highly automated techniques is crucial in the design of safety-critical real-time systems. Indeed, the motivation of the A-7E project was that the maintenance of the A-7E software had been labor-intensive and error-prone, in no small measure caused by the fact that the software program was basically a 16K-word cyclic executive written in assembly language. As a wet-behind-the-ears graduate student researcher, I was much enlightened by Dave's recognition of the larger problem in software maintenance, and I continue to work on the complete automation of the resource scheduler synthesis problem. Indeed, Dave's foresight remains relevant to today's problems; a recent example is the automation of the cyclic executive construction for the Air Information Management System of the Boeing 777 aircraft [1]. As embedded systems become more and more commonplace and affect the public's safety, Dave's foresight can only become more important.

Reference

1. A.K. Mok, D.C. Tsou, and R.C.M. de Rooij, "The MSP.RTL Real-Time Scheduler Synthesis Tool," in *Proceedings of 17th IEEE Real-Time Systems Symposium*, Washington, DC, December 4–6, 1996, pp. 118–128.

Scheduling Processes with Release Times, Deadlines, Precedence, and Exclusion Relations

Jia Xu and David Lorge Parnas

23.1 Abstract

We present an algorithm that finds an optimal schedule on a single processor for a given set of processes such that each process starts executing after its release time and completes its computation before its deadline, and a given set of precedence relations and a given set of exclusion relations defined on ordered pairs of process segments are satisfied. This algorithm can be applied to the important and previously unsolved problem of automated pre-run-time scheduling of processes with arbitrary precedence and exclusion relations in hard-real-time systems.

23.2 Introduction

We present an algorithm for solving the following problem: We are given a set of processes, where each process consists of a sequence of segments. Each segment is required to precede a given set of other segments. Each segment also excludes a given set of other segments, i.e., once a segment has started its computation it cannot be preempted by any segment in the set that it excludes. For each process, we are given a release time, a computation time, and a deadline. It is also assumed that we know the computation time and start time of each segment relative to the beginning of the process containing that segment.

Our problem is to find a schedule on a single processor for the given set of processes such that each process starts executing after its release time and completes its computation before its deadline, and all the precedence and exclusion relations on segments are satisfied.

Note that if we can solve the problem stated above, then we can also solve the special case where the release times and deadlines of each process are periodic, by solving the above problem for the set of processes occurring within a time period that is equal to the least common multiple of the periods of the given set of processes.

The algorithm presented here was designed to be used by a pre-run-time scheduler for scheduling processes with arbitrary precedence and exclusion relations in hard-real-time systems [3]. In such systems, precedence relations may exist between process segments when some process segments require information that is produced by other process segments. Exclusion relations may exist between process segments when some process segments must exclude interruption by other process segments to prevent errors caused by simultaneous access to shared resources, such as data, I/O devices, etc.

It has been observed that in many hard-real-time applications, the bulk of the computation can be confined to periodic processes where the sequencing and timing constraints are known in advance. That is, the release times and deadlines of processes besides the precedence and exclusion relations defined on them are known in advance. General techniques also exist for transforming a set of asynchronous processes into an equivalent set of periodic processes [16, 17]. Thus it is possible to use a pre-run-time scheduler to make scheduling decisions before run time. Pre-run-time scheduling has many advantages compared to run time scheduling: precious run time resources required for run time scheduling and context switching can be greatly reduced, and more important, it is easier to guarantee in advance that real-time deadlines will be met.

However, up to the present time, the automated pre-run-time scheduler for processes with arbitrary precedence and exclusion relations has remained "an unsolved problem" [3]. As will be discussed below, no algorithm previously existed for solving the problem of finding an optimal schedule for a set of processes with arbitrary release times, deadlines, precedence, and exclusion relations. In the past, designers of safety-critical hard-real-time systems have had to resort to ad hoc methods and perform pre-run-time scheduling by hand. Except for very simple problems, ad hoc and manual methods are prone to errors, are time-consuming, and often fail to find a feasible schedule even when one exists.

The algorithm presented here makes it possible to completely automate the task of pre-run-time scheduling processes with arbitrary precedence and exclusion relations. Currently we are working on producing a practical system that uses this algorithm to systematically search for a feasible schedule when given a set of release time, deadline, precedence, and exclusion relation parameters. Such a system would greatly facilitate the task of pre-run-time scheduling. It would virtually eliminate any possibility of errors in the computation of schedules. Not only would it be capable of finding a feasible schedule whenever one exists, it would also be capable of informing the user whenever no feasible schedule exists for a given set of parameters much faster and more reliably than any ad hoc or manual method. In the latter case, it could also provide the user with useful information on which parameters should be modified in order to obtain a feasible schedule. Such a system would be particularly useful for applications in which changes in the system often occur and schedules have to be frequently recomputed.

In [16], Mok treats in detail techniques which allow one to use a pre-run-time scheduler to make scheduling decisions before run time for both periodic and synchronous processes by replacing asynchronous processes with an equivalent set of periodic processes. Extensive surveys of scheduling problems and algorithms can be found in [2, 8, and 10]. For solving the problem of finding a feasible schedule for a set of processes where each process must execute between a given release time and deadline, all previously reported algorithms either solve the special case where each process consists of a single segment that does not allow preemptions or solve the special case where each process consists of a single segment that can be preempted by any other process. The latter case can be solved in polynomial time, even if n processors are used [11, 13]. In the former case, the problem is NP-complete in the strong sense, even if only one processor is used [6], which effectively excludes the possibility of the existence of a polynomial time algorithm for solving the problem. For special cases where all processes have unit computation time, and no preemptions are allowed, polynomial time algorithms have been obtained [4, 5, 7, and 18]. Several heuristics have also been proposed or studied for the former case [12, 9]. For solving the case where each process consists of a single segment that does not allow preemptions, and a single processor is used, an elegant implicit enumeration algorithm was presented in [14]. Another implicit enumeration algorithm of comparable efficiency is described in [1].

We do not know of any published algorithm that solves the more general problem where some portions of a process are preemptable by certain portions of other processes, while other portions of a process are not preemptable by certain portions of other processes. Such problems occur frequently in many real world situations. Since the major concern in a hard-real-time environment is meeting deadlines, none of the previously published algorithms was applicable to our problem, since assuming all processes are completely preemptable would allow simultaneous access to shared resources which could have disastrous consequences; whereas assuming all processes are completely nonpreemptable would seriously affect our ability to meet deadlines.

The problem as stated above can easily be proved to be NP-hard (even the special case where each process is composed of a single segment that excludes all other single segment processes is NP-hard). The objective of the work reported here was to find a feasible schedule whenever one exists for a given set of problem parameters. This requirement, together with the fact that the problem to be solved is NP-hard, effectively excludes all other types of solutions except solutions that implicitly enumerate all possible feasible schedules.

Although it is possible to construct pathological problem instances where the algorithm would require an amount of computation time that is exponentially related to the problem size, it is extremely unlikely that such pathological problem instances would occur in practical hard-real-time system applications. Our experience has shown that even with difficult problems of very large size, the algorithms can still provide an optimal solution within reasonable time.

One can easily see that our algorithm is also applicable to a wide range of practical problems that are not directly related to the field of computer science. Although we have adopted the terminology commonly used in computer science, readers familiar with the terminology of operations research may substitute the terms "job" or "task" for "process"; "machine" for "processor"; "processing time" for "computation time"; and "portions of a job that cannot be interrupted by portions of other jobs" for "segments that exclude other segments."

A very useful property of this algorithm is that at each intermediate stage of the algorithm a complete schedule is constructed. At the beginning, the algorithm starts with a schedule that is obtained by using an earliest-deadline-first strategy. Then it systematically improves on that initial schedule until an optimal or feasible schedule is found. Thus, even if we have to terminate the algorithm prematurely, it would still provide a complete schedule that is at least as good as any schedule obtained by using an earliest-deadline-first heuristic. Schedules obtained by using an earliest-deadline-first heuristic have the best known upperbound on lateness among all previously proposed heuristics for scheduling nonpreemptable processes with arbitrary release times and deadlines [9]. The earliest-deadline-first strategy is also optimal for scheduling processes that are completely preemptable [15]. Under any circumstance, for solving the problem of scheduling processes with arbitrary release times, deadlines, and precedence and exclusion relations defined on process segments, this algorithm should outperform any previously proposed heuristic.

In the next section, we provide an overview of the algorithm. Basic notation and definitions are introduced in Section 23.4. In Section 23.5 we show how to improve on a valid initial solution. In Section 23.6 we describe the strategy used to search for an optimal or feasible solution. The empirical behavior of the algorithm is described in Section 23.7. Finally, conclusions are presented in Section 23.8.

23.3 Overview of the Algorithm

From the computation time and start time of each segment relative to the beginning of the process containing that segment, and the release time, computation time, and deadline of each process, one should be able to compute the release time, computation time, and the deadline for each segment.

Our algorithm finds a valid schedule in which the lateness of all segments in the schedule is minimized, while satisfying a given set of *"EXCLUDE"* relations and a given set of *"PRECEDE"* relations defined on ordered pairs of segments. The set of *EXCLUDE* relations and the set of *PRECEDE* relations are initialized to be identical with those exclusion and precedence relations required in our original problem.

If the minimum lateness of all schedules is greater than zero, then no feasible schedule exists that will satisfy all deadline constraints. Otherwise, the algorithm will find a feasible schedule that meets all deadline constraints.

Our algorithm uses a branch-and-bound technique. It has a search tree where at its root node we use an earliest-deadline-first strategy to compute a schedule called a "valid initial solution" that satisfies the release time constraints and all the initial *EXCLUDE* and *PRECEDE* relations.

At each node in the search tree, we find the latest segment in the valid initial solution computed at that node. We identify two "expand" sets of segments G_1 and G_2 such that the valid initial solution can be improved on if either the latest segment is scheduled before a segment in the expand set G_1 or the latest segment preempts a segment in the expand set G_2.

For each segment in the expand sets G_1 and G_2, we create a successor node in which we add appropriate *PRECEDE* or *PREEMPT* relations, such that if a valid initial solution for the successor node is computed using those new additional relations, then the latest segment in the parent node would be scheduled before a segment in G_1 or preempt a segment in G_2 whenever possible.

For each node in the search tree, we also compute a lower bound on the lateness of any schedule leading from that node. The node that has the least lower bound among all unexpanded nodes is considered to be the node that is most likely to lead to an optimal solution—we always branch from the node that has the least lower bound among all unexpanded nodes. In case of ties, we choose the node with least lateness among the nodes with least lower bound.

We continue to create new nodes in the search tree until we either find a feasible solution, or until there exists no unexpanded node that has a lower bound less than the least lateness of all valid initial solutions found so far. In the latter case, the valid initial solution that has the least lateness is an optimal solution.

The ways in which we use *PRECEDE* and *PREEMPT* relations to either schedule the latest segment before a segment in the expand set G_1 or let the latest segment preempt a segment in the expand set G_2 cover *all* possible ways of improving on a valid initial solution. This guarantees that in the latter case, the solution is globally optimal rather than locally optimal.

In the following section, we shall formally define all the terms mentioned above.

23.4 Notation and Definitions

In order to solve the problem stated above, we first introduce the following definitions and notations:

Let the *set of processes* be denoted by P.

Each process $p \in P$ consists of a finite sequence of *segments* $p[0]$, $p[1],\ldots,p[n[p]]$, where $p[0]$ is the first segment and $p[n[p]]$ is the last segment in process p.

For each segment i, we define

- A release time $r[i]$;
- A deadline $d[i]$;
- A computation time $c[i]$.

It is assumed that $r[i]$, $d[i]$, and $c[i]$ have integer values.

Let the *set of all segments* belonging to processes in P be denoted by $S(P)$. Each segment i consists of a sequence of *segment units* $(i, 0)$, $(i, 1),\ldots$, $(1, c[i] - 1)$, where $(i, 0)$ is the first segment unit and $(i, c[i] - 1)$ is the last segment unit in segment i.

We define the *set of segment units of* $S(P)$:

$$U = \{(i, k) \mid i \in S(P) \wedge 0 \le k \le c[i] - 1\}.$$

Intuitively, a segment unit is the smallest indivisible granule of a process. Each segment unit requires unit time to execute, during which it cannot be preempted by any other process. The total number of segment units in each segment is equal to the computation time required by that segment.

A *schedule* of a set of processes P is a total function $\pi: U \to [0, \infty)$ satisfying the following properties:

1. $\forall t \in [0, \infty): |\{(i, k) \in U \mid \pi(i, k) = t\}| \le 1$.

2. $\forall (i, k_1), (i, k_2) \in U: (k_1 < k_2) \Rightarrow (\pi(i, k_1) < \pi(i, k_2))$.

3. $\forall p, i, j \in P, 0 \le i, j \le n[p]: (i < j) \Rightarrow (\pi(p[i], c[p[i]] - 1) < \pi(p[j], 0))$

Above, condition 1 states that no more than one segment can be executing at any time. Condition 2 states that a schedule must preserve the ordering of the segment units in each segment. Condition 3 states that a schedule must preserve the ordering of the segments in each process.

We say segment i *executes at time* t iff $\exists k, 0 \le k \le c[i] - 1: \pi(i, k) = t$.

We say *segment executes from* t_1 to t_2 iff $\exists k, \forall t, 0 \le k \le c[i] - 1, 0 \le t \le t_2 - t_1 - 1: \pi(i, k + t) = t_1 + t$.

We define the *start time* of segment i to be $s[i] = \pi(i, 0)$;

We define the *completion time* of segment i to be $e[i] = \pi(i, c[i] - 1) + 1$.

The *lateness of a segment* i in a schedule of P is defined by $e[i] - d[i]$.

The *lateness of a schedule of* P is defined by max $\{e[i] - d[i] \mid i \in S(P)\}$.

We define a *latest segment* to be a segment that realizes the value of the lateness of the schedule.

We introduce the *PRECEDE* relation and *EXCLUDE* relation on ordered pairs of segments together with the notion of a "valid schedule."

A *valid schedule* of a set of processes P is a schedule of P satisfying the following properties.

$\forall i, j \in S(P)$:

1. $s[i] \geq r[i]$
2. $(i\ PRECEDES\ j) \Rightarrow (e[i] \leq s[j])$
3. $(i\ EXCLUDES\ j \wedge s[i] < s[j]) \Rightarrow (e[i] \leq s[j])$

Above, condition 1 states that each process can only start execution after its release time. Condition 2 states that in a valid schedule, if segment i *PRECEDES* segment j, then under all circumstances, segment j cannot start execution before segment i has completed its computation. Condition 3 states that in a valid schedule, if segment i *EXCLUDES* segment j, then segment j is not allowed to preempt segment i. That is, if segment i started execution before segment j, then segment j can only start execution after segment i has completed its computation.

We initialize the set of *PRECEDE* relations and the set of *EXCLUDE* relations to be identical with the precedence and exclusion relations that must be satisfied in the original problem. In addition, in order to enforce the proper ordering of segments within each process, we let $p[k]$ *PRECEDE* $p[k + 1]$ for all $p \in P$, and for all k, $0 \leq k \leq n[p] - 2$. Thus, a valid schedule would satisfy all the release time, exclusion, and precedence constraints in the original problem.

A *feasible schedule* of a set of processes P is a valid schedule of P such that its lateness is less than or equal to zero.

An *optimal schedule* of a set of processes P is a valid schedule of P with minimal lateness.

The *adjusted release time* $r'[i]$ of segment i is defined by

1. $r'[i] = r[i]$, if $\not\exists j\colon j\ PRECEDES\ i$;

else

2. $r'[i] = \max \{r[i], r'[j] + c[j] \mid j\ PRECEDES\ i\}$

At any time, t, $t \in [0, \infty]$, we say segment "j is *ELIGIBLE* at t" iff:

1. $t \geq r'[j] \wedge \neg (e[j] \leq t)$
2. $\not\exists i\colon i\ PRECEDES\ j \wedge \neg (e[i] \leq t)$
3. $\not\exists i\colon i\ EXCLUDES\ j \wedge s[i] < t \wedge \neg (e[i] \leq t)$

The above definition guarantees that at any time t, if segment j *is ELIGIBLE at t*, then j can be put into execution at t, while satisfying all the properties of a valid schedule.

We also introduce a third relation that will be used in our algorithm—the *PREEMPT* relation on pairs of segments together with the notion of a "valid initial solution."

A *valid initial solution* for a set of processes P is a valid schedule of P satisfying the following properties:

$\forall t \in [0,\infty]$:

1. $\forall j:(\exists i:((i\ PREEMPTS\ j \wedge i\ is\ ELIGIBLE\ at\ t)$
   $\vee\ (d[i] < d[j] \wedge \neg\ (j\ PREEMPTS\ i)$
   $\wedge\ i\ is\ ELIGIBLE\ at\ t)$
   $\vee\ (d[i] = d[j] \wedge c[i] > c[j]$
   $\wedge \neg\ (j\ PREEMPTS\ i) \wedge i\ is\ ELIGIBLE\ at\ t))$
   $\Rightarrow \neg\ (j\ executes\ at\ t))$

2. $\exists i: i\ is\ ELIGIBLE\ at\ t$
   $\Rightarrow \exists i: i\ executes\ at\ t$

Above, condition 1 states that in a valid initial solution, if at least one segment i *PREEMPTS* segment j and i is *ELIGIBLE* at time t; or if at least one segment i has a shorter deadline than j and i is *ELIGIBLE* at time t and j does *NOT PREEMPT* i; or if at least one segment i has the same deadline but a longer computation time than j and i is *ELIGIBLE* at time t and j does *NOT PREEMPT* i, then segment j cannot execute at time t. Condition 2 states that in a valid initial solution, at any time t, if at least one segment is *ELIGIBLE*, then one segment should execute at time t. Condition 2 effectively guarantees that all segments will eventually be completed in a valid initial solution, provided that all relations on segments are "consistent" as defined below.

We define each pair of relations on segments indicated by an "x" in the following table to be *inconsistent*. All other pairs of relations on segments are *consistent*.

	i PC j	j PC i	i EX j	j EX i	i PM j	j PM i
i PC j:		x				x
i EX j:						x
i PM j:		x		x		x

i PC j : i *PRECEDES* j
i EX j : i *EXCLUDES* j
i PM j : i *PREEMPTS* j
x: inconsistent

In addition to satisfying release time, exclusion, and precedence constraints, a valid initial solution also satisfies execution priority constraints defined by the set of *PREEMPT* relations and deadlines.

Initially, we set the set of *PREEMPT* relations to be empty. New *PREEMPT* relations as well as new *PRECEDE* relations will be defined and used by the algorithm to reschedule the latest segment earlier in order to improve on existing valid initial solutions.

The following (simplified) procedure uses an earliest-deadline-first strategy to compute a valid initial solution in which release time constraints and a given set of *EXCLUDE*, *PRECEDE*, and *PREEMPT* relations are enforced:

$t \leftarrow 0$
while $\neg \ (\forall i : e[i] \leq t)$ **do**
   begin
      if $(\exists i : t = r'[i] \vee t = e[i])$ **then**
          begin
      Among the set
            $\{ \, j \,|\, j$ *is ELIGIBLE at t*
                   $\wedge \ (\nexists i : i$ *is ELIGIBLE at* $t \wedge i$ *PREEMPTS j*$)$
            $\}$
            select the segment j *that has min d[j]*.
            in case of ties, select the segment j that has max $c[j]$.
            put j into execution.
         end
         $t \leftarrow t + 1$
   end

A more detailed implementation of the procedure for computing a valid initial solution can be found in Appendix 23.A.

See Examples 1–5 in Appendix 23.C for examples of schedules corresponding to valid initial solutions.

23.5 How to Improve on a Valid Initial Solution

Let j be the latest segment in a valid initial solution. (If there exists more than one segment that has maximum lateness, then let j be the segment that completed last among those segments.)

Any nonoptimal schedule may be improved on only if j can be rescheduled earlier.

We define the set of segments $Z[i]$ recursively as follows:

1. $i \in Z[i]$;

2. $\forall k$:
    if $\exists l, l \in Z[i]$:
        $(e[k] = s[l] \wedge (\exists l', l' \in Z[i]: r'[l'] < e[k])$
        $\vee \ (s[l] < e[k] < e[i])$
    then $k \in Z[i]$

The properties of a valid initial solution imply that in any schedule that corresponds to a valid initial solution:

- $Z[i]$ is the set of segments that precede (and include) i in a period of continuous utilization of the processor;

- $e[i]$ is the earliest possible completion time for the entire set of segments $Z[i]$.

- Any nonoptimal schedule may be improved on only by scheduling some segment $k \in Z[j]$ such that $d[j] < d[k]$ later than the latest segment j.

As an example, in the valid initial solution of the root node of the search tree of Example 5: $D \in Z[D]$ from 1; $A \in Z[D]$ because $e[A] = s[D]$ $\wedge r'[D] < e[A]$; B, $C \in Z[D]$ because $s[A] < e[B]$, $e[C] < e[D]$. Thus, $Z[D]$ $= \{A, B, C, D\}$. $e[D]$ is the earliest possible completion time for the entire set of segments $Z[D]$—if any other order for the segments in $Z[D]$ is chosen, the last segment in that new order cannot complete before $e[D]$.

We define two *expand* sets G_1 and G_2 as follows:

$$G_1 = \{i \mid i \in Z[j] \wedge d[j] < d[i]$$
$$\wedge\, i\ EXCLUDES\ j$$
$$\wedge \neg (i\ PRECEDES\ j)$$
$$\wedge \neg (i\ PREEMPTS\ j)\}$$
$$G_2 = \{i \mid i \in Z[j] \wedge d[j] < d[i]$$
$$\wedge \neg (i\ EXCLUDES\ j)$$
$$\wedge \neg (i\ PRECEDES\ j)$$
$$\wedge \neg (i\ PREEMPTS\ j)$$
$$\wedge \exists l: (\exists k, t: 0 \le k \le c[l] - (1, 0$$
$$\le t < \infty : s[i] \le \pi(l, k) \le e[j])$$
$$*\%\ an\ execution\ of\ l\ occurs\ between\ i\ and\ j\%$$
$$\wedge\ (i\ PRECEDES\ l \vee i\ PREEMPTS\ l)\}$$

G_1 is the set of segments that, if scheduled after j, may reduce the maximum lateness.

G_2 is the set of segments that, if preempted by j, may reduce the maximum lateness.

As examples, the valid initial solution of the root node of the search tree in Example 1 can be improved on by scheduling $A \in G_1$ after the latest segment C. The valid initial solution of the root node of the search tree in Example 4 can be improved on if the latest segment E preempts $A \in G_2$. In example 4 $B \notin G_2$ because there exists D such that $B\ PRECEDES\ D$ and an execution of D occurs between B and E.

By making use of the fact that $e[i]$ is the earliest possible completion time of the entire set of segments $Z[i]$, we can compute a lower bound on the lateness of any valid initial solution satisfying a given set of *EXCLUDE*, *PRECEDE*, and *PREEMPT* relations with the following formula:

let $K[i] = \{k \mid k \in Z[i] \wedge k \neq i \wedge d[i] < d[k] \wedge \neg (k \; PRECEDES \; i)$
    $\wedge \neg (k \; PREEMPTS \; i)\}$
if $K[i] = \varnothing$
then $LB[i] = e[i] - d[i]$
else $LB[i] = e[i] + \min \{GAP[k,i] - d[k] \mid k \in K[i] \}$ where
    if $\neg (k \; EXCLUDES \; i)$ then $GAP[k, i] = 0$
    else $GAP[k, i] = \max \{0, -s[k] + \min \{r'[l] \mid$
        $l \in Z[i] \wedge k \neq l \wedge s[k] < s[l] \leq s[i] \wedge \neg (k \; PRECEDE \; l)\}\}$
$LB_1[i] = \min \{LB[i], e[i] - d[i]\}$

$LB_2[i] = r'[i] + c[i] - d[i]$

lowerbound $= \max \{LB_1[i], LB_2[i] \mid i \in S(P)\}$

The lowerbound function can be derived by observing the following: if the set $K[i]$ is empty then the lateness of i, i.e., $e[i] - d[i]$, cannot be improved on. This is because if any other segment $k \in Z[i]$ where $d[k] \leq d[i]$ is scheduled last, then k would be at least as late as the lateness of i. If k EXCLUDEs i and $s[k] < min\{r'[l] \mid s[k] < s[1] \leq s[i]\}$, then from the properties of a valid initial solution, scheduling k after i would leave a gap in the new schedule that starts at $s[k]$ and ends at $\min \{r'[l] \mid s[k] < s[1] \leq s[i]\}$. Note that l could be equal to i, and the lateness of the new schedule would be at least $e[i] - d[k]$ plus the gap size. $LB_2[i]$ is a trivial lowerbound on the lateness of any segment i.

23.6 Searching for an Optimal or Feasible Solution

We now define a search tree that has as its root node the valid initial solution that satisfies all the *EXCLUDE* and *PRECEDE* relations in the original problem specification.

At each node in the search tree we compute the lowerbound and two expand sets G_1 and G_2. Let segment j be the latest segment in the valid initial solution computed at that node.

For each segment $k \in G_1$, we create a successor node that corresponds to a new problem, in which we assign a new relation j *PRECEDES* k. If we apply the procedure above and compute a new valid initial solution in which the new relations are enforced, then segment k will be scheduled later than segment j in the new schedule.

For each segment $k \in G_2$, we create a successor node that corresponds to a new problem, in which for all segments l such that k *EXCLUDES* l and an execution of l occurs between k and j, we assign the relation l *PRECEDES* k, and for all segments q such that k does *NOT EXCLUDE* q and an execution of q occurs between k and j, we assign the relation q *PREEMPTS* k and the relation j *PREEMPTS* k. We let each successor node inherit all relations assigned to any of its predecessor nodes. If we apply the procedure above and compute a new valid initial solution in which the new relations are enforced, then segment k will be preempted by segment j in the new schedule if possible. After generating the valid initial solution for each new successor node, we test it for optimality. If the optimal solution is not discovered among any of the resulting problems, then we proceed to create new successor nodes in a similar manner. We use a strategy of branching from the node with the least lowerbound. In case of ties, we choose the node with least lateness among the nodes with least lowerbound.

The steps of the algorithm are as follows:

(For a more detailed implementation of the algorithm see Appendix 22.B.)

Step 0: Compute an initial valid solution and the corresponding lowerbound. Find the latest segment j and its lateness. If its lateness equals its lowerbound then stop—the schedule is optimal. Otherwise, call the node corresponding to the schedule of the parent node.

Step 1: Find the expand sets of G_1 and G_2 and create $|G_1| + |G_2|$ new child nodes. For each node corresponding to a segment k in G_1, assign a new relation j *PRECEDES* k. For each node corresponding to a segment k in G_2, for all segments l such that k *EXCLUDES* l and an execution of l occurs between k and j, assign a new relation l *PRECEDES* k, and, for all segments q such that k does *NOT EXCLUDE* q and an execution of q occurs between k and j, assign the relation q *PREEMPTS* k and the new relation j *PREEMPTS* k.

Let each child node inherit all relations assigned to any of its predecessor nodes.

Recompute a valid initial solution, lowerbound and find the latest segment and its lateness for each child node.

Step 2: If steps 3 and 4 have been performed for all child nodes, then close the parent node and go to step 5.

Otherwise, select the child node with the least lateness.

Step 3: Set minlateness $\leftarrow$ min {minlateness, lateness (childnode)}.

If minlateness is less than or equal to the last lowerbound of all open nodes then **stop**—the solution is optimal.

Step 4: If lateness (childnode) = lowerbound (childnode) then close this child node and return to step 2—this solution is locally optimal.

If minlateness is less than lowerbound (childnode) then close this child-node—this node will never lead to a solution that is better than the current minlateness.

Return to step 2.

Step 5: Select among all open nodes the node with the least lowerbound, in case of ties, select the node with least lateness. Call this node the parent node and go to step 1.

(See examples 1–5 in Appendix 23.C.)

If a feasible schedule is considered sufficient, to achieve more efficiency, instead of terminating the algorithm only when a minimum lateness schedule has been found, one may terminate the algorithm as soon as a feasible schedule in which all deadlines are met is found. One could also adopt a strategy of terminating the search whenever a schedule has been found such that its lateness is within a prespecified ratio of optimal. An upperbound on that ratio can be computed with the formula $(lateness - L)/L$ where L is the least lowerbound of all nodes belonging to the open node set.

23.7 Empirical Behavior of the Algorithm

We have written a program in Pascal that implements the algorithm described above.

Observation of the empirical behavior of the algorithm indicated that this algorithm consistently generated significantly fewer nodes than one of the best algorithms reported so far that solves the special case where each process consists of only one segment that excludes all other segments [14].

We restricted ourselves to comparing the number of nodes generated for an identical problem sample, because this is the major factor that determines the size of the problem that can be effectively computed—it is basically this number that will grow exponentially when the problem size increases.

By comparing the two algorithms on sample problems corresponding to the special case where each process consists of only one segment that excludes all other segments, we found that for problem sizes of 25 (number of segments), our algorithm frequently generated 25 percent fewer nodes than the algorithm reported in [14]. When the problem size doubled to 50, our algorithm frequently generated 44 percent (approximately $1 - (1 - 0.25)^2$) fewer nodes. When we doubled the problem size again, the difference became even greater—their algorithm was unable to terminate after generating several tens of thousands of nodes, while our algorithm terminated on the same problem sample after generating only a few thousand nodes. It was also observed that for all problem samples of the general case (arbitrary exclusion relations defined on segments) that we constructed, solving them with our algorithm always generated fewer nodes before an optimal schedule was found than if all segments excluded each other (which corresponds to the special case).

Thus the performance of our algorithm on the general case in terms of the number of nodes generated should be much better than the performance reported in [14] when solving the special case.

23.8 Conclusions

The major contribution of our algorithm is that it solves a very general and important problem that no other reported algorithm is capable of solving. It is the first algorithm that is able to systematically search for an optimal or feasible schedule that satisfies a given set of release time, deadline, precedence, and exclusion constraints defined on process segments. The algorithm can be applied to the important and previously unsolved problem of automated pre-run-time scheduling of processes with arbitrary precedence and exclusion relations in hard-real-time systems.

With our algorithm it is possible to take into account the cost of context switching. All we need to do is add to the computation time of each segment the following: 1) the time required to save the status of a preempted segment, 2) the time required to load a new segment, and 3) the time required to restart a preempted segment. This is because the only possible time where a process switch may take place is either at the adjusted release time or at the completion time of a segment. Furthermore, each segment can only preempt any other segment once. Hence we can always "charge" the cost of a context switch to the preempting segment so that all deadlines will be met. (See [15] for a similar argument for the earliest-deadline-first strategy.)

When implementing this algorithm, it may be advantageous to make space-time tradeoffs to match available resources. If our major constraint is space instead of time, we might consider only storing at each node partial information that is different from the information stored at its ancestor nodes, then whenever we need complete information to proceed at a certain node, we use the information stored at its ancestor nodes to reconstruct the complete information required at that node. For example, we only stored new *PRECEDE* and *PREEMPT* relations at each node when implementing our algorithm, which resulted in a significant saving of space without seriously affecting computation time.

One may also include an initial problem parameter verification stage that performs a preliminary analysis of all the initial problem parameters and modifies or rejects if necessary any problem parameters that are either redundant or inconsistent with other parameters prior to using this algorithm.

We note that this algorithm can be easily generalized to the case where exclusion regions within each process overlap or are embedded within each other.

For future work, we will explore ways of generalizing this algorithm to solve the problem of scheduling processes with release times, deadlines, precedence, and exclusion relations on n processors. Another interesting direction for future work would be to explore ways of generalizing this algorithm to solve the problem with additional resource constraints [19].

References

1. J. Carlier, "Probleme a une machine," Institute de Programmation, Univ. Paris VI, manuscript, 1980.

2. E.G. Coffman, Jr., *Computer and Jobshop Scheduling Theory*, New York: Wiley-Interscience, 1976.

3. S.R. Faulk and D.L. Parnas, "On sychronization in hard-real-time systems," *Commun. ACM*, vol. 31, March 1988.

4. M.R. Garey and D.S. Johnson, "Scheduling tasks with non-uniform deadlines on two-processors," *J. ACM*, vol. 23, July 1976.

5. ——, "Two-processor scheduling with start-times and deadlines," *SIAM J. Comput.*, vol. 6, September 1977.

6. ——, "*Computers and Intractability: A Guide to the Theory of NP-Completeness*. San Francisco, CA: Freeman, 1979.

7. M.R. Garey, D.S. Johnson, B.B. Simons, and R.E. Tarjan, "Scheduling unit-time tasks with arbitrary release times and deadlines," *SIAM J. Comput.*, vol. 10, May 1981.

8. M.J. Gonzalez, Jr., "Deterministic processor scheduling," *Comput. Surveys*, vol. 9, September 1977.

9. D. Gunsfield, "Bounds for naïve multiple machine scheduling with release times and deadlines," *J. Algorithms*, vol. 5, 1984.

10. E.L. Lawler, J.K. Lenstra, and A.H.G. Rinnooy Kan, "Recent developments in deterministic sequencing and scheduling: A survey," *In Proc. NATO Advanced Study and Research Institute on Theoretical Approaches to Scheduling Problems*, Durham, England, July 1981; also in *Deterministic and Stochastic Scheduling*, M.A.H. Dempster et al., Eds. Dordrecht, The Netherlands: D. Reidel.

11. C.L. Lui and J.W. Layland, "Scheduling algorithms for multiprogramming in a hard-real-time environment," *J. ACM*, vol. 20, January 1973.

12. G.K. Manacher, "Production and stabilization of real-time task schedules," *J. ACM*, vol. 14, July 1967.

13. C. Martel, "Preemptive scheduling with release times, deadlines, and due dates," *J. ACM*, vol. 29, July 1982.

14. G. McMahon and M. Florian, "On scheduling with ready time and due dates to minimize maximum lateness," *Oper. Res.*, vol. 23, 1975.

15. A.K. Mok and M.L. Dertouzos, "Multiprocessor scheduling in a hard-real-time environment," in *Proc. 7th IEEE Texas Conf. Computing Systems*, November 1978.

16. A.K. Mok, "Fundamental design problems of distributed systems for the hard-real-time environment," Ph.D. dissertation, Dept. Elec. Eng. Comput. Sci., MIT, Cambridge, MA, May 1983.

17. ———, "The design of real-time programming systems based on process models," in *Proc. IEEE Real-Time Systems Symp.*, December 1984.

18. B. Simons, "Multiprocessor scheduling of unit-time jobs with arbitrary release times and deadlines," *SIAM J. Comput.*, vol. 12, May 1983.

19. W. Zhou, K. Ramamrithan, and J. Stankovic, "Preemptive scheduling under time and resource constraints," *IEEE Trans. Comput.*, August 1987.

Acknowledgments

We are grateful to E. Margulis and K.C. Sevcik for helpful comments on earlier drafts. Helpful comments and suggestions from the anonymous referees are gratefully acknowledged.

Appendix 23.A

An Implementation of the Procedure for Computing a Valid Initial Solution

The following procedure computes a valid initial solution in which the release time constraints and a set of EXCLUDE, PRECEDE, and PREEMPT relations are satisfied:

```
lastt :=   · any negative value >;
lastseg := · any segment index >;
idle := true ;
for each segment i do
     begin
         started[i] := false;
         completed[i] := false;
         comptimeleft[i] := c[i];
         s[i] := -1;
     end;
   t := 0;
   while not ( for all segments i; completed[i] = true) do
   begin
       t := min { t | t > lastt and (( exists i: t = r'[i] ) or
           ((idle = false) and (comptimeleft[lastseg] = t - lastt )))
                 } ;
       if idle = false then
     begin
       % in the valid initial solution computed by the procedure: %
       let segment lastseg execute from lastt to t;
       comptimeleft[lastseg] := comptimeleft[lastseg] - (t - lastt );
       if comptimeleft[lastseg] = 0 then
           begin
               completed[lastseg] := true;
               e[lastseg] := t;
           end;
   end;
   S ← { j | j is ELIGIBLE and no other segment i exists
             such that i is also ELIGIBLE and i
             PREEMPTS j
      }
```

```
    if S is empty then idle := true
        else
            begin
                idle := false;
                S1 ← { j | d[j] = min { d[i] | i in S } }
                select segment x such that c[x] =
                 max { c[i] | i in S1 }:
                if not started[x] then
                    begin
                        started[x] := true;
                        s[x] := t;
                    end;
                    lastseg := x;
        end;
    lastt := t;
end;
```

Above, "lastt" is the last time that the procedure tried to select a segment for
execution. "lastseg" is the segment that was last selected for execution. "idle"
indicates whether there was any segment selected at lastt. "started[i]" indicates
whether segment i had started execution. "completed[i]" indicates whether segment i had completed execution. "comptimeleft[i]" is the remaining computation
time of segment i.

Appendix 23.B

An Implementation of the Main Algorithm

```
begin {main }
   nodeindex := 0
   initialize(PC(nodeindex), EX)
   PM(nodeindex) ← ∅
   optimal := false;
   feasible:= false;
   opennodeset ← ∅
   if consistent(PC(nodeindex), EX, PM (nodeindex)) then
   begin
      schedule(nodeindex) ← validinitialsolution(PC(nodeindex),
         EX, PM(nodeindex))
      leastlowerbound := lowerbound(nodeindex)
      if lateness(nodeindex)  = least lowerbound then
         optimal := true;
      if lateness(nodeindex) ≤ 0 then
         feasible := true;
      if not (optimal or feasible) then
      begin
         opennodeset ← {nodeindex}
         minlateness := lateness(nodeindex);
         minlatenode := nodeindex;
         while not(optimal or feasible or spacetimelimitsexceeded)
            do
         begin
            lowestboundset ← {1 | lowerbound(1) = leastlowerbound}
            select parentnode such that:
                  lateness(parentnode) =
                     min{lateness(i) | i ∈ lowestboundset }
            j := latestsegment(schedule(parentnode))
            firstchildnode := nodeindex + 1
      for each segment k ∈ G₁(parentnode)
         begin
            nodeindex := nodeindex + 1
            PC(nodeindex) ← PC(parentnode) ∪ {(j,k)}
         end
      for each k ∈ G₂(parentnode)
```

```
      begin
          nodeindex := nodeindex + 1
          PC(nodeindex) ← PC(parentnode)
          for all l such that:
              k EX l and an execution of l
              occurs between k and j in schedule(parentnode):
              begin
                  PC(nodeindex) ← PC(nodeindex) ∪ {(l,k)}
              end
          PM(nodeindex) ← PM(parentnode) ∪ {(j,k)}
          for all q such that:
              not(k EX q) and an execution of q
              occurs between k and j in sched-
                ule(parentnode);
              begin
                  PM(nodeindex) ← PM(nodeindex) ∪ {(q,k)}
              end
      end
  opennodeset ← opennodeset - {parentnode}
  if not (optimal or feasible) then
  for childnode := firstchildnode to nodeindex do
  begin
      if consistent(PC(childnode), EX, PM(childnode))
          then
      begin
          schedule(childnode) ←
            validinitialsolution(PC(childnode), EX. PM(childnode))
          if lateness(childnode) < minlateness then
          begin
              minlateness := lateness(childnode);
              minlatenode := childnode;
          end;
          if lateness(childnode) ≤ 0 then
              feasible := true
          else
              if minlateness > lowerbound(childnode) then
                  opennodeset ← opennodeset ∪ {childnode}
          end;
      end;
      leastlowerbound ← min{lowerbound(i) | i∈ opennodeset}
      if opennodeset = ∅ or (minlateness ≤ leastlowerbound)
          then
              optimal := true;
  end;
  minlateschedule := schedule(minlatenode)
      end;
  end;
end.
(end of algorithm)
```

In the algorithm above, a node in the "opennodeset" is a node that does not have successors, but may be selected as the node to be branched from next. "PC(nodeindex)" and "PM(nodeindex)" are, respectively, the set of *PRECEDE* relations and the set of *PREEMPT* relations associated with the node identified by "nodeindex." "EX" is the (constant) set of *EXCLUDE* relations. "schedule(nodeindex)" is the valid initial solution computed using PC(nodeindex), EX and PM(nodeindex). "lateness(nodeindex)" is the lateness of schedule(nodeindex). "lowerbound(nodeindex), G_1 (nodeindex), and G_2 (nodeindex)" are, respectively, the lowerbound and the two expand sets computed from schedule(nodeindex).

To achieve more efficiency, instead of terminating the algorithm only when a minimum lateness schedule has been found, the algorithm terminates as soon as a feasible schedule in which all deadlines are met is found; or, when a predefined space/time limit is exceeded.

Appendix 23.C

Examples 1–5

Example 23.C.1

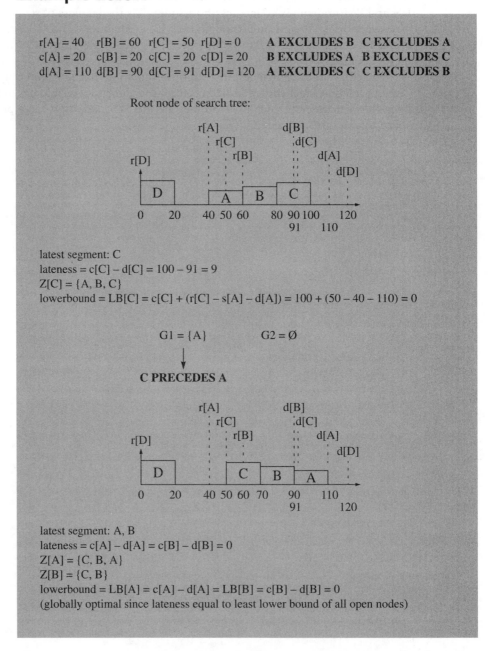

r[A] = 40   r[B] = 60 r[C] = 50 r[D] = 0   **A EXCLUDES B C EXCLUDES A**
c[A] = 20   c[B] = 20 c[C] = 20 c[D] = 20   **B EXCLUDES A B EXCLUDES C**
d[A] = 110 d[B] = 90 d[C] = 91 d[D] = 120   **A EXCLUDES C C EXCLUDES B**

Root node of search tree:

latest segment: C
lateness = c[C] − d[C] = 100 − 91 = 9
Z[C] = {A, B, C}
lowerbound = LB[C] = c[C] + (r[C] − s[A] − d[A]) = 100 + (50 − 40 − 110) = 0

G1 = {A}   G2 = Ø

C PRECEDES A

latest segment: A, B
lateness = c[A] − d[A] = c[B] − d[B] = 0
Z[A] = {C, B, A}
Z[B] = {C, B}
lowerbound = LB[A] = c[A] − d[A] = LB[B] = c[B] − d[B] = 0
(globally optimal since lateness equal to least lower bound of all open nodes)

Example 23.C.2

r[A] = 0   r[C] = 10   r[D] = 60   **A EXCLUDES B**
c[A] = 50   c[E] = 20   c[D] = 30   **B EXCLUDES C**
d[A] = 110 d[C] = 101   d[D] = 90

Root node of search tree:

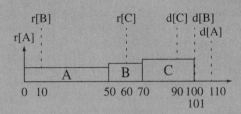

latest segment: C
lateness = c[C] − d[C] = 100 − 90 = 10
Z[C] = {A, B, C}
lowerbound = LB2[C] = r[C] + c[C] − d[C] = 60 + 30 − 90 = 0

G1 = {B}   G2 = {A}

                                  C PREEMPTS A
                                  B PRECEDES A
        C PRECEDES B

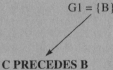

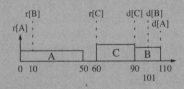

latest segment: B   latest segment: A, C
lateness = c[B] − d[B] = 110 − 101 = 9   lateness = c[A] − d[A] = c[C] − d[C] = C
Z[B] = {C, B}   Z[A] = {A, B, C}
lowerbound = LB[B] = c[B] d[B]   Z[C] = {C}
          = 110 − 109 = 9   lowerbound = LB[A] = c[A] − d[A]
(globally optimal since lateness equal to   = LB[C] − c[C] − d[C] = 0
least lower bound of all open nodes)   (globally optimal since lateness equal to
                                         least lower bound of all open nodes)

Example 23.C.3

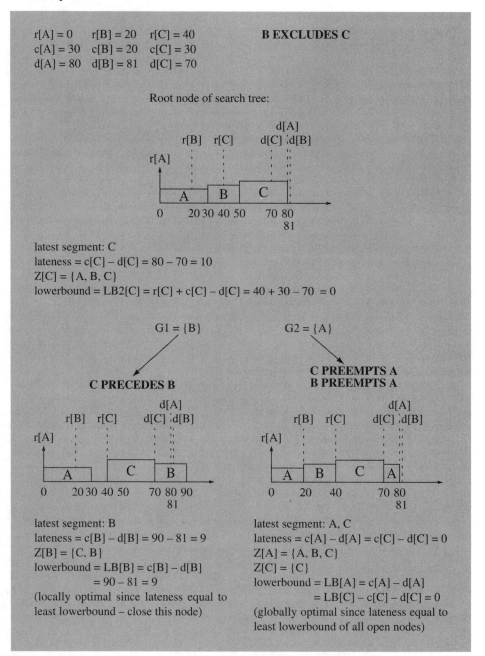

r[A] = 0   r[B] = 20   r[C] = 40   **B EXCLUDES C**
c[A] = 30   c[B] = 20   c[C] = 30
d[A] = 80   d[B] = 81   d[C] = 70

Root node of search tree:

latest segment: C
lateness = c[C] − d[C] = 80 − 70 = 10
Z[C] = {A, B, C}
lowerbound = LB2[C] = r[C] + c[C] − d[C] = 40 + 30 − 70 = 0

G1 = {B}   G2 = {A}

C PRECEDES B   **C PREEMPTS A**
                            B PREEMPTS A

latest segment: B
lateness = c[B] − d[B] = 90 − 81 = 9
Z[B] = {C, B}
lowerbound = LB[B] = c[B] − d[B]
              = 90 − 81 = 9
(locally optimal since lateness equal to
least lowerbound – close this node)

latest segment: A, C
lateness = c[A] − d[A] = c[C] − d[C] = 0
Z[A] = {A, B, C}
Z[C] = {C}
lowerbound = LB[A] = c[A] − d[A]
              = LB[C] − c[C] − d[C] = 0
(globally optimal since lateness equal to
least lowerbound of all open nodes)

Example 23.C.4

$r[A] = 0$ $r[B] = 1$ $r[C] = 60$ $r[D] = 40$ $r[E] = 90$ **A EXCLUDES D   C EXCLUDES E**
$c[A] = 30$ $c[B] = 40$ $c[C] = 30$ $c[D] = 10$ $c[E] = 50$ **A EXCLUDES B   C EXCLUDES D**
$d[A] = 161$ $d[B] = 51$ $d[C] = 90$ $d[D] = 91$ $d[E] = 140$ **B EXCLUDES C   D EXCLUDES E**
                                                           B PRECEDES D

Root node of search tree:

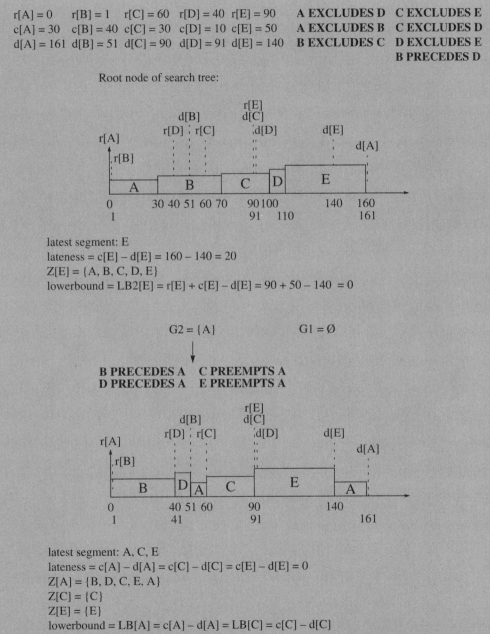

latest segment: E
lateness = $c[E] - d[E] = 160 - 140 = 20$
$Z[E] = \{A, B, C, D, E\}$
lowerbound = $LB2[E] = r[E] + c[E] - d[E] = 90 + 50 - 140 = 0$

G2 = {A}   G1 = Ø

B PRECEDES A   C PREEMPTS A
D PRECEDES A   E PREEMPTS A

latest segment: A, C, E
lateness = $c[A] - d[A] = c[C] - d[C] = c[E] - d[E] = 0$
$Z[A] = \{B, D, C, E, A\}$
$Z[C] = \{C\}$
$Z[E] = \{E\}$
lowerbound = $LB[A] = c[A] - d[A] = LB[C] = c[C] - d[C]$
              $= LB[E] = c[E] - d[E] = 0$
(globally optimal since lateness equal to least lowerbound of all open nodes)

Example 23.C.5

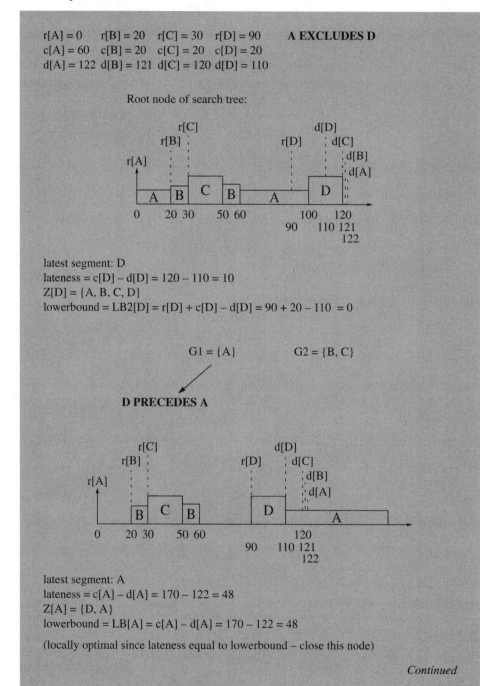

r[A] = 0   r[B] = 20   r[C] = 30   r[D] = 90   **A EXCLUDES D**
c[A] = 60   c[B] = 20   c[C] = 20   c[D] = 20
d[A] = 122   d[B] = 121   d[C] = 120   d[D] = 110

Root node of search tree:

latest segment: D
lateness = c[D] – d[D] = 120 – 110 = 10
Z[D] = {A, B, C, D}
lowerbound = LB2[D] = r[D] + c[D] – d[D] = 90 + 20 – 110 = 0

G1 = {A}   G2 = {B, C}

D PRECEDES A

latest segment: A
lateness = c[A] – d[A] = 170 – 122 = 48
Z[A] = {D, A}
lowerbound = LB[A] = c[A] – d[A] = 170 – 122 = 48

(locally optimal since lateness equal to lowerbound – close this node)

Continued

Example 23.C.5 *continued*

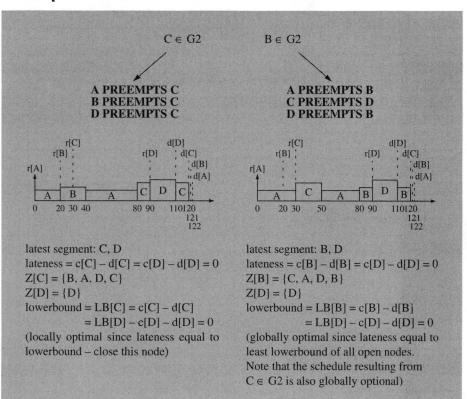

latest segment: C, D

lateness $= c[C] - d[C] = c[D] - d[D] = 0$

$Z[C] = \{B, A, D, C\}$

$Z[D] = \{D\}$

lowerbound $= LB[C] = c[C] - d[C]$
$= LB[D] - c[D] - d[D] = 0$

(locally optimal since lateness equal to lowerbound – close this node)

latest segment: B, D

lateness $= c[B] - d[B] = c[D] - d[D] = 0$

$Z[B] = \{C, A, D, B\}$

$Z[D] = \{D\}$

lowerbound $= LB[B] = c[B] - d[B]$
$= LB[D] - c[D] - d[D] = 0$

(globally optimal since lateness equal to least lowerbound of all open nodes. Note that the schedule resulting from $C \in G2$ is also globally optional)

Commentary

DAVID LORGE PARNAS, P. ENG

1. Should Researchers Publish Outside Their Speciality?

If the diverse papers in this section have anything in common, it is that they all, to some extent, deal with issues beyond my technical interests in software design and documentation. In addition to these papers, I have also written a few dozen guest editorials in a variety of newspapers; they are even further out of my area. Many of these have incited angry reactions. I have heard colleagues suggesting that such commentary is somehow inappropriate. They believe that scientists should restrict their comments to their field of expertise. I reject their opinion for two reasons:

- The right to comment belongs to all citizens. Scientists and other researchers do not lose their right to comment on topics just because they are educated in a different field. They are, however, obliged not to use their titles to suggest that they have expertise in areas where they are no better educated than others.

- One of the reasons that I have always been glad that I chose to pursue an Engineering education is that it has taught me how to return to fundamentals and analyse a problem using basic principles. Many of these articles are simply that—an application of basic principles to reach new conclusions and new insight.

The paper "Building Reliable Software in BLOWHARD" is a simple example. I wrote it as a panel position paper for a conference that seemed to be predicated on the assumption that the path to more reliable software required developing new programming languages. I questioned that assumption and wanted others to question it as well. A special language is neither sufficient nor necessary for better software. Often, the search for a better language is simply a diversion from the real problem.

It is interesting that this commentary, and several of the others, invoked a negative response. The paper was excluded from the original conference proceedings and was published (separately) only after I (and others) complained strongly about censorship.

2. Commenting on "Star Wars" and Other Missile Defence Systems

Papers 26 and 27 on the Strategic Defense Initiative (SDI) may well be my most widely read papers since they were written for, and read by, people with no education in Computer Science. They arose from a consulting appointment to a Pentagon committee. In this context I found that the military decision makers were assuming that the United States could eventually build a space-based missile interception system that decision makers could rely upon. I wanted those in charge to question that assumption. There is no reason to believe that the software for such a system would be trustworthy. This paper, too, evoked many angry responses as well as many supportive responses. It was the angry responses that convinced me that I had said something worth saying.

The idea of missile defence is current again at the time of this writing (2000). To many people's surprise, I no longer oppose the effort. When I wrote the original papers, I was convinced that investing so much effort in something that could not succeed would keep the United States from investing in weapons that were more likely to succeed. In the long run, it would have weakened the United States. My opinion of the technical feasibility has not changed. The arguments that I made are still valid. However, I no longer believe that weakening the United States is a bad thing. I am sure that this too will anger many people.

3. Barter

I have published two papers [1, 4] on what would today be called electronic commerce. However, these papers are different because they question one of the basic assumptions implicit in both electronic and other commerce, namely that every service or commodity can be assigned a price in a single currency. This is one of the basic assumptions of many areas of economics, and in conversations with economists I have found that many of them really don't like questioning that assumption. The second of these papers shows that if we insist on optimal solutions, the kind of "materialistic commerce" that it advocates is computationally infeasible. However, there is room for research on efficient algorithms for finding approximate solutions.

Some of my students have actually built trading systems of the kind described. However, it was never my goal to build practical barter systems. Instead, I wanted people to question their assumptions and see how the assumption of a single currency and uniform pricing eliminated some perfectly reasonable commercial deals. Moreover, I wanted to show countries with weak currencies that there was an alternative to using a strong (foreign) currency for international trade. While barter, even when computerised, is not always practical for retail, it can work for wholesale international trade.

4. Education

Some of my commentaries question common educational assumptions. Educators often do things out of habit, teaching the way they have always taught or teaching the way that they themselves were taught. Computer Science education has evolved without much planning; new research results have been inserted into our courses, often at the expense of older results from other fields. We also act as if teaching programming languages was the same as teaching how to program. We need to question these assumptions once in a while; older science and engineering disciplines have a lot to offer. In addition to the papers in this collection, readers might want to read [2, 3].

5. Computer Science Research

Many aspects of Computer Science research also deserve to be questioned. The pressure put on university teachers to "publish or perish" has caused many of them to lose sight of the obligations of researchers to the people who (ultimately) pay for that research. Many act as if publishing were an end in itself. Research is considered successful if it appears; the issue of whether it is ever used, or could be used, is considered irrelevant. I have repeatedly been told that the value of a paper is determined by whether the conclusions follow from the assumptions, not from the realism or accuracy of the assumptions.

We obtain much of our funding by creating the impression that the work that we are going to do will eventually have some practical value. In most countries, Computer Science is much better funded than other fields. Many researchers do not seem to take the implied obligations very seriously. There are many well-known papers that seem to have had little or no effect on the way that computer systems are designed and developed. The usual response of researchers is to blame their customers, that is, the software developers. I believe that this evades the issue. In other fields, customers (developers) will quickly respond to new research results with new development methods. We should all be asking why this does not happen in Computer Science and using the answers that we get to improve our "hit rate". The papers in which

I raise these issues have also invoked angry responses. We need to discuss research policy issues dispassionately.

6. Conclusion

Eventually, I would like to write a book full of nothing but commentaries. Too few of us question our assumptions; I unquestioningly assume that every assumption should be questioned.

References

1. Parnas, D.L., "The Impact of Money-Free Computer Assisted Barter Systems", University of Victoria Report No. DCS-48-IR, July 1985, 9 pgs.

2. Parnas, D.L., "Education for Computing Professionals", *IEEE Computer, vol. 23,* no. 1, January 1990, pp. 17–22. Also published in *Teaching and Learning Formal Methods,* eds. C. Neville Dean and Michael G. Hinchey, Academic Press, 1996, pp. 31–42.

3. Parnas, D.L., "Software Engineering Programmes Are Not Computer Science Programmes", *Annals of Software Engineering,* vol. 6, 1998, pgs. 19–37. Also reprinted (by request), in *IEEE Software,* November/December 1999, pp. 19–30.

4. Parnas D.L., Luo, Z.-Q., "On the Computational Complexity of the Maximum Trade Problem", *Acta Methematicae Applicatae Sinicae* (English Series), Volume 10, No. 4, 1994, pp. 434–440.

Introduction

James Horning

I found this little paper less entertaining in 1977 than I do now. In fact, I took it personally. I was the program chairman for the Conference on Language Design for Reliable Software and was very serious about the topic. I didn't appreciate a conference panelist coming in with a self-confessed farce to argue that the conference was misconceived, that we should not be investing our effort in designing new languages (such as CLU and ALPHARD) or language features (such as abstract data types and control abstractions).

Over the years I have learned that Dave Parnas often uses humor to make serious points, and that it's a mistake to let this get under your skin. Looking back, I can see that he was poking fun at both the self-importance of the designers and the lack of evidence for many of their claims. (It's still easy to write bad, unreliable programs in any language.) He was also raising the question of whether structuring and checking features in programming languages really attacked the major sources of software unreliability.

I still take language design and software reliability very seriously. The questions raised by this paper remain open. On the one hand, we have disappointingly little empirical evidence that elaborate or restrictive programming language features actually improve software reliability, or that today's languages are significantly better than those of 1977. On the other hand, we don't have a language extension mechanism and scope rules that come close to achieving the properties claimed for BLOWHARD. The "future papers" promised in Section 24.5 remain in the future (as does the implementation of ALPHARD).

Dave's four views of a programming language are still worthy of consideration by any language designer or evaluator—a nugget of serious content in a satirical piece.

Building Reliable Software in BLOWHARD

David L. Parnas

24.1 Introduction

This note is written as a position paper for a panel discussion at a conference titled "Language Design for Reliable Software". The position that it presents is that improvements in software reliability are best obtained by studying software design, not by designing new languages.

24.2 On "Building In"

The title of this paper is ambiguous. The subject could be a report on the methods that we have used to ensure the reliability of the software in the BLOWHARD[1] system. The title could equally well describe a discussion of the properties of the BLOWHARD language that help the BLOWHARD programmer to produce reliable programs.

The title was chosen in order to contrast *two alternative* approaches to "Language Design for Reliable Software".

One approach lies in the creation of "sophisticated" (i.e., "more complex than ALGOL 60") languages with many constructs that are intended to help in the process of program construction and verification. These are *built in* software.

An alternative approach lies in the creation of extremely simple languages, languages with very little built in. It is hoped that the simplicity of the tool will contribute more to the reliability of the product than would the omitted features.

If we are willing to build more in (using) the language, one can reduce the amount that must be built in (to) the language.

The optimal compromise is not known.

In designing BLOWHARD I have taken a rather extreme position. The remainder of this paper explains that position.

---

1. BLOWHARD is a new programming language. Its name is an acronym: Basic Language—Omnificent With Hardly Any Research or Development. Any similarity to languages living or not is purely coincidental.

24.3 Four Views of a Programming Language

When listening to discussions of programming languages I am always reminded of the old story of the blind men encountering an elephant. In my experience, there are four commonly held views of programming language. Each has an element of truth, but each overlooks important considerations.

1. *A Notation for the Description of Computations*   A programming language is a notation to be used to describe classes of computations. A computation is a sequence of state transformations. A single program describes a class that includes all computations that could be caused by the invocation of the program. This view is most eloquently described in [1, Chapter 1].

2. *A Convenient Way to Instruct a Computer*   The task of programmers is to tell a machine what to do. A programming language is a means for directing the computer that is more convenient than the language interpreted by the hardware alone.

3. *An Enforcer of Rules of Good Practice*   Computer folklore contains a great many suggestions about "structured" programming. A programmer using machine language is essentially unrestricted. The syntax of a programming language may prescribe restrictions on program organization. These may be enforced (or checked) by the compiler.

4. *A Means of Invoking Previously Written Programs*   The machine language programmer must compose his programs from the relatively simple commands provided to him by the hardware. The programmer using modern programming languages has available a more convenient "virtual" machine with commands for accessing arrays, calling subroutines, and other commonly used operations. These operations are implemented by programs that are built into the compiler.

24.4 Resolving Conflicts of Viewpoint in the Design of BLOWHARD

There are fundamental conflicts between the four viewpoints that we have sketched above. The first one demands a language with the simplicity of that used in [1]. The other three persuasions have led to the introduction of many features in languages that have been proposed at this conference.

In designing BLOWHARD I have attempted to find other mechanisms for achieving the goals associated with those three viewpoints that tend to lead to more complex languages.

- Rather than build previously written programs into the language, I have decided on an extremely simple Basic Language (BL). The ability to efficiently evoke one program from within the text of another is an extension mechanism that will be necessary anyway. If there is some program which cannot be invoked efficiently or reliably using the extension mechanism, it is a sign that the extension mechanism must be refined—not an excuse for adding a feature. Built-in features are held to a minimum in BLOWHARD.

■ I allow the users of my language to determine their own "structuring" (restricting) rules. Flexible scope rules allow a designer to enforce the rules [2]. There are no vigilante features in BLOWHARD.

■ I allow BLOWHARD users to define modules that use the machine language to exploit the machine. I depend upon his skill as a designer to use this power wisely. There is no programmer built into BLOWHARD. BLOWHARD performs no optimization.

24.5 What Is BLOWHARD?

BLOWHARD lives up to its name. It is a processor of empty statements. It claims to be omnificent and it is. The Basic Language component prevents nothing. The extension mechanism will be the subject of future papers.

24.6 Why This Farce?

BLOWHARD is obviously a farce. An alternative farce would have been a language with so much built into it that any system was but an invocation of one of its features. I view most of the languages at this conference as much closer to the latter than to BLOWHARD. In my view, the best language for reliable software is closer to BLOWHARD than to most other languages.

References

1. E.W. Dijkstra, *A Discipline of Programming,* Prentice-Hall, 1976.
2. Parnas, D.L., Shore, J.E., Elliot, W.D., "On the Need for Fewer Restrictions in Changing Compile-Time Environments," *Proceedings of the International Computing Symposium 1975,* North Holland, pp. 45–48.

Introduction

John Shore

Dave proposes in this paper that we build computer systems to facilitate barter—the exchange of goods and services without monetary prices.

I didn't even know about the paper before being asked to introduce it in this volume. Having now read it, I can say that I don't agree with most of it, and I don't think it has stood the test of time. Nevertheless, I really like the paper. It reminds me of two of Dave's qualities: his abilities as a consultant, and his approach to social issues that are important to him.

Dave is by far the best consultant I ever worked with. No matter what the subject, and whether we agreed on the basics, I welcomed his input because it was always thoughtful, always careful, and almost always surprised me in some interesting and useful way. This paper is typical. Computer Assisted Barter Systems (CABS) do have some advantages, but I don't think they will catch on because they are too much trouble. In the end, most people want to reduce value to some common denominator. On those few Internet barter sites that have sprung up (with nowhere near the success of eBay), one can usually spot such a common denominator, which is just money by another name. Nevertheless, reading the paper made me aware of money's disadvantages and convinced me that barter systems will have a growing role in international trade.

Dave has a strong social conscience. Like many, he's not shy about expressing his opinions. But, unlike most, Dave incorporates some of his social interests into his professional work. He does so by taking an engineering approach to the subject, whether it's ballistic missile defense, nuclear reactor safety, or the role of money in society. I asked Dave why he wrote this paper on CABS:

> I think that there are many things that we could be doing in this world that go undone because people think they need money. They actually need materials and people, not money. If you think in terms of barter you can see solutions to economic problems that you do not otherwise see.

I love interacting with Dave. He always makes you think, and he often makes you think in new ways.

The Impact of Money-Free Computer Assisted Barter Systems

David L. Parnas

25.1 Introduction

Computer Assisted Barter Systems (CABS) are computer systems designed to facilitate barter. They provide an opportunity to exchange goods and services without attaching dollar prices to them. Unlike traditional barter, trade may proceed without identifying pairs of traders as trading partners. A person wishing to do business enters one or more proposed trades into the system. Each proposed trade is a list of goods that the trader is willing to provide (products) and a list of goods that he expects in return (needs). The trader is aware that some of his trades may be rejected, others may be accepted. CABS process the data and determine which of the trades can be accepted. They give this information to the traders. The operator of the CABS then collects the products and delivers the needs. Traders need not know who receives their products or who supplied the goods that they receive in return.

Unlike other computerized trading systems, CABS do not introduce a primary currency that is used to price each of the goods. Each commodity is its own currency. Each individual trader makes his own evaluation of the relative value of various goods.

It is the purpose of this paper to suggest that, if they are developed properly (which will require a considerable amount of work), CABS can eliminate many of the ills of our monetary economy. The rest of this paper discusses the way that these systems can help. We propose that currency-free CABS can reduce unemployment, eliminate the fear of inflation, make better use of our resources, and increase the productive trade in our economy.

We discuss the influence of CABS in two main sections. Section 25.2 assumes that we are trading only goods and services that are presently available. Section 25.4 deals with the use of barter when dealing with goods and services that cannot be delivered until some time in the future. Later sections deal with some of the difficult issues that would have to be solved if we began to use CABS.

25.2 Money Versus Barter as a Mechanism for Exchanging Our Current Goods and Services

25.2.1 What Problem Was Money Intended to Solve?

We begin this discussion by asking a basic question, "Why did mankind invent money?" The answer is simple and, I believe, uncontroversial. Money was invented to help us to exchange goods and services. It is time to ask whether or not it is the best mechanism available for that purpose. Money was introduced as a medium of exchange when we did not have the technology that we have today. It is important to ask whether or not our new technology can solve the original problem in a better way.

Money is also used by some as a vehicle for the accumulation of wealth for the future. We consider this to be a secondary use both because there are alternative vehicles for saving and because money has not proven to be a good vehicle for long term saving. Successful investors have used material goods and facilities for that purpose.

25.2.2 How Money Constrains Our Economy

Money has been with us for so long, that we are not conscious of the mathematical assumption behind it. By assigning monetary values to goods, we are assuming that we all assign the same relative values to commodities. If a pair of shoes is priced at $2 and a sweater priced at $1, we are assuming that, for all people, in all situations, two sweaters are worth one pair of shoes. If a can of tomatoes is also $1, we are assuming that, for everyone, two cans of tomatoes are equal in value to a pair of shoes.

These assumptions are patently false. Our evaluations of the relative values of goods are not consistent. We do not make an exchange unless we feel that what we are receiving is worth more to us than what we are giving up. My relative evaluation of the worth of items A and B may not be the same as my evaluation of the relative worth of A and C—even if you think that B and C are equal in value.

The table below illustrates the importance of this observation. Each row in the table represents an exchange that someone is willing to make. The items that he is willing to give in the exchange are represented by positive numbers. An entry of +2 under "Kennels" means that he is willing to provide two kennels. An entry of −3 under "Puppies," means that he wants three puppies as part of the exchange.

	Puppies	Dog food	Kennels
Mr. Breeder	+20	−5	−6
Ms. Butcher	−15	+4	−1
Ms. Carpenter	−1	−2	+5
Mr. Pro	−3	+3	+2

One can evaluate this table in two ways. If one simply compares the goods offered with the set of goods wanted, one sees that all parties can make the exchanges that they have proposed. If one attempts to find a set of prices that make each exchange "fair", the table defines a set of linear equations in which the unknowns are the prices. Let p be the price of puppies, f the price of dog food, and k the price of kennels. The equations we get are

$$
\begin{aligned}
+20p &\ -5f &\ -6k &= 0 \\
-15p &\ +4f &\ -1k &= 0 \\
-1p &\ -2f &\ +5k &= 0 \\
-3p &\ +3f &\ +2k &= 0
\end{aligned}
$$

The only solution to the above equations is p = f = k = \$0.00. If we have to trade by assigning prices to goods, these trades are impossible.[1]

The conclusion that we can draw from this example is that our subconscious assumption that we can put a price, in a single currency, on every commodity is a constraint on our economy. We could have more trade and a more productive economy, if we were able to function without putting prices on things.

Some might argue that the example is misleading because the table presents inconsistent evaluations of the relative worth of goods. We argue that this is normal; our evaluations of the relative worth of goods are not consistent.

25.2.3 The Problem of Currency Supply

Money constrains our economy in quite a different way as well. In order for a modern money based economy to function the supply of money must be controlled. We now watch governmental and semi-governmental agencies go into lengthy and inconclusive discussions about the size of the money supply. There is almost always evidence that the supply is too large and evidence that it is too small—at the same time. When the supply is too large, the money loses in value. When it is too small, the economy is unnecessarily restricted because there is not enough money to allow business to flourish. We usually see both effects at once. It seems the amount of money in service should correspond exactly to the value of goods and services

---

1. It·is reasonable to ask if the equations should not actually be the inequations obtained by replacing each "=" with "≥". After all, each trader wants to get at least as much as needed to buy the goods that he wants. He would not object to getting more. Using inequations introduces extra variables and may allow a solution where there is no solution to the equations. Unfortunately, unless there is a source of extra money in the system, solving the inequations will not lead to satisfactory prices unless the solution satisfies the equations. If some people receive more than they pay out and nobody receives less, there will be more money in the system after the exchanges than there was at the start.

available for trade. It cannot. It is not just that no central banker has enough information to know what the magic amount is. The deeper problem is that the monetary values assigned to goods are arbitrary and meaningless. If we increase the money supply to correspond to an increase in the supply of a certain type of labor, it may result in inflation in the price of some other commodity. There is no way to label money and say that it can only be used for a particular commodity.

With CABS replacing money the problem of money supply goes away. CABS provide a multiple currency system in which there is a currency corresponding to each type of goods being traded and the amount of that currency corresponds to the supply of that commodity.

25.2.4 The Problem of Inflation

Many of our leaders and economists regard inflation as a major problem in our economy. Many governments have instituted harsh economic measures in order to reduce the rate of inflation. In some cases they have succeeded, but always at the cost of reduced economic activity, reduced employment, and great personal hardship for many people.

If we view the problem of inflation from the perspective offered by barter systems, we find that it is an artificial problem. If we have a barter system, i.e., if we do not attempt to put prices in a single currency on goods and services, there can be no inflation because there is no money to decline in value. We can, of course, have changes in the relative values of goods but that is not the same as inflation.

It is also possible to argue that the inconsistencies in the equations implied by the monetary model may lead to inflation. When we put prices on goods, a trader can use a few of the equations to determine that he is not getting the highest possible price for his goods. His goods are worth more in terms of one commodity than another. While some of the equations would tell him that he is getting a fair price, others may tell him that he is getting cheated. Naturally, he increases his price wherever possible. That can lead to the vicious cycle, which we know as inflation.

The widespread use of CABS could ameliorate the problem. First, there would be no need for harsh measures to prevent a decline in value of the universal currency. There is no such currency. Second, we would be less inclined to make trading decisions based on the assumption that the value of our goods could be expressed in a single universal currency. Rather than comparing prices, we would be asking only if each trade gave us something that was worth more *to us* than what we gave up in return.

25.2.5 A Computer "Matching" Service

In our present economy some trading opportunities are missed because people are unaware of the possibility of making them. Producer and consumer may not know about each other. When a trade would involve many parties, the chances of making the trade are further reduced. Even when some of the parties know of the availability of needed goods, they may be unable to purchase them because they have not been able to sell their own products. CABS can outperform other trading systems because they provide the centralized information needed to maximize trade. The old barter systems failed because of the unavailability of such information. Monetary systems do better than primitive barter, but not as well as could be done. The computer makes it possible to "do business" where it would have been very difficult and unlikely without it.

25.2.6 Maintaining Balance in a System

One of the illnesses of our monetary economy is trade imbalance. Money acts as a buffer and allows goods to be sold to people whose own products are not being purchased. Those people have a trade deficit and, eventually, can no longer serve as a market. The use of currency allows this destructive imbalance to continue until the problem is very difficult to correct.

Even more subtle is the problem of the trade surplus. A group may be selling more than it purchases. It takes in money in return for goods. They have the impression that they are getting richer but, when we view things in terms of the real materials that we are bartering, they are getting poorer. They are trading away more than they receive. The money that they receive in return is not bringing them anything that they want. If it did, they would not have a trade surplus.

CABS can be operated in such a way that the system remains in balance. You cannot purchase goods from a trader without selling some of yours in return. In effect, sellers are forced to buy from their customers. Barter keeps us aware of our interdependence. When we use barter it becomes clear that an economy in which one group buys without selling is not stable in the long run.

25.2.7 Allows a More Accurate Measure of Gain/Loss

The assumption that we can measure everything by a single scalar quantity often confuses us, leading us into deals that do not leave us materially better off. We may sell productive facilities or resources for dollars and watch with satisfaction as our bank balance grows. We may fail to notice that there is nothing that those dollars can buy us that is as valuable to us as the things that we exchanged for them.

Businessmen are very fond of talking about the "bottom line". They add up the costs and benefits of the alternatives and make decisions that maximize their gain. This sounds very rational but it is mathematically unsound. The "bottom line" is not a single scalar value; it must be a vector. Because there are no truly meaningful prices, the scalar or dollar sum is not meaningful. Information is lost whenever we try to represent vector quantities as scalars and the loss of that information leads to poor decisions.

To be truly rational in decision making, we must change our economics to a vector economics. Our needs and our inventory must be expressed in terms of vectors. Until we develop such a way of thinking we are deluding ourselves when we believe that we are using mathematical techniques to make good economic decisions.

Our measures of productivity and efficiency are also inadequate. It is simply not true that the process that produces goods with the minimum dollar outlay is the most efficient. It is not necessarily true that factories that use modern capital intensive techniques to save money have the highest productivity. Each situation must be examined in more detail using vectors to represent gain and loss. Dollar totals do not give us the necessary information. CABS would supply us with data which show the real costs of a deal.

25.3 Money Versus Barter for Future Sales?

It is not too difficult to see how barter can be used to exchange goods and services that are available now. Money, however, is often used by people who sell goods or services now but will not need the exchanges until some time in the future. We all save for the future (for our retirement, for a house, or for "hard times"). Money is used as a means of storing the value of our present offerings until we need something in the future. In this section we discuss how we can achieve this necessary function in a barter system.

A closely related problem is the production of goods that require a lengthy period of manufacture or for which equipment must first be built and installed. I may want to manufacture boards, but to do that I must build a factory and purchase equipment. I have nothing to trade for the equipment that I need to begin my work. In our monetary system, I can, if I have a good credit rating, borrow the money that I need to build the factory, and pay it back from the money that I earn selling my goods. We must ask how we can achieve this necessary function in a barter system.

One answer to these questions can be found in the financial pages of your daily newspaper. There you will find reports on a "futures" market. It is possible, today, to purchase grain that will not be grown until next summer. Some of the money obtained now is used to pay the costs of growing the grain.

Futures for various products can be bartered just as the products themselves can be bartered. Current goods and services can be bartered for the futures. This allows those who have an excess now to "save" or "invest" for their future. It also allows those who need goods and services not to obtain them by bartering away their future products.

In the following sections, I will argue that this scheme is preferable, in several ways, to our present system of saving and borrowing money.

25.3.1 Savings Can Be Targeted to Needs and Be Inflation-Free

It should be recognized that money is quite poor as a mechanism for saving for the future. It is only when money is used to store value that inflation does any damage. I cannot wear, live in, or eat money. Money's only value to me is for the goods that I can get for it. There have been periods in which inflation was so severe that a man's life savings would not buy a loaf of bread. Even forgetting such extremes, we see that no one is certain just how much money he must save because he does not know what will happen with prices and what he will be able to get when he needs his savings. This leads to insecurity and, consequently, to either excessive or insufficient saving. It leads to excessive saving when people choose to save well beyond their expected needs. It leads to insufficient saving when people, fearing that their savings will lose in value, choose to buy now instead.

With a well-developed system of "futures", savings could be expressed, not in terms of an arbitrary currency, but in terms of the goods that it can buy. We would know with certainty what our savings could buy us.

25.3.2 Borrowing Can Be "Future Sales" Eliminating Dangers for Both Parties

With our present system borrowing is a risky process for both lender and borrower. The future products may decline in price to a point where the borrower may not be able to repay the loan. For example, lumber prices may decline because of the use of other products in building, because of currency changes, or because of a decline in the demand for homes. The borrower may be unable to repay his loan. The lender may not get his investment back. This can happen because of factors entirely beyond the control of either borrower or lender. As a result, the borrower must charge high rates of interest; the lender must allow for much of his profit to go to the borrower in the form of interest.

If, instead of borrowing, the purchaser sells his future products, most of the risk (obviously not all) is eliminated. The products are sold, the borrower can fail only if he fails to produce what he promised.

With properly designed business insurance both the buyer of the future product and its producer can work with a minimum of risk and still be rewarded for their efforts.

Note that if there are no buyers for the future products, it is likely that the products should not be produced. Recall that, in a barter system, consumers can only "save" by purchasing future goods and service.

25.3.3 The Use of CABS Can Help in Economic Planning

The use of a futures market for both saving and borrowing facilitates one of the most basic problems of any economy—planning. In every industry, decisions must be made by guessing what consumers will want 1, 5, 10, or 20 years from now. Failures in this process are well known to everyone. With the sophisticated use of a futures market, the guesswork goes away. People are forced to think about what they will want in the future and to make commitments about their plans. In return for those commitments they will receive guarantees that their savings will buy what they have committed to buy. It is as good as theirs. With the introduction of reliable information about future plans, we will find our economy working with much greater efficiency.

25.3.4 Does Saving Using Futures Prevent People from Changing Their Plans?

Some may be concerned that if they save for something specific by buying futures, they cannot change their mind. That is not the case. The goods that they have purchased, or the futures themselves, can be bartered for other goods or other futures using CABS.

25.3.5 Does the Proposed System Require People to Make Predictions That Nobody Can Make?

Some may worry about their inability to predict their future needs for certain commodities, such as old age care. None of us knows whether or not we will require extensive nursing care in the future. It is here that insurance can play a role. We can buy insurance to cover those needs. The insurance companies will purchase the futures based on a statistical analysis that will be much more accurate than an individual's own predictions. The use of CABS does not change the basic needs of individuals for the security provided by insurance schemes.

25.4 What Would Barter Mean for Foreign Trade?

Foreign trade currently takes place with the aid of the monetary system and currency trading. If a country were using CABS rather than currency, how would foreign trade be handled? Again, the answer already exists—it is known as "counter-trade". Traders in different countries arrange to trade goods produced in one country for goods produced in another. This practice has developed (a) to protect the trades against unpredictable arbitrary swings in the value of one currency in terms of another, and (b) to allow nations that have shortages of "hard currencies" to trade. All of the problems that we have noted with a single currency system are exacerbated when there are several such arbitrary currencies involved. When foreign trades are priced in terms of a currency, the producer may find that currency swings have made the price too low. The purchaser may find that, in terms of his own economy, changes in exchange rates have made the price too high. By trading in terms of goods, both sides are protected from such swings. Nations whose own currencies are not worth much on the international scene, now choose to trade goods because neither values the currency offered by the other. CABS can make such deals easier to arrange.

In fact, all of the advantages of CABS on a local scale are to be found for international trade. The uncertainties of a single currency are multiplied when dealing in several. The arbitrariness of the prices is even more apparent when comparing two nations' economies. That currency can be a barrier to trade is applicable on an international scale as well as on a local scale.

As in the intranational situation, CABS keep trade in balance. Both trade surpluses and trade deficits can be argued to be harmful to an economy in the long run. In the first, a country gives but does not receive. In the second, it receives but goes into debt, eventually becoming unable to pay and selling a part of itself in order to survive.

CABS also make it possible for a nation to examine the effects of its international trade on its political freedom or sovereignty. We can look, not just at the arbitrary dollar amount of the trade, but at the net trade in certain kinds of goods. We can determine whether or not we could survive if the border were closed, i.e., if trade were used as a form of blackmail (as it often is). The mere fact that a land has a dollar trade surplus does not mean that it is independent; the fact that it has a trade deficit does not mean that it could not survive on its own. It depends on what we are trading, not just on how much.

25.5 Are CABS a Dream or Are They Current Technology?

In the spring term of 1985, ten groups of software engineering students at the University of Victoria built CABS as part of a software course. Some of these ran on central computers, others on "personal" computers. These systems provided a tangible demonstration of the concepts in this paper. They showed that simple CABS could be built by four people during a semester (while taking five courses). None of those systems could be considered a "production system" ready to serve large communities. They were available for demonstrations, but there is substantial software engineering work that must be done before one could use CABS with thousands of traders and commodities. While the construction of high capacity CABS and CABS networks is not trivial, it appears achievable with current software and computer technology.

25.6 Turning Theory into Practice

We have a theory that suggests that CABS can be useful, but there is a great deal of work to be done to put that theory into practice. Imagine that we have shown that electricity can be produced by moving a magnet near a wire and that that electricity can light lamps and cool refrigerators. Think of the problems that remain to be solved to go from that theory to the power distribution network that we have today. Those problems do not mean that there is something inherently wrong with the theory; they mean that there is a great deal of work needed to turn the theory into a practical tool. However, just as with the electrical theory, those developments can take place gradually; the monetary system can coexist with CABS. If the theory proves to be correct, the switch will take place gradually as implementation problems are solved.

By now it should be clear that CABS can be used to facilitate trade between people who produce tangible services and products for consumption by other individuals. It is certainly not obvious how to use these ideas for dealing with less tangible services, or services that are used by society as a whole. For example, it is not clear how one would use CABS to provide the services of a police chief, prime minister, or hospital administrator. We also should wonder how we can buy things that we have never seen, or buy futures from people we do not know.

In this section, we discuss a few of the problems that must be solved during this development.

25.6.1 Development and Enforcement of Standards

With CABS we must buy a pig in a poke. The full potential of the computer in this application cannot be realized if the purchaser must inspect the goods personally before agreeing to a trade. To make this kind of trade practical there must be a classification scheme based on clear standards for each kind of goods that we trade. This is not a new problem. Currently, there are many examples of business being done on the basis of such standards. However, more standards and more inspections will be needed if we expand this way of doing business.

25.6.2 The Burden of Detail

If we applied these ideas in their pure form, we would find shoppers and savers burdened with an incredible amount of detail. In making my personal purchases, I would have to keep track of the number of bars of soap I use currently and to estimate my needs for the future. Since my need for soap bars depends on the number of business trips I take and the number of soap bars that I find in hotels, this would be a difficult, and probably futile, exercise. Soap bars are only one of the hundreds of such items that would be involved in my barter for present and future needs. I certainly do not want to plan my life in that kind of detail.

The likely solution to this problem is a system of "market basket" certificates. In effect a specialized currency, a certificate would be equivalent to a well-defined mix of consumer goods. The issuer would guarantee that that exact mix could be purchased but would then allow those certificates to be exchanged for other items in his retail store at posted ratios. Consumers would pick the market basket closest to their expected needs, provided that they liked the selection of goods available at that retail store. These new kinds of currency would differ from money in two ways. First, they are based on consumer goods rather than gold or no standard at all. Second, we would have a choice of many of them; the system is not based on a single fragile currency.

25.6.3 Assurance of Reliability

Standards and inspections can help, but there is an additional problem in purchasing futures. How does the purchaser know that the goods will actually be produced? He pays now; will he get something in the future? Will it be what was promised? Bulk purchasers can buy futures now by investigating the seller and by risk sharing. Only the latter is practical for small purchasers. A system of insurers or guarantors with proper underwriting will have to be developed for these markets. Banks and investment brokers now conduct the investigations necessary to make such a system work. It can work in this new context.

25.6.4 Goods for Common or Shared Needs

There are many things that we need but cannot purchase as individuals. Among them are clean air and rain, clean streets, hospitals, parks, police protection, fire protection, water protection, legislatures, courts, colleges, universities, armies, coast guard, weather service, and jails. Our need for these products and services is just as real as our need for clothing or entertainment. The only difference is that the nature of these commodities prohibits individual ownership and purchase. We have to buy them as a society. Our modern society has more need for common or shared goods than did societies of the past.

If we can identify these products, they can be expressed as needs to CABS. The exchange for these societal needs must come from all of us. It is a political decision to decide how to share that load. It is no different in essence from the decisions we now make on taxation. Each of us is forced to purchase some proportion of these services; we do this by providing some services or products for which we receive no other compensation. CABS may help us to see taxation as payment for services and goods rather than punishment or overhead. However, CABS will also make us question the basis of our taxation. Currently we tax some exchanges heavily, others lightly, and some not at all. CABS will make us rethink the way we tax. That rethinking is long overdue. In CABS taxes could not be expressed in dollars but in goods and services. Taxpayers would be free to barter other goods for those needed to pay their taxes. Here again, the problem can be solved in theory, but some more work will be needed to make it practical.

25.7 What Would Be the Net Effect of the Use of CABS?

The most important effect of using CABS would be an increase in trade and production activity. We would get more done. If we use the system wisely, it would allow us to manage our resources better and to achieve more of the things that we want. At the moment we have many forms of productive capacity, including labor, that are being wasted even though we have needs and desires that they could satisfy. CABS would put them to work producing more for all of us. We would stop working only when there was nothing left to do or because of a shortage of real resources, not because of a shortage of money.

CABS would contribute to the "climate of confidence" sought by our government and business leaders. The obvious illness of an economy that wastes resources when we have need for them, the obvious meaninglessness of our currency, which changes in apparent value when someone in New York sneezes, leaves people uncertain and unwilling to invest. CABS would allow people to save and produce with confidence.

It should be clear that although there are substantial problems to be overcome, these are not computer problems. All classification, standardization, and quality control of the quantities being traded must take place outside of the computer system. The problem of guaranteeing the value of the futures, making sure that they are solid, needs study. The question of how to distribute the cost of shared services is a fundamental one that is independent of whether we use money or barter. Barter merely makes the issues starker. The purpose of this paper is not to argue that CABS should be installed tomorrow, but to argue that the theory has merit and an effort should be made to turn the theory into practice.

25.8 Can a Materialistic, "Rational", System Be Humane?

The arguments in this paper have been materialistic in two senses. First, they are materialist as contrasted to monetarist. We have argued that the real limitations on our ability to produce are material ones and that our currency system is keeping us from reaching those limits. Projects that appear too expensive when viewed in monetaristic terms, turn out to be completely feasible when viewed in terms of the material that the money is supposed to represent. Money is working as a kind of rationing mechanism, keeping us from achieving goals that a purely materialistic analysis would show to be achievable.

The paper is also materialistic in a more conventional sense. It has made no appeal to moral issues, questions of concern for poor people or unemployed people. We have made no value judgments except the assumption that more trade is a good thing. It is good, if we trade things that we do not want for things that we want.

However, we believe that this materialistic view makes it possible for us to make decisions on an ethical basis—it gives us choices that were not available to us before. When we measure everything in terms of a single abstract quantity, money, we unwittingly assume that our goal must be to maximize the amount of money that is circulating. For example, we find governments measuring their success by the GDP (Gross Domestic Product). This figure is calculated by using meaningless prices and is not a good measure of the success of an economy. When we study an economy whose production is measured by a vector rather than a scalar, we recognize that we lack what people in operations research call an "objective function". An objective function is a description of what we want to maximize. If it is not the dollar sum of our trade, what is it? That choice is an ethical one. By removing money as a source of confusion, CABS can allow us to make that choice. Eventually, we may find CABS to be a mechanism that allows communal goal setting while relying on individual enterprise to achieve those goals efficiently.

25.9 CABS and the Moral Illnesses in the Bishop's Report

In 1983 the Canadian Council of Catholic Bishops published a report describing our society as having a moral illness. It claimed that we were choosing to leave people in poverty and the misery of unemployment by our economic policies. The reply of leading politicians and establishment economists was that the bishops were poor economists. In effect, we were told that the goals of the bishops were laudable but that there was not enough money to do what they proposed. There is no moral illness in not doing something that cannot be done.

The possibility of using a modern form of barter supports the bishops' position. Money should not and need not be treated as a resource in our economy. Lack of money is not a real constraint; it is an artificial constraint. The fear of inflation is an artificial fear. We are able to get rid of those constraints and get everyone involved in our economy. It will be a moral illness if we do not try to do so.

Acknowledgments

I am grateful to Lillian L.N. Chik-Parnas and James Hamilton for asking some probing questions, which have strengthened this paper.

Introduction

David M. Weiss

In 1983 President Reagan appealed to the scientific and technological community to create a system to shield the United States population from a massive missile attack from the Soviet Union. Formally known as the Strategic Defense Initiative (SDI) the President's proposal became popularly known as Star Wars because a prime feature of the defense was space-based weapons and battle-management satellites.

In 1985, Dave became a public figure by renouncing funding from the Strategic Defense Initiative, denouncing those who accepted it, and repeatedly insisting that software developed to implement SDI would not be trustworthy. Until that time few in the computing community had paid much attention to the ethical issues involved in working on projects that were a source of risks to the public. (One notable exception was Computing Professionals for Social Responsibility, a nonprofit organization, formed in 1983, devoted precisely to such issues.) Dave's reputation as a computer science researcher and the political sensitivity of the SDI program quickly drew attention to his stance from the news media. After a few times I was only mildly surprised to hear his voice as he was interviewed on National Public Radio or to see his picture in a newspaper next to an article explaining his views on SDI.

"Software Aspects of Strategic Defense Systems," Paper 26, lays out the technical arguments that convinced Dave that we could not produce trustworthy SDI software. It reproduces eight short position papers that he wrote just before he resigned from the Strategic Defense Initiative Organization (SDIO) Panel on Computing in Support of Battle Management. These papers are intended for the general public and try to explain in nontechnical terms what differentiates software development from other forms of engineering. In many of these papers Dave did not completely succeed in making the technical issues understandable to the nontechnocrat. However, the central argument comes through well: We do not know how to build complex systems in such a way that we can be sure that they work properly the first time that they are put into use. The difficulty is considerably worsened for systems of a type that we have never previously built. In 1985, this was a point that Dave thought was unfamiliar to the public. With the widespread use of evidently unreliable personal computers today, this argument would be much easier to make.

Dave didn't rail just against the difficulties in building a missile defense system. His target was also the research that was funded by the SDIO. As a researcher competing for funds and as a taxpayer funding research, he protested the futility and the poor quality of the research. As he put it,

I am not a modest man. I believe that I have as sound and broad an understanding of the problems of software engineering as anyone that I know. If you gave me the job of building the system, and all the resources that I wanted, I could not do it. I don't expect the next 20 years of research to change that fact.

"SDI: A Violation of Professional Responsibility," Paper 27, describes the ethical principles that impelled Dave to take a stand, the technical reasoning that compelled him to believe that any SDI system would be untrustworthy, and the practical reasons that convinced him that SDI-funded research would not be useful in solving the many problems associated with building a population defense. Although I had seen many discussions about what would be necessary for software engineering to become a profession, never before had I seen a paper argue about the ethics of such a profession. Dave summarized a professional's responsibility in three short statements:

- I am responsible for my own actions and cannot rely on any external authority to make my decisions for me.
- I cannot ignore ethical and moral issues. I must devote some of my energy to deciding whether the task that I have been given is of benefit to society.
- I must make sure that I am solving the real problem, not simply providing short-term satisfaction to my supervisor.

Dave bolstered his arguments by pointing out his long-standing relationship as a contractor to the U.S. Navy, thereby indicating both his familiarity with weapons systems and his willingness to work on defense projects in the right circumstances. He notes the speciousness of the arguments that had been raised to counter his objections and briefly indicates the special problems associated with producing SDI software.

Dave's active stance against SDI resulted in continuing media interest in software engineering, in several public debates between Dave and computer scientists who disagreed with him, and in the Congressional Office of Technology Assessment including a section on battle-management software in their report to Congress on the feasibility of building SDI [1]. As a coauthor of this report, I had the opportunity to visit and talk with researchers and developers in companies and government laboratories working on SDI and with project managers within the SDIO. Nearly everyone knew the name David Parnas and the issues that he had raised. One Air Force officer in charge of software development for SDI told me that he was happy that Dave had raised these issues. The publicity about software problems had made it easier for him to get more funding.

The essential difficulties that Dave raised in his octet of papers persist today, and later events in missile defense technology have increased the currency of his arguments. The failures of the Patriot Missile System in the Gulf War, as documented by the U.S. General Accounting Office, illustrate the problems that occur when a battle situation differs from predicted behavior [2]. Recent failures of attempts to test interceptors against single incoming missiles under controlled conditions illustrate the difficulty of the interception task and the ease with which the offense can spoof the defense. Nonetheless, the lure of "an impenetrable missile defense system" continues to attract attention, money, and consistent failure, with little counterbalance from technologists. Dave's ethical stance is still a lonely one.

References

1. "SDI: Technology, Survivability, and Software," Congress of the United States, Office of Technology Assessment, May 1998.
2. "Operation Desert Storm: Evaluation of the Air War," United States General Accounting Office, July 1996.

Software Aspects of Strategic Defense Systems

David Lorge Parnas

26.1 Abstract

On 28 June 1985, David Lorge Parnas, a respected computer scientist who has consulted extensively on United States defense projects, resigned from the Panel on Computing in Support of Battle Management, convened by the Strategic Defense Initiative Organization (SDIO). With his letter of resignation, he submitted eight short essays explaining why he believed the software required by the Strategic Defense Initiative would not be trustworthy. Excerpts from Dr. Parnas's letter and the accompanying papers have appeared widely in the press. The editors of *American Scientist* believe that it would be useful to the scientific community to reprint these essays in their entirety to stimulate scientific discussion of the feasibility of the project.

26.2 Introduction

This report comprises eight short papers that were completed while I was a member of the Panel on Computing in Support of Battle Management, convened by the Strategic Defense Initiative Organization (SDIO). SDIO is part of the Office of the U.S. Secretary of Defense. The panel was asked to identify the computer science problems that would have to be solved before an effective antiballistic missile (ABM) system could be deployed. It is clear to everyone that computers must play a critical role in the systems that SDIO is considering. The essays that constitute this report were written to organize my thoughts on these topics and were submitted to SDIO with my resignation from the panel.

My conclusions are not based on political or policy judgments. Unlike many other academic critics of the SDI effort, I have not, in the past, objected to defense efforts or defense-sponsored research. I have been deeply involved in such research and have consulted extensively on defense projects. My conclusions are based on more than 20 years of research on software engineering, including more than 8 years of work on real-time software used in military aircraft. They are based on familiarity with both operational military software and computer science research. My conclusions are based on characteristics peculiar to this particular effort whose requirements are shown in Figure 26.1, not objections to weapons development in general.

In March 1983, President Reagan said, "I call upon the scientific community, who gave us nuclear weapons, to turn their great talents to the cause of mankind and world peace; to give us the means of rendering these nuclear weapons impotent and obsolete."

To satisfy this request the software must perform the following functions:

- Rapid and reliable warning of attack
- Determination of the source of the attack
- Determination of the likely targets of the attack
- Determination of the missile trajectories
- Coordinated interception of the missiles or warheads during boost, midcourse, and terminal phases, including assignment of responsibility for targets to individual sensors or weapons
- Discrimination between decoys and warheads
- Detailed control of individual weapons
- Evaluation of the effectiveness of each attempt to destroy a target

Figure 26.1 *The requirements of a strategic defense system.*

I am publishing the papers that accompanied my letter of resignation so that interested people can understand why many computer scientists believe that systems of the sort being considered by the SDIO cannot be built. These essays address the software engineering aspects of SDIO and the organization of engineering research. They avoid political issues; those have been widely discussed elsewhere, and I have nothing to add.

In these essays I have attempted to avoid technical jargon, and readers need not be computer programmers to understand them. They may be read in any order.

The individual essays explain

1. The fundamental technological differences between software engineering and other areas of engineering and why software is unreliable;

2. The properties of the proposed SDI software that make it unattainable;

3. Why the techniques commonly used to build military software are inadequate for this job;

4. The nature of research in software engineering, and why the improvements that it can effect will not be sufficient to allow construction of a truly reliable strategic defense system;

5. Why I do not expect research in artificial intelligence to help in building reliable military software;

6. Why I do not expect research in automatic programming to bring about the substantial improvements that are needed;

7. Why program verification (mathematical proofs of correctness) cannot give us a reliable strategic defense battle-management system;

8. Why military funding of research in software and other aspects of computing science is inefficient and ineffective.

This essay responds to the proposal that SDIO should be funded even if the ABM system cannot be produced, because the program will produce good research.

26.3 Why Software Is Unreliable

26.3.1 Introduction

People familiar with both software engineering and older engineering disciplines observe that the state of the art in software is significantly behind that in other areas of engineering. When most engineering products have been completed, tested, and sold, it is reasonable to expect that the product design is correct and that it will work reliably. With software products, it is usual to find that the software has major "bugs" and does not work reliably for some users. These problems may persist for several versions and sometimes worsen as the software is "improved." While most products come with an express or implied warranty, software products often carry a specific disclaimer of warranty. The lay public, familiar with only a few incidents of software failure, may regard them as exceptions caused by inept programmers. Those of us who are software professionals know better; the most competent programmers in the world cannot avoid such problems. This section discusses one reason for this situation.

26.3.2 System Types

Engineering products can be classified as discrete state systems, analog systems, or hybrid systems.

Discrete state or digital systems are made from components with a finite number of stable states. They are designed in such a way that the behavior of the system when not in a stable state is not significant.

Continuous or analog systems are made from components that, within a broad operating range, have an infinite number of stable states and whose behavior can be adequately described by continuous functions.

Hybrid systems are mixtures of the two types of component. For example, we may have an electrical circuit containing, in addition to analog components, a few components whose descriptive equations have discontinuities (e.g., diodes). Each of these components has a small number of discrete operating states. Within these states its behavior can be described by continuous functions.

26.3.3 Mathematical Tools

Analog systems form the core of the traditional areas of engineering. The mathematics of continuous functions is well understood. When we say that a system is described by continuous functions we are saying that it can contain no hidden surprises. Small changes in inputs will always cause correspondingly small changes in outputs. An engineer who ensures, through careful design, that the system components are always operating within their normal operating range can use a mathematical analysis to ensure that there are no surprises. When combined with testing to ensure that the components are within their operating range, this leads to reliable systems.

Before the advent of digital computers, when discrete state systems were built, the number of states in such systems was relatively small. With a small number of states, exhaustive testing was possible. Such testing compensated for the lack of mathematical tools corresponding to those used in analog systems design. The engineers of such systems still had systematic methods that allowed them to obtain a complete understanding of their system's behavior.

The design of many hybrid systems can be verified by a combination of the two methods. We can then identify a finite number of operating states for the components with discrete behavior. Within those states, the system's behavior can be described by continuous functions. Usually the number of states that must be distinguished is small. For each of those states, the tools of continuous mathematics can be applied to analyze the behavior of the system.

With the advent of digital computers, we found the first discrete state systems with very large numbers of states. However, to manufacture such systems it was necessary to construct them using many copies of very small digital subsystems. Each of those small subsystems could be analyzed and tested exhaustively. Because of the repetitive structure, exhaustive testing was not necessary to obtain correct and reliable hardware. Although design errors are found in computer hardware, they are considered exceptional. They usually occur in those parts of the computer that are not repetitive structures.

Software systems are discrete state systems that do not have the repetitive structure found in computer circuitry. There is seldom a good reason to construct software as highly repetitive structures. The number of states in software systems is orders of magnitude larger than the number of states in the nonrepetitive parts of computers. The mathematical functions that describe the behavior of these systems are not continuous functions, and traditional engineering mathematics does not help in their verification. This difference clearly contributes to the relative unreliability of software systems and the apparent lack of competence of software engineers. It is a fundamental difference that will not disappear with improved technology.

26.3.4 How Can We Understand Software?

To ameliorate the problems caused by this fundamental difference in technology two techniques are available: (1) the building of software as highly organized collections of small programs, and (2) the use of mathematical logic to replace continuous mathematics.

Dividing software into modules and building each module of so-called "structured" programs clearly helps. When properly done, each component deals with a small number of cases and can be completely analyzed. However, real software systems have many such components, and there is no repetitive structure to simplify the analysis. Even in highly structured systems, surprises and unreliability occur because the human mind is not able to fully comprehend the many conditions that can arise because of the interaction of these components. Moreover, finding the right structure has proved to be very difficult. Well-structured real software systems are still rare.

Logic is a branch of mathematics that can deal with functions that are not continuous. Many researchers believe that it can play the role in software engineering that continuous mathematics plays in mechanical and electrical engineering. Unfortunately, this has not yet been verified in practice. The large number of states and lack of regularity in the software result in extremely complex mathematical expressions. Disciplined use of these expressions is beyond the computational capacity of both the human programmer and current computer systems. There is progress in this area, but it is very slow, and we are far from being able to handle even small software systems. With current techniques the mathematical expressions describing a program are often notably harder to understand than the program itself.

26.3.5 The Education of Programmers

Worsening the differences between software and other areas of technology is a personnel problem. Most designers in traditional engineering disciplines have been educated to understand the mathematical tools that are available to them. Most programmers cannot even begin to use the meager tools that are available to software engineers.

26.4 Why the SDI Software System Will Be Untrustworthy

26.4.1 Introduction

In March 1983, the President called for an intensive and comprehensive effort to define a long-term research program with the ultimate goal of eliminating the threat posed by nuclear ballistic missiles. He asked us, as members of the scientific community, to provide the means of rendering these nuclear weapons impotent and obsolete. To accomplish this goal we would need a software system so well developed that we could have extremely high confidence that the system would work correctly when called upon. In this section I will present some of the characteristics of the required battle-management software and then discuss their implications on the feasibility of achieving that confidence.

26.4.2 Characteristics of the Proposed Battle-Management Software System

1. The system will be required to identify, track, and direct weapons toward targets whose ballistic characteristics cannot be known with certainty before the moment of battle. It must distinguish these targets from decoys whose characteristics are also unknown.

2. The computing will be done by a network of computers connected to sensors, weapons, and each other by channels whose behavior, at the time the system is invoked, cannot be predicted because of possible countermeasures by an attacker. The actual subset of system components that will be available at the time that the system is put into service, and throughout the period of service, cannot be predicted for the same reason.

3. It will be impossible to test the system under realistic conditions prior to its actual use.

4. The service period of the system will be so short that there will be little possibility of human intervention and no possibility of debugging and modification of the program during that period of service.

5. Like many other military programs, there are absolute real-time deadlines for the computation. The computation will consist primarily of periodic processes, but the number of those processes that will be required, and the computational requirements of each process, cannot be predicted in advance because they depend on target characteristics. The resources available for computation cannot be predicted in advance. We cannot even predict the "worst case" with any confidence.

6. The weapon system will include a large variety of sensors and weapons, most of which will themselves require a large and complex software system. The suite of weapons and sensors is likely to grow during development and after deployment. The characteristics of weapons and sensors are not yet known and are likely to remain fluid for many years after deployment. The result is that the overall battle-management software system will have to integrate a software system significantly larger than has ever been attempted before. The components of that system will be subject to independent modification.

26.4.3 Implications of These Problem Characteristics

Each of the following characteristics has clear implications on the feasibility of building battle-management software that will meet the President's requirements.

1. Fire-control software cannot be written without making assumptions about the characteristics of enemy weapons and targets. This information is used in determining the recognition algorithms, the sampling periods, and the noise-filtering techniques. If the system is developed without the knowledge of these characteristics, or with the knowledge that the enemy can change some of them on the day of battle, there are likely to be subtle but fatal errors in the software.

2. Although there has been some real progress in the area of "fail-soft" computer software, I have seen no success except in situations where (a) the likely failures can be predicted on the basis of past history, (b) the component failures are unlikely and are statistically independent, (c) the system has excess capacity, and (d) the real-time deadlines, if any, are soft, i.e., they can be missed without long-term effects. None of these is true for the required battle-management software.

3. No large-scale software system has even been installed without extensive testing under realistic conditions. For example, in operational software for military aircraft, even minor modifications require extensive ground testing followed by flight testing in which battle conditions can be closely approximated. Even with these tests, bugs can and do show up in battle conditions. The inability to test a strategic defense system under field conditions before we actually need it will mean that no knowledgeable person would have much faith in the system.

4. It is not unusual for software modifications to be made in the field. Programmers are transported by helicopter to Navy ships; debugging notes can be found on the walls of trucks carrying computers that were used in Vietnam. It is only through such modifications that software becomes reliable. Such opportunities will not be available in the 30–90 minute war to be fought by a strategic defense battle-management system.

5. Programs of this type must meet hard real-time deadlines reliably. In theory, this can be done either by scheduling at runtime or by preruntime scheduling. In practice, efficiency and predictability require some preruntime scheduling. Schedules for the worst-case load are often built into the program. Unless one can work out worst-case real-time schedules in advance, one can have no confidence that the system will meet its deadlines when its service is required.

6. All of our experience indicates that the difficulties in building software increase with the size of the system, with the number of independently modifiable subsystems, and with the number of interfaces that must be defined. Problems worsen when interfaces may change. The consequent modifications increase the complexity of the software and the difficulty of making a change correctly.

26.4.4 Conclusions

All of the cost estimates indicate that this will be the most massive software project ever attempted. The system has numerous technical characteristics that will make it more difficult than previous systems, independent of size. Because of the extreme demands on the system and our inability to test it, we will never be able to believe, with any confidence, that we have succeeded. Nuclear weapons will remain a potent threat.

26.5 Why Conventional Software Development Does Not Produce Reliable Programs

26.5.1 What Is the Conventional Method?

The easiest way to describe the programming method used in most projects today was given to me by a teacher who was explaining how he teaches programming. "Think like a computer," he said. He instructed his students to begin by thinking about what the computer had to do first and to write that down. They would then think about what the computer had to do next and continue in that way until they had described the last thing the computer would do. This, in fact, is the way I was taught to program. Most of today's textbooks demonstrate the same method, although it has been improved by allowing us to describe the computer's "thoughts" in larger steps and later to refine those large steps to a sequence of smaller steps.

26.5.2 Why This Method Leads to Confusion

This intuitively appealing method works well—on problems too small to matter. We think that it works because it worked for the first program that we wrote. One can follow the method with programs that have neither branches nor loops. As soon as our thinking reaches a point where the action of the computer must depend on conditions that are not known until the program is running, we must deviate from the method by labeling one or more of the actions and remembering how we would get there. As soon as we introduce loops into the program, there are many ways of getting to some of the points and we must remember all of those ways. As we progress through the algorithm, we recognize the need for information about earlier events and add variables to our data structure. We now have to start remembering what data mean and under what circumstances data are meaningful.

As we continue in our attempt to "think like a computer," the amount we have to remember grows and grows. The simple rules defining how we got to certain points in a program become more complex as we branch there from other points The simple rules defining what the data mean become more complex as we find other uses for existing variables and add new variables. Eventually, we make an error. Sometimes we note that error; sometimes it is not found until we test. Sometimes the error is not very important; it happens only on rare or unforeseen occasions. In that case, we find it when the program is in use. Often, because one needs to remember so much about the meaning of each label and each variable, new problems are created when old problems are corrected.

26.5.3 What Is the Effect of Concurrency on This Method?

In many of our computer systems there are several sources of information and several outputs that must be controlled. This leads to a computer that might be thought of as doing many things at once. If the sequence of external events cannot be predicted in advance, the sequence of actions taken by the computer is also not predictable. The computer may be doing only one thing at a time, but as one attempts to "think like a computer," one finds many more points where the action must be conditional on what happened in the past. Any attempt to design these programs by thinking things through in the order that the computer will execute them leads to confusion and results in systems that nobody can understand completely.

26.5.4 What Is the Effect of Multiprocessing?

When there is more than one computer in a system, the software not only appears to be doing more than one thing at a time, it really is doing many things at once. There is no sequential program that one can study. Any attempt to "think like the computer system" is obviously hopeless. There are so many possibilities to consider that only extensive testing can begin to sort things out. Even after such testing, we have incidents such as one that happened on a space shuttle flight several years ago. The wrong combination of sequences occurred and prevented the flight from starting.

26.5.5 Do Professional Programmers Really Use This Approach?

Yes. I have had occasion to study lots of practical software and to discuss programs with lots of professional programmers. In recent years many programmers have tried to improve their working methods using a variety of software design approaches. However, when they get down to writing executable programs, they revert to the conventional way of thinking. I have yet to find a substantial program in practical use whose structure was not based on the expected execution sequence. I would be happy to be shown some.

Other methods are discussed in advanced courses, a few good textbooks, and scientific meetings, but most programmers continue to use the basic approach of thinking things out in the order that the computer will execute them. This is most noticeable in the maintenance (deficiency correction) phase of programming.

26.5.6 How Do We Get Away with This Inadequate Approach?

It should be clear that writing and understanding very large real-time programs by "thinking like a computer" will be beyond our intellectual capabilities. How can it be that we have so much software that is reliable enough for us to use it? The answer is simple: Programming is a trial and error craft. People write programs without any expectation that they will be right the first time. They spend at least as much time testing and correcting errors as they spend writing the initial program. Large concerns have separate groups of testers to do quality assurance. Programmers cannot be trusted to test their own programs adequately. Software is released for use, not when it is known to be correct, but when the rate of discovering new errors slows down to one that management considers acceptable. Users learn to expect errors and are often told how to avoid the bugs until the program is improved.

26.5.7 Conclusions

The military software that we depend on every day is not likely to be correct. The methods that are in use in the industry today are not adequate for building large real-time software systems that must be reliable when first used. A drastic change in methods is needed.

26.6 The Limits of Software Engineering Methods

26.6.1 What Is Software Engineering Research?

We have known for 25 years that our programming methods are inadequate for large projects. Research in software engineering, programming methodology, software design, etc., looks for better tools and methods. The common thrust of results in these fields is to reduce the amount that a programmer must remember when checking and changing a program.

Two main lines of research are (1) structured programming and the use of formal program semantics, and (2) the use of formally specified abstract interfaces to hide information about one module (work assignment) from the programmers who are working on other parts. A third idea, less well understood but no less important, is the use of cooperating sequential processes to help deal with the complexities arising from concurrency and multiprogramming. By the late 1970s the basic ideas in software engineering were considered "motherhood" in the academic community. Nonetheless, examinations of real programs revealed that actual programming practice, especially for military systems, had not been changed much by the publication of the academic proposals.

The gap between theory and practice was large and growing. Those espousing structured approaches to software were certain that it would be easy to apply their ideas to the problems that they faced in their daily work. They doubted that programs organized according to the principles espoused by academics could ever meet the performance constraints on "real" systems. Even those who claimed to believe in these principles were not able to apply them consistently.

In 1977 the management of the Naval Research Laboratory in Washington, D.C., and the Naval Weapons Center in China Lake, California, decided that something should be done to close the gap. They asked one of the academics who had faith in the new approach (myself) to demonstrate the applicability of those methods by building, for the sake of comparison, a second version of a Navy real-time program. The project, now known as the Software Cost Reduction project (SCR), was expected to take two to four years. It is still going on.

The project has made two things clear: (1) much of what the academics proposed can be done; (2) good software engineering is far from easy. The methods reduce, but do not eliminate, errors. They reduce, but do not eliminate, the need for testing.

26.6.2 What Should We Do and What Can We Do?

The SCR work has been based on the following precepts:

1. The software requirements should be nailed down with a complete, black-box requirements document before software design is begun.

2. The system should be divided into modules using information-hiding (abstraction) before writing the program begins.

3. Each module should have a precise, black-box, formal specification before writing the program begins.

4. Formal methods should be used to give precise documentation.

5. Real-time systems should be built as a set of cooperating sequential processes, each with a specified period and deadline.

6. Programs should be written using the ideas of structured programming as taught by Harlan Mills.

We have demonstrated that the first four of these precepts can be applied to military software by doing it. The documents that we have written have served as models for others. We have evidence that the models provide a most effective means of technology transfer.

We have not yet proved that these methods lead to reliable code that meets the space and time constraints. We have found that every one of these precepts is easier to pronounce than to carry out. Those who think that software designs will become easy and that errors will disappear, have not attacked substantial problems.

26.6.3 What Makes Software Engineering Hard?

We can write software requirements documents that are complete and precise. We understand the mathematical model behind such documents and can follow a systematic procedure to document all necessary requirements decisions. Unfortunately, it is hard to make the decisions that must be made to write such a document. We often do not know how to make those decisions until we can play with the system. Only when we have built a similar system before is it easy to determine the requirements in advance. It is worth doing, but it is not easy.

We know how to decompose complex systems into modules when we know the set of design decisions that must be made in the implementation. Each of these must be assigned to a single module. We can do that when we are building a system that resembles a system we built before. When we are solving a totally new problem, we will overlook difficult design decisions. The result will be a structure that does not fully separate concerns and minimize complexity.

We know how to specify abstract interfaces for modules. We have a set of standard notations for use in that task. Unfortunately, it is very hard to find the right interface. The interface should be an abstraction of the set of all alternative designs. We can find that abstraction only when we understand the alternative designs. For example, it has proved unexpectedly hard to design an abstract interface that hides the mathematical model of the earth's shape. We have no previous experience with such models and no one has designed such an abstraction before.

The common thread in all these observations is that, even with sound software design principles, we need broad experience with similar systems to design good, reliable software.

26.6.4 Will New Programming Languages Make Much Difference?

Because of the very large improvements in productivity that were noted when compiler languages were introduced, many continue to look for another improvement by introducing better languages. Better notation always helps, but we cannot expect new languages to provide the same magnitude of improvement that we got from the first introduction of such languages. Our experience in SCR has not shown the lack of a language to be a major problem.

Programming languages are now sufficiently flexible that we can use almost any of them for almost any task. We should seek simplifications in programming languages, but we cannot expect that this will make a big difference.

26.6.5 What About Programming Environments?

The success of UNIX as a programming development tool has made it clear that the environment in which we work does make a difference. The flexibility of UNIX has allowed us to eliminate many of the time-consuming house-keeping tasks involved in producing large programs. Consequently, there is extensive research in programming environments. Here, too, I expect small improvements can be made by basing tools on improved notations but no big breakthroughs. Problems with our programming environment have not been a major impediment in our SCR work.

26.6.6 Why Software Engineering Research Will Not Make the SDI Goals Attainable

Although I believe that further research on software engineering methods can lead to substantial improvements in our ability to build large real-time software systems, this work will not overcome the difficulties inherent in the plans for battle-management computing for SDI. Software engineering methods do not eliminate errors. They do not eliminate the basic differences between software technology and other areas of engineering. They do not eliminate the need for extensive testing under field conditions or the need for opportunities to revise the system while it is in use. Most important, we have learned that the successful application of these methods depends on experience accumulated while building and maintaining similar systems. There is no body of experience for SDI battle management.

26.6.7 Conclusions

I am not a modest man. I believe that I have as sound and broad an understanding of the problems of software engineering as anyone that I know. If you gave me the job of building the system and all the resources that I wanted, I could not do it. I don't expect the next 20 years of research to change that fact.

26.7 Artificial Intelligence and the Strategic Defense Initiative

26.7.1 Introduction

One of the technologies being considered for use in the SDI battle-management software is artificial intelligence (AI). Researchers in AI have often made big claims, and it is natural to believe that one should use this technology for a problem as difficult as SDI battle management. In this section, I argue that one cannot expect much help from AI in building reliable battle-management software.

26.7.2 What Is Artificial Intelligence?

Two quite different definitions of AI are in common use today.

AI-1:   The use of computers to solve problems that previously could be solved only by applying human intelligence.

AI-2:   The use of a specific set of programming techniques known as heuristic or rule-based programming. In this approach human experts are studied to determine what heuristics or rules of thumb they use in solving problems. Usually they are asked for their rules. These rules are then encoded as input to a program that attempts to behave in accordance with them. In other words, the program is designed to solve a problem the way that humans seem to solve it.

It should be noted that the first definition defines AI as a set of problems; the second defines AI as a set of techniques. The first definition has a sliding meaning. In the Middle Ages, it was thought that arithmetic required intelligence. Now we recognize it as a mechanical act. Something can fit the definition of AI-1 today, but, once we see how the program works and understand the problem, we will not think of it as AI anymore.

It is quite possible for a program to meet one definition and not the other. If we build a speech-recognition program that uses Bayesian mathematics rather than heuristics, it is AI-1 but not AI-2. If we write a rule-based program to generate parsers for precedence grammars using heuristics, it will be AI-2 but not AI-1 because the problem has a known algorithmic solution.

Although it is possible for work to satisfy both definitions, the best AI-1 work that I have seen does not use heuristic or rule-based methods. Workers in AI-1 often use traditional engineering and scientific approaches. They study the problem and its physical and logical constraints and write a program that makes no attempt to mimic the way that people say they solve the problem.

26.7.3 What Can We Learn from AI That Will Help Us Build the Battle-Management Computer Software?

I have seen some outstanding AI-1 work. Unfortunately, I cannot identify a body of techniques or technology that is unique to this field. When one studies these AI-1 programs one finds that they use sound scientific approaches, approaches that are also used in work that is not called AI. Most of the work is problem specific, and some abstraction and creativity are required to see how to transfer it. People speak of AI as if it were some magic body of new ideas. There is good work in AI-1 but nothing so magic it will allow the solution of the SDI battle-management problem.

I find the approaches taken in AI-2 to be dangerous, and much of the work misleading. The rules that one obtains by studying people turn out to be inconsistent, incomplete, and inaccurate. Heuristic programs are developed by a trial and error process in which a new rule is added whenever one finds a case that is not handled by the old rules. This approach usually yields a program whose behavior is poorly understood and hard to predict. AI-2 researchers accept this evolutionary approach to programming as normal and proper. I trust such programs even less than I trust unstructured conventional programs. One never knows when the program will fail.

On occasion I have had to examine closely the claims of a worker in AI-2. I have always been disappointed. On close examination the heuristics turned out to handle a small number of obvious cases but failed to work in general. The author was able to demonstrate spectacular behavior on the cases that the program handled correctly. He marked the other cases as extensions for future researchers. In fact, the techniques being used often do not generalize and the improved program never appears.

26.7.4 What About Expert Systems?

Lately we have heard a great deal about the success of a particular class of rule-based systems known as expert systems. Every discussion cites one example of such a system that is being used to solve real problems by people other than its developer. That example is always the same—a program designed to find configurations for VAX computers. To many of us, that does not sound like a difficult problem; it sounds like the kind of problem that is amenable to algorithmic solution because VAX systems are constructed from well-understood, well-designed components. Recently I read a paper that reported that this program had become a maintenance nightmare. It was poorly understood, badly structured, and hence hard to change. I have good reason to believe that it could be replaced by a better program written using good software engineering techniques instead of heuristic techniques.

SDI presents a problem that may be more difficult than those being tackled in AI-1 and expert systems. Workers in those areas attack problems that now require human expertise. Some of the problems in SDI are in areas where we now have no human experts. Do we now have humans who can, with high reliability and confidence, look at missiles in ballistic flight and distinguish warheads from decoys?

26.7.5 Conclusions

Artificial intelligence has the same relation to intelligence as artificial flowers have to flowers. From a distance they may appear much alike, but when closely examined they are quite different. I don't think we can learn much about one by studying the other. AI offers no magic technology to solve our problem. Heuristic techniques do not yield systems that one can trust.

26.8 Can Automatic Programming Solve the SDI Software Problem?

26.8.1 Introduction

Throughout my career in computing I have heard people claim that the solution to the software problem is automatic programming. All that one has to do is write the specifications for the software, and the computer will find a program. Can we expect such technology to produce reliable programs for SDI?

26.8.2 Some Perspective on Automatic Programming

The oldest paper known to me that discusses automatic programming was written in the 1940s by Saul Gorn when he was working at the Aberdeen Proving Ground. This paper, titled "Is Automatic Programming Feasible?" was classified for a while. It answered the question positively.

At that time, programs were fed into computers on paper tapes. The programmer worked the punch directly and actually looked at the holes in the tape. I have seen programmers "patch" programs by literally patching the paper tape.

The automatic programming system considered by Gorn in that paper was an assembler in today's terminology. All that one would have to do with his automatic programming system would be to write a code such as CLA, and the computer would automatically punch the proper holes in the tape. In this way, the programmer's task would be performed automatically by the computer.

In later years the phrase was used to refer to program generation from languages such as IT, FORTRAN, and ALGOL. In each case, the programmer entered a specification of what he wanted, and the computer produced the program in the language of the machine.

In short, automatic programming always has been a euphemism for programming with a higher-level language than was then available to the programmer. Research in automatic programming is simply research in the implementation of higher-level programming languages.

26.8.3 Is Automatic Programming Feasible? What Does That Mean?

Of course automatic programming is feasible. We have known for years that we can implement higher-level programming languages. The only real question was the efficiency of the resulting programs. Usually, if the input "specification" is not a description of an algorithm, the resulting program is woefully inefficient. I do not believe that the use of nonalgorithmic specifications as a programming language will prove practical for systems with limited computer capacity and hard real-time deadlines. When the input specification is a description of an algorithm, writing the specification is really writing a program. There will be no substantial change from our present capability.

26.8.4 Will Automatic Programming Lead to More Reliable Programs?

The use of improved languages has led to a reduction in the amount of detail that a programmer must handle and hence to an improvement in reliability. However, extant programming languages, while far from perfect, are not that bad. Unless we move to nonalgorithmic specifications as an input to these systems, I do not expect a drastic improvement to result from this research.

On the other hand, our experience in writing nonalgorithmic specifications has shown that people make mistakes in writing them just as they do in writing algorithms. The effect of such work on reliability is not yet clear.

26.8.5 Will Automatic Programming Lead to a Reliable SDI Battle-Management System?

I believe that the claims that have been made for automatic programming systems are greatly exaggerated. Automatic programming in a way that is substantially different from what we do today is not likely to become a practical tool for real-time systems like the SDI battle-management system. Moreover, one of the basic problems with SDI is that we do not have the information to write specifications that we can trust. In such a situation, automatic programming is no help at all.

26.9 Can Program Verification Make the SDI Software Reliable?

26.9.1 Introduction

Programs are mathematical objects. They have meanings that are mathematical objects. Program specifications are mathematical objects. Should it not be possible to prove that a program will meet its specification? This has been a topic of research now for at least 25 years. If we can prove programs correct, could we not prove the SDI software correct? If it was proved correct, could we not rely on it to defend us in time of need?

26.9.2 What Can We Prove?

We can prove that certain small programs in special programming languages meet a specification. The word *small* is a relative one. Those working in verification would consider a 500-line program to be large. In discussing SDI software, we would consider a 500-line program to be small. The programs whose proofs I have seen have been well under 500 lines. They have performed easily defined mathematical tasks. They have been written without use of side effects, an important tool in practical programs.

Proofs for programs such as a model of the earth's gravity field do not have these properties. Such programs are larger; their specifications are not as neat or mathematically formalizable. They are often written in programming languages whose semantics are difficult to formalize. I have seen no proof of such a program.

Not only are manual proofs limited to programs of small size with mathematical specifications; machine theorem provers and verifiers are also strictly limited in the size of the program that they can handle. The size of programs that they can handle is several orders of magnitude different from the size of the programs that would constitute the SDI battle-management system.

26.9.3 Do We Have the Specifications?

In the case of SDI we do not have the specifications against which a proof could be applied. Even if size were not a problem, the lack of specifications would make the notion of a formula proof meaningless. If we wrote a formal specification for the software, we would have no way of proving that a program that satisfied the specification would actually do what we expected it to do. The specification itself might be wrong or incomplete.

26.9.4 Can We Have Faith in Proofs?

Proofs increase our confidence in a program, but we have no basis for complete confidence. Even in pure mathematics there are many cases of proofs that were published with errors. Proofs tend to be reliable when they are small, well polished, and carefully read. They are not reliable when they are large, complex, and not read by anyone but their author. That is what would happen with any attempt to prove even a portion of the SDI software correct.

26.9.5 What About Concurrency?

The proof techniques that are most practical are restricted to sequential programs. Recent work on proofs of systems of concurrent processes has focused on message-passing protocols rather than processes that cooperate using shared memory. There are some techniques that can be applied with shared memory, but they are more difficult than proofs for sequential programs or proofs for programs that are restricted to communication over message channels.

26.9.6 What About Programs That Are Supposed to Be Robust?

One of the major problems with the SDI software is that it should function with part of its equipment destroyed or disabled by enemy action. In 20 years of watching attempts to prove programs correct, I have seen only one attempt at proving that a program would get the correct answer in the event of a hardware failure. That proof made extremely unrealistic assumptions. We have no techniques for proving the correctness of programs in the presence of unknown hardware failures and errors in input data.

26.9.7 Conclusions

It is inconceivable to me that one could provide a convincing proof of correctness of even a small portion of the SDI software. Given our inability to specify the requirements of the software, I do not know what such a proof would mean if I had it.

26.10 Is SDIO an Efficient Way to Fund Worthwhile Research?

The subject of this section is not computer science. Instead, it discusses an issue of concern to all modern scientists: the mechanism that determines what research will be done. These remarks are based on nearly 20 years of experience with DoD funding as well as experience with other funding mechanisms in several countries.

26.10.1 The Proposal

In several discussions of this problem, I have found people telling me they knew the SDIO software could not be built but felt the project should continue because it might fund some good research. In this section I want to discuss that point of view.

26.10.2 The Moral Issue

There is an obvious moral issue raised by this position. The American people and their representatives have been willing to spend huge amounts of money on this project because of the hope that has been offered. Is it honest to take the attitude expressed above? Is it wise to have our policymakers make decisions on the assumption that such a system might be possible? I am not an expert on moral or political issues and offer no answers to these questions.

26.10.3 Is DoD Sponsoring of Software Research Effective?

I can raise another problem with this position. Is the SDIO an effective way to get good research done? Throughout many years of association with DoD I have been astounded at the amount of money that has been wasted on ineffective research projects. In my first contact with the U.S. Navy, I watched millions of dollars spent on a wild computer design that had absolutely no technical merit. It was abandoned many years after its lack of merit became clear. As a consultant for both the Navy and a number of contractors, I have seen expensive software research that produces very large reports with very little content. I have seen those large, expensive reports put on shelves and never used. I have seen many, almost identical efforts carried out independently and redundantly. I have seen talented professionals take approaches that they considered unwise because their "customers" asked for it. I have seen their customers take positions they do not understand because they thought that the contractors believed in them.

In computer software, the DoD contracting and funding scheme is remarkably ineffective because the bureaucrats who run it do not understand what they are buying.

26.10.4 Who Can Judge Research?

The most difficult and crucial step in research is identifying and defining the problem. Successful researchers are usually those who have the insight to find a problem that is both solvable and important.

For applied research, additional judgment is needed. A problem may be an important one in theory, but there may be restrictions that prevent the use of its solution in practice. Only people closely familiar with the practical aspects of the problem can judge whether or not they could use the results of a research project.

Applied research must be judged by teams that include both successful researchers and experienced system engineers. They must have ample opportunity to meet, be fully informed, and have clearly defined responsibilities.

26.10.5 Who Judges Research in DoD?

Although there are a few notable exceptions within DoD, the majority of those who manage its applied research program are neither successful researchers nor people with extensive system-building experience. There are outstanding researchers who work for DoD, but most of them work in the laboratories, not in the funding agencies. There are many accomplished system builders who work for DoD, but their managers often consider them too valuable to allow them to spend their time reviewing research proposals. The people who end up making funding decisions in DoD are very often unsuccessful researchers, unsuccessful system builders, and people who enter bureaucracy immediately after their education. We call them "technocrats."

Technocrats are bombarded with weighty volumes of highly detailed proposals that they are ill prepared to judge. They do not have the time to study and think; they are forced to rely on the advice of others. When they look for advice, they look for people that they know well, whether or not they are people whose areas of expertise are appropriate, and whether or not they have unbiased positions on the subject.

Most technocrats are honest and hard-working, but they are not capable of doing what is needed. The result is a very inefficient research program. I am convinced that there is now much more money being spent on software research than can be usefully spent. Very little of the work that is sponsored leads to results that are useful. Many useful results go unnoticed because the good work is buried in the rest.

26.10.6 The SDIO

The SDIO is a typical organization of technocrats. It is so involved in the advocacy of the program that it cannot judge the quality of the research involved.

The SDIO panel on battle-management computing contains not one person who has built actual battle-management software. It contains no experts on trajectory computations, pattern recognition, or other areas critical to this problem. All of its members stand to profit from continuation of the program.

26.10.7 Alternatives

If there is good research being funded by SDIO, that research has an applicability that is far broader than the SDI itself. It should be managed by teams of scientists and engineers as part of a well-organized research program. There is no need to create a special organization to judge this research. To do so is counterproductive. It can only make the program less efficient.

26.10.8 Conclusions

There is no justification for continuing with the pretense that the SDI battle-management software can be built just to obtain funding for otherwise worthwhile programs. DoD's overall approach to research management requires a thorough evaluation and review by people outside the DoD.

SDI: A Violation of Professional Responsibility

David Lorge Parnas

27.1 Introduction

In May of 1985 I was asked by the Strategic Defense Initiative Organization, the group within the Office of the U.S. Secretary of Defense that is responsible for the "Star Wars" program, to serve on a $1000/day advisory panel, the SDIO Panel on Computing in Support of Battle Management. The panel was to make recommendations about a research and development program to solve the computational problems inherent in space-based defense systems.

Like President Reagan, I consider the use of nuclear weapons as a deterrent to be dangerous and immoral. If there is a way to make nuclear weapons "impotent and obsolete" and end the fear of such weapons, there is nothing I would rather work on. However, two months later I had resigned from the panel. I have since become an active opponent of the SDI. This article explains why I am opposed to the program.

27.1.1 My View of Professional Responsibility

My decision to resign from the panel was consistent with long-held views about the individual responsibility of a professional. I believe this responsibility goes beyond an obligation to satisfy the short-term demands of the immediate employer. As a professional

- I am responsible for my own actions and cannot rely on any external authority to make my decisions for me.
- I cannot ignore ethical and moral issues. I must devote some of my energy to deciding whether the task that I have been given is of benefit to society.
- I must make sure that I am solving the real problem, not simply providing short-term satisfaction to my supervisor.

Some have held that a professional is a "team player" and should never "blow the whistle" on his colleagues and employer. I disagree. As the Challenger incident demonstrates, such action is sometimes necessary. One's obligations as a professional precede other obligations. One must not enter into contracts that conflict with one's professional obligations.

27.1.2 My Views on Defense Work

Many opponents of the SDI oppose all military development. I am not one of them. I have been a consultant to the Department of Defense and other components of the defense industry since 1971. I am considered an expert on the organization of large software systems, and I lead the U.S. Navy's Software Cost Reduction Project at the Naval Research Laboratory. Although I have friends who argue that "people of conscience" should not work on weapons, I consider it vital that people with a strong sense of social responsibility continue to work within the military/industrial complex. I do not want to see that power completely in the hands of people who are *not* conscious of social responsibility.

My own views on military work are close to those of Albert Einstein. Einstein, who called himself a militant pacifist, at one time held the view that scientists should refuse to contribute to arms development. Later in his life he concluded that to hold to a "no arms" policy would be to place the world at the mercy of its worst enemies. Each country has a right to be protected from those who use force, or the threat of force, to impose their will on others. Force can morally be used only against those persons who are themselves using force. Weapons development should be limited to weapons that are suitable for that use. Neither the present arms spiral nor nuclear weapons are consistent with Einstein's principles. One of our greatest scientists, he knew that international security requires progress in political education, not weapons technology.

27.2 SDI Background

The Strategic Defense Initiative, popularly known as "Star Wars," was initiated by a 1983 presidential speech calling on scientists to free us from the fear of nuclear weapons. President Reagan directed the Pentagon to search for a way to make nuclear strategic missiles impotent and obsolete. In response, the SDIO has embarked upon a project to develop a network of satellites carrying sensors, weapons, and computers to detect intercontinental ballistic missiles (ICBMs) and intercept them before they can do much damage. In addition to sponsoring work on the basic technologies of sensors and weapons, SDI has funded a number of Phase I "architecture studies," each of which proposes a basic design for the system. The best of these have been selected, and the contractors are now proceeding to "Phase II," a more detailed design.

27.2.1 My Early Doubts

As a scientist, I wondered whether technology offered us a way to meet these goals. My own research has centered on computer software, and I have used military software in some of my research. My experience with computer-controlled weapon systems led me to wonder whether any such system could meet the requirements set forth by President Reagan.

I also had doubts about a possible conflict of interest. I have a project within the U.S. Navy that could benefit from SDI funding. I suggested to the panel organizer that this conflict might disqualify me. He assured me that if I did not have such a conflict, they would not want me on the panel. He pointed out that the other panelists—employees of defense contractors and university professors dependent on DoD funds for their research—had similar conflicts. Readers should think about such conflicts the next time they hear of a panel of "distinguished experts."

27.2.2 My Work for the Panel

The first meeting increased my doubts. In spite of the high rate of pay, the meeting was poorly prepared; presentations were at a disturbingly unprofessional level. Technical terms were used without definition; numbers were used without supporting evidence. The participants appeared predisposed to discuss many of the interesting but tractable technical problems in space-based missile defense, while ignoring the basic problems and "big picture." Everyone seemed to have a pet project of their own that they thought should be funded.

At the end of the meeting we were asked to prepare position papers describing research problems that must be solved in order to build an effective and trustworthy shield against nuclear missiles. I spent the weeks after the meeting writing up those problems and trying to convince myself that SDIO-supported research could solve them. I failed. I could not convince myself that it would be possible to build a system that we could trust, nor that it would be useful to build a system we did not trust.

27.2.3 Why Trustworthiness Is Essential

If the United States does not trust SDI, it will not abandon deterrence and nuclear missiles. Even so, the U.S.S.R. could not assume that SDI would be completely ineffective. Seeing both a "shield" and missiles, it would feel impelled to improve its offensive forces in an effort to compensate for SDI. The United States, not trusting its defense, would feel a need to build still more nuclear missiles to compensate for the increased Soviet strength. The arms race would speed up. Further, because NATO would be wasting an immense amount of effort on a system it couldn't trust, we would see a weakening of our relative strength. Instead of the safer world that President Reagan envisions, we would have a far more dangerous situation. Thus, the issue of our trust in the system is critical. Unless the shield is trustworthy, it will not benefit any country.

27.3 The Role of Computers

SDI discussions often ignore computers, focusing on new developments in sensors and weapons. However, the sensors will produce vast amounts of raw data that computers must process and analyze. Computers must detect missile firings, determine the source of the attack, and compute the attacking trajectories. Computers must discriminate between threatening warheads and mere decoys designed to confuse our defensive system. Computers will aim and fire the weapons. All the weapons and sensors will be useless if the computers do not function properly. Software is the glue that holds such systems together. If the software is not trustworthy, the system is not trustworthy.

27.3.1 The Limits of Software Technology

Computer specialists know that software is always the most troublesome component in systems that depend on computer control. Traditional engineering products can be verified by a combination of mathematical analysis, case analysis, and prolonged testing of the complete product under realistic operating conditions. Without such validation, we cannot trust the product. None of these validation methods works well for software. Mathematical proofs verify only abstractions of small programs in restricted languages. Testing and case analysis sufficient to ensure trustworthiness take too much time. As E.W. Dijkstra has said, "Testing can show the presence of bugs, never their absence."

The lack of validation methods explains why we cannot expect a real program to work properly the first time it is really used. This is confirmed by practical experience. We can build adequately reliable software systems, but they become reliable only after extensive use in the field. Although responsible developers perform many tests, including simulations, before releasing their software, serious problems always remain when the first customers use the product. The test designers overlook the same problems the software designers overlook. No experienced person trusts a software system before it has seen extensive use under actual operating conditions.

27.3.2 Why Software for SDI Is Especially Difficult

SDI is far more difficult than any software system we have ever attempted. Some of the reasons are listed here; a more complete discussion can be found in an article published in *American Scientist* [2].

SDI software must be based on assumptions about target and decoy characteristics, and those characteristics are controlled by the attacker. We cannot rely on our information about them. The dependence of any program on local assumptions is a rich source of effective countermeasures. Espionage could render the whole multibillion-dollar system worthless without our knowledge. It could show an attacker how to exploit the inevitable differences between the computer model on which the program is based and the real world.

The techniques used to provide high reliability in other systems are hard to apply for SDI. In space, the redundancy required for high reliability is unusually expensive. The dependence of SDI on communicating computers in satellites makes it unusually vulnerable. High reliability can be achieved only if the failures of individual components are statistically independent; for a system subject to coordinated attacks, that is not the case.

Overloading the system will always be a potent countermeasure, because any computer system will have a limited capacity, and even crude decoys would consume computer capacity. An overloaded system must either ignore some of the objects it should track, or fail completely. For SDI, either option is catastrophic.

Satellites will be in fixed orbits that will not allow the same one to track a missile from its launch and destroy it. The responsibility for tracking a missile will transfer from one satellite to another. Because of noise caused by the battle and enemy interference, a satellite will require data from other satellites to assist in tracking and discrimination. The result is a distributed real-time database. For the shield to be effective, the data will have to be kept up-to-date and consistent in real time. This means that satellite clocks will have to be accurately synchronized. None of this can be done when the network's components and communication links are unreliable, and unreliability must be expected during a real battle in which an enemy would attack the network. Damaged stations are likely to inject inaccurate or false data into the database.

Realistic testing of the integrated hardware and software is impossible. Thorough testing would require "practice" nuclear wars, including attacks that partially damage the satellites. Our experience tells us that many potential problems would not be revealed by lesser measures such as component testing, simulations, or small-scale field tests.

Unlike other weapon systems, this one will offer us no opportunity to modify the software during or after its first battle. It must work the first time.

These properties are inherent in the problem, not in some particular system design. As we will see below, they cannot be evaded by proposing a new system structure.

27.4 My Decision to Act

After reaching the conclusions described above, I solicited comments from other scientists and found none that disagreed with my technical conclusions. Instead, they told me that the program should be continued, not because it would free us from the fear of nuclear weapons, but because the research money would advance the state of computer science! I disagree with that statement, but I also consider it irrelevant. Taking money allocated for developing a shield against nuclear missiles, while knowing that such a shield was impossible, seemed like fraud to me. I did not want to participate, and submitted my resignation. Feeling that it would be unprofessional to resign without explanation, I submitted position papers to support my letter. I sent copies to a number of government officials and friends, but did not send them to the press until after they had been sent to reporters by others. They have since been widely published.

27.4.1 SDIO's Reaction

The SDIO's response to my resignation transformed my stand on SDI from a passive refusal to participate to an active opposition. Neither the SDIO nor the other panelists reacted with a serious and scientific discussion of the technical problems that I raised.

The first reaction came from one of the panel organizers. He asked me to reconsider, but not because he disagreed with my technical conclusions. He accepted my view that an effective shield was unlikely, but argued that the money was going to be spent and I should help to see it well spent. There was no further reaction from the SDIO until a *New York Times* reporter made some inquiries. Then, the only reaction I received was a telephone call demanding to know who had sent the material to the *Times*.

After the story broke, the statements made to the press seemed, to me, designed to mislead rather than inform the public. Examples are given below. When I observed that the SDIO was engaged in "damage control," rather than a serious consideration of my arguments, I felt that I should inform the public and its representatives of my own view. I want the public to understand that no trustworthy shield will result from the SDIO-sponsored work. I want them to understand that technology offers no magic that will eliminate the fear of nuclear weapons. I consider this part of my personal professional responsibility as a scientist and an educator.

27.5 Critical Issues

Democracy can only work if the public is accurately informed. Again, most of the statements made by SDIO supporters seem designed to mislead the public. For example, one SDIO scientist told the public that there could be 100,000 errors in the software and it would still work properly. Strictly speaking, this statement is true. If one picks one's errors very carefully, they won't matter much. However, a single error caused the complete failure of a Venus probe many years ago. I find it hard to believe that the SDIO spokesman was not aware of that.

Another panelist repeatedly told the press that there was no fundamental law of computer science that said the problem could not be solved. Again, strictly speaking, the statement is true, but it does not counter my arguments.

I did not say that a correct program was impossible; I said that it was impossible that we could trust the program. It is not impossible that such a program would work the first time it was used; it is also not impossible that 10,000 monkeys would reproduce the works of Shakespeare if allowed to type for five years. Both are highly unlikely. However, we could tell when the monkeys had succeeded; there is no way that we could verify that the SDI software was adequate.

Another form of disinformation was the statement that I—and other SDI critics—were demanding perfection. Nowhere have I demanded perfection. To trust the software we merely need to know that the software is free of catastrophic flaws, flaws that could cause massive failure or that could be exploited by a sophisticated enemy. That is certainly easier to achieve than perfection, but there is no way to know when we have achieved it.

A common characteristic of all these statements is that they argue with statements other than the ones I published in my papers. In fact, in some cases SDIO officials dispute statements made by earlier panels or by other SDIO officials, rather than debating the point I made.

27.5.1 The "90%" Distraction

One of the most prevalent arguments in support of SDI suggests that if there are three layers, each 90% effective, the overall "leakage" would be less than 1% because the effectiveness multiplies. This argument is accepted by many people who do not have scientific training. However,

- There is no basis for the 90% figure; an SDI official told me it was picked for purpose of illustration.
- The argument assumes that the performance of each layer is independent of the others, when it is clear that there are actually many links.
- It is not valid to rate the effectiveness of such systems by a single "percentage." Such statistics are only useful for describing a random process. Any space battle would be a battle between two skilled opponents. A simple percentage figure is no more valid for such systems than it is as a way of rating chess players. The performance of defensive systems depends on the opponent's tactics. Many defensive systems have been completely defeated by a sophisticated opponent who found an effective countermeasure.

27.5.2 The "Loose Coordination" Distraction

The most sophisticated response was made by the remaining members of SDIO's Panel on Computing in Support of Battle Management, which named itself the Eastport group, in December 1985. This group of SDI proponents wrote that the system structures proposed by the best Phase I contractors, those being elaborated in Phase II, would not work because the software could not be built or tested. They said that these "architectures" called for excessively tight coordination between the "battle stations"—excessive communication—and they proposed that new Phase I studies be started. However, they disputed my conclusions, arguing that the software difficulties could be overcome using "loose coordination."

The Eastport Report neither defines its terms nor describes the structure that it had in mind. Parts of the report imply that "loose coordination" can be achieved by reducing the communication between the stations. Later sections of the report discuss the need for extensive communication in the battle-station network, contradicting some statements in the earlier section. However, the essence of their argument is that SDI could be trustworthy if each battle station functioned autonomously, without relying on help from others.

Three claims can be made for such a design:

- It decomposes an excessively large program to a set of smaller ones, each one of which can be built and tested.
- Because the battle stations would be autonomous, a failure of some would allow the others to continue to function.
- Because of the independence, one could infer the behavior of the whole system from tests on individual battle stations.

The Eastport group's argument is based on four unstated assumptions:

1. Battle stations do not need data from other satellites to perform their basic functions.
2. An individual battle station is a small software project that will not run into the software difficulties described above.
3. The only interaction between the stations is by explicit communication. This assumption is needed to conclude that test results about a single station allow one to infer the behavior of the complete system.
4. A collection of communicating systems differs in fundamental ways from a single system.

All of these assumptions are false!

1. The data from other satellites is essential for accurate tracking, and for discriminating between warheads and decoys in the presence of noise.
2. Each battle station has to perform all of the functions of the whole system. The original arguments apply to it. Each one is unlikely to work, impossible to test in actual operating conditions, and consequently impossible to trust. Far easier projects have failed.

3. Battle stations interact through weapons and sensors as well as through their shared targets. The weapons might affect the data produced by the sensors. For example, destruction of a single warhead or decoy might produce noise that makes tracking of other objects impossible. If we got a single station working perfectly in isolation, it might fail completely when operating near others. The failure of one station might cause others to fail because of overload. Only a real battle would give us confidence that such interactions would not occur.

4. A collection of communicating programs is mathematically equivalent to a single program. In practice, distribution makes the problem harder, not easier.

Restricting the communication between the satellites does not solve the problem. There is still no way to know the effectiveness of the system, and it would not be trusted. Further, the restrictions on communication are likely to reduce the effectiveness of the system. I assume that this is why none of the Phase I contractors chose such an approach.

The first claim in the list is appealing, and reminiscent of arguments made in the '60s and '70s about modular programming. Unfortunately, experience has shown that modular programming is an effective technique for making errors easier to correct, not for eliminating errors. Modular programming does not solve the problems described earlier in this paper. None of my arguments was based on an assumption of tight coupling; some of the arguments do assume that there will be data passed from one satellite to another. The Eastport Report, like earlier reports, supports that assumption.

The Eastport group is correct when it says that designs calling for extensive data communication between the battle stations are unlikely to work. However, the Phase I contractors were also right when they assumed that without such communication the system could not be effective.

27.5.3 Redefining the Problem

The issue of SDI software was debated in March 1986, at an IEEE computer conference. While two of us argued that SDI could not be trusted, the two SDI supporters argued that it did not matter. Rather than argue the computer science issues, they tried to use strategic arguments to say that a shield need not be considered trustworthy. One of them argued, most eloquently, that the President's "impotent and obsolete" terminology was technical nonsense. He suggested that we ignore what "the President's speechwriters" had to say and look at what was actually feasible. Others argue that increased uncertainty is a good thing—quite a contrast to President Reagan's promise of increased security.

In fact, the ultimate response of the computer scientists working on SDI is to redefine the problem in such a way that there is a trivial solution and improvement is always possible. Such a problem is the ideal project for government sponsorship. The contractor can always show both progress and the need for further work. Contracts will be renewed indefinitely!

Those working on the project often disparage statements made by the President and his most vocal supporters, stating that SDIO scientists and officials are not responsible for such statements. However, the general public remains unaware of their position, and believes that the President's goals are the goals of those who are doing the scientific work.

27.6 Broader Questions

27.6.1 Is SDIO-Sponsored Work of Good Quality?

Although the Eastport panel were unequivocally supportive of continuing SDI, their criticisms of the Phase I studies were quite harsh. They assert that those studies, costing a million dollars each, overlooked elementary problems that were discussed in earlier studies. If the Eastport group is correct, the SDIO contractors and the SDIO evaluators must be considered incompetent. If the Eastport group's criticisms were unjustified, or if their alternative is unworkable, *their* competence must be questioned.

Although I do not have access to much of the SDIO-sponsored work in my field, I have had a chance to study some of it. What I have seen makes big promises, but is of low quality. Because it has bypassed the usual scientific review processes, it overstates its accomplishments and makes no real scientific contribution.

27.6.2 Do Those Who Take SDIO Funds Really Disagree with Me?

I have discussed my views with many who work on SDIO-funded projects. Few of them disagree with my technical conclusions. In fact, since the story became public, two SDIO contractors and two DoD agencies have sought my advice. My position on this subject has not made them doubt my competence.

Those who accept SDIO money give a variety of excuses: "The money is going to be spent anyway; shouldn't we use it well?" "We can use the money to solve other problems." "The money will be good for computer science."

I have also discussed the problem with scientists at the Los Alamos and Sandia National Laboratories. Here, too, I found no substantive disagreement with my analysis. Instead, I was told that the project offered lots of challenging problems for physicists.

In November 1985, I read in *Der Speigel* an interview with a leading German supporter of Star Wars. He made it clear that he thought of SDI as a way of injecting funds into high technology and not as a military project. He even said that he would probably be opposed to participation in any deployment should the project come to fruition.

27.6.3 The Blind Led by Those with Their Eyes Shut

My years as a consultant in the defense field have shown me that unprofessional behavior is common. When consulting, I often find people doing something foolish. Knowing that the person involved is quite competent, I may say something like, "You know that's not the right way to do that."

"Of course," is the response, "but this is what the customer asked for."

"Is your customer a computer scientist? Does he know what he is asking?" ask I.

"No" is the simple reply.

"Why don't you tell him?" elicits the response:

"At XYZ Corporation, we don't tell our customers that what they want is wrong. We get contracts."

That may be a businesslike attitude, but it is not a professional one. It misleads the government into wasting taxpayers' money.

27.6.4 The Role of Academic Institutions

Traditionally, universities provide tenure and academic freedom so that faculty members can speak out on issues such as these. Many have done just that. Unfortunately, at U.S. universities there are institutional pressures in favor of accepting research funds from any source. A researcher's ability to attract funds is taken as a measure of his ability.

The president of a major university in the U.S. recently explained his acceptance of a DoD institute on campus by saying, "As a practical matter, it is important to realize that the Department of Defense is a major administrator of research funds. In fact, the department has more research funds at its disposal than any other organization in the country. . . . Increases in research funding in significant amounts can be received only on the basis of defense-related appropriations."

27.6.5 Should We Pursue SDI for Other Reasons?

I consider such rationalizations to be both unprofessional and dangerous. SDI endangers the safety of the world. By working on SDI, these scientists allow themselves to be counted among those who believe that the program can succeed. If they are truly professionals, they must make it very clear that an effective shield is unlikely, and a trustworthy one impossible. The issue of more money for high technology should be debated without the smoke screen of SDI. I can think of no research that is so important as to justify pretending that an ABM system can bring security to populations. Good research stands on its own merits; poor research must masquerade as something else.

I believe in research; I believe that technology can improve our world in many ways. I also agree with Professor Janusz Makowski of the Technion Institute, who wrote in the *Jerusalem Post*, "Overfunded research is like heroin, it leads to addiction, weakens the mind, and leads to prostitution." Many research fields in the United States are now clearly overfunded, largely because of DoD agencies. I believe we are witnessing the proof of Professor Makowski's statement.

27.6.6 My Advice on Participation in Defense Projects

I believe that it's quite appropriate for professionals to devote their energies to making the people of their land more secure. In contrast, it is not professional to accept employment doing "military" things that do not advance the legitimate defense interests of that country. If the project would not be effective, or if, in one's opinion, it goes beyond the legitimate defense needs of the country, a professional should not participate. Too many do not ask such questions. They ask only how they can get another contract.

It is a truism that if each of us lives as though what we do does matter, the world will be a far better place than it is now. The cause of many serious problems in our world is that many of us act as if our actions do not matter. Our streets are littered, our environment polluted, and our children are neglected because we underestimate our individual responsibility.

The arguments given to me for continuation of the SDI program are examples of such thinking. "The government has decided; we cannot change it." "The money will be spent; all you can do is make good use of it." "The system will be built; you cannot change that." "Your resignation will not stop the program."

It is true, my decision not to toss trash on the ground will not eliminate litter. However, if we are to eliminate litter, I must decide not to toss trash on the ground. We all make a difference.

Similarly, my decision not to participate in SDI will not stop this misguided program. However, if everyone who knows that the program will not lead to a trustworthy shield against nuclear weapons refuses to participate, there will be no program. Every individual's decision is important.

It is not necessary for computer scientists to take a political position; they need only be true to their professional responsibilities. If the public were aware of the technical facts, if they knew how unlikely it is that such a shield would be effective, public support would evaporate. We do not need to tell the public not to build SDI. We only need to help them understand why it will never be an effective and trustworthy shield.

References

1. Einstein, Albert, and Freud, Sigmund. *Warum Krieg?* Zurich: Diogenes Verlag, 1972.

2. Parnas, D.L., "Software Aspects of Strategic Defense Systems," *American Scientist*, September–October 1985: 432–40. Also published in German in Kursbuch 83, *Krieg und Frieden—Streit um SDI*, by Kursbuch/Rotbuch Verlag, March 1986; and in Dutch in *Informatie*, Nr. 3, March 1986: 175–86.

3. Parnas, D.L., "On the Criteria to Be Used in Decomposing Systems into Modules." *Communications of the ACM* **15**, 12 (1972): 1053–8.

4. Eastport Group, "Summer Study 1985," A Report to the Director—Strategic Defense Initiative Organization, December 1985.

5. "Wer kuscht, hat keine Chance," *Der Spiegel*, Nr. 47, 18 November 1985.

Introduction

Leonard L. Tripp

Dave reminds us that to call our discipline "software engineering" we must acknowledge and abide by the principles of engineering: technical, ethical, and, perhaps least understood in our profession, legal. What are the legal principles?

As a result of performing professional services, an engineer may become liable for injuries or damages caused by his/her negligence. A consulting engineer working in the construction industry may make an error in a plan that could result in a building failure. Or, an engineer working for a manufacturer could make an error in design that could result in a defective product. In either case, property might be damaged or someone might be injured, causing a claim to be made or a lawsuit to be filed against the engineer or the manufacturer.

The courts in England and in the United States have developed numerous rules governing negligence suits or actions. Among those rules are the four elements that the plaintiff must show in an action to prove his/her negligence case against the defendant. The four elements are

1. A duty that the defendant owed the plaintiff to conform to a certain standard of conduct as established by the law.
2. A breach of legal duty by the defendant.
3. The breach of duty must have a causal connection to the injury sustained by the plaintiff. The law requires that the breach of duty (the defendant's action or failure to act) must be the "proximate cause" of the harm suffered by the plaintiff.
4. Damage suffered by the plaintiff. Obviously, if the plaintiff has not sustained any personal injury or damage to his/her property, he/she is not entitled to recover any money from the defendant.

The law in recent years has drawn a clear distinction between the rules applying to the engineer working in construction or other consulting areas and the engineer working in manufacturing.

In order to show that a consulting engineer has breached his/her professional duty, the plaintiff must have an expert testify as to the standard of care that allegedly was breached. In most jurisdictions, the expert who testifies must practice the same profession as the defendant. Under professional liability law, an engineer is not the guarantor of a result. His/her only responsibility is to render services in accordance with applicable standards of his/her profession.

Under the laws of negligence, a manufacturer has a duty to produce a product that is not negligent in manufacture or design. In order for a plaintiff to prove negligence in design, he/she must show a standard and demonstrate how the manufacturer's design deviated from the standard. An expert witness for the plaintiff may testify that either a written or an informal standard had established certain design criteria, which were not met by the manufacturer.

In addition to legal principles, for software engineering to be recognized as a professional engineering discipline, the following elements need to be in place: initial professional education, accreditation, a recognized body of knowledge and standards, practicing professionals, a means for assessing competence of practicing professionals, a code of ethics, and an organized group of practicing professionals. The paper discusses most of the elements for software engineering to become a recognized profession. One of the key assumptions made in the paper is that software engineering, as a profession would be similar to traditional engineering disciplines.

The genesis of the ideas in the paper was discussed by Dave in 1985. At that time, the concept of software engineering as a professional discipline was in its infancy. In 1985 there was limited use of computers in safety-critical applications such as avionics systems on commercial transport planes. By the date of the paper publication (1995), several activities were progressing toward the professionalization of software engineering as a discipline. In 1993, the IEEE Computer Society and the ACM had formed a joint steering committee on "Software Engineering as a Profession." Its charter was "to establish the appropriate set(s) of criteria and norms for professional practice of software engineering upon which industrial decisions, professional certification, and educational curricula can be based." By 1998 the committee had overseen the development of a code of ethics and professional practice, a model accreditation criteria, a terminology baseline, and initial work in identifying a body of knowledge.

Today, undergraduate education in software engineering is starting to emerge. Programs exist in Australia, Canada, the United Kingdom, and the United States. The integration in 1998 of the Computer Science Accreditation Board into ABET is a major step in putting in place the mechanism for accreditation of software engineering educational programs in the United States. Since 1998 several jurisdictions, for example, the state of Texas and the province of British Columbia, have initiated processes to license engineers with a specialty in software. Progress is being made on identifying the body of knowledge for software engineering, developing criteria for evaluating relevant engineering experience, and specifying the elements of an undergraduate curriculum for software engineering.

Standards for software engineering were initiated by the IEEE Computer Society in 1976. The early standards focused on terminology, quality assurance concerns and documentation. The 1999 IEEE Collection of Software Engineering Standards contains more than forty standards in four volumes. In 1987 the ISO committee for software engineering standards was formed. Also, there are various ISO or IEC committees that produce software engineering-related standards for specific application areas such as aerospace, durability, functional safety, medical applications, nuclear power, and quality.

Dave's focus on the professional responsibility of a software engineer, both in word and in deed, sets a powerful example for the maturation of the discipline.

The Professional Responsibilities of Software Engineers

David Lorge Parnas

28.1 Abstract

Registered Engineers are expected to be aware of their responsibilities as professionals. Those who practice Software Engineering often enter that profession without either an engineering education or professional registration. This paper discusses professional responsibilities and ways to improve the level of professionalism among software developers.

28.2 Personal Responsibility, Social Responsibility, and Professional Responsibility

Since 1985 I have been involved in many discussions on the subject of the responsibility of Engineers and Scientists. In those discussions the phrases "Social Responsibility," "Personal Responsibility," and "Professional Responsibility" have been used almost interchangeably. It has taken me some time to understand the distinction.

My involvement with these issues began in 1985 when I found that I could not, in good conscience, continue to be a member of a U.S. Defense Department Committee advising on the Strategic Defense Initiative (SDI) also known as Star Wars [1, 2]. My first thoughts on the subject were simply about honesty. I felt the claims being made for the project were outrageous and it violated my sense of personal responsibility to participate in an activity that I felt to be dishonest. It was concern over *personal* responsibility that led me to resign. My second thoughts were about *professional* responsibility. I had accepted a professional obligation to serve as an advisor. Although I did not feel that the activity was honest, I did have an obligation to explain my concerns to my clients. I needed to let them know why the task that they had given the committee was one that could not be done. It was for this reason that I spent many days writing a carefully structured set of short essays, which I submitted as part of my letter of resignation. It was some weeks after those letters were written that I began to think about *social* responsibility. I reached the conclusion that the public, i.e., society as a whole, was being misled. It was concern about social responsibility that led me to agree to the publication of those resignation letters and, later, to accept many invitations to explain my views to the public. Today, I offer three definitions:

- *Personal Responsibilities* are those that are shared by all persons, no matter what their profession or educational background. These include basic obligations such as honesty in our dealings with others and concern for their well-being and feelings.

- *Professional Responsibilities* are additional responsibilities that we take on because we have become members of a particular profession such as medicine, journalism, or engineering. Each profession has developed a code of responsibilities for its members that goes beyond general personal responsibilities.

- *Social Responsibilities* are responsibilities toward society as a whole rather than toward other individuals. My view is that those of us who have received an extensive education from society have a debt to repay; we have to share our knowledge with that society when it can be of benefit to that society.

The primary subject of this paper is professional responsibility, but I wish to begin with a discussion of social responsibility, which is always part of professional responsibility.

28.3 The Social Responsibility of Scientists and Engineers

It is often said that, in the land of the blind, the one-eyed man is king. This saying is a bit anachronistic in a society that is organized along democratic lines, one in which the few remaining "royals" have very little power. However, it is even more important that scientists recognize that, in a world increasingly dependent on science and technology, they are the one-eyed ones and the majority of the world's decision makers are quite blind.

Many of the important decisions that our society must make in the next few years are technological issues. Consider the following examples:

- Can we reduce our energy expenditures without great disruption in people's lives?
- How urgent is the need to reduce the level of greenhouse gases?
- Should we build more nuclear power generating stations?
- Is it safe to allow nuclear power generating stations to be controlled by computers?
- Can technology help us to reduce the amount of the paper that we use?
- Is it safe to allow computers to control cars and trucks?

Decisions on each of these issues will be taken by people who are not scientists, but there are difficult scientific questions behind each of these "hot" issues. In each of these areas, it is unlikely that the "correct" choice will be made unless those who make the decisions have some understanding of the relevant scientific and technical facts.

Science and technology are the "black magic" of our age. Scientists and engineers are like wizards; their knowledge of arcane rituals and obscure terminology gives them an understanding that is not shared by the general public. The public, dazzled by the many visible achievements of modern technology, regard scientists as magicians who can solve any problem if given enough funds. Many scientists encourage the impression that we are wizards when they are asking for funds. The public, like the peasants of old, are so awed by technological advances that they make no attempt to understand the black magic.

Most public officials share this attitude. They too assume that there will be major issues in modern science that they simply cannot understand. They are prepared to be mystified and amazed. When forced to decide between conflicting positions, they make their judgments based on the apparent trustworthiness of the advocates rather than on the merit of the arguments. In most cases, established scientists have the attention of those in control, but, occasionally, a radical newcomer with a gift for rhetoric carries the day. Scientific topics often become fads only to quietly disappear when they are replaced by newer "miracles."

The feeling that science must be obscure and enigmatic, has often led to very poor policies by science funding agencies. At times, these seem to prefer obscure, mystical, poorly defined concepts over those that can be explained in terms of easily measured phenomena. Funding often goes to scientists who make dramatic promises instead of those who honestly explain the limitations of the technology and seek incremental improvements. On other occasions funding goes to work that is not science at all; in the name of "industrial relevance" our scientific agencies sometimes support development work that could better be done by industry itself.

In a world where science is treated as a branch of magic, the rewards often go to those who are illusionists, people who use sleight of hand and distraction to create the impression that there are easy answers to difficult problems. Even those entrusted by our governments with the task of administering science funding often allow themselves to be "snowed" by work that they think they cannot understand.

In such an environment, scientists with a sense of social responsibility must devote some of their time and energy to public education. Only if we remove the veil of mysticism that comes from our use of highly specialized jargon and obscure notation, can we expect informed decisions from our governments.

28.4 The Professional Responsibilities of Engineers

The title of this paper deals with Software Engineers. In this section, I take that phrase literally. I assume that the word "Software" in "Software Engineering" plays the same role as "Electrical" in "Electrical Engineering," i.e., that Software Engineers are Engineers. This assumption is, at best, questionable. Software Engineering is often the subject of some very shallow courses and books taught, not in Engineering Faculties but in Science Departments. Many people who have the title, "software engineer" in their jobs have no education in any technical field at all. Many others do not have an education that would satisfy the requirements of the Professional Engineering Associations in their home jurisdictions; few have bothered to apply for professional registration as Engineers. The standards in journals on software engineering are very low and many people in the field confuse software engineering with configuration management.

Blithely ignoring these sad facts, I base my assumptions on basic definitions. An Engineer is someone who uses advanced knowledge of Science, Mathematics, and Technology to build objects for use by others. By this basic definition, most of those who call themselves either programmers or software engineers, are Engineers. The facts mentioned above simply imply that they are underqualified, unlicensed, and often unprofessional. This may leave them unaware of their professional responsibilities, but it does not relieve them from those obligations.

28.4.1 Why Do We Have Licensed Professional Engineers?

The notion of the licensed professional is an old one, dating back to when engineers built bridges, steam engines, etc. Our present system of licensing engineers was introduced for the following reasons:

- Products such as roads, bridges, elevators, power plants, etc. are potentially dangerous. Incompetent designs can endanger the lives, health, or property of both users and the public at large.

- Those who purchase or commission the design of such products are usually unable to judge the competence of the person or persons that they hire to do the work for them.

- The competent, conscientious, and disciplined members of any profession have an interest in making sure that potential customers and the public are able to distinguish between themselves and others who may claim to be able to do a job. Bad work by a few damages the reputations and business prospects of all.

■ Financial pressures may tempt employers or customers to follow unsafe or unwise practices, and introduce devices that could fail and endanger others. The design of certain devices should be done by people who have accepted professional obligations that go beyond loyalty or obedience to an employer or customer.

Today, most jurisdictions have legislation establishing Associations of Professional Engineers and giving them the right to grant recognition to people they deem competent to practice Engineering. Government regulations often require that certain products be produced or approved by a recognized Professional Engineer. Professional Engineers are obligated to follow rules of good practice and to object strongly, whenever they see such rules violated.

For most Professional Engineers, licensing involves two stages: (1) completion of an educational program that has been accredited by a national body, and (2) passing an examination on the issue of professional responsibility and the legal obligations of a Professional Engineer.

28.4.2 Why Should Software Engineers Be Different?

The phrase "Software Engineering" became popular in the late 60s as a result of a growing concern about what was then, optimistically, called "the software crisis." NATO sponsored two important conferences on the topic in Munich. Although the word "Engineering" was used, few of those who attended were Professional Engineers. The concerns of those who attended the Software Engineering conferences in the late 60s were technical or scientific ones rather than the types of issues discussed above. At that time, few Engineers recognized the potential importance of software in their profession; they often regarded programming as a simple, technician-level task akin to stringing wires. Professional Engineering societies, dominated by people who were used to physical products did not take the phrase "Software Engineering," very seriously. Engineers were assumed to be people who produced physical products not programs.

As a result of this neglect by the Professional Engineers, Software Engineering developed *outside* of the Engineering Community. It has been left to Computer Science departments and taught by people who are not themselves Professional Engineers. Because so many of the problems experienced in software development manifest themselves as problems of project management, courses titled Software Engineering are not technical courses like those on other engineering subjects; they are often courses on project management, project scheduling, version control, etc.

28.5 What Are the Obligations of the Engineer?

Whole books have been written on this subject and this paper is not going to cover it. I focus on a few obligations that I think are particularly important for software engineers.

28.5.1 Accept Individual Responsibility

A Professional Engineer accepts responsibility for design decisions and must not approve inappropriate designs even if ordered to do so. As a professional, the engineer is not a "team player" and must object openly to decisions that violate professional standards. Professional standards have priority over obligations to employer or customer.

28.5.2 Solve the Real Problem

A Professional Engineer is expected to make sure that the technical problem being solved is the client's real problem. Engineers are expected to have a precise description of a problem before they work on its solution and to consult customers and other experts about that description to make sure that they know what they are trying to achieve. Engineers are expected to look at the "whole problem" not just at the technical problems that are their specialty.

28.5.3 Be Honest About Capabilities

There are problems for which there are no appropriate technological solutions. An Engineer is expected to report that fact rather than accept contracts to do something that cannot or should not be done. For example, feasibility studies should not be undertaken when you are already certain that the job is not feasible.

28.5.4 Produce Reviewable Designs

Although Engineers accept individual responsibility for their work, they also know that no individual is infallible and that often their work is so important that it must be reviewed by others. An engineer must document and explain each design in ways that help the reviewers and must view inspections as tools to help improve the quality of their products.

28.5.5 Maintainability

Usually, an Engineer is involved in the initial development of a product, but the product continues in use after the design team has moved on to new projects. It is the responsibility of the Engineer to produce a product that can be maintained by others. Both the structure of the product and the documentation must be designed so that maintenance is possible and practical.

28.6 Professional Practice in Software Development

Earlier in my professional career, I did a lot of consulting with software development organizations. It will surprise nobody who knows me to hear that I was often quite critical of designs that I was asked to review and evaluate. I was, and continue to be, distressed by the poor design of many commercial programs, but I was even more distressed by answers that I received when I pointed out the disadvantages of certain design decisions.

- "Of course it's wrong, but that is what my boss told me to do."
- "We already know the answer, but they will pay us $1,000,000 for the study."
- "It's not the right way, but it's the way the customer wants it."
- "At XYZ Corporation, we don't tell our customers that they're wrong, we take their contracts."
- "That's not the real problem, but it is what they asked us to do."
- "We can't give them what they need, but we'll do the best we can."
- "We've got a deadline; we'll worry about maintainability when we get that contract."
- "We don't like people criticizing our designs!"

Such remarks did not come from Professional Engineers; they came from programmers who were doing work that should have been done by Engineers who were conscious of their professional responsibilities.

It is clear to everyone in the field that most programs are not designed so that they are easily reviewable or maintainable.

28.7 A Simple Example, Pacemakers

The heart pacemaker is one of the wonders of today's medical technology. It allows people who would have been the prisoners of a weak or unreliable body to live full, nearly normal, lives. While it is obvious that the life of the owner depends on the reliability of the device, the fact that the owner may be driving a car means that the public safety is affected as well. Thus, this tiny, seemingly innocuous, device has the properties of devices that are usually the product of professional engineers.

28.7.1 Software That Is Close to One's Heart

Although the early pacemakers were simply self-contained, sealed, battery-driven, pulse generators, they have evolved to be surprisingly sophisticated software-controlled devices. They have a number of operating modes, and a tiny telemetry system that allows them to be adjusted by an external device (called a programmer). Modern pacemakers collect data and, when requested, transmit statistics that allow the doctor to know how well they have served the patient. Most include sensors that observe the patient's natural heart function and generate pulses only when the natural heart rate falls below some specified limit. More sophisticated devices adjust that limit to the patient's activity level.

The whole sophisticated computer system must be packaged in a sealed unit about the size of a large coin. It is expected to operate in a hostile environment (the human body) for about a decade. Service is expensive; the device is replaced by surgery.

28.7.2 What Should Be Done

In other publications [3], I indicated what should be done for such critical software. The programmers should have been given a precise description of the operating environment and the conditions that can arise. A document describing the device as "black box" should have been produced and reviewed by both engineers and doctors to make sure that the real problem was accurately described. The code should have been documented in a way that permitted systematic review and revision [4]. The doctor should have been supplied with well-organized precise documentation that explained the behavior of the device to him. Some would argue that the code should have been subject to formal proof.

28.7.3 What Seems to Be Done

This section reports my personal experience with one such device. I have not done the study necessary to be sure that this is typical, but all of my information suggests that it is. Briefly, my expectations were not met!

I first became conscious of a possible "software engineering" problem when I observed the surgeon, with the help of a specially trained technician trying to perform a test on the device. The device "refused" the surgeon's command and neither the surgeon nor the technician was able to figure out why. The surgeon found another way to get the information he wanted. Concerned that the device might contain a software "bug" I asked for a copy of the medical material and, after several hours, found a footnote explaining the behavior. It was located far from where you would expect to find the information. The location of the information was so unlikely, that when I went to show it to the surgeon, it took 30 minutes to find it a second time.

I managed to visit the manufacturer and meet the Engineer responsible for the design. Although he could explain the hardware aspects in great detail, he relied on a programmer, who could not be found, to explain the code. The hardware, and its manufacturing process had been subject to careful documentation and scrutiny. The programming was viewed as a trivial task and had not been subject to the same discipline.

As a result of the failure to document and review properly, the device in question has some fundamental weaknesses. For example, the activity sensor is actually a motion sensor and often increases heart rate when the owner is sitting in a vehicle and subject to externally induced motion. The range of adjustments provided does not allow for some conditions encountered in use. The problem that was solved was not the real problem. The software was considered self-documenting; a new programmer would have great difficulties inducing the intended structure from the code. In other words, this was a typical software product.

In this application the hardware is the product of professional engineers. The System Engineering and Software development were carefully, but not professionally, done. The behavior of the overall system was determined in large part by the software, but the programmers had no precise statement of requirements and did not know the requirements.

This case is typical. Engineers rarely take programming seriously; they view it as something rather trivial, mastering the syntax of a programming language, and trust it to people who are not Professional Engineers. Engineers who do write programs, have not been educated for the task. They usually know little about either Computer Science or programming methods. They just write code the way that it was written 30 years ago.

28.8 Other Concerns

Some Professional Engineers in Australia made me cognizant of a more general problem. As active members of their professional engineering society, they take their responsibilities seriously. However, they are required to use computerized tools written by people who are not members of that, or any similar, society. They feel uncomfortable putting their professional stamp on a product developed using software that doesn't carry the stamp of approval of someone with similar professional qualifications. "How," they ask, "can we put our professional approval on a product that was designed with the help of programs whose package carries a disclaimer?"

They felt that those who write software for use by Professional Engineers should be Professional Engineers.

28.9 The "Know How" Isn't There

If you take the time to talk to the people who develop software for use by others, you will find that they do not know how to do the things that would be required by good professional standards. They may recognize the need for a precise requirements statement, but they don't know how to write one. They may recognize the need for reviewable design documentation, but they don't know how to do that either. The will to do a better job is there, but the ability, the knowledge necessary to do the work properly is not usually present.

28.10 How to Improve the Level of Professionalism in Software Development

If you, like I, feel that we should be increasing the level of Professionalism in Software Engineering, that Software Engineers should have the same consciousness of the professional responsibilities that other Engineers have, there are two things you should do.

28.10.1 Work with Professional Engineering Societies

Although there are occasional discussions within IFIP member societies about accreditation of Computer Science programs, such efforts have never produced rigorous accreditation standards and there are no requirements that someone producing important software be a graduate of such a program. I believe that this is the wrong approach. Rather than get into a jurisdictional dispute with Engineering groups on who sets the standards for software engineering, we should work with those groups to establish standards for a new "flavor" of Engineer, either "Software Engineer" or "Computer Engineer." We should take advantage of the experience that these groups have in setting professional standards; we should try to use existing legislation to enforce those standards. The basic standards for the professional behavior of Software Engineers are the same as those for other engineers. It is only the underlying technology, scientific knowledge, and mathematics that are different.

In the future, all Engineers will have to know more about digital technology and discrete mathematics and some of the differences will disappear.

28.10.2 Work for Accreditation of Software Engineering Programs

In my country, Canada, Computer Engineering programs must meet standards that are close to those in place for Electrical Engineers. Computer Engineering, including Software Engineering, is considered to be a branch of

Electrical Engineering. This has limited the evolution of the programs so that it no longer fits the marketplace. Computer Engineers now know more than necessary about electrical hardware and less than they need to know of Computer Science and Discrete Mathematics. It is time to develop standards for educational programs that can stand on their own rather than fit into the EE curriculum pattern. Accreditation is an essential component in efforts to improve the professional practice of Engineers. Unless we can get the accreditation committees to understand the needs of Software Engineering, we can make little progress.

28.10.3 Develop Educational Programs

If the accreditation committees were ready to work with us, we would not be ready to work with them. There is little agreement on the essential knowledge required of those practicing Software Engineering. Some programs teach nothing more than programming languages, others stress process management, a few focus on programming methods. None of these programs recognizes the broad knowledge required of an engineer specializing in systems in which software plays an important role. Moreover, most programs are so fixated on teaching the latest technology, that they fail to provide the fundamental knowledge necessary to follow and understand future developments. Above all, we need to remember that Engineering is not management. Both Engineering and Management are honorable professions, but they are quite distinct. Our present programs and literature confuse them.

References

1. Parnas, D.L., Software Aspects of Strategic Defense Systems, *American Scientist*, Vol. 73, No. 5, September–October 1985, pp. 432–440. Also published in Comm. of the ACM, 28, 12, December 1985, pp. 1326–1335. Dutch—Informatie, *jaargang* 28, 3, March 1986, pp. 175–186., Japanese—SEKAI, no. 6, 1986, pp. 298–319. German—Software Wars, in Kursbuch 83, Krieg und Frieden–Streit um SDI. Published by Kursbuch/Rotbuch Verlag, March, 1986. Also a partial translation "Wie Kunstliche Blumen," in *Frontal*, May/June 1986, p. 46. Hebrew—Explaining Preparation of Military Strategic Software, *Maaseh Hoshev*, April 1986, p. 3 by Information Processing Association of Israel. Translated into Swedish—Programvaruaspekter pa strategiska for svarssystem, *Zenit*, Issue No. 94, Winter 1986/87, pp. 66–82. Reprinted in *Computerization & Controversy: Value Conflicts & Social Choices*, edited by Charles Dunlop & Rob Kling, Academic Press, Boston, March 1991.

2. Parnas, D.L., "SDI: A Violation of Professional Responsibility," *ABACUS*, vol. 4, no. 2, Winter 1987, pp. 46–52. Reprinted in "The Name of the Chamber was Peace," *Science for Peace*, Samuel Stevens and Co., Toronto and Fort Meyers, 1988. Also reprinted in *A Computer Science Reader—Selections from ABACUS*, edited by Eric A Weiss, Springer-Verlag, 1987, pp. 46–52. (QA 76.24 C658.) Also reprinted in *COMPUTER STUDIES: Computers in Society*, edited by

Kathryn Schellenberg, Dushkin Publishing Group, 1988. (ISBN 0-87967-727-9) Also reprinted in *Ethical Issues in Engineering,* by Deborah G. Johnson, Prentice-Hall, 1991, p. 15–25. (ISBN 0-13-290578-7)

3. Parnas, D.L., Madey, J., "Functional Documentation for Computer Systems Engineering (Version 2)," CRL Report 237, Communications Research Laboratory, McMaster University, (to appear in *Science of Computer Programming*).

4. Parnas, D.L., Madey, J., Iglewski, M., "Formal Documentation of Well-Structured Programs," CRL Report 259, Communications Research Laboratory, McMaster University, September 1992, 37 pgs.

Introduction

Victor R. Basili

Do software systems age analogously to humans? As usual Dave Parnas asks a provocative question and provides well-informed insight in answering it. Although humans age from within, software systems age from without, that is, they no longer keep up with the user's ever-changing needs for them. They age because what is expected from them changes over time, and when we try to update them to meet those changing needs, we do not change them appropriately.

To make progress in transforming software development into software engineering, we must observe the development process and reflect on what we observe. We must then build models that allow us to reason about what we observe and thereby find ways to improve it. This paper represents a set of observations by someone with a keen perception about how software systems evolve, how they are maintained, and what we might do to slow the aging process. It gives us a model for thinking about the evolution of software systems.

One might compare this approach with one that uses data as the observation and abstraction mechanism. For example, Manny Lehman has also observed system evolution and has tried to capture his observations in empirical models, using data to help understand and predict the "aging" of systems. Observation is fundamental to both approaches, as it is to any discovery process. One basic difference is the use of data as the observation and abstraction mechanism, as opposed to qualitative insight. A major strength of Parnas's approach is the attempt to understand and classify the specific types of problems and to recommend potential solutions for each class of problem, rather than to quantify the results. A major strength of the empirical approach is the ability to produce quantitative predictive models.

As a set of insights, this paper is a real contribution to how we view software evolution. Because there has not been quantitative validation of these insights, they provide valuable hypotheses for researchers in empirical studies.

The pity is that there is not enough observation in software engineering, especially observation that allows us to build both insights and models! Insights of special interest to me in this paper include the following:

- The need to employ "solid engineering" in the software maintenance process—at the very least requiring the same good concepts expected for good software development. This point cannot be made strongly enough.
- The need to characterize the kinds of changes anticipated, so that the design can take these into account. Although this is not the first time Dave has discussed this issue, it remains for me one of the fundamentals I

learned from his writings. The need to specify, as part of any requirements document, the anticipated evolution of the system is basic information necessary for the design. There may be a very large number of good designs for a given system, but that number shrinks dramatically the minute you try to make the first change.

- The need to read good designs as a means of learning how to design. Unfortunately, there are not enough good designs available for educational purposes.

- The need to review designs from several points of view. This idea has influenced the work in our research group in building document- and notation-specific, goal-oriented, focused reading techniques. For example, Perspective-based reading [1] is an attempt at supplying technical support for reading requirements documents.

Can we stop the software aging process? Probably not. But it certainly appears that there are opportunities to retard it.

Reference

1. F. Shull, I. Rus, and V. Basili, "How Perspective-Based Reading Can Improve Requirements Inspections," *IEEE Computer,* Vol. 33, No. 7, July 2000.

Software Aging

David Lorge Parnas

29.1 Abstract

Programs, like people, get old. We can't prevent aging, but we can understand its causes, take steps to limit its effects, temporarily reverse some of the damage it has caused, and prepare for the day when the software is no longer viable. A sign that the Software Engineering profession has matured will be that we lose our preoccupation with the first release and focus on the long-term health of our products. Researchers and practitioners must change their perception of the problems of software development. Only then will Software Engineering deserve to be called Engineering.

29.2 What Nonsense!

I can easily imagine the reaction of some computer scientists to the title of this paper.

> Software is a mathematical product; mathematics doesn't decay with time. If a theorem was correct 200 years ago, it will be correct tomorrow. If a program is correct today, it will be correct 100 years from now. If it is wrong 100 years from now, it must have been wrong when it was written. It makes no sense to talk about software aging.

Like many such statements, the imagined quote is true but not really relevant. Software products do exhibit a phenomenon that closely resembles human aging. Old software has begun to cripple its once-proud owners; many products are now viewed as a burdensome legacy from the past. A steadily increasing amount of effort is going into the support of these older products. Like human aging, software aging is inevitable, but like human aging, there are things that we can do to slow down the process and, sometimes, even reverse its effects.

Software aging is not a new phenomenon, but it is gaining in significance because of the growing economic importance of software and the fact that increasingly, software is a major part of the "capital" of many high-tech firms. Many old software products have become essential cogs in the machinery of our society. The aging of these products is impeding the further development of the systems that include them.

The authors and owners of new software products often look at aging software with disdain. They believe that, if the product had been designed using today's techniques, it wouldn't be causing problems. Such remarks remind me of a young jogger scoffing at an 86-year-old man (who, unknown to the jogger, was a champion swimmer into his 50s) and saying that he should have had more exercise in his youth. Just as we will all (if we are lucky) get old, software aging can, and will, occur in all *successful* products. We must recognize that it will happen to our products and prepare for it. When old age arrives, we must be prepared to deal with it.

The purpose of this paper is to explain how an abstract, mathematical product can age and then to review some of the approaches to dealing with it.

29.3 The Causes of Software Aging

There are two, quite distinct, types of software aging. The first is caused by the failure of the product's owners to modify it to meet changing needs; the second is the result of the changes that are made. This "one-two punch" can lead to rapid decline in the value of a software product.

29.3.1 Lack of Movement

Over the last three decades, our expectations about software products have changed greatly. I can recall the days when a programmer would "patch" a program stored on paper tape by using a glue and paper. We were all willing to submit large decks of cards and to wait hours or days for the job to compile and run. When interactive programming first came in, we were willing to use cryptic command languages. Today, everyone takes on-line access, "instant" response, and menu-driven interfaces for granted. We expect communications capabilities, mass on-line storage, etc. The first software product that I built (in 1960) would do its job perfectly today (if I could find a Bendix computer), but nobody would use it. That software has aged even though nobody has touched it. Although users in the early 60s were enthusiastic about the product, today's users expect more. My old software could, at best, be the kernel of a more convenient system on today's market. Unless software is frequently updated, its users will become dissatisfied and they will change to a new product as soon as the benefits outweigh the costs of retraining and converting. They will refer to that software as old and outdated.

29.3.2 Ignorant Surgery

Although it is essential to upgrade software to prevent aging, changing software can cause a different form of aging. The designer of a piece of software usually had a simple concept in mind when writing the program. If the program is large, understanding that concept allows one to find those sections of the program that must be altered when an update or correction is needed. Understanding that concept also implies understanding the interfaces used within the system and between the system and its environment.

Changes made by people who do not understand the original design concept almost always cause the structure of the program to degrade. Under those circumstances, changes will be inconsistent with the original concept; in fact, they will invalidate the original concept. Sometimes the damage is small, but often it is quite severe. After those changes, one must know both the original design rules, and the newly introduced exceptions to the rules, to understand the product. After many such changes, the original designers no longer understand the product. Those who made the changes, never did. In other words, *nobody* understands the modified product. Software that has been repeatedly modified (maintained) in this way becomes very expensive to update. Changes take longer and are more likely to introduce new "bugs". Change induced aging is often exacerbated by the fact that the maintainers feel that they do not have time to update the documentation. The documentation becomes increasingly inaccurate thereby making future changes even more difficult.

29.4 Kidney Failure

A problem that is often confused with, but is distinct from, software aging, is the system slow down caused by failure to release allocated memory. Files may grow and require pruning. Sometimes a memory allocation routine may not release all the space that has been allocated. Slowly, swap and file space are diminished and performance degrades. This problem is often a congenital design failure and can strike at any age; but it may also be the result of ignorant surgery or exacerbated by changing usage patterns. Nonetheless, it is more easily cured than the "aging" that is the subject of this paper. A dialysis type process may intervene and clean up the file system and memory, improved routines may cause the cleanup to occur rapidly and the software may be considered completely "cured".

29.5 The Costs of Software Aging

The symptoms of software aging mirror those of human aging: (1) owners of aging software find it increasingly hard to keep up with the market and lose customers to newer products; (2) aging software often degrades in its space/time performance as a result of a gradually deteriorating structure; (3) aging software often becomes "buggy" because of errors introduced when changes are made. Each of these results in real costs to the owner.

29.5.1 Inability to Keep Up

As software ages, it grows bigger. This "weight gain" is a result of the fact that the easiest way to add a feature, is to add new code. Modifying existing code to handle the new situations is often difficult because that code is neither well understood nor well documented. As the size of a program increases, sometimes by one or two orders of magnitude over a period of several years, changes become more difficult in a variety of ways. First, there is more code to change; a change that might have been made in one or two parts of the original program, now requires altering many sections of the code. Second, it is more difficult to find the routines that must be changed. As a result, the owners are unable to add new features quickly enough. Customers may switch to a younger product to get those features. The company experiences a notable drop in revenue; when they bring out a new version, it is of interest to a dwindling customer base. If they do attempt to keep up with the market, by increasing their work force, the increased costs of the changes and the delays lead to further loss of customers.

29.5.2 Reduced Performance

As the size of the program grows, it places more demands on the computer memory, and there are more delays as code must be swapped in from mass storage. The program responds more slowly; customers must upgrade their computers to get acceptable response. Performance also decreases because of poor design. The software is no longer well understood and changes may adversely affect performance. A younger product, whose original design reflected the need for recently introduced features will run faster or use less memory.

29.5.3 Decreasing Reliability

As the software is maintained, errors are introduced. Even in the early years of industry, observers were able to document situations in which each error corrected introduced (on average) more than one error. Each time an attempt was made to decrease the failure rate of the systems, it got worse. Often the only choice was to abandon the product or at least to stop repairing bugs. I have been told of older software products in which the list of known, but not yet repaired, bugs exceeded 2000 entries.

29.6 Reducing the Costs of Software Aging

Inexperienced programmers can often be recognized by the elation that they show the first time that they get correct results from a program. "I'm done; it works!" is the shout of a new programmer who has just had a successful first demonstration.[1] The experienced programmer realizes that this is just the beginning. They know that any serious product requires extensive testing,

---

1. Students get this "rush" with their first error-free compilation.

review, and revision after the first successful run. The work that is invested by responsible, professional organizations after the first successful run and before the first release is usually much greater than that required to get the first successful run. However, even experienced programmers focus on that first release. Our experience with software aging tells us that we should be looking far beyond the first release to the time when the product is old.

Too many papers at software engineering conferences focus on the problems of getting to the first release. Too many papers focus on the management issues (e.g., configuration management and control). Dealing with software aging requires more than "patient management"; it requires solid engineering. It is the purpose of the remainder of this paper to consider what actions we might take to reduce the costs associated with Software Aging.

29.7 Preventive Medicine

Since software aging is such a serious problem, the first question we must ask is what we can do to delay the decay and limit its effects.

29.7.1 Design for Success

The first step in controlling software aging is applying the old slogan, "design for change." Since the early 70s we have known how to design software for change. The principle to be applied is known by various names, e.g., "information hiding," "abstraction," "separation of concerns," "data hiding," or most recently, "object orientation." To apply this principle one begins by trying to characterize the changes that are likely to occur over the "lifetime" of the product. Since we cannot predict the actual changes, the predictions will be about classes of changes, e.g., revised expression representation, replacing of the terminal with a new type, changes in the user interface, change to a new windowing system, etc. Since it is impossible to make everything equally easy to change, it is important to estimate the probabilities of each type of change. Then one organizes the software so that the items that are most likely to change are "confined" to a small amount of code, so that if those things do change, only a small amount of code would be affected. In spite of the simplicity of this principle and in spite of its broad acceptance, I do not see much software that is well designed from this point of view. It is worthwhile to examine some of the reasons for the industry's failure to apply this principle.

■ Many textbooks on software mention this technique,[2] but they cover it in a superficial way. They say that one should hide, or abstract from "implementation details," but they do not discuss or illustrate the pro-

---

2. It is so well accepted, that textbooks often fail to point out the places where the idea first appeared.

cess of estimating the probability of change for various classes of changes. The principle is simple; applying it properly requires a lot of thought about the application and the environment. The textbooks do not make that clear.

■ Many programmers are impatient with such considerations; they are so eager to get the first version working or to meet some imminent deadline, that they do not take the time to design for change. Management is so concerned with the next deadline (and so eager to get to a higher position) that future maintenance costs don't have top priority.

■ Designs that result from a careful application of information hiding are quite different from the "natural" designs that are the result of most programmers' intuitive work. The programmers' intuition is to think about steps in the data processing, not likely changes. Even when told to associate each module with a "secret," something that is likely to change that should be encapsulated, they use "secrets" of the form, "how to ..." and make each module perform some step in the processing, often violating the information hiding principle in the process.

■ Designers tend to mimic other designs that they have seen. They don't see many good applications of information hiding. One example of information hiding design is [9].

■ Programmers tend to confuse design principles with languages. For example, they believe that one cannot apply "object-oriented" ideas without an "object-oriented" language. Even worse, they think that one has applied the techniques, if one has used such a language.

■ Many people who are doing software development, do not have an education appropriate to the job. Topics that are "old hat" to those who attend this conference are unknown, or vague jargon, to many who are writing software. Each industry has its own software conferences and many programmers in each industry work as if their problems were unique.

■ Software Engineering researchers continue to preach to the converted, to write papers for each other, and to ignore what is happening where the majority of software is written. They assume that "design for change" is an old problem, not one that requires further work. They are wrong!

Thus, although the principle of information hiding was first enunciated in the early 70s (and illustrated even earlier), it is rare to find a software product that was properly designed from this point of view. The code is often clever, efficient, and correct; it performs rather amazing functions, but rarely is it designed to be easily changed. The problem is not that nobody knows how to do it, but that most programmers don't do it. I suspect that some programmers think that their program will be so good that it won't have to be changed. This is foolish. The only programs that don't get changed are those that are so bad that nobody wants to use them. Designing for change is designing for success.

29.7.2 Keeping Records—Documentation

Even when the code is designed so that changes can be carried out efficiently, the design principles and design decisions are often not recorded in a form that is useful to future maintainers. Documentation is the aspect of software engineering most neglected by both academic researchers and practitioners. It is common to hear a programmer saying that the code is its own documentation; even highly respected language researchers take this position, arguing that if you use *their* latest language, the structure will be explicit and obvious.

When documentation is written, it is usually poorly organized, incomplete, and imprecise. Often the coverage is random; a programmer or manager decides that a particular idea is clever and writes a memo about it while other topics, equally important, are ignored. In other situations, where documentation is a contractual requirement, a technical writer, who does not understand the system, is hired to write the documentation. The resulting documentation is ignored by the maintenance programmers because it is not accurate. Some projects keep two sets of books; there is the official documentation, written as required for the contract, and the real documentation, written informally when specific issues arise.

Documentation that seems clear and adequate to its authors is often about as clear as mud to the programmer who must maintain the code 6 months or 6 years later. Even when the information is present, the maintenance programmer doesn't know where to look for it. It is almost as common to find that the same topic is covered twice, but that the statements in the documentation are inconsistent with each other and the code.

Documentation is not an "attractive" research topic. Last year, I suggested to the leader of an Esprit project who was looking for a topic for a conference, that he focus on documentation. His answer was that it would not be interesting. I objected, saying that there were many interesting aspects to this topic. His response was that the problem was not that the discussions wouldn't be interesting, the topic wouldn't *sound* interesting and would not attract an audience.

For the past five or six years my own research, and that of many of my students and close colleagues, has focused on the problems of documentation. We have shown how mathematical methods can be used to provide clear, concise, and systematic documentation of program design [3, 4]. We have invented and illustrated new mathematical notation that is much more suited to use in documentation, but no less formal [5–7]. The reaction of academics and practitioners to this work has been insight-provoking. Both sides fail to recognize documentation as the subject of our work. Academics keep pointing out that we are neglecting "proof obligations"; industrial reviewers classify our work as "verification" which they (often correctly) consider too difficult and theoretical. Neither group can see documentation as an easier, and in some sense more important topic than verification. To them, documentation is that "blah blah" that you have to write. In fact, unless we can solve the documentation problem, the verification work will be a waste of time.

In talking to people developing commercial software we find that documentation is neglected because it won't speed up the next release. Again, programmers and managers are so driven by the most imminent deadline, that they cannot plan for the software's old age. If we recognize that software aging is inevitable and expensive, that the first or next release of the program is not the end of its development, that the long-term costs are going to exceed the short term profit, we will start taking documentation more seriously.

When we start taking documentation more seriously, we will see that just as in other kinds of engineering documentation, software documentation must be based on mathematics. Each document will be a representation of one or more mathematical relations. The only practical way to record the information needed in proper documentation will be to use formally defined notation.

29.7.3 Second Opinions—Reviews

In engineering, as in medicine, the need for reviews by other professionals is never questioned. In the design of a building, a ship, or an aircraft, there is always a series of increasingly precise design documents and each is carefully reviewed by others. Although the topic of design reviews is widely discussed by software engineering lecturers, it is quite astounding to see how often commercial programs are produced without adequate review. There are many reasons for this:

- Many programmers have no professional training in software at all. Some are engineers from other fields; some are "fallen scientists" who learned programming incidentally while getting their education. Some were mathematicians, and some came from nontechnical backgrounds. In many of those areas, the concept of preparing and holding a design review is nonexistent.

- Even among those that have Computer Science degrees many have had an education that neglected such professional concerns as the need for design documentation and reviews. The emphasis is on the mathematics and science; professional discipline is not a topic for a "liberal" education.

■ Most practitioners (and many researchers) do not know how to provide readable precise documentation of a *design*, as distinct from an implementation. No precise description, other than the detailed code, is available for review. Design reviews early in a project, when they would do the most good, are reduced to chat sessions because there are no detailed design documents to discuss.

■ Much software is produced as a cottage industry, where there are no people who could serve as qualified reviewers and there is no funding to hire outside reviewers.

■ Software is often produced under time pressure that misleads the designers into thinking that they have no time for proper reviews.

■ Many programmers regard programming as an "art" and resent the idea that anyone could or should review the work that they have done. I have known programmers to quit working because they resented the fact that their work would be subject to review.

For any organization that intends to maintain its software products over a period of years, reviews are essential and must be taken more seriously than is now usual. In particular, to ameliorate the problems of software aging, every design should be reviewed and approved by someone whose responsibilities are for the long-term future of the product. Reviews by people concerned with maintenance should be carried out when the design is first proposed and long before there is code. A discussion of how to review design documents can be found in [2].

29.7.4 Why Software Aging Is Inevitable

Even if we take all reasonable preventive measures, and do so religiously, aging is inevitable. Our ability to design for change depends on our ability to predict the future. We can do so only approximately and imperfectly. Over a period of years, we will make changes that violate our original assumptions. Documentation, even if formal and precise, will never be perfect. Reviews will bring out issues that the designers miss, but there are bound to be issues that the reviewers miss as well. Preventive measures are worthwhile, but anyone who thinks that this will eliminate aging is living in a dream world.

29.8 Software Geriatrics

Prevention is always the best medicine, but we still have to deal with old software. This section outlines several things that can be done to treat software aging that has already occurred.

29.8.1 Stopping the Deterioration

If software has been maintained for some time without much concern for the issues raised here, a marked deterioration will be observed. The first step should be to slow the progress of the deterioration. This is done by introducing, or recreating, structure whenever changes are made. The principles of design mentioned earlier, can be used to guide change and maintenance as well. If a design decision about the system is changed, the new data structure or algorithm can be hidden (encapsulated) in a way that makes any future changes of that aspect of the system easier. Careful reviews must ensure that each change is consistent with the intent of the original designers, that the original design concept is not violated by the new changes.

Stopping the deterioration is, like many other things in Software Engineering, much easier to say than to do. Many companies have allowed cancerous growth to go on unchecked in their software, for years. When times are good, growth is rapid and there is no obvious reason to be cautious. The result is that a single project may exist in many versions, each with subtly different structures and based on slightly different assumptions. When the period of rapid growth is over, every change must be made many times and the maintainers get confused by the profusion of almost alike versions. Someone has to do a serious study of all of those versions and record the differences. Then a team will have to agree on the proper structure and all versions will have to be forced into that mold. In a time when things are not going well, it is difficult to get enough staff to do the job properly.

New documents must be created and reviewed. The code must then be checked to make sure that it has been made consistent with these new documents. Such a process might take several years and during that time demands for changes and corrections will continue to come in. Nipping the growth in the bud is by far preferable. Retrenchment is always painful.

29.8.2 Retroactive Documentation

A major step in slowing the aging of older software, and often rejuvenating it, is to upgrade the quality of the documentation. Often, documentation is neglected by the maintenance programmers because of their haste to correct problems reported by customers or to introduce features demanded by the market. When they do document their work, it is often by means of a memo that is not integrated into the previously existing documentation, but simply added to it. If the software is really valuable, the resulting unstructured documentation can, and should, be replaced by carefully structured documentation that has been reviewed to be complete and correct. Often, when such a project is suggested, programmers (who are rarely enthusiastic about any form of documentation) scoff at the suggestion as impractical. Their interests are short-term interests, and their work satisfaction comes from running programs. Nonetheless, there are situations where it is in the owner's best interest to insist that the product be documented in a form that can serve as a reference for future maintenance programmers.

A pleasant side effect of documentation efforts is often the improvement of the software. The formal documentation that we recommend requires a detailed and systematic examination of the code and often reveals bugs, duplicate or almost alike functions, and ways to improve performance. In a recent experiment, I asked an undergraduate student to produce documentation for a piece of software that was no longer functional. The author had left our country. Although the student was not asked to find bugs, the systematic analysis necessary to create the formal documentation forced him to look at each routine carefully. He suggested some changes and the software is now functional—and well documented for future changes.

29.8.3 Retroactive Incremental Modularization

Although all software experts now admit the importance of modularization, and most large programs do have some units that are considered modules, a good understanding of the principles of modularization is rarely reflected in the code. Modularization requires more than simply identifying subroutines, or small groups of procedures and calling them modules. Each module must comprise all the programs that "know" (are based on) a particular design decision that is likely to change. Recognizing things that are likely to change requires experience, and successfully hiding or confining knowledge of a design decision to one module requires skills and understanding that are rare. Still programmers who understand information hiding and abstraction can usually find code segments that should be modules and collect them into units. A consultant who views the software with fresh eyes can often show how the job is done. Doing so greatly eases the future maintenance of the code. Often these improvements can be made at little cost as a side effect of changes that have to be made anyway.

29.8.4 Amputation

Occasionally, a section of code has been modified so often, and so thoughtlessly, that it is not worth saving. Large sections can be discarded and replaced by artificial "stumps" which perform the function in some other way. Amputation is always a difficult and controversial decision. Those who have created the old code are not willing to admit that it is not worth keeping. Again, consultants are often helpful, if they can be fully informed. They don't have the emotional attachment to the code that the authors might have.

29.8.5 Major Surgery—Restructuring

When a large and important family of products gets out of control, a major effort to restructure it is appropriate. The first step must be to reduce the size of the program family. One must examine the various versions to determine why and how they differ. If one can introduce modules that hide those differences, agree on (and document) standard interfaces for those modules, and then make those changes in the various versions, one can collapse the versions into a single system that differs only in a few modules. Replacing the old versions with the restructured ones, allows future changes to the shared code to be shared by many versions. In many situations, the separate versions can be combined into one by introducing "switches" that are checked at run-time to determine which version of behavior is wanted. This introduces a small amount of run-time inefficiency but greatly reduces the size of the maintenance staff. I have seen a few organizations that were able to offer what appeared to be a broad family of products by distributing a single piece of code and setting hidden switches to create systems that appear to be quite different. The maintenance costs of these organizations are much lower than they would be if they had separate versions. Unfortunately, some of their customers found the switches and were able to enjoy the benefits of features that they had not purchased. In spite of this, I suspect that the software manufacturer was ahead because of reduced maintenance costs.

29.9 Planning Ahead

If we want to prevent, or at least slow down, software aging, we have to recognize it as a problem and plan for it. The earlier we plan for old age, the more we can do.

29.9.1 A New "Life Style"

It's time to stop acting as if "getting it to run" was the only thing that matters. It is obviously important to get a product to the customer quickly, but we cannot continue to act as if there were no tomorrow. We must not let today's pressures result in a crippled product (and company) next year. We cannot do good work under stress, especially the constant stress of a 25-year crisis. The industry itself must take steps to slow down the rapid pace of development. This can be done by imposing standards on structure and documentation, making sure that products that are produced using "short cuts" do not carry the industry "seal of quality".

29.9.2 Planning for Change

Designs have to be documented, and carefully reviewed, before coding begins. The programs have to be documented and reviewed. Changes have to be documented and reviewed. A thorough analysis of future changes must be a part of every product design and maintenance action. Organizations that are bigger than a few people should have a professional, or a department, devoted to reviewing designs for changeability. They should have the power to veto changes that will get things done quicker now but at a great cost later.

29.9.3 If It's Not Documented, It's Not Done

If a product is not documented as it is designed, using documentation as a design medium [1], we will save a little today, but pay far more in the future. It is far harder to recreate the design documentation than to create it as we go along. Documentation that has been created after the design is done, and the product is shipped, is usually not very accurate. Further, such documentation was not available when (and if) the design was reviewed before coding. As a result, even if the documentation is as good as it would have been, it has cost more and been worth less.

29.9.4 Retirement Savings Plans

In other areas of engineering, product obsolescence is recognized and included in design and marketing plans. The new car you buy today, is "old hat" to the engineers who are already working on future models. The car is guaranteed only for a (very) limited time and spare parts are available only for prescribed periods. When we buy a car we know that it will age and will eventually have to be replaced. If we are wise, we begin to plan for that replacement both financially and by reading about new developments. The manufacturers show similar foresight. It is only in the software industry where people work as if their product will "live" forever. Every designer and purchaser of software should be planning for the day when the product must be replaced. A part of this planning is financial planning, making sure that when the time comes to install or develop a new product, the funds and the people are there.

29.10 Barriers to Progress

If we are going to ameliorate the problem of aging software, we are going to have to make some deep changes in our profession. There are four basic barriers to progress in Software Engineering. These are attitudes and assumptions that make it impossible for research to make a difference.

29.10.1 A 25-Year Crisis?

I first heard the term "software crisis" 25 years ago and have heard it used to describe a current problem every year since then. This is clearly nonsense. A crisis is a sudden, short-term, serious emergency. The so-called "software crisis" is certainly serious, but it is neither sudden nor short-term. It cannot be treated as if it were a sudden emergency. It needs careful long-term therapy. "Quick and easy" solutions have never worked and will not work in the future. The phrase "software crisis" helps in dealing with certain funding agencies, but it prevents the deep analysis needed to cure a chronic illness. It leads to short term thinking and software that ages quickly.

29.10.2 "Our Industry Is Different"

Software is used in almost every industry, e.g., aircraft, military, automotive, nuclear power, and telecommunications. Each of these industries developed as an intellectual community before it became dependent upon software. Each has its own professional organizations, trade organizations, technical societies, and technical journals. As a result, we find that many of these industries are attacking their software problems without being aware of the efforts in other industries. Each industry has developed its own vocabulary and documents describing the way that software should be built. Some have developed their own specification notations and diagramming conventions. There is very little cross-communication. Nuclear industry engineers discuss their software problems at nuclear industry meetings, while telecommunications engineers discuss very similar problems at entirely different meetings. To reach its intended audience, a paper on software engineering will have to be published in many different places. Nobody wants to do that (but promotion committees reward it).

This intellectual isolation is inappropriate and costly. It is inappropriate because the problems are very similar. Sometimes the cost structures that affect solutions are different, but the technical issues are very much the same. It is costly because the isolation often results in people reinventing wheels, and even more often in their reinventing very bumpy and structurally weak wheels. For example, the telecommunications industry and those interested in manufacturing systems, rarely communicate but their communication protocol problems have many similarities. One observes that the people working in the two industries often do not realize that they have the same problems and repeat each other's mistakes. Even the separation between safety-critical and non-safety-critical software (which might seem to make sense) is unfortunate because ideas that work well in one situation are often applicable in others.

We need to build a professional identity that extends to people in all industries. At the moment we reach some people in all industries but we don't seem to be reaching the typical person in those industries.

29.10.3 Where Are the Professionals?

The partitioning of people and industries with software problems is a symptom of a different problem. Although we have lots of people who are paid to write software, we don't have software engineers in the sense that we have aeronautical, electrical, or civil engineers. The latter groups are primarily people who have received a professional education in the field in which they work, belong to professional societies in that field, and are expected to keep up with that field. In contrast, we find that software in the nuclear field is written by nuclear engineers who have learned a programming language, software in the telecommunications field is written by communications engineers and electrical engineers, software in the automated manufacturing field is written by mechanical engineers, etc. Programming engineers in those industries do not think of themselves as a profession in the sense that aeronautical or nuclear engineers do. Moreover, they have not received a formal education in the field in which they are now working. We find that engineers who write programs know far too little about computing science, but computer science graduates know far too little about engineering procedures and disciplines. I often hear, "anybody can write a program" and it's true, but programs written in an unprofessional way will age much more rapidly than programs written by engineers who have received an education in the mathematics and the techniques that are important to program design [8].

29.10.4 Talking to Ourselves

Researchers have to start rethinking their audience. All too often, we are writing papers to impress our colleagues, other researchers. Even worse, if we try to write a paper for the practitioner, the referees complain if we include any basic definitions or problems. We end up writing papers that are read by our fellow researchers but not by many others. We also spend too little time finding out what the practitioners know, think, and need. In Faculties of Engineering, professional practice is recognized as essential to good teaching and research. In many Science faculties, it is viewed simply as a way to make some extra money. This is one of many reasons why I believe that Computer Science Departments would function better if they were always part of an Engineering Faculty.

29.11 Conclusions for Our Profession

1. We cannot assume that the old stuff is known and didn't work. If it didn't work, we have to find out why. Often it is because it wasn't tried.

2. We cannot assume that the old stuff will work. Sometimes widely held beliefs are wrong.

3. We cannot ignore the splinter software engineering groups. Together they outnumber the people who will read our papers or come to our conferences.

4. Model products are a must. If we cannot illustrate a principle with a real product, there may well be something wrong with the principle. Even if the principle is right, without real models, the technology won't transfer. Practitioners imitate what they see in other products. If we want our ideas to catch on, we have to put them into products. There is a legitimate, honorable, and important place for researchers who don't invent new ideas but, instead, apply, demonstrate, and evaluate old ones.

5. We need to make the phrase "software engineer" mean something. Until we have professional standards, reasonably standardized educational requirements, and a professional identity, we have no right to use the phrase, "Software Engineering."

References

1. Hester, S.D., Parnas, D.L., Utter, D.F. "Using Documentation as a Software Design Medium", *Bell System Technical Journal*, 60, 8 October 1981, pp. 1941–1977.

2. Parnas, D.L., Weiss, D.M., "Active Design Reviews: Principles and Practices", *Proceedings of the 8th International Conference on Software Engineering*, London, August 1985. Also published in Journal of Systems and Software, December 1987.

3. Van Schouwen, A.J., Parnas, D.L., Madey, J., "Documentation of Requirements for Computer Systems," presented *at RE '93 IEEE International Symposium on Requirements Engineering*, San Diego, CA, 4–6 January 1993.

4. Parnas, D.L., Madey, J., "Functional Documentation for Computer Systems Engineering (Version 2)," CRL Report 237, CRL-TRIO McMaster University, September 1991, 14 pgs. (to be published in *Science of Computer Programming*).

5. Parnas, D.L., "Tabular Representation of Relations," CRL Report 260, CRL. McMaster University, October 1992, 17 pgs.

6. Janicki, R., "Towards a Formal Semantics of Tables," CRL Report 264. CRL McMaster University, September 1993, 18 pgs.

7. Zucker, J.I., "Normal and Inverted Function Tables," CRL Report 265, CRL, McMaster University, December 1993, 16 pgs.

8. Parnas, D.L., "Education for Computing Professionals," *IEEE Computer*, vol. 23, no. 1, January 1990, pp. 17–22.

9. Parnas, D.L., Clements, P.C., Weiss, D.M., "The Modular Structure of Complex Systems," *IEEE Transactions on Software Engineering*, March 1985, Vol. SE-11 No. 3, pp. 259–266. Also published *in Proceedings of 7th International Conference on Software Engineering*, March 1984, pp. 408–417.

Introduction

Richard Kemmerer

In 1995, Dave received the International Conference on Software Engineering's "Most Influential Paper" award. At each ICSE, this award is given for a paper from the 10th previous ICSE, which, in this case, was ICSE-7. Dave used the occasion to say that most of the work presented at ICSE, as well as most of the work published in IEEE Transactions on Software Engineering, was not of interest to practicing engineers who were writing software. Furthermore, he stated that the ideas expressed in these papers were not used by the "vast army of people who write programs as part of their professional activities." He felt strongly that using the term "influential" for this award was questionable.

What made Dave's point so plausible was that, of the total of seven awards that had been made, he was coauthor of two, and he included both of these papers among those that he deemed to be not used by practicing software engineers. He did state that one of the papers that had previously won this award did describe a system that practicing programmers used. However, he felt that the paper itself did not matter.

As expected, this paper and Dave's associated acceptance talk generated strong reactions at ICSE-17. More important, the ideas that Dave expressed here set the tone for ICSE-18 the following year in Berlin. Before the first day of the ICSE-18 conference Dave was interviewed for the conference newsletter, "Windows on the World" (WOW). In that interview he continued his campaign by expressing his concern about "the growing gap between the 'real world' of software development and the researchers who report results at ICSE and in IEEE TSE." He suggested that "ICSE should become a conference where the academic papers and the industrial papers are mixed and mutually relevant."

Of course, Dave's comments at ICSE-18 provoked a number of heated responses that were published along with his interview in the first issue of WOW. There were responses from the ICSE-18 Program cochairs and the conference chair and from the ICSE Steering Committee chair. There was also a response from the organizers of ICSE-19, which was scheduled for the next year in Boston. The responses varied from partial agreement to outrage. (You can retrieve this issue of WOW from http://cis.cs.tu-berlin.de/~icsewow/.)

The theme for ICSE-19, "Pulling Together," was probably influenced by Dave's talk at ICSE-17. However, ICSE-19's theme was broader in the sense that it intended to pull together different disciplines, as well as researchers and practitioners.

Dave's concern about the gap between real world programmers and researchers is still relevant today. At the recent ICSE 2000 there was no "Most Influential Paper" award, an omission that was not an oversight.

On ICSE's "Most Influential" Papers

David Lorge Parnas

30.1 Background

The International Conference on Software Engineering has established a tradition of looking back ten conferences and selecting papers that have stood the test of time. The remarks below were prepared in connection with an acceptance speech at ICSE 17 where two colleagues and I received the award for the best paper of ICSE 7.

30.2 What Are the Best Papers of Our Most Important Software Engineering Conference?

The following seven papers have won a "best paper" retrospective award from the International Conference of Software Engineering, the major conference devoted to Software Engineering. When these awards were first given, they were called "Most Influential Paper" awards and this is what has stimulated the remarks that follow the list.

ICSE 1—September 1975
> Marc J. Rochkind, "The Source Code Control System"

ICSE2—October 1976
> William A. Wulf, Ralph L. London, Mary Shaw, "An Introduction to the Construction and Verification of Alphard Programs"

ICSE 3—May 1978
> David Lorge Parnas, "Designing Software for Ease of Extension and Contraction"

ICSE 4—September 1979
> Walter F. Tichy, "Software Development Based on Module Interconnection"

ICSE 5—March 1981
> Mark Weiser, "Program Slicing"

ICSE 6—September 1982
> S.J. Greenspan, J. Mylopoulos, A. Borgida, "Capturing More World Knowledge in the Requirements Specification"

ICSE 7—March 1984
> D.L. Parnas, P.C. Clements, D.M. Weiss, "The Modular Structure of Complex Systems"

My observation, when studying this list (which includes two papers that I helped to write), is that *at most* one of these papers could be considered influential. There is now a vast army of people who write programs as part or all of their professional activities. Most of those professional programmers have never read any of these papers and do not use the ideas explained in these papers. The one exception, the first paper, describes a system that practicing programmers do use. In that case, it is probably true that the system was influential, but the paper itself didn't matter.

The sad fact is that most Engineers actually writing code do not come to these conferences. They also do not read *IEEE Transactions on Software Engineering,* the main journal in our field. Computer professionals do not read our literature because it does not help them to do their job better. These papers may be very good papers, they may have influenced other researchers, but they have not significantly changed the way that programs are written. There are exceptions (of course) and they "prove" the rule by being exceptions.

These are strong statements, not backed by data, but I say them with confidence. My contacts with the many people who actually produce software professionally leave me no doubt. The people who come to ICSE are exceptional; they are not typical of those who produce software. Even the practitioners who do attend tell me that they do not find much that is useful in these conferences. The people I meet in the nuclear industry, the medical equipment industry, and the telephone industry are more typical of practicing professionals. They have learned to program by learning a language, an operating system, and perhaps some application software, They believe that this is all the information that they need. They have rarely, very rarely, been exposed to the ideas that we call "Software Engineering." Few read papers such as those above or do the kinds of things suggested in ICSE papers. Those who are Engineers often have some other area of engineering as their professional identity. They think of themselves as Mechanical Engineers, Electrical Engineers or perhaps Nuclear Engineers, but not as Software Engineers. They go to conferences in those fields, not to ours. The nonengineers in the field identify themselves as "programmers" and read manuals, books on specific systems, or glossy trade magazines, but not our papers.

30.3 We Must Be Doing Something(s) Wrong!

It is easy for us to say that the practitioners are doing something wrong—they are ignoring us, "the learned researchers." However, if we want to influence the way that software is written, we have to admit that *we* are doing something wrong. Otherwise it is beyond our capability to fix the problem. I have a list of things that we, the SE research clique, should reconsider.

30.3.1 We Are Talking to Ourselves

Most of our papers are written in the tradition of science, not engineering. We write up the results of our research for readers who are also researchers, not for practitioners. We base our papers on previous work done by other researchers, and often ignore current practical problems. In many other engineering fields, the results of research are reported in "how to" papers. Our papers are "this is what I did" papers. We describe *our* work, how *our* work differs from other people's work, what we will do next, etc. This is quite appropriate for papers directed to other researchers, but it is not what is needed in papers that are intended to influence practitioners. Practitioners are far more interested in being told the basic assumptions behind the work, than in knowing how this work differs from the work by the author's cohorts in the research game.

30.3.2 We Are Ignoring Engineering Organizations

If we take the "Engineering" in "Software Engineering" seriously, we must also take the organizations operating in the rest of Engineering seriously. They should be our natural allies. They have faced similar problems in the past and have goals that are similar to ours. Just as we are trying to raise the level of professionalism in software development, the Professional Engineering societies were formed to assure a high level of professionalism in traditional Engineering fields.

What the Professional Engineering societies have done is to identify the basic information and skills that should be known by every Engineer in each of the Engineering specialties. Having identified this information, they make sure that each accredited institution presents that information to its students and that every Professional Engineer has learned those ideas. In our field, no such minimum education has been identified and there is no meaningful accreditation process. At this conference we have heard an eloquent talk by a graduate of one of our leading institutions, who reported as new, observations that were reported at least 20 years ago.

Professional Engineering societies are supported by legislation in most jurisdictions and they have well thought-out accreditation and examination procedures, etc. These mechanisms assure them the attention of their members, students, and university teachers. We need those facilities to do our job and it makes no sense to try to develop similar mechanisms on our own.

In the last few years, it has become clear to me that there is a distressing lack of communication between those in Software Engineering and those in traditional Engineering fields. Traditional Engineers do not understand our work and most of us do not understand what they do.

The Engineering societies need to understand that professional programmers require more than simple knowledge of the language, support software, and operating system. They need to increase the level of understanding of software expected of the Professional Engineer. They also, and this is quite distinct, need to recognize the need for Professional Engineers specialized in computer systems, just as they recognized the needs for other new specialties in the past. Engineers have always underestimated the difficulty of writing software; unreliable software is the result.

However, we need to understand that a Software Engineer has to understand a lot more than the things that we talk about. Just as a Chemical Engineer must know more than Chemistry, there are many areas of traditional Engineering that are relevant to the work of Software Engineers.

Above all, we need to stop the competition between societies of Computing Professionals and Societies of Professional Engineers for the right to identify people as Software Engineers. They need us and we need them.

30.3.3 We Are Ignoring History

There has been a great deal of progress in Engineering in the last few centuries. Early bridges were built by a trial-and-error (learn-from-experience) process not unlike our present programming styles. Early power system developers did their work without the mathematical models developed by people like Steinmetz and regarded such work as irrelevant theory. Doesn't this sound familiar? However, new methods in Engineering were not adopted as a result of the kinds of things we are trying in Software Engineering. Engineers use methods if they work. They did not expect "controlled experiments" (nearly impossible in studying design methods) before using Kirchoff's laws. University teachers taught Nyquist's methods because they obviously made the Engineer's job easier. It wasn't necessary for Gauss or Kirchoff to form "User Groups" or write "Ten Commandment" style articles to sell their ideas. The ideas sold themselves. Like the proverbial "better mousetraps," good methods spread. We are putting too much effort into selling methods that are not yet ready. If they were ready, we would not have to sell them. We should be putting our efforts into testing and improving our technology, not into high pressure sales.

30.3.4 We Are Becoming "Snake Foot" Salespeople

In Chinese there are sayings about "putting feet on a snake." Snakes have evolved to function quite well without feet and adding feet would not be doing them a favor. I fear that some of the things that we are asking practitioners to do when developing software fall into that category; they don't help and may interfere with the ability of designers to work under tight constraints. What I see is a great many people who have become very talented entertainers and after-dinner speakers, but they are hucksters. They write "papers" that are sales brochures, often inaccurate and sloppy. I remember sitting in shock as one such "expert," a Professor at a European university, sold his "do it naturally" philosophy by such statements as

- Ants invented "just-in-time" manufacturing because they have no warehouses.
- If you go to a party and drink, you can then go to your office and write a program of 5000 lines overnight and it will be correct without testing.
- The important thing is to have "team spirit" (generated by standing in a circle and holding hands); disciplined development methods don't matter.

On the other side, I have watched advocates of new methods make the claim that mathematical methods can allow you to write programs that are right the first time (without testing) while displaying slides with programs that would not pass even a simple test.

30.4 We Need to Change Something

If those are some of the things that we are doing wrong, what can we do about it? Here are a few ideas:

- Recognize that Software Engineering is a branch of Engineering. Software Engineering is treated as part of Computer Science, but that is no more true than Chemical Engineering is a branch of Chemistry. Chemical Engineering is treated as a profession quite different from that of chemistry. If you look at the curricula in that field, you will see why.
- Distinguish conferences for researchers from conferences for practitioners. Researchers need to talk to each other, but to achieve our goals we really need to address practitioners properly. Conferences for practitioners might well be modeled on the Pacific Northwest Software Quality Conference where the program committee is dominated by practitioners who want to listen, not by researchers who want to talk. ICSE would do well to follow that model. We also need to remember that the distinction is between researchers and practitioners, not between people who work for universities and people who work for industry. Lots of researchers work in industry.
- Start a dialogue with the Professional Engineering societies. Perhaps the head of the VDI (Association of German Engineers) could address the next ICSE in Berlin.
- Stop misusing the word "Engineer." When I attend ICSE conferences I am constantly reminded of a housekeeper, who used to tell me that she was going to "engineer a good dinner tonight." At ICSE 17, I stayed in a hotel that sent an "Engineer" to change a light bulb in my room. He failed on his first try! Engineering is a profession; entry into the profession requires extensive training and is carefully controlled. We cannot

make up new fields such as "Requirements Engineering" or "Reliability Engineering" whenever it suits our purposes. In fact, it is my observation that Professional Engineers rarely use "engineer" as a verb. When we understand the meaning of the term "Engineering," we won't offer one-term courses titled Software Engineering.

30.5 Conclusions

It would not be very gracious to "accept" an award by implying that it is not worth very much. That is not the message of my remarks. I am quite proud of having won this award twice and display the awards prominently. My point is not that the papers are not good papers, but simply that they have not been influential. I hope that others will begin to think about why we are not influencing the way that programming is done and make some further suggestions.

Introduction

Daniel Hoffman

I first encountered David Parnas when I was a student in a graduate software engineering course at the University of North Carolina. Dave taught the course with Fred Brooks, alternating lectures. Brooks's trained speaking style and dramatic use of imagery was strikingly different from Parnas's quiet, almost shy presentation of his ideas. From Brooks I learned about the importance of people in software engineering and in all aspects of life. From Dave, I learned an engineering approach to software development. I learned to value the use of mathematics in software and to prefer simple, old ideas to complex, new proposals. I learned that precise specification and systematic verification are essential in any engineering approach to software. I learned to refuse to accept vague ideas and to be suspicious of proposals that have not been tried on real-world problems.

Because I went to graduate school after spending five years as a software developer in industry, I was familiar with the so-called software crisis. Much of the software was late, over budget, unreliable, and expensive to maintain. Worse, it was just plain unsuitable for the task at hand, reminding me of the old joke about the three clothing sizes in the army: too big, too small, and utterly ridiculous. This paper concerns a second software crisis: a crisis in software education. We have taught programming to generations of undergraduates without teaching sound fundamentals. This situation is unsatisfying to students and teachers alike and has had a negative impact on the reputation of Computer Science (CS) departments within their universities. Further, this educational software crisis contributes heavily to the critical difficulties we see in software development and to the lack of progress in identifying the fundamentals necessary for professionalization of software engineering.

This paper describes the fundamentals appropriate for teaching programming in accredited, undergraduate software engineering programs. According to Dave: "Professional engineers are expected to use discipline, science, and mathematics to assure that their products are reliable and robust. We should expect no less of anyone who produces programs professionally." Selecting fundamentals is always a difficult task. There is inevitably far too much material to teach, and, because each candidate topic has loyal adherents, omitting any topic offends someone. Clear criteria for selection are needed in this emotionally charged situation. Dave's emphasis on professional programs provides the focus necessary for success, a focus not currently available to those designing CS programs.

To identify the fundamentals, Dave first considers the current approaches in CS. Usually, the choice of programming language is the most important and visible decision in the course. Then the focus becomes language syntax and semantics. Such courses produce students who program with a "try it and see" approach and who do not know that there is any alternative. They are not taught material that will be useful throughout their careers. The course textbook is typically out of date before graduation. While some courses do teach mathematical fundamentals, the treatment is highly theoretical. The material remains current but is applied to only the simplest programs. Students doubt that the material is practical; their doubts are confirmed when they see that it is not applied anywhere else in the curriculum.

Dave rejects both the typical focus on language syntax and semantics and the theoretical, but impractical approach. He selects material from discrete mathematics, making careful choices based on simplicity and practicality. For example, he restricts his treatment of logic to finite sets and uses finite state machines as the model of computation. Finite sets and FSMs are sufficient because no digital computer has infinite state. Determining the equivalence of two Turing machines is undecidable. With FSMs, however, many problems are intractable but none is undecidable. If scientific interest is the issue, then infinite sets and Turing machines are the clear choice. If simplicity and utility are the driving force, then finite sets and FSMs are far better. Parnas favours simplicity and utility, selecting a small body of mathematics that is both sufficient to support disciplined programming and easily accessible to any student who can handle first-year university calculus.

Anyone familiar with the work of Harlan Mills will recognize his pervasive influence in this paper. Thus the lack of any reference to Mills' published work is a serious omission, which I am pleased to correct. Of particular relevance are Mills' pioneering work on a practical mathematical basis for programming [1, 2] and the superb course materials prepared by Mills and others at the University of Maryland [3].

References

1. H.D. Mills, "The new math of computer programming," *CACM*, January 1975.

2. R.C. Linger, H.D. Mills, and B.I. Witt, *Structured Programming: Theory and Practice*. Addison-Wesley, 1979.

3. H. Mills, V. Basili, J. Gannon, R. Hamlet, *Principles of Computer Programming: A Mathematical Approach*, Allyn and Bacon, Boston, 1987.

Teaching Programming as Engineering

David Lorge Parnas

31.1 Introduction

In spite of unheralded advances in computer hardware and software, most of today's introductory programming courses are much like courses taught 30 years ago. Although the programming languages have changed, we continue to equate teaching programming with teaching the syntax and semantics of programming languages. This paper describes a different approach being taken in the Faculty of Engineering at McMaster University. Our course emphasizes program design rather than language syntax, insisting that the program design is something distinct from the detailed code. It allows students a choice of programming languages for use in their laboratory work. Students learn a mathematical model of programming and are to use that model to understand program design, analysis, and documentation. Considerable effort is spent on teaching the students how to apply what they see as "theory" in practice.

31.2 Programming Courses and Engineering

Professional engineers are expected to use discipline, science, and mathematics to assure that their products are reliable and robust. We should expect no less of anyone who produces programs professionally.

In most jurisdictions, engineers are expected either to be graduates of carefully accredited university programs or to have passed exams that demonstrate that they have the knowledge that they would have obtained in such a program. It is unfortunate that there is no corresponding registration process for those who design programs.

This paper treats programming as an engineering discipline and describes a course that is intended to teach the fundamental knowledge that should be expected of any professional programmer. Because we believe in teaching good programming design habits from the start, this is our student's first course in programming. Unfortunately, many students come to university having learned to use a computer in high school or elsewhere. With rare exceptions those students have learned to program intuitively and resist learning a new, more disciplined, approach.

31.3 The Important Characteristics of Programming Courses

For many years, the first question asked about any introductory programming course for engineers was "What programming language do you teach?" If one examines the many textbooks available for such courses, one finds that at least half of the book, and usually more, is simply a description of the syntax and interpretation of a particular language. The situation is exactly as if courses on circuit design were dominated by a description of one model of oscilloscope. We seem to have forgotten that our task is to teach students how to design programs, not the characteristics of one or two human artifacts.

Engineering educators have long known that their students must be prepared to work in rapidly changing fields. We have recognized that the educational program must stress fundamentals—science, mathematics, and design discipline—so that graduates will find their education still valid and useful late in their careers. Most of the books that I used in my own engineering education are still correct and relevant, several decades later. In contrast, many introductory programming books are considered out of date before the students who use them have graduated.

The approach taken by those who teach programming differs greatly from the approach taken by those who teach engineering. All aspects of computing have developed very rapidly and will continue to do so. Instead of reacting to rapid change by focusing on fundamentals, programming books and courses try to keep up with the latest developments. Each new language, each new operating system, each new database package, each new windowing system, and each new programming fad give rise to another wave of books. The few books that claim to focus on fundamentals are highly theoretical. Instead of learning the latest tools, students are given theories that, while they don't go out of date, do not seem relevant to the task of programming.

The subject matter of most introductory programming courses is material that many engineers of previous generations learned on their own. Just as we did not have courses devoted to the use of slide rules, we did not need an academic course to learn FORTRAN. In fact, many students of my generation found that a one-week evening course, offered by the computer center (without credit), was sufficient as an introduction to the tools that were available.

If we are to include a course on programming as part of a university education, we must focus on programming fundamentals and their application, not on tools.

31.4 The Role of Mathematics in Engineering

One of the clear differences between typical programming courses and most engineering courses is that the programming courses neither teach, nor make much use of, mathematics.

Those who do not have an engineering education often do not realize how much mathematics is taught to engineers. At my university, approximately 30 percent of an engineer's education is devoted to things that are explicitly titled mathematics. There is also a great deal of mathematics taught in specialized engineering courses. The ability to use mathematics is one of the things that differentiates professional engineers from technicians.

In engineering education we emphasize the concept of professional responsibility. Engineers are taught from their first day at university, that their products must be "fit for use." They learn that they cannot rely on intuition alone. Much of their education is devoted to learning how to perform both mathematical analysis and carefully planned testing of their products. My own engineering education included approximately as much mathematics as would have been taken by a mathematics major and, at my alma mater, many of the courses were the same ones taken by the mathematics majors. However, we did not learn math as an "end" but as a "means." We learned how to use mathematics in developing and analyzing product designs.

In spite of the fact that, in every other area of engineering, students are expected to learn the relevant mathematics, most programming courses treat the mathematics of programming as if it were (a) too difficult and (b) not relevant to programming. Moreover, many of those who advocate the use of mathematical methods in analyzing programs disparage the use of testing. They treat complementary methods of assuring quality as if they were alternatives. Students should be taught how to use mathematics, together with testing, to increase the reliability of their programs.

In fact, the mathematics needed to understand modern programming techniques is elementary and entirely within the capability of anyone who can learn differential and integral calculus. That includes all engineers and scientists.

31.5 The Role of Programming in Engineering, Business, and Science

There is no longer any question about whether or not engineering, business, and science students should take courses in programming. Computers and software are now ubiquitous in those fields. Many engineering products include computers and software; most others are designed and analyzed using computers. Hardly a week passes in which we do not hear some anecdote about the failure of an engineering product caused by an error either in the software contained in the product or in the software used to design it. Since people rarely talk loudly about their failures, we can assume that these anecdotes are just the "tip of the iceberg." The question is no longer "Do we teach our students about programming?" but "What do we teach our students about programming?" Educators should insist that courses on programming be more substantive than is currently the case.

31.6 The Content of Most "Standard" Programming Courses

It is time to question the intellectual content of many courses in computing. We need to ask whether these courses are comparable to other engineering, mathematics, or science courses. The typical programming course simply teaches about a programming language, an artifact designed by a few fallible human beings. Most of the time is spent on things that are neither mathematical truths nor facts about the world; they are just human design decisions. Such courses are analogous to teaching about a particular calculator, including the location of its buttons, how to turn it on, how to change the display, etc. I often hear complaints that many of these courses teach almost the same artifacts that were taught 30 years ago; computer scientists think that we should teach more modern languages than FORTRAN. I believe that the teaching of "old" languages is not the real problem; the real problem is that the subject of the course is an artifact, any artifact.

At my university, we were teaching two distinct courses under a single number (to preserve the illusion that we had a common first year for all engineering students). One "section" was a FORTRAN course; the other, a course in Pascal. Because these two languages are quite different, the material taught to one section differed greatly from material taught to the other. For example, Pascal users learn about records; FORTRAN users do not. In fact, the concept of a record is an important one that can be used in FORTRAN even though the language has no explicit facilities for it; if one group of students should learn about records, so should the other.

31.7 Programming Courses Are Not Science Courses

We must recognize another difference between engineering education and the education of scientists and mathematicians. In engineering schools there is great emphasis on design, i.e., on how to invent useful things. Science courses can focus on science, i.e., on facts about the world. Like engineering courses, programming courses should emphasize how to apply those facts. This has very practical implications. Every course is limited in the amount of contact and student time; when we choose to stress the application of science, we are choosing not to teach certain facts or theories that might be interesting and elegant for all involved.

As part of a course in programming, students must learn problem-solving skills. They must learn how to formulate problems, how to decompose a problem into smaller problems, how to integrate solutions, etc. The emphasis in many courses taught in Computer Science departments is quite different. Computer Scientists are interested in programming languages (and the science of programming), for their own sake. There is more emphasis on the syntax and semantics of a language, than on how to use the language or how to decide when to use them. Computer Scientists are also interested in models of programming and often teach automata theory, language theory, etc. in introductory courses. The material is elegant and has great intellectual value; there is rarely emphasis on how to use it. In Engineering courses we teach theory and models, but the emphasis is always on the application of what we teach to design problems. Design and analysis may be viewed as complementary skills. Design is inherently creative and most of the things we can teach about design are heuristics, things that don't always work. Because a heuristic, intuitive, design process often yields designs that are "almost right" (i.e., wrong), solid, disciplined analysis of the results of the design process is essential. In Engineering, mathematics is most often used as a means of design analysis. In contrast, many Computer Scientists talk about systematically deriving programs from specifications. Program derivation is analogous to deriving a bridge from a description of the river and the expected traffic. Refining a formal specification to a program would be like refining a blueprint until it turned into a house. Neither is realistic; the creative steps in design are absolutely essential. This is as true in programming as it is in any other area of Engineering. Engineers have learned to make a clear distinction between the product itself and a description of it. This distinction seems to have been lost in the Computer Science literature on programming. Mathematical tradition, in which formulae are the products, has led computer scientists to view programs and their mathematical descriptions as if they were the same things.

Those who chose Engineering as a career path are often people with a fairly pragmatic view of life. They appreciate mathematics that is simple and elegant, but they want frequent assurance that the mathematics is useful. It is important to show them how to use a mathematical concept, not simply to teach them the definitions and theorems. In engineering mathematics, the emphasis has always been more on application of theorems than on proofs. Computer Science has followed the approach taken by mathematicians. When most Computer Scientists design a course, they will discuss proof of correctness more than they discuss design.

31.8 A New Approach to Teaching Programming

We are currently teaching a novel programming course for all first year engineering students. It differs from conventional programming courses in two ways:

- The early part of the course teaches basic mathematics of programming with emphasis on the use of mathematics to describe what a program does, or must do. Programming assignments are expressed as mathematical specifications. Students learn to compare programs with mathematical descriptions.

- We stress that the programming language is not the subject of the course. Students are given a choice of programming languages that can be used in the laboratories. Two of the three lectures per week are taught in an algorithmic notation based on Dijkstra's guarded commands [1, 4]. The third, a "laboratory" lecture, uses a "real" language. Currently we offer FORTRAN and C. Lectures are scheduled so that students who wish to do so can attend both C and FORTRAN lectures. A system of bonus points rewards students who learn both languages. The lectures present the same algorithms. Students see every algorithm at least twice, once in pseudocode, once in FORTRAN or C.

Our course emphasizes both the creative steps in programming and the analytical steps needed to confirm the correctness of a design. Students are taught a "divide and conquer" approach to programming in which problems are systematically reduced to simpler problems and programs can be inspected in a disciplined, systematic way.

31.9 The Mathematics Needed for Professional Programming

This section describes the mathematical content of this first course on programming. Although the material would be familiar to any Computer Scientist, it will be unfamiliar to most Engineers; most engineers have not kept up with developments in Computer Science or software design methods.

31.9.1 Finite State Machines

The first step in getting students to take a professional approach to programming is to get rid of the "giant brain" and "obedient servant" views of a computer. It is essential that students see computers as purely mechanical devices, capable of mathematical description. Students learn that "remembering" or "storing" data is just a state change and are then taught to analyze simple finite state machines to verify that they accomplish specified tasks. The Moore-Mealy model is used. Students are also taught how to design finite state machines to perform simple tasks. We do not present the usual "automata theory." The emphasis is on understanding how the machines function and on designing them. A simulator is provided so that students can test their designs. The use of the state machine concept allows students to take a disciplined approach to designing systems that process sequences of data.

31.9.2 Sets, Functions, Relations, Composition

We present a naïve set theory in which all sets consist of a finite number of elements selected from previously defined finite universes. It is important to present the students with examples of the use of these concepts and exercises in their use. We want the students to know far more than the definitions and the algebraic laws; we ask them to use the concepts to provide precise models of real-world situations. We show how state machines can be described by a pair of mathematical relations and how to use the operations of union, intersection, negation, and relational composition. This is the first step toward describing programs using functions and relations.

31.9.3 Mathematical Logic Based on Finite Sets

In the first two sections, finite state machines and sets have been kept not just finite, but small, so that they could all be described by enumeration. The next step is to point out that these are unrealistically small sets, that it is not practical to describe most sets by enumeration, and that we must be able to make general statements about classes of states. We then introduce an interpretation of classical predicate logic in which expression denotations are finite sets and show how to use predicate calculus to characterize sets, including functions and relations. By restricting the definitions to finite sets, we eliminate all the problems that Mathematicians and Computer Scientists find interesting and can focus on the use of these concepts in program design.

We define the logic formally, but unlike most Computer Science and Mathematics courses, we do not give proof rules. Instead we give the evaluation rules, which are much simpler. We use logic to describe program behavior, not to prove theorems.

The logic allows use of partial functions (defining all primitive predicates on undefined values to be *false*). It is important to provide numerous examples in which the students use predicate logic to characterize the states of something real. Arrays (viewed as partial functions) provide a rich source of examples such as, "Write a predicate that is *true* if array A contains a palindrome of length 3." We repeatedly use the mathematics to say things about programs, and teach students to use, as contrasted to prove theorems about, logic [3].

31.9.4 Programs as "Initial States"

We briefly present an unconventional view of programming as picking the initial state of a finite state machine. This helps to explain such concepts as table-driven programs, interpreters, etc. It allows us to explain von Neumann's insight about the interchangeability of program and data and the practical implications of his contributions. We show practical examples of "trade-offs" made by moving decision logic between program and data, e.g., introducing table-driven programs.

31.9.5 Programs as Descriptions of State Sequences

Next, we present a more conventional view of programs as descriptions of a sequence of state changes. This concept is presented abstractly; we do not give any programming language notation for describing the sequences.

31.9.6 Programs Described by Functions from Starting State to Stopping State

After pointing out that programs can be characterized as either terminating or nonterminating, we indicate that our course focuses on programs that are intended to terminate after computing some useful values. We explain how the most important characteristics of programs can be described by a mathematical relation between its starting-states and stopping-states. The exact model used is LD-relations [1, 4]. We provide examples in which the students use relations to describe distinct sets of sequences that are equivalent in the sense of having the same set of (start-state, final-state) pairs. We show how these relations can be used to describe a class of programs that are equivalent (in the sense of getting the same answers) but may differ in the algorithms that they use. We show that this allows a mathematical description of a program that is simpler and easier to understand than the program itself because it omits information about the intermediate states in the state sequences.

31.9.7 Tabular Descriptions of Functions and Relations

We extend the notation of predicate calculus by introducing 2-dimensional tableaux, which we call simply tables, whose entries are predicate expressions or terms. We show that these are equivalent to more conventional notation, but much easier to read. Students are given many examples in which we describe mathematical functions using these tables [2]. Figure 31.1 is an example of a complete specification of a program.

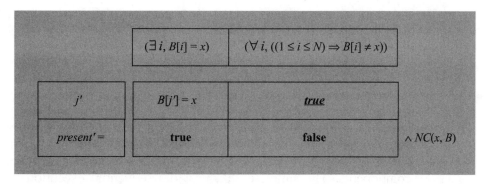

Figure 31.1 *Specification of a programming assignment.*

31.10 Teaching Programming with This Mathematical Background

Although we teach a lot of mathematics, the purpose of the course is teaching students to program well. We must teach them to use the mathematics. We stress four points: (1) postponing program design until one has a precise statement of the requirements, (2) producing a precise program design before starting detailed coding, (3) constructing programs from components rather than simply "writing" the lines down in execution order, and (4) detailed checking of algorithms using a "divide and conquer" philosophy.

31.10.1 Programming Professionally

Students are taught that they should never begin coding until they have a precise description of the program that they are trying to produce. All programs are introduced, not just with a natural language description, but with a mathematical description of the required behavior.

31.10.2 Program Construction

A main theme of the course is that engineers should *not* program by "thinking like a computer"; they should not plan the steps to be followed by the computer in the order that the computer will follow them. Instead, they are told that their job is to assemble new programs from previously constructed "building-blocks," simpler programs. They are reminded that, if they are successful, their products will later be used as components of still larger programs. They are also taught that they may have to deal with programs that are thousands, even millions, of lines long. They cannot expect to understand all lines of the program. They must have precise "blackbox" descriptions of the program building blocks. They are shown how to use mathematical descriptions instead of examining the code for the programs they will use as building blocks.

31.10.3 A Simple Language of Program Constructors

To keep the main lectures "language-neutral" we introduce a stripped-down notation for describing programs. The syntax is shown in Figure 31.2. The language is introduced in a way consistent with the idea that we are constructing programs from building blocks. The language provides four "constructors" or "constructs" that are used to construct programs from components. The simplest, ";", provides sequential execution. The others provide conditional execution, alternatives, and iteration. The programming notation is defined using the mathematical concepts taught earlier [4]. We begin with very simple programs and continue, always using the "divide and conquer" discipline, to construct programs that solve more complex engineering problems. The students see every program twice, first developed systematically in the program planning notation, then translated into the programming language of their choice. A discipline of program design is stressed in every example. We systematically decompose a problem into simpler problems, then construct the complete solution from the components. We show how this program design notation, together with the mathematics, provides a method of analysis that can be used to validate a design.

Students are shown how to systematically determine whether or not a design covers all cases and does the right thing in each case. Although we never talk of "correctness proofs," we do use correctness concepts to explain programs. For example, we usually identify an "invariant" when explaining

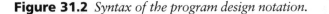

```
<simple program::= <primitive program> | (<program>) | it <program> ti

<guard>::= <boolean expression>

<guarded program>::= <guard> <simple program>

<guarded program list>::= <guarded program> | <guarded program list>
        | <guarded program>

<composed program>::= <simple program>; <simple program>
        | <composed program>; <simple program>

<program>::= <simple program | <composed program> | <guarded program list>

<primitive program>::= <expression> | <assignment> | • | ☞ | skip | abort | init
```

Figure 31.2 *Syntax of the program design notation.*

a loop and demonstrate that the invariant is maintained by an execution of the body of the loop. We demonstrate how thinking in terms of "invariants" makes it unnecessary to try to enumerate all the execution sequences that might arise. Students learn these concepts in a language-independent way and come to understand that they can be applied in any imperative programming language.

31.10.4 Turning Designs into Programs

The course stresses a separation between algorithm design and detailed implementation. The Program Design Notation is used to develop and analyze the algorithm. Students are then required to translate the design into correct code in FORTRAN or C and to test those programs thoroughly. Both the language lectures and the tutorials stress that there must be a correspondence between the running program and the pseudocode so that the latter serves as documentation for the former. We tell the students about studies that show that this "design and then code" process greatly reduces errors in program design. Points are deducted if they have not kept the two versions of their program in correspondence. Homework assignments are specified using the tabular notation. Each problem must be done twice. The students must first do it using the program design notation and have that solution checked by the syntax checker that we provide. They then translate the program into the language that they are using in their laboratory work. This must be tested thoroughly. Both versions are graded. We have learned that the tutorials and the grading must stress that the pseudocode is used for a preliminary design before the coding. If we don't enforce this, students fall back to their high school habits, write the running code using intuitive methods, and then write the "design" as an afterthought.

31.10.5 Tests

The first test deals entirely with mathematical concepts and state machines. The second tests the student's ability to match pseudocode programs with mathematical specifications. In the third, the student deals with more complex programs and specifications. In the second and third test and the final exam, students are also asked to match pseudocode programs to programs in their chosen "real" language.

Because it is impossible to grade 400 student programs accurately, we actually ask students to complete programs, using a multiple choice format, so that there is only one correct answer and the tests can be graded mechanically.

31.11 Experience

The course has been taught three times, each time to about 400 first-year engineering students. In the first year there was strong student resistance to the change. Students who turned to upper-year students for help found that they were being asked to learn more than the students in previous years. "Why do we have to learn this when they did not?" was a frequent remark. Some of the strongest resistance came from students with previous computer experience; they thought that they already "knew" how to program (often in Basic) and did not need to be taught theory, design methods, or mathematics. However, at the end of the term many confessed that they now understood the material and could not explain their original resistance.

In the second year, there was much less resistance, but students learned the "theory" without applying it to practice. Many students observed that they could learn the program design aspects without actually running C or FORTRAN programs. We discovered a great deal of copying of those by the end of the term. By the third year, we felt we had the basic material correct and focused on changing the delivery so that students would see the connection between the design lectures and producing working programs. We made several changes:

- We changed our illustrative examples to illustrate the practical relevance of the methods. For example, instead of using recognizers to explain state tables, we had a series of problems on the mode control in a bicycle computer.

- We provided consultants in the computer labs to help people who got stuck because of "mysterious" details about the compiler languages. We did this to remove any excuse for copying another student's work. In previous years students justified copying by claiming that they had no other source of help.

- We introduced a "laboratory exam" in which students were required to debug a simple program under supervision of Teaching Assistants (TAs). Students were given a correct pseudocode design for the program a week before the exam but had to find the errors in the C or FORTRAN in "real time."

- We changed our grading procedure to increase the likelihood of detecting copying and treated all copying as academic dishonesty.

- We introduced carefully worked out tutorial sessions in which problems similar to the assignments were solved using exactly the methods called for in the design lectures. The TAs who presented these tutorials were carefully selected for their familiarity with the design method and mathematics.

Some instructors from other courses complained after the second year saying that we were teaching theory not programming. In part, this was justified. The students who had cheated on their homework did not learn how to get a program to run. However, an instructor whose classes included both students from the old, language-oriented, course, and students from the new course, found that the students from the old course were equally weak on the practical aspects. Computer assignments are far too easy to copy. Busy students will cheat to buy time.

Instructors in other subjects, e.g., chemical engineering or civil engineering, were also resistant because the material was new to *them*. One department accused us of teaching "recent research" claiming that "finite state machines" were an example of recent theoretical advances; discussion revealed that they had never seen that half-century old concept. We often forget how little people in other areas understand about the advances made in computer science and programming methods in the last 30 years. They still program in the same way that people programmed 30 years ago. To be successful in such an environment, those who hope to upgrade programming courses must devote more effort than we did to the education of their colleagues.

Our goal is to improve students' ability to program in any language throughout their careers. It will be years before we can know how well we have succeeded.

31.12 Conclusions

Programming should be taught as if it were engineering because it is engineering. We should not be satisfied with teaching the detailed characteristics of one of today's tools. To prepare students for the rapidly changing world of computing, we must focus on fundamentals and design discipline. First year engineering students can be taught the mathematics and discipline necessary for professional programming.

It is difficult to teach students with programming experience and novices in one class. We must choose between boring the experienced and confusing the novices.

References

1. Parnas, D.L. (1983) A Generalized Control Structure and Its Formal Definition. *Communications of the ACM*, 26(8):572–581, August.

2. Parnas, D.L. (1992) *Tabular Representation of Relations*, CRL Report 260, Communications Research Laboratory, McMaster University, October.

3. Parnas, D.L. (1993) Predicate Logic for Software Engineering. *IEEE Transactions on Software Engineering*, 19(9):856–862, September.

   4. Parnas, D.L. and Wadge, W.W. (1986) *Less Restrictive Constructs for Structured Programs*, Technical Report 86–186, Computer and Information Science Department, Queen's University, Kingston, Ontario, Canada, October (available from the author).

Acknowledgments

These thoughts have been strongly influenced by H.D. Mills and N.G. de Bruijn. I am also deeply grateful to Professor E.M. Williams, former head of the Department of Electrical Engineering at Carnegie Institute of Technology (now deceased), for having taught me his philosophy of engineering education. Referees have contributed to clarification of an earlier version of this paper. Brian Bauer, Dennis Peters, Ruth Abraham, and Preeti Rastogi made wonderful contributions in the third year.

Introduction

Victor R. Basili

This paper represents a position I have heard Dave argue on many occasions, with a great deal of passion: the need for the education of "software engineers" as engineers. Dave was trained as an engineer and so is able to see the engineering issues more clearly than most computer scientists.

It is a hard position to sell for a number of reasons:

- It is counter to the way software engineering grew up in computer science departments. Computer scientists have a mathematics mentality, rather than a scientific one, much less an engineering one.

- There are a large number of practicing software engineers who do not think of themselves as "engineers" in the true sense of that word and would not be willing to retrain.

- It would require a great deal of change in university education on the side of both computer science departments and engineering departments. Who has the required training in software engineering to teach it?

I believe that the basis of the problem is that software engineering is still an immature discipline and has not really emerged as a separate discipline from computer science. Computer science has a recommended curriculum of courses, supported by both professional societies—the IEEE Computer Society and the ACM—that includes "software engineering" as part of it. But software engineering in that context is more programming than engineering.

To create a separate discipline, a branch of engineering of the same status as electrical or civil engineering, would require a discipline that can do a better job of characterizing its problem space and recognizing potential solutions along with their limits. It would contain sets of engineering solutions that have been validated in practice and are supported by models that allow us to reason about their use.

Too much of software engineering education today is still "watch what I do and then do it," rather than specifying the problem and reasoning about potential solutions from a set of validated options.

Maybe the principles we hold today need to be better specified, integrated, validated, and embodied as engineering models before we can teach them. That would provide us with the materials and the people who can create and teach a sound engineering program.

Software Engineering: An Unconsummated Marriage

David Lorge Parnas

32.1 Software Engineering Education

When discussing the risks of using computers, we rarely mention the most basic problem: most programmers are not well educated for the work they do. Many have never learned the basic principles of software design and validation. Detailed knowledge of arcane system interfaces and languages is no substitute for knowing how to apply fundamental design principles.

The year-2000 problem illustrates my point. Since the late 1960s, we have known how to design programs so that it's easy to change the amount of storage used for dates. Nonetheless, thousands of programmers wrote millions of lines of code that violated well-accepted design principles. The simplest explanation—those who designed and approved that software were incompetent!

We once had similar problems with bridges and steam engines. Many who presented themselves as qualified to design, and direct the construction of, those products did not have the requisite knowledge and discipline. The response in many jurisdictions was legislation establishing engineering as a self-regulating profession. Under those laws, before anyone is allowed to practice engineering, they must be licensed by a specified professional engineering association. These associations identify a core body of knowledge for each engineering specialty. Accreditation committees visit universities frequently to make sure engineering programs teach the required material. The records of applicants for a license are examined to make sure they have passed the necessary courses. After acquiring supervised experience, applicants must pass additional examinations on the legal and ethical obligations of engineers.

When NATO organized two famous conferences on software engineering three decades ago, most engineers ignored them. Electrical engineers, interested in building computers, regarded programming as something to be done by others—either scientists who wanted the numerical results or mathematicians interested in numerical methods. Engineers viewed programming as a trivial task, akin to using a calculator. To this day, many refer to programming as a "skill" and deny that engineering principles must be applied when building software.

The organizers of the NATO conferences saw things differently. Knowing that the engineering profession has always been very protective of its legal right to control the use of the title "engineer," they hoped the conference title would provoke interest. They recognized that

- Programming is neither science nor mathematics. Programmers are not adding to our body of knowledge; they build products.
- Using science and mathematics to build products for others is what engineers do.
- Software is a major source of problems for those who own and use it. The problems are exactly those to be expected when products are built by people who are educated for other professions and believe that building things is not their "real job."

Unfortunately, communication between engineers and those who study software hasn't been effective. The majority of engineers understand very little about the science of programming or the mathematics that one uses to analyze a program, and most computer scientists don't understand what it means to be an engineer.

Today, the problems that motivated the engineering legislation are rampant in the software field.

Over the years, engineering has split into a number of specialities, each centered on a distinct area of engineering science. Engineering societies must now recognize a new branch of engineering—software engineering—and identify its core body of knowledge. Just as chemical engineering is a marriage of chemistry with classical engineering areas such as thermodynamics, mechanics, and fluid dynamics, software engineering should wed a subset of computer science with the concepts and discipline taught to other engineers.

Software engineering is often treated as a branch of computer science. This is akin to regarding chemical engineering as a branch of chemistry. We need both chemists and chemical engineers but they are very different. Chemists are scientists; chemical engineers are engineers. Software engineering and computer science have the same relationship.

The marriage will be successful only if the engineering societies, and computer scientists come to understand that neither can create a software engineering profession without the other. Engineers must accept that they don't know enough computer science. Computer scientists must recognize that being an engineer is different from being a scientist, and that software engineers require an education very different from their own.

Introduction

John Shore

This little gem masquerades as a conventional "thank you for the award" speech (1999 ACM–SIGSOFT Outstanding Researcher Award), written as an appreciation of four people who taught Dave the most about software engineering research: Everard Williams, Alan Perlis, Leo Finzi, and Harlan Mills.

Dave goes well beyond conventional acknowledgments. By describing clearly what he learned from these teachers, Dave communicates his own beliefs about the conduct of software engineering research, and by implication summarizes what's wrong with much work in the field. This was quite intentional. When I asked Dave about the paper, he wrote:

> I was in Japan for an ICSE to receive the award and found myself wondering why I disagreed with so many of the papers. I wanted to comment about the disagreements but the only space for me on the program was the "thank you for the award" space.

Dave pointedly remarks in the paper that none of the four teachers was educated as a computer scientist—all came from backgrounds in engineering and mathematics. From them he learned that an engineer's practice should be based on sound scientific and mathematical principles (the title "Engineer" shouldn't be applied merely to people who build things, whether houses or programs). And he learned that intellectual discipline and mathematical rigor could be applied to software.

The papers in this volume show that Dave learned his lessons well. His teachers would be proud of him.

Who Taught Me About Software Engineering Research?

David Lorge Parnas, P. Eng.

33.1 Whom to Thank?

I am honoured and grateful to have received the ACM–SIGSOFT Outstanding Researcher Award for 1998 and want to express my thanks. I am obviously grateful to the members of the award committee, but I also want to thank four of the people who taught me how to do research.

None of the four was educated as a computer scientist. Two taught engineering and had little to do with computers; the other two were mathematicians who turned to computing. The four were Everard M. Williams, longtime head of the Department of Electrical Engineering at Carnegie Institute of Technology (now Carnegie Mellon); Alan J. Perlis, founding head of Carnegie's Computer Science Department and the first winner of the Turing prize; Leo A. Finzi, an internationally known Electrical Engineering researcher; and Harlan Mills a mathematician best known for the work he did while an IBM Fellow. Since all have passed away, I can express my thanks to them only by attempting to convey their teachings to others.

33.2 Everard M. Williams

When I entered university I believed that I would learn how the universe worked; I thought that the search for scientific knowledge would satisfy me throughout my life. Two years as a physics student gave me a different picture of what scientists did. Many of my teachers were involved in a project whose goal was to get a more accurate estimate of the weight of the electron. I began to wonder if I really would enjoy approaching the "secrets" of the universe, one decimal place at a time. It was at this time that I met Everard Williams who convinced me that solving engineering problems offered the same intellectual challenges as scientific research and then asked, "If you want to solve hard problems, why not work on those that produce something useful?" He helped me to understand that while I would never discover the ultimate secrets of the universe, I could contribute by building better, safer, and less expensive products. Although, today, I appreciate the immense value of basic scientific research much more than I did at that time, I am still glad that my personal choice was engineering.

One of the most important lessons that Williams taught me was the meaning of "Engineer." In its primary meaning, the word is a noun, not a verb. As a verb it is only a vague term that refers to the broad variety of things that engineers do. More important, he taught me that "Engineer" is not a job description, but a title describing the holder's qualifications. One doesn't become an engineer by being assigned a task, but by successfully completing an education, obtaining relevant experience, demonstrating one's competence, and agreeing to subscribe to a code of ethics. The academic degree certifies that one has endured the education; in many jurisdictions, it is licensing or registration that certifies that one has the complete set of qualifications and has accepted the responsibility of applying one's knowledge to improve the safety and well-being of the public.

Williams believed that the mechanisms for accreditation of educational programmes and licensing of individual practitioners were at the heart of engineering; it is those licensing standards that give meaning to the word "Engineer." He stressed that we should not use the title "Engineer" to describe anyone who builds things, but only to refer to those whose education and experience prepared them to base their practice on sound scientific and mathematical principles. Although Williams had no interest or expertise in software, it was from him that I learned to object when people use the phrase "Software Engineering" to describe the activities of the majority of today's programmers. The use of scientific principles and engineering discipline when designing software is not common today. Williams would say that the title "Software Engineer" should be reserved for the graduates of future *accredited* Software Engineering programmes.

This understanding of the word "engineering" has always guided my research. I knew that a qualified engineer has been taught the science and mathematics necessary to design and inspect products. When I began teaching programming, I saw that we did not have the required knowledge in a form that could be communicated to students; in our teaching we showed people programmes and taught them syntax, but we did not teach them how to design or analyse programs. My research is dedicated to discovering knowledge that should be taught to software engineers.

Williams taught me a lot about the nature of engineering research. In his teaching he stressed that the primary task of an engineer was designing and that, while pure scientists could study any topic of interest, engineering researchers should focus on gaining knowledge that helped people to design better products. He taught us that for engineering research it was essential to know how design was presently done; only then could one look for better ways to do the job. It was because of his lessons that I chose to spend a few of my years working in industry and that I always endeavor to find out how programs are actually being written.

Williams always stressed the importance of mathematics. He did not believe in "cut and try" approaches or the use of "rules of thumb" (heuristics). He stressed that it was our responsibility as Engineers to do the analysis needed to be *sure* that the design was correct. He used countless examples to demonstrate why Engineers should not follow rules blindly, but must understand the basis of those rules and know their limitations. Williams stressed things that my mathematics teachers neglected. For example, he stressed the importance of always having precise definitions of the physical interpretation of mathematical variables. Without such definitions, sound mathematics can be used to produce unsound products. Good mathematics stands on its own, without physical interpretation, but a good *application* of mathematics requires a precise understanding of what the terms mean in the real world.

Williams also taught me what the word "specification" means to engineers. He made it clear that a "specification" must be a precise statement of requirements, one that left no doubt about what was required and what was not. I don't think he would have appreciated the use of "specification" in today's Software Engineering (SE) literature where it is sometimes used to refer to models, or to very impractical designs. Neither models nor designs allow us to distinguish required behavior from incidental properties of the description provided.

Williams taught what many today would call "process," but did it in a way that is very different from what I hear at SE conferences. He taught process by following a disciplined process when he showed us how to design. He never simply showed us a completed design; he showed us how to arrive at it. However, he wasted no time on empty words about process. He taught "process" by setting a good example, but never discussed process formally.

33.3 Alan J. Perlis

Alan Perlis was the first of my teachers who was interested in programming, and it was his excitement that inspired my interest. He took a topic that seemed dull when taught by others and showed us how much more there was to programming than finding the right command. He was the first to show me that the intellectual discipline and mathematical rigour that I enjoyed in engineering, could also be applied to software. However, his most important contribution was to make it clear that sound methods made programming fun. Over the years I have seen many intuitive (nonsystematic) approaches to programming; they make programming seem like drudgery. Without Perlis's demonstration of deeper approaches to programming, I don't think I would have become interested in software.

Perlis showed us how to go straight to the heart of a problem, to ignore the irrelevant or unimportant details, to pay little attention to the arbitrary choices made by others, to focus on essentials. He had a direct, sometimes brutal, way of saying things—a way that left no room for doubt on where he stood. If you had an idea, he tried to poke holes in it. It didn't matter what your idea was, he would try to show you where it was weak. He was a serious researcher, determined to get real results, but, in spite of his seriousness, he had a great sense of humour and was able to use humour to make his point as well.

It was from Alan Perlis that I first learned the value of pure mathematics. He made it clear that when choosing either students or colleagues, there was often more value in a mathematics course than in a computer science course. The mathematics that he liked was so clean that it was powerful, so abstract that it could be applied to a variety of real problems. Perlis taught me to go to math books, rather than computer science papers or texts, for help. I follow that advice today.

Perlis also taught me the importance of not bending the truth. In watching him answer questions, I learned the importance of never defending the indefensible. When he, or his students, had done something wrong, he never defended it—simply explained why it had been an error and moved forward from there. Often, I have watched other researchers take years to retreat from a silly idea, and thought how lucky I was to have Alan Perlis as my teacher.

On the other hand, Alan Perlis never backed down from what he perceived to be the truth. If his research had shown him something that went against "conventional wisdom," he would not give in to the pressure to conform. He never followed fads. Interested in programming languages and compilers, he either ignored or poked fun at, those he considered unworthy of study. I remember him speaking out against very powerful forces that were proposing a new programming language called "NPL" (later "PL/I"), spontaneously calling it the Needless Programming Language. We know today that he was right. He would be equally rough on many of today's languages.

Perlis taught me that if a research question in computing is relevant now, it must have been relevant 20 years ago, and would be relevant 20 years from now. To this day, that rule guides me in selecting what I study.

Finally, although he worked together with some of the early founders of AI, he taught me not to pay much attention to that work. I will never forget his reference to AI researchers as "illusionists," people who are trying to create the *illusion* of intelligence. From him I learned to look for methods that would get the job done reliably, not mechanisms that were modeled on the way that people or animals *appear* to solve a problem. If we trust a computer to solve a problem, it should solve it better, or more reliably, than humans. Imitating human behavior is not the path to reliable software.

33.4 Leo Aldo Finzi

Leo Finzi was a classically trained engineer interested in classical electrical engineering problems such as transformers, motors, and transmission lines. He was not a person to turn to the computer to solve design problems. He preferred symbolic mathematics to numerical calculations. He felt that it was possible to waste a lot of time writing programmes when one should have spent that time thinking more about the problem. He once told us that his data supported the observation that a computer was equivalent to a toilet. He observed his students trying to solve a problem, would see them growing increasingly uncomfortable, and then hear them say, "I am going to solve this on the computer." They would then disappear for a while. When they returned they seemed more comfortable and said that the time had been spent productively. However, they still had not solved the problem. Often, when I see SE researchers building tools rather than analyzing the problem, I think that if they had been Finzi's student, they might have remembered that joke and spent more time defining the problem before deciding to build a tool. Finzi shared with my other teachers a talent for using humour and unconventional teaching techniques to get his ideas across.

Finzi taught us that we were designing in a multidimensional space and repeatedly showed us that no single metric (or figure of merit) could capture what was meant by "good design." He showed us that, even for simple devices like transformers, he could show us a set of designs in which every design was, by some metric, better than the others. He also showed us it was always possible to design a product that had a good value of a metric, but was still a lousy design. While he taught us the importance of measurement and numerical figures of merit, he taught us something more important, namely that we must measure what counts, and not resort to counting whatever happens to be easy to measure.

Finzi was also a strong advocate of the importance of mathematics in engineering. His students often spent hours with mathematical problems. However, we learned to apply mathematics, not to prove theorems. He also taught us the value of finding "closed form" expressions for mathematical functions, and the importance of choosing notation that fits the class of functions we are using. When I look at the lengthy, axiomatic specifications of relatively simple systems that one finds in "formal methods" papers, I often wonder what would have happened if those authors had been students of Finzi because Finzi had a marvelous sense of what could, and could not, be used in practical design.

Finzi was also a devoted educator who spent a lot of his time making sure that the Engineering curriculum focused on material that engineers would find useful during lengthy careers. He fought frequent battles with the science departments to get them to refrain from including the latest results in their courses if the new material was taught at the cost of the fundamental knowledge that was needed by engineers.

33.5 Harlan D. Mills

Harlan Mills was never formally my teacher, but I learned a great deal by working with him and watching him. He took what my other teachers had taught me about mathematics and showed me how it worked.

I vividly recall watching him serve as judge in a student paper contest at a major conference. He told his audience about a conversation he had had with his father when he decided to do postdoctoral work at the Institute for Advanced Studies in Princeton, N.J. He told his father that he wanted to go to a place filled with great people like von Neumann and Einstein because he wanted to look in their wastebaskets. They published only one or two tightly worded papers a year and he wanted to see what they threw out. When he looked in their wastebaskets he found that:

- they often threw out more in a day than they published in a year, and
- although they published carefully organized and worded papers, they discarded material that was "stream of consciousness" and verbose.

His final word to the students was that, after reading their papers, he was sure that if he visited their offices their wastebaskets would not be very full. After hearing that story I resolved to publish less and discard more. My wastebasket today is electronic, and rarely emptied, but it is rapidly expanding.

Mills, like Alan Perlis, taught me how "old" mathematics could be more useful than new computer science and the importance of putting techniques on a sound mathematical basis. He was often able to spot errors in mathematical models by checking very basic properties in the definitions. Often his colleagues, particularly those who were not mathematicians, interpreted his confident application of standard mathematical ideas as brilliance.

Mills found fresh ways to solve old problems with old mathematical ideas. For example, I was inspired by his explanation of why we did not need to find loop invariants to verify loops. He simply told us to verify the equivalence of two functions. Although one of my favorite papers is Mills's "The New Math of Computer Programming" [1], the lesson that I learned from Mills is that the mathematics of programming isn't at all new.

The focus of Mills's work was on how to design. In that way, he was more of an engineer than a mathematician. He knew and used mathematics, but he never lost sight of the fact that our job was to help programmers design better software. Mills gave us procedures for coming up with good programs. Like Everard Williams, he taught us about "process" but always by showing us both what to do and how to do it. He was very good at giving inspirational talks, but he didn't stop after saying the encouraging words; he went on to show us how to do what he preached.

One of Mills's most important lessons had to do with the difference between management and engineering. He did not try to tell us how to manage unmanageable projects; he showed us how to make projects manageable. He understood that only well-designed and well-documented software could be managed properly; he taught us how to design products in ways that made management easier. Today, when so many papers discuss software engineering as if the problem was simply project management, I miss Harlan Mills.

33.6 Conclusions

Although two of these teachers knew nothing about programming and none was a computer scientist, all had important things to teach us about Software Engineering. I could not have won this prize without them.

References

1. Mills, H.D. "The New Math of Computer Programming" *Communications of the ACM*, Vol. 18, No. 1, pp. 43–48, January 1975.

Bibliography

Bibliography

1. Parnas, D.L., "Kirchhoff's Laws", Programmed Text, Electrical Engineering Department, Carnegie Institute of Technology, Pittsburgh PA., 1960, 43 pgs.

2. Parnas, D.L., "Elementary Calculus: Programmed Study Material", Computation Center, Carnegie-Mellon University, Pittsburgh PA., 1962.

3. Strauss, J.C., Parnas, D.L., Snelsire, R., Wallach, Y., "A Design-Emphasis Problem-Solving Experience", Electrical Engineering Department, Carnegie Institute of Technology, Pittsburgh PA., 1963, 129 pgs.

4. Parnas, D.L., "System Function Description-Algol", (Ph.D. thesis), Computation Center, Carnegie-Mellon University, Pittsburgh PA., February 1965, 100 pgs.

5. Parnas, D.L., "A Language for Describing the Functions of Synchronous Systems", *Communications of the ACM*, 9, 2, February 1966, pp. 72–75.

6. Parnas, D.L., "On the Use of the Computer in Engineering Education Without a Programming Prerequisite", *Journal of Engineering Education*, April 1966, pp. 313–315.

7. Parnas, D.L., "On the Preliminary Report of C3S", (letter to the editor), *Communications of the ACM*, 9, 4, April 1966, pp. 242–243.

8. Parnas, D.L., "On Facilitating Parallel and Multi-Processing in Algol", (letter to the editor), *Communications of the ACM*, 9, 4, April 1966, p. 257.

9. Parnas, D.L., Richardson, L.C., Kohl, W.H., "Preliminary Version—An Introduction to Boole–66", Computation Center, Carnegie-Mellon University, Pittsburgh PA., September 1966, 23 pgs.

10. Parnas, D.L., "State Table Analysis of Programs in an Algol-Like Language", *Proceedings of the 1966 National ACM Conference*, Thompson Book Co., Washington, D.C., pp. 391–400.

11. Parnas, D.L., "Sequential Equivalents of Parallel Processes", Carnegie Institute of Technology, Pittsburgh PA., February 1967, 38 pgs.

12. Parnas, D.L., Darringer, J.A., "SODAS and a Methodology for System Design", *Proceedings of AFIPS 1967 Fall Joint Computing Conference*, pp. 449–474.

13. Parnas, D.L., "On Improving the Quality of Our Technical Meetings", (letter to the editor), *Communications of the ACM*, 11, 8, September 1968, pp. 537.

14. Parnas, D.L., "On Operating Computer Systems and Simulation Systems", *Computer Science Research Review 3*, Carnegie-Mellon University, December 1968, pp. 23–27.

15. Parnas, D.L., "More on Simulation Languages and Design Methodology for Computer Systems", *Proceedings of SJCC*, 1969, pp. 739–743.

16. Parnas, D.L., "On the Use of Transition Diagrams in the Design of a User Interface for an Interactive Computer System", *Proceedings of the 1969 National ACM Conference*, pp. 379–386.

17. Parnas, D.L., "On Simulating Networks of Parallel Processes in Which Simultaneous Events May Occur", *Communications of the ACM*, 12, 9, September 1969, pp. 519–531.

18. Parnas, D.L., "The Application of Modelling to System Development and Design", *International Computing Symposium*, ACM European Chapters, Vol. IV, May 1970, pp. 137–147.

19. Parnas, D.L., "Research Problems in the Area of Operating Systems", M.B.L.E. Laboratoire de Recherches, Brussels, September 1970, 4 pgs.

20. Parnas, D.L., "Review of Dynamic Protection Structures", (B.W. Lampson, *Proceedings AFIPS 1969 FJCC*), *Computing Reviews*, 12, 1, January 1971, pp. 29–30.

21. Parnas, D.L., "Review of Productivity of Multiprogramming Computers—Progress in Developing an Analytic Prediction Method", D.J. Lesser, *Computing Reviews*, 12, 1, January 1971, pp. 30.

22. Courtois, P.-J., Heymans, F., Parnas, D.L., "Concurrent Control with Readers and Writers", *Communications of the ACM*, 14, 10, October 1971, pp. 667–668.

23. Parnas, D.L., "Information Distributions Aspects of Design Methodology", *Proceedings of IFIP Congress '71*, 1971, Booklet TA-3, pp. 26–30.

24. Parnas, D.L., "A Technique for Software Module Specification with Examples", *Communications of the ACM*, 15, 5, May 1972, pp. 330–336.
    - Republished in *Writings of the Revolution,* edited by Edward Nash Yourdon, Yourdon Press, 1982, pp. 5–18.
    - Also in *Software Specification Techniques* edited by N. Gehani and A.D. McGettrick, AT&T Bell Telephone Laboratories, 1985, pp. 75–88 (QA 76.7 S6437).
    - Translated into Russian, "*Danniye v yazikach programmirovania*" Moscow, Mir (Publishing House), 1984, pp. 9–24.

25. Parnas, D.L., Habermann, A.N., "Comment on Deadlock Prevention Method", *Communications of the ACM*, 15, 9, September 1972, pp. 840–841.

26. Parnas, D.L., "On the Criteria to Be Used in Decomposing Systems into Modules", *Communications of the ACM*, 15, 12, December 1972, pp. 1053–1058.
    - Translated into Japanese, *BIT*, vol. 14, no. 3, 1982, pp. 54–60.
    - Republished in *Classics in Software Engineering*, edited by Edward Nash Yourdon, Yourdon Press, 1979, pp. 141–150.
    - Republished in *Great Papers in Computer Science*, edited by Phillip Laplante, West Publishing Co, Minneapolis/St. Paul 1996, pp. 433–441.

27. Parnas, D.L., "Sample Man-Machine Interface Specification—A Graphics-Based Line Editor", In *Display Use for Man-Machine Dialog* (eds. W. Handler, J. Weizembaum), Carl Hanser Verlag, Munchen, 1972, pp. 33–52.

28. Parnas, D.L., "A Course on Software Engineering Techniques", in *Proceedings of the ACM SIGCSE*, Second Technical Symposium, 24–25 March 1972, pp. 1–6.

29. Courtois, P.-J., Heymans, F., Parnas, D.L., "Comments on a Comparison of Two Synchronizing Concepts", *Acta Informatica*, 1, 1972, pp. 375–376.

30. Parnas, D.L., "Some Conclusions from an Experiment in Software Engineering Techniques", *Proceedings of the 1972 FJCC*, 41, Part I, pp. 325–330.

31. Parnas, D.L., Price, W.R., "The Design of the Virtual Memory Aspects of a Virtual Machine", *Proceedings of the ACM SIGARCH-SIGOPS Workshop on Virtual Computer Systems*, March 1973, 7 pgs.

32. Parnas, D.L., Gerhardt, D., "Window: A Formally-Specified Graphics-Based Text Editor" Carnegie-Mellon University, June 1973, 34 pgs.

33. Parnas, D.L., Robinson, L., "A Program Holder Module", Carnegie-Mellon University, June 1973, 48 pgs.

34. Parnas, D.L., "Review of Protection Systems and Protection Implementations", (Needham, R. M. *Proceedings AFIPS 1972 Fall Joint Computer Conference*, Vol. 41, Part I), *Computing Reviews*, 14, 12, December 1973, p. 582.

35. Parnas, D.L., Price, W.R., "Design of a Non-Random Access Virtual Memory Machine", *Proceedings of the International Workshop On Protection in Operating Systems*, Paris, August 1974, 14 pgs.

36. Parnas, D.L., "On a 'Buzzword': Hierarchical Structure", *IFIP Congress '74*, North Holland Publishing Company, 1974, pp. 336–339.

37. Parnas, D.L., "Review of a Comparison of Two Synchronizing Concepts", (Brinch Hansen, Per., *Acta Informatica* 1, 3), *Computing Reviews*, 15, 6, June 1974, pp. 203–204.

38. Cooprider, L.W., Courtois, P.J., Heymans, F., Parnas, D.L., "Information Streams Sharing a Finite Buffer: Other Solutions", *Information Processing Letters*, 3, 1, July 1974, pp. 16–21.

39. Parnas, D.L., "On a Solution to the Cigarette Smokers' Problem (Without Conditional Statements)", *Communications of the ACM*, 18, 3, March 1975, pp. 181–183.

40. Babich, A., Grason, J., Parnas, D.L., "Significant Event Simulation", *Communications of the ACM*, 18, 6, June 1975, pp. 323–329.

41. Parnas, D.L., Siewiorek, D.L., "Use of the Concept of Transparency in the Design of Hierarchically Structured Systems", *Communications of the ACM*, 18, 7, July 1975, pp. 401–408.

42. Parnas, D.L., Shore, J.E., Elliott, W.D., "On the Need for Fewer Restrictions in Changing Compile-Time Environments", *Proceedings of the International Computing Symposium 1975*, North Holland Publishing Company, pp. 45–48.

43. Parnas, D.L., "Software Engineering or Methods for the Multi-Person Construction of Multi-Version Programs", in *Programming Methodology*, (eds. G. Goos, J. Hartmanis), Lecture Notes in Computer Science 23, Springer Verlag, Berlin, 1975, pp. 1–11.

44. Parnas, D.L., "The Influence of Software Structure on Reliability", *Proceedings International Conference on Reliable Software*, April 1975, Los Angeles, CA., pp. 358–362.
    ■ Reprinted with improvements in Yeh, R., *Current Trends in Programming Methodology (I)*, Prentice Hall, 1977.

45. Parnas, D.L., Handzel, G., "More on Specification Techniques for Software Modules", Report BS I 75/1, Fachbereich Informatik, Technische Hochschule Darmstadt, April 1975, 16 pgs.

46. Parnas, D.L., "Evaluation Criteria for Abstract Machines with Unknown Applications", *ACM Computer Architecture News*, 4, 3, September 1975, pp. 2–9.

47. Parnas, D.L., "On the Design and Development of Program Families", *IEEE Transactions on Software Engineering*, Vol. SE-2, No. 1, March 1976, pp. 1–9.

48. Parnas, D.L., "Some Hypotheses About the 'Uses Hierarchy' for Operating Systems", Technical Report, Technische Hochschule Darmstadt, Darmstadt, West Germany, March 1976, 26 pgs.

49. Parnas, D.L., Shore, J.E., Weiss, D., "Abstract Types Defined as Classes of Variables", *Proceedings Conference on Data: Abstraction, Definition, and Structure*, Salt Lake City, March 1976, pp. 22–24. Reprinted in NRL Memorandum Report 7998, April 22, 1976, pp. 1–10.

50. Parnas, D.L., Würges, H., "Response to Undesired Events in Software Systems", *Proceedings of Second International Conference on Software Engineering*, October 1976, pp. 437–447.

51. Parnas, D.L., Handzel, G., Würges, H., "Design and Specification of the Minimal Subset of an Operating System Family", *Presented at 2nd International Conference on Software Engineering*, October 1976.
    ■ Also in *IEEE Transactions on Software Engineering*, SE-2, 4, Dec. 1976, pp. 301–307.

52. Parnas, D.L., Bartussek, W., Handzel, G., Würges, H., "Using Predicate Transformers to Verify the Effects of 'Real' Programs", UNC Report No. TR-76-101, October 1976, 36 pgs.

53. Encarnacao, J., Fink, B., Horbst, E., Konkart, R., Nees, G., Parnas, D.L., Schlechtendahl, E.G., "A Recommendation on Methodology in Computer Graphics", Kernforschungszentrum Karlsrue 2394, February 1977, 49 pgs.

54. Parnas, D.L., "Building Reliable Software in Blowhard", ACM *Software Engineering Notes*, 2, 3, April 1977, pp. 5–6.

55. Parnas, D.L., "The Use of Precise Specifications in the Development of Software", *Proceedings of the IFIP Congress '77*, 1977, North Holland Publishing Company, pp. 861–867.

56. Parnas, D.L., "Further Excerpts from the ACM SIGTRANS Notices", ACM *Software Engineering Notes*, 2, 5, October 1977, pp. 6–7.

57. Bartussek, W., Parnas, D.L., "Using Assertions About Traces to Write Abstract Specifications for Software Modules", UNC Report No. TR77-012, December 1977, 26 pgs.
    ■ Also in Lecture Notes in Computer Science (65), *Information Systems Methodology, Proceedings ICS*, Venice, 1978, Springer Verlag, pp. 211–236.
    ■ Also in *Software Specification Techniques* edited by N. Gehani and A.D. McGettrick, AT&T Bell Telephone Laboratories, 1985, pp. 111–130 (QA 76.6 S6437).

58. Parnas, D.L., "Use of Abstract Interfaces in the Development of Software for Embedded Computer Systems", NRL Report No. 8047, June 1977, 30 pgs.
    ■ Reprinted in Infotech State of the Art Report, Structured System Development, Infotech International, 1979.

59. Parnas D.L., "Some Software Engineering Principles", Infotech State of the Art Report on Structured Analysis and Design, *Infotech International*, 1978, 10 pgs.

60. Parnas D.L., "Designing Software for Ease of Extension and Contraction", *IEEE Transactions on Software Engineering*, March 1979, pp. 128–138.
    ■ Also in *Proceedings of the Third International Conference on Software Engineering*, May 1978, pp. 264–277.

61. Parnas, D.L. et al., "Software Engineering Principles", NRL Course Notes, 1976, 7, 8, 9, 80, 1, 3 (available from NTIS).

62. Parnas, D.L., "The Non-Problem of Nested Monitor Calls", *ACM Operating Systems Review*, 12, 1, January 1978, pp. 12–14.

63. Parnas, D.L., "Another View of the Dijkstra-DMLP Controversy", *ACM Software Engineering Notes*, 3, 4, October 1978, pp. 20–21.

64. Heninger, K., Kallander, J., Parnas, D.L., Shore, J., "Software Requirements for the A-7E Aircraft", NRL Report 3876, November 1978, 523 pgs.

65. Parnas, D.L., Review of "Measuring Improvements in Program Clarity" by R.D. Gordon, (*IEEE Transactions Software Engineering*, SE-5, 2, March 1979, pp. 79–90) in *Computing Reviews*, 21, 1, January 1980, p. 31.

66. Parnas, D.L., "Research Problems in Programming Methodology", *In Research Directions in Software Technology*, Peter Wegner (Ed.), MIT Press, 1979, pp. 352–385.

67. Parnas, D.L., "The Role of Program Specifications", in *Research Directions in Software Technology*, Peter Wegner (Ed.), The MIT Press, 1979, pp. 364–370.

68. Parker, R.A., Heninger, K.L., Parnas, D.L., Shore, J.E., "Abstract Interface Specifications for the A-7E Device Interface Modules", NRL Report 4385, November 1980, 176 pgs.

69. Britton, K.H., Parker, R.A., Parnas, D.L., "A Procedure for Designing Abstract Interfaces for Device Interface Modules", *Proceedings of the 5th International Conference on Software Engineering*, March 1981, pp. 195–204.

70. Parnas D.L., "An Alternative Control Structure and Its Formal Definition", IBM Technical Report TR FSD-81-0012, August 1981, 41 pgs.

71. Hester, S.D., Parnas, D.L., Utter, D.F., "Using Documentation as a Software Design Medium", *Bell System Technical Journal*, 60, 8, October 1981, pp. 1941–1977.

72. Britton, K.H., Parnas, D.L., "A-7E Software Module Guide", NRL Report 4702, Dec. 1981, 35 pgs.

73. Britton, K.H., Clements, P., Parnas, D.L., "Interface Specifications for the SCR (A-7E) Extended Computer Module", NRL Report 4843, Jan. 1983 (revised as item 86).

74. Parnas D.L., "Software Engineering Principles", University of Victoria Report No. DCS-29-IR, February 1983, 14 pgs.

75. Clements P.C., Parnas, D.L., Weiss, D.M., "Enhancing Reusability with Information Hiding", *Proceedings of the Workshop on Reusability in Programming*, September 1983, pp. 240–247 (revised as item 103).

76. Clements, P.C., Faulk, S.R., Parnas, D.L., "Interface Specifications for the SCR (A-7E) Application Data Types Module", NRL Report 8734, August 1983, 31 pgs.

77. Parnas D.L., "A Generalized Control Structure and its Formal Definition", *Communications of the ACM*, 26, 8, August 1983, pp. 572–581 (modification of item 70).

78. Faulk, S.R., Parnas, D.L., "On the Uses of Synchronization in Hard-Real-Time Systems", *Proceedings of Real-Time Systems Symposium*, Arlington, Virginia, 6–8 December 1983, pp. 101-109, IEEE Cat. No. 83CH1941-4.

79. Parnas, D.L., Clements, P.C., Weiss, D.M., "The Modular Structure of Complex Systems", *IEEE Transactions on Software Engineering*, March 1985, Vol. SE-11 No. 3, pp. 259–266 (special issue on the 7th International Conference on Software Engineering).
    - ■ Also published in *Proceedings of 7th International Conference on Software Engineering*, March 1984, pp. 408–417.

■ Reprinted in IEEE Tutorial: "Object-Oriented Computing", Vol. 2: *Implementations,* edited by Gerald E. Peterson, IEEE Computer Society Press, IEEE Catalog Number EH0264-2, ISBN 0-8186-4822-8, 1987, pp. 162–169.

80. Clements, P.C., Parnas, D.L., "Experience with a Module Interface Specification Technique", *Proceedings of International Workshop on Models and Languages for Software Specification and Design,* 30 March 1984, Orlando, Florida, pp. 70–73.

81. Parnas, D.L., "Author's Response Regarding an Alternative Control Structure and Its Formal Definition", (Technical Correspondence), *Comm. of the ACM,* 27, 5, May 1984, pp. 498–499.

82. Parnas, D.L., Wadge, W., "A Final Comment Regarding an Alternative Control Structure and Its Formal Definition", (Technical Correspondence), *Comm. of the ACM,* 27, 5, May 1984, pp. 499, 522.

83. Clements, P.C., Parker, R.A., Parnas, D.L., Shore, J., "A Standard Organization for Specifying Abstract Interfaces", NRL Report 8815, June 1984, 19 pgs.

84. Parnas, D.L., "Is ADA Too Big?", (Technical Correspondence), *Communications of the ACM,* 27, 11, November 1984, p. 1155.

85. Parnas, D.L., "Software Engineering Principles", *INFOR, Canadian Journal of Operations Research and Information Processing,* Vol. 22, no. 4, November 1984, pp. 303–316 (revised version of item 74).

86. Parnas D.L., Weiss, D.M., Clements, P.C., Britton, K.H., "Interface Specifications for the SCR (A-7E) Extended Computer Module", NRL Memorandum Report 5502, December 1984, 129 pgs. (major revision of item 73).

87. Parnas, D.L., Woolsey, J.R., "An Introduction to the Extended Computer", University of Victoria/IBM Technical Report No. 2, February 1985, 7 pgs.

88. Parnas D.L., Clements, P.C., "A Rational Design Process: How and Why to Fake It", Presented at the *TAPSOFT Joint Conference on Theory and Practice of Software Development,* Berlin, 25–29 March, 1985.
■ Also published as University of Victoria/IBM Technical Report No. 3, February 1985, 18 pgs.

89. Parnas, D.L., Weiss, D.M., "Active Design Reviews: Principles and Practices", *Proceedings of the 8th International Conference on Software Engineering,* London, August 1985.
■ Also published in *Journal of Systems and Software,* December 1987.

90. Parnas, D.L., "Predicative Programming", Technical Correspondence (refereed), *Communications of the ACM,* 28, 5, May 1985, pp. 534–536.

91. Parnas, D.L., "The Impact of Money-Free Computer-Assisted Barter Systems, University of Victoria Report No. DCS-48-IR, July 1985, 9 pgs.

92. Parnas, D.L., "More on Is ADA Too Big?", (Technical Correspondence), *Communications of the ACM,* 28, 7, July 1985, pp. 753.

93. Parnas, D.L., Software Aspects of Strategic Defense Systems, American Scientist, Vol. 73, No. 5, Sept.–Oct. 1985, pp. 432–440 (revised version of University of Victoria Report No. DCS-47-IR).
■ Also published in *Communications of the ACM,* 28, 12, December 1985, pp. 1326–1335.
■ Translated into Dutch, *Informatie, jaargang* 28, 3, March 1986, pp. 175–186.

- Translated into Japanese, *SEKAI,* no. 6, 1986, pp. 298–319.
- Translated into German, *Software Wars,* in Kursbuch 83, Krieg und Frieden—Streit um SDI. Published by Kursbuch/Rotbuch Verlag, March, 1986. Also a partial translation, "Wie Kunstliche Blumen", in *Frontal,* May/June 1986, p. 46.
- Translated into Hebrew, *Explaining Preparation of Military Strategic Software,* Maaseh Hoshev, April 1986, p. 3 by Information Processing Association of Israel.
- Translated into Swedish, *Programvaruaspekter pa strategiska for svarssystem,* Zenit, Issue No. 94, Winter 1986/87, pp. 66–82.
- Reprinted in *Computerization & Controversy: Value Conflicts and Social Choices,* edited by Charles Dunlop & Rob Kling, Academic Press, Boston, March 1991.

94. Parnas, D.L., Clements, P.C., "A Rational Design Process: How and Why to Fake It", *IEEE Transactions on Software Engineering,* Vol. SE-12, No. 2, February 1986, pp. 251–257 (revised version of item 88).
   - Republished in *Great Papers in Computer Science,* edited by Phillip Laplante, West Publishing Co, Minneapolis/St. Paul 1996, pp. 442–451.

95. Parnas, D.L. (with the help of Dieter Brehde), "Warum SDI Betrug ist" im Stern Nr. 15, 3 April 1986.

96. Parnas, D.L., "Star Wars and the Scientific Community", *Alternatives,* April 1986, pp. 27–31.

97. Parnas, D.L., "The Star Wars Nightmare", *South,* July 1986, p. 117.

98. Parnas, D.L., letter, "Star Wars Software", *Science,* 25 July 1986, p. 403.

99. Parnas, D.L., "Why I Won't Work on Software for SDI", *The World & I,* no. 6, 1986, pp. 573–575.

100. Parnas, D.L., Wadge, W., "Less Restrictive Constructs for Structured Programs", Technical Report No. 86–186, Queen's, Kingston, Ontario, September 1986, 16 pgs.

101. Parnas, D.L., "SDI: A Violation of Professional Responsibility", *ABACUS,* vol. 4, no. 2, Winter, 1987, pp. 46–52.
   - Reprinted in "The Name of the Chamber Was Peace", *Science for Peace,* Samuel Stevens and Co. Toronto and Fort Meyers, 1988.
   - Reprinted in *A Computer Science Reader—Selections from ABACUS,* edited by Eric A. Weiss, Springer-Verlag, 1987, pp. 46–52 (QA 76.24 C658).
   - Reprinted in *COMPUTER STUDIES: Computers in Society,* edited by Kathryn Schellenberg, Dushkin Publishing Group, 1988 (ISBN: 0-87967-727-9)
   - Reprinted in *Ethical Issues in Engineering,* by Deborah G. Johnson, Prentice Hall, 1991, pp. 15–25 (ISBN: 0-13-290578-7)

102. Parnas, D.L., "SDI: 'Red Herrings' Miss the Boat", *Computer IEEE,* (Letter to the Editor) vol. 20, no. 2, February 1987, pp. 6–7.

103. Clements, P.C., Parnas, D.L., Weiss, D.M., "Enhancing Reusability with Information Hiding", IEEE Tutorial "Software Reusability" edited by Peter Freeman, IEEE Computer Society Press, IEEE Catalog #EH0256-8, ISBN: 0-8186-0750-5, 1987, pp. 83–90 (revised version of item 75).
   - Reprinted in *Software Reusability,* edited by Ted J. Biggerstaff and Alan J. Perlis, Volume I, pp. 141–157, Addison-Wesley, 1989.

104. Parnas, D.L., "Warum ich an SDI nicht mitarbeite: Eine Auffassung beruflicher Verantwortung", *Informatik-Spektrum*, Band 10, Heft 1, Februar 1987, pp. 3–10.
    - Extracted in *Tagesanzeiger Magazin*, Zurich, 27 June 1987 Warum ich nicht mehr mitmache.

105. Parnas, D.L., "STAR WARS: Lesson for Canada", published in *The Whig Standard Magazine*, Kingston, Ontario, Canada, 3 October 1987, pp. 5–9.

106. Parnas, D.L., "Computers in Weapons: The Limits of Confidence", Chapter 7 in *Computers in Battle: Will They Work?* David Bellin and Gary Chapman (editors) published by Harcourt Brace Jovanovich Inc., NY 1987, 362 pgs. (ISBN: 0-15-121232-5).

107. Parnas, D.L., "U.S. Military Planners View Canada the Way Boxers View Their Gloves", in *If You Love This Country, Facts and Feelings on Free Trade,* assembled by Laurier LaPierre, McClelland and Stewart, Toronto, 1987, pp. 169–176 (ISBN: 0-7710-4697-9 soft cover).

108. Parnas, D.L., "Star Wars: Dream or Nightmare", *Proceedings of the 37th Pugwash Conference on Science and World Affairs* in Gmunden am Traunsee, Austria, 1–6 September 1987, pp. 388–394.
    - Japanese translation, in *SEKAI*, no. 12, 1987, pp. 201–211.
    - Chinese translation by M.S. Ng *Ming Pao Monthly, Hong Kong*, #284, Vol. 24, Issue 8, August 1989, pp. 91–95.

109. Parnas, D.L., van Schouwen, J., Kwan, P., Fougere, S., "Evaluation of the Shutdown Software for Darlington (SDS-1)", Interim Report for the Atomic Energy Control Board, 16 Nov. 1987, 69 pgs.

110. Faulk, S.R., Parnas, D.L., "On Synchronization in Hard-Real-Time Systems", *Communications of the ACM*, 31, 3, March 1988, pp. 274–287.
    - Reprinted in *Real-Time Systems: Abstractions, Languages, and Design Methodologies*, Chapter 6, pgs. 621–634. Krishna M. Kavi (editor), published by IEEE Computer Society Press, Los Alamitos, CA, 1992, 660 pgs., (ISBN: 0-8186-3152-X).

111. Parnas D.L., Kwan, S.P., van Schouwen, J., "Evaluation Standards for Safety-Critical Software", Technical Report No. 88-220, Queen's Kingston, Dept. of CIS, May 1988, 34 pgs.
    - Published in the *Proceedings of the International Working Group on Nuclear Power Plant Control and Instrumentation*, IAEA NPPCS Specialists' Meeting on Microprocessors in Systems Important to the Safety of Nuclear Power Plants, by the International Atomic Energy Agency, London, United Kingdom, 10–12 May 1988.
    - Also in *Software Development: Tips and Techniques*, Papers from Information Management Conference, U.S. Professional Development Institute, Silver Spring, MD, 1989, pp. 311–350.
    - Published in the *Proceeding of the Seventh International Conference on Testing Computer Software*, San Francisco, June 18–21, 1990, pp. 89–117.

112. Parnas, D.L., Smith, D.G., Pearce, T., "Making Software Documentation More Practical", study carried out for Bell-Northern Research (BNR). Technical Report No. 88-236, Queen's University, Dept. of Computing & Information Science, Nov. 1988, 53 pgs.

113. Parnas, D.L., "Why Engineers Should Not Use Artificial Intelligence", *Proceedings of the CIPS Edmonton '87 Conference*, Edmonton, Alberta, November 16–19, 1987. Published in *Intelligence Integration,* J. Schaeffer and L. Stewart (editors), Dept. of Computing Science, University of Alberta, pp. 39–42 (ISBN: 0-88864-858-8)
    - Substantial revision published in *INFOR*, vol. 26, no. 4, 1988, pp. 234–246.

114. Xu, J., Parnas, D.L., "Scheduling Processes with Release Times, Deadlines, Precedence, and Exclusion Relations", *IEEE Transactions on Software Engineering*, vol. 16, no. 3, March 1990, pp. 360–369.
    ■ Also Technical. Report CS-88-11, Dept. of Computer Science, York University, Sep. 1988, 26 pgs.
    ■ Also in *Advances in Real-Time Systems*, John A. Stankovic and Krithi Ramamritham (editors), IEEE Computer Society Press, 1993 pp. 140–149 (ISBN: 0-8186-3792-7).

115. Parnas, D.L., "Can We Tolerate Software Errors?", *Proceedings of the IFIP 11th World Computer Congress*, San Francisco, 28 August–1 September 1989. Published in Information Processing '89, G.X. Ritter (editor), North Holland 1989, p. 502 (ISBN: 0-444-88015-1)

116. Parnas, D.L., "On Artificial Intelligence and Expert Systems—Myths, Legends, and Facts", *Proceedings of the IFIP 11th World Computer Congress*, San Francisco, 28 August–1 September 1989. Published in *Information Processing '89*, G.X. Ritter (editor), North Holland, 1989, pp. 1145–1146 (ISBN: 0-444-88015-1).

117. Parnas, D.L., "Education for Computing Professionals", *IEEE Computer*, vol. 23, no. 1, January 1990, pp. 17–22.
    ■ Also published in *Teaching and Learning Formal Methods*, C. Neville Dean and Michael G. Hinchey (eds.), Academic Press, 1996, pp. 31–42.
    ■ Also published as Technical Report 89-247, Queen's University, Dept. of Computing & Information Science, March 1989.

118. Parnas, D.L., "On the Cruelty of Really Teaching Computer Science—Response to E.W. Dijkstra", *Communications of the ACM*, vol. 32, no. 12, December 1989, pp. 1405–1406.

119. Parnas, D.L., Wang, Y., "The Trace Assertion Method of Module Interface Specification", Technical Report 89-261, Queen's, Kingston, TRIO, October 1989, 39 pgs.
    ■ Also accepted (subject to reorganisation) by *IEEE Transactions on Software Engineering*.

120. Parnas, D.L., "Inspection Will Not Be Enough", *Proceedings of the 38th Pugwash Conference on Science and World Affairs* in *Dagomys*, USSR, 29 August–3 September 1988, pp. 211–212 (published 1989).

121. Parnas, D.L., "Documentation of Communications Services and Protocols", Technical Report 90-272, Queen's University, TRIO (Telecommunications Research Institute of Ontario), February 1990, 4 pgs.
    ■ Published in *Formal Description Techniques II*, S.T. Vuong (editor), North-Holland Publishing Co., 1989, pp. 277–280 (ISBN: 0-444-88544-7), Proceedings of IFIP TC/WG 6.1 Second International Conference on Formal Description Techniques for Distributed Systems and Communications Protocols, *FORTE '89*, Vancouver, 5–8 December 1989.

122. Parnas, D.L., "On Iterative Constructs", *ACM Transactions on Programming Languages and Systems*, (Technical Correspondence), vol. 12, no. 1, January 1990, pp. 139–141.

123. Parnas, D.L., "Herr Parnas, Moechten Sie die Welt Retten", *Wissenschaft und Frieden*, vol. 5, no. 1, February 1987, pp. 17–20.

124. Parnas, D.L., "Computing Science vs. Engineering Education", *EDUCATIONews (IEEE)*, vol. 3, no. 1, April 1990, pp. 3–5.

125. Parnas, D.L., "Education for Computing Professionals", *Proceedings of International Conference on Computing and Information, ICCI'90*, Niagara Falls, Ontario, May 1990.
   ■ Published in *Advances in Computing and Information*, S.G. Akl, F. Fiala, W. Koczkodaj (editors), Canadian Scholars' Press Inc, 1990, p. xi (ISBN: 0-921627-70-X).

126. Parnas, D.L., Asmis, G.J.K., Kendall, J.D., "Reviewable Development of Safety Critical Software", *The Institution of Nuclear Engineers*, International Conference on Control & Instrumentation in Nuclear Installations, 8–10 May 1990, Glasgow, United Kingdom, paper no. 4:2, 17 pgs.

127. Parnas, D.L., van Schouwen, A.J., Kwan, S.P., "Evaluation of Safety-Critical Software", *Communications of the ACM*, vol. 33, no. 6, June 1990, pp. 636–648 (substantially revised version of item 111).
   ■ Published in *Advances in Real-Time Systems*, John A. Stankovic and Krithi Ramamritham (eds), IEEE Computer Society Press, 1993 pp. 34–46 (ISBN: 0-8186-3792-7).

128. Parnas D.L., Madey, J., "Functional Documentation for Computer Systems Engineering", Technical Report 90–287, Queen's University, TRIO (Telecommunications Research Institute of Ontario), September 1990, 14 pgs.
   ■ Reproduced in CANDU Computer Conference, sponsored by the CANDU Owner's Group, November 11–13, 1990.

129. Parnas, D.L., "Functional Specifications for Old (and New) Software", *Proceedings of the 20th GI Jahrestagung*, Stuttgart, Germany, 10 October 1990, edited by Prof. A. Reuter, Informatik Fachberichte 257, Springer-Verlag, Berlin, 12 pgs.

130. Parnas, D.L., Madey, J., "Functional Documentation for Computer Systems", *Colloque sur l'inge'nierie de la qualite*, Le Centre, Montreal, 4–5 October 1990, 7 pages.

131. Parnas, D.L., Asmis, G.J.K., "Quality Assurance for Safety-Critical Software", *CIPS '90 Information Technology Conference*, Edmonton, Alberta, 24 October 1990, 12 pgs.

132. Parnas D.L., Asmis, G.J.K., Madey, J., "Managing Complexity in Safety-Critical Software", *ACM Conference on Critical Issues*, McLean, VA, 6 November 1990, 10 pgs.

133. Parnas, D.L., "Stellungnahme: Wissenschaft im Krieg–Krieg in der Wissenschaft", *Wissenschaft im Krieg–Krieg in der Wissenschaft*, Schriftenreihe des Arbeitskreises Marburger Wissenschaftler fuer Frieden, (Martina Tschimrt, Heinz-Wemer Goebel, eds.), Marburg, Germany 1990.

134. Parnas D.L., Asmis, G.J.K., Madey, J., "Assessment of Safety-Critical Software", Proceedings of the 9th Annual Software Reliability Symposium, by the IEEE Reliability Society, Denver Chapter, Colorado Springs, Colorado May 2–3 1991 (modified version of item 132).
   ■ Also Technical Report 90–295, Queen's, Kingston, TRIO (Telecommunications Research Institute of Ontario), December 1990, 13 pgs.

135. Parnas, D.L., "Who Assesses the Assessors?", (comments on the CommACM "Self-Assessment on Concurrency"), *Comm ACM*, vol. 34, no. 2, Feb. 1991, pp. 19–20.
   ■ Translated into Spanish, "Quien evalua a los evaluadores?" *Novatica* vol. XVIII., num. 97, 1992, pp. 58–60.

136. Parnas, D.L., Asmis, G.J.K., Madey, J., "Assessment of Safety-Critical Software in Nuclear Power Plants", *Nuclear Safety*, vol. 32, no. 2, April–June 1991, pp. 189–198 (modified version of item 134).

137. Xu, J., Parnas, D.L., "On Satisfying Timing Constraints in Hard-Real-Time Systems", Proceedings of *ACM SIGSOFT '91 Conference on Software for Critical Systems*, New Orleans, 4–6 December 1991, pp. 132–146.
    ■ Published in the IEEE Transactions on Software Engineering, Vol. 19, No. 11, January 1993, pp. 70–84.

138. Xu, J., Parnas, D.L., "Pre-Run-Time Scheduling of Processes with Exclusion Relations on Nested or Overlapping Critical Sections", *The Eleventh Annual IEEE International Phoenix Conference on Computers and Communications (IPCCC-11)* April 1–3, 1992, Scottsdale, AZ.

139. Parnas, D.L., "Responsibilities of Scientists in a Complex Society", *Proceedings of the 40th Pugwash Conference on Science and World Affairs* in Egham, UK, 15–20 Sept. 1990, pp. 627–637.
    ■ Also published in *Towards a Secure World in the 21st Century. Annals of Pugwash* 1990, Edited by Joseph Rotblat and Frank Blackaby. Taylor & Francis 1991, UK, pp. 337–348.

140. Parnas, D.L., Madey, J., "Functional Documentation for Computer Systems Engineering" published in *Science of Computer Programming* (Elsevier) vol. 25, number 1, October 1995, pp. 41–61 (substantially revised version of item 128).
    ■ also CRL Report 309, McMaster University, TRIO, September 1991, 14 pgs.

141. Parnas, D.L., Korsman, J.A., "The Systematic Construction of Precise Software Documents", *"Colloque sur l'inge'nierie de la qualite"*, Ottawa, 16–17 October 1991, pgs. 17.1–17.11.

142. Parnas D.L., "Predicate Logic for Software Engineering", CRL Report 241, McMaster University, TRIO (Telecommunications Research Institute of Ontario), Feb. 1992, 8 pgs.

143. Parnas, D.L., "Never Again: Reflections on the War Against Iraq", *Peace Magazine*, vol. VIII, issue II, March 1992.

144. Parnas, D.L., "Getting Serious About Computer System Documentation", *Proceedings of Tenth Annual Software Reliability Symposium*, Denver, Colorado, June 25–26, 1992, pp. 1–8.

145. Parnas D.L., Luo, Z.-Q., "On the Computational Complexity of the Maximum Trade Problem", CRL Report 254, McMaster University, CRL (Communications Research Laboratory) July 1992, 8 pgs (for revised version see item 176).

146. Parnas, D.L., "The Responsibilities of Scientists in a Changing World", published in *Erdsicht-Global Change*, Kunst-und Ausstellungshalle der Bundesrepublik Deutschland, Verlag Gerd Hatje, June 1992, pp. 155–168.
    ■ Also in German "Die Verantwortung der Wissenschaftler in einer sich verändernden Welt" in Erdischt-Global Change. Reprinted "FIFF Kommunikation", Mai 1993.
    ■ Also in Spanish "La responsabilidad de los cientificos en un mundo cambiante" in Erdischt-Global Change, 1995, pp. 147–160.

147. Courtois P.-J., Parnas D.L., "Documentation for Safety-Critical Software", presented at the IAEA Specialists' Meeting on Software Engineering in Nuclear Power Plants, Chalk River, Ontario, Canada, 9–11 September 1992.
    ■ Published in IAEA Specialist's Meeting on Software Engineering in Nuclear Power Plants: Experience, Issues and Directions, February 1993, pgs. 11–29 (revised as item 148).

148. Courtois P.-J., Parnas D.L., "Documentation for Safety-Critical Software", *Proceedings of the 15th International Conference on Software Engineering*, Baltimore, MD, 17–21 May 1993, pgs. 315–323 (revised version of item 147).

149. Parnas D.L., "Evaluation Procedure for Safety-Critical Software", *De Ingeneuze Informatika, op weg naar 2001*, Proceedings of the meeting on ten years of computer engineering in Holland.

150. Parnas D.L., Madey, J., Iglewski, M., "Formal Documentation of Well-Structured Programs", CRL Report 259, McMaster University, Communications Research Laboratory, TRIO (Telecommunications Research Institute of Ontario), September 1992, 37 pgs.

151. Parnas, D.L., "Tabular Representation of Relations", CRL Report 260, McMaster University, Communications Research Laboratory, TRIO (Telecommunications Research Institute of Ontario), October 1992, 17 pgs.

152. Parnas, D.L., Wang, Y., "Trace Rewriting Systems", CRL Report 247, McMaster University, Communications Research Laboratory, TRIO (Telecommunications Research Institute of Ontario), October 1992, 16 pgs.

153. Parnas, D.L., Madey, J., "Documentation of Real-Time Requirements", in *Real-Time Systems: Abstractions, Languages, and Design Methodologies*, pgs. 48–56. Krishna M. Kavi (editor), IEEE Computer Society Press, Los Alamitos, CA, 1992, 660 pgs. (ISBN: 0-8186-3152-X).

154. van Schouwen, A.J., Parnas, D.L., Madey, J., "Documentation of Requirements for Computer Systems", Proceedings of '93 *IEEE International Symposium on Requirements Engineering*, San Diego, CA, 4–6 January 1993, pp. 198–207.

155. Parnas D.L., Wang, Y., "Simulating the Behaviour of Software Modules by Trace Rewriting Systems", *Proceeding of the 15th International Conference on Software Engineering*, Baltimore, MD, 17–21 May 1993, pgs 14–23 (revised version see item 174).

156. Parnas, D.L., "On Software Engineering Programmes", *Proceedings of the National Workshop on Software Engineering Education*, Toronto, ON, 31 May 1993, pgs 115–119.

157. Parnas, D.L.,. Wang, Y., "Trace Rewriting Systems", *Proceedings of the Third International Workshop, CTRS-92*, Pont-a-Mousson, France, July 1992.
    ■ Also published in *Conditional Term Rewriting Systems*, M. Rusinowitch, J.L. Remy (eds.), Springer-Verlag, 1993, pp. 343–356 (ISBN: 3-540-56393-8).

158. Parnas, D.L., "Mathematics of Computation for (Software and Other) Engineers", *Bulletin of the European Association for Theoretical Computer Science*, No. 51, October 1993, pgs. 249–259.
    ■ Also in *Proceedings of the Third International Conference on Algebraic Methodology and Software Technology*, University of Twente, Netherlands, June 21–25, 1993.
    ■ Also in *Proceedings of the First IMA Conference on Mathematics of Dependable Systems*, University of London, England, September 1993.
    ■ Also in *Mathematics of Dependable Systems*, edited by Chris Mitchell and Victoria Stavridou, Claredon Press, Oxford, 1995, pp. 209–224 (small revisions).

159. Parnas, D.L., "Some Theorems We Should Prove", *Proceedings of 1993 International Meeting on Higher Order Logic Theorem Proving and Its Applications*, The University of British Columbia, Vancouver, BC, August 10–13, 1993, pgs 156–163.

160. Courtois, F., Parnas, D.L., "Formally Specifying a Communications Protocol Using the Trace Assertion Method", CRL Report 269, McMaster University, CRL (Communications Research Laboratory), TRIO (Telecommunications Research Institute of Ontario), July 1993, 19 pgs.

161. Iglewski, M., Madey, J., Parnas, D.L., Kelly, P. "Documentation Paradigms (A Progress Report)", CRL Report 270, McMaster University, CRL (Communications Research Laboratory), TRIO (Telecommunications Research Institute of Ontario), July 1993, 45 pgs.

162. Parnas, D.L., "Forward" in *Digital Woes: Why We Should Not Depend on Software*, by Lauren Ruth Wiener, published by Addison-Wesley, pp. ix–xiii, (ISBN:0-201-62609-8), September 1993.

163. Engel, M., Kubica, M., Madey, J., Parnas, D.L., Ravn, A.P., van Schouwen, A.J., "A Formal Approach to Computer Systems Requirements Documentation", in *Hybrid Systems*, Grossman R.L., Nerode A., Ravn A.P., Rischel H. (eds.), Lecture Notes in Computer Science 736, Springer-Verlag, 1993, pp. 452–474.

164. Parnas, D.L., "Predicate Logic for Software Engineering", *IEEE Transactions on Software Engineering*, Vol. 19, No. 9, September 1993, pp. 856–862 (substantively enhanced version of item 142).

165. Parnas, D.L., "Can We Make Software More Trustworthy?", in *"Na 30 jaar informatie"* Proceedings of a symposium held in Apeldoorn, Holland on 22 June 1989, Informatie–Maandblad voor Gegvensverwerking.

166. Parnas, D.L., "Software Aging", in *Proceedings of the 16ᵗʰ International Conference on Software Engineering*, Sorrento, Italy, May 16–21, 1994, IEEE Press, pp. 279–287.

167. Parnas, D.L., "Mathematical Descriptions and Specification of Software", *Proceedings of IFIP World Congress 1994*, Volume I, August 1994, pp. 354–359.

168. Parnas, D.L., "Professional Responsibilities of Software Engineers", *Proceedings of IFIP World Congress 1994*, Volume II, August 1994, pp. 332–339.
    ■ Reprinted in *"Softwaretechnik Trends"* Band 14, Heft 3, pp. 3–10, November 1994, Gesellschaft fuer Informatik.

169. Parnas, D.L., "Inspection of Safety-Critical Software Using Function Tables", *Proceedings of IFIP World Congress 1994*, Volume III August 1994, pp. 270–277.

170. Parnas, D.L., "Teaching Programming as if It Were Engineering", *Proceedings of the 1994 Annual Meeting of the American Society for Engineering Education., Edmonton AB.*

171. Peters, D., Parnas, D.L., "Generating a Test Oracle from Program Documentation", *Proceedings of the 1994 International Symposium on Software Testing and Analysis (ISSTA)*, August 17–19, 1994, pp. 58–65.

172. Parnas, D.L., "Creating Insecurity!", in *World Security, the New Challenge* by Canadian Pugwash Group, pp. 74–95, published by Dundern Press Ltd., 1994, ISBN: 0-88866-952-6.

173. Bauer, B., Parnas, D.L., "Experience with the Use of Precise Documentation", CRL Report 293, McMaster University, CRL, TRIO, August 1994, 12 pgs.

174. Parnas D.L., Wang, Y., "Simulating the Behaviour of Software Modules by Trace Rewriting Systems", *IEEE Transactions of Software Engineering*, Vol. 19, No. 10, October 1994, pp. 750–759 (revised version of item 155).

175. Parnas, D.L., Madey, J., Iglewski, M., "Precise Documentation of Well-Structured Programs", *IEEE Transactions on Software Engineering*, Vol. 20, No.12, December 1994, pp. 948–976 (substantively enhanced version of item 150).

176. Parnas D.L., Luo, Z.-Q., "On the Computational Complexity of the Maximum Trade Problem", *Acta Methematicae Applicatae Sinicae* (English Series) Volume 10, No. 4, 1994, pp. 434–440 (revised version of item 145).

177. Bauer, B., Parnas, D.L., "Applying Mathematical Software Documentation—An Experience Report", in *Proceedings of the Tenth Annual Conference on Computer Assurance*, National Institute of Standards and Technology, Gaithersburg, MD, June 25–29, 1995, pp. 273–285 (substantively enhanced version of item 173).

178. Parnas, D.L., "On ICSE's 'Most Influential Papers'", *ACM Software Engineering Notes*, vol. 20, no 3, July 1995, pp. 29–32.

179. Parnas, D.L., "Language-Free Mathematical Methods for Software Design—Extended Abstract", in *ZUM '95: The Z Formal Specification Notation*, 9th International Conference of Z Users, Limerick, Ireland, September 1995, Bowen J.P., Hinchey M.G. (eds.), Lecture Notes in Computer Science 967, Springer-Verlag, 1995, pp. 3–4.

180. Parnas, D.L., "The Future of Formal Methods in Industry—Position Statement", in *ZUM '95: The Z Formal Specification Notation*, 9th International Conference of Z Users, Limerick, Ireland, September 1995, Bowen J.P., Hinchey M.G. (eds.), Lecture Notes in Computer Science 967, Springer-Verlag, 1995, p. 238.

181. Parnas, D.L., "Teaching Programming as Engineering", in *ZUM '95: The Z Formal Specification Notation*, 9th International Conference of Z Users, Limerick, Ireland, September 1995, Bowen J.P., Hinchey M.G. (eds.), Lecture Notes in Computer Science 967, Springer-Verlag, 1995, pp. 471–481.

182. Parnas, D.L., "Using Mathematical Models in the Inspection of Critical Software", in *Applications of Formal Methods*, Hinchey M.G., Bowen J.P. (eds.), Prentice Hall International Series in Computer Science, 1995, pp. 17-31.

183. Parnas, D.L., "Geleitwort", in Baber, R.L., *Praktische Anwendbarkeit mathematisch rigoroser Methoden zum Sicherstellen der Programmkorrektheit*, Walter de Gruter, 1995, pp. v–vi.

184. Parnas, D.L., "A Logic for Describing, not Verifying, Software", *Erkenntnis* (Kluwer), volume 43, No. 3, November 1995, pp. 321–338.

185. Janicki, R., Parnas, D.L., Zucker, J., "Tabular Representations in Relational Documents", in "*Relational Methods in Computer Science*", Chapter 12, Ed. C. Brink and G. Schmidt. Springer Verlag, pp. 184–196, 1997 (ISBN 3-211-82971-7).
    ■ Also published as CRL Report 313, McMaster University, CRL TRIO, November 1995.

186. Parnas, D.L., "Why Software Jewels Are Rare", in *IEEE Computer*, Vol. 29, No. 2, February 1996, pp. 57–60.

187. Pakula, A., Parnas, D.L., "The Dayton Accord—Pro and Con and Pro and Con", *Peace Magazine*, March/April 1996, pp. 16–22.

188. Shen H., Zucker J.I., Parnas, D.L., "Table Transformation Tools: Why and How", *Proceedings of the Eleventh Annual Conference on Computer Assurance (COMPASS '96)*, published by IEEE and NIST, Gaithersburg, MD., June 1996, pp. 3–11.

189. Parnas, D.L., "Mathematical Methods: What We Need and Don't Need", in *IEEE Computer*, Vol. 29, No. 4, April 1996, pp. 28–29 (In roundtable "An Invitation to Formal Methods").

190. Parnas, D.L. "Teaching Programming as if It Were Engineering", published in *Teaching and Learning Formal Methods*, eds. C. Neville Dean and Michael G. Hinchey, Academic Press, 1996, pp. 43–55 (Substantively modified version of item170).

191. McMaster University Software Engineering Research Group, "Table Tool System Developer's Guide" CRL Report 339, McMaster University, CRL (Communications Research Laboratory), TRIO (Telecommunications Research Institute of Ontario), January 1997.

192. McMaster University Software Engineering Research Group, "Appendices to the Table Tool System Developer's Guide" CRL Report 340, McMaster University, CRL (Communications Research Laboratory), TRIO (Telecommunications Research Institute of Ontario), January 1997.

193. Singh, B., Viveros, R., Parnas, D.L., "Software Reliability Using Inverse Sampling", CRL Report 351, McMaster University, CRL (Communications Research Laboratory), TRIO (Telecommunications Research Institute of Ontario), August 1997, 23 pgs.

194. Parnas, D.L., "Software Engineering: An Unconsummated Marriage", *Communications of the ACM*, 40, 9, September 1997, pg. 128.

195. Parnas, D.L., "Software Engineering: An Unconsummated Marriage (Extended Abstract)", in *Software Engineering—ESEC/FSE '97*, Zurich, Switzerland, September 1997, Jazayeri, M., Schauer, H., (eds.), Lecture Notes in Computer Science 1301, Springer-Verlag, 1997, pp. 1–3. Simultaneously published as Volume 22, Number 6 of *Software Engineering Notes*, Nov. 1997

196. Parnas, D.L. "Precise Description and Specification of Software", in *Mathematics of Dependable Systems II*, edited by V. Stavridou, Clarendon Press, 1997, pp. 1–14.

197. Aspray, W., , Keil-Slawik, R., Parnas, D. L. (editors) *"The History of Software Engineering"* Dagstuhl-Seminar-Report 153, Schloss Dagstuhl, Internationales Begegungs-und Forschungszentrum fuer Informatik, Universitaet Saarbruecken, Germany

198. Peters, D., Parnas, D.L., "Using Test Oracles Generated from Program Documentation", *IEEE Transactions on Software Engineering*, Vol. 24, No. 3, March 1998, pp. 161–173.

199. Parnas, D.L., Lawton, A., "Precisely Annotated Hierarchical Pictures of Programs", *CRL Report 359*, TRIO, Communication Research Laboratory, McMaster University, March 1998.

200. Parnas, D.L., "Software Engineering Programmes are not Computer Science Programmes", *Annals of Software Engineering*, vol. 6, 1998, pgs. 19–37. Also available as *CRL Report 361*, Communication Research Laboratory, McMaster University, April 1998.

201. Parnas, D.L., ""Formal Methods" Technology Transfer Will Fail", *Journal of Systems and Software*, Vol. 40, No. 3, pp. 195–198, 1998.

202. Xu, J., Parnas, D.L., "Priority Scheduling Versus Pre-Run-Time Scheduling", Proceedings of the *23rd IFAC/IFIP Workshop on Real Time Programming, WRTP'98*, Shantou, Guandong Province, P.R. China, 23–25 June, 1998. Revised version published as 210.

203. Parnas, D.L., "Successful Software Engineering Research", *ACM Software Engineering Notes*, Vol. 23, No 3, May 1998, pp. 64–68.

204. Parnas, D.L., "Who Taught Me About Software Engineering Research", *ACM Software Engineering Notes*, Vol. 23, No 4, July 1998, pp. 26–28.

205. Parnas, D.L., "Some Perspective on Refinement", *Program Development by Refinement— Case Studies Using the B Method*, Sekerinski, E., Sere, K. (eds.), Springer-Verlag, pp. xix– xxiv, ISBN 1-85233-053-8.

206. Parnas, D. L., Peters, D. K., "An Easily Extensible Toolset for Tabular Mathematical Expressions", to appear in *Proceedings of the Fifth International Conference on Tools and Algorithms for the Construction and Analysis of Systems (TACAS '99)*, 22–26 March 1999 Amsterdam, Netherlands.

207. Kreyman, K., Parnas, D.L., Qiao, S. "Inspection Procedures for Critical Programs that Model Physical Phenomena" CRL Report 368, TRIO, Communication Research Laboratory, McMaster University, February 1999, 15 pgs.

208. Parnas, D.L., "Myths and Methods: Is There a Scientific Basis for Y2K Inspections?" in the *Proceedings of the OECD Nuclear Energy Agency International Workshop: "Impact of the Year 2000 on the Nuclear Industry"*. Also available as CRL Report 369, Communications Research Laboratory, McMaster University, February 1999, 8 pgs.

209. Parnas, D.L., "Myths about Y2K Inspections", *Communications of the ACM*, 42, 5, May 1999, pg. 128.

210. Xu, J., Parnas, D.L., "Priority Scheduling Versus Pre-Run-Time Scheduling", Revised version of 200. To appear in *"Journal of Real-Time Systems"*.

Biographies

Joanne Atlee is an associate professor of computer science at the University of Waterloo. She received her B.S. in computer science and physics from the College of William and Mary in 1985, and her graduate degrees in computer science from the University of Maryland (M.S. in 1988 and Ph.D. in 1992). Her primary research interests are practical formalisms for specifying and analyzing software requirements and coordination models for composing features and resolving interactions. Other interests include formal methods, computer-aided verification, software architecture and design, and software engineering education.

Victor R. Basili is a professor of computer science at the University of Maryland, College Park; the Executive Director of the Fraunhofer Center in Maryland; and one of the founders and principals in the Software Engineering Laboratory (SEL). He works on measuring, evaluating, and improving the software development process and product and has consulted for many organizations. Dr. Basili has authored over 150 journal and refereed conference papers, has served as editor-in-chief of the IEEE Transactions on Software Engineering and as program chair and general chair of the 6th and 15th International Conferences on Software Engineering, respectively. He is coeditor-in-chief of the *International Journal of Empirical Software Engineering*, published by Kluwer. He is an IEEE and ACM Fellow.

Barry W. Boehm is TRW Professor of Software Engineering, and director, Center for Software Engineering, University of Southern California. He has served as director of the DARPA Information Science and Technology Office, and as director of the DDR&E Software and Computer Technology Office. He was chief scientist of the Defense Systems Group at TRW, and head of the Information Sciences Department at the Rand Corporation. His research focuses on an approach for integrating a software system's process, product, property, and success models. His contributions include the Constructive Cost Model (COCOMO), the Spiral Model of the software process, and the Theory W (win-win) approach to software management and requirements determination. He is an AIAA Fellow, an ACM Fellow, an IEEE Fellow, an INCOSE Fellow, and a member of the National Academy of Engineering.

Kathryn Heninger Britton is a senior technical staff member in IBM's Application Integration Middleware division (Research Triangle Park, NC). Since joining IBM in 1981, Ms. Britton has contributed to IBM's network architecture with a focus on two-phase commit protocols and multiprotocol networking. She has also worked on the development of several software products for networking and mobile computing. She has served as IBM's representative to the X/Open XNET working group. Prior to working for IBM, Ms. Britton worked for the Naval Research Laboratory, collaborating with David Parnas on software engineering research and technology transfer. Ms. Britton holds a bachelor's degree in English from Stanford University and two master's degrees, one in computer science, from the University of North Carolina at Chapel Hill.

Paul Clements is a senior member of the technical staff at Carnegie-Mellon University's Software Engineering Institute (SEI). His interests there include software architecture and design and software product-line practices. He is the author or coauthor of over 30 papers on software engineering, a book on software architecture, two forthcoming books on software architecture, and a forthcoming book on software product lines. Before joining the SEI in 1994, he was a computer scientist at the Naval Research Laboratory, where for a time he was the principal investigator of the Software Cost Reduction (A-7E) Project, begun by David Parnas and David Weiss.

Pierre-Jacques Courtois has degrees in electrical engineering and nuclear physics and a doctorate in applied sciences. He is a professor of computer science in the engineering department of the Catholic University of Louvain-la-Neuve in Belgium. Formerly with the Philips Research Laboratory in Brussels, he has been working for the last ten years at the Belgian authorized inspection agency for nuclear installations, where he is in charge of the assessment of safety-critical software-based systems used in nuclear power plants. He has been consultant to the OECD and to the IAEA (International Atomic Energy Agency, Vienne) for promoting guidance on the design and validation of software important to nuclear safety. He is chairman of the European Commission nuclear regulator task force on licensing issues of nuclear safety-critical software.

Stuart Faulk received his B.A. from Cornell University and his Ph.D. in computer science from the University of North Carolina at Chapel Hill. He is currently on faculty at the University of Oregon with the Department of Computer and Information Science where he is director of the Oregon Software Engineering Research Center. He recently served as chief architect of the state-wide Oregon Master of Software Engineering. Previously, he served as principal investigator for the Consortium Requirements Engineering project at the Software Productivity Consortium and as project head for the Software Cost Reduction Project at the U.S. Naval Research Laboratory. His research interests include software product-lines, software requirements methodology, software engineering for high-assurance systems, and network quality of service.

Dan Hoffman received his B.A. degree in mathematics from the State University of New York, Binghamton, in 1974, and the M.S. and Ph.D. degrees in computer science in 1981 and 1984, from the University of North Carolina, Chapel Hill. From 1974 to 1979 he worked as a commercial programmer/analyst. He is currently an associate professor of computer science at the University of Victoria, Canada. His research area is software engineering, emphasizing automated software testing. Dr. Hoffman has taught software engineering in academia and industry for more than ten years. He spent the 1992–93 year on leave at Tandem Computers, Inc., working on software inspection and automated class testing, and the 1998–99 year on sabbatical at Bell Laboratories, Lucent Technologies, doing research in software product lines.

Jim Horning is director of the Strategic Technologies and Architectural Research Laboratory (STAR Lab) at InterTrust Technologies Corporation. Previously, he was a founding member and senior consultant at Digital's Systems Research Center (DEC/SRC), a research fellow at Xerox's Palo Alto Research Center (PARC), and a founding member and chairman of the University of Toronto's Computer Systems Research Group (CSRG). He is a member and past chairman of IFIP's Working Group 2.3 (Programming Methodology). He is a coauthor of two books: *Larch: Languages and Tools for Formal Specification* (1993) and *A Compiler Generator* (1970). He wrote his first computer program in 1959 and received his Ph.D. in computer science from Stanford University ten years later. He is a fellow of the ACM.

Ralph Johnson is on the computer science faculty of the University of Illinois at Urbana-Champaign. He has been studying how object-oriented programming changes the way software is developed. He has worked on several projects, including frameworks for operating systems, drawing editors, music synthesis, and business transaction processing. He is coauthor of the book *Design Patterns: Elements of Reusable Object-Oriented Design*, winner of the 1994 Software Productivity Award. He was one of the originators of the software patterns movement, organizing the first conference on patterns, as well as writing many of the first papers on the subject. He believes that software will never become engineering until there are catalogs of designs that can be reused, and so he has been documenting these designs, both as frameworks and as patterns.

Richard A. Kemmerer is a professor in the Department of Computer Science at the University of California, Santa Barbara, where he served as chairman for four years. His research interests include formal specification and verification of systems and computer system security and reliability. His current research projects are in intrusion detection, efficient infinite state model checking, and secure mobile code. He is a fellow of the IEEE, a governing board member of the IEEE Computer Society, and a fellow of the Association for Computing Machinery. He is a past editor-in-chief of *IEEE Transactions on Software Engineering* (1996–1999). Dr. Kemmerer received his B.S. degree in mathematics from the Pennsylvania State University in 1966, and his M.S. and Ph.D. degrees in computer science from UCLA in 1976 and 1979, respectively.

John McLean is the director of the Naval Research Laboratory's Center for High Assurance Computer Systems, where his primary research interests are formal methods and computer security. McLean is an associate editor of *Distributed Computing,* of the *Journal of Computer Security,* and of *ACM Transactions on Information and System Security.* He is a senior research fellow of the University of Cambridge's Centre for Communications Systems Research and was on the Scientific Advisory Committee of Cambridge's Isaac Newton Institute Program in Computer Security, Cryptology, and Coding Theory. McLean graduated from Oberlin College in 1974 with a B.A. in mathematics. He received his Ph.D. in philosophy and his M.S. in computer science in 1980 from the University of North Carolina at Chapel Hill.

Ali Mili holds a Ph.D. from the University of Illinois at Urbana-Champaign (1981) and a Doctorat es-Sciences d'Etat from the Université Joseph Fourier de Grenoble, France (1985). His research interests are in software engineering and range from technical to managerial aspects. He has authored or coauthored four books, ten book chapters, and about 150 articles in journals and conference proceedings. His fifth book, dealing with software reuse, will be published by John Wiley and Sons; it is coauthored with Drs. H. Mili (UQAM), Sh. Yacoub (HP Labs), and E. Addy (Logicon).

Aloysius K. Mok received his B.S. in electrical engineering and his M.S. and Ph.D. degrees in computer science, from the Massachusetts Institute of Technology. Since 1983, he has been on the faculty of the Department of Computer Sciences at the University of Texas at Austin where he is currently Quincy Lee Centennial Professor of Computer Sciences. Professor Mok has done extensive research on real-time systems design and has consulted for both government and industry on many technical issues in real-time embedded computing. His current interests include research in an integrated approach to the design of real-time fault-tolerant and secure systems, network-centric computing, and knowledge-based systems with timeliness constraints. Professor Mok is a past chairman of the Technical Committee on Real-Time Systems of the IEEE.

John Shore was educated at Yale (B.S. in Physics) and the University of Maryland (Ph.D. in Theoretical Physics). He spent seventeen years at the Naval Research Laboratory performing R&D in mathematics, computer science, and electrical engineering. He was the founder of Entropic, Inc., the leading international supplier of software tools for speech R&D, and the developer of commercial technology for speech recognition and synthesis. Entropic was acquired by Microsoft in 1999. Dr. Shore is the author of many technical papers in information theory, signal processing, and computer science. He also wrote *The Sachertorte Algorithm and Other Antidotes to Computer Anxiety* (Viking Press, 1985; Penguin Books, 1986). Dr. Shore is presently an independent consultant and author.

Daniel P. Siewiorek, Buhl Professor of Computer Science and Electrical and Computer Engineering at Carnegie Mellon University, is currently Director of the Human Computer Interaction Institute. He helped to produce the Cm* multiprocessor system and has contributed to the dependability design of 24 commercial computer systems. He has published over 400 technical papers and eight text books. Siewiorek received his B.S. from the University of Michigan and his M.S. and Ph.D. from Stanford University, all in electrical engineering. He was elected an IEEE Fellow in 1981 for contributions to the design of modular computer systems. In 1988 he received the Eckert-Mauchly Award for his contributions to computer architecture. He was elected as a member of the 1994 Inaugural Class of ACM Fellows and was elected to the National Academy of Engineering.

Leonard L. Tripp is a technical fellow at the Boeing Company, involved in processes, standards, and tools for airborne software. He is the chair of the Professional Practices Committee of the IEEE Computer Society. Leonard was the 1999 president for the IEEE Computer Society. He has developed software engineering standards since 1982, and chaired the IEEE Software Engineering standards committee from 1992 to 1998. He served as the Head of the U.S. delegation to the ISO committee on software engineering standards from 1993 to 1998. He is the author of three books and 45 technical papers.

Maarten van Emden. After undergraduate work in electrical engineering and mathematics, Maarten van Emden completed his Ph.D. thesis in information theory and data analysis at the University of Amsterdam. He has held research positions at the IBM T.J. Watson Research Laboratory and the University of Edinburgh. In Canada, at the University of Waterloo and the University of Victoria, he has taught and published in logic programming, artificial intelligence, and software engineering. His current work is in constraint processing, engineering computation, and object-oriented software design.

John van Schouwen completed his masters degree in computer science at Queen's University in 1990. He worked as a research assistant on the evaluation of the Darlington shutdown system software while at Queen's from 1987 through 1990. From 1990 to 1991, he worked for the Telecommunications Research Institute of Ontario. John has been working for Nortel Networks from 1991 to the present. During that time he has worked on software documentation, software process development, development and experimentation on software specifications, and development of maintenance systems for telecommunications products.

Bill Wadge was trained in mathematics and mathematical logic at the University of British Columbia (B.A.) and the University of California, Berkeley (Ph.D.). Since then, however, his teaching and research have been primarily in computer science. He has been a faculty member at the University of Waterloo, the University of Warwick (UK), and, since 1983, at the University of Victoria (Canada). He is especially interested in the application of mathematical logic to practical problems of computer science, most recently in using intentional (possible worlds) logic as a framework for versioning systems for programs, Web pages, and other kinds of digital documents.

Jim Waldo is a distinguished engineer with Sun Microsystems, where he is the lead architect for Jini technology. Within Java Software, Jim's research has included object-oriented programming and systems, distributed computing, and user environments. Before joining Sun, Jim spent eight years at Apollo Computer and Hewlett-Packard. While at Hewlett-Packard, he led the design and development of the first Object Request Broker and was instrumental in getting that technology incorporated into the first OMG CORBA specification.

David M. Weiss is Director of Software Technology Research at Avaya Laboratories, where he conducts and guides research into ways of improving the effectiveness of software development. Formerly he was Director of Software Production Research at Bell Laboratories. He has also served as CTO of PaceLine Technologies and as Director of Reuse and Measurement at the Software Productivity Consortium. At the Congressional Office of Technology Assessment he was coauthor of an assessment of the Strategic Defense Initiative, and he was a visiting scholar at the Wang Institute. He originated the GQM approach to software measurement as his Ph.D. thesis at the University of Maryland, was a member of the A-7 project at the Naval Research Laboratory, and devised the FAST process for product-line engineering. He has also worked as a programmer and mathematician.

Credits

Chapter 1. Bartussek, W., Parnas, D.L., "Using Assertions About Traces to Write Abstract Specifications for Software Modules", University of North Carolina at Chapel Hill. Report No. TR77-012, December 1977, pp. 111–130.

Chapter 2. Wadge, W. and Parnas, D. Less Restrictive Constructs for Structured Programs. Unpublished.

Chapter 3. Parnas, D.L., "Predicate Logic for Software Engineering", Copyright 1993 IEEE. Reprinted, with permission, from *IEEE Transactions on Software Engineering,* Vol. 19, No. 9, September 1993, pp. 856–862.

Chapter 4. Janicki, R., Parnas, D.L., Zucker, J., "Tabular Representations in Relational Documents", in *Relational Methods in Computer Science*, Chapter 12, C. Brink and G. Schmidt (editors). Springer Verlag, KG. ISBN 3-211-82971-7 1977. pp. 184–196.

Chapter 5. Parnas, D.L. "Precise Description and Specification of Software", in *Mathematics of Dependable Systems II*, edited by V. Stavridou, Clarendon Press, 1997. pp. 1–14.

Chapter 6. Heninger, K.L., "Specifying Software Requirements for Complex Systems: New Techniques and Their Application", Copyright 1980, IEEE. Reprinted, with permission, from *IEEE Transactions on Software Engineering,* SE-6, January 1980. pp. 2–13.

Chapter 7. Reprinted with permission of the Association for Computing Machinery. Parnas, D.L., "On the Criteria to be Used in Decomposing Systems into Modules", Communications of the ACM, 15, 12, December 1972. pp. 1053–1058.

Chapter 8. Parnas, D.L., "On a 'Buzzword': Hierarchical Structure", IFIP Congress 74, North Holland Publishing Company, 1974. pp. 336–339.

Chapter 9. Reprinted with permission of the Association for Computing Machinery. Parnas, D.L., Siewiorek, D.L., "Use of the Concept of Transparency in the Design of Hierarchically Structured Systems", Communications of the ACM, 18, 7, July 1975, pp. 401–408.

Chapter 10. Parnas, D.L., "On the Design and Development of Program Families", Copyright 1976, IEEE. Reprinted, with permission, from *IEEE Transactions on Software Engineering,* Vol. SE-2, No. 1, March 1976, pp. 1–9.

Chapter 11. Parnas, D.L., Shore, J.E., Weiss, D., "Abstract Types Defined as Classes of Variables", Proceedings Conference on Data Abstraction, Definition, and Structure, Salt Lake City, March 1976, pp. 22–24. Reprinted in NRL Memorandum Report 7998, April 22, 1976, pp. 1–10.

Chapter 12. Parnas, D.L., Wuerges, H., "Response to Undesired Events in Software Systems", Proceedings of Second International Conference on Software Engineering, October 1976, pp. 437–447.

Chapter 13. Parnas D.L., "Some Software Engineering Principles", Infotech State of the Art Report on Structured Analysis and Design, Infotech International, 1978, 10 pgs.

Chapter 14. Parnas D.L., "Designing Software for Ease of Extension and Contraction", Copyright 1979, IEEE. Reprinted, with permission, from *IEEE Transactions on Software Engineering,* March 1979, pp. 128–138.

Chapter 15. Britton, K.H., Parker, R.A., Parnas, D.L., "A Procedure for Designing Abstract Interfaces for Device Interface Modules", Proceedings of the 5th International Conference on Software Engineering, March 1981, pp. 195–204.

Chapter 16. Parnas, D.L., Clements, P.C., Weiss, D.M., "The Modular Structure of Complex Systems", Copyright 1985, IEEE. Reprinted, with permission, from *IEEE Transactions on Software Engineering,* March 1985, Vol. SE-11 No. 3, pp. 259–266 (special issue on the 7th International Conference on Software Engineering).

Chapter 17. Parnas, D.L., Weiss, D.M., "Active Design Reviews: Principles and Practices", Proceedings of the 8th International Conference on Software Engineering, London, August 1985.

Chapter 18. Parnas, D.L., Clements, P.C., "A Rational Design Process: How and Why to Fake It", Copyright 1986, IEEE. Reprinted, with permission, from *IEEE Transactions on Software Engineering,* Vol. SE-12, No. 2, February 1986, pp. 251–257.

Chapter 19. Parnas, D.L. "Inspection of Safety Critical Software using Function Tables", Proceedings of IFIP World Congress 1994. Volume III" August 1994, pp. 270–277.

Chapter 20. Reprinted with permission of the Association for Computing Machinery. Courtois, P.J., Heymans, F., Parnas, D.L., "Concurrent Control with Readers and Writers", Communications of the ACM, 14, 10, October 1971. pp. 667–668.

Chapter 21. Reprinted with permission of the Association for Computing Machinery. Parnas, D.L., "On a Solution to the Cigarette Smokers' Problem (Without Conditional Statements)", Communications of the ACM, 18, 3, March 1975. pp. 181–183.

Chapter 22. Reprinted with permission of the Association for Computing Machinery. Faulk, S.R., Parnas, D.L., "On Synchronization in Hard-Real-Time Systems", Communications of the ACM, 31, 3, March 1988, pp. 274–287.

Chapter 23. Xu, J., Parnas, D.L., "Scheduling Processes with Release Times, Deadlines, Precedence and Exclusion Relations", Copyright 1990, IEEE. Reprinted, with permission, from *IEEE Transactions on Software Engineering,* vol. 16, no. 3, March 1990, pp. 360–369.

Chapter 24. Reprinted with permission of the Association for Computing Machinery. Parnas, D.L., "Building Reliable Software in Blowhard", ACM Software Engineering Notes, 2, 3, April 1977. pp. 5–6.

Chapter 25. Parnas, D.L., "The Impact of Money-Free Computer Assisted Barter Systems, University of Victoria Report No. DCS-48-IR, July 1985, 9 pgs.

Chapter 26. Parnas, D.L., Software Aspects of Strategic Defense Systems, American Scientist, Vol. 73, No. 5, Sept.–Oct. 1985, pp. 432–440.

Chapter 27. Parnas, D.L., "SDI: A Violation of Professional Responsibility", Springer-Verlag, New York, Inc., ABACUS, vol. 4, no. 2, Winter, 1987, pp. 46–52.

Chapter 28. Parnas, D.L. "Professional Responsibilities of Software Engineers", Proceedings of IFIP World Congress 1994, Volume II" August 1994, pp. 332–339.

Chapter 29. Parnas, D.L., "Software Aging", in Proceedings of the 16th International Conference on Software Engineering, Sorento, Italy, May 1994, Copyright 1994 IEEE. Reprinted with permission from IEEE Press, pp. 279–287.

Chapter 30. Reprinted with permission of the Association for Computing Machinery. Parnas, D.L., 'On ICSE's "Most Influential Papers"', ACM Software Engineering Notes, vol. 20, no 3, July 1995, pp. 29–32.

Chapter 31. Reprinted from *Teaching and Learning Formal Methods,* C. Neville Dean and Michael G. Hinchey (editors). "Teaching Programming as if it were Engineering", Parnas, D.L. pp. 43–55. Copyright 1996, by permission of the publisher Academic Press.

Chapter 32. Reprinted with permission of the Association for Computing Machinery. Parnas, D.L., "Software Engineering: An Unconsummated Marriage", Communications of the ACM, 40, 9, September 1997, pg. 128.

Chapter 33. Reprinted with permission of the Association for Computing Machinery. Parnas, D.L., "Who Taught Me About Software Engineering Research", ACM Software Engineering Notes, Vol. 23, No 4, July 1998, pp. 26–28.

Index

Note: *Italicized page locators refer to figures.*